Y0-BER-894

LIBRARIES
&
CULTURE

LIBRARIES

&

CULTURE

Proceedings of
Library History Seminar VI

19-22 March 1980
Austin, Texas

Edited by
Donald G. Davis, Jr.

University of Texas Press

Reprinted from *Journal of Library History,* Volume 16, Numbers 1 & 2

Library of Congress Cataloging in Publication Data

Library History Seminar (6th : 1980 : Austin, Texas)
    Libraries & culture.

    "Reprinted from Journal of library history,
volume 16, numbers 1& 2."
    Includes index.
    1. Library science—Congresses. 2. Libraries—
History—20th century—Congresses. 3. Culture—
Congresses. 4. Libraries and society—Congresses.
I. Davis, Donald G. II. Journal of library history
(University of Texas at Austin) III. Title.
Z665.L67 1980   020   81-13015
ISBN 0-292-74632-6   AACR2

Copyright © 1981 by the University of Texas Press

Printed in the United States of America

Contents

Foreword

The addresses and papers that follow will document some of the intellectual challenge and delight that characterized Library History Seminar VI, "Libraries & Culture," held in Austin, Texas, on 19-22 March 1980. Their presentation to responsive audiences represented the culmination of nearly eighteen months of planning and preparation. Their publication here will no doubt encourage wider reflection on the themes, issues, and finer points raised by the speakers.

When the first such seminar convened nineteen years before, 2-4 November 1961 in Tallahassee, the seventeen participants included the six speakers. Succeeding conferences—held in 1965, 1968, 1971, and 1976—have grown in attendance and in sophistication. LHS VI was the first such seminar under the sponsorship of the University of Texas at Austin, where the *Journal of Library History* has been edited and published since 1976. The Graduate School of Library Science and the Division of Continuing Education shared the major responsibility, supported by the American Library Association's Library History Round Table and Beta Phi Mu, the international library science honorary society, both the national organization and the Beta Eta chapter in Austin.

In the early stages of planning the program committee, comprised of the *JLH* editorial board and Arthur P. Young of the Library History Round Table, decided that in contrast to recent seminars, LHS VI would aim for the broadest possible chronological and geographical scope as reflected in the breadth of topics, the most open competition in submitted proposals, and the widest possible appeal to a variety of persons interested in the history of collected graphic records.

From the 109 prospectuses resulting from the call for papers, 31 were selected and divided into 13 sessions. The spectrum of topics is unusual even for an interdisciplinary field, as a glance at the table of contents will reveal. The papers range from "Ancient Burials of Metal Documents in Stone Boxes—Their Implications for Library History" to "Chinese Libraries during and after the Cultural Revolution" and from "Book Collecting in Counter-Reformation Italy: The Library of Gian Vincenzo Pinelli (1535-

1601)" to "Frances Newman: Librarian and Novelist." The varied backgrounds and perspectives of the speakers likewise contributed to general interest. Although prepared commentators initiated discussion in about half of the sessions, limitation of space has not allowed for printing their remarks here despite the spice they added to the live meetings. The aim of the evening plenary sessions, addressed by Elspeth Rostow, David Davies, and Neil Harris, was to place the historic role of libraries in a broad and general context that would complement the more focused papers presented during the day.

The fact that more than 100 librarians, historians, bibliographers, library school faculty members and students, and generally interested persons attended the sessions seemed to support the optimism of the seminar's planners. Since the seminar itself has received thorough news coverage in the library press, nothing descriptive need be added here. Summary accounts, descriptive and evaluative, appear in *American Libraries* (May 1980), *Library Journal* (1 June 1980), *JLH* (Summer 1980), and *Texas Libraries* (Fall 1980).

Although the speakers and the editor have made every effort to provide accurate copy for these proceedings, the editor and the sponsoring entities do not presume responsibility for the entire contents. The variety of subjects treated by authors with dissimilar academic preparation and divergent points of view ensured, and continues to ensure, provocative, and even controversial, responses from others. The cause of library history will be well served if readers will consider these papers critically, engage in further research, prepare papers of their own—or, at least, forward their thoughtful comments for inclusion in the "Communications" section of *JLH*. As John Cole of The Center for the Book at the Library of Congress expressed it in his concluding remarks, "Concrete steps have been taken toward expanding the horizons of library history," including the attempt of the speakers "to view their subjects broadly, to pay attention to context—social, cultural, and intellectual." He perceptively suggested that, along with other major conferences, 1980 appears to have been a critical year in establishing a new level of interest in the history and role of books and libraries.

This introduction would be more incomplete than it is, were not thanks rendered to those who gave so freely of their time and energy to guarantee the success of LHS VI. The local arrangements helpers, though indispensable, are too numerous to list individually. However, two persons deserve special mention with regard to this compilation. Janet Fisher of the University of Texas Press gave every encouragement in publication of these proceedings and Betsy Vantine, *JLH* editorial assistant, gave up her summer to help copyedit them. *Vox audita perit, littera scripta manet.*

Fall 1980   *Donald G. Davis, Jr.*
                                                     Seminar Coordinator

The bookplate belonging to John Andrews's Library dated 1774.
Courtesy of the British Museum

THE BOOKPLATE

While hunting information for his doctoral dissertation, A. M. Fazle Kabir discovered two interesting items used by an enterprising shopkeeper in Bengal two centuries ago. One is an advertisement dated 7 October 1780, which describes the difficulties faced by a proprietor of a lending library in a large community with an unsettled population—such as Calcutta was for a long time. The other is the bookplate used by that proprietor to identify books in his circulating library. It is featured on the cover of this issue of the *Journal of Library History*.

In addition to the rather usual (for the time) well-nourished classical figures surrounding the stylized library alcove, the bookplate contains several words and numbers. "UTILE DULCI"—the useful with the agreeable—is at the top; "Calcutta 1774" is just below the banner; almost hidden in the lower left is the artist's name, "Shepperd sc."; and at the foot is "Iohn Andrews's / Circulating Library."

Fazle Kabir found answers to some questions I asked in the February 1968 issue of the *Journal of Asian Studies* (27:335–338) in "Bengali Types and Their Founders."

Shepperd (or Shepherd) was the 21-year-old engraver for the English East India Company's (EEIC) mint located at Hooghly, about 30 miles north of Calcutta. Adjacent was the Dutch East India Company's (DEIC) jurisdiction in Chinsurah, Charles Wilkins, EEIC mint superintendent, was responsible for munitions, coinage, other metal products, and, later, types. At or near the mint, Shepperd designed and etched the metal plate used to produce the bookplate for the circulating library in Andrews's Calcutta establishment, which dealt in liquors and various other fine imports (including books) for sale. The circulating library was supported by quarterly subscriptions. I would believe it was located in the (present) Dalhousie Square area. Not far distant, James Augustus Hicky, printer and publisher, announced most of what we know about the Andrews shop in *Hicky's Bengal Gazette*, issued 29 January 1780 through 5 January 1782 only. Hicky was too outspoken for Government to tolerate longer.

A few years earlier, two young men attending Harrow were courting the same young woman. Splicing the *Dictionary of National Biography*'s comments on each, when Richard Brinsley Sheridan was chosen, Nathaniel Brassey Halhed (then at Oxford) decided to enter EEIC service. He was posted at the Hooghly establishment (and later married the daughter of the DEIC governor at Chinsurah). Though it was not his first publication, in 1778 there appeared *Bodhaprakāśaṁ śabdaśāstraṁ . . . A Grammar of the Bengal Language by Nathaniel Brassey Halhed. . . . Printed at Hoogly in Bengal M DCC LXXVIII.*

A Grammar of the Bengal Language, long acclaimed as the first book printed in Bengal, is the first book produced anywhere in the world to use bengali types. I reported in 1968 that *A Grammar* lauds Wilkins, the mint superintendent, for his exceptional type production. The Bengali blacksmith, Panchanan Karmakar, and the die sinker, Joseph Shepperd, are overlooked completely.

John Clark Marshman was only six or seven years old when he came with his parents to Serampore. The Baptist missionaries, or the Serampore Trio, and their children soon learned to know the local printing establishments, and I have no reservations concerning Marshman's statement in his *The Life and Times of Carey, Marshman, and Ward: Embracing the History of the Serampore Mission*, 2 vols. (London: Longman, Brown, Green, Longmans, and Roberts, 1859). On page 159 of the first volume he wrote, "The first Book in which Bengalee types were used was Halhed's Bengalee Grammar, printed at Hooghly at the press established by Mr. Andrews, a bookseller, in 1778." The *1778*, of course, belongs with the title. Though on EEIC property, within the fortifications needed for a mint, this was a private printery: Mr. Andrews's

Press. After the success of *A Grammar of the Bengal Language* it required some steady persuasion to convince the Company to sponsor its own print shop—for even one year. They soon found it advantageous.

No more than one press was necessary in 1774, and there was but one other in the Presidency of Bengal before 1780—that of Charles Wilkins for the EEIC. When John Andrews had begun printing (both copperplate engravings and small business papers using letterpress) has not been learned. The *Grammar* was certainly *not* his first venture! Nor do we seem to know when Andrews opened his circulating library in Calcutta: it could well have been in 1774, or earlier. He would travel with the tides (the usual manner) between Calcutta and Hooghly to attend affairs in the two locations.

Early in the 1780s a young Scot, John Borthwick Gilchrist, arrived in Bengal and became interested in the Urdu (Hindoostanee/Hindustani) language. He requested permanent retirement from the EEIC's Medical Service in order to devote himself to production of a diglot dictionary. This I have discussed in the Fall 1978 *JLH* cover article (13:466–468). Gilchrist began publishing in the late 1780s, but it was 1 August 1798 when he signed his preface. On page xlii of the preface to *A Dictionary, English and Hindoostanee . . .* (Calcutta: several publishers, 1787–1798), Gilchrist wrote clearly that Shepperd had not only helped him with the Urdu types but had assisted Charles Wilkins through the entire process of making and using non-Western types—with not a word of thanks.

On page 75 of Holmes and Company's *The Bengal Obituary* (Calcutta: Baptist Mission Press, 1848) is the Joseph Shepperd notice. Burial had been in South Park Street Burial Ground, Calcutta. In 1970 I visited that cemetery. Few eighteenth-century stones remain, either in their original positions or side-by-side against the compound walls. The Shepperd memorial was nowhere to be found. The same day I visited St. John's Church, the old Anglican Cathedral, for which Shepperd had engraved some plates for the cornerstone-laying ceremony. All such plates were missing. Only the holes, into which rivets had been sunk, remained.

Adding further to Kabir's article, on my return to Carey Library in 1968, I found a four-volume set of Thomas Carte's *A General History of England* (London, 1752). The verso of each volume's title page bears a stamped ownership mark: "John Andrews / Houghley 1799." In 1799, John Andrews was alive and well, residing in the twin communities he had long known—not in Calcutta. Did he then have a small press operating at Hooghly/Chinsurah? It would be interesting to know, for these large villages were soon to be the scene of some exciting local literary activity that included translation, compilation, printing, and publishing. A bit of this is in my paper "The Literary Hussain Family of Chinsurah/Hooghly, 1800–1850," included in *Proceedings of the 1978 Southwest Conference on Asian Studies*, edited by Lester J. Bilsky (Little Rock, Ark., 1979), pages 150–162.

The bookplate that my 1960/61 Dacca University student, now Dr. Fazle Kabir, found is very likely the oldest extant piece of print (an engraving) from the first press established in Bengal. What other small pieces of business paper were produced at Mr. Andrews's shop? And when, exactly, did it begin operation?

Katharine Smith Diehl
Seguin, Texas

The Diary of the Human Race: Libraries in a Troubled Age

Elspeth Rostow

From the moment I accepted your invitation to speak this evening, I have been somewhat uneasy. As an outsider, a user rather than a librarian, I have always stood in awe of your profession. The quintessential librarian remains for me the first one I recall meeting: I was perhaps four years old, walking across the Columbia University campus with my father. Looking up, I saw a majestic figure striding along with a walking stick in his hand, using the curved handle to decapitate such dandelions as had the poor taste to grow beside the path. It was, of course, the director of the Columbia libraries. Perhaps later on I became a fairly docile borrower because in the back of my mind I could still hear the swish of that cane as it beheaded an offender.

This respectful, even cowed, attitude was in no way altered by a headline in a recent *New York Times*: "The Humble Librarians Are Humble No More." Humble? If the long-dead Columbia librarian was humble, what indeed have his descendants become in the 1980s? Veritable juggernauts of destruction!

To make matters still more tense, I know, as I am sure you do, that Mao Tse-tung began his professional life as a librarian. As an assistant at the university library in Peking at $8.00 a month, Mao reported that his job was so modest that to most readers "I didn't exist as a human being." A biographer reports that "many whose names Mao had to register as they came in were famous leaders of the literary renaissance" but (in Mao's words) "they had no time

Elspeth Rostow *is dean, Lyndon B. Johnson School of Public Affairs, University of Texas at Austin.*

Journal of Library History, Vol. 16, No. 1, Winter 1981
© 1981 by the University of Texas Press   0275-3650/81/010008-08$01.15

to listen to an assistant librarian speaking southern dialect."[1] How Chairman Mao solved his humility problem is now history. Perhaps it also shows the potential for upward mobility in the soul of all librarians.

Libraries, whether Chinese or American, are an index to the cultures within which they exist. In common with universities, libraries operate on several planes: as reservoirs of knowledge; as resources; and as clues to the level of culture. On the one hand, they provide a repository of what has been discovered, imagined, or hoped; on the other, they serve as arenas within which the minds of each generation can grapple with the tasks of the present and attempt to cope with the future. It is to the issue of the library as connective tissue, tying what has been to what lies ahead, that I should like to address myself this evening. I do so with a concerned perception of the peril in which libraries in the United States stand as the turbulent decade of the 1980s opens.

As you know well, the American preoccupation with libraries dates from the very beginning of colonization. Samuel Eliot Morison, discussing the intellectual life of seventeenth-century New England, emphasized the value that early New Englanders attached to the books they brought with them as symbols and ties to the culture now behind them across the seas. The elder William Brewster, for example, left over 400 different prized works when he died in 1644.[2] Morison points out that, although college graduates were inevitably more disposed than others to be book owners, "a surprisingly large proportion of the population" owned books, including "farmers, fishermen, servants, and poor widows."[3] A town library began in Boston as early as 1656; colleges were founded around donations of books. It was reported (although not by Sam Morison, who was rarely interested in events that took place as far south as Connecticut) that volumes destined to become the Yale College Library were distributed in several towns before the decision was made to locate the college in New Haven. Citizens of the hamlets of Branford and Guilford, perhaps anxious to obtain the revenues they anticipated from selling beer to future undergraduates, were so outraged at the decision to place the college in New Haven that they blew up some of the bridges separating their towns from the lucky winner in order to keep the books from reaching their destination. Morison guesses that by 1700 about ten thousand separate titles may have existed in New England alone and "that the number of copies of each work would range from several thousand of the Bible, and several hundred of the more popular works of puritan divinity, down to a single copy of the less common works."[4]

The competition between Massachusetts and Virginia for library primacy caused Morison to refer to the "odious and highly inaccurate comparisons between New England and Virginian libraries in the early volumes of the *William and Mary College Quarterly*." Morison is at pains to point out that the largest library found inventoried in Virginia had somewhat over two hundred titles, as contrasted with nearly twice the number in various New England private collections.[5]

Despite Morison's evocation of a learned fisherman to match the more traditional classical blacksmith, both the possession of books and the use of libraries was relatively limited in the colonial period—limited by income and by education. It remained for the booming nineteenth century, filled with the buoyancy of growth, to extend the thrust of literacy and with it the concept that through education and its handmaiden, the library, the individual could grow both in understanding and in marketable competence. As public schools spread the capacity to read to the children of newly arrived peasants, literacy opened the doors and windows of libraries to second-generation immigrants: first to the Irish and then to the immigrants who flowed in after the 1880s from southern and eastern Europe. Libraries provided new roots for those whom Oscar Handlin called "the uprooted." In Handlin's words, the immigrants were "accused of their poverty." To correct it, they were urged quickly to learn about the country into which they had been thrust and above all to learn about "the Anglo-Saxon conception of righteousness, law, and order."[6] For the old or even the middle-aged immigrant, the shock of alien status never wholly eased. For the young, the task of becoming American was somewhat less painful. The process begun in the schools could be continued through the books to which they now had access and the free public libraries from which they could borrow them. In New York, Chicago, Boston, the library became a vehicle of escalation, a way out of the slum.

(A great-aunt of mine, a librarian working on the lower east side of New York during World War I, reported her amazement at the condition of some of the books returned from the hands of borrowers. The pages, she said, were often as "limp as rags—as if they had been fingered over and over again." I recall asking whether the books were returned dirty. "No," she answered, "they simply looked exhausted.")

American communities in the nineteenth and twentieth centuries slowly became aware that budgets for libraries, although they needed to be defended in terms of cost, could be justified in terms of social returns. The tie between a reading population and a population that would potentially vote right also had an appeal to certain politicians. This somewhat eased the issue of funding. One former immigrant, a Scottish bobbin boy of talent and ambition, among his many benefactions endowed over 2,800 libraries. As Andrew Carnegie pointed out in 1889 in his essay *The Gospel of Wealth*, it was appropriate that rich men should plow back into society some of the benefits that they had received from it. Endowing libraries was a nice way of clarifying the relationship between the *quid* and the *quo.*

By the time Carnegie, the Johnny Appleseed of libraries, died in 1919, the United States had become a mature industrial society. The tradition of college libraries, pioneered by Harvard and Yale, had proliferated to land grant colleges across the country. The tradition of town or city libraries had become a characteristic of communities from one ocean to another; and local governments, with varying degrees of enthusiasm, regarded library budgets as a constant. Notably absent throughout this period was any federal enthusiasm for libraries—with the outstanding exception of the Library of Congress. It was inevitable that Thomas Jefferson would regard the establishment of a national library, largely to serve the interests of the legislature, as of prime importance. After 1870, when the Copyright Act required that all copyright material be deposited in the Library of Congress, a new era in preserving the current flow of intellectual output in this country was inaugurated. The magnificent collection inspired by Jefferson in time was opened to the public and, through interlibrary loan, to widening circles of readers throughout the country. But federal support for libraries as a collectivity remained at low level until fairly recently.

The correlation between economic growth and support of libraries is close. An ebullient, upsurging society may take pleasure in watching libraries grow numerous, may hail the introduction of new technologies, and may absorb attendant costs with relatively little pain. A mature society with productivity increasing can slice a bit of its growing national pie and hand it to librarians. Look back for example at the euphoric prose that accompanied the legislation of the 1960s. It is poignant to reread accounts of the enthusiasm with which new efforts af federal funding were greeted in that now-distant decade.

But we must forego nostalgia and settle down to sober contemplation of the rough times ahead in the eighties. As in so many other areas, inflation is the great enemy of the American library as the decade of the eighties opens. Inflation, of course, wears a thousand faces. It may come disguised as Proposition 13. It may surface in sharply escalating costs for paper or mailing. It is reflected in tightened municipal budgets. It gallops along in the form of escalating labor costs and it renders acutely painful libraries' constant need to cope with the products of the new information explosion. Every community has its horror story. Everyone is aware in one way or another of the strain on the library fabric.

To readers, the impact of inflationary pressures and the budget squeeze looks somewhat different. At a time of increasing library use, suddenly borrowers are confronted with shortened hours and reduced services. Already conditioned to the ubiquitous paperback, discouraged by what appears to be bureaucratic indifference to their own timetables, flooded with information coming across the tube in their living rooms, they have the potential to turn into non–library-users. To be sure, the figures are heartening: they suggest that this habit has not appealed to many Americans. The danger, nonetheless, remains. Two years ago a visiting professor at Yale, concerned with the range in quality of the student papers he received, began to inquire, both of his best and his worst students, how much time each had devoted to reading during grammar school days. The professor's unscientific conclusions, as he reported them to me, established a firm correlation between the great readers and the top students in his class, with the reverse equally true. I should add that he discovered that those who did the very best had found novels of extraordinary interest, perhaps because of the novel's capacity to enlarge the inevitably limited horizon of a single human experience. The fact that the visiting professor to whom I allude is named Howard Cosell is an interesting but irrelevant fact. As a footnote, I should add that Mr. Cosell himself was a voracious reader as a young man. (I do not hear you clamoring to know who was Howard Cosell's favorite novelist but I will tell you anyway—Thomas Hardy.)

Shall we blame the plight of the libraries on technology? No. One of my distinguished colleagues at the University of Texas, Denise Schmandt-Besserat, has pushed back the date of the invention of writing significantly through her recent discoveries of which you may have read in *Scientific American*.[7] I feel sure that the use of the clay tablets some 11,000 years ago, about which Professor Schmandt-Besserat writes, must have evoked some opposition at the time. (After all, it could have been argued, man had survived fairly well since the dawn of time without such technological change.) As we have subsequently managed to adjust to the printing press and the cornucopia of inventions that followed it, so, I believe, will we be able to deal with the information explosion, with the need for books in machine-readable form, with the panoply of costly technology that confronts us now. But to say that we will absorb the psychological impact of such changes is not to say that we are at present able to deal with the costs that will go with them. In short, it is not technology that should concern us, but rather policy.

It was thus with some concern that I read President Carter's speech to the White House Conference on Libraries and Information Services in November 1979. I was interested to learn that the Carter family has always read books at the dining room table. I was pleased that the president still holds card number five in his home town library and uses it regularly. And I was reassured that he believes that an enlightened public is to be encouraged. However, I listened in vain for a commitment on his part to take the lead in increasing the percentage of federal support for libraries, which now hovers at around 5 percent. His speech ended with the words—"you can remember that you've got a friend in the White House." Fine. But perhaps the test will be in the reaction President Carter gives to the reports that derive from the November White House Conference. Equally significant will be the legislative response to the proposal for a National Library Act approved on a bipartisan basis by Senators Pell and Javits. The dean of a public affairs school should be dispassionate in respect to the merits of these proposals. A dean, however, may be permitted to underline the importance of the debate.

Yet the question of funding for libraries in an age of inflation will not be solved by itself. Libraries are simply the victims of a public failure that affects the whole society—namely, the failure to develop a strategy to deal with inflation, to master the energy crisis, to increase productivity, and, in the end, to turn this country from a worried dependency of OPEC into the energy-exporting, highly productive society we have been in the past and could be again.

Thus my message is in one sense a bleak one. Only within the context of an overall economic and political strategy for the eighties that yields steady growth without inflation can the problem of funding for libraries be solved. A short-run victory on a given piece of library-tied legislation may be welcomed, but it will not be sufficient. Without the surge of productivity of that era, the legislation of the Johnson period would not have occurred. By the same token, there is no reason for short-run optimism in the contemplation of a decade where increasing raw material prices, uncontrolled costs, and pressures on the taxpayer may be expected to make even the most desirable social programs appear at worst unpopular and at best deferrable. This is the price to be paid for the multiple role of the library. Just as the library provides the information with which problems may be solved, it also reflects on its shelves man's frequent failure to solve the great dilemmas he confronts. There are pages in the diary of the human race that are acutely painful to read; they do not necessarily come at the end of the volume.

However, my short-run pessimism about the easy solubility of the problems facing American libraries is matched by longer-run optimism. I am currently serving with forty-eight other members on a Commission to delineate a National Agenda for the Eighties. As I look at the task facing the Commission, a central requirement obviously is to construct a national strategy of the kind just described. It must be directed, first, to a multifaceted approach to the energy problem that would radically reduce oil imports; second, to an increase in productivity; and third, to the restoration of an innovative thrust in a country that has lost primacy in this area to other societies, notably Japan. In addition to economic issues, an overall national political strategy is needed to deal with the dilemmas of party breakdown, special interest politics, and a frustrated, truculent, and tendentious America. A national, social, and cultural strategy is also required, one that would deal with the substance of that important cliché the "quality of life" and would emphasize within it the importance of an information policy that would be commensurate with the needs on economic and political levels. All of this means that we require a sharp break from the counterproductive trends of the 1970s.

An international strategy would be the fourth pillar that I would hope to see raised in a design for surmounting the decade's difficulties and establishing in this contentious world a reasonable degree of stability and resumption of progress toward arms control. A good part of the international strategy, too, must be economic—for most of the world is in the grip of an energy crisis even greater than the one confronting the United States.

Are these strategies conceivable? Certainly. A study of the past demonstrates, as Toynbee emphasized, that the survival of a society is a function of several variables: the educated intelligence of its individual members, a level of challenge high enough to stimulate invention and innovation, yet a challenge capable also of yielding answers within the forseeable future.

These are the four strategic elements that face us in this decade; there is nothing in their nature or in a reading of the American past to suggest the impossibility of their solution. Inevitability, however, is not one of the elements of the package. We have seen societies fall, as well as rise.

If we *can* succeed in designing and executing these strategies, the American library will inevitably be a significant piece in the mosaic. If we fail, all the lobbying in the world and all the professional competence available will not permit the library to continue its multiple functions at an optimal level. However, if we do succeed, the American library will inevitably play a significant part in the attainment of strategic goals. Success will mean that the foundation will have been laid for a future in which libraries can fulfill to the limit their vital contribution to the life of this society.

Notes

1. Anne Fremantle (ed.), *Mao Tse-tung: An Anthology of His Writings* (New York: New American Library, 1962), p. xxiii.

2. Samuel Eliot Morison, *The Intellectual Life of Colonial New England* (Ithaca: Cornell University Press, 1960), p. 133.

3. Ibid., p. 141.

4. Ibid., p. 149.

5. Ibid., p. 133.

6. Oscar Handlin, *The Uprooted: The Epic Story of the Great Migrations That Made the American People* (New York: Grosset and Dunlap, 1951), p. 273.

7. Denise Schmandt-Besserat, "The Earliest Precursor of Writing," *Scientific American* 238, no. 6 (June 1978): 50-59.

Libraries and the Two Cultures

David W. Davies

The word *culture* has a Latin root, and is found in a number of modern languages. In English the word has several meanings. In earlier times perhaps the most common use was in connection with agriculture, but in the Elizabethan age the agricultural use of the word was extended, so that people spoke of manuring the mind, by which they meant its preparation and training. In the nineteenth century two interesting uses of the word developed. First, the word was used in the sense in which Matthew Arnold used it, that is, to denote an acquaintance with the best that had been known and said in the world; and second, the new discipline of anthropology used the word to mean the whole congeries of ways in which a particular people construct buildings, manufacture artifacts, worship deities, make war and love, raise children, and live with one another.[1] Logically, culture in Matthew Arnold's sense of the word is a segment of the culture known to the anthropologists, but there is some advantage here in considering the two cultures, Arnold's and the anthropologists', separately.

Although culture in Arnold's sense of the word was defined in the nineteenth century, people in the remote past had sought an acquaintance with the best that had been known and said in the world, or some segment of such an acquaintanceship. With us the pursuit of culture has involved the use of books, but culture in Arnold's sense, and of a high order, has existed without books. The culture of ancient Greece was at first an oral culture. The

David W. Davies *is librarian emeritus of Honnold Library, Claremont Colleges, Claremont, California.*

Journal of Library History, Vol. 16, No. 1, Winter 1981
© 1981 by the University of Texas Press   0275-3650/81/010016-12$01.10

plays of the dramatists were listened to and remembered, and perhaps the historians recited their chronicles as Herodotus is said to have done. Plato, a man of the fifth century who lived on into the fourth, had no use for the newfangled vogue for books. He avowed that he would never write one. He characterized books as dead things, They provided no interplay of mind; they inhibited questions and answers. They were of little importance, said Plato, in states with healthy constitutions, and only flourished in states with luxurious constitutions.[2] Despite Plato, the number of books in the world has continued to grow, and those books have been gathered into collections, or libraries, which must necessarily have guardians and keepers, thus making it possible for most of us here to earn our scanty bread.

The person pursuing culture not only uses libraries, but he or she may not achieve culture without libraries. The culture seeker may use laboratories, or museums, visit natural monuments, or dig on the sites of ancient cities, but sooner or later the seeker must go to a library and there study carefully the accounts of others who have worked in the same segment of culture. In the Western world the pursuit of culture usually, but not always, has been considered a laudable activity. In revolutionary times it has occasionally gone into eclipse, but that by definition is an abnormal condition. Culture was a laudable pursuit in Greece, and continued to be so in pagan Rome, but when Rome was Christianized, a startling revolutionary event, culture was at a discount. If early Christians were living according to the precepts of Christ they were leading the ideal life, and accordingly the Christians had no need to know the best that had been said and thought in the pagan world and were better off without such knowledge. Inevitably culture went out of fashion, and libraries as a concomitant of culture perished. There were said to be twenty-eight public libraries in Rome in the fourth century, but all of them disappeared, and the great library at Alexandria was destroyed by a Christian mob of the fifth century, rather than by the Muslims as is sometimes said.[3]

The culture of the ancient world was kept alive by such men as Cassiodorus, and what has been called the anti-Christian *fronde*.[4] Classical texts as well as Christian works were copied and preserved in monasteries, even though few monasteries had libraries or *scriptoria*. Still, even in that remote outpost of the Western world, the British Isles, between the years 597 and 1066 in one library or another one could read the *Golden Ass* of Apuleius, Pliny's *Natural History*, and Homer's *Odyssey*, as well as works by Hippocrates, Juvenal, Persius, Proclus, Propertius, Pythagoras Quintilius, Sallust, Seneca, Suetonius, Terence, Tacitus, Varro, Virgil, Vetruvius, Cato, Cicero, Dioscorides, Cassiodorus, and other less well known writers.[5] The seekers after learning in medieval Europe were not numerous, and those who went to libraries to pursue learning were far outnumbered by those who went there for plunder; but with the renascence, culture regained its former honored place, and in the centuries following the renascence up into the nineteenth century, some part, probably a small part, of the rich and the wellborn continued to seek an acquaintance with the best that had been known and utilized libraries, which became progressively better. Still, the mass of the people, those of interest to the anthropologist, used libraries very little. For them the valued and necessary depositories of documents were not libraries but public record offices, where land titles, contracts between individuals, court records, certificates of births, deaths, and marriages, and such other documents as citizens or officials wished to make of public record were deposited. Great numbers of the clay tablets recovered from the ruins of ancient cities in the Tigris and Euphrates valleys were found in single mounds. Some of these collections were libraries. The Assyrian kings had clay tablet libraries of religious, mythological, magical, literary, scientific, legal, historical, and astronomical works. More often the hoards of tablets represented official records and commercial correspondence. The tablets recorded transfers of land, contracts for the purchase of cattle, tax rolls, court cases, lists of prisoners and of booty. Such hoards of tablets were the remains of public record offices, or the business correspondence of merchants.[6]

Writing in fact was used for religious, commercial, and governmental purposes before it was used for cultural ends, and religious archives and official records were preserved before cultural works were gathered together and preserved. The primary position of the public record collection in early civilizations is attested by the fact that the first Greek public library is said to have been established in 350 B.C., when Lycurgus sponsored a measure whereby it was ordered that henceforth copies of the works of the great dramatists were to be preserved in the state archive or public record office.[7]

A great number of papyri, perhaps 60,000, has been preserved, but only a few are genuine gems of literature. The papyri that have been preserved are, as in the case of the clay tablets, the vestiges of past official record collections.[8] A considerable number of papyri has survived from the first centuries of Christianity. One such papyrus states that Emperor Hadrian has instituted a fund to maintain the children of a certain town. A petition is accordingly presented for an allowance for a child from this fund.[9] In another instance, owners of land that has been inundated by the Nile are eligible for a tax deduction. In accordance with the law the village scribe has checked and verified certain claims for such a deduction.[10] Another document states that a couple who are named have been divorced. It is recorded that the dowry has been repaid to the father of the wife, and both parties to the divorce renounce all claims upon the other.[11] A commodity broker, a dealer in futures, gives a receipt for a large quantity of beans. The beans are to be delivered to the buyer at a future date at a stipulated price.[12] Isadora, the castanets dancing girl, with two companion dancing girls, agrees to make a certain number of appearances. Her wages are to be paid partly in money and partly in kind. The entrepreneur agrees also to place two donkeys at the disposal of the women for their transportation.[13]

The public record offices of the early eras of civilization were succeeded by the record offices of western Europe. There is a very scant literature, if any, on the history of public record offices. Much of what is available is included in histories of libraries because the authors of those histories have thought it unimportant to distinguish between libraries, which carry the best that has been said and known in the world, from record offices, in which the official records necessary for the lives of the people and the conduct of government are filed. The record offices preserved the documents essential to the creators and conveyors of culture in the anthropological sense, and they are as essential to that culture as are libraries to Matthew Arnold's culture. It is perhaps worth noting that not only are libraries crucially important to seekers after culture in Arnold's sense of the word, but those seekers spend a large segment of their time in libraries. Public record offices, though vitally necessary to the conveyors of culture in the anthropological sense, only occasionally impinge directly on the activities of the teeming multitude. The bulk of the activities of the people as a whole is unrecorded, and the techniques and routines that make their activities possible are seldom described and preserved in records.

In France in the Merovingian era there were large numbers of Greeks, Jews, and Syrians settled in French cities. There were, for example, in 576 more than five hundred Jews living in the city of Clermont. In 585 the population of Orléans was said to consist of Latins, Syrians, and Jews. In 589 the population of Narbonne was

composed of Goths, Romans, Jews, Greeks, and Syrians. In 591 a
a member of the Syrian colony in Paris purchased the bishopric of
that city and filled the ecclesiastic posts with his fellow country-
men. History textbooks do not have much to say, if anything, of
the migration of Jews, Syrians, and Greeks to French cities in the
sixth century, but we can deduce who those émigrés were. Greg-
ory, in his Frankish chronicle, speaks of the merchant guilds in
Gallic towns, and his contemporary, Venantius Fortunatus, mentions the wines of Gaza, Crete, Samos, and Cyprus, which in his
time were to be found on the dinner tables of aristocratic Franks.
From such evidence, and other scraps of information, it becomes
clear why the natives of the Near East were in Frankish territory:
they were merchants, and they were there to make a living.[14]
One might wish to know more about the trade between Merovingian France and the Near East. What articles, in addition to wines,
were traded? What trade routes were followed? What was the volume of the trade? Was this commerce exclusively in the hands of
the guilds? If one wishes for such knowledge, probably one will
wish in vain. Such information was confidential, or else so common and so widely known that no one saw the necessity of writing
it down.

In the early years of the seventeenth century, to take another
example, there was a spate of European travelers to Iran, or Persia
as it was then called. The travelers, gentlemen adventurers, ambas-
sadors, and religious missionaries, left accounts of their travels that
are well known to historians. But if one reads the accounts with
care it is obvious that the chroniclers were traveling routes that
had been known to European merchants for decades, if not for
centuries.[15] Those who wrote accounts of their travels stayed at
inns that catered to European merchants; they were guided by
natives who made their living by guiding Western merchants; and
the travelers bought their supplies from vendors who gained a
livelihood by supplying such traders. In our own early West, Fremont, whose travels are amply recorded, is known as the "pathfinder," but everyone with an interest in the American West
knows that the pathfinder was guided along his route by the
beaver traders and trappers.

Not only have the vast numbers of traders remained anonymous
through centuries, but those who made the articles of commerce
are as anonymous as the merchants who sold the articles. Some
years ago in London there was an exhibition of tools used by the
artisans of ancient Rome: trowels, spokeshaves, planes, hammers,
files, saws, and chisels. The remarkable fact that immediately

struck the visitor to the exhibition was how little the shape of
tools had changed. It is doubtful that toolmakers learned to make
tools by reading books; it is highly probable that they learned
their craft by being apprenticed to toolmakers, and how those
articles ought to be shaped, how balanced and tempered, was
knowledge passed down through generations of toolmakers. If
the continuity were lost, the artisans of a later age had the artifacts of the earlier times as models. Each article or tool was slowly, very slowly, changed so that it was handier to use and more
efficient. Almost every American family has an axe. The handle
of that common object has a very uncommon shape. It is comfort-
able to the hand; it curves in one direction and then in the other,
varying in thickness and in cross-section. It is not easy to identify
the designing genius who made the first axehandle. Perhaps, even
probably, there was none, only an artisan or many artisans saw
how the handle could be improved and changed it until it attained
its present shape.

The traders of Merovingian France, the makers of tools, and the
designers of axehandles are largely anonymous, but there is no
reason to conclude that their lives were nasty, brutish, and short;
that they were rude, illiterate, and untaught. They corresponded
with associates, bought land, made contracts, were married, had
children, and these facts were in all probability recorded by nota-
ries, or records were deposited in public record offices, or letters
were filed in commercial houses, records that have now been lost
or else are still extant and neglected. The myriads of activities that
make up the culture of a people are only slightly described in
books, and the reading of books has had little to do, speaking
generally, with shaping those activities. Experience, tradition, accumulated wisdom and the lack of it, handed down from generation to generation, have been the chief agencies.

The two cultures—the one vast, energetic, teeming with the life
of millions, the other confined to a relatively small subgroup—existed side by side; the small group relying on libraries for what was
essential to their lives, and the people as a whole, insofar as they
needed documents, relying on record offices. Both groups were
literate, both were intelligent. It did not seem unnatural up until
the nineteenth century that there should be a small group with the
time and means to read books and pursue culture, and a mass of
people whose active lives required that only a minor segment of
their time should be devoted to creating and reading documents
and records. But in the nineteenth century, nudged along by the
fact that thousands of upper-class French had recently been made

shorter by a head, as an Elizabethan might put it, the European upper classes, among them those devoted to culture, became suddenly solicitous for the well-being of the millions who were the bearers and creators of the anthropologists' culture.[16] It was a little difficult to be solicitous about merchants and artisans, but those below them were susceptible to solicitude, and so there blossomed among the upper classes a concern for the well-being of the poor, the unfortunate, and the unskilled. An effort was made by some of the leisure class to attend to a wide variety of the needs of the lower social orders, those who would do good banding together to achieve good works.

"This is the age of Societies," Macaulay remarked; "There is scarcely one Englishman in ten who has not belonged to some Association for distributing books, or for prosecuting them, for sending invalids to the hospitals, or beggars to the treadmill; for giving plate to the rich or blankets to the poor." The diversity of the aims of the societies referred to by Macaulay is indicated by their names. Some of them are:

The Association for the Relief of the Manufacturing and
    Labouring Poor;
Philanthropic Society, St. George's Fields, for Children of
    Criminal Parents and Young Delinquents;
Marine Society for Educating Poor Destitute Boys to the
    Sea;
School for Soldiers' Girls, at Chelsea, supported by Ladies;
The Society for Giving Effect to His Majesty's Proclamation
    against Vice and Immorality;
The Society for Promoting Christian Knowledge;
The Society for Promoting Religious Knowledge by Distribut-
    ing Books among the Poor;
The British Society for the Encouragement of Servants;
The Society for Giving Religious Instruction to the Negroes
    in the West Indies;
The Society for Giving Bibles to Soldiers and Sailors;
Society for the Relief of Poor Pious Clergymen;
Royal Institution for Applying the Arts to the Common
    Purposes of Life;
Welsh Hospital for Decayed Natives of Wales;
Magdalen Hospital for the Admission of Seduced Females;
Society for the Support of Poor Artists and Their Widows;
Society for the Support of Decayed Musicians, Their Widows
    and Children;

Society for the Relief of Decayed Actors;
ABC-darian Society for the Relief of Decayed Schoolmasters;
Society for the Relief of Authors in Distress;
Society for Bettering the Condition, and Increasing the
    Comforts of the Poor;
Charitable Society for Industrious Poor.[17]

Generally the efforts of the upper classes in Britain to aid the
lower classes took on a familiar nineteenth-century pattern. How
could one aid the natives of darkest Africa? The answer was simple. Send them Christian missionaries and make them more like us.
How could one aid the benighted native women of Hawaii? The
answer was simple. Dress them in housedresses so that they will
look more like us. The answer to the question "How can one aid
the lower orders in Britain?" was equally simple. Have them read
the books we read so they will think and act as we do. Those
below the leisure class in the social hierarchy were not, in fact,
behindhand in their reading. Those of the middle class were
diverting themselves with middling good fiction and a great deal of
religious reading. The poor and the working classes were reading
penny ballads and unbelievably bad fiction. The upper classes concentrated their efforts to do good on the lower classes. These were
the people who were to change their reading and become more
like the upper classes. A very prestigious society, the Society for
the Diffusion of Useful Knowledge, was formed, designed to induce artisans to read improving books. It is a mild statement to say
that the books on useful knowledge published by the Society were
not a success. The books sold, but all of the evidence available
points to the fact that they were bought by professional people
and by ladies and gentlemen rather than by working people. The
Society also published a series for working people called the Library of Entertaining Knowledge, which included such titles as
*Insect Architecture, The Elephant Principally Viewed in Relation
to Man, Two Volumes on Paris and Its Historical Scenes,* a volume
on the Elgin Marbles, one on Egyptian antiquities, and another on
the unfortunate city of Pompeii. The idea was that a docker, after
a hard day in the rain and wind on the London docks, would come
home and, if not up to a treatise on the mechanics of the steam
engine, would relax with a volume on Egyptian antiquities. It appears that not many, if any, dockers did so relax. A little over
thirty years after the Society for the Diffusion of Useful Knowledge began, a writer in *Blackwood's Magazine* asked the rhetorical
question "Who now remembers the Society for the Diffusion of

Useful Knowledge?" The writer recalled somewhat sheepishly the efforts on behalf of the lower classes. "Those unfortunate masses. . . . " he wrote. "How we laboured to bring ourselves down to the capacity of that unknown intelligence, the working man. How we benevolently volunteered to amuse him in a profitable and edifying way by histories and descriptions of the ingenious crafts, and nice accounts of how they make pins, and laces and china, or how a steam engine is put together."[18]

The nineteenth century also saw the beginning not only of books for the working classes but of libraries for workers and the lower classes. Beginning about 1820, mechanics' institutes were formed, and after them lyceums, intended not for mechanics, but for lesser-skilled workers, and these, too, had libraries. Settlement houses were founded, which gave courses for the poor and the downtrodden, and they also had libraries; and in England there were active movements to place circulating libraries in the tenements of the poor.[19]

Tenement libraries have disappeared. Such mechanics' institutes and lyceums as survive in Britain have become middle-class clubs. The fault of the nineteenth-century uplift movement was that it neglected a pattern of society that was thousands of years old. It neglected to note carefully the culture of a people as an anthropologist would examine it, and assumed that the culture of the upper-class few ought to be the culture of the people as a whole; that the library, the indispensable tool for culture in Arnold's sense, must be indispensable for all activities of the national culture. It was a bizarre and unreasonable assumption. It would be unreasonable to expect that Isadora, the castanets dancing girl, after concluding her contract with her latest employer and filing it with the local scribe, should then repair to the library at Alexandria, and there be transformed into a nice bluestocking lady, studying to ascertain the best that had been known and said in the world. It would be odd if the Syrian merchant, who with great labor had succeeded in bringing a shipment of Samos wine to Merovingian Paris, should then seek out the nearest monastic library, there to study the writings of classical antiquity. The typical life patterns of merchants and dancing girls did not, and probably now do not, include systematic visits to libraries. It is not in their life style.

The nineteenth-century uplifters neglected the fact that the age-old and necessary depository of documents in any culture was the public record office, and that such offices were created before libraries of the best thoughts were created, that societies could and did develop a high degree of culture with public record offices but without libraries. It is perhaps true that the bookish tend to make the mistake of the nineteenth-century uplifters. How does one improve the lot of the unbookish? How does one bring sweetness and light to the butcher, the baker, the corporation accountant; to jet pilots, generals, and general contractors? The answer is simple: by making them bookish, of course. The error is a common one. The lament of the professor in *My Fair Lady* was, men being such splendid chaps, why could women not be like them? It is assumed by the intellectual and the artistic that their culture is better than the culture of the people as a whole, and that their culture ought to be extended to the people as a whole. It is not easy to account for the assumption that the life of a critic is in all cases better than that of a cabinetmaker. It is difficult to find reliable statistics that would lead one to such a belief. There is a dearth of evidence proving that the cultured are more generous, just, courageous, kind, content, and magnanimous than are the uncultured.

These observations are not intended to disparage either culture seekers or the indispensable adjunct to culture seeking, libraries. The happy few who seek culture and seek out libraries enjoy almost universal approbation, and rightly so, for theirs is an arduous life. They are in libraries day after day, month after month, year after year. They are there on Washington's birthday, and Lincoln's birthday, on the fourth of July, Ground Hog Day, Sadie Hawkins Day, and Guy Fawkes Day. They labor in silence and in solitude. Their life is known in some degree to all who are here. They put in ten dreary hours to be rewarded by ten minutes of exaltation, but they persist in their labors because they know that culture is acquired in no other way; and, despite the promises of the primrose pathers in education, there can be no other way. But the makeup of societies and cultures that are thousands of years old is not much influenced by the small number who seek culture, nor the onward and upward spirit of the nineteenth century. Libraries remain peripheral in the culture of the people as a whole. The teeming multitude, a large segment of it highly literate, files briefs in law courts, land titles in the county recorder's office, and baptismal records in the church. Those who compose it correspond voluminously as individuals and as corporations. They belong in a pattern of culture that is as legitimate as our own and of far greater antiquity. When at leisure they may go to the library or they may relax in contemplation of the awesome skills of the Astros, the Rangers, the Cowboys, and the Oilers. It would be more in the traditional pattern if they did the latter.

Notes

1. Neither the *New English Dictionary* nor the *Century Dictionary* gives uses of the word *culture*, in the senses in which the word is used here, before the nineteenth century. The two cultures described here are not identical with the two cultures of C. P. Snow.
2. *Seventh Epistle*; *Protagoras*, 329; *Phaedras*, 275.
3. James Westfall Thompson, *Ancient Libraries* (Hamden, Conn.: Archon Books, 1962), p. 23.
4. Ibid., p. 41.
5. J. D. A. Ogilvy, *Books Known to the English, 597-1066* (Cambridge, Mass.: Medieval Academy of America, 1967), passim.
6. About 3,000 Sumerian tablets have been discovered that are literary compositions. There are hundreds of thousands of legal records, wills, business papers, and court decisions. David Diringer, *The Alphabet: A Key to the History of Mankind* (New York: Philosophical Library, 1948), p. 49; Samuel Noah Kramer, *History Begins at Sumer* (Garden City, N.Y.: Doubleday, 1959), pp. xix-xx.
About 4,000 tablets were discovered near the ancient city of Nuzi. These were family or temple archives. Edward Chiera, *They Wrote on Clay: The Babylonian Tablets Speak Today* (Chicago: University of Chicago Press, 1938), p. 177. The tablets discovered at Tell El-Amarna were largely diplomatic correspondence, ibid., p. 202 ff. A large number of tablets discovered near the ancient city of Caesarea belonged to a large group of Assyrian merchants who had settled in that part of Asia Minor, ibid., p. 212. In the great temple of Boghaz-Keui, the ancient capital of Hattushash, 10,000 fragments of clay tablets were discovered. These were the official archives of the Hittite Kingdom. Ernst Doblhofer, *Voices in Stone: The Decipherment of Ancient Scripts and Writings* (New York: Collier, 1971), p. 166.
7. Thompson, *Ancient Libraries*, p. 21.
8. M. David and B. A. van Groningen, *Papyrological Primer* (Leyden: E. J. Brill, 1965), p. 5.
9. Ibid., p. 22.
10. Ibid., p. 34.
11. Ibid., p. 47.
12. Ibid., p. 82.
13. Ibid., p. 94.
14. Nils Åberg, *The Occident and the Orient in the Art of the Seventh Century*, 3 vols. (Stockholm: Wahlström and Widstrand, 1943-1947), part 3, *The Merovingian Empire* (1947), pp. 18-19.
15. The reader is referred to the author's *Elizabethans Errant: The Strange Fortunes of Sir Thomas Sherley and His Three Sons . . .* (Ithaca, N.Y.: Cornell University Press, 1967).
16. The reader is referred to the author's *Public Libraries as Culture and Social Centers: The Origin of the Concept* (Metuchen, N.J.: Scarecrow Press, 1974). It is noted in the work referred to that there were instances in which workers themselves sought to form libraries that would bring them culture, but the efforts by workers were a small fraction of the total effort to bring culture to the lower classes.
17. The present writer's *An Enquiry into the Reading of the Lower Classes* (Pasadena, Calif.: Grant Dahlstrom, 1970), p. 31.

18. Ibid., p. 41.
19. There is an account of such libraries in the writer's *Public Libraries as Culture and Social Centers.*

Cultural Institutions and American Modernization

Neil Harris

I am delighted to be attending this conference, and addressing you tonight. But I do so with some trepidation. Knowing next to nothing about the history of libraries, I speak to those who know almost everything. I expect, therefore, to be both abstract and opinionated.

In preparation, however, I did some homework, reviewing recent literature treating the history of American libraries and renewing acquaintance with a set of classic texts. I was certainly unprepared for the vigorous, intense, and complex scholarly squalls I soon encountered. The names of Michael Harris, Dee Garrison, John Colson, Elaine Fain, and Phyllis Dain are familiar to you all, but they introduced to me some fascinating debates concerning purpose and policy in our public library movement. I followed the discussion from the philosophy of Andrew Carnegie through the cultural values of New York immigrant groups. Running through most of the contributions was a concern, voiced again and again, that American library historians join (or rejoin) the main body of our historiography, share its critical methods, and participate in its major issues. The urgency of this demand grew so self-conscious as occasionally to seem self-defeating. Nevertheless, however telescoped, the recent debate has indeed aided this task of reintegration.

This change in historiographical emphasis, however, has not been accomplished without cost. And that cost may be an understanding of the complex relationship between the founding of our

Neil Harris *is professor of history at the University of Chicago.*

Journal of Library History, Vol. 16, No. 1, Winter 1981
©1981 by the University of Texas Press   0275-3650/81/010028-20$02.00

cultural institutions and the ongoing efforts to modernize national society. By bridging the historiographical gap with an ideological connection, the controversy gains strength but the subject is occasionally obscured. I am, I must admit, uncomfortable with the term *modernization*, particularly when it is applied to modern American history. It has become something of a buzzword among social scientists, and when coupled with detailed historical models it inevitably begs some questions. But I know of no surrogate for this notion of a society developing rituals, values, skills, legal relationships, structures, expectations, life experiences, functional to fundamental economic and technological changes.[1] In America the modernized world would be dominated by the principles of industrial capitalism and mass democracy; accompanying the shift were inevitable rearrangements in work and leisure, family and class structures, savings and consumption patterns.

I believe that historical understanding of our cultural institutions involves making sense of their position within this broad movement. The status, rhetoric, and strategies of the founders and early administrators suggest their concern, from one standpoint or another, with this relationship. But before we can examine the connections, we must contend with a significant historiographical shift that has taken place among cultural historians within the last two decades, a more combative and critical stance toward our institutions, which has served as a bridge for the public library debate to enter the larger arena. This shift has sharpened our vision, but also, in some cases, distorted our aim. Having abandoned one set of presentist dead ends, we may be constructing another. Let me specify my observations by moving through three different but related subjects this evening. First, identifying and accounting for the massive historiographical change I have just referred to. Secondly, raising some questions about its conclusions and their relationship to modernization. And third, most briefly, reflecting upon the connection between history and contemporary policy debates.

Twenty-five years ago most histories of cultural institutions were self-confident and optimistic. Almost any institution that had managed to survive—zoo, hospital, library, museum, college, professional society—was admired, a tribute to sacrificing founders bent on combining the democratic genius with obvious needs for enlightenment, recreation, standardization, or reform. It was a credit, also, to patient clients and supporters who nurtured these institutions when they were young and vulnerable, and saw them mature into strong and influential entities, capable of commissioning, or at least sustaining, a historical narrative.

These were, in the large, company histories. Their authors were not unaware of larger currents of argument, or the multiplication of scholarly monographs. Indeed, they supplemented their observations with references to major figures like Beard, Turner, Parrington, Schlesinger, Fish, and others. Charles Beard's notion, for example, that social and cultural institutions were not automatic responses to challenge but rested on intent, analysis, and deliberation, all deserving scrutiny, helped stimulate historical investigation of subjects like the museum and the library, neglected because taken for granted.[2] Any number of institutional historians were sustained by the status of the new scientific history introduced from Europe through the seminar system, which had led to rigorous analysis of the evolution of American political instruments like the town meeting, universal suffrage, federalism, and party competition. Fond in their early days of employing "germ" metaphors to indicate their concern with institutional roots, these historians happily drew on the prestige and comprehensiveness of the Spencerian persuasion, that grafting of Darwinian theory to social analysis. These institutional narratives were as much influenced by the genial determinism of evolutionary history as was the better-known new political and economic history. Primary energy frequently went into cataloguing the predisposing factors encouraging the creation of an institution. Judgment was exercised by evaluating their comparative strength.

This is not to say that these historians presented no conflicts or tensions. Some cultural institutions were begun too late, and perished because they were unequal to the occasion or to the problem. Others were born too early, and had to await refunding or reformulation. There was occasional veniality, mismanagement, and fanaticism. Useful changes could arouse bitter resistance, and there was always the presence of conservatives moving too slowly or radicals moving too fast. But in general there were few guiding questions to help shape what inevitably became a homogeneous, affirmative, and noncritical literature, concerned with demonstrating an almost teleological necessity for the emergence of particular institutions, and supplying a wealth of detail that permitted some kind of chronological organization to emerge.

This, I repeat, was the condition of a broad range of institutional history in the fields of education and culture. If intellectual whiggism was inevitable, immense amounts of labor reconstructed long-buried traditions and helped preserve and organize invaluable records. While burdened with the tasks of simply creating coherent narratives, these historians often managed quite evocatively to summarize the eloquent calls to arms that initially activated so many of the organizations they described. And their texts still form the substantive basis of our current knowledge. What they did not do was supply any set of tests, questions, or arguments that could be extracted and applied to other areas or other institutions. Despite their sensitivity to ongoing historical generalizations, the books were institution-specific in all but the blandest ways. And, to some extent, they were out of touch with popular opinion and revisionist historiography at large, both of which raised questions about the motives, conduct, and impact of many of these same institutions.

Thus Thorstein Veblen, for example, had been able to turn upside down this benevolent and affirmative evolutionism into an ironic and uproarious set of juxtapositions; these colored popular consciousness, and even sophisticated historians who concentrated on other areas accepted Veblenian notions of conspicuous consumption and pecuniary emulation. But institutional historians tended to ignore such critiques when they examined single subjects or communities. They were sealed off from this critical tradition. Indeed, the Veblenian polemic did not really service serious intellectual investigation; if it supported anything, it nourished a vague, often unspecified set of grievances about the character of our high culture, making it out to be forbidding, irrelevant, vulgar, or self-interested. There seemed little connection between popular attitudes to libraries, universities, museums, and schools and the histories written about them, partly, perhaps, because the density of detail and repetition of argument gave institutional histories little interest to the lay public.

But then something happened. Beginning, perhaps, in the late 1950s, quickening in the 1960s, and multiplying still further in the 1970s, a set of speculations, investigations, and monographs transformed what I take to have been a somewhat sluggish field into one of the liveliest arenas of historical debate, so comprehensive and sharply etched that it affected both public conceptions and the work of scholars in other disciplines. Dozens of books and many times that number of articles spelled out, in these years, a set of critical and sometimes hostile questions about the beneficence, disinterestedness, and effectiveness of some of our most revered cultural institutions, applying in their examinations a range of new techniques and an international context. Listing these books and articles in their entirety or even in numbers suggesting their influence would be tedious; let me recount a few titles, however, to indicate their variety of subject matter: Daniel Calhoun, *Professional Lives in America* (1965); Roger Lane, *Policing the City* (1967); Michael Katz, *The Irony of Early School Reform* (1968); David Rothman, *The Discovery of the Asylum* (1971); Anthony Platt, *The Child-Savers* (1969); David F. Noble, *America by Design* (1977); Marvin Lazerson, *Origins of the Urban School* (1971); Stanley Schultz, *The Culture Factory*; Helen L. Horowitz, *Culture and the City* (1976); Jerold Auerbach, *Unequal Justice* (1976); Laurence R. Veysey, *The Emergence of the American University* (1965).[3] There are forthcoming monographs on the history of American hospitals, baseball and sports management, prisons, and other subjects, which promise to continue this critical tradition and to provoke renewed controversy and debate. And this, of course, is in addition to the heated discussions among library historians, and the biographical research that in some instances has contributed to the revisionist thrust. What happened to produce a historiographical movement with so broad a sweep, so many common concerns, and such powerful effects? There are a number of reasons that deserve exploration. Many of these fall within the profession itself, growing rapidly in number during these same years, fed on one end by expanding Ph.D. programs producing larger numbers of dissertations, and nourished on the other by growing college and university systems meant to provide ultimate employment for the new scholars.

But growth was merely one of the general conditions. There were others more specific. First of all came the appearance of classic texts, books that became exemplary and influential as a result of their cogency, persuasiveness, and obvious applications. One of these books appeared in 1960, during the early years of the larger historiographical movement; its contribution to revisionism is interesting the attacks mounted by radical historians some years later. That was Bernard Bailyn's *Education in the Forming of American Society*, which helped make American educational history one of the shock fronts for radical speculation about institutional history, a model-bringer to many other areas of historical research. Bailyn's impact came about not only through his specific arguments about early American educational history or his exploration of the social functions of formal institutions. These were important. But it was his commentary upon the historiographical tradition he confronted that gave his book such special status, his concern with the depressing effects of historical plenitude.

Bailyn was, after all, evaluating a field rich with monographs and syntheses. But despite the scale of historical research, we had "almost no historical leverage on the problems of American education. The facts, or at least a great quantity of them, are there, but they lie inert; they form no significant pattern."[4] The reason for this, Bailyn argued, again in terms that had great meaning for institutional historians generally, was that the history of education had been written and taught by educationists, by missionaries whose scholarly activity constituted a demonstration of the theoretical and procedural centrality of their own institutions. Thus the schools were "self-contained entities whose development had followed an inner logic and an innate propulsion." The restriction of educational history to formal instruction, argued Bailyn, resulted from a conviction that "the past was simply the present writ small. It differed from the present in the magnitudes and arrangement of its elements, not in their character. The ingredients of past and present were the same. . . . They had no capacity for surprise." These creators of institutional history "lacked the belief, the historian's instinct, that the elements of their world might not have existed at all for others, might in fact have been inconceivable to them, and that the real task is to describe the dawning of ideas and the creation of forms—surprising, strange, and awkward then, however familiar they may have become since—in response to the changing demands of circumstance." Institutions represented solutions to problems then, rather than predetermined or preordained symbols of progress. Their origins were not understood because scholars approached them with condescension. Seeking familiarity "in an unfamiliar past," these historians "had no choice but to accept crude facsimiles, deceptive cognates." This foreshortening produced a past differentiated from the present "mainly by its primitivism, the rudimentary character of the institutions and ideas whose ultimate development the writers were privileged to know so well."[5] Such condescension exaggerated the quaintness of the institutional ancestry, and sacrificed indispensable historical leverage.

I think Bailyn's remarks offer an exceptionally perceptive glimpse into the structure of the earlier historiography, into the relationship between the authors' assumptions and their modes of investigation. In the opening pages to his book Bailyn did far more than open up the question of public education, or insist upon the need to integrate questions of family structure, denominationalism, economic activity, and land ownership with educational theory. He also provided a charter of liberation for historians who wished to escape the constraints professional loyalties had imposed upon institutional history. The peculiar combination of presentism and condescension that Bailyn diagnosed would survive in newer, more disguised forms; Bailyn's call for approaching earlier social history with respect for difference, complexity, and surprise was not invariably obeyed. But his suggestion that institutions be examined, not necessarily as revelations of cultural strength but also as demonstrations of social weakness, building upon the disintegration of traditional structures, would help color the working world of institutional historians for the next twenty years.

There were other classic texts besides Bailyn's, some of them produced in Europe by a group of French and British historians, who had broadened the subject matter of historical investigation to include activities and values that had never quite attained legitimacy in the United States, ranging from what would later be known as material culture to the study of alchemy, magic, witchcraft, and mental disease. In the pages of some of their journals, particularly *Annales* and *Past and Present*, and the work of Braudel, Bloch, E. P. Thompson, and Brian Harrison, a set of traditions was being created that would feed later institutional work.[6]

Their texts, in fact, bring up a second source for this historiographical revolution, and that was the steadily easier communication, during these twenty years, between historians and their colleagues in the humanities and social sciences. Interdisciplinary fashions now pervaded university curricula and foundation grants, and inevitably affected the character of historical research. Taste for other fields was catholic, and many of the trends had little to do with institutional history. But many of them did, particularly in anthropology, political science, and sociology. I need mention only the names of Simmel, Parsons, Lévi-Strauss, Lazarsfield, Adorno, Mannheim, Foucault, Goffman, Durkheim, and Gramsci to give some sense of their scope and variety. Increasingly, historians were arming themselves with theoretical insights before constructing research projects, and using them to help form a narrative strategy. While such influences produced many different outcomes, the heavy concern with mass society and collective behavior and the role of Marxist social science, so rich a source for European thinking, both proved eminently useful to historians of culture. With the assumption of a more critical view of the development of society and a conviction that institutions reflected, in some measure, both the level of economic organization and the division of power, a range of new questions was opened up. Individual institutions could be placed within a landscape acknowledging their particularity but assigning them specific functions. Ideal types provided a set of standards, a scale system by which to weigh the impact of everything from professional associations and learned societies to newspapers and museums. Although the social sciences were used more heavily for certain classic areas of economic and social history, it was inevitable that the integrated social view they encouraged should stimulate new thinking about the evolution of culture itself.

All this was aided by still another historiographical stimulus, the creation of sophisticated generalizations that reworked the periodization of American history, and that drew upon the social sciences. Instead of relying upon once sacrosanct political subdivisions, historians like Richard Hofstadter and Robert Wiebe, George Mowry and Henry May, Gabriel Kolko and Sam Hays, provided new benchmarks to separate generations of people and generations of institutions.[7] The functions of status revolutions, efficiency ideals, bureaucratic management, and technological imperatives invaded histories of politics, judicial decision making, industrial growth, and urban government, inviting once again new statements about the symbolic function and intended role of the cultural institutions.

To all of these historiographical influences—supplemented by the growing popularity of methods like prosopography—must be added new social and professional attitudes held by many American scholars coming to intellectual maturity during the 1960s and 1970s. Replacing an older set of satisfactions with the development of major cultural institutions, a sense of victories won and successes gained, were a long list of discontents, suspicions, and criticisms. These focused on the unequal distribution of power within American life, the continued exploitation of minorities, the power of sexual discrimination, the military adventurism of American governments, the enormous power of advertising and corporate influence, and the co-optation, by those with economic and political power, of cultural institutions that had once appeared to be independent or at least neutral. Indeed many protesting intellectuals in the sixties and seventies took it as their mission to demystify relationships between power and culture so as to indicate the overwhelming strength of the establishment and its capacity to shape any set of values or institutions. Classic figures in American political or social reform from Horace Mann and John Dewey to Jane Addams and Walter Lippmann were redefined and reclassified as futile or paradoxical gestures in the face of a larger movement of economic rationalization. Modernity was seen as a set of repressions, exerted through the same instruments of culture that had once been portrayed as liberating or enlightening. Social control was the goal of the powerful, fear of disorder or revolution their anxiety, and civilization but another name for the translation of their obsession with order. The free market, mobility, individualism, and equality were basically rhetorical strategies, for they contained contradictory tendencies that could never be simultaneously achieved.[8]

This bundle of dissatisfactions, which built upon undeniable frustrations and realistic fears, was as influential upon historians as earlier consensual satisfactions had been. Obviously it did not affect all who wrote institutional history, nor all professionals who traced the evolution of their specialties. But it posed a set of dynamic questions for institutional historians. Instead of a success story, one could now develop tragic failure, institutions exploiting and even worsening the plight of those whom they claimed to serve and benefit. Created by privilege, cultural institutions serviced the needs of privilege. There did not need to be villains or evildoers in this process, cardboard caricatures who had for so long dominated late nineteenth century political history. That was the beauty of the new arguments. For there was self-delusion as well as purposiveness involved, not only on the part of founders and donors but also of professionals and administrators. Teachers, principals, doctors, lawyers, hospital administrators, university professors, settlement house workers, guidance counselors, librarians, may indeed have believed in the social utility of their labor, the neutrality or beneficence of their professional standards, or the value of their social prejudices. But in fact such individual commitments were not the crucial aspects of the larger institutional effects. Whether or not their planners and governors realized it, such institutions expressed, through their rituals of use, their appearance, their patterns of consumption, their presentation of values and information, the driving needs of an economic system that required the maintenance of unequal power distributions, passively satisfied labor forces, punctual, obedient, industrious workers and ambitious, hungry, manipulable consumers.[9] The logic of cultural institutions—those concerned with instruction, certification, indoctrination, and entertainment—was conservative and designed to strengthen the system as it was already structured.

The monographs and syntheses concerned with a revisionist interpretation of these institutions ranged far back in American history, some of them confronting the colonial period, others exam-

ining the Age of Jackson and the purported radical democracy of
free school and asylum reformers like Dorothea Dix and Horace
Mann. But the period enjoying most attention was the late nineteenth and early twentieth centuries, when wealth, need, urban
growth, and immigration combined to create the system of cultural institutions that still survives in the form of public school systems, universities, libraries, museums, and professional and learned
associations. It was a period of special ingenuity and creativity so
far as the shaping and direction of cultural institutions are concerned, but also one of extraordinary instability and social unrest.
Thus the very institutional creativity could be explained in terms
of the special challenges conservatives faced, the intensity of their
anxieties being related to the increasing pace of foreign immigration, violent strikes, the spectre of international socialism, and a
new political radicalism. Many of these institutions had to invent
the very diseases they were meant to treat, because without a
sense of social defects they could hardly be justified. So juvenile
delinquency became popular as a device for justifying the institu-
tionalization of potentially dangerous youngsters from unstable or
broken families. And mental disease was specified and redefined in
an effort to remove other sources of social instability.

Institutions with overtly compulsory aims—schools, hospitals,
prisons, asylums—do not exhaust the larger category. What of
those in which attendance was more voluntary, or whose certification was a response to individual ambition or mobility? Zoos, libraries, museums, universities, professional societies, all multiplied
rapidly during the Progressive Era.[10] Here some of the new history
has been particularly valuable in categorizing the variant forms
that emerged and tying them to specific social needs: coping with
the vast increase of information and of records, with the requirements of expert training, particularly in the sciences, with the development of professionally specialized subcultures, and providing
avenues of instruction, amusement, diversion, or inspiration for an
increasingly urbanized industrial population.[11]

It is here that we come to the question that interests me most,
and for which, I add, I have no easy answer. How instrumental
were these new cultural institutions in meeting the social needs of
a modernizing society, in lubricating the economic and political
engines of progress? The assumption, unspoken in many cases, of
some contemporary cultural historians is that, in fact, these institutions were supported by monied or politically powerful elites
because they would contribute to the security and efficiency of
the community as a whole. One historian of the library movement

concludes that public library support was "one of the movements of urban reform designed to cope with the problems of industrialized society. Seeking orderly cohesion, library leadership was essentially conservative in purpose and sought to impose the cultural and social norms of the upper class." But were the cultural and social norms of this class appropriate to American modernization or not? For Dee Garrison goes on to say that the result of this movement was an estrangement between the public library and the working-class community, a divorce between library ideology and reality, an emphasis upon critical functions and irrelevant if traditional values. "Like other custodians of culture in this era," she concludes, "the librarian tended to resist, rather than to facilitate, the coming of modern values."[12] With this last statement I agree. Many of the custodians of culture, although not all, did resist modern values. But what, in fact, are such values? The only indication given in this context is that modern values have something to do with democratic reality.

But if we include modernization in the category of the modern, we must also examine, among other things, first, the increasing specialization of social and economic functions, the new professionalism with its lengthened training periods and modes of certification; second, the greater emphasis, in production, advertising, and marketing, upon mass consumption and the creation of hungry and manipulable consumers; third, a secularizing insistence upon rationality and bureaucratic efficiency rather than sentiment or religion as the source for social reform and the basis for human relationships; fourth, a bias toward national integration, economic, social, and cultural, and an increasing reliance upon planning; and finally, an ever-larger role for government as arbiter, standard-setter, rate-fixer, regulator, and taxer. Occupational specialization, consumer orientation, efficiency-based values, national integration, and governmental supervision: these were all aspects of the modernizing process, well under way by the early twentieth century.

And this, I believe, introduces a new complexity. For these objectives were not necessarily inherently democratic, nor, on the other hand, were they associated with the upper-class elites, resistant to majoritarian democracy. If libraries, museums, or universities questioned or resisted some of these trends, they were not necessarily seeking to redress the distribution of power. They or their organizers were rather engaged in a struggle to govern the course of this modernization and the organizational logic of the modern world. We are less aware of this fact than we should be, because many of the new institutional studies do not clearly reconstruct the old alternatives, or suggest the kinds of choices institutions represented. Goals and motives were highly mixed, and subservience to political establishment was not the invariable result.

One of the cultural revisionists has, rather eloquently, reminded us how easily misinterpretation can develop. Anthony Platt, introducing a second edition of his book, *The Child Savers: The Invention of Delinquency*, eight years after its initial publication, confessed that he had failed to relate the movement to other institutions of the new welfare state, or to explain the timing of its appearance, its sources of support, or the nature of the opposition. "Criticism," Platt concluded, in self-reproach, "no matter how well documented and substantiated, is an insufficient basis for action unless it is grounded in an overall conceptual framework and a thorough understanding of history."[13] By criticizing reformers who created the juvenile court system, his book seemed to imply that they alone were responsible for its unpleasant consequences, and that more enlightened people could have constructed a better system. Drawing such an inference, Platt insisted, was improper, for it ignored the actual alternatives of the day.

It is this recovery of alternatives, of both the symbolic and practical implications of institution-founding, that will constitute its real integration with the larger field. The evocation of complexity and surprise, ambition and anxiety, which Bailyn described, seems called for. From my own work I believe that many cultural institutions were formed to reshape aspects of modernization, in the name of traditional values. But these values often sat uncomfortably with the new lords of business and commerce, the political power brokers, and the new professionals and efficiency experts. Just as we have rediscovered the power of the domestic sphere as an alternative as well as a helpmeet to worldliness, so the nature of culture as a value system in itself must help shape the new institutional history. Here the names of Carlyle, Ruskin, Morris, and Arnold are vitally important as spokesmen for an ideology that was, in part, anti-industrial and antimodernist.[14] This ideology contained, to be sure, particularly in its English manifestation, elements of what is now labeled elitism, and greeted democracy skeptically as the spread of political democracy.

But in important ways this antidemocratic sentiment was diverted, in America, toward a concern with personal fulfillment and individualistic moral and aesthetic standards. We are just beginning to understand, for example, the powerful dimensions of that large

and multifaceted artistic movement that paralleled the official
American Renaissance of McKim, Mead and White, and Daniel
Burnham, and has been labeled the Arts and Crafts Movement.
Here, for several decades, a search for personal expression and a
revulsion against aspects of the new industrialization combined to
produce widespread activity in the creation and consumption of
furniture, glass, pottery, printing, weaving, and bookbinding, activities representing a defection from the mass-produced trends of
the new factories, department stores, and mail-order houses.[15] In
various cities like Chicago, Detroit, and Boston, members of the
movement were involved in the policymaking of the new libraries
and museums. We know, moreover, that some businesspeople were
openly hostile to the goals of collegiate liberal education. The insistence upon common instruction in art, history, philosophy, literature, and science as sources of personal integration, critical
thought, and social harmony, was opposed by advocates of voca-
tionalism. It is true that many apologists for liberal culture held
conservative social goals. But they also argued that colleges and
universities could strengthen values resistant to efficiency-oriented
modern trends. The paradox that lay at the heart of Progressive
educational methods—socialization to a competitive socioeconomic order through immersion within a cooperative, comprehensive
school society—affected many other cultural institutions as well.

And so did the knowledge that this might produce critical discontent with the arrangements of modern life. Both adaptation
and resistance were mingled. Thus American museums were born,
in part, from anxiety about the poverty of American design, the
apparent inability to compete effectively with European makers of
jewelry, silver, furniture, and textiles. Businesspeople were interested in developing the taste of both artisan and customer, and
comprehensive historical exhibitions of the applied arts could
help. The museum was an aid to early industrial design training,
and the museum movement can be seen as part of a modernizing
impulse toward improving American productive efficiency.[16] But
museums were also places to display masterpieces whose transcen-
dent aesthetic standards suggested something else, a world where
economic competition did not set values, and where the experience of the art encounter substituted, in its own fashion, for an
earlier generation's religious passion. The culture of the museum,
like the culture of the church, contained both sources of accommodation and sources of resistance to dominant social modes and
values.[17] Thus Josiah Royce (a central figure in R. Jackson Wilson's *In Quest of Community*), an opponent, like J. Mark Baldwin

and G. Stanley Hall, of regimentation, standardization, and modern rootlessness, sought in provincial museums, regional folklore, and the city beautiful a revival of local loyalties to limit the ongoing social disintegration.[18] Along with the museum, the university, the learned society, and the library combined in volatile quantities the modern era's capacity to gather, organize, and manipulate experience in the interest of modernity, and the same era's infatuation with the simpler verities of an earlier day.

Such division of loyalties may account for the arresting combinations of internal efficiency and external archaicism characteristic of the richer institutions. The newborn universities' dedicated researchers worked in laboratories modeled on medieval chapter houses, or in quadrangles that sought the instant appeal of antiquity. The libraries' efficient stack and delivery systems stood alongside muraled reading rooms or cloister courts, whose paint and marble instilled a sense of ages past to the visitor. The temple-like museums developed new labeling and display methodologies. It was not always clear whether such institutions were to be engines of culture, as one historian described the museum, or temples of culture, generators or asylums.[19]

Henry James, describing his return visit to America in 1904, caught this sense of institutional strain as he toured the Boston Public Library in Copley Square. Noting the hostility of social democrats to the survival of penetralia, so necessary, in James's view, for study and meditation, he was caught by the splendor of the Library building, the main staircase with its "amplitude of wing and its splendour of tawny marble, a high and luxurious beauty," bribing the visitor to enter a courtyard and inner arcade that, "when the afternoon light sadly slants," seemed like "one of the myriad gold-coloured courts of the Vatican."

This was all fine, but James was also caught by the Boston concern with amusing children on rainy afternoons in this great palace, "so many little heads bent over their story-books that the edifice took on at moments the appearance . . . of a lively distributing-house of the new fiction for the young." James found the notes of cloistered reserve and busy service to be bewildering. Could one, he asked rhetorically, "snatching the bread-and-molasses from their lips, cruelly deprive the young of rights in which they have been installed with a majesty nowhere else approaching that of their American installation?" Labeling such a question abysmal, he fled from the library straight to the Museum of Fine Arts, where he found only temporary consolation.[20]

What we can see then, in the foundation of our cultural institutions, are divided loyalties concerning the character of national modernization. Were our libraries, museums, and universities, or our theater companies, motion pictures, and paintings, to stand for anything in particular, to provide standards of reference to measure the character of progress or to raise questions about the values of punctuality, hard work, and consumer salvation? Or were they primarily instrumental in character, designed to respond to socioeconomic needs rather than to question them, to speed the socialization of the dispossessed, to aid the efficiency of production and consumption sought by major interests? This choice of strategy, which I have reduced, I fear, almost to the level of caricature, affected almost every level of institutional operation, from physical location and architectural style to ease of access, budgetary emphasis, and relationship to public authority. The choices cut in many directions. Service orientation might aid the mobility and self-education of ambitious immigrants, eager to participate in the larger culture; or it might simply satisfy the light reading needs of overworked clerks. Physical grandeur might inspire; or then again it might intimidate. Those institutions seeking simultaneously to be everything to everybody might find their resources dangerously overstrained. Institutions rarely contained representatives of only one point of view, and rarely maintained any single policy with total consistency over long periods of time. As we learn more from minute books, trustee meetings, newspaper accounts, dedicatory rhetoric, and abandoned plans, we will find more discrepancy, confusion, and uncertainty than some historians might have us believe. Coexisting within these institutions were unstable mixtures of preservation and popularization, dogmatism and tolerance, opposition to and acquiescence in mass taste. From an early date there is a surprising blending of high and popular culture in unlikely places such as Carnegie Hall, the Chicago Art Institute, and the Library of Congress. Whether the popular was acknowledged out of respect for its integrity or from a desire to reshape it is not always clear. But these institutions adopted a stance toward modernity that was both more skeptical and more probing than easy wisdom would suggest.

Before we can be sure of any conclusions we must know more about the history of libraries, museums, and universities as cultural institutions. I offer this summary as only one organizing device. But I offer it also because as a user of these institutions, particularly the library, I am not always encouraged by new statements of purpose. Increasingly, the road of total accommodation seems to be the preferred strategy, accommodation, that is, to directly utilitarian ends. Since our cultural institutions depend upon public subsidy, popular opinion must be a significant force in shaping policy. But not the only force. American popular opinion is itself affected by many factors, including the impact of political, institutional, and corporate advertising; it is not always either consistent or continuous. Private resources, endowments, self-perpetuating boards were once hedges against sudden shifts of opinion. They were often, admittedly, used to support unenlightened, narrow, and patronizing policies. But not always. The increasing insistence that institutions be cost-effective shifts the balance.

The older dream of bibliophilic grandeur is now passing from the scene. It was both a dream and a nightmare, as Jorge Luis Borges reminds us in his ironic, chilling, and mysterious tale "The Library of Babel." "Man, the imperfect librarian, may be the work of chance or of malevolent demiurges; the universe [which others call the Library], with its elegant endowment of shelves, of enigmatic volumes, of indefatigable ladders for the voyager, and of privies for the seated librarian, can only be the work of a god."[21] The image of the eternal stacks ebbs, replaced by intercommunicating data banks, whose network maintenance now dominates professional planning. Increasingly, inquiries must be packaged in content-specific terms; scholarly browsing, without apparent purpose, will be more difficult.

The approach to knowledge was once meant to possess, in itself, existential meaning. The encounter with the book, like the encounter with art, was supposedly distinguishable from commercial or industrial transactions. The cultural center, the art complex, was presented as an alternative world. This separation of spheres, I repeat, can be defined as acknowledgement that modern existence requires fragmented, atomized life sectors, specially shaped by distinctive purposes. Or it can be seen as a statement of resistance to the logic of modern commercial and work values. In any event, I believe that our earlier institutions were poised between a commitment to and a suspicion of the coming of modernity. The tension was accepted, by some, as a source of strength. Our present posture, perhaps through technological or fiscal imperatives, is more accommodative.

I confess that the more thought I have given this problem, the less certain I have become of any conclusions. Contemporary libraries and museums are classification systems that reflect our modern capacity to dominate experience by indexing and subdividing it. We can command the art and the knowledge of civilizations distant in time and space, but our very appetite for information and our rage for order can reduce and even trivialize their character, by deracinating belief systems and responses to experience.

On one level, then, the library and the museum are supreme tributes to the modernizing spirit, the same spirit that has produced a human-dominated nature, and specialized industrial societies governed by bureaucracies absorbed with the tasks of regulating and rationalizing the conduct of life.

But on another level, despite the fact that they are conceits, contrived assumptions of power, these institutions can be asylums of experience as well. They were once given semireligious powers of legitimation. In their expressive gestures, libraries, museums, and universities, archaic as they sometimes may have been, represented possible challenges to the new way of life. To understand more fully the nature of this symbolism we must, I believe, cast off formulas that make some ends seem more or less democratic or enfranchising. We must see the creation of these institutions as responses to a world grown surprising, bewildering, and disintegrating. In so doing, we can avoid a new Manicheanism, which threatens an exciting moment of historical research.

Notes

1. There is a vast literature relating to modernization theory. For one example of its application to American history, and some references to this literature, see Richard D. Brown, *Modernization: The Transformation of American Life, 1600–1865* (New York: Hill and Wang, 1976).
2. See the reference to Beard in one of these institutional histories: Gwladys Spencer, *The Chicago Public Library: Origins and Background* (Chicago: University of Chicago Press, 1943), p. xiii.
3. Daniel H. Calhoun, *Professional Lives in America: Structure and Aspiration, 1750–1850* (Cambridge, Mass.: Harvard University Press, 1965); Roger Lane, *Policing the City: Boston, 1822–1885* (Cambridge, Mass.: Harvard University Press, 1967); Michael B. Katz, *The Irony of Early School Reform: Educational Innovation in Mid-Nineteenth Century Massachusetts* (Cambridge, Mass.: Harvard University Press, 1968); David J. Rothman, *The Discovery of the Asylum: Social Order and Disorder in the New Republic* (Boston: Little, Brown, 1971); Anthony M. Platt, *The Child Savers: The Invention of Delinquency* (Chicago: University of Chicago Press, 1969, 1977); David F. Noble, *America by Design: Science, Technology, and the Rise of Corporate Capitalism* (New York: Knopf, 1977); Marvin Lazerson, *Origins of the Urban School: Public Education in Massachusetts, 1870–1915* (Cambridge, Mass.: Harvard University Press, 1971); Stanley K. Schultz, *The Culture Factory: Boston Public Schools, 1789–1860* (New York: Oxford University Press, 1973); Helen L. Horowitz, *Culture and the City: Cultural Philanthropy in Chicago from the 1880's to 1917* (Lexington, Ky.: University Press of Kentucky, 1976); Jerold S. Auerbach, *Unequal Justice: Lawyers and*

Social Change in Modern America (New York: Oxford University Press, 1976); Laurence R. Veysey, *The Emergence of the American University* (Chicago: University of Chicago Press, 1965). These books, of course, vary enormously in method and point of view, and to them must be added many other monographs, and a growing literature on the impact of nineteenth-century professionalism and the organizational needs of modern society. Many of these are conveniently referred to in the notes to chapter 1 of Dee Garrison, *Apostles of Culture: The Public Librarian and American Society, 1876-1920* (New York: Free Press, 1979), pp. 248-250.

4. Bernard Bailyn, *Education in the Forming of American Society: Needs and Opportunities for Study* (Chapel Hill: University of North Carolina Press, 1960; New York: Vintage Books, n.d.), p. 4.

5. Ibid., pp. 9-11.

6. These influences, and interdisciplinary sources, are fully discussed by James A. Henretta, "Social History as Lived and Written," *American Historical Review* 84 (December 1979): 1293-1322.

7. Some of the influential texts here are Richard Hofstadter, *The Age of Reform: From Bryan to F.D.R.* (New York: Knopf, 1955); Robert H. Wiebe, *The Search for Order, 1877-1920* (New York: Hill and Wang, 1967); George E. Mowry, *The California Progressives* (Berkeley: University of California Press, 1951); Henry F. May, *The End of American Innocence: A Study of the First Years of Our Own Time, 1912-1917* (New York: Knopf, 1959); Gabriel Kolko, *The Triumph of Conservatism: A Re-interpretation of American History, 1900-1916* (Chicago: Quadrangle, 1967); and Samuel P. Hays, *The Response to Industrialism, 1885-1914* (Chicago: University of Chicago Press, 1967).

8. See, for example, various anthologies of essays containing examples of these attitudes: Barton J. Bernstein (ed.), *Towards a New Past: Dissenting Essays in American History* (New York: Pantheon, 1968); Alfred F. Young (ed.), *Dissent: Explorations in the History of American Radicalism* (DeKalb: Northern Illinois University Press, 1968); Alfred F. Young (ed.), *The American Revolution: Explorations in the History of American Radicalism* (DeKalb: Northern Illinois University Press, 1976); Irwin Unger (ed.), *Beyond Liberalism: The New Left Views American History* (Waltham, Mass.: Xerox College Pub., 1971). See also many of the articles published in *Radical History Review* (1975-); *Marxist Perspectives* (1978-).

9. Among the many texts that have reexamined the shaping of American culture are Christopher Lasch, *The New Radicalism in America, 1889-1963: The Intellectual as a Social Type* (New York: Knopf, 1965); James Weinstein, *The Corporate Ideal in the Liberal State, 1900-1918* (Boston: Beacon, 1968); Samuel Haber, *Efficiency and Uplift: Scientific Management in the Progressive Era, 1890-1920* (Chicago: University of Chicago Press, 1964); Carol S. Gruber, *Mars and Minerva: World War I and the Uses of Higher Learning in America* (Baton Rouge: Louisiana State University Press, 1975); Ann Douglas, *The Feminization of American Culture* (New York: Knopf, 1977); Stuart Ewen, *Captains of Consciousness: Advertising and the Social Roots of the Consumer Culture* (New York: McGraw-Hill, 1976). See also recent work in the *Journal of Interdisciplinary History* (1970-); *Journal of Social History* (1967-); *Past and Present* (1952-).

10. In addition to many of the works already cited, several essays during the past few years have concentrated on the conservative objectives of the

new professionals and the new institutions; among others, see Paul Finkel-
man, "Class and Culture in Late Nineteenth-Century Chicago: The Founding
of the Newberry Library," *American Studies* 16 (Spring 1975): 5-22; Marvin
E. Gettlemen, "Philanthropy as Social Control in Late Nineteenth-Century
America: Some Hypotheses and Data on the Rise of Social Work," *Societas*
5, no. 1 (Winter 1975): 49-59; Robert W. Rydell, "The World's Columbian
Exposition of 1893: Racist Underpinnings of a Utopian Artifact," *Journal of
American Culture* 1 (Summer 1978): 253-275; also, Kenneth L. Kusmer,
"The Social History of Cultural Institutions: The Upper-Class Connection,"
Journal of Interdisciplinary History 10, no. 1 (Summer 1979): 137-146.

11. For summaries of recent thinking and research, and references to the
literature on professionalization and institution-founding during this period,
see the essays in Alexandra Oleson and John Voss (eds.), *The Organization of
Knowledge in Modern America, 1860-1920* (Baltimore: Johns Hopkins University Press, 1979). There has also been important research on the development of cultural institutions in Victorian Britain. See particularly H. E.
Meller, *Leisure and the Changing City, 1870-1914* (London and Boston:
Routledge and Kegan Paul, 1976); Peter Bailey, *Leisure and Class in Victorian
England: Rational Recreation and the Contest for Control, 1830-1885* (London: Routledge and Kegan Paul; Buffalo, N.Y.: University of Toronto Press,
1978); many of the essays in H. J. Dyos and Michael Wolf (eds.), *The Victorian City: Images and Realities* (London and Boston: Routledge and Kegan
Paul, 1973); Robert W. Malcolmson, *Popular Recreations in English Society,
1700-1850* (Cambridge: Cambridge University Press, 1973).

12. Dee Garrison, "Rejoinder," *Journal of Library History* 10, no. 2 (April
1975): 112, 115-116. I do find, in Dee Garrison, *Apostles of Culture*, many
indications of the complexity of analyzing cultural relationships. See particularly pages 60-63.

13. Anthony M. Platt, *The Child Savers* (2nd ed.), pp. xii-xiv.

14. In the vast literature that deals with these figures and their broad influence, students of American culture should find the following books particularly helpful: Roger B. Stein, *John Ruskin and Aesthetic Thought in
America, 1840-1900* (Cambridge, Mass.: Harvard University Press, 1967);
Kermit Vanderbilt, *Charles Eliot Norton: Apostle of Culture in a Democracy*
(Cambridge, Mass: Belknap Press of Harvard University Press, 1959); Raymond Williams, *Culture and Society, 1780-1950* (London: Chatto and Win-
dus, 1958); Philip Henderson, *William Morris, His Life, Work and Friends*
(London: Thames and Hudson, 1967); Lionel Trilling, *Matthew Arnold* (New
York: Norton, 1939); John Tomsich, *A Genteel Endeavor: American Culture
and Politics in the Gilded Age* (Stanford, Calif.: Stanford University Press,
1971); E. P. Thompson, *William Morris: Romantic to Revolutionary* (London: Lawrence and Wishart, 1955).

15. For more on this movement, see Susan Otis Thompson, *American
Book Design and William Morris* (New York and London: Bowker, 1977);
Freeman Champney, *Art and Glory: The Story of Elbert Hubbard* (New
York: Crown, 1968); John Crosby Freeman, *The Forgotten Rebel: Gustav
Stickley and His Craftsman Mission Furniture* (Watkins Glen, N.Y.: Century
House, 1966); Oscar Lovell Triggs, *Chapters in the History of the Arts and
Crafts Movement* (Chicago: Bohemia Guild of the Industrial Art League,
1902); David H. Dickason, *The Daring Young Men: The Story of the Ameri-
can Pre-Raphaelites* (Bloomington: University of Indiana Press, 1953); Joy H.

Colby, *Art and a City: A History of the Detroit Society of Arts and Crafts* (Detroit: Wayne State University Press, 1956); Anthea Callen, *Women Artists of the Arts and Crafts Movement, 1870-1914* (New York: Pantheon, 1979); Herbert Peck, *The Book of Rookwood Pottery* (New York: Crown, 1968); Diane Chalmers Johnson, *American Art Nouveau* (New York: Abrams, 1979); Paul Evans, *Art Pottery of the United States: An Encyclopedia of Producers and Their Marks* (New York: Scribner's, 1974).

16. This connection is discussed in Neil Harris, "The Gilded Age Revisited: Boston and the Museum Movement," *American Quarterly* 14, no. 4 (Winter 1962): 545-566.

17. On this point, see Neil Harris, "Museums, Merchandising, and Popular Taste: The Struggle for Influence," in Ian M. G. Quimby (ed.), *Material Culture and the Study of American Life* (New York: Norton, 1978), pp. 140-174.

18. R. Jackson Wilson, *In Quest of Community: Social Philosophy in the United States, 1860-1920* (London and New York: Oxford University Press, 1970), p. 165.

19. Daniel M. Fox, *Engines of Culture: Philanthropy and Art Museums* (Madison: State Historical Society of Wisconsin, 1963).

20. Henry James, *The American Scene* (Bloomington and London: Indiana University Press, 1968), pp. 249-252.

21. Jorge Luis Borges, "The Library of Babel," *Ficciones* (New York: Grove, 1962), pp. 80-81.

Ancient Burials of Metal Documents in Stone Boxes—Their Implications for Library History

H. Curtis Wright

Archaeological digs have amply documented this custom, observed by the Mesopotamian kings, of burying among the substructures of the temples or palaces they built or restored such things as clay nails, cones, barrel cylinders, and stone or metal tablets, on which they inscribed a permanent record of their labors.[1]

Before and after Persepolis

Old Persian studies got a new lease on life in 1926, "when an inscription of Darius was found at Hamadan, in duplicate on gold and silver tablets."[2] The inscription, wrongly thought to be "wholly novel as to its form and content," was discovered in an old foundation "between two square hewn stones which had been carefully prepared to receive it."[3] The find, which established the exact location of ancient Ecbatana, also elicited Herzfeld's prediction that "we may expect with certainty the discovery of similar documents in the excavations at . . . Persepolis" and elsewhere.[4]

H. Curtis Wright *is associate professor of library and information sciences at Brigham Young University.*

Journal of Library History, Vol. 16, No. 1, Winter 1981
©1981 by the University of Texas Press   0275-3650/81/010048-23$02.20

This prophecy was fulfilled in September 1933, when Herzfeld discovered that "two shallow, neatly made stone boxes with [sealed] lids, each containing two square plates of gold and silver, had been sunk into the bedrock beneath the walls at the corners of . . . the apadana," the multicolumned audience hall of the palace at Persepolis.[5] The plates, which bore the same inscription as their counterparts from Hamadan, "were laid down, probably in the presence of Darius, in 515-16 B.C." They were retrieved 2,500 years later in perfect condition, "the metal shining as the day it was incised."[6] There were then six metallic copies of the same inscription, three complete sets of duplicates proclaiming the majesty of Darius and the vastness of his kingdom.[7] Four more gold tablets found at Hamadan bear similar inscriptions issued by Ariaramnes, Arsames, Artaxerxes II, and Darius II.[8]

The Persepolis plates constitute the high point in a long tradition of concealed metallic documents, which persists from Sumerian to Alexandrian times. The stone boxes found in holes cut into rock foundations prove conclusively that the plates were building deposits. The Darius inscription on gold and silver tablets is therefore "of the same type as the foundation inscriptions on metal tablets of Warad Sin of Larsa [1834-1823 B.C.], of . . . the wife of Rim-Sin [1822-1763 B.C.] . . . , of Tukulti-Ninurta I [1244-1208 B.C.], and of Sargon II [721-705 B.C.]."[9] Metallic foundation inscriptions are older than that, however, possibly reaching as far back as Early Dynastic II (ca. 2700-2500 B.C.).[10] The stone chest may be older still, if an object dated 2900 B.C. or earlier, which was found in a temple at Tell Brak, is actually an "early dynastic foundation box."[11] The metallic foundation inscription lived on until the crash of the Late Assyrian Empire (ca. 626-609 B.C.), when it perished because the Neo-Babylonians followed other documentary procedures. It was briefly resurrected from the Late Assyrian past by the Achaemenid dynasty of Persia (539-331 B.C.),[12] only to die once more when Alexander the Great fired the palace at Persepolis. It surfaced yet again at Alexandria in the excavations of a granite box for holding the writings of a late Greek author,[13] and dozens of small metallic plates from the foundations of the Serapis Temple, which housed the Serapeum Library.[14] It remains, then, only to review the history of metallic foundation inscriptions before and after the Darius plates, and to summarize their significance for library history.

Before Persepolis

The history of foundation deposits provides too many boxes and documents to discuss each one separately. This paper therefore reviews that history only in relation to (1) *three Neo-Sumerian kings*, whose peg deposits probably led to the later burials of metal documents in stone boxes, and (2) *nine subsequent rulers*, including one Kassite, one Chaldean, two Amorite, and five Assyrian kings, who ruled from the nineteenth through the seventh centuries B.C.

The stone box loaded with metal documents is probably derived from the peg deposits of the Neo-Sumerian Renaissance at Mari in the Ur III period (ca. 2100-2000 B.C.).[15] Parrot uncovered "six foundation deposits" of King Niwar-Mer, which had been imbedded in the materials used to construct an ancient building. Four of these deposits, "placed very precisely at its corners, identified the building as the Ninhursag Temple, thanks to the inscribed bronze plates" that they included.[16] Three of the four corners in the temple of Dagan have also given up the foundation deposits of King Ishtup-Ilum, which definitely suggest a development toward the stone box of Darius. They were found "inside the wall . . . in a rectangular space" carefully prepared to receive them.[17]

> In one corner of this rectangle was placed a box made of two square stone slabs. The lower slab had a square depression, in which a bronze plaque . . . was placed. A bronze spike . . . was thrust through holes in the [inscribed] bronze plaque and the stone slab, and into the mud brickwork beneath. A second stone slab, of the same size as the first but without the depression or hole, was placed over the first.[18]

The several deposits of King Apil-kin were concealed in the boxlike cavities of false bricks placed beneath the foundations themselves. The king had concealed two inscribed bronze plates beneath the inner doors of the *sahuru*, a small entrance hall leading to the "Lions' Temple," which he had built behind the Temple of Ninhursag. He had actually "made a box by hollowing out one of the rough bricks in the footings beneath the foundation."[19]

Warad-Sin (1834-1823 B.C.) and Rim-Sin (1822-1763 B.C.) are "the only Larsa kings who used peg deposits";[20] but both of these rulers were involved with either the boxes or the documents of the metallic tradition. While clearing a small temple site in southeastern Ur, Woolley dug into the remains of an old wall. About six inches below its highest remaining surface, he uncovered "a box of burnt brick contrived in the mud-brick core of the wall." The box contained "an intact foundation-deposit consisting of the copper figure of the king" and a "brick-shaped inscribed steatite tablet." The statuette and the tablet bore the same inscription, which stated that "the temple was dedicated to En-ki, the water god of Eridu, . . . by Rim-Sin king of Larsa."[21] The excavation disclosed no metal tablets, however, and none are known from Rim-Sin; but Simat-Innana, "one of the wives of Rim-Sin," did deposit inscribed limestone and copper tablets in the foundations of a Larsa temple.[22] No deposits actually made by Warad-Sin have ever been recovered, and the same is true of Kurigalzu II (1345–1324 B.C.). But excavation of the later Ningal Temple, which was built about 650 B.C. and subsequently remodeled by Nabonidus (555–539 B.C.), has produced a pair of steatite and copper tablets from each of those rulers. This reburial of tablets from the Amorite and Kassite dynasties by the last Neo-Babylonian king proves that Warad-Sin and Kurigalzu II included metallic inscriptions in their building deposits.[23]

After Kurigalzu II, the Assyrian kings more or less monopolized the use of metallic foundation inscriptions until the breakup of their empire (ca. 600 B.C.). There is an interesting reburial by Shalmaneser III of a complicated bowl-deposit containing small gold and silver plates from Shalmaneser I and Tukulti-Ninurta I, which straddles most of the Middle Assyrian period (ca. 1363–859 B.C.).[24] Similar tablets "were used from the time of Shalmaneser I onwards."[25] The most complicated foundation deposits of Mesopotamia come from the later Ishtar Temple restored by Tukulti-Ninurta I (1244–1208 B.C.), who dedicated its twin shrines to Asshuritu and Dinitu. These deposits from Assur constitute "a very elaborate combination of [inscribed] slabs and tablets, large and small, of various mateials," installed with "a lavish use of beads and nondescript fragments of stone."[26] The complex arrangements of the twenty-seven documents from the two shrines of this temple defy verbal description; but those from the larger shrine were partially disposed as follows:

First three lead blocks were placed upon the mud brick subfoundation; two small inscribed tablets of gold and silver and a tiny square of sheet copper were placed on the middle block. A few baked bricks were laid along the wall face to make a level

bed for the stone slab. Glass beads, fragments of stones, and . . .
twigs or bits of wood were strewn over these objects, and the
limestone slab was placed over them. . . . Mats were laid over the
block, and . . . [near] its rear edge were placed more valuable
trifles, including beads and . . . bits of ivory. On this "cushion"
of beads and mortar went two more gold and silver tablets, and
a square of sheet gold. Then the fourth lead block was laid over
the lot and the construction of the wall continued in mud
brick.[27]

An important pair of gold and silver *plaquettes* have survived
from Assurnasirpal II (883–859 B.C.).[28] They were very probably
found at Nineveh in the Temple of Nabu, the god of learning,
writing, scribes, and secretaries.[29] These documents present Assurnasirpal II as saying explicitly: "I laid the foundations of the
palace at the city of X, the foundations of my royal residence, on
tablets of silver and gold."[30] The actual wording of these tablets
means "to establish the foundations on documents."[31] Bottéro
knows of "only one other formula somewhat like this one." It
occurs "in the Prism [text] describing the thirtieth year of Assurbanipal," who says of the Nergal Temple at Kutha: "In a favorable
month, on a propitious day, I established its subfoundation on
GULA oil, that fine oil, and upon tablets of silver and of gold."
This statement, Bottéro notes, incorporates "the same verb (*addi*),
the same preposition (*ina*), and the same mention of gold and
silver tablets as in our text."[32] It suggests that foundation documents are not merely inscriptions discovered in foundations: they
are documents bearing witness to the founding of royal and religious buildings on *writing*, which was known anciently as the
"King's Secret"–a mysterious something giving him both the right
and the power to rule.[33] The regal habit of building upon inscriptions, furthermore, probably symbolized the original founding of
the temple, the palace, and the city-state upon the written word.[34]
    The inscribed stone box "appears for the first time in the reign
of Assurnasirpal II [883–859 B.C.]."[35] All previous examples of
boxes were either uninscribed or directly incorporated into the
structure of some building. In 1929, however, "a damaged stone
box bearing an inscription" by Assurnasirpal II showed up in
Philadelphia.[36] The box came from the ancient city of Apqu, also
known as Bumariyah or Tell Abu-Maria, "some twenty miles west
of Mosul, near Telefar," in Iraq.[37] It was pieced together by E. A.
Speiser, who "identified it as a foundation-box, and deciphered

the [long] cuneiform inscription" on its sides and lid.[38] Since the
gold and silver tablets of Assurnasirpal II may also have come from
Apqu, "it is possible that they were [originally] enclosed in the
foundation box."[39] Another stone box inscribed by Assurnasirpal
II was retrieved from "a mound called Balawat," supposedly the
ancient Imgur-Bel near Nineveh, "about fifteen miles to the east of
Mossul."[40] Rassam described it as "a stone coffer with a lid, containing two tablets of stone covered with inscriptions."[41] It was
apparently taken from the entrance to a burnt-out temple chamber, where Rassam also found, lying on a marble altar, "an inscribed marble tablet of the same size and shape as the other
two."[42] Because the stone box had exactly enough room for this
third tablet, he concluded that it had been removed from the box
and placed on the altar for reading. The cavity of this box was
large enough to hold three tablets "twelve-and-a-half inches long,
eight wide, and two-and-a-half thick."[43] It was a massive marble
chest, whose great weight, though unspecified, was sufficient to
tax Rassam's ingenuity in transporting it to Mossul.[44] There is still
another ninth-century example of this kind from Shalmaneser III
(858-824 B.C.). This stone box is engraved on three sides, but beyond that, very little is known of it.[45] Excavations at Nimrud and
Arslan Tash have also disclosed six or seven inscribed "Assyrian
statues of deities holding square boxes" in their arms.[46] Their inscriptions state that "they were set up for . . . Nabu," the learned
god of the written word, who was also known as "the perfect
scribe."[47] These statues "are close chronologically to the boxes of
Assurnasirpal II and Shalmaneser III," and Mallowan has suggested
that their boxes "might have been meant to hold tablets, in view
of Nabu's association with writing and scholarship."[48]

The metallic foundation inscription flourished under the Neo-
Assyrian kings. It is therefore no surprise that "the depositing of
inscribed documents was greatly elaborated in Sargon II's palace at
Khorsabad."[49] Victor Place "was intrigued by the unusual thickness [nearly 26 feet] of one of its dividing walls." On digging into
the wall he found "a stone box, whose lid had been broken by the
weight of the wall . . . ; and in it he discovered five foundation tablets" on which Sargon II had "described the building of Khorsabad" from scratch.[50] "One of the tablets was made of gold, another of silver, the third of bronze, a fourth of lead, and the last" of
a mysterious "white material" that has proven harder to identify.[51] The lead tablet and the inscribed stone box,[52] which completed this series of foundation documents from Khorsabad, dis-

appeared in the infamous shipwreck of collections on 23 May
1855, "in which so many of the archaeological materials gathered
by the French were lost."[53]
The metallic foundation inscription perished with the fall of the
Neo-Assyrian empire (ca. 626–609 B.C.). It "was not adopted by
the Neo-Babylonian rulers," who preferred "clay cylinders, the
only type of inscribed building deposit used in their time."[54] The
years between 626 and 609 B.C. thus mark a chronological datum
before which foundation documents were inscribed on metals but
not after. "The custom was briefly revived by the Achaemenids,"
who intentionally resurrected it from the Neo-Assyrian past.[55] It
died for the second time in 331 B.C., when the Persian empire was
toppled by Alexander the Great; but it also underwent a second
resurrection, this time in the great city of Alexandria.

The Alexandrian Echo of Persepolis

Archaeology is problematic at Alexandria, where "excavation
has yielded, and can yield, but little material for its reconstruction
at any period."[56] There are two major causes for this.

> The first is a general subsidence, probably of about four metres,
> which has taken much of the coastal region of the ancient city
> beneath sea level. . . . This subsidence is complicated by a sec-
> ond, man-made difficulty. . . . Intense building activity [since
> ca. 1850] has created a new and wholly artificial coastline, to a
> depth of some three hundred metres [990 feet] at its widest
> extent.[57]

The stratigraphy and ceramic sequences of Alexandria have thus
been largely disrupted, as most of the "fill" for the modern city
was taken from the ancient city, sherds and all.[58] These artificial
conditions "exclude any possibility of accurate determination of
the contours of the most important part of the city."[59] Excavators
have therefore been forced to concentrate on the east and west
sides of Alexandria, the former containing its ancient cemeteries
and the latter its famous Temple of Serapis. "The Serapeum," as a
matter of fact, "is the *only* excavated temple" in the city; and its
foundation deposits "may reasonably be described as the most important archaeological find of the Ptolemaic period [ever] made
in Alexandria."[60] It is therefore disconcerting to learn that "not
only Parsons, *The Alexandrian Library* . . . , but also serious works
like the *Handbuch der Bibliothekswissenschaft* . . . or the *Ge-*

55

schichte der Textüberlieferung . . . [have] failed to take notice of the excavations."[61]

On 23 August 1943, Alan Rowe discovered "a set of ten foundation plaques bearing bilingual inscriptions in hieroglyphs and Greek stating that Ptolemy III had built the Temple and the Sacred Enclosure for Serapis." They were found in a hole sunk into a rock foundation beneath the southeast corner of the Serapeum at Alexandria. The set included: (1) three metal plates of gold, silver, and bronze; (2) five opaque glass plates; (3) a tablet made of faience; and (4) a mud tablet, apparently uninscribed.[62] The find was repeated on 31 December 1944, when a "similar set of ten plaques of Ptolemy III" was taken from another deposit hole in the foundation trench under the southwest corner of the same temple.[63] The inscriptions, materials, and arrangements of the plaques were essentially the same as before, as was the actual find-spot.[64] "The holes themselves were filled with sand after the plaques had been laid at the bottom and then covered over with limestone foundation blocks which were later removed by unknown persons" who dug up the foundations without disturbing the foundation trenches.[65] Rowe also announced "part of a foundation deposit in a small hole cut in the rock discovered on 30th October, 1945," from which "the gold, silver, bronze and . . . [some] opaque glass plaques had been removed in ancient times."[66] The remaining glass plaques bore "black ink inscriptions . . . , Greek on one side and hieroglyphic on the other." As these inscriptions were identical to those previously found, and since the early finds were uniformly alike, Rowe concluded that the deposit originally contained "ten plaques as in the *temenos* corners."[67] This find led to the discovery of ten more deposit holes, which enabled the Greco-Roman Museum to distinguish three separate structures in the same general area of the Serapeum, the early "Ptolemaic and [later] Roman temples of Serapis and a [small] Ptolemaic Shrine of Harpocrates."[68] There were eight deposit holes in the Shrine of Harpocrates alone, each meant to hold "ten plaques, which were placed in pairs of two [deposits] in every corner."[69] The Museum also discovered north of these deposit holes "the rock-cut holes for two other deposits," which may belong to the Harpocrates Shrine or to "the southern part of an adjacent Ptolemaic shrine."[70] These holes and their deposits were so skilfully hidden that they could not be detected unless the surface of the foundation trench was brushed.[71] The inscription on one of the gold plates "indicates that the shrine was made by Ptolemy IV (221-203 B.C.)" and dedicated to Harpocrates, the son of Serapis and Isis.[72] Rowe thus found thirteen rock-cut holes in all, from which he actually retrieved forty-three foundation tablets made of glass, metal, and clay.[73] If these were all foundation holes, and if their deposits were indeed uniform, they should originally have contained 130 tablets—65 of glass and 13 each of gold, silver, bronze, faience, and mud. Other deposits doubtless remain in the northern foundation trenches of the Serapeum Enclosure and its temples, where they cannot be excavated because they lie beneath the modern Bab Sidra Cemetery.[74] Similar foundation documents are also known from clandestine excavations in Alexandria and from various other sources.[75] Evidence for the Serapeum remains confusing, to say the least;[76] but thanks to Alan Rowe and the foundation plaques, five definite conclusions can now be drawn from it: (1) the buildings and grounds of the Serapeum, known as its *temenos*, were located on the west side of Alexandria where Pompey's Pillar now stands;[77] (2) the Temple of Serapis was built within the Serapeum Enclosure at its north end;[78] (3) the Shrine of Harpocrates, also inside the Enclosure, was a later adjunct to the southwest corner of the Serapis Temple;[79] (4) Ptolemy III Euergetes (246-221 B.C.) built the Serapeum Enclosure and its Temple of Serapis;[80] and (5) the Shrine of Harpocrates was built by Ptolemy IV Philopator (221-203 B.C.).[81]

There are some hints about stone boxes in Alexandria. The third deposit from the Harpocrates Shrine, for example, "was once enclosed in a kind of plaster box," whose remains were found by Rowe.[82] Rectangular limestone coffers were also kept in niches in the long underground passages beneath the Roman Serapeum, "which Botti thought might be Ptolemaic in origin."[83] But the best evidence is the discovery, in 1847, of a granite box bearing the inscription DIOSKURIDES G TOMOI, "For Three Volumes by Dioscurides."[84] Discovered "in the garden of the Consulate General of Prussia," it was wrongly interpreted at first as "confirming the location of the great library in the same place."[85]

> Recently, while digging for some stones to use as building materials, someone discovered a small block of granite 17 1/2 inches long, by 15 1/2 inches wide and high. A cavity had been hewn in this block for holding papyrus rolls. . . . This cavity is 10 inches long by 8 inches wide and 3 inches deep. . . . Thus there would have been room for three rolls.[86]

This granite box, which weighed over 380 pounds, was "already lost in 1848."[87] The grounds where it was found had been purchased by the Prussian consul general to Alexandria, Antonio de Laurin of Austria, "who apparently conducted some [amateur] excavations there. . . . [But] no one knows what became of the artifacts from these digs. Unfortunately, they could have fallen into the hands of Cassavetti," an unscrupulous character who may have made a killing from the box on the antiquities market.[88] Whatever its fortunes, the whereabouts of the granite box remains completely unknown;[89] and partly for that reason it was long thought to be an out-and-out hoax: an uncritical account of the box was the only one ever published, as it was subsequently ignored by serious scholars.[90] Breccia, for example, repudiated the stories that he had discovered the box, that it was made to hold ten rolls instead of three, and so on.[91] It had been noticed briefly in 1848 by J. A. Letronne, who was quoting an excerpt from the letter written by Sir Anthony Charles Harris to Samuel Birch on 28 December 1847.[92] But this notice was ignored by virtually everyone until the daughter of A. C. Harris, almost three decades after his death, delivered some of his notebooks to the Greco-Roman Museum in 1896.[93] Botti, who was then director of the Museum, was thus able "to find the note which, as the files of Sir Antonio de Laurin had been scattered and his papers destroyed by a fire in 1892, takes on the value of an original source."[94] The description and drawing of a heavy granite box by the scholarly Harris was impressive. "Although his note cannot be given the authority of a meticulous epigraphic copy . . . , no one familiar with the usual exactitude of his notebooks" could flippantly dismiss the box or "doubt that the inscription was faithfully reproduced by him."[95] So some of the scholars began to reassess the box. Reinach, for example, wrote about it in a spirit of atonement for his previous skepticism.[96] The box itself, however, which was too cumbersome to be typical,[97] must have been created for a special purpose of some sort.[98] There was also a question about the actual shape of the box, because the visual proportions of the drawing by Harris did not fit the measurements he provided for it.[99]

The inscription of the granite box is dated, on rather tenuous palaeographical evidence, between 220 B.C. and 140 A.D.[100] The most difficult problem with the inscription, however, is probably its referent: which Dioscurides is meant? There are eight or nine possibilities and no sure method of selecting the right one, although the choices can be narrowed somewhat if Reinach's dates are accepted.[101] His favorite is Dioscurides Pedanius, the one-book author of the *De Materia Medica*, for whom he argues somewhat speciously at great length.[102] My own choice would be Dioscurides Epigrammaticus, the brilliant student of Callimachus, for whom I can present no better evidence, perhaps, than wishful thinking; but he certainly cannot be disqualified by the ultimate in scholarly "objectivity"—Reinach's assertion that "light poetry would be out of place in such a heavy chest"![103]

The Significance of All This for Library History

The antecedents of the foundation inscriptions from Alexandria must be Macedonian, Greco-Roman, Mesopotamian, or Egyptian, or some combination thereof. Greco-Roman influence may be ruled out immediately, however, as foundation deposits of this kind have never been attested for any Greek or Roman building;[104] and the influence of Egypt, which is unquestionably at work in the Serapeum, must be evaluated by others.[105] But we are badly mistaken, I think, if we insist on deriving the accomplishments of the Ptolemies from their Greek or Egyptian subjugates. It is above all else Macedon's own cultural force and long-standing openness to the peoples and influences of Mesopotamia that best account for those accomplishments. "The Ptolemies traced their descent from Dionysus,"[106] who was regarded as the father of Serapis himself.[107] Dionysus, be it remembered, was known as the interloper god from western Asia, who forced his way into the Olympic pantheon through Macedonia and Thrace.[108] When the aging Euripides left Attica in a huff, disgusted with the smart-alec intellectuals of Athens, he withdrew to Macedonia in the rustic mountain country of hillbilly Greece; and there, in the northern backlands of the wild, wild West, he wrote the *Bacchae*, a play about the fundamentally irreconcilable conflict of the Apollonian and Dionysiac "gospels" in ancient Greece.[109] The awesome issues raised here by Euripides have not been resolved to this day. But the Macedonians, although fascinated with the sophic traditions of Apollonian Greece, never swerved from their fierce devotion to the mantic Dionysus. And that, I think, is the basic fact that must always be remembered in evaluating the influences of Macedon, Mesopotamia, and Egypt upon the Ptolemies.

It is difficult for the modern mentality to comprehend the sacral outlook of the ancient mentality. When a king runs a foundation trench, lays down a permanent record of his authority and dominions inscribed on stone tablets or metal plates, and erects a building on top of it, what is he really doing? He is saying in the language of a dramatized ritual enactment that every aspect of human civilized culture—the civilizing tendency itself, which gives birth to the temple, the palace, the city-state, his entire kingdom, and even to his own powers—is built upon the written document. Could there possibly be a better way of saying it? The foundation inscription was not used for communicating in any ordinary sense of the word.[110] It was nevertheless the backbone of the Mesopotamian documentary system. The royal inscriptions, written either by the kings or under their direct supervision, included both the foundation tablets or other forms of building inscriptions and their historical elaborations, which were known as "annals" or "chronicles."[111] The inscription "was a secondary element in Early Dynastic foundation deposits." Its use increased with the decline of the peg, however, and "the inscription began to take on more importance." As time wore on, these "building deposit inscriptions became both longer and more numerous," thus leading everywhere to the historical document and "in Assyria [to] the literary prism."[112] The documents derived from building inscriptions, furthermore, "must be taken to reflect literary patterns."[113] The royal inscriptions of Assyria thus include such things as chronicles, long-winded invocations, paeans, triumphal hymns, poetic language, and episodic narratives. It is "only when the royal inscriptions are linked with their literary background," therefore, that "their diversification and . . . stylistic changes [can] be explained."[114] Nabonidus even "enlivens inscriptions with dialogues" in which gods, kings, priests and common laborers participate. He also "quotes in scholarly fashion the texts of the documents his workmen had excavated from the ruins of temples," just as Assurbanipal repeatedly includes "descriptions of his training and . . . achievements as a scholar and a soldier." All of this demonstrates "the continuity and tenacity of a living literary tradition"—distinct from the scribal tradition "preserved in the royal library of Nineveh"—which makes it necessary for the would-be writer of Mesopotamian literary history "to consult these living, changing royal inscriptions."[115] These two literary traditions, the regal and the scribal, were for the most part intertwined in Mesopotamia. They may have shared a common origin; if they did, it was probably the stereotyped formulas of the ancient foundation inscription: an invocation of the god, the names and accomplishments of the king, mention of something (like a temple, kingdom, or so forth) built upon the civilizing function of writing, a curse on anyone desecrating the foundation document, and blessings for those who honor it.[116]

The most important development in Assyrian literature is to
be found in the royal inscriptions. These were modelled on the
old Babylonian building inscription. . . . From this fixed form
the Assyrians developed the long historical inscriptions on
which our knowledge of . . . Mesopotamia is largely based. By
elaborating the titles of the king, and giving a more discursive
account . . . of the dedication, the scribes were able to give general accounts of the principal events of their time. . . . Thus
arose the general account of a king's exploits. The next step was
to arrange the events in their chronological sequence. . . . Finally . . . each year or each campaign was elaborately and separately described, and then a complete history of the reign . . . [was]
recorded on clay or stone with all the literary art of which the
writer was capable. . . . The building inscription remains, [but]
the annalistic element is entirely new. . . . The annals of the Assyrian kings from Sargon onwards deserve to be classed with the
most important literary works in cuneiform.[117]

If the history of librarianship is reduced to library history, the
substance of this paper has little relevance to it. There is more to
carpentry than the history of boards and shingles. Why, then, must
librarianship be regarded as so much bibliographic lumber? The
history of books and libraries is the history of *instruments*, like
the history of hammers, nails, saws, tool cribs, and lumberyards. It
can therefore have only instrumental relevance to librarianship,
which must *use* communicative instruments of one kind or another in order to do its job. But the history of librarianship is not
the history of its instruments; it is the history of societal information systems in which *ideas* are expressed and recognized by means
of communicative instruments—such as bard traditions, marked
arrows, cattle brands, metal plates, stone tablets, clay cylinders,
palm leaves, papyrus rolls, waxed boards, parchment codices,
paper books, microforms, magnetic tapes, data banks, printouts,
computer terminals, and who knows what all. The information
systems of the ancient Near East are thus an integral part of the
history of librarianship. They were based on "the marvelous function of writing as the great synthesizer," for the old Egyptians and
Mesopotamians knew instinctively that "to write is to synthesize."[118] We have forgotten all that in our insane commitment to
the scientific analysis of everything. There is therefore no critical
librarianship today, no comprehensive synthesis of knowledge in
which anything that is known can be located and correlated with
everything else that is known. We have pushed Humpty Dumpty

off the wall and watched him shatter into thousands of little bits and pieces; and we have descended on the pieces and broken them down into progressively smaller bits and pieces. But we cannot put him together again because we find it much easier to analyze than to synthesize. The modern age has no House of Life, no temple where its knowledge records can be copied and discussed and studied as a whole.

Ancient records come to us not in single books but in whole libraries. These are not mere collections but organic entities . . . representing every department of human knowledge. . . . There is no aspect of our civilization that does not have its rise in the temple, thanks to the power of the written word. In the all-embracing relationships of the Divine Book everything is relevant. Nothing is really dead or forgotten; every detail belongs in the picture, which would be incomplete without it. Lacking such a synthesizing principle, our present-day knowledge becomes ever more fragmented, and our universities and libraries crumble and disintegrate as they expand. Where the temple that gave it birth is missing, civilization itself becomes a hollow shell.[119]

And that, it would seem, should have at least minor significance for the history of librarianship.

Notes

1. J. Bottéro, "Deux tablettes de fondation, en or et en argent, d'Assurnasirpal II," *Semitica* 1 (1948): 20.
2. R. G. Kent, "The Present Status of Old Persian Studies," *Journal of the American Oriental Society* 56 (1936): 209. This journal is henceforth abbreviated as *JAOS*.
3. Ernst Herzfeld, "Eine neue Darius-Inschrift aus Hamadan," *Deutsche Literaturzeitung* 47 (1926): 2105.
4. Ibid.
5. Richard S. Ellis, *Foundation Deposits in Ancient Mesopotamia*, Yale Near Eastern Researches, no. 2 (New Haven and London: Yale University Press, 1968), p. 104. See also Kent, "Present Status of Old Persian Studies," p. 212, and J. P. Barden, "Xerxes a Doughty Warrior until He Met the Greeks," *University of Chicago Magazine* (February 1936): 25.
6. Ibid.
7. Ernst Herzfeld, *Altpersische Inschriften*, Erster Ergänzungsband zu den archaeologischen Mitteilungen aus Iran (Berlin: D. Reimer, 1938), pp. 18–19: "All these tablets—one gold and one silver from Hamadan, two gold and two silver from Persepolis—were discovered *in situ*. . . . The texts of the gold tab-

lets from Hamadan and Persepolis vary only in the line arrangements imposed by different formats. The Persepolis tablets underlie the issuance of this 'edition,' whose unconventional writing [of a particular word] . . . shows that all of its copies were created from one and the same *Urtext* in a central office. Darius had undertaken simultaneous building projects in Persepolis, Susa, and Ecbatana, and the administration of these buildings was a unified thing."

8. See Roland G. Kent, "The Oldest Old Persian Inscriptions," *JAOS* 66 (1946): 206–212, for Ariaramnes; A. V. Pope, "Recently Found Treasures . . . : Archaemenid Gold Objects," *Illustrated London News*, 17 July 1946, pp. 58–59, for both Arsames and Artaxerxes II; and H. H. Paper, "An Old Persian Text of Darius II (D2Ha)," *JAOS* 72 (1953): 169–170. See also R. G. Kent, *Old Persian: Grammar, Texts, Lexicon*, 2nd ed. rev., American Oriental Series, vol. 33 (New Haven: American Oriental Society, 1953), pp. 107, 111–112.

9. S. Smith, "Inscription of Darius on Gold Tablet," *Journal of the Royal Asiatic Society* (1926): 433. Henceforth abbreviated as *JRAS*.

10. See the graphic summary of foundation documents in Ellis, *Foundation Deposits*, illus. 36.

11. M. E. L. Mallowan, "Excavations at Brak and Chagar Bazar," *Iraq* 9 (1947): plate 48, no. 6, following p. 87. The object is called "an alabaster foundation box" in ibid., p. 54. It is further described as a "foundation box, white limestone, measuring 51 x 23 x 17 cm. This box, which had been pulled to pieces by plunderers, was reconstituted and photographed on the spot where it was found. . . . It consisted of eight blocks and originally contained two, or possibly four, compartments. The separate blocks were riveted together and stuck with white lime mortar. . . . If the Brak foundation box belonged to the Eye-Temple of the Jamdat Nasr [or late protoliterate] period [3100–2900 B.C.], it is the earliest object of its type so far discovered, and the absence of its contents is a grievous loss," ibid., pp. 195–196.

12. Ellis, *Foundation Deposits*, pp. 104, 161.

13. Discussed by A. J. Reinach, "DIOSKOURIDES G TOMOI," *Bulletin de la Société Royale d'Archéologie d'Alexandrie* 11 (1909): 350–370.

14. See Alan Rowe, *Discovery of the Famous Temple and Enclosure of Serapis at Alexandria*, Supplément aux Annales du Service des Antiquités de l'Egypte, cahier no. 2 (Cairo: Institut Français d'Archéologie Orientale, 1946), passim. Cited henceforth as Rowe, *DTES*.

15. According to Hallo's revision of Porada, the Neo-Sumerian period (2300–2000 B.C.) includes both of the periods known as Post Akkadian (2300–2100 B.C.) and Ur III (2100–2000 B.C.), William W. Hallo and William Kelly Simpson, *The Ancient Near East: A History* (New York: Harcourt Brace Jovanovich, 1971), pp. 36–37 and n. 16, p. 77. For the history of peg deposits, see chapter 3 of Ellis, *Foundation Deposits*, pp. 46–93.

16. André Parrot, "Les Fouilles de Mari: Sixième Campagne (Automne 1938)," *Syria* 21 (1940): 5. "In each case a bronze plate . . . was placed directly on the mud bricks. Each plate had a short inscription in one corner. In the center of each was a round hole through which was thrust vertically a bronze peg. . . . A slab of wood about the same size as the metal plate was put on top, and a miscellaneous collection of small objects . . . was placed beside it," Ellis, *Foundation Deposits*, p. 58.

17. Parrot, "Fouilles de Mari: Sixième Campagne," p. 20.

18. Ellis, *Foundation Deposits*, p. 59.

19. Parrot, "Fouilles de Mari: Sixième Campagne," p. 6. "In this box a bronze plate had been deposited without being nailed down. It was encased in wood, as the cavity was larger than the metal plate. A plank, cut to the exact dimensions of the *cachette*, covered both the plate and its framework. A mat was then placed over the whole thing, the hiding place with its hollow brick was concealed, the brick foundation was laid atop all this as though nothing had happened, and construction continued," ibid., pp. 6-7.

20. Ellis, *Foundation Deposits*, p. 150.

21. C. Leonard Woolley, "Excavations at Ur, 1929-30," *Antiquaries Journal* 10, no. 4 (October 1930): 323 and pl. 38.

22. C. J. Gadd, "Babylonian Foundation Texts: 1. Limestone and Copper Tablets of a Wife of Rim-Sin," *JRAS* (1926): 679.

23. C. Leonard Woolley, "Excavations at Ur, 1924-1925," *Antiquaries Journal* 5, no. 4 (October 1925): 368. See also A. Leo Oppenheim, *Ancient Mesopotamia: Portrait of a Dead Civilization* (Chicago: University of Chicago Press, 1964), pp. 152-153, 163; C. Leonard Woolley, *The Ziggurat and Its Surroundings*, Ur Excavations Series 1, vol. 5 (New York: British Museum and the University of Pennsylvania Museum, 1939), p. 63; Woolley, "Excavations at Ur, 1924-1925," p. 370, fig. 3, and pl. 36, 1; and Ellis, *Foundation Deposits*, pp. 95, 160.

24. Ibid., pp. 97-98. The burial of this *Schalenkapsel* (with pictures of the three bowls, a technical description of the plates, and a sectional drawing of the whole package) is discussed by Walter Andrae, *Die jüngeren Ischtar-tempel in Assur*, Wissenschaftliche veröffentlichung der deutschen Orient-Gesellschaft, 58 (Leipzig: J. C. Hinrichs, 1935), pp. 51-54.

25. Ellis, *Foundation Deposits*, p. 160.

26. Ibid., pp. 138, 160. For the whole story of these deposits, see Andrae, *Die jüngeren Ischtar-tempel in Assur*, pp. 37-51, figs. 14-17, and pls. 1-3, pls. 17-25.

27. Ellis, *Foundation Deposits*, p. 98.

28. These little "platelets" are described by Bottéro, "Deux tablettes," pp. 25-32.

29. The excavators of the Nabu Temple, after listing their "chief finds during 1927-8," were also shown "two small plaques—one in gold, the other in lead—inscribed with a text of Ashurnasirpal, indicating that he had decorated the palace of the city Apki for his abode." But they declined to discuss the plaques further, "as it would trench too far on the possessor's rights," R. Campbell Thompson and R. W. Hutchinson, "The Excavations on the Temple of Nabu at Nineveh," *Archaelogia* 79 (1929): 108, 109, n. 1. According to Ferris J. Stephens, "The Provenience of the Gold and Silver Tablets of Ashurnasirpal," *Journal of Cuneiform Studies* 7, no. 2 (1953): 73, "it seems probable that these were our gold and silver tablets. The silver piece might easily be mistaken for lead since it has indentations on the reverse giving the appearance of softness in the metal. It is of course possible that there was also a lead copy of the inscription. . . . The note of Thompson and Hutchinson is included in the report of finds in 1927-8. This may be taken as the date of the discovery of the pieces."

30. From lines 7-9 of whichever tablet is transliterated and translated by Bottéro, "Deux tablettes," pp. 25-26. "This is one of the few instances in which . . . a term [actually] used in a building deposit text refers to the objects on which it is written," Ellis, *Foundation Deposits*, p. 100.

31. "Etablir les fondations sur des documents," Bottéro, "Deux tablettes," p. 30.

32. Ibid., adding that "*temmenu* is also basically the synonym of *ussu*." The cuneiform sentence under discussion is fully analyzed by Essad Nassouhi, "Prisme d'Assurbanipal daté de sa trentième année, provenant du temple de Gula à Babylone," *Archiv für Keilschriftforschung* 2 (1924/25): 97–106.

33. Hugh Nibley, "Genesis of the Written Word," in Truman Madsen (ed.), *Nibley on the Timely and the Timeless: Classic Essays of Hugh W. Nibley*, Religious Studies Monograph Series, no. 1 (Salt Lake City, Ut.: Publishers Press, 1978), p. 120.

34. I have discussed this occurrence in the first half of the fourth millennium B.C. in "Before and After the Permanent Temple," H. Curtis Wright, *The Oral Antecedents of Greek Librarianship* (Provo, Ut.: Brigham Young University Press, 1978), pp. 43–64. For its recurrence *mutatis mutandis* in the West, see also "The Age of Revolution," ibid., pp. 94–107.

35. Ellis, *Foundation Deposits*, p. 100.

36. "A Foundation-Box from Tell Abu-Maria in Iraq," *Art and Archeology* 30, no. 5 (November 1930): 190.

37. E. M. Speiser, "Translation of the Foundation-Box from Tell Abu-Maria," *Art and Archeology* 30, no. 5 (November 1930): 190–191.

38. Ibid., p. 190. For the decipherment, see ibid., pp. 190–191.

39. Stephens, "Provenience of the Gold and Silver Tablets," p. 74.

40. H. Rassam, "Excavations and Discoveries in Assyria," *Transactions of the Society of Biblical Archaeology* 7 (1882): 45. Henceforth abbreviated as *TSBA*. Only "the upper side of the box was inscribed," Ellis, *Foundation Deposits*, p. 101. For the inscription, see E. A. W. Budge, "On a Recently Discovered Text of Assurnatsir-pal, B.C. 885," *TSBA* 7 (1882): 59–82; E. A. W. Budge and L. W. King (eds.), *Annals of the Kings of Assyria* . . . (London: British Museum, 1902–   ), vol. 1, pp. 167–173; and Daniel David Luckenbill, *Ancient Records of Assyria and Babylonia*, 2 vols. (Chicago: University of Chicago Press, 1926/27), vol. 1, pp. 194–196. Henceforth cited as Budge and King, *AKA*; and Luckenbill, *ARAB*.

41. Rassam, "Excavations and Discoveries in Assyria," p. 53.

42. Ibid., pp. 54–55. The chamber turned out to be part of the Temple of Machir.

43. Budge, "Recently Discovered Text of Assurnatsir-pal," p. 59.

44. Rassam, "Excavations and Discoveries in Assyria," p. 54.

45. Ellis, *Foundation Deposits*, p. 101. For the text from this box, see O. Schroeder, *Keilschrifttexte aus Assur historischen Inhalts*, Wissenshaftliche Veröffentlichung der deutschen Orient-Gesellschaft, 16, 37 (Leipzig: J. C. Hinrichs, 1911–1922), vol. 2, p. 66; and W. Andrae, *Die Festungswerke von Assur: Textband*, Ausgrabungen der deutschen Orient-Gesellschaft in Assur, A: Baudenkmäler aus assyrischer Zeit, 2; Wissenschaftliche Veröffentlichung der deutschen Orient-Gesellschaft, 23 (Leipzig: J. C. Hinrichs, 1913), p. 175. For its transliteration with a German translation, a drawing, and a photograph, see ibid., pp. 174–175 and pl. 104. For its English translation, see Luckenbill, *ARAB*, vol. 1, p. 251 (items 703–705). This box is also discussed in *Die Welt des Orients* 1 (1947–1952): 387–388, which I have not seen.

46. Ellis, *Foundation Deposits*, pp. 105–106.

47. M. E. L. Mallowan, *Nimrud and Its Remains*, 3 vols. (London: Collins, 1966), vol. 1, pp. 260, 261, 351–352, n. 48.

48. Ellis, *Foundation Deposits*, p. 106. Cf. M. E. L. Mallowan, "The Excavations at Nimrud (Kalhu), 1955," *Iraq* 18 (1956): 7; and Mallowan, *Nimrud and Its Remains*, vol. 1, pp. 260–261.

49. Ellis, *Foundation Deposits*, p. 101. Khorsabad, also known as Dur-Sharrukin, was the "capital of Assyria, founded by Sargon II (721–705 B.C.), twelve miles northeast of Nineveh. . . . The city had been built toward the end of the reign of Sargon and seems to have been maintained as seat of a governor for nearly a century thereafter," Oppenheim, *Ancient Mesopotamia*, p. 393.

50. M. Pillet, *Khorsabad: Les Découvertes de V. Place en Assyrie* (Paris: Editions E. Leroux, 1918), p. 84. I have not seen the basic account of this discovery by Victor Place, *Ninive et l'Assyrie* . . . , 3 vols. (Paris: Imprimerie Impériale, 1867–1870), vol. 1, pp. 61–63; vol. 2, pp. 267, 303–307; vol. 3, pls. 4, 77. This source should by all means be consulted if possible.

51. Pillet, *Khorsabad*, p. 84.

52. The box "had a lid with a cuneiform inscription," Ellis, *Foundation Deposits*, p. 102.

53. Pillet, *Khorsabad*, p. 87; and Luckenbill, *ARAB*, vol. 2, p. 56. The first four tablets, which were brought out of Assyria by Place himself, are presently in the Louvre Museum. As the box and the leaden tablet were too heavy for inclusion in his personal luggage, however, Place loaded them on the rafts that were supposed to bring the products of his digs down the Tigris River to Bassora. But the rafts capsized at Qurnah and everything was lost, including the leaden tablet and the stone box with its broken lid-inscription. See Pillet, *Khorsabad*, p. 85; Jules Oppert, *Expédition scientifique en Mesopotamie* . . . , 2 vols. (Paris: Imprimerie Impériale, 1868/69), vol. 2, p. 343; Ellis, *Foundation Deposits*, p. 102; F. Lenormant, "Les Noms de l'airain et du cuivre . . . ," *TSBA* 6 (1878): 337; and D. G. Lyon, *Keilschrifttexte Sargon's Königs von Assyrien (722–705 v. Chr.)* . . . , Assyriologische Bibliothek (Leipzig: J. C. Hinrichs, 1883), p. xii. This may be the most tragic loss of archaeological artifacts in the history of archaeology.

54. Ellis, *Foundation Deposits*, p. 104. "Building deposits in this [Neo-Babylonian] period were limited almost entirely to clay cylinders," ibid., p. 157.

55. Ibid., pp. 104, 161. Evidence for the disruption of this tradition by the Neo-Babylonians is also provided by the Achaemenid jewelers, who deliberately followed Neo-Assyrian rather than Neo-Babylonian practices. See J. B. Bury, S. A. Cook, and F. E. Adcock, *The Assyrian Empire*, The Cambridge Ancient History, 3 (Cambridge: At the University Press, 1929), p. 109.

56. P. M. Fraser, *Ptolemaic Alexandria*, 3 vols. (Oxford: Clarendon Press, 1972), vol. 1, p. 8.

57. Ibid., vol. 1, pp. 8–9. Cf. ibid., vol. 2, p. 20, n. 34.

58. See ibid., vol. 1, p. 9.

59. Ibid., vol. 1, p. 10.

60. Ibid., vol. 1, pp. 27–28. Italics mine.

61. Rudolf Pfeiffer, *History of Classical Scholarship from the Beginnings to the End of the Hellenistic Age* (Oxford: Clarendon Press, 1968), p. 102, n. 2.

62. Rowe, *DTES*, p. 1. For a tabular description of the plaques and a drawing and photograph of the foundation hole, see ibid., pp. 4–7 and pl. 1.

63. Ibid., p. 3.

64. Ibid., p. 5.

65. Ibid.

66. Ibid., p. 51 and n. 2.

67. Ibid.

68. Ibid.

69. Ibid., p. 54 and pl. 16.

70. Ibid., p. 59 and pl. 16.

71. A. Rowe, "A Contribution to the Archaeology of the Western Desert: III," *Bulletin of the John Rylands Library* 38 (1955/56): 160. Henceforth cited as *BJRL*.

72. Rowe, *DTES*, p. 55.

73. Rowe, "Archaeology of the Western Desert: IV," p. 160; *BJRL* 39 (1956/57): 489. I have not been able to determine the distribution of these materials among the 43 plaques, as Rowe tends to discuss them in clusters.

74. Ibid., p. 505, and the map opposite p. 492; and Rowe, *DTES*, p. 54, n. 1, pl. 17.

75. These include the inscribed gold plates from Canopus and from the old Bourse excavations, which are discussed in W. M. F. Petrie, *Naukratis, Pt. I: 1884-5*, Third Memoir of the Egypt Exploration Fund (London: Trübner, 1886), p. 32; M. N. Tod, "A Bilingual Dedication from Alexandria," *Journal of Egyptian Archaeology* 28 (1942): 53-56 and pl. 6; H. B. Walters, *A Guide to the Department of Greek and Roman Antiquities in the British Museum*, 6th ed. (London: Trustees of the British Museum, 1928), pp. 108-109; and Rowe, *DTES*, pp. 10-13. Several others are described by J. J. Clère, "Deux nouvelles plaques de foundation bilingues de Ptolémée IV Philopator," *Zeitschrift für Ägyptische Sprache und Altertumskunde* 90 (1963): 16-22, who generalizes about Alexandrian foundation deposits: they are usually "bilingual foundation plaques made of different materials, notably of gold and silver [or bronze], and of opaque glass or pottery. The plaques made of the last two materials are usually found in clusters of several exemplars, whereas each deposit has only one exemplar of the plaques made from each of the different metals," ibid., p. 16.

76. Since "the debris in the Serapeum area has generally been turned over and over again," for example, "no reliable evidence for dating levels is to be obtained from it in most cases," Rowe, *DTES*, p. 42. Cf. Fraser, *Ptolemaic Alexandria*, vol. 1, pp. 36, 37; vol. 2, pp. 89 n. 190, 91 n. 191.

77. A. J. B. Wace, "Recent Ptolemaic Finds in Egypt," *Journal of Hellenic Studies* 65 (1945): 106, 108. Henceforth cited as *JHS*.

78. Ibid., p. 108.

79. Ibid.

80. Ibid., pp. 106, 108. Cf. Pfeiffer, *History of Classical Scholarship*, p. 102.

81. Wace, "Recent Ptolemaic Finds," p. 108.

82. Rowe, *DTES*, p. 56.

83. Ibid., pp. 34-35, 36, fig. 7. Botti felt, however, that these limestone coffers were for holding human or animal remains, not for holding documents, ibid., p. 35. Rowe also refers to one of the sons of Cheops who retrieved an inscription "from a hidden chest in the temple of Hermopolis," but he does not specify the material of the chest, ibid., p. 15, n. 1, citing Petrie, *Naukratis, Pt. I: 1884-5*, p. 32. This raises the whole issue, which I am not prepared to investigate, of Egyptian foundation deposits.

84. This inscribed granite box is discussed in detail by A. J. Reinach, "DIOSKOURIDES G TOMOI," *Bulletin de la Société Royale d'Archéologie d'Alexandrie* 11 (1909): 350-370, which we shall follow closely. This journal is henceforth abbreviated as *BSRAA*.

85. Ibid., p. 351, citing Mahmoud Pacha El Falaki's account of his researches in 1865/66. The discovery of a granite box in the garden of the Prussian consulate proves only that a granite box was discovered in the garden of the Prussian consulate, nothing more. On this topographical controversy, see ibid., pp. 350-352, 354-358, 369; and Fraser, *Ptolemaic Alexandria*, vol. 2, p. 31, n. 77: "Reinach . . . showed that this chance find had no significance for the history or the site of the Library." This topographical fallacy has nevertheless been advocated by André Bernand, *Alexandrie la Grande* (Paris: B. Arthaud, 1966), p. 116: "Il est donc parfaitement possible que ce monument indique l'emplacement de l'ancienne bibliothèque, partie du Musée." Serious objections remain to such a view.

86. Reinach, "DIOSKOURIDES," pp. 355-356. On the dimensions of the box, see also ibid., p. 353, and G. Botti, *Plan de la ville d'Alexandrie à l'époque ptolémaïque* . . . (Alexandria: L. Carrière, 1898), p. 65.

87. Fraser, *Ptolemaic Alexandria*, vol. 2, p. 31, n. 77. The box weighed 173 kilograms, or 380.6 lbs., Reinach, "DIOSKOURIDES," pp. 357, 367.

88. Ibid., p. 354, adding that de Laurin was the Austrian consul general until 1852. "Mrs. Penelope de Laurin remembers, writes Botti, some digs by her late husband on these grounds. Roughly speaking, he could have found there such things as sphinxes, inscriptions, marble busts, and mummies," ibid.

89. Cf. ibid.: "One regrets . . . that nothing is known of the fortunes of the granite block found on these premises in 1847."

90. "A published account appeared only in the passage following Mahmoud Pacha El Falaki's explanation of his researches in 1865-66 for the records of Napoleon III," ibid., pp. 350-351. "There is not the slightest hint of the discovery discussed by Brugsch with Mahmoud El Falaki" in writers like Puchstein, Dziatzko, Susemihl, or even in Brugsch himself, ibid., p. 352. For the published account, see Bey Mahmud, *Mémoire sur l'antique Alexandrie, ses faubourgs et environs découverts par les fouilles* . . . (Copenhagen: 1872), p. 53. This work, despite its French appearance, is in Arabic.

91. See Reinach, "DIOSKOURIDES," p. 350; and the two notices by E. Breccia, *Bulletin de la Société Archéologique d'Alexandrie* 10 (1908): 250-252, and 18 (1921): 62-64.

92. See J. A. Letronne, *Revue Archéologique* 5 (1848): 758. I have not been able to lay hands on this article. The portions of the letter cited by Letronne appear in Reinach, "DIOSKOURIDES," pp. 353-356. See also above, n. 86, and Botti, *Plan de la ville d'Alexandrie*, p. 64.

93. Reinach, "DIOSKOURIDES," p. 353, n. 1: "Harris' notebooks were acquired in 1896 by Botti from the daughter of the English Counsul," that is, from the daughter of A. C. Harris.

94. Ibid., pp. 352-353. This note, found on p. 39 of his cahier 11, was "discovered precisely as copied into his notebooks" by Harris, ibid., p. 253.

95. Ibid., pp. 360 and 350 (for the drawing). The scholarly reputation of A. C. Harris was apparently beyond reproach, although I have been unable to find out very much about him. "His name remains attached to the famous hieratic papyri and to the discourse of Hyperides against Demosthenes, both of which he discovered," ibid., p. 353, and cf. ibid., p. 368. For a bibliogra-

phy of over seventy scholarly articles about the Harris papyri, see Dieter
Jankuhn, *Bibliographie der hieratischen und hieroglyphischen Papyri*, Göt-
tinger Orientforschungen: Reihe 4, Ägypten 2 (Wiesbaden: O. Harrassowitz,
1974), pp. 48-51.

96. Cf. Reinach, "DIOSKOURIDES," pp. 369-370: "Is it . . . brash to
think that the granite box, brought to light in 1847, will one day take its
rightful place in front of the door to the New Museum Library at Alexandria?
Can these few pages at least draw attention to such a precious monument and
dissipate the doubts and legends surrounding it? I have personally contributed
too much to the propagation of legends and shared too many of these doubts
not to hope, by way of reparation, that I have established the reality and
demonstrated the importance of the granite box which contained the work
of Dioscurides." Cf. ibid., p. 350.

97. See ibid., p. 357: "Such an inconvenient arrangement, where three
rolls would have required a granite box weighing at least 380 pounds, could
not have been adopted in a library of 700,000 volumes or so." That would
have required well over 200,000 of these "boxes," ibid., p. 355. "Granite is
not only the heaviest material anyone could choose but also the most difficult to engrave and the most expensive. It is difficult to imagine the organizers of temple libraries . . . bringing . . . the thousands of blocks . . . necessary
for even the smallest libraries where each work required such a box. . . . No
one could invoke the furnace in order to explain the disappearance of so
many tons of granite; and you would be pressed even harder to explain their
presence, for granite was apparently used at Alexandria only for very prestigious monuments," ibid., p. 363. Cf. E. Breccia, *Alexandrea ad Aegyptum*
. . . (Bergamo: Istituto Italiano d'Arti Grafiche, 1922), p. 94: "We have only
to think of the enormous weight and of the great difficulty of working granite to persuade ourselves that it is impossible for such book-cases to have been
used in the Library of the Ptolemies, which possessed hundreds of thousands
of rolls."

98. See Reinach, "DIOSKOURIDES," pp. 364, 366-369.

99. Reinach removes this difficulty by doubling the measurements given
by Harris and providing another sketch of his own, ibid., pp. 350, 370 and n.
1. The sketch by Harris also appears in Botti, *Plan de la ville d'Alexandrie*,
p. 65.

100. Reinach, "DIOSKOURIDES," pp. 359-361. The dating is mostly
based on Harris's rendering of sigma by its lineal rather than its round form,
the former being common before, the latter after, the Roman annexation of
Alexandria. This study needs redoing, I think, by someone competent to
judge the scanty available evidence.

101. Ibid., p. 361: "Those who admit these epigraphical limitations are . . .
justified in rejecting the identification of our Dioscurides with three other
writers of the same name." Reinach also eliminates two more candidates
whose written works, if they existed at all, were never popular, ibid., pp.
361-362. But even that leaves three or four writers with the same name, any
one of which could be associated with the granite box.

102. See ibid., pp. 357-363, for Reinach's argument, which is essentially
that Pedanius was the only Dioscurides famous enough to be recognized by
his name alone, without reference to his works. This long argument may reflect nothing more than a preference for the Dioscurides associated with the

famous magical papyri discovered by A. C. Harris. It may, in fact, be ultimately traceable to Harris himself.

103. The Alexandrian selection of poetry from this Dioscurides, which includes only his best stuff, amounts to "about forty epigrams in the Greek
Anthology, some based on the work of his predecessors Asclepiades, Callimachus, and Leonidas. Eight deal with famous poets; many are paradoxical
anecdotes. The rest—save one hate poem—are lively love poems in the sharp-
est epigrammatic style," The Oxford Classical Dictionary, 2nd ed., ed. N. G.
L. Hammond and H. H. Scullard (Oxford: Clarendon Press, 1970), p. 353.
For this poetry see The Greek Anthology: Hellenistic Epigrams, ed. A. S. F.
Gow and D. L. Page, 2 vols. (Cambridge: At the University Press, 1965), vol.
1, pp. 81-96 (lines 1463-1772); vol. 2, pp. 235-270.

104. I was told this in 1966 by the late D. W. Bradeen, professor of ancient history in the classics department of the University of Cincinnati. Cf.
the cautious statement by Wace in Rowe, DTES, p. 18: "At present the evidence about foundation deposits made when a Greek temple was built is un-
satisfactory. No certain case is known and as a rule it has not been the practice of excavators of Greek sites to look for foundation deposits in connection with Greek temples" (italics mine). This statement is repeated in Rowe,
"Archaeology of the Western Desert: III," p. 160, n. 1. Architecturally speaking, moreover, the Serapeum "follows the Egyptian rather than the Greek
custom," as only one instance of "a Ptolemaic sanctuary with buildings constructed in the Greek style has been found in Egypt," namely, the sanctuary
discovered beneath the ruins of the great Basilica at Hermopolis Magna.
"Nothing like this has yet been found at Alexandria," Wace, "Recent Ptolemaic Finds," pp. 108, 109.

105. I have been remarkably unsuccessful in trying to find my way around
in things Egyptian. This is, I think, no place for amateurs unless expert guidance is available. There are, I understand, foundation deposits, metallic documents, and stone boxes in Egypt, although I have never been able to get a
solid line on them. But see H. Curtis Wright, "Metallic Documents of Antiquity," Brigham Young University Studies 10 (1970): 473; and Rowe, DTES,
pp. 13-15. Rowe derives everything from Egypt because he apparently knows
nothing of Mesopotamia, as in his discussion of Palestine, ibid., pp. 18-19.

106. N. G. L. Hammond and G. T. Griffith, A History of Macedonia, 2
vols. to date (Oxford: Clarendon Press, 1972-   ), vol. 2, p. 17. The new
Satyrus fragment (Oxyrhynchus Papyrus no. 2465) "is concerned with the
names of the demes in Ptolemaic Alexandria. There the Bacchiad genealogy is
traced backwards from Bacchis, king of Corinth, . . . to Aletes, . . . and from
Aletes . . . to Antiochus. . . . The mother of Antiochus was Deianeira, who
was the daughter of Dionysus and Althaea. It was because of this lineage that
two demes of Alexandria were named Deianeiris and Althaeis," ibid. The
Bacchiadae of Macedon "traced their line back to Heracles and so to Dionysus. . . . Thus Dionysus was the founder of the Bacchiad family," from whom
the Ptolemies were descended, ibid.

107. For the marble inscription discovered by Botti, which identified
Serapis (Serapeion) as the son of Dionysus, see Rowe, "Archaeology of the
Western Desert: IV," p. 499.

108. For a good introduction to Dionysus, see Lewis Richard Farnell, The
Cults of the Greek States, 5 vols. (Chicago: Aegaean Press, 1971), vol. 5, pp.

85-324. "The first chorus of the *Bacchae* is full of names recalling the Asiatic cult of Dionysis," W. K. C. Guthrie, *Orpheus and Greek Religion: A Study of the Orphic Movement*, rev. ed. (New York: Norton, 1966), p. 147, n. 40.

109. Much of which is discussed by E. M. Blaiklock, "The Natural Man," *Greece and Rome* 16 (1947): 49-66. See also Guthrie, *Orpheus and Greek Religion*, p. 114: "Euripides himself makes no secret of the fact that he is fascinated by the thrilling service of the Thracian god, so much so that his play the *Bacchae* is our richest source of information on the cult. . . . If the orgiastic worship of the Thracians was received with opposition, as in many parts of Greece it was, this opposition was largely fed by feelings of contempt for the Thracians themselves, who to Greek eyes were barbarians and beyond the pale." That goes for the Macedonians, too, who were more or less one with the Thracians in Greek eyes.

110. See Ellis, *Foundation Deposits*, pp. 166-167; and Oppenheim, *Ancient Mesopotamia*, p. 26: "Only a small fraction of these documents was written for the purpose of recording and conveying information to be read; on the contrary, they were buried carefully in the foundations of temples and palaces or engraved in other inaccessible places." Cf. ibid., pp. 146-148.

111. On the identification of annals and chronicles in Assyria, see Carl Roebuck, *The World of Ancient Times* (New York: Scribner, 1966), pp. 143-144.

112. Ellis, *Foundation Deposits*, p. 120. Other evidence for this development is the discovery of two tablets (one with a building inscription, the other bearing Shalmaneser's annals) from the same foundation deposit in the city wall of Assur, and the Achaemenid deposits, which follow the Mesopotamian pattern but include no building inscriptions at all, ibid., pp. 101, 104, 162. The literary prism often presents massive amounts of historical information, as in the clay prism of Assurbanipal, which contains "the annals of his reign (668-626 B.C.). The original has ten sides; is 19 1/2 inches high, and contains 1,303 lines of writing," Hormuzd Rassam, *Asshur and the Land of Nimrod* . . . (New York: Eaton and Mains, 1897), opp. p. 218.

113. Oppenheim, *Ancient Mesopotamia*, p. 148.

114. Ibid., pp. 148-149.

115. Ibid., pp. 149-150, including all quotations back to the previous superscript. Assurbanipal "succeeded in assembling in Nineveh what has every right to be called the first systematically collected library in the ancient Near East. . . . [This] collection is representative of the main body, if not the entire content, of the scribal tradition," ibid., p. 15.

116. These fixed ingredients of the recipe for creating foundation inscriptions are listed in Bury, Cook, and Adcock, *The Assyrian Empire*, p. 111.

117. Ibid., pp. 111-112, adding that the building inscription was first converted into a historical record in Assyria.

118. Madsen (ed.), *Nibley on the Timely and the Timeless*, p. 114.

119. Ibid., pp. 114-116.

Methods of Reference in Cassiodorus

James W. Halporn

Now that palaeographers of the Latin bookhand in Late Antiquity and the Middle Ages have to a large extent achieved the goals they had aimed at since the time of Jean Mabillon, namely the dating of hands and the localization of scripts, they have turned their attention to a subject that has always concerned the bibliographers of the printed book. Now the student of the manuscript book considers the actual format: its shape, its size, the *mise en page* of the text, and all matters of what may be called generally external appearance. Several recent scholars call this kind of study the "typology of the book."[1] I cannot in fact speak of *a* typology, since I am going to deal with a single text by one author, fashioned in a format created by that author himself, a type of format that was never to my knowledge used again in the history of the medieval book. Although this form of book was sui generis, its origin and its later vicissitudes offer an important chapter in the presentation of intellectual thought in Late Antiquity and the early Middle Ages.

The work is the *Psalm Commentary* of the sixth-century Latin church father, Cassiodorus.[2] Perhaps because we have viewed the importance of writers from the standpoint of the intellectual content of their writings and the freshness of their philosophical and religious insights, we have given Cassiodorus short shrift. It has become a truism that Cassiodorus had very little importance in the transmission of late antique and early Christian culture to the

James W. Halporn *is professor of classical studies and comparative literature at Indiana University.*

Journal of Library History, Vol. 16, No. 1, Winter 1981
©1981 by the University of Texas Press   0275-3650/81/010071–20$01.80

medieval period.[3] Although Cassiodorus's writings are simply the products of a patient and uncritical compiler of basically Augustinian thought, it is unjust to disregard his attempt to make the learning of antiquity available to a Christian audience of limited education, and it is unfair to neglect his genuine contribution to the analysis of a complex text for a number of educational purposes. What I shall attempt to do briefly is to show how Cassiodorus, by the organization of the *Psalm Commentary* and by the use of a system of marginal symbols, was able to present to his students a handbook from which they could learn the rudiments of the liberal arts through the study of Divine Scripture. The importance of the *Psalm Commentary* in the Western intellectual tradition rests on its function as a self-help manual for the individual reader.

At the beginning of his *Institutiones*, Cassiodorus tells about his plan for a Christian school for advanced study. He recalls now (in the 560s A.D.) that in the 530s he had tried, with the aid of Pope Agapetus, "to collect money for expenses to enable the Christian schools in the city of Rome to employ learned teachers, from whom the faithful might gain eternal salvation for their souls, and the adornment of fine, pure eloquence for their speech." Unfortunately, he continues, the wars in Italy made the realization of this project impossible.[4] Indeed, soon after the close of Cassiodorus's political career as praetorian prefect in the court of the Ostrogoth kings of Italy, at the beginning of A.D. 540, Belisarius, the general of the Eastern Empire, captured the Ostrogoth capital of Ravenna. He sent the Ostrogoth king, his wife, and members of his court, including Cassiodorus, to Constantinople.[5]

Cassiodorus took some early sections of his *Psalm Commentary* with him to the East. By the beginning of A.D. 548, while he was still in Constantinople, Cassiodorus finished this work, which he had based largely on St. Augustine's *Enarrationes in Psalmos*, and dedicated it to Pope Vigilius.[6] In A.D. 554, Cassiodorus returned to Italy and went to his estates in the south, where he founded a monastery at Vivarium.[7] At this time he was preparing the first draft of his bibliographical guide, the *Institutiones*, and he used the opportunity to include in the *Psalm Commentary* references to the literature discussed at greater length in the other work.[8] It is clear, then, that between A.D. 560 and 570 Cassiodorus revised, edited, and made a number of bibliographical additions to the *Psalm Commentary*, consisting of books that had come to his attention since writing the original work. All evidence suggests that he entered these citations as marginal notes in the three codices into which he had now divided the *Psalm Commentary*.[9] In effect, he pointed his reader to other relevant works in the collection of the library at Vivarium.

Beyond its value as a work of edification, Cassiodorus intended the *Psalm Commentary* to show "that the teachers of secular letters afterwards transferred to their pursuits some characteristic qualities which come from Sacred Scripture."[10] In a sense, the entire commentary is offered as proof of a view Cassiodorus had taken from Augustine, that all secular learning in the arts and sciences is derived from the Bible.[11] This curious approach had two results. First, it enabled the Christian scholar to avoid the guilty conscience that had afflicted earlier Christian teachers and writers, the most famous case being that of St. Jerome, who dreamt he was accused of being a Ciceronian rather than a Christian.[12] Now the scholar begins with the assumption that it is the pagans who have stolen from the Bible.[13] Second, and more importantly for Cassiodorus, living in those parlous times when learning seemed to be rapidly disappearing in the West, he could use his commentary to serve the needs of the late antique student who had no effective access to higher education, and had to rely entirely on the books at his disposal.

How then did Cassiodorus design his commentary to serve these needs? He presents the commentary in the same form used for centuries in Greek and Roman education. That is to say, he maintains the fiction by which the commentator frames his remarks as if he were interpreting a speaker's words for an audience that was listening without fully understanding. As the Greek commentator on a tragedy or comedy instinctively treats the characters as if they were alive and spoke their own minds, Cassiodorus presents the Psalmist as a personage speaking to us directly.[14] Although Cassiodorus interprets the text line by line in the same manner in which Servius comments on Vergil,[15] the format of his commentary breaks with this tradition, and for the first time in Latin antiquity a commentary is presented as one to be read in private and in silence. For the *Psalm Commentary* of Cassiodorus is a book written for the eye, not the ear; for the individual reader, not for oral presentation in the classroom. When we recall that Augustine's *Enarrationes in Psalmos*, which Cassiodorus used as his model, are a collection of sermons on the psalms, we can begin to appreciate the revolutionary method of teaching that this work presents.

Cassiodorus's task was to enable his reader to see at a glance that the psalms contained all divine as well as secular wisdom and at the same time allow him to glean such learning of the arts and sciences as he needed or desired. In the majority of the manuscripts of the *Psalm Commentary* a list of marginal *notae* precedes the preface of the work.[16] From the position of these *notae* even before any mention of the title of the work, it is clear that they were a late addition to the commentary. We can see these *notae* clearly in a ninth-century German manuscript from the monastery of Weissenburg, now in the library at Wolfenbüttel (plate 1).[17] Cassiodorus heads the list of *notae* with a two-sentence description: *Diversas notas more maiorum certis locis aestimavimus affigendas. Has cum explanationibus suis subter adiunximus, ut quidquid lector voluerit inquirere per similitudines earum sine aliqua difficultate debeat invenire—*"I decided to add various critical marks to specific places in the text. I added below these critical marks with a key to them, so that whatever the reader wishes to study in this text he may find easily by locating the like symbols." Cassiodorus leaves the reader to understand that these critical marks will appear somewhere in the text. But why does Cassiodorus, normally so prolix a writer, not explain in more detail the specific functions of each of the symbols?

It is simply because the use of such symbols had been prevalent in ancient books since the third century B.C., when critical marks were invented by the Greek scholars in Alexandria for the purpose of relating their commentaries to the texts that were studied. Although the Byzantine manuscripts would give the impression that the commentaries were written in the margins of the books containing the text,[18] in fact the papyri have made it clear that the commentaries (or ὑπομνήματα as they are technically called, to distinguish them from the marginal comments known as σχόλια) were separate from the texts.[19] Since line numbers were not available to the ancient scholar, this was the only easy way to tie text and commentary together (much as we still can use daggers and asterisks, themselves Alexandrian inventions, for footnote references).

One of these Alexandrian symbols can be seen, for example, in a second-century A.D. papyrus of a Greek play (London BL Pap. 3036), found by the Egyptian Exploration Society in the town of Oxyrhynchus.[20] Opposite the eleventh line on the papyrus is the symbol "χρ" in monogram form. This is an abbreviation of the word χρῆσις, and is used here to mark a passage suitable for quotation.

A fuller set of *notae* is set out in the so-called *Anecdoton Romanum*, which contains the symbols used by the Alexandrian

75

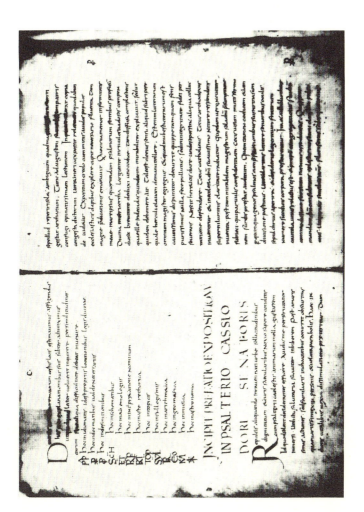

Plate 1 *WOLFENBÜTTEL Herzog August Bibliothek Cod. Guelf. 4 Weissenburg, fol. 1ᵛ–2.* Reproduced with the permission of the Herzog August Bibliothek, Wolfenbüttel.

scholar Aristarchus in his edition of the poems of Homer.[21] These
symbols and their explanations can be seen in the facsimile of
folio 3 of the manuscript now at Rome, Biblioteca Vittorio Em-
manuele gr. 6 of the ninth or tenth century.[22] The *Anecdoton* begins with a brief sentence: "It is necessary that those who come
upon them know the signs (σημεῖα) of Aristarchus affixed to the
lines of Homer." A set of symbols follows:

the διπλῆ ἀπερ ἱστικτος (like the close of angular brackets)—
"the undotted diplē";
the διπλῆ περιεστιγμένυν—"the dotted diplē";
the ὀβελός (like the printed dash)—"the obelus (or spit)";
the ἀστερίσκος καθ᾿ ἑαυτόν—"the asterisk by itself";
the ἀστερίσκος μετὰ ὀβελοῦ—"the asterisk and obelus";
the ἀντίσιγμα (like a reversed *C*)—"the reversed *S*";
the ἀντίσιγμα περιεστιγμένον—"the dotted reversed *S*";
the κεραύνιον (like a serifed *T*)—"the (lightning) bolt."

These symbols are invariably used for text-critical questions, to be
answered in the relevant place in the separate commentary. In all
cases the presence of these signs in an ancient text meant that the
text was so marked to make a separate commentary accessible to
the user of the text. The symbols are not used to explain, point to,
or consider anything in the text, no more than our footnote numbers do.[23]

A similar, but more extensive, list of critical symbols appears in
a Latin manuscript, Paris BN lat. 7530, the *Anecdoton Parisinum
de notis*, which gives illustrations and explanations of critical signs
that it states were used by Aristarchus and his Roman successors.[24] This set includes the chi-rho in monogram form found in
the London papyrus discussed above. It is explained here as being
set down to make a note of anything as the commentator wished
(almost equivalent to our *N.B.*). In his *Institutiones*, Cassiodorus
mentions a set of *notae* that have the same functions as those described above.[25]

In the *Psalm Commentary*, however, Cassiodorus adapted this
traditional scheme of marginal symbols for new ends. In contrast
to the Alexandrian system of marginal symbols, which presents
pointers from the text to separate commentaries (much like modern footnotes), Cassiodorus used essentially the same apparatus to
point from a general topic to the particular instance in the text.
Cassiodorus introduced the marginal *notae* in the *Psalm Commentary* to serve as an indexing system. By means of his indexing

symbols, Cassiodorus intends to show that the way to the eloquence of secular literature and of secular thought in general is through Scripture. He also wants the reader to be able to find in an easy way such passages in his commentary that refer to peculiarities of Biblical Latin, that discuss orthodox and heretical opinions, and that will tell something about the arts and the sciences.

The signs of reference no longer simply deal with matters outside the text, or suggest some doubts about the text. The *notae* now have been transformed into a new scheme that will enable the reader to gain an education formerly possible only through a study of the secular texts themselves. Cassiodorus is, of course, quite aware that the terminology of the liberal arts and sciences is not present in Scripture. As he says, "they are found clearly *in virtute sensuum, non in effatione verborum*." That is, these terms are all in the psalms in a potential way and must be brought to the surface for men's contemplation in the same way as we draw a tasty fish from the deep, one never before seen by human eyes (*ExpPs*, Praefatio XV.94ff.).

The *notae*, then, are the instruments by which the reader's attention is drawn to this information in the text of his commentary. To make the list of symbols even clearer to the reader, one entire group of manuscripts shows the symbols and, in addition, gives an example for the use of each of them taken from relevant portions of the *Psalm Commentary* itself. This group of manuscripts can be recognized by the presence of these expansions of the *notae* and from the fact that the text of the preface begins with the word *Respuissem* instead of the form *Repulsis*. These expansions, which can be seen in Munich Bayerische Staatsbibliothek Clm. 6253 (plate 2), do not go back to Cassiodorus. There is no doubt that they come from an Insular model, since in the explanation for the symbol used for etymologies (ET; fol. 1ᵛ, col. 2 at the bottom) all of these manuscripts read *his* for *autem* in two places (fol. 2, col. 1, lines 1 and 5: *calix his et* and *Calix his dictus est*), obviously the result of a misunderstanding by the scribe of the parent of these codices of the Insular symbol for *autem*, which is like a hooked form of minuscule *h* (ɦ).

Heading the list of *notae* (plate 1) is a symbol Cassiodorus had already mentioned in the *Institutiones* (I.xxvi.2 [p. 67.23 Mynors]). It consists of the letters *PP* surmounted by a diplē. Cassiodorus uses this symbol to mark those means of expression that are either peculiar to biblical Latin or represent a biblical way of speaking. The symbol appears in the margin to the text discussing Psalm 23:5: "he shall receive a blessing from the Lord and mercy

78

Plate 2   *MUNICH Bayerische Staatsbibliothek Clm. 6253, fol. 1ᵛ–2.*
Reproduced with the permission of the Bayerische Staatsbibliothek, München.

from God his savior." Cassiodorus remarks that it seems odd that we should receive the blessing first and mercy second. But such variation, he says, is often found in the psalms, and he refers us to Psalm 66:2, where both arrangements occur in the same verse: "May God have mercy on us and bless us; may he let his face shine upon us and have mercy on us" (*ExpPs*, Ps. 23. 105-112).

The chi-rho symbol is used by Cassiodorus *"in dogmatibus valde necessariis."* We find the symbol in Schaffhausen Stadtbibliothek Min. 78, fol. 17ᵛ (plate 3) set in the margin next to a passage cited from St. Augustine's *Tractate on the Gospel of John*, which discusses the human and divine nature of Christ (*ExpPs*, Ps. 2.34-40). Again and again throughout the *Psalm Commentary* we find this symbol used to mark Cassiodorus's polemics against heretics, especially those who deny the Trinity or who confuse the nature of the Second Person. From the use that Cassiodorus makes of the chi-rho symbol we can assume that he may have regarded it as standing not for *chresimon* ("useful"), but as a version of the chi-rho symbol for Christianity or Christ, a symbol used most famously by the emperor Constantine on his military standards.

Perhaps the most complicated of the symbol usages is that of the definition sign. It clearly consists of the Greek letter *omega* with a superscribed Greek *rho* (see plates 1 and 4). It is an abbreviation of the Greek word ὡραῖον ("timely"). The sign does not appear among the Aristarchan symbols, nor in the *Anecdoton Parisinum*, nor in Isidore. It is found, however, in a list of *notae* in MS Florence Biblioteca Mediceo-Laurenziana 59.38, a fifteenth-century Greek manuscript, and is explained there as follows: "the ὡραῖον is set by those passages in which the expression is very fine or the thought is embellished or both qualities excel."[26] Cassiodorus uses the symbol in three ways:

1. To define words. In plate 3, fol. 17ᵛ bottom, it stands in the margin next to a definition of *figura* (*ExpPs*, Ps. 2.67-71).

2. To offer definitions of a metaphorical kind. In discussing Psalm 56:2: "in the shadow of your wings I shall hope," Cassiodorus defines the shadow of the wings as the covering the mother hen gives to her chicks, comparing a passage in Matthew (23:37): "O Jerusalem, Jerusalem! . . . How often would I have gathered thy children together, as a hen gathers her young under her wings. . . . " (*ExpPs*, Ps. 56.64-71).

3. Finally, Cassiodorus uses this symbol in his discussion of the types of definition distinguished by the rhetoricians; these are taken from the work on definition by the Latin rhetorician of the fourth century, Marius Victorinus.[27]

80

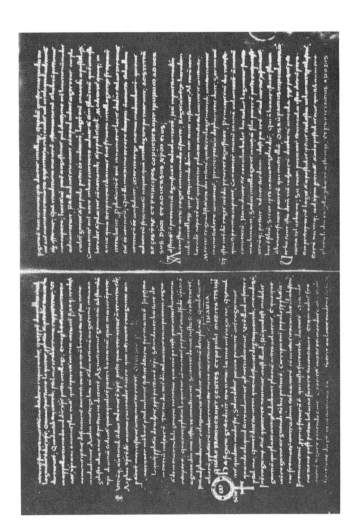

Plate 3 *SCHAFFHAUSEN Stadtbibliothek Min. 78, fol. 17ᵛ–18.*
Reproduced with the permission of the Stadtbibliothek, Schaffhausen.

81

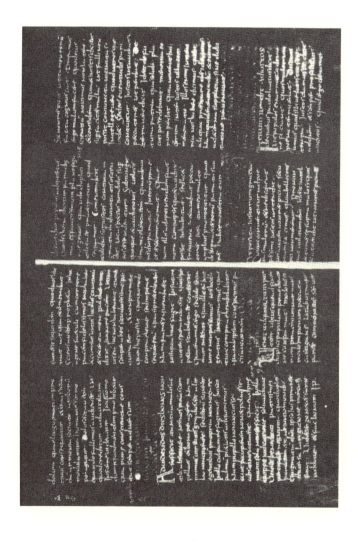

PARIS BN lat. 12239, fol. 144ᵛ–145.

Plate 4 Reproduced with the permission of the Bibliothèque nationale, Paris.

Cassiodorus next takes a term from grammar and rhetoric, *schema* (SCHE), which he defines as "a figure of speech in an arrangement of words set out in an attractive way" (*ExpPs*, Ps. 1. 321-322). He refers to such *schemata* in the *Commentary* either as *schema* or *figura*, and often gives the Greek term before offering the Latin, following a common procedure of Latin grammarians. See plate 3, fol. 17ᵛ, where Cassiodorus defines *erotema/interrogatio* (*ExpPs* Ps. 2.53-56).

The symbol *ET* is used to mark some examples of Cassiodorus's favorite type of language analysis, the etymology. He defines etymology at *ExpPs*, Ps. 1. 112-114. First he gives the Latin equivalent, *veriloquium*, and then the definition: "etymology is a brief statement, showing by certain resemblances of sound from what word the word sought comes." Many of his etymologies, like those of most other ancient Latin philologists, contain delightful absurdities.[28] Proceeding systematically through the grammatical categories, Cassiodorus now sets down a symbol for a subdivision of etymology, the interpretation of names, by which he means biblical (that is, Hebrew) names, with explanations taken from St. Jerome's work on the subject or from St. Augustine's *Enarrationes*.[29]

From grammar, Cassiodorus turns to rhetoric, first setting down a general *nota*, and then separate *notae* for two specific terms, *topica* (the basis of an argument; defined at *ExpPs* Ps. 144. 342-344) and *syllogismus*. The *RT* symbol covers a number of observations from the study of rhetoric:

1. At Psalm 31:4 it marks a metaphor: "spine" stands for "pride" (*ExpPs*, Ps. 31. 126-127).

2. At Psalm 26:13, Cassiodorus marks a passage with this symbol in which he refers to the oratorical *status collectivus* (*ExPs*, Ps. 26.270-273).

3. At Psalm 32:4, Cassiodorus says that the Psalmist is beginning to run through praises of the Lord in the *genus demonstrativum*, a kind of oratory that concerns itself with the praise or blame of some individual (cf. *Institutiones* II.ii.3 [p. 98.12-13 Mynors]), and he marks the passage in the margin with *RT* (*ExpPs*, Ps. 32.99-101).

When we come to arithmetic, geometry, music, and astronomy, we do not find much more than what we might expect in a late antique study of science, what Marrou less charitably calls "erudition."[30] The symbol *AR* is set beside a passage in the conclusion to Psalm 26. Cassiodorus, after having found a mystical meaning in the numbers of the first twenty-five psalms, suddenly, in a fit of weariness, says frankly that he cannot find any specific meaning in the number of this psalm, or in the numbers of the next two, either. He suggests that students take up the task of finding the meanings, perhaps by separating the number into parts, turning 26 into 20 and 6; 27 into 3 times 9. Since the Lord has fashioned "everything in weight, number and measure" (Wisdom 11:21), these mysteries can be discovered (*ExpPs*, Ps. 26.295-311).

The symbol for geometry (*GEO*) appears, for example, in Paris BN lat. 12240, fol. 310ᵛ-311 (plate 5) where Cassiodorus takes up (in reference to Psalm 95:13) the question of how it is that Scripture here refers to the world as the *orbis terrae* (or *terrarum*), giving the sense that the world is round, and in Psalm 106:3 speaks of the four cardinal points (east, west, north, south), and, finally, in Matthew 24:31 speaks of the four corners of the earth. How do we deal with the circle and the square? We follow the principles of geometry, says Cassiodorus, and inscribe a square within a circle (*ExpPs*, Ps. 95. 311-335).

The symbol for music (Ḿ) appears at all discussions of musical instruments in the psalter and also in passages like that in Psalm 33:14: "Keep your tongue from evil and your lips from speaking guile" (seen in plate 4 from Paris BN lat. 12239, fol. 144ᵛ, col. 1), where Cassiodorus suggests that the harmony of tongue and lips creates human speech (*ExpPs*, Ps. 33.247-250).

Finally, Cassiodorus picks up the ancient critical mark, the asterisk, and uses it to symbolize the study of astronomy (*asteriskos* is, of course, the diminutive of the Greek word for "star," ἀστήρ). Mention of the moon at Psalm 71:5 (see plate 6 from Paris BN lat. 12240, fol. 135ᵛ) leads Cassiodorus to remark that the moon does not have its own light, but takes its light from the sun (*ExpPs*, Ps. 71.147-150).

Cassiodorus also supplied his readers with other aids to make the use of the text simpler. Thus, the first verse of each psalm is marked by an ansate cross placed in the margin (see plate 3, next to the opening of Psalm 2: *Quare fremuerunt gentes et populi meditati sunt inania*). This device, which consists most often of a multicolored circle containing the Greek letter *omega* surmounting a cross, appears in most manuscripts of the *Psalm Commentary*.[31] In the alphabetical psalms (for example, Psalms 33 and 36, inter alios), the manuscripts show in the margin a tracing of the Hebrew letter and the name of the letter written in small uncials. In Paris BN lat. 15304, fol. 176ᵛ (plate 7), next to the beginning of verse 32 of Psalm 36 we see the name of the letter "ZADECH" and below it the Hebrew letter. So, too, in Paris BN lat. 12239, fol. 144ᵛ

84

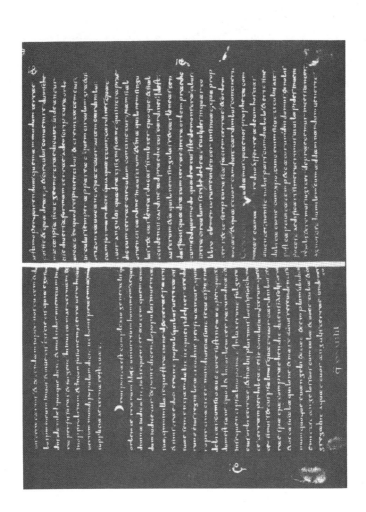

Plate 5 *PARIS BN lat. 12240, fol. 310ᵛ–311.* Reproduced with the permission of the Bibliothèque nationale, Paris.

85

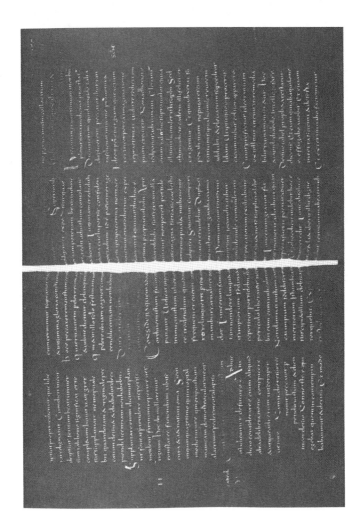

PARIS BN lat. 15304, fol. 176ᵛ–177.

Plate 7 Reproduced with the permission of the Bibliothèque nationale, Paris.

(plate 4), col. 1, the margin shows "<S>AMECH" and the letter form next to verse 15 of Psalm 33; in col. 2, "AGIN" and the letter form next to verse 16; on fol. 145, col. 2 "TZADECH" and the letter form next to verse 18.[32]

We have seen, then, how Cassiodorus used this method of reference to make the Book of Psalms available to the student for private study. In spite of his allusions now and again to "listeners" (for example, *ExpPs*, Ps. 71.453: *auditores eximii*), which belong to the entire tradition of annotation that assumes a speaker and a listener in addition to the commentator, the work is set up to be read by the individual. This, among other reasons, is why Cassiodorus has divided the text into three volumes each containing fifty psalms, the format of the majority of the manuscripts of this text. The *notae* Cassiodorus has taken over from the tradition of annotation have now been put to a new use. No longer are they symbols that link the text under discussion with a separate commentary; now they are signs that serve as an index to the content of the very commentary in which they are present. The reader who, like the Venerable Bede, wants to find out about, say, the figures of speech, can simply run down the margins of the codices containing the *Psalm Commentary* and pick out passages containing the necessary information. The commentary thus becomes a source of secular learning. And this process is exactly the one Bede followed, it seems, when he excerpted Cassiodorus's commentary for his own textbook, *De schematibus et tropis*.[33] The editor of the *editio princeps* of the *Psalm Commentary*, Johann Heynlin von Stein, in addition to listing the *notae* and marking them in the text, clearly also used them in fashioning the index, *Notabilium dictorum et expositorum annotatio*, which precedes the text of the commentary (plate 8).

Writing the *Psalm Commentary* in an age when political and social unrest made the idea of a formal Christian education an unachievable dream, Cassiodorus realized that the future of education lay in the students themselves and not in the availability of a school. With the idea in mind he determined to invent a new type of book, the first self-help manual for independent study. It is a little difficult to assess the effect of Cassiodorus's innovative ideas on Christian education and his practical approach to the presentation of the traditional disciplines of the liberal arts and sciences within a completely Christian framework. As I said at the beginning, Cassiodorus's work stands alone. No great tradition of textbook writing grew out of it. Perhaps Cassiodorus's system of indexing symbols can best be seen as a noble experiment, which for

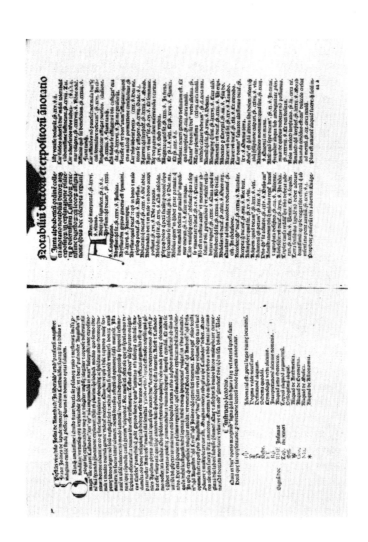

Plate 8 *Cassiodori Clarissimi Senatoris in Psalterium expositio (Basel: J. Amerbach, 1491), fol. as 1ᵛ–aa 2.*

many cultural and historical reasons was not further imitated and developed. Nevertheless, when the history of the textbook is written, perhaps Cassiodorus will receive his proper appreciation and a deserved place of honor.[34]

Notes

1. Such a study is subsumed under the wider discipline referred to by the French term *codicologie* (anglicè, "codicology"). For the classic discussion of this term by one of the founders of the discipline, see Alphonse Dain, *Les Manuscrits*, 2nd ed. (Paris: Les Belles Lettres, 1964), pp. 76ff. Although Dain objected to including the study of the "architecture" of the book under this rubric, reserving this field to the palaeographer, his restrictions of the term have not found favor in the scholarly world. His initial broad definition suits my purposes best: "codicology is the scholarly study which has as its object the manuscripts themselves, and does not concern itself with their scripts." Recent work in this area for the period earlier than Cassiodorus has been done by Eric G. Turner, *The Typology of the Early Codex* (Philadelphia: University of Pennsylvania Press, 1977), and for the later period by Léon Gilissen, *Prolégomènes à la codicologie: Recherches sur la construction des cahiers et la mise en page des manuscrits médiévaux* (Gand: Story Scientia, 1977).

2. The unreliable modern edition is that in the *Corpus Christianorum*, Series Latina, vols. 97-98 (Turnhout: Brepols, 1958), edited by M. Adriaen. Future references to the *Psalm Commentary* (hereafter referred to as *ExpPs*) will be made to this edition and its lineation.

3. Typical is the comment of James O'Donnell, *Cassiodorus* (Berkeley: University of California Press, 1979), p. 251: "But was Cassiodorus influential? Have we seen anything to indicate that his ideas themselves had any greater life in the middle ages, that his educational scheme itself took root and thrived? We have not." The monastic foundation at Vivarium in South Italy to which he dedicated the last years of his life disappeared soon after his death. A useful summary concerning the fate of the texts from Vivarium can be found in Pierre Courcelle, *Late Latin Writers and Their Greek Sources*, trans. Harry E. Wedeck (Cambridge, Mass.: Harvard University Press, 1969), pp. 376ff.

4. Cassiodori Senatoris *Institutiones*, ed. R. A. B. Mynors (Oxford: Clarendon Press, 1937 [1961]), I, Praefatio, p. 3.

5. O'Donnell, *Cassiodorus*, pp. 106, 130.

6. *ExpPs*, Praefatio 10-28, 121-124; Ps. 138.548-552. See also O'Donnell, *Cassiodorus*, pp. 131ff.

7. O'Donnell, *Cassiodorus*, p. 193.

8. P. Lehmann, "Cassiodorstudien," *Erforschung des Mittelalters*, 5 vols. (Stuttgart: Hiersemann, 1959), II, pp. 41ff., dates this draft to A.D. 562.

9. *ExpPs*, Praefatio 32-38. He had also divided his working copy of the psalms into three codices; see *Institutiones* I.iiii.4 (pp. 21.20-22.5, Mynors).

10. *Institutiones* I.iiii.2 (p. 21.5-7, Mynors); see also *ExpPs*, Ps. 6.94-100.

11. *ExpPs*, Praefatio XV ("*De eloquentia totius legis divinae*"), 45-91.

12. Jerome, *Ep.* 22.30 (to Julia Estochium). See J. N. D. Kelly, *Jerome:*

His Life, Writings, and Controversies (New York: Harper and Row, 1975), pp. 41ff.

13. No longer need the Christian scholar employ a tortured exegesis of Exodus 3:22 (see also Exodus 12:36): "But every woman shall borrow of her neighbour, and of her that sojourneth in her house, jewels of silver, and jewels of gold, and raiment: and ye shall put them upon your sons, and upon your daughters; and ye shall spoil the Egyptians."

14. W. G. Rutherford, *A Chapter in the History of Annotation* (London: Macmillan, 1905), p. 9; Reinhard Schlieben, *Christliche Theologie und Philologie in der Spätantike* (Berlin: de Gruyter, 1974), pp. 14ff.

15. H.-I. Marrou, *Saint Augustin et la fin de la culture antique*, 4th ed. (Paris: E. de Boccard, 1958), pp. 24f.

16. These marginal *notae* disappeared from scholarly attention because the seventeenth-century editor, J. Garet, omitted them from his edition (Magni Aurelii Cassiodori Senatoris . . . *Opera omnia*, 2 vols. [Rouen: L. Billaine and A. Dezallier, 1679], vol. 2, coll. 1–503; reprinted in J.-P. Migne, *Patrologia Latina* 70 [1865], coll. 9–1056). They were mentioned in the modern literature first by A. Reifferscheid, "Mitteilungen aus Handschriften," *Rheinisches Museum* 23 (1868): 131ff., who did not seem to know that the *notae* had already been printed in the *editio princips* of the *Psalm Commentary* (Basel: J. Amerbach, 1491; Hain 4574).

17. Wolfenbüttel Herzog August Bibliothek Cod. Guelf. 4 Weissenburg; first quarter of the ninth century, fol. 1^V.

18. For a Latin example of a marginal commentary, see the fourth or fifth-century A.D. Bembine Terence (Vatican City Vat. lat. 3226 [CLA 1.12]). A convenient facsimile of fol. 107^V (containing Terence, *Adelphoe* 763ff. with commentary) appears in Franz Ehrle and Paul Liebaert, *Specimina codicum latinorum Vaticanorum*, 2nd ed. (Berlin: de Gruyter, 1932), pl. 2 c. For *marginalia* in late antiquity, see A. R. Natale, "*Marginalia*: La scrittura della glossa dal V al IX secolo," in *Studi in onore di Carlo Castiglioni*, Fontes Ambrosiani 32 (Milan: Giuffrè, 1957), pp. 619–623.

19. E. G. Turner, *Greek Papyri: An Introduction* (Oxford: Clarendon Press, 1968), p. 121.

20. Facsimile in E. G. Turner, *Greek Manuscripts of the Ancient World* (Oxford: Clarendon Press, 1971), pp. 56f., pl. 27.

21. The text appears in G. Dindorf (ed.), *Scholia Graeca in Homeri Iliadem*, 6 vols. (Oxford: Clarendon Press, 1875), vol. 1, pp. xliiif. For Aristarchus and his use of symbols in his edition of, and commentary on, Homer, see Rudolf Pfeiffer, *History of Classical Scholarship from the Beginnings to the End of the Hellenistic Age* (Oxford: Clarendon Press, 1968), p. 218.

22. R. Devreese, *Introduction à l'étude des manuscrits grecs* (Paris: Klincksieck, 1954), pl. XVI.

23. The Greek church father, Origen, used some of these symbols (the asterisk and obelus) in his edition of the Old Testament, the Hexapla Bible, to mark passages where the Hebrew and Greek differed; see M. F. Wiles, "Origen as Biblical Scholar," in P. R. Ackroyd and C. F. Evans (eds.), *The Cambridge History of the Bible*, 3 vols. (Cambridge: Cambridge University Press, 1963–1970), vol. 1, pp. 457f.

24. For the text, see G. Funaioli (ed.), *Grammaticae Romanae Fragmenta* (Leipzig: Teubner, 1907), vol. 1, pp. 54ff.; for a modern redrawing of the symbols, see K. Büchner, "Überlieferungsgeschichte der lateinischen Literatur des Altertums," in *Geschichte der Textüberlieferung*, 2 vols. (Zürich: Atlantis

91

Verlag, 1961), vol. 1, p. 329. For a discussion of this document and its relation to the Roman scholar of the Republican period, L. Aelius Stilo, see S. F. Bonner, "Anecdoton Parisinum," *Hermes* 88 (1960): 354-360.

25. *Institutiones* I.xxvi (p. 67, Mynors); there is also a set of symbols listed in Isidore's *Etymologies* I.xxi, with explanations. Some of the terms are the same as those in the *anecdota*; a few have reference to Christian texts.

26. C. Wachsmuth, "Ueber die Zeichen und einige andere Eigenthümlichkeiten des *codex Venetus* der Ilias," *Rheinisches Museum* 18 (1863): 181. Why Cassiodorus should have chosen this symbol to mark definitions is still unclear to me.

27. Marius Victorinus, *De definitionibus*, ed. T. Stangl (1888), reprinted in Pierre Hadot, *Marius Victorinus: Recherches sur sa vie et des oeuvres* (Paris: Études Augustiniennes, 1971), pp. 331-362; for a list of definitions taken from Victorinus by Cassiodorus in his *Psalm Commentary*, see Hadot, p. 365.

28. Thus, at *ExpPs*, Ps. 2.319-320, he cites *"Terra autem dicta est a terendo, quod commeantium gressibus atteratur"*; which comes, in the final analysis, from Varro, *De lingua latina*. See H. Erdbrügger, *Cassiodorus, unde etymologias in Psalterii commentario prolatas petiuisse putandus sit* (diss., Jena, 1912).

29. Jerome, *Liber Interpretationis Hebraicorum Nominum*, ed. Paul de Lagarde, *Corpus Christianorum*, Series Latina 72 (Turnhout: Brepols, 1959), pp. 57ff.

30. Marrou, *Saint Augustin*, pp. 105ff.

31. Among the oldest manuscripts (i.e., pre-Caroline), we find this marker of the ansate cross in Paris BN lat. 12239, 12240, 12241 (*Codices Latini Antiquiores: A Paleographical Guide to Manuscripts Prior to the Ninth Century*, ed. E. A. Lowe, 11 vols [Oxford: Clarendon Press, 1934-1971], vol. 5, nos. 638, 639); Paris Bibl. Ste. Geneviève 55 (ibid., no. 694); Wolfenbüttel Herzog August Bibliothek Cod. Guelf. 14 + 24 Weissenburg (*Codices Latini Antiquiores*, ed. E. A. Lowe [Oxford: Clarendon Press, 1959], vol. 9, no. 1384).

32. "PHE" in verse 17 has been cut off in photographing the inside margin of the page.

33. See the edition of this treatise by C. B. Kendall, *Bedae Venerabilis Opera*, Pars I: *Opera Didascalica, Corpus Christianorum*, Series Latina 123 A (Turnhout: Brepols, 1975), pp. 142ff.

34. I wish to thank Professor Victor H. Yngve of the Graduate Library School, University of Chicago, for his helpful and incisive comments on the preliminary draft of this paper.

Stoic Influences in Librarianship: A Critique

Victor H. Yngve

This paper is a little different from some of the other papers in
this conference in that it looks to the future as well as to the past.
I started out with the problems of the future of librarianship and
information science generally, and have spent many years on them.
But the future must bear a continuity with the present. Attempted
solutions to problems in librarianship are simply proposed answers
to the perceived problems, needs, and aspirations of the present.
Thus anyone working on problems of the future needs to try to
understand the present out of which these problems and their
perceptions as problems have grown. Now it should come as no
surprise to historians that I have found that the present can only
be understood as a continuation and direct outgrowth of the past.
As an information scientist I have had to become a historian.

This paper, then, is a celebration of our deep indebtedness to
the thought and culture of ancient Greece, and at the same time it
sounds a warning to information scientists that some of the lessons
we have learned from the Greeks are being blindly and unthinking-
ly misapplied today, to the detriment of clear thinking about library problems.[1]

Although Greek thought and Greek culture played a pivotal
role in the development of Western thought, and their influence
can be seen everywhere today, it must be recognized that they do
represent an older time, older values, and an older culture. The
modern era, removed by over a hundred generations, has seen the

Victor H. Yngve *is professor of information science at the University of Chicago.*

Journal of Library History, Vol. 16, No. 1, Winter 1981
© 1981 by the University of Texas Press   0275-3650/81/010092-14$01.25

emergence of the scientific revolution. Today we are to some extent asking different questions and making decisions on the basis of a different set of values. Therefore we would do well to examine carefully and reassess especially those parts of that great cultural heritage that we tend to take for granted, as they may be anachronistic or inapplicable in a more modern system of thought.

The Theory of the Sign

Of fundamental importance to our topic is the theory connecting words, thoughts, and things, the theory of the sign that we know from Plato, Aristotle, and especially the Stoics. The influence of the ancient Greek theory of the sign manifests itself today in the "common-sense" that is enshrined in the everyday language we employ when talking about writing, content, knowledge, language, the diffusion of ideas, and so on. Its influence is likewise evident in current philosophical conceptions and in the way we think about librarianship.

A good place to start in considering the theory of the sign is with Plato, who discussed in his interesting dialog *Cratylus* the relation of names to the things named. The discussion turns on the question of whether everything has a right name of its own by nature, or whether the only correctness of names comes from convention or agreement. Underlying the discussion there appears to be a presumption of a one-to-one pairing of names and things, the important issue simply being how to determine for each thing its true and proper name. Thus it was seen as a disturbing factor that words had changed from former times by adding, subtracting, transposing, and changing letters "until finally no human being can understand what in the world the word means."[2]

Aristotle, in a remarkably epigrammatic passage at the beginning of his book *On Interpretation*, says that words *directly symbolize* mental experiences, while mental experiences are the *images* of things. The conception of three related elements, here called words, mental experiences, and things, has been incorporated with little change in successive views of the sign relation right up to the present day (see figure 1). Aristotle believed that although words are different in different languages, the mental experiences they symbolize and the things of which the mental experiences are the images are universal, that is, the same for everybody.[3] Modern opinion, however, is to the contrary. It is now widely understood in cultural anthropology and linguistics that mental experiences are not the same for all. They may be quite different in different

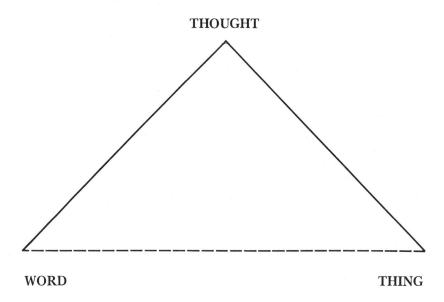

THOUGHT

WORD   THING

Figure 1

The ancient Greek theory of the sign expressing the relation between words, thoughts, and things is still influential in philosophy, linguistics, and psychology, but is often inappropriately invoked in these disciplines and in library and information science and the study of communication. Ambiguity is a problem in this theory. The diagram is adapted from Ogden and Richards. The terms used in the text for *words*, *thoughts*, and *things* according to the various authors are:

	words	*thoughts*	*things*
Plato	names	—	things named
Aristotle	words	mental experience	things
Stoics	signifier	signified	thing referred to
	sound (grammatical)	thing indicated (logical)	real object
Apollonius	form	meaning	
Ogden and Richards	symbol	reference	referent

cultures. There are no absolutes in the realm of concepts, a point that classifiers of knowledge need to remember.

Although the impact of Aristotle in recent centuries is widely acknowledged, the Stoic impact has often been underestimated because we have received it indirectly, the original writings having been lost. Of the three parts of Stoic philosophy—logical, physical, and ethical—the logical part, which included the theory of the sign, was central, for it considered how one arrives at truth, and without it ethics and physics could not express themselves.[4] The Stoic theory of the sign, developed between about 300 B.C. and 150 B.C., went far beyond Aristotle. It represents, to my mind, one of the most spectacular achievements of ancient Greece.

The Stoics opposed Aristotle on many points, but they accepted the basic three-element conception of the sign. According to Sextus Empiricus (c. A.D. 200), the Stoics said that:

> Three things are linked together, the thing signified [*sēmaino-menon*] and the thing signifying [*sēmainon*] and the thing referred to [*tugkhanon*]; and of these the thing signifying is the sound [*phōnē*] ("Dion," for instance); and the thing signified is the actual thing indicated thereby, and which we apprehend as existing in dependence on our intellect, whereas the barbarians although hearing the sound do not understand it; and the thing referred to is the external real object, such as Dion himself. And of these, two are bodies—that is, the sound and the thing referred to—and one is incorporeal, namely the thing signified and expressible [*lekton*], and this too is true or false.[5]

Note that the term "barbarian" refers to people who speak languages other than Greek, so that, as with Aristotle, the speech sounds would be different in different languages, and the thing signified, the thought that we apprehend, has the character of logical truth and falsity and would thus be universal.

The Stoic theory of the signified, of mental experiences, included a logic differing from Aristotelian logic in that it was a logic of propositions rather than of classes and a theory of inference schemas rather than of logically true matrices. It included discussions of propositions, their constituent subjects and predicates, active and passive, genera and species, arguments, moods, syllogisms, and fallacies. Their logical theory was similar in certain respects to the modern theories of Frege and Carnap. The prolific third-century B.C. Stoic Chrysippus was probably the greatest logician of ancient times.[6] The accidents of history by which

Aristotle has been preserved from the fourth century B.C., but the Stoic writings from the third and second centuries have been lost to us, give one pause regarding the problems of preserving the written record over long periods of time.

Whereas the Stoic theory of the signified, of concepts, thoughts, or mental experiences, was logical in character, the Stoic theory of the signifier, of speech sounds or words, was of a grammatical nature. It had three levels. The first level was called *phonē* [voice], which was defined as a percussion of the air or as the proper object of the sense of hearing. It was essentially a level of phonetic substance. The second level was called *lexis* [diction]. Diction is voice reducible to writing. The difference between diction and voice is that diction is articulate. The elements of diction are the twenty-four letters or phonemes. It was recognized that a given representation at the level of diction could ambiguously represent two or more distinct senses at a higher level. Differences of dialect, and barbarisms or mispronunciations, were treated at the level of diction. Diction was a phonemic and phonotactic level. The third level was called *logos* [speech]. The level of speech was a grammatical level having the parts of speech as elements, five parts of speech being distinguished. The difference between speech and diction is that speech is always semantic, it means something, whereas at the level of diction one can have meaningless nonsense forms. Solecisms or grammatical errors were treated at the level of speech. It was the level of speech in the theory of the signifier that directly signified the thoughts or meanings at the level of logic (*lekton*) in the theory of the signified. Thus a verb (*rhēma*) at the level of speech signifies an isolated predicate (*asyndeton katēgorēma*) at the level of logic. In the scope of this discussion it is impossible to do justice to the elegance and detailed sophistication of the Stoic grammatical and logical theory of the sign.

The Stoic theory of the sign became the philosophical foundation for grammar in the ancient world, and it remains the philosophical foundation of linguistics today. The conduit of Stoic thinking on the theory of the sign has been mainly the grammatical tradition, propagated through Greek and Latin grammar, and studied in grammar schools right up to modern times. The concepts of signifier and signified, of form and meaning, are basic in the works of the very influential Alexandrian of the second century A.D. Apollonius Dyscolus.[7] In Rome, Stoic philosophy became very popular. The close similarity of early Latin grammars to Stoic models has been clearly demonstrated.[8] Some of these early grammars with strong Stoic influence, such as Donatus and Priscian, served in the school for well over a millennium, right up to modern times. Thus although the original Stoic writings are lost to us, the Stoic view of what grammar is all about, and with it the Stoic theory of the sign, has survived in a very strong tradition in the schools, handed on through a hundred generations of school-children. In the process the ideas have become common coin in Western thought. They have entered our everyday language in the expressions we use when talking about language and meaning. As a result they seem so natural, so compelling, and so much a part of common sense as to be beyond question. Today, however, they need to be questioned.

A measure of the current influence of the Stoic theory of the sign can be obtained by considering that it was embraced explicit-ly by Ferdinand de Saussure, the founder of structural linguistics in the beginning of the century.[9] It was the cornerstone of the contributions of the influential philosopher Charles Sanders Peirce.[10] It figured centrally in the widely read book *The Meaning of Meaning*, by C. K. Ogden and I. A. Richards, who introduced there the well-known triangle of reference with the corners labeled symbol, reference, and referent, standing explicitly for word, thought, and thing (see figure 1).[11] Later, Charles Morris made his reputation in connection with the theory of the sign.[12] It has been championed by Roman Jakobson, the elder statesman of linguis-tics,[13] and has been tacitly or explicitly accepted by nearly all modern linguists. Recently there has been launched a whole new discipline or intellectual movement called semiotics, which is es-sentially the general study of the theory of the sign and its appli-cations.[14] The nearly universal acceptance of this 2,300-year-old theory, which I wish to question in some of its applications, is due in large part, I believe, to the pressure of tradition. It is so deeply entrenched in our everyday life, in the way we talk about talk and think about thought, that it seems completely natural and self-evident.

The Problem of Ambiguity

Of the various criticisms that can be brought to bear against the theory of the sign, I want to concentrate on just one. It is the problem of ambiguity.

The theory of the sign is designed to cover the standard case of one-word/one-meaning, yet we observe in fact that a given word may stand for several different meanings. This fact was, of course, known to the ancients. Chrysippus himself wrote at least seven-

teen books on ambiguity.[15] But basically the theory was not
equipped in the beginning to handle ambiguity, and it still can't.
Ogden and Richards, to give just one modern example, take as the
first of their "canons of symbolism": "One Symbol stands for one
and only one Referent."[16] They qualify it before too many pages
have gone by, however, by saying that when a symbol seems to
stand for two or more referents, such as top (mountain) and top
(spinning), we must regard it as two or more symbols, which are to
be differentiated in order to guard against the most obvious kind
of ambiguity.[17] This dodge of defining the problem out of existence for the sake of preserving an ancient theory is unfortunate.
Its continued prevalence in the literature seems to me to be an intellectual scandal of major proportions. It does nothing to comfort
someone who has looked up *run* in the dictionary and has found
several dozen senses differentiated there. If they all are spelled the
same and sound the same, how are we to differentiate them when
they are used? How is it that when someone uses the word *run* in
the presumably uncontrolled vocabulary of English, I can almost
invariably tell which sense is meant? The theory of the sign offers
no adequate explanation. Furthermore, it can easily be shown that
no word ever corresponds to the supposed standard case of one-
word/one-meaning. *Napoleon Bonaparte* is not only the name of
the historical figure: it could well be the name of a pet poodle.
Penicillin does not only refer to the antibiotic drug: a hospital
patient can use it to refer to the nurse who appears at the door
by saying *Come in, Penicillin.*

Some authors have elaborated the view that we can resolve ambiguities by taking into account the context, that is, the surrounding words. Grammarians have pointed out that the grammatical or
syntactic constraints in the sentence serve to restrict the possible
senses of the individual words, thus the noun-verb ambiguity of
walk is resolved by context in *the walk* and *to walk*. But decades
of work on the mechanical translation of language have shown
rather conclusively that taking the grammatical context into account is in itself inadequate for resolving ambiguities.

Some students of language have maintained that ambiguities can
be resolved by taking into account the context of situation, including the speaker and listener, the physical setting, the topic of
conversation, and numerous other such factors. Others have said
that pragmatic and functional factors must be taken into account,
that is, what the speaker intends to accomplish with his utterance,
and what he does accomplish from the hearer's point of view. But
the fact remains that the theory of the sign, which can but poorly

accommodate grammatical considerations of the verbal context, has no place at all for considerations of the context of situations or of pragmatic or functional considerations related to speakers and listeners.

If we retain the theory of the sign, the everyday facts of ambiguity pose an insuperable problem. Yet this ancient theory, originally designed as a philosophical theory of knowledge, lives on, nourished by the tradition, and continues to be resorted to even today in certain applications not contemplated by the Greeks.

An Alternative Model

What is needed is a better theory, not only for modern linguistics but, as I shall show, for facing important problems in librarianship. A possible candidate, and the one I favor, is what I call human linguistics, to distinguish it from the familiar linguistics of language. Human linguistics is a scientific discipline focused on people, individually and in groups, rather than a philosophical or grammatical discipline focused on language. Human linguistics is defined as the scientific study of how people communicate. Although a full treatment would require many chapters, and thus can not be given here, it is possible to describe rather briefly just those aspects of the theory that are relevant to our topic of the problem of ambiguity.

Since the focus of human linguistics is not on the scholastic conception of language, but rather on people, there is need for a theoretical construct corresponding to the person. This construct is called the *communicating individual*. The communicating individual is defined as an abstraction in linguistics that includes just those properties of the person required to account for his communicative behavior. It is thus a theoretical abstraction representing a concrete reality. Corresponding to observations of this reality, no two communicating individuals need be exactly the same: similarities and differences of individuals are handled in terms of same and different properties. Human linguistics is thus not a philosophical or grammatical discipline, but a natural science. This being the case it is possible to treat the communicating individual as a system in a way parallel to the systems approaches in the other sciences.

There is also need in human linguistics for a theoretical construct corresponding to groups of communicating individuals. This construct is called a *linkage*. The linkage is a system defined over a definite group of individuals who are the participants, over a definite stretch of time, together with the necessary channels, props, and settings, that carries out communicative behavior in such a way as to develop and maintain certain communicative properties at the system level. A typical linkage might be composed of two individuals, participant A and participant B, interacting through a channel (see figure 2).

Individuals and linkages are systems defined in part by their *properties*. Properties are set up on the basis of observational and experimental evidence in a manner paralleling standard practice in other sciences. Properties are thus theoretical constructs postulated on the basis of evidence. Proposed generalizations can then yield predictions that can be tested against further observational evidence. The human linguistics proposal is thus a proposal for a scientific discipline involving the usual interplay of observation and theory.

When people communicate it is physical energy that is carried in the channel. If the individuals are speaking to each other it is sound energy. If gestures and facial expressions are important, light energy is also involved. The energy in the channel is measurable by physical instruments. This picture differs markedly from the usual one in the linguistics of language following the theory of the sign. In this picture the channel carries only energy. It specifically does not carry speech sounds, words, symbols, sentences, meanings, content, or signs of any kind. The usual conception that it does makes no physical sense.

Then how can we account for the fact that person A can tell person B something? Don't we have to assume that the meaning is transmitted from A to B? No. The energy in the channel has no significance by itself. Any significance it may have is relative to the individuals involved. A has certain properties. These properties and their changes describe what A is doing when he speaks. The sound energy that is transmitted reflects some of these properties and their changes. It reflects the conditions of the speaker A. Any significance it may have at this point, then, is located in the speaker and described in terms of his properties and their changes. The listener B also has properties, some of which are sensitive to the incoming sound energy. These properties, and the changes reflecting the incoming energy, describe how B is affected by the incoming energy, how he understands it. Any significance the incoming energy may have at this point is located in the listener B. If A says *run* meaning a run of good luck, and B hears *run* and understands

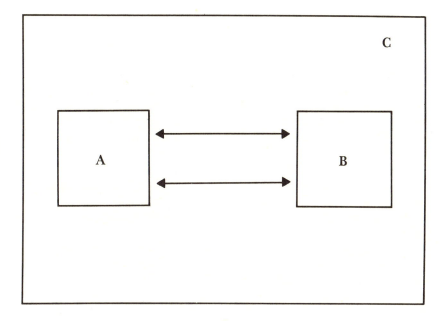

Figure 2

The human linguistics approach to communicative behavior between two individuals in a linkage treats the individuals A and B and the channel as systems and the linkage C as a system composed of the individuals and the
channel. It then studies the properties of the systems, and does not invoke
the ancient and misleading theory of the sign. In this theory ambiguity is not
a problem.

a run in a silk stocking, the meanings or understandings are entirely in A and in B. The channel transmits only the sound energy of *run*, nothing more.

Now we know from observation that an item like *run* is understood differently under different contexts of situation. According to the point of view proposed here, these different contexts of situation are active only in the individual participants—the speaker and the listener. But the usual theories of speakers and listeners are intellectually based on the theory of the sign, which has no place for the context of situation. Semantic theories, for example, would have the speaker and listener consult their internal dictionaries. Grammatical theories would have them consult their internal grammars. Structural linguistic theories emphasize the selective function in a paradigm. This is Saussure's paradigmatic axis. Theories following the communication theory of Shannon make use of an allied concept called selective information.[18] It is not widely realized that the theory of the sign is inadequate as a foundation for a theory of communication.

In a system-theory approach to the properties of the individual, on the other hand, the changing context of situation is encoded in the changing properties of the individual. It is thus easily possible to comprehend that an individual could respond differently at different times to the same input energy if his properties were different. One can also easily comprehend in a system-theory approach that speaking and understanding both involve changes in the properties of the individuals that we interpret as changes in the context of situation. Syntactic, semantic, and pragmatic considerations can all be taken into account in this same way.

The theory of the individual that makes these things possible postulates that the properties of the individual include a repertoire of dimensions or *categories* along which the momentary state or *conditions* of the individual can change with time. There is also a repertoire of *procedures*, each of which, when triggered, will effect a change of condition of one of the categories of the individual. Each procedure has its own complex triggering conditions involving a number of categories, and possibly also certain input energies. Thus when specified conditions are met, a procedure is triggered, and as a result one of the conditions is changed. Categories, conditions, and procedures are supported by *basic properties*.

The context of situation is taken into account, then, in the resolution of ambiguity, in the following way: when certain conditions obtain in the properties of the speaker, certain procedures are triggered, and *run*, for example, is produced in one of its senses. Now if the listener has been following what the speaker has been saying, he will have some *mutuality* of properties with those of the speaker, and certain conditions will then obtain also in the listener, with the result that selected procedures will be triggered in the listener to constitute the appropriate understanding of *run*. The coordinated execution of these procedures in the speaker and listener changes the conditions of the speaker and listener in a coordinated way so that not only does appropriate understanding take place, but also the listener continues to follow and to stay "with it" so that future items can continue to be understood appropriately. In this way we see how a system theory not based on the theory of the sign can account for communication and the resolution of ambiguities.

A Library Application

Let us consider as an example what happens when a library patron approaches the reference desk with a question. According to the usual theory of communication based on the theory of the sign, on logic, and on the linguistics of language, the reference librarian, together with the available reference materials and services, would be viewed as a gigantic data base filled with true and unambiguous propositions. The patron, in querying this data base, would pose a simple unambiguous question. The reference librarian would match portions of the question against the propositions in the data base and retrieve the proposition or propositions that answer the question. The unreality of this as a picture of what really happens is obvious, yet one often finds it put forward as a theoretical picture of question answering, or information retrieval. It betrays the origins of the theory of the sign in the Aristotelian-Stoic theory of knowledge, a philosophical enterprise having little to do with how people really communicate.

The predictions of human linguistics theory would be quite different. With a focus on the properties of the individuals involved—the patron and the reference librarian—we predict the importance of the initial mutuality of properties they have, that is, how well they know each other. If they know each other well, there may be enough mutuality that the reference librarian will understand immediately what the patron is asking. But if not, we would expect some initial difficulties. The question would likely appear vague and ambiguous to the librarian, although it may be quite clear to the patron. We would predict, then, the necessity for a dialog by means of which the required mutuality would gradually be developed. If all goes well this would eventually result in the librarian understanding what the patron wants well enough to attempt an answer. We see that the human linguistics theory, contrary to the theory of the sign, predicts the necessity of what has aptly been called negotiating the question, and provides a principled basis for a theory of what is actually observed to take place.

This is only one example of the inadequacy of the theory of the sign as a basis for approaching library problems. Other examples could be given. I should like to urge in conclusion that the philosophy of librarianship not be based on the ancient theory of the sign, inherited from the Greek culture of 2,300 years ago or more. That was designed for a different purpose. It should instead be based on modern scientific principles. It is time to move away from a reliance on the ancient philosophical theory of the representation of knowledge, with its presumptions of universality, of one-word/one-meaning, and of independence from the context of situation. These are false and misleading in many library applications. We should turn instead to a proper scientific understanding of how people communicate.

Notes

1. This is a report of some of the results of research on communication that has occupied me for more than a decade. A fuller report will be published soon as a book under the title *Human Linguistics: The Scientific Study of How People Communicate*. I should like to thank my colleague on the panel, James W. Halporn, for his kind comments that have helped me to clarify some of the footnotes to this paper, and Mary Grathwol for insightful comments that have helped me to clarify the body of the paper and figure 1. Any remaining flaws are my own responsibility.

2. Cratylus 414 d: ... ὥστ᾽ ἐπεμβάλλοντες πολλά ἐπί τά πρῶτα ὀνόματα τελευτῶντες ποιοῦσιν μηδ ἄν ἕνα ἀνθρώπων συνεῖναι ὅτι ποτέ βούλεται τό ὄνομα. The translation is by H. N. Fowler, *Plato: With an English Translation*, vol. 6 (London: W. Heinemann; New York: G. P. Putnam's Sons, 1926), p. 106.

3. On interpretation 1, translated by E. M. Edghill in Richard McKeon (ed.), *The Basic Works of Aristotle* (New York: Random House, 1941), p. 40. The relevant quote is: "Spoken words are the symbols of mental experience and written words are the symbols of spoken words. Just as all men have not the same writing, so all men have not the same speech sounds, but the mental experiences, which these directly symbolize, are the same for all, as also are those things of which our experiences are the images."

4. Sources for Stoic philosophy have been collected in Hans von Arnim (ed.), *Stoicorum Veterum Fragmenta*, 4 vols. (Leipzig: B. G. Teubner, 1903–1924), hereafter cited as *SVF*. The best single connected ancient source for the Stoic theory of the sign is the article on Zeno in the third-century A.D.

Lives by Diogenes Laertius. For a very approximate translation, see R. D. Hicks, *Lives of Eminent Philosophers*, 2 vols. (London: Heinemann; New York: G. P. Putnam's Sons, 1925), vol. 2.

5. *SVF* II.166. Translation slightly altered from *Adv. Log.* II.11,12 in R. G. Bury (trans.), *Sextus Empiricus*, 4 vols. (Cambridge, Mass.: Harvard University Press, 1933-1949), vol. 2.

6. A reconstruction of Stoic logic is given in Benson Mates, *Stoic Logic*, University of California Publications in Philosophy vol. 26 (Berkeley and Los Angeles: University of California Press, 1953).

7. Richard Schneider and Gustav Uhlig (eds.), *Grammatici Graeci*, 4 vols. (Leipzig: B. G. Teubner, 1878-1911), part 2. I understand that an English translation is being prepared for publication by Fred Householder. The later influence of Apollonius Dyscolus is discussed at page xxii in the German translation by Alexander Buttman (Berlin: Ferd. Dümmlers Verlagsbuchhand-lung Harrwitz und Grossmann, 1878). It is also now thought that the widely used textbook attributed to Dionysius Thrax was actually based on the work of Apollonius. For this, see Jan Pinborg, "Classical Antiquity," in Thomas Sebeok (ed.), *Current Trends in Linguistics* 13: 69-126 (The Hague: Mouton, 1975).

8. Karl Barwick, *Remmius Palaemon und die römische Ars Grammatica*, *Philologus* Supplbd. 15.2 (Leipzig: Dieterich'sche Verlagsbuchhandlung, 1922).

9. Ferdinand de Saussure, *Course in General Linguistics*, ed. Charles Bally and Albert Sechehaye in collaboration with Albert Riedlinger, trans. Wade Baskin (New York, Toronto, and London: McGraw-Hill, 1966). The material dates from Saussure's lectures between 1906 and 1911.

10. See, for example, Justus Buchler (ed.), *Philosophical Writings of Peirce* (New York: Dover, 1955).

11. *The Meaning of Meaning: A Study of the Influence of Language upon Thought and of the Science of Symbolism* (New York: Harcourt Brace, 1923). Their famous triangle diagram, which is the only diagram in the book, is on page 11.

12. Charles Morris, *Signs, Language, and Behavior* (New York: Prentice-Hall, 1946).

13. See, for example, his "Quest for the Essence of Language," in Roman Jakobson, *Word and Language*, vol. 2 of *Selected Writings* (The Hague and Paris: Mouton, 1971).

14. See, for example, the writings and editorial projects of Thomas Sebeok.

15. As shown in the partial catalog of his works in Diogenes Laertius VII 193. We can only guess as to their content.

16. Ogden and Richards, *Meaning of Meaning*, p. 88.

17. Ibid., p. 91.

18. Claude E. Shannon, "A Mathematical Theory of Communication," *Bell System Technical Journal* 27 (1948): 379-423.

An Idea of Librarianship: An Outline for a Root-Metaphor Theory in Library Science

Joseph Z. Nitecki

Introduction

One of the dimensions of growth is its complexity. Most often, the bigger or older the institution, the more intricate its organization, the more elaborate its goals, and the more involved its ways for meeting these goals.

This principle seems to apply fully to librarianship, whether it is considered a discipline, an institution, or a service. To understand better the nature of modern librarianship, a two-fold approach is suggested.[1]

First, one should look at librarianship as a general discipline and study its essential characteristics as a whole, rather than limit such study to some specialized aspects of that discipline. Library science and information science are both subspecies of the same basic intellectual approach; we refer to that theoretical discipline as "metalibrarianship."

Second, we ought to identify basic components of librarianship by reducing the complexity of the field to its simplest parts, the "roots" of that discipline. Since the complexity encompasses more than just the structure of physical library buildings and collections, the term "roots" refers not to empirically verifiable facts or measurable entities, but rather to the relationships between these facts or entities and to their interpretations. Hence, the suggested metalibrarianship is tentatively defined in this paper as a disci-

Joseph Z. Nitecki *is director of libraries at the State University of New York at Albany.*

Journal of Library History, Vol. 16, No. 1, Winter 1981
© 1981 by the University of Texas Press   0275-3650/81/010106–15$01.30

pline, the study of relationships between three basic components of knowledge (or information) transfer: the generic book (B); its subject matter, or knowledge (K); and its readers, or users (U), considered simultaneously as an actual process of information transfer, the impact of that process on its participants, and an expression of the meaning of knowledge or information transferred.

Methodology: Epistemological Assumptions

There is no single, all-inclusive philosophical explanation of all phenomena. Instead, different schools of philosophy offer their own hypothetical speculations about the universe. It is proposed that the theory of metalibrarianship, as an eclectic discipline, can also be formulated in terms of selected philosophical hypotheses, each providing a comprehensive view of metalibrarianship, offered from a different vantage point. In this approach, I base my model on Pepper's theory about philosophies, which he calls "world hypotheses."[2]

My model is also hypothetical. It provides a conditional explanation of metalibrarianship, based on a series of provisional assumptions about its nature in terms of three of Pepper's five world hypotheses: the mechanism, expanded contextualism, and formism.[3] These three world hypotheses provide a theoretical interpretation of the entire field: *mechanism* by structuring information processes, *contextualism* by interpreting psychological aspects of these processes, and *formism* by relating all processes to the overall mission of metalibrarianship. Individually, each interpretation offers a microscopic view of one of the dimensions of metalibrarianship, and only together do they present a macroscopic survey of the whole field.

The basic difference between Pepper's world hypotheses approach and my own adaptation of that philosophical methodology is in the interpretation of the concept of "root metaphor," and in the interrelationships between the world hypotheses.

In metalibrarianship, the primary root metaphor is the relationship between B, U, and K (that is, the generic book, its user, and knowledge contained in the book), analyzed within the framework of the three world hypotheses, each formulated in terms of its own, secondary root-metaphor: machine-like, quantitative properties in proceduralism; pragmatic, contextual relations viewed in terms of "an act in the context"; and the qualitative, conceptual aspects of relations perceived in terms of the root metaphor of similarity.

Furthermore, the concept of wholism in the model interrelates the three subtheories, while Pepper considers each world hypothesis as an independent, whole-in-itself interpretation of the total universe.

Wholism in metalibrarianship implies complete interdependence between the three subtheories; a change affecting one dimension of the B-U-K relationship has impact on the B-U-K relationships in the other two dimensions. Together, the three dimensions are interpreted as the fundamental levels of metalibrarianship.

In our model, each concept of metalibrarianship, B, U, and K, is accepted as a given, internally undefined "black box," transplanted from other disciplines. Hence, the approach applies equally to readers of books, listeners of music, or viewers of the visual arts. It does not matter whether the carrier of information refers to a printed book or its filmed version; or whether the message is presented in the form of a philosophical treatise, technical report, or poetic insight. Instead, our model concentrates on these aspects of relations that are essential in any conceptual communication, irrespective of the type of message, its carrier, or recipient.

Metalibrarianship as a System: Logical Assumptions

"Metalibrary system" is defined as a set of concepts that interrelates users' needs for information with the means available to them to obtain that information. The system provides a generalization of relations between the component parts of the discipline, without destroying their internal unity.

Essential to this approach is the relationship between the basic concepts, not the specific properties of these concepts. We subscribe to the proposition that human knowledge is defined as "relations known"; the world around us is perceived as a physical or conceptual relationship between objects, events, or concepts, formulated by comparing or contrasting the acquired knowledge with the knowledge of something else either better understood or more familiar to us.

In our model, the relationship is analyzed on two different, although fully interrelated levels: (a) internal relationships between the three primitive terms, B, U, and K; and (b) external relationships between sets of B-U-K, each set considered within its own dimension of metalibrarianship (figure 1).

The internal, primary relationships are determined by their own structural laws, while the secondary, external relationships are described in terms of different secondary root metaphors of each

109

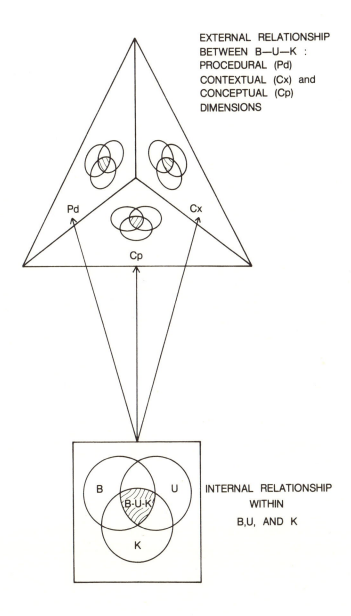

FIG. 1. TWO LEVELS OF RELATIONSHIP IN THE THEORY OF
METALIBRARIANSHIP.

dimension (procedural, contextual, and conceptual). The former provides a definition of the essence of relationships, the latter describes the impact of these relationships on various activities in the field.

(a) The internal B-U-K relationship is analyzed within its two distinct stages, static and dynamic.

A static model is considered in terms of the four constituents of the B-U-K: (1) the *need*, expressing the user's awareness of the necessity to attain certain goals; (2) specific *goals* sought by the user; (3) *means* to achieve them; and (4) the feeling of *goal-fulfillment*.

The relationships between these four constituents are in turn determined by their own attributes: *efficiency* of selected means in reaching the goals; *satisfaction* resulting from the fulfillment of needs; and *lacuna*, indicating a disparity between the goals sought and their fulfillment.

Fundamental relationships between the constituents and their attributes are expressed by three laws: (1) *Law of Structure*, stating that the conceptual relationships between the basic constituents (that is, need, goal, means, and goal-fulfillment) define a metalibrary system at any given point; (2) *Operational Law*, stipulating that the operational interrelationship between the primitive terms B, U, and K defines a given metalibrary system in terms of the quantitative characteristics of each term; and (3) *Valuational Law*, maintaining that the valuational interrelationship between the attributes (that is, efficiency, satisfaction, and lacuna) in any given metalibrary system defines the qualitative characteristics of each primitive term, with goal-fulfillment as a common denominator.

In a dynamic stage, changes are expressed by three major principles. (1) *Principle of Internal Change*: a given system, in which needs, means, and goals are fixed, will change so as to either increase or decrease the total complexity of its subsystems (that is, satisfaction, efficiency, and achievement). A positive change increases, while a negative change decreases the number of such relations. (2) *Corollary Principle*: a system will not normally move from a state of equilibrium, since it balances the degree of satisfaction, efficiency, and accomplishment, with their counterparts, dissatisfaction, waste, and lacuna. (3) *Principle of External Change*: any change in the formators (needs, means, and goals) affects the basic metalibrary system and induces further changes by altering placement of equilibrium.

(b) External relationships between different B-U-K subsytems describe the B-U-K behavior within each dimension of metalibrarianship.

In the *procedural* dimension, the relations are considered functions of particular sets of quantitative characteristics, associated respectively with the book (B), its user (U), and the book content (K). These entities are organized around the secondary root metaphor of the machine, interpreting all relationships in terms of natural, physical properties of B-U-K, such as the format of the book, the illustrations used to explain its content, or the level of the reader's education or interest.

The procedural approach refers to the technical, engineering processes in acquisition, classification, storing, and handling of information material; it aims at the efficiency in B-U-K processes. This approach determines the methods of metalibrary operations.

The relationships in the *contextual* dimension of metalibrarianship are formulated around the secondary root metaphor of a total given event, interpreting the impact of the particular context of information transfer on its receiver, the carrier, and the message itself. This approach provides a pragmatic evaluation of consequences of any action or decision made in the metalibrary operations.

The rational, *conceptual* level of metalibrarianship concentrates on the logical relationship between the intangible attributes of each B-U-K relationship evaluated qualitatively. The root metaphor of this approach is the similarity between actual relations and an ideal, potential concept of knowledge transfer. The conceptual approach formulates the purposes of metalibrary operations, and is important in library planning activities.

Each of the approaches just outlined has its own theoretical limitations. Proceduralism is limited to the description of operations, since its *modi operandi* are based on quantitative aspects of B-U-K relations. This approach cannot, by itself, explain the reasons for these relations.

The contextual emphasis on the context of specific, current events limits its ability to forecast future changes in the B-U-K relationships.

The conceptual approach offers a theoretical explanation based on an intuitive perception of the totality of such relationships. However, since the relations between the primitive terms are dynamic, the insight obtained from these relations is always temporary, changing with each new configuration of B-U-K.

Together, the three approaches balance each other's limitations, offering a model of metalibrarianship as a unified discipline that can be procedurally quantified, conceptually qualified, and contextually tested in actual operations.

The analogy between the structure of the proposed model and the things modeled, in our case, the library-oriented information phenomena, can be verified directly or indirectly in at least two different ways: statistically, by measuring the coefficient of changes, resulting from the quantitive rearrangements within the B-U-K relationships; and methodologically, by structural corroboration of the degree of inclusiveness (that is, the scope of the model), and the extent of logical consistency (that is, the level of precision provided by the model).

Philosophical Framework

A possible contribution of our model to the theory of library science can be illustrated by a brief summary of the roles it can fulfill in structuring and interrelating various missions and activities in metalibrarianship.

(1) Metalibrary Discourse

Each dialogue in metalibrarianship consists of an actual, procedural sequence of stimulus-response activities, utilized in achieving particular informational ends; a possible, contextual environment, suitable for need-fulfillment activities; and a necessary and minimal conceptual relationship between the actual and possible conditions in metalibrary communication.

The procedural level of communication refers to the methods used in finding needed material, the contextual level reflects the search strategy, and the conceptual level interfaces the processes of information retrieval with the users' needs for information.

The end product of a discourse in metalibrary communication is a new metaphorical relationship established between the description of some aspects of reality, recorded physically in the carriers of information, and that reality's perception in the minds of the interpreters of the description. The discourse is satisfactory if it meets the users' needs by expanding or modifying their conceptual perception of reality.

(2) Ethical Relativism

In metalibrarianship, as in any other discipline, policies are formulated and actions are undertaken to accomplish some specific goals. A theory of metalibrarianship must, therefore, address itself to the ethical issues examining reasons for choosing given goals, or for accepting certain standards as guides in decision-making processes. Likewise, the concept of "goodness" of metalibrary services, or "rightness" of metalibrary policies must be evaluated in terms of basic premises, expressing specific philosophical attitudes toward the expected metalibrary role in the community.

In proceduralism, the statement "this book is good" is interpreted as meaning that a particular book is good for some specific, identifiable reasons. Thus, in our example, a book can be considered good for the quality of its reproductions; its subject matter may be acceptable because of the style in which it is written, or because the level of presentation matches the interest of its readers well. A given book is desirable because of its characteristics.

The conceptual values are formulated in terms of qualitative properties, which, although not measured physically, can be grasped intuitively. "This book is good" in conceptual interpretation means that it has some intrinsic values, approaching the ideal norm of "goodness" as it is expressed in the mores of our society, or in our own personal beliefs. For example, a given book may be praised or criticized for its presentation of a given style of life, depending on the ethical philosophy professed by the society. Conceptually, a good book expresses the value standards of its readers.

In the contextual interpretation of ethical concepts, the value judgments are not of things or of acts, but of the attitudes toward them. "This book is good" expresses an attitude toward that book by its readers or critics. Contextualism is not concerned with properties of books but with books' overall impact on their readers. Thus, a book arguing for a given style of life may be effective only if it creates some significant reaction in the reader. In this analysis, the book is good only if it is stimulating, if it has some intellectual impact on its readers.

It is important, however, to stress again that a value judgment based on any one of the above root metaphors alone is professionally prejudicial, or at least incomplete, because it expresses a value structure of only one of the basic philosophical viewpoints.

Together, empirically identified values in proceduralism, examined in terms of the socially conceptualized ideal values and verified in the actual informational transfer, constitute the bases for a comprehensive value theory in metalibrarianship.

(3) Sociological Realism

The extent of metalibrary involvement in the affairs of the community can be defined in terms of its attitude toward public interest. Public interest expresses the community's concepts of the common good, the effectiveness of the means used to achieve it, and the capability of social institutions, such as the library or information center, to reconcile conflicting group interests.

Conceptually, public interest is conceived as a criterion for developing public policies. It is defined as a function of an ultimate, ideal good sanctioned by the society. Thus, in a statement "reading is in the public interest" reading is assumed to have some intrinsic, qualitative properties that are of value to the members of a given society. Consequently, the librarian is here considered as an educator, disseminating the communally held values.

In proceduralism, public interest becomes a mandate given to social institutions to provide an efficient mechanism for reaching the ultimate good. The mechanism itself is value-neutral and equally available to all group interests. A statement "free library service is in the public interest" assumes that the concepts of "free service" have some characteristics directly contributing to efficiency in achieving the goals prescribed by the community, in our case, by providing information services that are economically accessible to everybody.

The role of the librarian is here conceived as that of a custodian of culture, protecting its resources and providing effective access to them.

In contextualism, public interest is interpreted as a process of balancing conflicting group interests. It is defined as an activity yielding to a common good that, in turn, is determined by a majority rule and consensus of the community. In the statement "a censor-free library service is in the public interest" the concept of "censor-free service" is considered to be in the public interest not because of some unique characteristics it may express, but simply because it fits the philosophical criteria of democracy. In this sense, the librarian acts as a broker, mediating between conflicting demands by referring to a generally accepted public interest.

(4) Metalibrary Metaphors

The subject matter of metalibrarianship can be considered in terms of a constantly changing metaphorical relationship between given and newly perceived dimensions of knowledge. These rela-

115

tionships are evident in two primary metalibrary functions: to assist the users in discovering concepts new to them; and to provide necessary resources for expanding the users' understanding of the concepts they have already discovered.

The following three diagrams exemplify these relations. In the first illustration (figure 2), the B-U-K encompasses the total, untapped but potentially available relationships, which can be actualized by bringing together a book on a desired subject with its reader. Here the Book-User relation (BU) represents the message (ME), the User-Knowledge (UK) stands for the receiver of the message (R), while the Book-Knowledge (BK) becomes an emerging concept (CO). Thus, an initially passive B-U-K relationship is transformed metaphorically into an active dialogue, CO-ME-R, initiated by the process of reading a book.

Our second illustration (figure 3) interrelates the theory of metalibrarianship with its practice. In this diagram the three hypotheses represent different levels at which metalibrarianship is perceived. The distinction between them expresses different hypotheses of each dimension.

This approach brings together the three seemingly incompatible components of metalibrarianship into one interrelated system. It also correlates the theoretical definition of metalibrarianship with its practical functions: to procure informational resources, to provide services, and to diffuse acquired knowledge.

And finally, our third illustration (figure 4) describes a metaphorical environment in metalibrarianship, allowing for a new insight into reality. This model illustrates the very concept of a root-metaphor theory in metalibrarianship.

The diagram interrelates the B-U-K relationships, defined in each of the metalibrary functional hypotheses, at three levels of communication, from the mere description of the message (D), through the acquaintance with the meaning of that message (A), into its interpretation (I). This relationship, in turn, explains different levels of apprehension of the knowledge communicated through its carriers: from an extrinsic, procedural description of the external relations in B-U-K (DA), through the contextual, intrinsic relationship between B-U-K (AI), culminating in a new insight into the essence of these relations (DI). It combines the unknown with an already known aspect of knowledge in the form of a just learned new relationship (DI).

Conclusion: A Plea for a New Frame of Mind

116

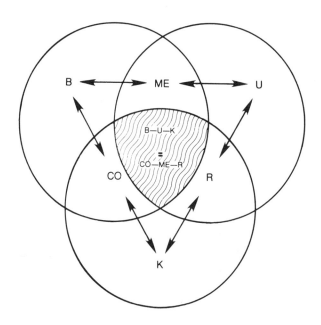

Fig. 2. METAPHORISM OF METALIBRARY RELATIONS

117

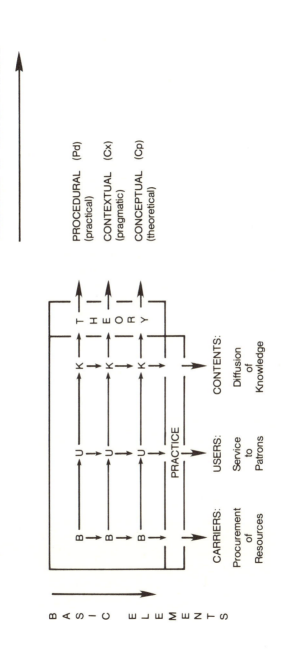

FIG. 3. PRACTICE AND ⊃RY OF METALIBRARIANSHIP.

118

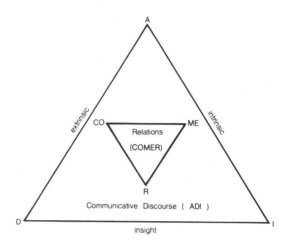

FIG 4. CONCEPTUAL ROOT - METAPHOR MODEL
IN METALIBRARIANSHIP

METAPHORICAL RELATIONSHIPS:
  CO: Concept
  ME: Meaning of the Concept (message)
  R: Response to the Message

COMMUNICATIVE DISCOURSES:
  A: Acquaintance (Intuitive Awareness)
  D: Description of the Meaning (Metaphoric)
  I: Interpretation of the Meaning (Symbolic)

LEVELS OF THE MEANING COMMUNICATED:
  Extrinsic: Description of the external relations (A - D)
  Intrinsic: Description of the internal relations (A - I)
  Insight: Description of the meaning of these
             relations (D - I)

*(The Journal of Library History, Philosophy and Comparative Librarianship,*Vol. 14, No. 1, Winter 1979, p. 36.)

The reality around us can never be fully apprehended, since it consists of constantly changing relationships between things in space, events in time, and concepts in our minds. Each known relationship becomes a seed for a potentially unlimited series of new relationships waiting to be discovered.

Metalibrarianship, as a discipline, is responsible not only for preserving the imprints of relations once discovered, but also for facilitating their rediscovery by new generations, giving each one of us an opportunity to make our own contribution to human knowledge by discovering new, not yet comprehended relations.

We all know, more or less, what metalibrarianship is about. What we do not fully realize is what it means, or could mean, since its meaning is metaphorical. It shifts with our involvement in the subject matter of metalibrarianship. Hence, the field is an open-ended discipline, its horizons expanding with each discovery of new relations.

Notes

1. I am indebted to Dr. Barbara McCrimmon for her valuable editorial comments.
   The following of my studies provide detailed analyses of the hypotheses reviewed in this essay: the relationship of definition of "good" to Pepper's classification of metaphysical theories (master's thesis, Roosevelt University, 1959); the concept of public interest in the philosophy of librarianship; the implications of a multiple approach (master's thesis, University of Chicago, 1963); "Public Interest and the Theory of Librarianship," *College and Research Libraries* 25, no. 4 (July 1964): 269-278, 325; "Reflections on the Nature and Limits of Library Science," *Journal of Library History* 3, no. 2 (April 1968): 103-119; "Repartee: Reply of Mr. Nitecki to Mr. Fairthorne," *Journal of Library History* 3, no. 4 (October 1968): 369-374; "Toward a Conceptual Pattern in Librarianship: A Model," *General Systems Bulletin* 2, no. 11 (June 1970): 2-16, also in: *Resources in Education* (ERIC no. ED 126897, December 1976); "On the Modality of Discourse in the Theory of Librarianship," unpublished manuscript, 1979 (available from ERIC, no. ED 171267); "Metaphors of Librarianship: A Suggestion for a Metaphysical Model," *Journal of Library History* 14, no. 1 (Winter 1979): 21-42; "Conceptual Dimensions of Library Management," *Journal of Library Management* 1, no. 2 (Summer 1980).
2. Stephen C. Pepper, *World Hypotheses: A Study in Evidence* (Berkeley: University of California Press, 1957).
3. Originally, Pepper identified four major world hypotheses: mechanism, formism, contextualism, and organicism. The root metaphor of organicism, the integration, is a kind of a refined "historical event" of contextualism, explaining away the time element from its contextualistic formulation. The fifth root metaphor, selectivism, is based on a root metaphor of the purposive, self-regulating act, resembling Whitehead's "actual occasion," and in-

terpreted by him as the "basic concrete actuality": Stephen C. Pepper, *Concept and Quality: A World Hypothesis* (La Salle, Ill.: Open Court, 1967), p. 5.

Founder of the Vatican Library: Nicholas V or Sixtus IV?

David Mycue

The Vatican Library, historians agree, came into being during the last half of the fifteenth century. The date of that event and the name of the founder depend upon what historian one reads. Since most historians credit either Pope Nicholas V (1447-1455) or Pope Sixtus IV (1471-1484), this paper will delve into the motives both popes had to establish the Library and the actions that they took to bring it about.[1] Is it possible that the Library had two founders within a generation?

That the papacy possessed no library worthy of the name when the Renaissance began will surprise few, once they recall the destructive invasions of the early Middle Ages and the feuds of powerful Roman families thereafter.[2] Owing to losses during the 1300s, when the headquarters of the papacy had been located in southern France, Pope Eugenius IV (1431-1447) possessed only 340 books,[3] which Nicholas V inherited upon Eugenius IV's death. Nicholas enlarged the collection; for that reason, as well as his being acknowledged as the first Renaissance pope, most historians have termed him the founder of the Vatican Library.[4]

If he deserves that title, his motive for establishing the Library is clear: his love of books. Nicholas, as Tommaso Parentucelli Sarzana, was born into poverty and grew up while his parents were in exile. His father died when he was nine, but Tommaso's mother kept him in school, for he was something of a prodigy. He became a master of arts at eighteen; then did private tutoring in Florence

David Mycue *is assistant director, budget and technical services, McAllen Memorial Library*.

Journal of Library History, Vol. 16, No. 1, Winter 1981
©1981 by the University of Texas Press   0275-3650/81/010121-13$01.15

until he had earned enough money to return to the university at Bologna, where he earned a doctor of theology degree while working part-time as a servant of the bishop of Bologna, Nicholao degli Albergati.

Recognizing the young man's ability, Bishop Albergati employed him to manage the Albergati household. Shortly thereafter, the bishop ordained Parentucelli as a priest; and when Albergati received a position in the foreign relations department of the Vatican, Father Parentucelli went along. For many years afterward, Albergati acted as a papal emissary throughout western Europe, although he was often so ill that Parentucelli had to perform many of his duties. When Albergati died, Pope Eugenius appointed Parentucelli to the bishopric of Bologna, but kept him at Rome, where his talents deeply impressed the pope. As a reward for high-quality work, Eugenius made Parentucelli a cardinal nine months after he had become a bishop. Less than a year after that promotion Eugenius died, and the college of cardinals voted Cardinal Parentucelli to succeed him.[5]

As Pope Nicholas V, he immediately began doing what he said he would do if he were wealthy—buying books and constructing lovely buildings. While working his way through college he had met the Florentine banker Cosimo de' Medici, who employed him to draw up a booklist for a library that Cosimo was building as part of the Dominican monastery of San Marco in Florence. The booklist achieved great respect among bibliophiles as the San Marco library gained recognition as the best in Italy. Consequently, the list became the basis for private collections of nobles in several Italian city-states, where the wealthy, to offset the stigma of usury and to display their riches, were promoting numerous cultural activities. Library building, as a result, was becoming a fad in fifteenth-century western Europe.[6]

Enthroned on St. Peter's chair, Nicholas expanded his youthful hobby of book collecting into a major Vatican enterprise. Under the direction of his longtime friend Fiorentino Vespasiano da Bisticci, a Florentine bookseller, book scouts from the Vatican scoured Europe for manuscripts while intellectuals throughout Italy were hired to copy manuscripts, to translate Greek works into Latin, to write new works, or to give public lectures on the liberal arts.[7] Rome swelled in an intellectual ferment during Nicholas V's papacy. As those activities proceeded, Nicholas added the accumulating manuscripts to the existing collection.

While he developed his library plans, he kept the rare books in his bedroom; the rest he placed in eight upright bookcases in a nearby room. Although his love of expensive binding later led to charges that his motivation was that of an aesthete, a dilettante, or an antiquarian, his appointment of Giovanni Tortelli as his special librarian offers another view. Up to then, and ever since 1318, the title "librarian of the pope" had been held by the pope's personal confessor, always a priest of the San Augustin order, who merely cared for the pope's prayerbooks. Nicholas continued the tradition, but the official librarian kept doing the same job while Tortelli worked on the library collection.

Before Nicholas V's papacy, Tortelli had earned a high reputation among academics for having compiled a dictionary and for having translated lives of the saints from the Greek. He was busy inventorying the growing number of books in the Vatican Palace when Nicholas died in 1455, his library plans still on the drawing-board even though they had become his top priority project during those final years. It would have been "a wonderful work could he have accomplished it; but, forestalled by death, he left it unfinished," mourned Vespasiano.[8] Tortelli soon found himself relegated to the position of a minor Vatican functionary, which he remained until his death in 1466.[9]

If founders are those who originally conceive of an idea, whether or not they carry it out, then Pope Nicholas V was a founder, as were other popes before him. His colleague, Aeneas Sylvius Piccolomini, later Pope Pius II (1458-1464), thought that Nicholas had tried to accomplish too much, and thus left numerous projects undone.[10] Nevertheless, the forces motivating Nicholas to institute a Vatican Library require analysis. True, personal inclination and the prevailing culture of humanism played a share in Nicholas's motives, yet the papacy of Pius II casts doubts that they were the main factors. Pius never finished the library project, nor did he take an interest in the collection.

On the surface, his unconcern appears curious. Before becoming pope, he had been a more famous humanist than Nicholas; and after reaching that high office, Pius did not abandon humanism. He not only retained most of the humanists working for the Vatican, but hired more, among them Bartolomeo Sacci de Piadena Platina. Pius valued good books and collected them with as much relish as Nicholas. In doing so, Pius built a considerable private library, but he did not contribute his books to the papal collection as Nicholas had done. Instead, Pius willed them to his family, which—three hundred years later—sold many of them to the Holy See. Pius had been born to a family of great landowners in the village of Corsignano, which he renamed Pienza in his own honor

after using papal resources to build in its center several large buildings, including a private residence for himself, and to restore the
declining fortunes of his family. Years later, his nephew, upon becoming Pius III (1503), converted the Pienza cathedral chapterhouse into the Piccolomini Library to preserve his uncle's books.[11]

When Nicholas was dying, he told friends why he had devoted
so much energy to promote learning as a major papal policy. It
was, he explained, actually a public relations stunt. Through it, he
hoped to restore the influence of the Catholic church after its decline in prestige. The power of the church had evaporated before
he had taken office, and spiritual concerns were being ridiculed in
Renaissance Europe. All that was left was for the pope to take
the lead in the revival of learning to channel it into proper directions.[12]

Whatever the merits of such a policy, the three popes who followed him saw no need to continue it. During the next sixteen
years, the collection received no new accessions, and many of its
volumes disappeared. Following Nicholas as pontiff, Calixtus III
(1455-1458), a Spaniard and the first Borgia pope, disliked Rome
and its culture. Although well-read in his youth, he was very old
when elected pope. Vespasiano considered him senile, a report
that one may discount; but it is clear that Calixtus was ignorant of
affairs beyond his expertise as a canon lawyer.

When, as pope, he first viewed Nicholas V's books, Calixtus exhibited amazement that many were encased in rich bindings. The
only books that he had previously seen had been bound in canvas
covers and written on linen that had been stitched together. Com-
plaining that Nicholas had squandered the patrimony "of the
Church of God" on books, Calixtus, according to Vespasiano,
threw away the Greek ones while giving others to his friends and
servants.[13] Nevertheless, humanists at Rome, some of whom were
pleading with Calixtus to value the library, continued to prosper
during his short reign and during the next one under Pius II, when
humanism, if not library-building, was surely looked upon with a
fond eye. Humanists, by this time, had become an integral part of
the papal bureaucracy. They had evolved into a new class at Rome,
divided from the nobles and clergy, yet mingling and influencing
both.[14]

It was, therefore, a shock to Vatican humanists when Pope
Eugenius's nephew, Pietro Barbo, succeeded Pius II as Pope Paul
II (1464-1471). Although he was occupied as a Venetian business-
man when his uncle was elected to the papacy, Barbo at once felt
the call to the priesthood. His rise in the church hierarchy was,

predictably, rapid. As pope himself, he dismissed nearly all the Vatican humanists in an economy move. Paul II's hobby was collecting rare gems, not books. "He was," recalled Platina, "a great enemy and despiser of human learning, branding those for heretics that gave their minds to it. . . . "[15] Clearly, Platina disliked Paul, who had fired him from the position that Platina had obtained under Pius II. For acting as a leader of the dismissed humanists, Platina was jailed twice by Paul, whose troubles with the disgruntled group ceased when he died of a heart attack on 28 July 1471.[16]

The subsequent election of Francesco della Rovere as Pope Sixtus IV proved a great blessing for humanists. Della Rovere, like Pope Nicholas, came from a poor family; according to some accounts his father was a fisherman or a cloth trader, but the facts about his background are obscure. As a boy, Francesco entered the Franciscan order, obtaining a doctorate in 1444. Twenty years later, owing to his talents in oratory and writing, he rose to the generalcy of the order, much through the help of the scholarly Cardinal John Bessarion, who in the 1450s had chosen Father della Rovere as his personal confessor. The men became close friends, forming with like-minded scholars what might be termed an underground study group during Pope Paul II's anti-intellectual pontificate. Owing to Bessarion's recommendation, however, Paul named della Rovere a cardinal of the church in 1467.[17] Four years later, as pope, Sixtus ordered Vatican officials to reassemble Nicholas V's collection. He then issued a papal bull excommunicating anyone who did not return within forty days books belonging to the church.

Vespasiano hailed Sixtus IV's reign as opening a new epoch for humanity. On 17 December 1471, Sixtus commissioned architects to construct a Vatican Library. He planned that it would adjoin the Apostolic Palace, but his numerous projects to renew decaying Rome soon raised so many complications that he suspended the Library building plan. Whatever the reason, the suspension remained in effect until 1475, after the death of Bishop Giovanni Andrea del Bussi, who, as a priest of the San Augustin order, had held the honorary title of librarian of the pope. Bussi was a classical scholar, and his scholarly work (together with his efforts to promote the new art of printing) proved too intense to permit him the energy for pushing through the Library construction.

About three weeks after Bussi's death, Sixtus broke tradition by nominating to the vacant post Platina, a layman, who, together with Sixtus, had been a member of Bessarion's study group.[18]

Four months later, on 15 June 1475, Sixtus officially appointed
"Bartholomeum Platinam scriptorem et familiarem nostrum" as
papal librarian. The same day, Sixtus issued his bull *Ad Decorem
Militantis Ecclesie*, the actual birth certificate of the Vatican Library. In that bull, he promised that the Vatican treasury would
from then on permanently finance maintenance of the Library. He
also directed Platina to supervise the project, work that began at
once along with cataloging the collection by subject and alphabeti-
cally by author. The result was the first library catalog of the
papal collection, since all previous booklists had been drawn up to
document the monetary value of the books for the benefit of the
papal treasury. Platina also received orders from Sixtus to oversee
the restoration of ancient manuscripts and the transcription of
new manuscripts. To accomplish all that, Sixtus put Platina in
charge of the library custodians.

Sixtus's strong directives inspired humanists, but—as usual with
grand enterprises—financial realities intervened, forcing him to
cancel plans to construct a special building for the Library. He
established it, instead, in a series of rooms located in a basement
wing of the Vatican Palace. Nicholas V had erected the wing for
another purpose (the storing of grain and wine) and, perhaps, had
one of the rooms decorated for reasons yet unknown. Thus in a
way Nicholas was unknowingly the builder of the Vatican Library.[19]

The physical work of turning the basement into a library began
in September 1475 and was completed during 1481, but the Library had been open to the public for some time before. As opposed to the few dozen humanists who had been privileged to
consult Nicholas V's books, under Platina's administration the
register of the Vatican Library is replete with names, many of
whom would achieve scholarly renown during the sixteenth century. Platina's lending regulations were lenient; even tourists in
Rome could borrow books.[20]

Why did Sixtus do it? There is little doubt that he hoped to establish the best library in Italy. He had been deeply influenced by
humanistic circles in Italian universities, where he had taught theology before joining the general staff of the Franciscans. Humanists applauded his efforts as the library project went on.[21] Though
some historians do not rank him as a humanist, he achieved a "vast
reputation" among humanists. He was well aware of the worth of
libraries.[22]

That point can be graphically illustrated. Close inspection of the
Vatican Library interior reveals that it is similar to a library built

by Domenico Malatesta Novello at Cesena, in Romagna, during 1452. Malatesta ordered it constructed as part of a Franciscan monastery, which General della Rovere probably visited later during his inspection trips. The influence of the Cesena library, called the Malatestiana, grows even clearer through other sources. Upon ascending the papal throne, Sixtus appointed as his physician Giovanni di Marco, who in 1473 gave his books to the Malatestiana. Previously, Marco had been the official town doctor of Cesena and personal physician to Domenico Malatesta.

Marco's passion for books may have been a spark that initiated Sixtus's library plans, just as Marco's ideas certainly were critical in motivating Malatesta to establish the library not only for the monastery but also as a town public library, permanently endowed by Malatesta in 1464, a precedent, perhaps, for Sixtus IV's similar action for the Vatican Library a decade later. As a close friend of Cosimo de' Medici, Malatesta had modeled the Malatestiana on the library of San Marco after Nicholas approved building the Cesena library in a May 1450 bull. The connection between the libraries of San Marco, Cesena, and the Vatican is close for both popes, Nicholas and Sixtus.[23]

The Franciscan influence on Sixtus to found the Vatican Library does not end with the Malatestiana. Ironically, the religious order founded under rules that its members could not own, or even read, books was soon transformed by Francis of Assisi's successor, Bonaventure, into an order of book lovers. The necessity to compete with the Dominicans and to preach effectively led, in the 1300s, to the library at Assisi becoming the grandest in Italy. Popes in that period often deposited in it valuable books from the Vatican; the Assisi library thus served as an unofficial papal book depository. Elsewhere, Franciscan libraries grew so large that other prelates, such as the bishop of Durham, England, Richard Aungerville de Bury, complained that the Franciscans were monopolizing books. Nicholas V had spurred the growth by threatening, in a 1451 edict, to excommunicate a citizen of Assisi if he did not turn over to the order certain books that had been donated. Sixtus IV, in 1472, granted two hundred years' indulgences to all who contributed books or helped repair the Assisi library. And it was Sixtus, significantly, who canonized Bonaventure.[24]

The fact that Nicholas intended to establish a Vatican Library is no reason to credit him for having done so. His dream for it never came close to partial achievement. Thinking and willing do not constitute the act of founding. Sixtus not only revived the dream but carried it out. Sixtus commanded that the manuscripts be set in order under professional guidelines, and he set aside a place for the preservation of written material. Only Sixtus guaranteed the collection a steady flow of funds. Platina, by all accounts, acted as a true library administrator. He was the first to receive the title "librarian of the Holy See" after he had worked some time under the more humble designation "librarian of the pope." Following his death on 21 September 1481 and up to the mid-1500s, people referred to the institution as the Sistine Library. Conversely, Tortelli was not a librarian; he was a scholar employed to inventory manuscripts on a short-term basis.[25] Even after Platina's death, Sixtus continued to support the Library; for example, he appointed another librarian within a month of Platina's death in the bull *Romanus Pontifex*, which renewed all the guarantees, and he greatly increased the custodians' income.[26] Nicholas created no institution; he merely willed his books, about 1,200, to the Vatican collection, which—under Sixtus—rose to 3,650 volumes.[27]

Could the motivations of either Nicholas or Sixtus be discovered from sociological analysis? Both popes were from the lower class; and, not having grown up in a family mansion, they looked upon the Vatican as home. Other popes during the Renaissance were raised in palaces, probably much better than the run-down Vatican. Both Nicholas and Sixtus tried to beautify it, to impress upon it their own personalities, as one does with one's home. Nicholas left his books to the Vatican rather than to his family. Sixtus did likewise.

Sixtus's background is so vague that historians have speculated that he was ashamed of it. As a young man, he had befriended a family who, though unrelated and living in another town, used the same surname as he. While climbing the ranks of the church hierarchy along with the well-to-do, who made up the largest segment of clerical leaders, Sixtus and the Rovere family began considering themselves related. He looked upon them as his adopted loved ones. When he needed a coat of arms to keep up with his colleagues, the Rovere family was glad to grant the favor to their strong, intelligent adopted uncle. Later, he made several of their members cardinals. One of them may have caused the suspension of the Library project in 1472 by convincing Sixtus that his library ought to be a private one located within a family mansion that the cardinal was constructing, but that work ended when the cardinal died suddenly in 1474. The Vatican, as time went on, became Sixtus's true home.

Though historians consider his motives political—to overawe his subjects by carrying out stupendous projects—certainly choices other than library-building would have been simpler and perhaps more effective. The one class that would have been impressed were the humanists, hardly an influential group, as Paul II's open disdain of them demonstrated. If Sixtus's motive were ostentation, he would have discontinued the entire project when it became evident that funds were insufficient for erecting a grand building for the Library and that a basement would have to do for the collection. That Sixtus's heart, as opposed to cold calculation, was in the Library project is indicated by his granting indulgences for the benefit of the Assisi library and by his founding of another library in Rome within the chapterhouse of St. Peter's basilica, an effort that would have done little to increase his prestige or to intimidate the masses. The Vatican Library was not Sixtus's "showpiece." It was, rather, his home piece.[28]

Both Nicholas and Sixtus overcame their backgrounds; few popes during the Renaissance, or later, arose from such circumstances. Most, like Pius II, took pride in their deep family roots. Until Nicholas became pope, it was traditional for papal collections to be considered the personal property of the incumbent. Nearly always, they were willed by pontiffs to their heirs. Despite the example set by Nicholas and Sixtus, they were unable to break that tradition. During the sixteenth and seventeenth centuries, the Vatican collection grew very slowly; many Vatican officials appropriated for themselves the church documents and manuscripts they handled. Private libraries throughout Italy still house materials that once belonged to the Vatican.[29]

Nicholas and Sixtus knew that their blood relatives would have appreciated neither the contents nor the intellectual value of books. After the reigns of those popes, however, the wealthy regained the papal throne, and their families valued the written word. The Vatican Library is an accident of birth, the birth of two men into the ranks of the poor and their rebirth in the Vatican Palace, which cried out for the comforts and the atmosphere intelligent people prefer to be surrounded with: knowledge in its physical form, a library to share, the living thoughts of the great minds of the past. The Vatican Library is the product of the most wonderful gift of the Renaissance to the modern world—human love, with which both Nicholas and Sixtus were filled.

Notes

1. Eugène Müntz and Paul Fabre, *La Bibliothèque du vaticane au XVe siècle d'après des documents inédits: Contributions pour servir à l'histoire de*

l'humanisme (Paris: E. Thorin, 1887), p. 35; Ludwig Pastor, *The History of the Popes, from the Close of the Middle Ages: Drawn from the Secret Archives of the Vatican and Other Original Sources*, trans. Frederick Ignatius Antrobus and Ralph Francis Kerr, 3rd ed., 40 vols. (London: Kegan Paul, Trench, Trübner, 1906-1953), vol. 2, p. 214.

2. Ethel D. Roberts, "Notes on Early Christian Libraries in Rome," *Speculum* 9 (1934): 190-194; Anselmo Maria Albareda (comp.), *Miniatures of the Renaissance: Catalogue of the Exhibition* . . . (Vatican City: Biblioteca Apostolica Vaticana, 1950), pp. 5-8.

3. Jeanne Bignami-Odier, *La Bibliothèque Vaticane de Sixte IV à Pie XI: Recherches sur l'histoire des collections de manuscrits* (Vatican City: Biblioteca Apostolica Vaticana, 1973), pp. 3-4; John Willis Clark, "On the Vatican Library of Sixtus IV," *Proceedings of the Cambridge Antiquarian Society with Communications Made to the Society* n.s. 4, no. 41 (1899): 14; John Linus Paschang, *The Popes and the Revival of Learning: A Dissertation* . . . (Washington, D.C.: Catholic University of America, 1927), p. 14; Dorothy M. Robathan, "The Catalogues of the Princely and Papal Libraries of the Italian Renaissance," *Transactions and Proceedings of the American Philological Association* 64 (1933): 146; Owen Chadwick, *Catholicism and History: The Opening of the Vatican Archives* (Cambridge and New York: Cambridge University Press, 1978), pp. 6, 13.

4. Eugène Müntz, "L'héritage de Nicholas V," *Gazette des Beaux-arts: Courrier Européen de l'Art et de la Curiosité* 15 (April 1877): 417-420; Bignami-Odier, *La Bibliothèque Vaticane*, pp. 9-10; Anonymous [William Oldys, according to William H. Robinson, catalog no. 40], *A Critical and Historical Account of All the Celebrated Libraries in Foreign Countries* . . . (London: Jolliffe, 1739), pp. 147-148; Paul Fabre, "La vaticane de Sixte IV," *Mélanges d'Archéologie et d'Histoire* 15 (December 1895): 455; Klemens Loffler, "Papst Nikolaus V. als Bücherfreund," *Zeitschrift für Bücherfreunde: Organ der Gesellschaft der Bibliophilen* n.s. 1, pt. 1 (April–September 1909): 174-175.

5. Fiorentino Vespasiano da Bisticci, *Renaissance Princes, Popes and Prelates: The Vespasiano Memoirs, Lives of Illustrious Men of the XVth Century*, trans. William George and Emily Waters (New York: Harper and Row Torchbook, 1963), pp. 30-33, 37-40; Bartolomeo Sacci di Piadena Platina, *The Lives of Popes from the Time of Our Saviour Jesus Christ to the Death of Paul II*, ed. W. Benham (anon. trans.), 2 vols. (London: Griffith, Farran, Okeden and Welsh [1888-1893]), vol. 2, p. 236; Pius II (Aeneas Sylvius Piccolomini), *Memoirs of a Renaissance Pope: The Commentaries of Pius II*, ed. Leona C. Gabel (New York: Putnam, 1959), p. 68.

6. Giorgio Vasari, *The Lives of the Painters, Sculptors, and Architects*, trans. A. B. Hinds, 4 vols. (London: Dent; New York: Dutton, 1927), vol. 1, pp. 319-320; Vespasiano da Bisticci, *Memoirs*, pp. 37-38; E. H. Gombrich, "The Early Medici as Patrons of Art," in *Italian Renaissance Studies: A Tribute to the Late Cecilia M. Ady*, ed. Ernest Fraser Jacob (London: Faber and Faber, 1960), pp. 281-285; Berthold L. Ullman and Philip A. Stadter, *The Public Library of Renaissance Florence: Niccolò Niccoli, Cosimo de' Medici and the Library of San Marco* (Padua, Italy: Antenore, 1972), p. xi; James F. O'Gorman, *The Architecture of the Monastic Library in Italy, 1300-1600: Catalogue with Introductory Essay*, Monographs on Archeology

and the Fine Arts, 25 (New York: New York University Press for the College Art Association of America, 1972), pp. 12-14, 19-20, 57-58.

7. Platina, *Lives of Popes*, vol. 2, pp. 248-249; Vespasiano da Bisticci, *Memoirs*, p. 50; Joseph Hilgers, "Zur Bibliothek Nikolaus V," *Zentralblatt für Bibliothekswesen* 19 (January-February 1902): 1-2.

8. Vespasiano da Bisticci, *Memoirs*, pp. 48-50, 422-423; Platina, *Lives of Popes*, vol. 2, pp. 248, 250; Bignami-Odier, *La Bibliothèque Vaticane*, p. 5; Jean Baptiste Cardinal Pitra (comp.), *Analecta novissima spicilegii solesmensis altera continuatio: de epistolis et registris Romanorum Pontificum* (Farnborough, Eng.: Gregg, 1967), pp. 347-349; Girolamo Mancini, "Giovanni Tortelli cooperatore di Niccolò V nel fondare la Biblioteca Vaticana," *Archivio Storico Italiano* 78, no. 2 (1920): 209-211; Domenico Zanelli, *La Biblioteca Vaticana della sua origine fino al presente* (Rome: Tipografia delle belle arti, 1857), p. 10; Eva Mathews Sanford, "Giovanni Tortelli's Commentary on Juvenal," *Transactions and Proceedings of the American Philological Association* n.s. 4, no. 41 (1899): 14-15; Revilo P. Oliver, "Giovanni Tortelli," in *Studies Presented to David Moore Robinson on His Seventieth Birthday*, ed. George Emmanuel Mylonas, 2 vols. (St. Louis, Mo.: Washington University, 1951-1953), vol. 2, pp. 1257-1258, 1271.

9. Ibid., vol. 2, p. 1262; Mancini, "Giovanni Tortelli," pp. 257-267.

10. Pius II, *Memoirs*, p. 68.

11. Platina, *Lives of Popes*, vol. 2, pp. 271-273; Bignami-Odier, *La Bibliothèque Vaticane*, pp. 12-13; Neil Ritchie, "Aeneas Silvius Piccolomini: Humanist and Pope," *History Today* 29 (July 1977): 434-443.

12. John B. Toews, "Formative Forces in the Pontificate of Nicholas V, 1447-1455," *Catholic Historical Review* 54, no. 2 (July 1968): 283.

13. Vespasiano da Bisticci, *Memoirs*, pp. 186-187; Francesco Martorell, "Un inventario della biblioteca di Calisto III," in *Miscellanea Francesco Ehrle . . .*, 5 vols. (Rome: Biblioteca Apostolica Vaticana, 1924), vol. 5, pp. 166-168; Mancini, "Giovanni Tortelli," pp. 250-254.

14. John W. O'Malley, "The Vatican Library and the Schools of Athens: A Text of Battista Casali, 1508," *Journal of Medieval and Renaissance Studies* 7, no. 2 (Fall 1977): 273; John Addington Symonds, *Renaissance in Italy: The Revival of Learning* (New York: Holt, 1908), pp. 215-217.

15. Platina, *Lives of Popes*, vol. 2, pp. 275-276, 296; William Joseph Lancaster, "Pope Sixtus IV (1471-1484): Humanist and Artists at His Court" (history thesis, University of Illinois at Champaign/Urbana, 1967), p. 12.

16. Platina, *Lives of Popes*, vol. 2, pp. 277-279, 286-292; Joseph Dommers Vehling, *Platina and the Rebirth of Man* (Chicago: Hill, 1941), pp. 65-72.

17. Vespasiano da Bisticci, *Memoirs*, p. 136 n.; Egmont Lee, *Sixtus IV and Men of Letters* (Rome: Edizioni di storia e letteratura, 1978), pp. 12-15, 17, 20-21, 24.

18. Pitra, *Analecta*, pp. 347-349; Fabre, "La vaticane de Sixte IV," pp. 472, 473 n.; José Ruysschaert, "Sixte IV, fondateur de la Bibliothèque vaticane (15 juin 1475)," *Archivum historiae Pontificiae* 7 (1969): 515-516; Lee, *Sixtus IV*, pp. 24, 110, 120-122.

19. Sixtus IV (Francesco della Rovere), "Ad decorem militantis Ecclesie," *Archivum historiae Pontificiae* 7 (1969): 523-524; Ruysschaert, "Sixte IV," pp. 515, 519; Theodor Gottlieb, *Ueber mittelalterliche Bibliotheken* (Leipzig:

O. Harrassowitz, 1890), pp. 234–236; G. Borghezio, "La Biblioteca Vaticana," in *Enciclopedia Italiana di scienze, lettere ed arti* (Milan: Rizzoli, 1937), vol. 34, p. 1045; Franz Ehrle, "Bibliothektechnisches aus der Vatikana," *Zentralblatt für Bibliothekswesen* 33 (July–August 1916): 12; Bignami-Odier, *La Bibliothèque Vaticane*, p. 20; Toby Yuen, "The 'Bibliotheca Graeca': Castagno, Alberti, and Ancient Sources," *Burlington Magazine* 112 (November 1970): 725–726, 733, 735.

20. Müntz and Fabre, *La Bibliothèque du vaticane*, p. 141; Albareda, *Miniatures*, p. 14; Clark, "Vatican Library of Sixtus IV," pp. 17, 19–20, 24–25, 27–28, 35–36, 38–39, 46, 48–49, 52–56, 59–60.

21. Robert Flemmyng, "Meditations at Tivoli," trans. George Bruner Parks in his *The English Traveller to Italy: The Middle Ages (to 1525)* (Rome: Edizioni di storia e litteratura, 1954), pp. 603–604; Lancaster, "Pope Sixtus," pp. 35–37, 80.

22. Ruysschaert, "Sixte IV," pp. 514–515; Lancaster, "Pope Sixtus," pp. 36–37.

23. Antonio Domeniconi, *La Biblioteca Malatestiana* (Rome: Doretti-Udine, 1962), pp. 9–19; Anonymous, "Monumenti: La Biblioteca Malatestiana Cesena," *L'Architettura: Chronache e Storia* 4 (February 1959): 704–706; John Willis Clark, "Notes on Chained Libraries at Cesena, Wells, and Guildford," *Proceedings of the Cambridge Antiquarian Society with Communications Made to the Society* 8, no. 34 (1891): 2–6; Constantine Klukowski, "Legal Documents Referring to Franciscan Libraries up to 1517," in *Librarianship and the Franciscan Library: Franciscan Educational Conference, 1947* (Washington, D.C.: Capuchin College, 1948), pp. 195–196, 204; Desiderius Wawro, "Discussion," ibid., p. 391.

24. Saint Francis d'Assisi, *Writings*, trans. Benen Fahy (Chicago: Franciscan Herald Press, 1964), pp. 34, 45, 63; Richard Aungerville de Bury, *The Philobiblon* (Berkeley: University of California Press, 1948), pp. 52–54; Saint Bonaventure, *Life of Saint Francis* (London: Dent, 1904), pp. 113–114; O'Gorman, *Architecture of the Monastic Library*, pp. 4–5; John Lenhart, "Franciscan Libraries of the Middle Ages," *Librarianship and the Franciscan Library*, pp. 351–359, 374, 377; Klukowski, "Legal Documents," pp. 194, 197–199, 203, 206–207, 209, 211, 213–214, 223–226, 298, 391; John Richard Humpidge Moorman, *A History of the Franciscan Order from Its Origins to the Year 1517* (Oxford: Clarendon, 1968), pp. 184–185, 367–368; K. W. Humphreys, *The Book Provisions of the Medieval Friars, 1215–1400* (Amsterdam: Erasmus Booksellers, 1964), pp. 46–48; John Richard Humpidge Moorman, "Early Franciscan Art and Literature," *Bulletin of the John Rylands Library* 27 (June 1943): 351–352.

25. Pietro Guidi, "Pietro Demetrio Guazzelli da Lucca, il primo custode della Biblioteca Vaticana (1481–1511) e l'inventario dei suoi libri," in *Miscellanea Francesco Ehrle* 5: 198; Ruysschaert, "Sixte IV," pp. 516–519; Gottlieb, *Ueber mittelalterliche Bibliotheken*, pp. 234–236; Fabre, "La vaticane de Sixte IV," p. 472; Mancini, "Giovanni Tortelli," pp. 208–222; Bignami-Odier, *La Bibliothèque Vaticane*, pp. 21–22, 320.

26. Robert Montel, "Un bénéficier de la basilique Saint-Pierre de Rome: Demetrius Guasselli, 'custode' de la Bibliothèque vaticane († 1511)," *Mélanges de L'Ecole Française de Rome*, 85, no. 2 (1973): 429–438; Guidi, "Pietro Demetrio Guazzelli," pp. 199–207; John Willis Clark, *The Care of Books: An Essay on the Development of Libraries and Their Fittings, from*

the *Earliest Times to the End of the Eighteenth Century*, 2nd ed. (Cambridge, Eng.: University Press, 1902), p. 199; O'Gorman, *Architecture of the Monastic Library*, pp. 44-45.

27. Eugène Cardinal Tisserant and Theodore Wesley Koch, *The Vatican Library: Two Papers* (Jersey City, N.J.: Snead and Company, 1929), p. 5; Fabre, "La vaticane de Sixte IV," p. 472; Pastor, *History of the Popes*, vol. 4, p. 434.

28. Herman Jean de Vleeschauwer, *Encyclopaedia of Library History*, 2 vols. (Pretoria, South Africa: n.p., 1955), vol. 1, p. 43, vol. 2, p. 85; Lee, *Sixtus IV*, pp. 26, 117, 120-122, 144, 202-203; Montel, "Un bénéficier," p. 438; Vespasiano da Bisticci, *Memoirs*, p. 139 n.

29. Chadwick, *Catholicism and History*, pp. 10-11.

Libraries and Printers in the Fifteenth Century

Barbara Halporn

Although libraries have always been important customers of the book trade, their contribution to the developing commerce in books in the early period of printing as a source of printable manuscripts is less conspicuous. In fact, early editors and publishers rarely acknowledged the aid of libraries as suppliers of manuscripts.[1] Rather, publishers often boasted of their wide search for manuscripts for a publication without mentioning the libraries to which they were indebted for their base texts. Since the publication of the works of living authors was less common in the incunable period than the printing of standard scholarly works of earlier times,[2] libraries, both capitular and monastic, became an important source of manuscripts for the early printer-publisher. From as early as the ninth century it was a well-established procedure in many monastic houses to lend books outside the walls on the permission of the head administrator and the receipt of a pledge, commonly money or a book of equal value. Loans among the houses of the same order were common and apparently fairly easy to obtain. So regular was interlibrary lending of this sort that the statutes of a number of monasteries set out their policy on making loans outside the monastery.[3] After the invention of movable type, the fledgling publishing industry made new demands on library resources for the purpose of copying and printing. The loan

Barbara Halporn *is subject librarian at Indiana University.*
The research for this paper was done in part with the generous support of an Advanced Study Fellowship granted by the Council on Library Resources for the year 1976/77.

Journal of Library History, Vol. 16, No. 1, Winter 1981

of materials for copying and dissemination by a secular, commercial agent marked a new era of cooperation and collaboration between libraries and the business world. It was fortunate both for the growth of the early book trade and for the printer-publishers engaged in it that these ecclesiastical curators of the written intellectual heritage of the West accepted and promoted the new art of printing immediately and enthusiastically. They regarded printing much as Brother Dominick in the delightful television commercial sees Xerox, as "a miracle."[4]

The publishers of printed texts who wanted to provide books for their large ecclesiastical clientele, that made up a large segment of the reading public in the fifteenth century,[5] needed widespread connections within the monastic world and the world of secular letters as well if they were to succeed in the marketplace. In addition to offering an identifiable audience, this group comprised a pool on which publishers could draw for advice on what works should be printed, for editorial expertise, and for access to library collections. One fifteenth-century publisher who grasped the possibilities of the new invention and was able to capitalize on the need for theological texts was Johann Amerbach, who worked as a printer and publisher in Basel, Switzerland, for some thirty-five years. Amerbach based his publishing program on theological works—patristic authors in particular—with a fair representation of humanistic authors, juristic works, and school texts to round out the list. In the course of conducting his active publishing business, Amerbach carefully and deliberately preserved the letters he received, most of which relate to some aspect of the book trade.[6] Very few letters written by Amerbach himself remain, and we must supply their content from the replies that he preserved. Although there are some interruptions in the continuity of the correspondence, this collection, beginning in 1481 and ending with Amerbach's death in 1513, presents us with a rare glimpse of the day-to-day workings of an early publishing house.[7]

The letters to Amerbach reveal an intellectual community of fellow printers, poets, scholars, teachers, and students from all over Europe and England who shared the printer's eagerness to get manuscript books into print. Amerbach published a number of books independently as well as a number of large-scale publications in collaboration with other printers, which required them to search the libraries of western Europe for manuscripts to provide a base text for printer's copy. In all of these publishing ventures—those undertaken independently and those undertaken jointly—the task of locating suitable manuscripts, then acquiring them either by borrowing or copying, and the preparation of a base text often involved years of effort before the printing began. Amerbach hoped to bring out alone or in conjunction with other printers complete editions of the works of the patristic authors, St. Augustine, St. Ambrose, St. Jerome, and Cassiodorus, along with the Biblical commentary of Hugo de Sancto Charo. These ambitious plans to publish collected editions of such prolific authors for the first time required an outlay of capital and staying power that few printers of the period could muster. For that reason Amerbach joined in partnership with Anthoni Koberger of Nuremberg, who supplied capital and handled the distribution of a number of these large-scale publications. In order to grasp the scope of such plans, we must forget the National Union Catalog and the printed catalogs of the national libraries of Europe. We must also set aside our notions of bibliographic citation, even our notions of authorship. In 1495 the hopeful borrower of a treatise by St. Ambrose or St. Augustine, for example, had little choice but to write to numerous libraries inquiring about their holdings, or to send an agent or go personally to libraries to look for the desired works.[8] The Amerbach correspondence documents this cumbersome process many times. In the early 1490s, when Amerbach was preparing his edition of the works of St. Ambrose for the press, he sent a letter to the Carthusian house in Strassburg inquiring about their holdings of the patristic author. Hoping perhaps to speed the reply, he had sent several gift books for the monastery library. The curator, Dr. Kaysersberg, supplied Amerbach with a list of works identified by short title owned by the Carthusian library (AK I:21). He also included a list of the holdings of the Augustinian and Dominican houses in Strassburg. Kaysersberg indicates whether the books are printed or are in manuscript. It is interesting from a bibliographic standpoint that he mentions the place of publication of the two printed works to help identify them. In response to similar inquiries, several letters from Alexius Stab, curator of the library of the Benedictine house at St. Blasien, survive. The letters tell us more than simply whether the library at St. Blasien did or did not have a particular work. Indirectly, they furnish a thumbnail sketch of the curator of the library of St. Blasien. It is impossible not to be impressed by the eagerness of this late fifteenth century librarian to contribute to the greater distribution of information and knowledge that printing promised. Despite the density of his language we cannot fail to see that Alexius Stab had caught the excitement in the air over the great possibilities that print held for the world of learning. He wanted to be involved in the great new venture even in a modest way. His negative reply to Amerbach's request is tinged with regret: "You write that you were informed that there are editions [of Petrarch] in the library of St. Blasius of the Black Forest. Accordingly you wanted me to find out. I looked over the collection with great care as you wished. Again and again I took up the task. I found nothing that would meet your needs after going through separate treatises fairly quickly. Since I cannot help you, please forgive me and do not think that laziness triumphed over labor. Please believe that those manuscripts are not in our library . . . for I have searched for the volumes in the oldest catalogs of books and satisfied myself that we do not have them" (AK I:35).

Some twelve years later Amerbach had not forgotten Stab's spirit of cooperation and once again called on him for help in preparing the collected edition of St. Jerome. Stab reports on an assignment "I have carried out an agreeable duty toward St. Jerome by carefully making a collection [of his works]. By no small labor on my part I have found the works by inquiring around for them. Such as they are I am sending them to you. . . . " (AK I: 371). In July of the following year Stab writes to make the embarrassing confession that Amerbach's agent ". . . visited our library unexpectedly, and happily and under a lucky star had found the letter of St. Jerome to Sunnia and Fretela about the emendation of the Psalms that I recently looked for at your request but was unable to find" (AK I:424).

If Alexius Stab was willing and quick to put the library of St. Blasien at Amerbach's disposal, he represents but one attitude of curators of libraries of the period, who differed considerably in their readiness to make their collections available to the printer. Moreover, individuals in the printing fraternity were not above practicing deceit if necessary to get hold of a desired manuscript book. We find, for example, Adolf Rusch, a printer from Strassburg, writing to Amerbach in 1485: "I am sending what I consider the finest manuscript containing the *Instituta* and *Collationes* [of Cassian] together. I want you to keep it very clean because if it should in any way be stained I would be considered untrustworthy, for I promised that I just wanted to keep it at home to copy it. Return it immediately after it has been used because I can have it until the Feast of Martin and no longer" (AK I:14).[9] Little wonder then that curators of library collections were suspicious from time to time of the intentions of their borrowers from the secular community. On the whole, however, the printers and publishers represented in the Amerbach correspondence recognized the necessity of treating borrowed books with great care and of following the restrictions on use that the lending library established. Printers who hoped to survive in this business valued and cultivated good relationships with the libraries from which they borrowed, since the fate of future publishing endeavors also depended on their good will and cooperation.

Between 1495 and 1502 Amerbach collaborated with Anthoni Koberger of Nuremberg[10] in the publication of a seven-volume edition of the Bible with Hugo de Sancto Charo's commentary.[11] Koberger financed the search for manuscripts and handled the shipment of manuscripts to Amerbach in Basel, who was in charge of the editorial work and the printing. His letters to Amerbach often suggest strained relations with the owners of the borrowed manuscripts. He wrote in December 1497 to say: "I have learned that you received the books from Maulbronn. God be praised they reached you safe and sound. Please, Hans, kindly keep them safe and clean so that we may again borrow. See to it that no mishap befall them. Since their Lordships, the Nuremberg Council, wrote vouching for me it would cause me great difficulty should there be complaint about the books entrusted to me on their Lordships' signature."[12] A couple of years later Koberger wrote to Amerbach to request the return of exemplars no longer needed. All was not well. Koberger mentioned that the abbot at Heilsbronn had complained about how badly the books on loan were treated and had indicated that they would not lend any more (Hase 30). Conversely, Amerbach (to judge by Koberger's replies) repeatedly asked for more manuscripts and criticized the quality of copies he received. In his search for suitable manuscripts to compile the first printed edition of Hugo's Biblical commentary, Koberger spared no expense or effort. The library at Heilsbronn had a rare complete text of the extensive work. Early in publishing the Hugo commentary Koberger suffered a major setback when the library at Heilsbronn recalled from him their complete text, the greatest treasure of their collection.[13] Koberger reports to Amerbach: "I am sending you . . . a small barrel containing eighteen volumes [of the Hugo commentary] with which you can make do for a while. . . . I had a complete copy but had to give it back to the monastery since they could not do without it. Also they would not allow us to enter corrections in it or to make a copy of it. I still hope, however, to succeed in this" (Hase 2). Although they refused Koberger the use of the copy in 1495, a new abbot who took charge a few years later relented and loaned him several volumes.[14] The fears that their books might receive harsh treatment were confirmed, however, and in 1500 the Heilsbronn monastery library again refused loans to Koberger and Amerbach. Koberger's letter of July 1500 reveals the breakdown in good relations with the library there. "I have written to you to send back the exemplars that you no longer need. Since they will not loan me other copies, I am returning the several that are now out; the abbot at Heilsbronn has learned how carelessly the copies were treated and that they will not be fit for use" (Hase 30). Damage to manuscripts could occur in rough handling at the print shop, but it was even more likely to occur in transit.

At the same time that he was involved with compiling, editing, and printing Hugo's commentary with Koberger, Amerbach began to assemble texts for his first collected edition of the works of St. Augustine.[15] In this case Amerbach himself took responsibility for financing the search for manuscripts, as well as for the editorial work and printing. He asked a number of friends and acquaintances scattered around Europe to watch for suitable manuscripts, but the main work of locating manuscripts was the charge of Augustinus Phrygius Dodo, canon of the monastery of St. Leonard in Basel. Acting as Amerbach's agent, Phrygius Dodo traveled from library to library investigating the manuscript resources of each and commissioning scribes to copy those works needed for the printed edition. A letter from Prior Walramus of Boedingen gives a clear picture of how the process worked. Phrygius Dodo asked Prior Walramus to assemble and have copied works of St. Augustine borrowed from another monastery of the same order. Walramus directed a group of scribes in making copies of the eleven volumes of Augustine's works. The letter is essentially a bill for services rendered. Walramus begins by spelling out the agreement and quotes the promises made by Phrygius Dodo as follows: "Because the holy prior of Boedingen [Walramus] was so helpful to me and a loyal worker, I . . . pledge on behalf of Master Johann to send you the works of St. Augustine, all that have been and are to be printed, and the works of St. Ambrose likewise. . . . Also because Prior Walramus gave the prior at Sieberg half a gold florin for a bereta in return for his lending us eleven volumes, I will repay him with the book *De scriptoribus ecclesiasticis* for that half florin" (AK I:61).[16] In pressing his claim with Amerbach, Prior Walramus goes on to say, "As Brother Augustinus may well have told you we have as yet few books and we do not have money to buy them." He stresses the problems his scribes had in copying from very old manuscripts and explains how they dealt with problems of spelling and unfamiliar foreign terms. This exchange of printed books and a bit of money for copies of manuscripts was repeated numerous times as Amerbach gradually assembled the text of St. Augustine for printing.

The letters to readers published as prefatory material in early printed editions more often served the interests of advertising than truth. They are often self-congratulatory statements by the publisher or letters of endorsement from well-placed friends. It is common to see in this genre extravagant statements of the publisher's attention to the accuracy of the text and descriptions of heroic efforts to locate manuscripts and provide editorial expertise. Amerbach's letters to the reader in his edition of St. Augustine are written in the spirit of this tradition. He describes with epic grandeur his efforts to provide a full and satisfactory text of all of Augustine's works, but he also records his difficulties and failures. He warns the reader that he has included some works spuriously attributed to St. Augustine and that he was forced to omit some treatises entirely because no copy could be located. He explains, further, that there may be errors that "I would have charged to me and my ignorance and lack of knowledge, though not entirely, but also to the very old and corrupt exemplars and semi-gothic letters and to faded scripts, to the lack of a large supply of exemplars, and in the case of some works to the availability of only a single copy and that obtained with difficulty" (AK I:294). Although these public letters may overstate the case, the private correspondence does support Amerbach's claim to have investigated the libraries of Germany, France, and Italy in order to present the best text possible.

Libraries were both the benefactors and beneficiaries of the new art. We can see that early in the era of printing curators of monastic libraries took an active interest in the development of the new technology and promoted its use and growth as a means to serve the needs of the scholarly community better. Even discounting the hyperbole that is characteristic of the epistolary style of the period, we can see in the letters to Amerbach that the curators of monastic libraries felt genuine enthusiasm about the usefulness of printed works. They were also realistically concerned about jeopardizing the safety of their collections, acquired slowly and at great cost, for the purpose of transforming manuscript books into print. It is quite clear that the manuscript book did not lose its value in the eyes of the librarian or scholar just because a printed copy could be placed alongside it. Librarians wanted their original manuscripts returned and wanted to receive a complimentary copy into the bargain. If printing was responsible for the destruction of manuscripts as is often suggested, it probably occurred through the hazards of shipping rather than through deliberate mistreatment or neglect.

In the light of what we know from these letters to be the hard realities of the situation, I would like to consider for a moment the claims commonly made by publishers of the incunable period of having provided the best manuscripts possible, expertly edited and corrected and accurately printed. It is easy to look at these monumental editions of the fifteenth century, which were produced by the combined efforts of the commercial and scholarly communities, and to judge the achievement as seriously flawed when viewed from the standpoint of modern textual criticism. In fairness, therefore, it is doubly important to look at the obstacles that early publishers faced in preparing any printed edition, and to see that the problems in producing a multivolume edition were further magnified. Chance played a very important part in what manuscripts were used for any printed edition. Scholarly publishers had, for the most part, to settle for what they could get. Laboring under the inadequacy of bibliographic information and limited access to library collections, the early publishers' first thought was for completeness. They could have been only dimly aware of the problems of establishing a critical text. Judged, however, in terms of what was available to him, it seems to me that Johann Amerbach did not fall far short of the generous assessment of his contemporaries, who remark on the accuracy of his editions and his contribution to the republic of letters and who address him as *princeps calcographorum*—foremost among printers.

Notes

1. Karl Schottenloher, "Handschriftenforschung und Buchdruck im XV. und XVI. Jahrhundert," *Gutenberg Jahrbuch* 6 (1931; Nedeln Liechtenstein: Kraus Reprint, 1973): 73-106.

2. Elizabeth Eisenstein outlines the debate on this subject in *The Printing Press as an Agent of Change*, 2 vols. (Cambridge: Cambridge University Press, 1979), vol. 1, p. 168, n. 12.

3. Ladislaus Buzás, *Deutsche Bibliotheksgeschichte des Mittelalters*, Elemente des Buch- und Bibliothekswesens, Bd. 1 (Wiesbaden: Ludwig Reichert Verlag, 1975), p. 56; and Klemens Loeffler, *Deutsche Klosterbibliotheken*, 2nd ed., Bücherei der Kultur und Geschichte, Bd. 27 (Bonn and Leipzig: K. Schroeder, 1922), pp. 40ff. Loeffler further suggests, "Im allgemein waren aber die Klosterbibliotheken schon des Mittelalters im dem Sinne auch öffentlich, daβ sie einem fremden Besucher nicht leicht verschlossen wurden."

4. Conrad Leontorius frequently calls printing a divine art: for example, letter 66, *Die Amerbachkorrespondenz*, vol. 1, ed. Alfred Hartmann (Basel:

Verlag der Universitätsbibliothek, 1942), p. 75. This collection will be referred to hereafter in the text as AK followed by the numbers of the volume and letter.

5. Rudolf Hirsch, *Printing, Selling and Reading 1450-1550*, 2nd printing, (Wiesbaden: O. Harrassowitz, 1974), p. 128.

6. *Die Amerbachkorrespondenz*, vol. 1, contains the letters written to Johann Amerbach between 1481 and 1513.

7. In referring to Amerbach, I use the terms "publisher" and "printer" interchangeably since he functioned sometimes as a printer, sometimes as a publisher in the sense that we use those terms today.

8. E. J. Kenney, *The Classical Text: Aspects of Editing in the Age of the Printed Book*, Sather Classical Lectures 44 (Berkeley: University of California Press, 1974), pp. 75ff.

9. Cassian's *Institutes*, a work of 208 leaves, was printed in a matter of weeks if Amerbach met Rusch's request to return it by St. Martin's Day.

10. Lucien Febvre and Henri-Jean Martin call Koberger "perhaps the most powerful publisher of his day" because of the size and extensiveness of his commercial operation and connections: *The Coming of the Book: The Impact of Printing 1450-1800*, ed. Geoffrey Nowell-Smith and David Wootton, trans. David Gerard (London: N.L.B., 1976), p. 124 (translation of the 1958 ed.). The alliance with Koberger was undoubtedly one of Amerbach's greatest assets.

11. Hain 3175; *Gesamtkatalog*, 4285.

12. Oskar von Hase, *Die Koberger* (Leipzig: Breitkopf und Härtel, 1885), letter no. 17. Koberger's letters to Amerbach are published in an appendix, "Briefbuch der Koberger." Referred to hereafter in the text as Hase.

13. P. Ruf (ed.), *Mittelalterliche Bibliothekskataloge Deutschlands und der Schweiz*, Bd. 3 T. 1 (Munich: Beck, 1932), pp. 202, 208.

14. O. von Hase, *Die Koberger*, p. 91.

15. Two articles give detailed accounts of the first collected edition of St. Augustine: Victor Scholderer, "The First Collected Edition of Saint Augustine," *The Library* 5th ser., 14, no. 1 (March 1959): 46-49, reprinted in *Fifty Essays in Fifteenth- and Sixteenth-Century Bibliography*, ed. Dennis E. Rhodes (Amsterdam: Hertzberger, 1966), pp. 275-278; J. de Ghellinck, "La première édition imprimée des 'Opera Omnia S. Augustini,'" in *Miscellanea J. Gessler*, 2 vols. (Louvain, 1948), vol. 1, pp. 530-547. Scholderer deals with the problems involved in the production of the edition. J. de Ghellinck takes up in some detail the constitution of the text and the issues of textual criticism related to this edition.

16. *De scriptoribus ecclesiasticis* is the bio-bibliography of Johannes Trithemius, published by Amerbach in 1494 (Hain 15613).

Book Collecting in Counter-Reformation Italy: The Library of Gian Vincenzo Pinelli (1535–1601)

Marcella Grendler

The name Gian Vincenzo Pinelli is not exactly a household word today, not even among historians of the Italian Renaissance. This was not always so. Four hundred years ago every Italian and most non-Italian scholars would have reacted to the name Pinelli with enthusiasm and appreciation. For he possessed one of the best, perhaps *the* best, private library in Italy in the second half of the sixteenth century. He not only collected books and manuscripts, but he put them at the disposal of every serious reader, and personally encouraged scholars in every imaginable field. To complement his library, he assembled materials for scientific research: mathematical and astronomical instruments, globes, maps, collections of fossils and metals, even a large botanical garden.

Pinelli belonged to a noble family that came originally from Genoa.[1] His parents settled in Naples, where Gian Vincenzo was born in 1535. Independently wealthy and intellectually precocious, Gian Vincenzo left Naples for Padua at the age of 23. Padua was the ideal place for a scholar and future bibliophile. It not only provided the stimulation of a first-rate university, but it boasted an excellent botanical garden as well. Nearby Venice remained the center of the Italian book trade in the second half of the sixteenth century, and the focal point of Greek learning in Italy. Pinelli arrived in Padua in 1558 and, save for a necessary trip or two, he remained there until his death in 1601.

Pinelli did not need to travel; for forty years, European scholars

Marcella Grendler *is the Cavagna Project bibliographer at the University of Illinois at Urbana-Champaign.*

Journal of Library History, Vol. 16, No. 1, Winter 1981
©1981 by the University of Texas Press   0275-3650/81/010143–09$00.90

came to visit him in Padua, or at least corresponded with him. He opened his home and library to every intellectual, and his house constituted an informal academy where visitors to Padua could be sure of intelligent conversation and a lively exchange of ideas. By sixteenth-century standards, Gian Vincenzo was an extraordinarily self-effacing *erudito*. At a time when learning and ego often went hand in hand, he remained personally modest, while totally open and affable to his friends. He was at his best in promoting the scholarly or personal interests of others, and his gentle character made possible friendships with intellectuals of the most diverse sorts—the difficult Tasso; the avid, rather selfish fellow collector Fulvio Orsini; the irascible humanist Sperone Speroni; and, among foreigners, the distinguished Lipsius and De Thou. Galileo must be considered Pinelli's most famous visitor; Gian Vincenzo helped to bring him to the Studio di Padova, and Galileo stayed in Pinelli's house while he prepared his first lectures.

Pinelli wrote thousands of letters to friends across Italy and the rest of Europe; he annotated hundreds of manuscripts and books, and filled many notebooks with observations, but he published nothing. Then, as now, the unpublished scholar was destined to oblivion. His lack of publications was one reason why his fame did not last beyond the early seventeenth century. The other reason, a sad one, was the dispersal of his magnificent library. Unlike his friend Fulvio Orsini, who willed his collection to the Vatican and thereby obtained institutional protection and an assured future for his manuscripts and books, Gian Vincenzo left his library and scientific collections to a nephew. They were thus subject to the vagaries of personal fortune. First, a servant plundered the collection. Next, the Venetian government confiscated "sensitive" materials dealing with the Venetian state.[2] Then the nephew, Cosmo Pinelli, died on 31 October 1602, only fourteen months after Gian Vincenzo's demise. The nephew's project to establish the library in Naples as a living memorial to his uncle died with him. The most serious misfortune occurred at sea, late in 1604, as the Pinelli collections were en route to Naples. Off the coast of Fermo (south of Venice on the Adriatic coast), Turkish pirates attacked the ship. Disappointed in their search for valuables, they threw overboard the scholarly treasures: chests of books, mathematical instruments, and portraits. Of thirty-three chests, only twenty-two were recovered. The surviving portion of the library did not fare well at Naples, for it lay neglected in a building with a leaky roof for several years while Cosmo's widow quarreled with the guardians of her young son's estate. She finally permitted the collection to be sold at auction in Naples in 1608.

Anthony Hobson, an English scholar, has published a fascinating account of the auction based on documents he found in the Ambrosiana.[3] The business agents of Cardinal Federigo Borromeo, in an atmosphere of intrigue and intense rivalry with the Neapolitan Jesuits, put in the last bid before the auctioneer's candle went out, and thus acquired the Pinelli books and manuscripts for 3,050 *scudi d'oro*. One of Borromeo's men circulated a false rumor that the collection had immediately been sent north by land. In fact, he kept it in Naples, hiding the manuscripts under and behind his own bed, while awaiting the safest possible transport: the Genoese fleet returning to its home port. His secrecy tells us not only how little book buyers trusted one another, but also the contemporary reputation of the Pinelli collection, even in a dilapidated and reduced state. One would like to say that the story ended well, but it seems clear that the collection was further broken up. In accordance with instructions that have not survived, Borromeo's agents resold many of the printed volumes in Naples because they did not think them valuable enough to warrant the cost of shipment. In 1609, all of Pinelli's surviving manuscripts and a selection of his books finally completed their circuit of Italy. They arrived in Milan, where they joined the new Biblioteca Ambrosiana, founded by Borromeo.

Because his manuscripts survive in the Ambrosiana, Pinelli has not been totally forgotten. A twentieth-century scholar, Adolfo Rivolta, included a brief study of his life, library, and intellectual interests as an introduction to a catalogue of Pinelli's Latin and vernacular manuscripts. Pinelli's Greek codices are described in an excellent catalogue of the Ambrosiana Greek manuscripts done by Martini and Bassi in 1906.[4] Although the Pinelli manuscript collection still needs some scholarly attention, the majority of its contents are known. But until recently, precise information on the size, breadth, and depth of the printed collection was, as for so many great libraries of the past, quite fragmentary.

In the last few years, two early seventeenth century handwritten inventories of both the manuscripts and printed books have come to light. Each is valuable in its own way, and they make it possible to reconstruct the magnificent library that was once Pinelli's. One inventory comes from Venice—Biblioteca Nazionale Marciana, Mss. Italiani, Classe X, 61 (6601). It dates from 1604, and was made as a record of the estate inherited by

Cosmo Pinelli's young son. The second inventory comes from the Ambrosiana itself—Ms. B 311 Sussidio. Before the purchase, Borromeo's agents had been given limited access to the library, only enough to assure them of its desirability. So, quickly but carefully they compiled a catalogue in Naples in early 1609, to inform the cardinal in detail of the treasures he had acquired, and perhaps to serve as a guide in choosing what printed books would be kept and what would be resold. It apparently has been in the Ambrosiana since 1609, uncatalogued and unnoticed until an employee came upon it about 1970.

These inventories present an embarrassment of riches to the scholar. I know at present of no other large sixteenth-century Italian private library for which we possess so complete a knowledge of the contents and mentality of its owner. The only other example that comes to mind is Pinelli's friend Fulvio Orsini, whose library and its acquisition were brilliantly studied in the nineteenth century by Pierre de Nolhac.[5] But not all of Orsini's book inventories survived. Pinelli's do—and the two versions complement one another in the information that they provide.

The Marciana inventory of 1604 documents the library before the pirates' attack. It serves as the most complete record of what Pinelli's library once was. The inventory catalogues a splendid collection of 6,428 printed volumes and 738 manuscripts. The entries for printed works are fairly complete, permitting in most instances identification of the work if not the specific edition. Manuscript entries are less satisfactory, often too brief to be useful. The "After Pirates" catalogue offers a more complete description of individual books and manuscripts. The inventory contains approximately 5,400 printed volumes—a thousand fewer than set out from Venice five years earlier. (The most obvious loss was hundreds of French political pamphlets, which perished at sea, were damaged in Naples, or were quietly eliminated before the sale.) The manuscripts are listed in greater number and in more detail than in the earlier inventory—some 576 Latin and vernacular, and 254 Greek manuscripts. Pinelli's Greek collection is actually larger, at least 338 manuscripts; as the compilers of the inventory apparently could not read Greek, manuscripts without an index in Latin escaped inventory even though they arrived at the Ambrosiana.[6]

Pinelli's manuscripts and printed works united to form a coherent collection. The subject matter included everything that interested Renaissance scholars: the ancient Greek and Latin classics of philosophy, mathematics, science, drama, poetry, and rhetoric; classical and Renaissance history; the church fathers, liturgical works, and scholastic theology; botany, medicine, astronomy, astrology, law, Italian popular literature, poetical theory, and political pamphlets from the French wars of religion. The printed volumes ranged from incunables to works published in 1601, the year of Pinelli's death. A substantial minority of the books came from non-Italian publishers. Thus, in addition to the expected Latin, Greek, and Italian, the major European vernaculars plus Hebrew, Syriac, and Arabic were represented. As one might expect, Pinelli owned more copies of Aristotle than of any other author. The manuscripts ranged from the fourth to the sixteenth century; the most famous is surely the "painted Homer," the earliest surviving illustrated copy of the *Iliad*, dating probably from the fourth century A.D.[7] Among the later manuscripts are many works by sixteenth-century authors, often Pinelli's friends, and numerous volumes of Gian Vincenzo's own correspondence and notebooks. It is clear that some of his papers—his own inventories of his collections, for example—are missing, and the survivors are in disorder.

The extant correspondence reveals a great deal about Pinelli the collector. Gian Vincenzo had a lifelong habit of retaining every useful scrap of paper, so that despite pirates and careless custodians, much remains to document the acquisition of his collection. A bibliophile in the great Italian tradition, Pinelli was a worthy predecessor to the better-known Antonio Magliabecchi (1633–1714), whose books and manuscripts enrich the National Library of Florence. Pinelli was an indefatigable and orderly collector. For printed books, publishers' catalogues from Venice and the Frankfurt book fairs provided him with basic information on new publications. For both new and older editions, he also asked his numerous correspondents in Italy and northern Europe for publication information and their opinion on the quality of given editions. Many works came as personal gifts from the author, although the majority of his acquisitions were made through professional booksellers. So far as major authors were concerned, Pinelli obviously aimed to possess a copy of every worthwhile edition, particularly the Greek and Latin classics. As a result he possessed many copies —often both manuscript and printed—of individual authors, and was aware of the relative quality of various editions. For example, as early as 1572 he counseled a Venetian friend on the best printed versions of Ptolemy's *Geography*. He already owned seven editions, and offered comments on their relative quality.[8]

Life was not always easy for a collector of Pinelli's generation.

He built up his library during a period of relatively effective book censorship in Italy. The earliest Italian censorship laws dated from the late 1540s, and at first they had little practical effect. But by the 1570s the Counter-Reformation was at its height, and church and state joined together to censor prohibited materials effectively. Not only the law but the enforcement machinery for keeping banned volumes out of Italy functioned well. That is, the state arranged that imported merchandise be searched for prohibited materials by customs officials and Holy Office agents. Serious collectors like Pinelli had a commitment to European-wide learning, but many books written by non-Italian scholars who happened to be Protestants had been placed on the Index of Forbidden Books and there was, practically speaking, no way of getting permission to read or possess these forbidden books.

With a bit of discretion, however, books banned in Italy could be purchased abroad, at the Frankfurt book fairs, for example, and sent clandestinely, or somehow included in a shipment of legitimate titles to Italy. A bookseller whose name occurs frequently in Pinelli's correspondence was Pietro Longo, who specialized in transporting books between northern Europe and Venice. Eventually he was discovered, tried, and executed by the Venetian Inquisition in 1588, the only Venetian member of the book trade to suffer such a fate. In Venice, Pinelli and his friends patronized the bookstore of Francesco Ziletti, a publisher and bookseller who sold prohibited books from northern Europe under the counter, and was fined for doing so by the Holy Office in 1582.[9]

Pinelli's French connection—an ex-Florentine called Jacopo Corbinelli—supplied some forbidden titles as well as French political pamphlets.[10] Corbinelli, a political exile with literary pretensions, enjoyed his commission as Pinelli's liaison with French publishers, booksellers, and intellectuals. He served Pinelli from 1566 through the 1580s, even after he had established himself on the literary scene and in court circles. Although Corbinelli spent most of his time in Paris, he maintained contact with the Protestant printer Henri Estienne of Geneva, whose scholarly publications were vital to Pinelli's collection, and oversaw their shipment to Gian Vincenzo. Books intended for Pinelli were often sent to another man called Abbate del Bene in Padua, who, despite his ecclesiastical name, was a layman and for a time was attached to the university in some capacity. There were sometimes difficulties with the authorities. When a problem arose in the Italian segment of the network, Corbinelli quickly and boldly pointed out the injustice of the book seizure and suggested that Pinelli should defend his interests. In 1570 a consignment of books from France fell into the hands of some monks from Mantua, who apparently turned them over to the authorities. This prompted a letter from Corbinelli to Gian Vincenzo, from Paris, 8 February 1570, arguing that a man like him ought to be permitted to hold any kind of book that would advance the learning of wise men.[11] Such a statement of principle, born of exasperation, or at least long-distance boldness, is rare in this period, in which discretion was the watchword. When the matter dragged on into the summer of 1570, Corbinelli suggested that if the books had been brought to the Inquisitors of Padua, a man like Pinelli should have no difficulty in getting them back, although he admitted that some were Huguenot histories and banned in France.[12] There is no indication how the matter ended.

Corbinelli's bravura crumpled when trouble occurred at his end of the network. Some years later, in September 1579, Catherine de' Medici's agents arrested his courier, a valet of the duc d'Anjou. The material intended for Pinelli was innocuous, but a book on the religious wars carried by the valet belonged to Corbinelli himself. Afraid to be considered "too curious in certain things," in his letters Corbinelli reveals his anxiety during the next months while he awaited Catherine de' Medici's vengeance. The vengeance never materialized, and by January 1580, Corbinelli was himself again, speculating on who had the book and whether he might retrieve it.[13] This was Corbinelli's only serious scare. On the whole, Pinelli and his associates seem to have encountered no serious difficulties in their quest for banned and legitimate books.

I am not suggesting religious deviation on Pinelli's or his friends' part, but rather a determined devotion to learning that led to quiet contraventions of the censorship laws in the most discreet way possible. They were more serious, obviously, than the carton of undeclared cigarettes we smuggle across the border, but evidently not a serious matter of conscience for a man of Pinelli's commitment to learning. Some, perhaps most, of the prohibited works Pinelli acquired are included in the 1604 inventory. I say "some," because I suspect that a portion may have been either removed or stolen before 1604. Some of the Venetian materials were already missing, for example, by the time the Venetian government inspected the library. The 1604 inventory lists at least seventy-three prohibited titles by non-Italian authors, including Erasmus, Bodin, Agrippa, Conrad Gesner, Sebastian Muenster, Paracelsus, Ramus, and Rabelais—works of literature or learning, not religious deviation. Among prohibited Italian authors, Pinelli held twelve titles of

Aretino, Boccaccio, Antonio Brucioli, Ortensio Lando, Machiavelli, Pomponazzi, and Pier Paolo Vergerio, in eighteen copies. I suspect that these numbers are low, because an early record of Pinelli's holdings, dating from 1565 to 1570 (Ms. Amb. 0 249 sup., pte. 2) already included nine Erasmus titles, whereas the 1604 inventory has only four, and seven copies of Machiavelli versus five in the later inventory. The Pinelli collection was, of course, in continual flux, and Gian Vincenzo himself may have eliminated some prohibited volumes.

Pinelli's forbidden books attest the continuing determination of some Italian intellectuals to remain abreast of the best of contemporary learning. Gian Vincenzo and others of his generation were intellectual polymaths, interested in every scholarly field, desiring knowledge for its own sake rather than for its contemporary relevance: detached scholars, in a word. Even if in sixteenth-century Italy the life of the mind had replaced the active life of the Quattrocento, one has the impression that the search for the "word" was as exciting to Pinelli's generation as it had been for Leonardo Bruni's. Antiquarianism, philological humanism, and the encyclopedic quest for knowledge characterized the Venetian/Paduan intellectual circles of Pinelli's time. Gian Vincenzo and his friends passed with ease from Provençal poetry to geography to Aristotelian philosophy to the exchange of spring bulbs, and they leave the modern scholar panting in their wake. Whether or not Gian Vincenzo reveals himself an original thinker remains to be seen; at the least, he emerges as the quintessential Renaissance bibliophile, a late but worthy representative in a tradition that goes back to Petrarch. An encyclopedic quest for knowledge and the willingness to devote great resources of time and money to his quest enabled him to amass an enviable library. Pinelli, in effect, practiced the profession of creating a library with the same dedication that other Renaissance figures gave to philosophy, literature, and art.

Notes

1. Biographical information comes from Paolo Gualdo, *Vita Joannis Vincentii Pinelli* (Augsburg, 1607), repd. William Bates (ed.), *Vitae selectorum aliquot virorum* (London, 1681), pp. 314–378; and Adolfo Rivolta, *Catalogo dei codici pinelliani dell' Ambrosiana* (Milan: Tipografia Pontificia archivescovile S. Giuseppe, 1933), pp. xvii–lxxx.

2. Venice, Archivio di Stato, Secrete, Archivio Proprio di G. V. Pinelli. The materials all dealt with Venetian public affairs, foreign and domestic: *relazioni, avvisi*, letters, descriptions, and so forth. All Venetian noble families would have some of this material; it was also sought after by non-Venetians, although the government opposed, when it could, its circulation.

151

3. Anthony Hobson, "A Sale by Candle in 1608," *Bibliographical Society* (1971): 215-233.

4. See Rivolta, *Catalogo*; Emidio Martini and Dominico Bassi, *Catalogus Codicum graecorum Bibliothecae Ambrosianae*, 2 vols. (Milan: U. Hoepli, 1906).

5. Pierre de Nolhac, *La Bibliothèque de Fulvio Orsini: Contributions à l'histoire des collections d'Italie et à l'étude de la Renaissance* (Paris: E. Bouillon and E. Vieweg, 1887).

6. At least 338 Greek manuscripts belonging to Pinelli survive in the Abrosiana. See my "A Greek Collection in Padua: The Library of Gian Vincenzo Pinelli," *Renaissance Quarterly* (forthcoming).

7. Biblioteca Ambrosiana, Ms. F 205 inf. olim B 88 sup.

8. Bib. Amb., Ms. G 272 inf., 3^r-4^r; Padova, 4 marzo 1572. The friend was Alvise Mocenigo of Venice.

9. On Longo and Ziletti, see Paul Grendler, *The Roman Inquisition and the Venetian Press, 1540-1605* (Princeton, N.J.: Princeton University Press, 1977), ch. 6. Longo is mentioned in Pinelli's correspondence: Bib. Amb., Ms. S 105 sup., 8^r (1576); 126^v-127^r, 148^v (1581); Ms. G 271 inf., 19^r (1584). Ziletti is mentioned in Ms. G 272 inf., 66^r (1578); Ms. S 105 sup., 37^v, 46^r (1579); 90^r, 94^r, 97^r (1582); and a 1582 letter from him to Pinelli, 66^r-66^v.

10. On Corbinelli, see Rita Calderini De Marchi, *Jacopo Corbinelli et les érudits Français d'après la correspondance inédite Corbinelli-Pinelli (1566-1587)* (Milan: U. Hoepli, 1914).

11. Bib. Amb., Ms. B 9 inf., 114^r, Parigi, 8 feb. 1570 " . . . oltre ch'io credo che voi habbiate facultà di tenere ogni sorta libro, che a' savi et bene edificati no' può servire se no' a più solida et più perfetta eruditione nella verità."

12. Bib. Amb., Ms. B 9 inf., 123^r-124^r; 10 luglio 1570, Parigi.

13. Bib. Amb., Ms. T 167 sup., 41^r-53^r; 8 letters from 25 September 1579 to 16 January 1580; quote, 49^r.

Libraries, Books, and the Nature of America: The Creation of the Smithsonian Institution

Jean V. Matthews

To the historian, the founding of the Smithsonian Institution is one of those key episodes that, as James Henretta has recently suggested, manifests many of the "intellectual currents extant in the larger society." It reveals a number of conflicting ideas and attitudes about the nature of the young republic, the role of government in the support of "high" culture, and the relationship of the scholar to society. In 1836 Congress accepted a bequest of over $500,000 from the estate of the English gentleman-chemist, James Smithson, to establish in Washington an institution for "the increase and diffusion of knowledge among men." Since the disposition of the fund was the responsibility of the national government, the precise use to which it was to be put had to be seen as a political statement. In a decade of intermittent debate in Congress and in the press, politicians, journalists, interested scholars, and scientists canvassed the responsibility of government toward the life of the mind and the more specific problem of what *kinds* of intellectual pursuits American needed—an issue that involved implicit national self-definition. The controversy, which lasted well beyond the passing of the act of establishment, served as a rallying point for those whose notion of civilization demanded that the nation recognize the existence and value of an intellectual elite. It also brought into the open much resentment and suspicion toward the elitism of esoteric scholarship and at the same time exposed a

Jean V. Matthews *is assistant professor of history at the University of Western Ontario.*

Journal of Library History, Vol. 16, No. 1, Winter 1981
© 1981 by the University of Texas Press   0275-3650/81/010152–14$01.25

growing rift between the defenders of the unified scholarship of
the eighteenth century and the vigorous "new men" of the exact
sciences.[1]

The feeling that society does not sufficiently appreciate one's
activities is probably a normal accompaniment of the scholarly
life. It seems to have been particularly strong, perhaps with more
than usual justification, in Jacksonian America. "In such a country
and such an age," lamented George Perkins March, a considerable
scholar himself, "the mere scholar hath no vocation." Society had
"no rewards" for the scholar, complained the *Dial*, "society rewards none but those who will do its work." While it was possible,
even desirable, for a gentleman to be incidentally a scholar, it
was hard to be a "mere" scholar without considerable private
resources, psychological as well as material. The mid-1840s, however, witnessed a growing self-assertiveness among American scholars and scientists ready to defend the authority of the disciplined
intellect against the "intuitive genius" of Jacksonian man. Yearn-
ing for "that appreciation and notice which should ever attend
upon merit," they were becoming bolder in demanding that the
nation provide them with the same kind of facilities and recognition that European governments accorded their learned men. "A
literary class is gradually forming itself into a distinct order"
claimed the historian George Washington Greene in 1837, "opening
for many new springs of wealth, for all new sources of enjoy-
ment." However, since it was "still dependent upon the other
classes of society for its subsistence and its success," the key question was: "how far is our community prepared to supply the
savants?"[2]

Smithson's bequest offered an opportunity to put that question
to the test. But its disposition was not a matter of top priority for
Congress and it was not until the mid-1840s that the legislators
were prodded into setting aside some time from debating the annexation of Texas and the claims to Oregon to deal with their responsibility for the "increase and diffusion of knowledge." Proposals for the bequest had included the foundation of a national
university and John Quincy Adams's pet project of a national
observatory, but as the debate dragged on, there was a noticeable
disposition both in and outside of Congress to assume that the
knowledge to be diffused was of a practical kind pertaining to
technology, useful inventions, and a manipulative approach to
nature.[3] The assumption that "practical science" constituted the
knowledge essential for a democratic community lay behind the
two bills that finally, between 1844 and 1846, brought the con-

gressional debate to a resolution. The Senate had turned over the problem to its Library Committee, and in December 1844, its chairman, the old Jacksonian Benjamin Tappan of Ohio, brought in a bill proposing a conglomerate institution, part museum, part technical school, part agricultural experiment station. It would have a library consisting of works relating "to the ordinary business of life" and from time to time it might issue publications "in popular form, on the sciences and on the aid they bring to labor."[4]

However, Tappan's Whig colleague on the Committee, the flamboyant lawyer-orator from Massachusetts, Rufus Choate, had radically different ideas. A bibliophile who had given up adolescent dreams of becoming a college professor, Choate saw in the Smithsonian fund the opportunity to make a dramatic contribution, materially and symbolically, to the needs of American scholars. What such people needed, especially the increasing number being drawn into historical research, was libraries. It had become a commonplace to echo Fisher Ames's claim that Gibbon's *Decline and Fall* could never have been written in the United States because no American library could have supplied his sources. In an elaborate speech in January 1845, Choate denounced Tappan's "somewhat narrow utilitarianism" and suggested that the bulk of the fund be used to establish a "grand and noble public library; one which, for variety, extent, and wealth, shall be, and be confessed to be, equal to any now in the world." Quoting extensively from the *North American Review* and repeating the Gibbon example, he insisted that only the national government was in a position to meet "the actual literary and scientific wants" of the country. Spending two-thirds of the annual income on books for twenty-five years should build up a representative collection of works on the model of a good modern library like that of the University of Göttingen, and thus remove the major barrier preventing the American scholar from equaling the European: lack of materials for research.[5]

There was still a certain resistance to the whole idea of government endorsement of any kind of cultural or intellectual activity. "The Constitution did not give us charge of the mind and genius of the American people," protested William Allen, Democratic senator from Ohio (coiner of the catchy "54'40 or fight" slogan apropos of Oregon), "we have no right to presume that the people are so ignorant that we ought to legislate for enlightening them." Nevertheless, the Senate accepted all of Choate's proposed amendments and attached most of the income to the founding of a comprehensive library. In the House, however, the amended bill ran into the opposition of the chairman of the Select Committee on the Smithsonian Bequest, Tappan's friend and fellow Democrat, the communitarian social reformer Robert Dale Owen, and expired. Owen reopened the question in the next session with a new bill of his own. Noting Smithson's "utilitarian simplicity and practical benevolence," he retained the essential features of Tappan's proposal and added his own pet project, a normal school for training public school teachers in order to improve the "world-subduing" and "republican" science of primary education.

The library cause was now taken up in the House by Choate's old Dartmouth classmate, the Whig polymath George Perkins Marsh of Vermont, who presented, as the *New Englander* said unkindly, "before the eyes of some of our western members, what many of them have never seen, the spectacle of a living scholar." Like Choate, Marsh saw in the bequest a unique opportunity for Americans to take their "proper place among the nations of the earth, not merely as a political society, but as patrons of knowledge and the liberal arts." Aided by John Quincy Adams, Marsh swung the House back to the idea of a great national library. At last all but four of the Whig representatives, with the addition of thirty-three Democrats, voted for a bill erecting a building in the Mall including a museum and an art gallery, but allowing the greater part of the income, "not exceeding an average of $25,000 annually, for the gradual formation of a library composed of valuable works pertaining to all departments of human knowledge."[6]

Round one of the Smithsonian battle thus concluded with the triumph of the Choate/Marsh axis. It had been fought essentially between those who wished to throw national support behind humane scholarship as essential to high civilization and those who demanded some clear and widespread "cash value" in social benefit from intellectual activity. It had been a question of to what extent the federal government should emulate the traditional patronage of princes, of how far the United States shared the traditional concerns of Western civilization, and how far it was a new and unique society with its own inherent virtue, needing neither complication nor mental stimulation. Choate and Marsh both spoke from within the Federalist/Whig tradition of the purposive state, but both realized it was necessary to demonstrate that a great library would not really be an elite institution, "an anti-republican monopoly," nor was the scholar a protected drone who contributed nothing of value to society. Marsh hastened to point out that scholars had in fact played a vital leadership role in Western history: "Columbus was a learned scholar, and Luther but a studious monk. . . . Our own independence was declared and maintained by scholars." The American scholar, he hastened to add, disciplined by the selfless search for truth, was, of course, quite different from the atheist intellectuals who had fomented the French revolution. Thus the scholar could be seen as a man of action, but in the safest possible way. Choate skirted the awkward democratic question of who would benefit from the library with the metaphor of organic nationalism: aid to the learned would somehow indirectly stimulate and raise the whole "American Mind": the "whole culture of the community" would be "raised and enriched."[7]

The exponents of the library plan quite deliberately linked the idea of a great library with European high culture. The whole idea of a national library was to enable American scholars to compete with their European counterparts, to enable American culture to equal European culture, on European terms. Neither Choate nor Marsh, nor the scholarly community for whom they spoke, saw any incompatibility between American freedom and republican purity and the more developed culture of Europe. While rejoicing that the United States was spared "those vast inequalities of fortune, that elaborate luxury, that fantastic and extreme refinement," Choate acknowledged that he felt a "pang of envy and grief that there should be one drop or one morsel more of the bread or water of intellectual life tasted by the European than by the American mind. Why should not the soul of this country eat as good food and as much of it as the soul of Europe? . . . Are we afraid that the stimulated and fervid faculties of this young nation will be oppressed and overlaid? Because we have liberty which other nations have not, shall we reject the knowledge which they have and which we have not?"[8]

When, in the next session of Congress, Owen brought in his own counterproposal, he took up Choate's challenge, and both the substance and the tone of his remarks indicate how the pretensions of the scholar could still touch a sensitive nerve.

It grieves me not that the fantastic taste of some epicure in learning may chance to find on the book shelves of Paris some literary morsel of choice and ancient flavor . . . I feel no envy if we republicans are outdone by luxurious Europe in some high-seasoned delicacy of the pampered soul. . . . Men have we; a people; a free people, self respecting, self-governing . . . bravely battling their onward way; treading, with liberty at their side, the path of progressive improvement, each step upward and onward—onward to the great goal of public virtue and social equality.[9]

Scholarship was a species of "luxury"—a concept that played a prominent role in traditional republican theory. Luxury, whether in the form of physical or mental riches, enervated and emasculated, destroyed moral fiber and increased class distinctions. From Owen's point of view, to attempt to equal Europe in traditional scholarship was to misconceive the nature of America, whose essence was a commitment to equality. The education of the masses supported that equality; encouragement of the higher mental development of the few subverted it. The library advocates were anxious to appropriate all the glories of the European past, and saw the library as a storehouse of civilization condensed: "the whole past speaking to the present and the future." For Owen, on the other hand, the past was something from which America was emerging as from a chrysalis, progressively divesting itself of outmoded ideas and prejudices. Thus a book was only of value in so far as it embodied information or ideas still considered valid. Like many others in the debate he doubted that there were enough books worth buying with $25,000 per annum. The "clouds of idle verbiage," the "loads of ostentatious technicalities," the "bloated book-gatherings that sleep in dust and cobwebs on the library shelves of European monarchies" had little worth saying to a modern people, who had learnt to refine real knowledge into the "slender pamphlet, the popular tract, the cheap periodical." To the "practical" men who supported Owen's opposition to a great library, books and libraries were "musty," antiquarian, "asleep in dust and cobwebs," "to be wondered at more for their extent than for their usefulness," associated with the dead hand of the past and aristocratic exclusiveness; their users, desiccated pedants or pampered epicures.[10]

In the face of this kind of attitude, the success of Choate and Marsh in getting the greater part of the bequest appropriated for the purchase of books was not only a practical victory but a symbolic one. A great library on the Mall, created by Congress, an "exponent of civilization, permanent, palpable, conspicuous, useful," could be seen as the deliberate adherence of the young republic to the traditions of Western civilization. As a "prestige-granting agency," Congress seemed to have validated, with national approval, the pursuit of scholarship. While the library would clearly have been useful to at least some American scholars, its importance lay more in the symbolic triumph it represented for particular kinds

of intellectual activity, bestowing upon them a "public designation of respectability" and affirming that they were "American"
as well as traditional.[11]

However, although the library proponents had won a victory for
scholarship against the utilitarians, they were to find the fruits of
that victory snatched away from them. The implementation of the
Smithsonian act was the duty of a Board of Regents appointed by
Congress. The Democratic Speaker of the House bypassed a furious Marsh and appointed Owen instead. The other major library
proponent, Rufus Choate, was a member of the Board, but he left
the Senate in 1845 and, absorbed with a busy legal career in Boston, did not take any active part in the work of the Regents after
the first year. The most dynamic member turned out to be Alexander Dallas Bache, the superintendent of the U.S. Coast Survey
and champion of the needs of the small but growing body of
American scientists. Smithson had, after all, been a chemist, and
Bache had seen in the Smithsonian bequest a providential windfall
for basic scientific research. Whatever Congress might have decided, he was not about to let it slip through his fingers. As a first
step he persuaded the Board to appoint as secretary the officer
who would be in day-to-day control of the Institution, his old
friend, the Princeton physicist Joseph Henry. Henry came with a
completely worked out program for the "increase and diffusion of
knowledge" that had very little to do with a library, or with the
museum and art gallery Congress had also designated as part of the
new Institution. Henry intended that the bulk of the income
should be spent on the encouragement of original research. The
"real working men" of science were to be given the opportunity to
publish their findings in prestigious volumes to be called the
Smithsonian Contributions to Knowledge. Henry's list of suitable
fields for publication included history and ethnology, but the list
was dominated by physics, chemistry, and meteorology.[12]

A dismayed Choate managed to effect a compromise in which
at least half the income would go toward a library—the rest on
what Henry always called "the *active* operations." This arrangement would not go into effect until the building was completed,
in several years, and meanwhile the management of the Institution
was at the discretion of its secretary. In addition, the man Choate
had wanted as secretary, Charles Coffin Jewett, the librarian of
Brown University, was to be appointed assistant secretary in
charge of the library. On this basis a precarious equilibrium was
maintained for a few years, but Jewett, who resented being relegated to the passive principle in the Smithsonian cosmos, grew in-

creasingly discontented. Every year Henry and the majority of the Regents voted smaller appropriations for the purchase of books: in 1853 it was $874.00. In March of 1853, as the building neared completion, the Regents on Henry's request formally abrogated the Choate compromise and recommended that in future the distribution of the income be left entirely to the discretion of the Board on the recommendation of the secretary. Henry then dismissed Jewett, with whom his relations had become increasingly strained, and Choate sent a formal letter of resignation to Congress, charging that Henry had perverted the will of the legislature.[13]

Jewett's dismissal and Choate's resignation sparked a flurry of controversy in the press, not only arguments for and against Henry's management, but a revival of sallies against "abstruse studies which are incomprehensible to the generality of men." Both houses of Congress appointed committees of enquiry. The Senate committee supported Henry; the head of the House committee, Charles W. Upham, the future historian of Salem witchcraft, was a library supporter and Choate's friend, but he could not carry his colleagues, and the committee issued two conflicting reports. The House refused to take any action and the whole controversy petered out. The newspapers lost interest almost as quickly and only a few periodicals were still reviewing the affair by mid-1855. Benjamin Peirce in the *American Journal of Science and Arts* concluded cheerfully that the policy of the institution was "heartily approved by the whole scientific interest of this country and appears to be favourably regarded by a large share of our best scholars and literary men."[14]

Nevertheless, the second round in the Smithsonian battle had revealed the beginnings of a split within the ranks of the learned, between the scientists and the traditional scholars. The astronomer Benjamin Gould tried to downplay this aspect as the deliberate mischief-making of interested individuals: "first to create a discord regarding the Institution between the purely scientific and purely literary men in the nation; and, when this was found impossible, to create an impression in the public mind that such discord existed." This was rather disingenuous; the library advocates did feel put upon and edged out by the scientists of the Smithsonian. The Smithsonian question, one pro-library Regent expostulated to Congress, had "become one of physical science versus everything else."[15]

During the congressional debates the defenders of "useful" knowledge had been inclined to associate "the improvement of the condition of the human races and particularly of the common people" with "the great sun of science." More readily than books or libraries it seemed that science could be allied with life, vigor, and democracy. Marsh, one of the last people to write both natural and cultural history, had protested what he perceived as an imperialistic claim that only experimental and applied science provided worthwhile knowledge. "I must be permitted to express my dissent from the doctrine . . . which confines all knowledge, all science, to the numerical and quantitative values of material things. . . . I should hope that at this time, and in this place, one might safely venture a plea in behalf of that higher knowledge which serves to humanize, to refine, to elevate, to make men more deeply wise. . . . " In the previous session, William C. Rives of Virginia had made a similar protest. He had noted with surprise observations made in the course of the debate that seemed "to imply that moral science is not knowledge and that nothing but what are regarded as the natural sciences . . . is knowledge." Were "the legislators of this country, who are so deeply concerned in the destinies and progressive civilization of the human race, to regard the science of government and legislation as no part of human knowledge?"[16]

To the rigorous new scientists, however, this did appear to be the case. For Joseph Henry, the apostle of science, "knowledge," strictly speaking, could only be the product of the scientific method of experimentally verifying an hypothesis, enabling one not only to explain but to predict. Only knowledge defined thus could actually be said to "grow" and to produce *new* "truths." Charles Jewett, writing to Henry in November 1847 and skirting around the differences between them, caught the distinction. "One who has the interests of learning really at heart can most cheerfully cooperate. . . . " he wrote, and then crossed out "learning" and replaced it with "knowledge" between quotation marks. Many years later, in 1870, Henry, by now the venerable head of a distinguished institution, was questioned by a British parliamentary committee on the publication policy of the Smithsonian. He related that a number of papers on philosophy had been submitted, "but the answer is, what are the evidences that they are true? and the rule is to publish no unverified speculations." T. H. Huxley asked him whether if one of Kant's *Critiques* had been submitted, he would have published it. The answer was no—because of "the indefiniteness of the subject."[17]

Much as Henry and his allies might despise the conception of science held by the democratic utilitarians, they did not hesitate to borrow their language. Henry's metaphor of "active operations," with its connotations of vigor, masculinity, and progress, put the proponents of traditional scholarship on the defensive. The scholar encumbered by musty books seemed a timid soul beside the stripped-for-action scientist. As a Henry supporter in the *Southern Literary Messenger* remarked loftily, "Authority, which is the tutelary genius of the Library, has in truth often arrested the progress of scientific exploration, raising barriers which only the undisciplined force of some intrepid thinker has availed to overthrow." Given the rhetorical milieu of the mid–nineteenth century, humanist scholars realized that it was necessary to repudiate the slur of passivity, to insist that libraries were not the mere "hiving" of knowledge. "The publication of books and the assumption of researches have been called 'active operations,'" complained the exasperated pro-library Regent James Meacham, "as if everything else were in comparison but standstill." Like the researcher in the physical sciences, scholars also tried to identify themselves with the nationally validated heroic figure of the pioneer, subduing the wilderness and pushing back the frontier. Choate insisted that the scholar in the library must also be seen as a frontiersman, planting himself "along the line of demarcation between what is known and what is unknown," making "this the base of operations for extending the conquests of science and enlarging the boundaries of human knowledge."[18]

The field in which they might most obviously do so was history, and the library advocates increasingly came to see history as the exemplar of progressive knowledge outside the physical sciences. As in those disciplines, researches could be made, new "facts" uncovered, and possibly "laws" deduced. Furthermore, as explorers of the national past in particular, the American historians demonstrated their vital role in the republic. American history not only offered as exciting a field for discovery as the physical universe, but one whose implications for national identity and for human existence in general were infinitely more important. Marsh in the House had pointed out that the cultivation of history was particularly necessary in a democracy. Jewett told a conference of librarians that Americans must begin to reexamine the past and rewrite history "from our own American standpoint." Thus a great national library was particularly necessary because it would make possible a real uncovering of the American past. Both Meacham and Upham, in their last-ditch defense of the library idea, pointed out that a national library would have the unique opportunity to collect all the material pertaining to the nation's history. "The annals of all other countries," Upham told Congress, were either lost or "shrouded in fable, . . . but ours, during their whole duration, are within the range of unclouded history. The great social, moral, and political experiment here going on to test the last hope of humanity is capable of being described in clear and certain records."[19]

This emphasis on history made clearer the gap between the scholars and the scientists on the function of books. Belonging to disciplines that progressed, like America itself in Owen's vision, by sloughing off its ancestry, the scientists thought in terms of a compact working library of current works. What the Smithsonian needed, said the Regents' report in support of Henry, was "not a collection of everything which learned dullness and literary folly as well as real wisdom and sound science have put into print—a vast and unwieldy repertory, in which the trash as well as the precious may be found—but a library of valuable books." Historians, on the other hand, were hoarders, to whom anything and everything might be valuable, however slight its intrinsic worth. Scholars, echoed by Jewett in his annual reports, continually hammered home the idea that every country should have at least one library that should aim at possessing every book published, "one great literary depot where no books should be esteemed as *trash*," which would preserve not only the costly, but works "of *too little value* in the common estimation, to be found elsewhere, down even to the smallest tracts."[20]

Looking back on the period a generation later, Benjamin Silliman marked the year 1845 as the beginning of a "revival of learning" and a "great Scientific Awakening." High on his list of contributing causes was the founding of the Smithsonian, which opened up opportunities for research and placed "the scientific workers of America in intimate fellowship with their co-workers in all parts of the civilized globe." The movement to improve American libraries also grew stronger during the fifties, and in 1854 both the new Boston Public Library with Jewett as its librarian and the Astor Library in New York were opened. After the Civil War the Library of Congress expanded to become the kind of national central library that Choate and Jewett had envisaged. In the years to come, both traditional scholarship and scientific research would receive increasing, though fluctuating, public endorsement and support. Still, humanistic scholars were aware that the struggle over the Smithsonian, which had begun as a battle against the utilitarians, had ended in another kind of skirmish, which they had lost. Justin Winsor, Jewett's successor at the

Boston Public Library, writing to the historian Herbert Baxter Adams in 1888, recalled the early years of the Smithsonian as a fight between science and "literature," and that "science beat." It had been a symptomatic victory. Far more than the traditional scholar, the scientist, with an aura of masculine mastery and a forward thrust into the future, would be able to capture the national imagination. The laboratory, rather than the library, would seem more truly to reflect the "nature" of America.[21]

Notes

1. James Henretta, "Social History as Lived and Written," *American Historical Review* 84 (December 1979): 1293-1322. Smithson's will and the debate over its acceptance in the 24th Congress is reprinted in William J. Rhees, *The Smithsonian Institution: Documents Relative to Its Origin and History, 1835-1899*, 2 vols. (Washington, D.C.: Government Printing Office, 1901), vol. 1, pp. 5-6, 125-143. See also Howard S. Miller, *Dollars for Research: Science and Its Patrons in Nineteenth-Century America* (Seattle: University of Washington Press, 1970), p. 15.

2. George Perkins Marsh, *Human Knowledge: A Discourse Delivered before the Massachusetts Alpha of the Phi Beta Kappa Society, at Cambridge, August 26, 1847* (Boston: C. C. Little and J. Brown, 1847), p. 3; "The Art of Life—The Scholar's Calling," 1 (October 1840): 175-182, quotation, p. 177. John Carroll Brent, *Letters on the National Institute, Smithsonian Legacy, the Fine Arts and Other Matters Connected with the Interests of the District of Columbia* (Washington, D.C.: J. and G. S. Gideon, 1844), p. 61. See also J. F. Jackson, "American Scholarship," *Knickerbocker* 28 (July 1846): 1-13, for similar demands. George Washington Greene, "Libraries," *North American Review* 45 (July 1837): 116-149, quotation, p. 138. Greene later held the first chair of American history to be created in the United States at Cornell in 1871. For the psychological and social difficulties entailed in this kind of withdrawal from the business and professional life that was socially validated, see Donald Fleming, "American Science and the World Scientific Community," *Journal of World History* 8, no. 3 (1965): 666-673.

3. The democratic and utilitarian implications associated with the study of "things not words" produced a tendency to regard scientific knowledge as merchandise, discrete facts or discoveries rendered immediately available to the marketplace of public acceptance. The Smithsonian Institution, proposed William Darlington, the Pennsylvania physician, should become a kind of intellectual supermarket, "a great national warehouse of knowledge, where everyone might find something suited to his wants, and to which he could freely resort whenever he became conscious of his necessities": "A Plea for a National Museum and Botanic Garden . . . 1841," in William J. Rhees, *The Smithsonian Institution: Documents Relative to Its Origins and History* (Washington, D.C.: Smithsonian Institution, 1880), pp. 903, 907.

4. Tappan's bill is in Rhees, *Documents, 1835-1899*, pp. 276-280.

5. Choate in the Senate, 8 January 1845, in Rhees, *Documents, 1835-1899*, pp. 280-293. The Ames remark is quoted in "Literary Institutions.—University.—Library," *North American Review* 8 (December 1818): 191-200;

by Greene in the *NAR* article referred to in note 2 (Choate quoted both these articles extensively); by Judge Joseph Story in a Phi Beta Kappa address and in the *NAR* 71 (1850): 186. See also Jesse H. Shera, *Foundations of the Public Library: The Origin of the Public Library Movement in New England, 1629-1855* (Hamden, Conn.: Shoe String Press, 1965; first pub. 1949), pp. 206-209.

    6. Allen in the Senate, 21 January 1845, in Rhees, *Documents, 1835-1899*, pp. 313, 315. Owen's bill is in ibid., pp. 321-331; review of Marsh's speech on the Smithsonian in *New Englander* 4 (October 1846): 605-607; Marsh in the House, 23 April 1846, in Rhees, *Documents, 1835-1899*, p. 378; the final act is in ibid., pp. 429-430.

    7. Choate, in Rhees, *Origins*, pp. 291-293; Marsh, in ibid., pp. 383-384; almost thirty years earlier a writer in the *NAR* had complained in similar tones of what appeared to be a neurotic super-independence of Europe. All civilized nations had their great libraries. "We alone will take upon ourselves to do without them; either despising the literary character, or undertaking to invent over again the arts and sciences, and re-write the books of all other countries and ages," "Literary Institutions.—University.—Library," p. 200.

    8. Choate, in Rhees, *Origins*, pp. 292-293.

    9. Owen in the House, 22 April 1846, in Rhees, *Documents, 1835-1899*, pp. 333-350, quotations, pp. 343-344.

    10. Choate, in Rhees, *Origins*, p. 287; Owen, in ibid., pp. 341-349; Rhees, *Documents, 1835-1899*, pp. 332-388 passim. The importance of the idea of culture, science, scholarship as forms of "luxury" can be seen in the fact that a speaker before the National Institution for the Promotion of Science (founded 1840) found it necessary to insist that "generations at least must pass away, before the turning point of civilization is reached, beyond which refinement sinks into luxury, and luxury becomes the harbinger of a decaying empire": J. R. Ingersoll, "National Institute," *American Review* 2 (1845): 235-255; quotation, p. 255.

    11. Choate, in Rhees, *Origins*, p. 286. For a discussion of political action as symbolic and designed to produce public acceptance of status, see Joseph Gusfield, *Symbolic Crusade: Status Politics and the American Temperance Movement* (Urbana: University of Illinois Press, 1969 [1963]), ch. 7. The phrases "prestige-granting agency" and "public designation of respectability" are from p. 176.

    12. For Henry's appointment and the initial compromise over the library, see Howard S. Miller, *Dollars for Research*, pp. 14-21. The phrase "real working men of science" is from a letter from Henry to Bache, 9 August 1838, quoted in Miller, p. 9.

    13. Joseph A. Borome, *Charles Coffin Jewett* (Chicago: American Library Association, 1951), pp. 43-84. Henry did encourage Jewett in a scheme to create a great union catalogue of all American public and college libraries, fulfilling the same function for the scholarly world as the "active operations" did for science: the facilitation of research. The report of the committee of Regents considering the abrogation of the compromise is in . . . *The Smithsonian Institution: Journals of the Board of Regents, Reports of Committees, Statistics, etc.*, ed. William J. Rhees (Washington D.C.: Smithsonian Institution, 1879), pp. 101-112. One of the committee, James Meacham of Vermont, submitted a minority report, printed separately, *Report of Hon. James Meacham . . . on the Distribution of the Income of the Smithsonian Fund*

(Washington, D.C.: Smithsonian Institution, 1854). Choate's letter of resignation is in Rhees, *Documents, 1835-1899*, pp. 511-512.

14. For the interest of the press, see *New York Daily Times*, 6 and 19 January 1855; *Boston Daily Advertiser*, 23, 25, 29 January 1855; *Boston Atlas*, 27, 29, 30, 31 January; 9 February; 5, 6, 12 March 1855; *Boston Post*, 27 January; 5, 7, 13, 21, 22 February 1855. For Henry's vision for the Smithsonian and his dispute with Jewett, see Wilcomb E. Washburn, "Joseph Henry's Conception of the Purpose of the Smithsonian Institution," in Whitfield J. Bell, Jr., et al., *A Cabinet of Curiosities: Five Episodes in the Evolution of American Museums* (Charlottesville: University Press of Virginia, 1967), pp. 106-166; *National Intelligencer*, 3 March 1854, and articles in the *Christian Examiner* (November 1854): 385-395; *Putnam's Monthly* 4, no. 20 (August 1854): 121-131; *Southern Literary Messenger* 21, no. 8 (August 1855): 457-471. The reports of the committees of both houses of Congress are in Rhees, *Documents, 1835-1899*, pp. 580-584, 557-574; Benjamin Peirce, "The Smithsonian Institution," *American Journal of Science and Arts* 20, 2nd series (July 1855): 17.

15. Miller, *Dollars for Research*, p. 15; Benjamin Gould, *The Smithsonian Institution* (Boston, 1855), pp. 29-30; Meacham in the House, 5 March 1855, in Rhees, *Documents, 1835-1899*, p. 597.

16. Rhees, *Documents, 1835-1899*, pp. 362, 385; Marsh in the House, in Rhees, *Documents, 1835-1899*, pp. 375, 383; Rives in the Senate, in ibid., p. 299.

17. Joseph Henry, "Programme of Organization of the Smithsonian Institution," in *Third Annual Report of the Board of Regents* . . . (Washington, D.C.: U.S. Government Printing Office, 1849), p. 17; Jewett to Henry, 16 November 1847, Bache papers, Smithsonian Institution archives; "Examination of Professor Henry by the English Government Scientific Commission . . . 1870," *Journals of the Board of Regents*, p. 790. See also Geoffrey T. Hellman, *The Smithsonian: Octopus on the Mall* (Philadelphia: Lippincott, 1967), pp. 63-64.

18. "Smithson's Bequest: Its Objects and Issues," *Southern Literary Messenger* 21 (August 1855): 457-471; quotation, p. 463; Meacham, in Rhees, *Origins*, p. 697; Choate, ms. report to the Smithsonian, n.d., Choate MSS, Houghton Library, Harvard.

19. Marsh, in Rhees, *Origins*, p. 271; Jewett Opening Address, in *Proceedings of the Librarians' Convention Held in New York City, September 15, 16, and 17, 1853* (rpd. Cedar Rapids, Iowa: W. H. Murray [at the Torch Press], 1915), p. 15; Report of Charles W. Upham to the House, 3 March 1855, in Rhees, *Documents, 1835-1899*, pp. 557-574; quotation, p. 572.

20. James A. Pearce, Report of the Regents' Committee, Journal of the Board of Regents, 20 May 1854, in *Smithsonian Miscellaneous Collections* (Washington, D.C.: Smithsonian Institution, 1880), vol. 18, p. 109; (Jewett), *National Intelligencer*, 14 April quoted in William Dawson Johnston, *History of the Library of Congress* (Washington, D.C.: Government Printing Office, 1904), vol. 1, p. 304; and George Livermore, *North American Review* 71 (July 1850): 185-189.

21. Benjamin Silliman, "American Contributions to Chemistry," *American Chemist* (August-September 1874): 70-114; ref., pp. 93-94; Winsor to Adams, 18 April 1888, quoted in Borome, *Charles Coffin Jewett*, p. 106.

Archival Resources and Writing Immigrant American History: The Bund Archives of the Jewish Labor Movement

Norma Fain Pratt

Introduction

Increasingly, historians in the United States are engaging in intensive new research into the specific histories of European immigrant cultures, including the intricate immigrant adjustments to American life in the late nineteenth and early twentieth centuries. Social historians, in particular, now value efforts to reconstruct the immigrant past and the significant ensuing Americanization, or rather the acculturation processes, which transformed immigrant cultures and contributed to the evolution of present American society.[1]

There are several interrelated reasons for scholars' exploration into the ethnic American past. First, in the late 1960s and 1970s, many second- and third-generation Italians, Jews, Irish, and Poles, for example, openly avowed a special immigrant heritage that they believed still existed within their communities; these children of immigrants expressed a sense of continuity with their past culture. Thus, for many people, the ideal of America as a melting pot was replaced by the concept of the United States as a culturally pluralistic society. Contemporary historians who accepted this new interpretation began to investigate the complex roots of the multicultural dimensions present in American society.[2] Second, there

Norma Fain Pratt *is professor of history at Mt. San Antonio College, Walnut, California, and currently visiting professor of women's history and American labor history at Sarah Lawrence College, Bronxville, New York.*

Journal of Library History, Vol. 16, No. 1, Winter 1981
©1981 by the University of Texas Press   0275-3650/81/010166-11$01.00

was a nostalgic curiosity about the recent past among young scholars. The original immigrant generation of the turn of the century faded from personal memory and scholars searched for their own heritage—the world of their grandmothers and grandfathers.[3] Third, and of a somewhat more general character, was the fact that interest in American social history made historians who might not have been especially concerned with immigrants more aware of such groups. Social historians sought out and uncovered new areas and new subjects, the formerly invisible subjects of history— the family, women, children, the working classes, and the immigrants.[4] And finally, the recent interest in the European ethnic past has a current function. The continuing immigration of peoples into the United States from Europe, Latin America, and Asia has sent social scientists back into the past looking for guides to historical patterns in the immigrant adjustments to American life.

Although historians are now interested in immigrant history, it is no simple matter to find comprehensive, systematically collected sources on this subject. Unfortunately, immigrants rarely kept good records. The vast numbers of immigrants—Russians, Poles, Italians, Jews, Hungarians, Finns—who came to the United States in the nineteenth and early twentieth centuries were poor and not highly educated. Their lives were so overwhelmingly immediate that there was little interest in preserving either the record of daily regularities or the amenities of special cultural expressions. In order to record the present for posterity, it is necessary to have the idea of the present as significant and as an important link in the process of creating the future. Therefore, for the most part, the record of immigrant life exists in bits and pieces. There are personal records (diaries, family albums, memorabilia); institutional records (club and immigrant society events or organizational minutes); and government records (census, school attendance, or voting statistics). However, it is only in the last decade or so that immigrant historical societies composed of professional academics have been founded and there are still only a few universities that have initiated immigrant archival collections.[5]

The History of the Jewish Labor Bund Archives

One of the most rare immigrant collections in the United States is the Archives of the Jewish Labor Bund, presently located at 25 East 78th Street in New York City. These Archives are exceptional because of their age, because of their comprehensiveness, and especially because of their founders' intention to preserve the present for the future, based upon a set of philosophic principles. The Archives are an invaluable treasure for American historians. The collection grew gradually and organically. Originally the Bund Archives were established in Geneva, Switzerland, in 1899 to serve as the archive-library of the then illegal social democratic organization, the Jewish Labor Bund of Russia, Poland, and Lithuania (founded in 1897). The Archives' founders were two Russian Jewish revolutionaries, John Mill and Tsemakh Kopelson, who had fled their native land to avoid political arrest. They founded the Archives in Geneva, the haven for socialist emigrés from many European countries and a safe place against unexpected tsarist search and seizure.

Thus, from their inception, the Bund Archives were created and administered by self-conscious intellectuals and activists with a purpose in mind—in fact, several purposes. The Bund Archives were meant to preserve documents such as pamphlets, newspapers, correspondence, and posters from destruction by adversaries (that is, the tsarist police); to keep records of achievements for future generations—and that included cultural achievements such as notices of theatrical and musical performances, books of poetry and fiction, and other events related to Jewish working-class culture; and to be a center of information and socialist education on matters concerning Jewish politics and economics.[6]

After their original foundation in Geneva, the Archives' history itself continued to be an intriguing chapter in Jewish immigrant history. Before the Archives emigrated to the United States in the late 1940s, the trials and tribulations of Eastern European Jewish socialism were mirrored in the fate of the Archives.[7] Thus, between 1899 and the First World War the Archives remained situated in Geneva and served the illegal Bund organization in Russia (which in that period included Poland) as a depository for its revolutionary materials. After the First World War and the 1917 Russian Revolution, the Bund became a legal socialist political party in the newly created republic of Poland. In Russia, however, the Bund was unwelcome because of its opposition to Bolshevik control. The Bund's opposition to Russian communism brought it into an alliance with other European social democratic parties; for instance, the Bund became a member of the Labor and Socialist International in 1930. Much earlier, in 1919, the Archives were moved from Geneva to Berlin and the collection was installed in the building of the Vorwaerts, which also housed the administrative headquarters of the German Social Democratic Party (SPD).[8] Here, in the years before the Second World War, the collection

169

continued to grow with contemporary materials documenting the
development of Jewish political and cultural life throughout Eastern Europe, including materials on the Zionist movement, with
which the Bund had considerable disagreement.

When Hitler came to power in 1933 the fascists occupied the
building of the SPD and confiscated its properties. As a way of
saving the Archives, the Bund collection was sold nominally to the
French government, and the French ambassador in Berlin ordered
them crated and transferred to France. Between 1933 and 1940
the Archives were housed in Paris. But during the occupation of
the French capital, the Archives were confiscated by the Nazis;
they were presumed to have been destroyed. After the liberation
of Paris in 1945, however, a major portion of the Archives surprisingly was recovered in crates that the Germans had tossed into
an open field several miles from the city, apparently as part of
their own evacuation.[9]

In the late 1940s, the Archives were transported to New York
City, miraculously having survived the European conflagration.
The collection was housed on the fifth floor of a former Madison
Avenue mansion, purchased by Frank Z. Atran, a member of the
Bund who had emigrated to the United States before the Second
World War and who had become wealthy. Until the present day,
the Bund Archives have remained the private collection of the
Jewish Labor Bund organization, whose administrative central
offices also were moved to New York after World War II. Besides
the few rooms where the collection is kept, a small reading room
is open free to scholars daily from 10 a.m. to 5 p.m. The Archives
are financed solely by the Bund, by small private endowments,
and by the Trade Union Council, representing eight major unions
affiliated with the AFL-CIO. The budget is extremely modest, and
the cramped quarters and problems of document preservation have
become a cause of considerable dismay to scholars concerned with
the invaluable archival materials. In 1978 an Academic Advisory
Committee of the Archives was established in order to involve
scholars in the general academic community with archival planning. The Committee is now composed of forty-six scholars—
historians, sociologists, linguists, and economists—from the United
States and abroad, representing educational institutions in California, Illinois, New York, Oklahoma, and Connecticut including
scholars from Hebrew University (Israel), McGill University (Canada), and Oxford University (England).[10]

The Eastern European Collection

In order to write the history of Jewish immigration in America, it is important to be able to reconstruct the Jewish past in Europe. The Archives have unique collections of Eastern European materials in various languages; for instance, in Yiddish, Hebrew, Russian, Polish, Ukrainian, and Lettish as well as some Western European materials in Spanish, French, and English. With these materials, the researcher can begin to develop the cultural, political, intellectual, and economic aspects of European life in the nineteenth and twentieth centuries. The documents deal with both Jewish and non-Jewish themes. The Bund's Eastern European collection contains materials in various forms: manuscripts (reports of meetings; conferences and conventions; the correspondence of leaders and active workers; unpublished literary works); proclamations; legal and illegal brochures, periodicals, and books; placards and photographs; statistical information and clippings about hundreds of Eastern European towns and cities; and biographic information on writers and political figures. The scope of the Eastern European archival collection encompasses the socialist and labor movements of the nineteenth and twentieth centuries. For example, among many other topics the following subjects were listed in the description *A Great Collection: The Archives of the Jewish Labor Movement* (New York, 1965):

(1) The General Jewish Labor Bund of Russia, Poland, and Lithuania

(2) The Russian Social Democratic movement—from *Osvobozhdenie truda* and *Soyuz Russkikh S. D.* to the Mensheviks and Bolsheviks

(3) The Populist movement in Russia and particularly the Yiddish literature of the Socialist Revolutionaries

(4) The Polish Socialist Party and its Jewish section: the Social Democrats of Poland and Lithuania; *Proletariat* and other groups of the Polish labor movement

(5) Poale Zion, Socialist Territorialists, and other Russian-Polish Zionist groups

(6) The Lettish Social Democratic Party; the Georgian, Armenian, Ukrainian Social Democratic Party

(7) Anarchists, particularly Jewish anarchists

(8) Revolutionary movements in the universities and high schools in Russia

(9) The 1905 revolution in Russia

(10) Pogroms and Jewish self-defense groups

(11) Russian, Polish, and Jewish communist parties in Russia and other Eastern European countries
(12) International Socialist Labor Movement, Second and Third Internationals
(13) The trade union movement in independent Poland (1919–1939)
(14) Jewish political parties in independent Poland
(15) Cultural movements among Jews, particularly *Zisho* (Central Yiddish School Organization in Poland)
(16) Statistics on the economic situation of Jews in Eastern Europe
(17) Biographies of writers and communal leaders
(18) Information on the annihilation and resistance of Jews in Europe during World War II.[11]

During the last twenty years, scores of books, articles, doctoral dissertations, and research papers relevant to an understanding of the Jewish experience in Europe before and during the Jewish mass immigration to the United States (1880 to 1924) have been written largely on the basis of the Bund's archival resources. For example, Ezra Mendelsohn, *Class Struggle in the Pale: The Formative Years of the Jewish Workers' Movement in Tsarist Russia* (Cambridge: Cambridge University Press, 1970); Henry Tobias, *The Jewish Labor Bund in Russia from Its Origins to 1905* (Stanford, Calif.: Stanford University Press, 1972); and Nora Levin, *While Messiah Tarried: Jewish Socialist Movements, 1871–1917* (New York: Schocken Books, 1977) are all scholarly works based upon archival material that explain and interpret the social and political development of Eastern European Jewry. Until the 1970s, books on Eastern European Jews, that population from which such a vast number of immigrants came to the United States, were exceedingly rare.

The American Jewish Collection

Within a few years of settling in New York, the Bund's archivists began to collect material relating to American Jewish history, particularly to trade unionism, socialist and communist movements, and Yiddish culture. The Archives, for example, now possess publications, documents, protocols, and correspondence from crucial periods in the development of the International Ladies Garment Workers' Union and its various locals; of the Amalgamat-

ed Clothing and Textile Workers of America, its main office and
various branches; of the United Hebrew Trade; of the Workmen's
Circle; and of the Jewish Labor Committee. The Archives also have
a rare and extensive collection of the Yiddish-language labor press
in the United States as well as considerable holdings in the radical
and labor-related literary Yiddish avant-garde press dating from
the 1880s to the present.

Much of the American Jewish collection has yet to be utilized
by scholars, particularly those researchers interested in the social
history of Jewish immigration. The field of social historical research and writing is still quite new to most American Jewish historians. Potentially, there are important studies to be made. For
instance, American social historians of immigration are now not
just interested in describing immigrant institutions, but rather are
more concerned with the methods employed by immigrant groups
(men, women, young, middle-aged, old, rich, poor, and so on) to
maintain an ethnic loyalty while simultaneously inculcating new
American identities. The Bund's collection of the Workmen's
Circle (*Arbeter ring*), a Jewish labor fraternal organization founded at the beginning of the twentieth century, would be an excellent source for such a study. Not only do the archival holdings include detailed materials on the social services programs of the
Workmen's Circles, but there is a good deal of material dealing
with educational, social, and cultural activities related to the actions of the men, women, and children who participated in the
Yiddish-language schools, in the summer camps, and in the *Folks-
bene*, Yiddish folk theater.[12] With this kind of information, social
historians can ask new questions about the changes in family life,
leisure habits, political ideals, and social values.

Recently three books in and around American Jewish history
have been published that used the Archives' materials: Irving
Howe's *World of Our Fathers* (New York: Harcourt Brace Jovano-
vich; Simon and Schuster, 1976); Paul Avrich's *An American
Anarchist: The Life of Voltairine De Cleyre* (Princeton, N.J.:
Princeton University Press, 1978); and my own *Morris Hillquit: A
Political History of an American Jewish Socialist* (Westport, Conn.:
Greenwood, 1979).

Special Concerns of the Contemporary Archives

The Archives face some special concerns as a private institution
that nevertheless openly serves the general academic community.
As mentioned earlier, originally the Archives were created to be an

information center for a Jewish socialist organization, although even from the beginning the collection included an extraordinarily broad spectrum of political and social materials. Most of the material has been available to serious students and scholars for public use. On the average, over 100 persons visit the Archives annually— many for extended periods of time. Nevertheless, some of the materials in the Archives are considered to be especially rare and important for understanding modern Jewish history. Therefore, certain documents dealing with Eastern European Zionism, with the Holocaust, and with internal Bund organizational politics can only be consulted at the discretion of the Bund archivists. Often, such materials are not catalogued.

Also, the inaccessibility of some documents at the Bund Archives is due to financial factors. For instance, the Archives contain at present between 2,500 and 3,000 feet of materials, of which one-third is manuscript. Approximately one-third of the total book holdings and more than a third of the manuscript collections have not been catalogued. Lack of funds is primarily responsible for these cataloguing problems.

There is still another problem related to the accessibility of materials, in this case a problem especially relevant to the social historian. Materials dealing with social history are not readily indicated in the catalogue system, mainly because in the past the Archives have focused their catalogue system upon political topics. For instance, the researcher who wants to investigate the role of Jewish women in the American labor movement must consult vast amounts of indirectly related materials before hitting upon relevant information. Of course, this is part of a historian's detective work and adventure in any archival situation. However, archives that have so much to offer the social historian ought to reflect this fact in their cataloguing systems. Again, funds are a central consideration.

One of the significant ways cataloguing limitations have been transcended at the Archives has been through personal librarianship. At the Bund Archives, the archivists function as scholars and intellectuals; they adhere to a tradition started by the founders, John Mill, Zemach Kopelson, Arcady Kremer, David Machlin in Geneva and Franz Kursky in Berlin and Paris. In the United States, David Meyer acted as the director of the Archives in the late 1950s and 1960s. Subsequently, Sholom Hertz, a historian with an impressive publication list of his own works, and Hillel Kempinski have guided scholars through the complexities of archival life. They are dedicated to explaining to visiting scholars the nature of the collection and the historical import of all its materials. Doing research at the Archives often is like participating in an excellent seminar where scholars of various disciplines and backgrounds review their ideas with each other and with the archivists.

Hillel Kempinski's personal librarianship, in particular, has inspired and delighted many scholars. He has received enthusiastic praise for his erudition and helpfulness in the dedication of books and also in some recent popular articles about the Archives. Hannah Koevary, for example, in her article "A Lost Outpost of Yiddish Culture" gave her impressions of this unique archivist:

> Sitting inside, bent over piles of papers, pamphlets, books and journals, is [the Archives'] director, Hillel Kempinski . . . a short man with strong, good looking features, greets me with flashing eyes and a warm smile. Before long he is deep in conversation, gesturing in all directions as he spews forth a monologue composed of names, facts, books, jokes, prayers and quotations from the widest range of sources. Sartre mixes with the Rambam, while Kafka meets Rabbi Akiva; Bialik, Tshernikovsky, Heidegger, Freud, the Vilna Gaon, the Baal Shem Tov: all are characters in Kempinski's vision.
>
> Kempinski is rarely alone. Usually another person sits with him at the long wooden table. One never knows who he or she might be. They come from around the world, yet all are one in their pursuit of knowledge, whether it be from the archives or its director.[13]

When Stefan Kanfer—author of a historical novel about the Nazi extermination of European gypsies, *The Eighth Sin* (New York: Random House, 1978), and author of another article on the Archives—asked Kempinski what he thought his title at the Archives was, the Bund archivist replied: "What is a title? To me all titles are at the same time too small and too large. I clean up the rooms. I file papers. I answer inquiries. I help writers." In this article Kanfer goes on to say, "No historian worthy of the name can write about labor movements, about 19th century Jewry, about socialism without consulting the two-thousand-odd linear feet of the Bund files and their archivists."

While the enthusiasm, intelligence, and dedication of the Bund archivists are important factors in overcoming the problems of cataloguing, the archivists cannot always overcome an equally difficult stumbling block—the linguistic limitations of most American researchers. It is true, as Kanfer also wrote, that the rich collections lie " . . . whispering on shelves and in great red envelopes, crowded in drawers, crammed in cabinets, waiting to speak to anyone who cares to listen."[14] Unfortunately for most American historians, however, their knowledge of Hebrew, Yiddish, Polish, Russian, and other languages is limited, and the materials are therefore inaccessible to them. Perhaps, one day, translations and other related aids will be developed at the Archives.

The Bund Archives can be likened to an immigrant, coming to America and settling here, who possesses a vast treasury of European Jewish heritage. Like other immigrants, the Archives have changed and grown by incorporating the American experience; and the Archives have transformed their environment by offering European perspectives on the past and the present. Their history continues into the future.

Notes

1. See, for example, the *Journal of Ethnic Studies* and the *Journal of Social History*.

2. There now is a considerable literature on European-American ethnic history. One of the earliest books to set the interpretative stage for further research was Nathan Glazer and Daniel Moynihan, *Beyond the Melting Pot: The Negroes, Puerto Ricans, Jews, Italians and Irish of New York City* (Cambridge, Mass.: MIT Press, 1963). For an introductory bibliography on ethnic studies, see Salvatore J. LaGumina and Frank J. Cavaioli, *The Ethnic Dimension in American Society* (Boston: Holbrook Press, 1974).

3. Irving Howe, *World of Our Fathers* (New York: Harcourt Brace Jovanovich; Simon and Schuster, 1976) is a recent best seller about the Eastern European Jewish immigration.

4. For an excellent article exploring ethnicity, women, and work, see Virginia Yans McLaughlin, "Patterns of Work and Family Organization: Buffalo's Italians," *Journal of Interdisciplinary History* 2, no. 2 (Autumn 1971): 299-314.

5. One of the best sources for new information on archival collections, especially at universities and colleges, is the *Immigrant History Newsletter* issued by the Immigrant History Society at the Minnesota Historical Society, St. Paul, Minnesota.

6. The basic information in English about the history of the Bund Archives and their collection is to be found in a pamphlet, *A Great Collection: The Archives of the Jewish Labor Movement* (New York: Bund Archives of the Jewish Labor Movement, 1965). For information on recent activities of the Archives, see *Bulletin of the Bund Archives of the Jewish Labor Movement* 1, no. 29 (Summer 1979).

7. See A. Menes, "Der Franz Kurski Archiv," *Zukunft* (January 1953), for a further discussion of the Bund Archives and Eastern European Jewish history.

8. Although the Archives were housed in the administrative offices of the SPD, the Bund's political life was entirely independent of the German party.

9. *A Great Collection*, pp. 2-7.

10. The Academic Advisory Committee of the Bund Archives includes co-chairmen Arcadius Kahan (University of Chicago) and Henry Tobias (University of Oklahoma) and Benjamin Nadel, executive director. The members of the AAC are: George J. Alexander, Abraham Ascher, Paul Avrich, Daniel Bell, Lipman Bers, Hasye Cooperman, Lucy S. Dawidowicz, Alexander Erlich, Victor Erlich, Joseph R. Fiszman, Jonathan Frankel (Israel), Jules Gelernt, Zvi Gitelman, Feliks Gross, Leopold H. Haimson, Michael Harrington, Paula Hyman, David Joravsky, Edward L. Keenan, Joseph C. Landis, Arthur Lermer (Canada), Nora Levin, Michael M. Luther, Ezra Mendelsohn (Israel), Eurgene Orenstein (Canada), Moshe Perlmann, Richard Pipes, Samuel Portnoy, Norma Fain Pratt, Shimon Redlich, Albert Resis, Moses Rischin, Leon Rosten, Jeremiah Schneiderman, Martin Segal, Robert Seltzer, Leon Shapiro, Harold Shukman (England), Isaiah Trunk, David Weinberg, Charles Woodhouse, Marvin S. Zukerman.

11. *A Great Collection*, pp. 12-14.

12. For a discussion about the Workmen's Circle collection in the Bund Archives, see *Bulletin of the Bund Archives of the Jewish Labor Movement* 1, no. 20 (February 1965). There have been eight bulletins issued by the Bund with articles and summaries in English about the Archives' collection.

13. Hannah Koevary, "A Lost Outpost of Yiddish Culture," *Jewish Look*, (November 1974): 19.

14. Stefan Kanfer, "The Yiddish Time Machine," *Present Tense* 3, no. 2 (Winter 1976): 13-15.

Thomas Bennet and the Origins of Analytical Bibliography

William L. Williamson

In the library of our host institution today, a famous collection brings together rare forgeries that, prior to their exposure, had been a major basis for Thomas J. Wise's reputation as dean of the world's bibliographers. The unmasking of this fraud dramatically demonstrated the power of the New Bibliography, a tool of scholarship developed and refined by three men, A. W. Pollard, W. W. Greg, and R. B. McKerrow. Sophisticated analysis of the book as a physical object meant finding answers based upon tangible, objective evidence to questions that previously had been tackled largely upon the basis of impressionistic literary judgments. Much praise has been showered upon the New Bibliography as a distinctive advance of the twentieth century.

With this view in mind, it is startling to read the assertion of so eminent a bibliographer as the late W. A. Jackson that a work published in 1715 ranks well with the bibliographical studies of the present day.[1] This assertion suggests that one man, working without the benefit of learning added during an intervening two centuries of scholarship and, presumably, without interaction with knowledgeable colleagues, was able to develop the essentials of a scholarly technique and to apply it in ways that match the achievements of capable twentieth-century scholars. So intriguing a suggestion invites study.

The man whose work was so highly praised was Dr. Thomas Bennet and his book was a study of the Thirty-Nine Articles of

William Landram Williamson *is professor of library science at the University of Wisconsin—Madison.*

Journal of Library History, Vol. 16, No. 1, Winter 1981
© 1981 by the University of Texas Press   0275-3650/81/010177–10$00.95

Religion, that is, of the basic statement of faith of the Church of England, adopted in 1571.[2] Bennet focused upon a specific question, namely the authenticity of the opening words of the Twentieth Article, "The Church Hath Power to Decree Rites or Ceremonies and Authority in Controversies of Faith." Brief though this so-called Controverted Clause is, its importance as a basis for the Church's jurisdiction and powers is self-evident. The issue of its authenticity was raised by the existence of copies, some containing and some lacking the Clause. The anomaly occurred most directly in copies of the English-language edition printed in the year 1571, even though those very copies appeared to have been produced in the same printing office and, at least in part, from the same setting of type. This sort of question is one that the New Bibliography in the twentieth century is well equipped to investigate. In the eighteenth century, only Bennet sought to use printing evidence to answer it.

For the study of Bennet's skills, evidence comes from two periods: around 1715 when he wrote his book and around 1571 when the Articles received parliamentary approval and the copies were published that directly presented the anomaly of the Controverted Clause. Bennet used eight of those copies.

To locate, in the latter part of the twentieth century, specific books published four centuries earlier and used by a particular man two hundred and fifty years earlier sounds a difficult task, but it is somewhat easier than might be thought, because Bennet gathered together as many copies as he could find and persuaded their owners to donate them to the library of St. John's College, Cambridge. Considering only those eight copies, six were in established libraries in 1715 and five of them remain so today. Of the other two, which were in private hands in 1715, one remains unknown. The last of the eight was the most interesting and important of them all, for it was one that Bennet had borrowed from Gilbert Burnet, bishop of Salisbury, and used as the master text against which he compared all other English-language copies. The last record of it was in the auction catalog of the bishop's library, which was sold in 1716. All systematic search for it was unavailing, but, by a miraculous coincidence, a London bookseller in 1973 offered in his catalog a copy of the 1571 Articles, and I had the luck to be able to buy it. Close study demonstrates incontrovertibly that it is the very copy Bennet used as his master text, unknown for 257 years.[3] Once these works were available for study, it was possible to assess Bennet's skills.

Anyone who follows Bennet's bibliographical footsteps must

soon learn respect before his diligence and humility before his accuracy. The heart and bulk of his reply consisted of a detailed collation of eighteen copies of the Articles, five of them in Latin and thirteen in English. His method was to reproduce exactly the text of one master copy in each language and then to record, in footnotes on the same page, every variation to be found in every other copy. Having reported the details of his evidence, he then analyzed it and gave his conclusions. Bennet's account demonstrates that he was well informed about the printing practices of his day. Although, he said, "Every Boy that has served a few Months at the Trade, will satisfy any of my readers" of the correctness of his conclusions, he nevertheless explained the printing technicalities in considerable detail. He spoke in printer's language when he denied that a certain period missing from one particular copy "was either dropt out of Chace, or drawn by the Ball."[4] One copy had the peculiarity that it was made up of sheets from two different printings, an anomaly that the layman might not understand immediately (although anyone who has run off documents consisting of more than one or two pages has had the experience of having sets left over, lacking only a single page to make them complete). In printing, this is so frequent that printers have a term, the "waste," for those incomplete sets. Bennet carefully explained how a printer, when next he came to print that particular work, would customarily run off extra copies of the missing sheet, thus, as printers say, "perfecting the waste" of the previous printing.

Bennet chose his bibliographical evidence judiciously and presented it in great detail. Among the sorts of evidence he used were watermarks, color of ink, ornamental title frames, battered type, loose, compressed, and irregular setting of type, and, most importantly, the printing practices that explained the many differences he found among individual copies of works that purported to be exactly the same. The most sophisticated demonstration of his knowledge came in his analysis of the order of succession in printing of those critical eight copies of the 1571 English-language edition. His case in regard to his first major point is representative. The first three copies, he said, were, "of the very same Impression . . . [as] is evident from the Workmanship." He explained:

> When a Book is reprinted, tho' the Compositor follows a printed Copy, and sets Page for Page, yet constant experience proves, that he will sometimes drive out, and at other times get in, a Word or a Syllable in a Line, or perhaps a Line in a Page. He will also very frequently, perhaps several times in a Line, in

spight [*sic*] of all his Care, set wider or closer than the Copy he
follows. None that knows any thing of Printing, can doubt of
these Matters.

The three copies under consideration, Bennet said, showed none
of these variations. "The Distance between Words is exactly the
same throughout; nor is there one Letter driven out or got in, in
any one Line of either the Title or the Body of any one Article
from the first to the last."[5] Such a result could have come about
only if all three copies had been printed from the very same setting of type. Yet each copy differed from every other in details
that Bennet explained and used to prove the order in which they
had been printed, as, in similar fashion, he did for all eight copies.
Proving that the four that contained the Controverted Clause preceded the four that lacked it, he concluded that the first group
contained the authentic text and the second reflected wrongful
tampering.

Although Bennet's final conclusion may be questioned, his skills
regarding printing technology and his understanding of the power
of printing evidence to clarify the meaning of text are beyond
doubt. Clearly he merits Jackson's praise as an accomplished analytical bibliographer.

With assurance that Jackson's conclusion is justified, the fundamental question arises that must engage the attention of all who
are interested in creativity, this most mysterious and interesting
and important question of all: How does a man create something
new to the world and why does he do so? The answer, according
to the assumptions of our day at least, must lie in the circumstances of the times and in the character of the man. Although less
is known of Bennet than one would wish, a résumé of his life together with attention to major religious, political, and scholarly
issues of his day may help to understand this question.

Thomas Bennet was born in the cathedral city of Salisbury in
1673, midway in the reign of Charles II. During the years when
Bennet was a schoolboy, England was recovering from the deep
wounds left by the Civil War and particularly by the execution of
Charles I, an event that left the whole nation shocked and unsettled. The trauma had special meaning for the Church of England,
whose own legitimacy and power were intimately tied up with
those of the monarchy. Even after the Restoration, the Church
had to tolerate religious diversity, from the Catholics on the right
to the Dissenters on the left, in order to avoid the deadly conflicts that had fragmented the society earlier in the century. Public

officials who were not Anglican communicants were allowed nevertheless to hold their positions if they took the sacrament at periodic intervals—a practice known as Occasional Conformity. In such ways the nation maintained a careful balance.

By 1688, when Bennet was approaching the age of fifteen, the political and religious situation had changed. James II, despite his known adherence to Catholicism, had been cordially accepted as his brother's successor on the assumption that he would preserve the religious settlement. Soon, however, he began to display the extraordinarily poor judgment that led him to grant exemptions from the requirements of Occasional Conformity and to force the appointment of Catholics to important positions. Reluctant though the English were to return to rebellion, they feared the restoration of Catholicism, an anxiety that became alarm when the birth of James's son raised the specter of a renewed Catholic line. Resolute leaders supported James's Protestant daughter and her Dutch husband in an invasion that forced James into exile and allowed the couple to take the throne jointly as William and Mary.

Just at the period of these exciting events, young Bennet went up to St. John's College, Cambridge, where he was admitted as a "sizar," that is, as a student who performed tasks for one of the Fellows of the College in return for the privilege of study. Bennet did well. He proceeded to his bachelor's and master's degrees, took orders as a clergyman, and received appointment in the College as Fellow and Tutor himself. Before the end of the century, this son of the lower middle class had an assured place in the University. Soon he was playing an active part in the affairs of the institution. Of special importance was his appointment to the board of curators of the Cambridge University Press.

As curator, Bennet was associated with Richard Bentley, the leading figure of the Press at that time. Bentley was a protagonist in the scholarly dispute immortalized by Jonathan Swift as the Battle of the Books. King's Librarian and, after 1700, Master of Trinity College, Bentley championed the cause of the Moderns, who advocated use of exact evidence in scholarly investigation, against the Ancients, who argued that truth and beauty, being embodied in the Greek and Latin classics, were to be sought by emulating the masters of the past. Bentley's *Dissertation on the Letters of Phalaris*, with its dazzling demonstration of a command of languages, linguistics, history, and the whole of classical literature, remains one of the landmarks of scholarship. Remarks we hear today about the New Bibliography are paralleled by the authoritative conclusion that Bentley's work pioneered "a new criticism which, by a scientific method, was to bring accurate philological knowledge into relation with historical research."[6] Surely the excitement of the great debate of those years was a lively part of the conversation of Bennet and his associates at Cambridge.

The application of empirical evidence to a question of scholarly interest is characteristic of investigations that began to be carried forward not simply in the classics but in many fields of study during the years around the turn of the eighteenth century. Under the rubric Natural Philosophy, leaders of the Church were investigating topics in geology and paleontology as aspects of cosmology, the fundamentally theological question of the creation of the earth. The churchmen who wrote on these topics affirmed sincerely their purpose to glorify God by a study of His works—Bennet himself said, "When you search after Truth, you are always in the Presence of that God who is Truth it self."[7] But the result was to turn them from philosophical speculation toward natural history, a process that much later produced Charles Darwin and his alarming conclusions.[8]

The point that is important to note about these matters is that empirical evidence was becoming important in scholarship during these years when young Thomas Bennet was entering the world of learning. His own writing dealt with topics of religious interest, particularly those that excited controversy. During the years between 1699 and 1708, the Cambridge University Press published seven of his books, including an "Answer" to dissenters, a "Confutation" of both popery and Quakerism, and a "Discourse" on schism, prayer, and baptism. His books became leading texts for students needing to understand complex theological questions and, as a consequence, Bennet became the Press's best-selling author. Most of his books went through three editions and one went into a fourth. Since each edition required an entirely new setting of type, Bennet perforce had the very special opportunity to participate repeatedly in planning for new printings and the instructive necessity to read proofs many times. His intimate knowledge of printing appears to stem from these circumstances as well as from his work as a curator of the Press in a day when the curators made the most minute decisions about the physical makeup of the books to be published.[9]

Although Bennet retained his links with Cambridge, in 1700 he moved the center of his activities to Colchester, where he became rector of St. James's Church. Now aged 27, he had good cause to feel pleased with himself. Indeed the move to Colchester came about in peculiar circumstances—he journeyed there to visit a friend who was the rector, only to discover that his friend had died. Bennet was asked to preach the funeral oration, and he so moved the congregation that they asked for his appointment to the vacancy. He once said of himself that he had the best preaching voice in England, and the results suggest that his opinion may have been justified. Rising from modest beginnings, he seems to have had nothing but success, and by 1700 he was a published author, an ordained minister, a Fellow of one of the great colleges, and a man of some acquaintance among the leading scholars. The move to Colchester confirmed him in a position that fed his self-esteem. Described as "tall, strong, and haughty,"[10] he was also successful, accomplished, and apparently ambitious. His early days at Colchester were unusually prosperous, with a church that was so popular and dominant that it gave him an excellent income of £300 annually. The prosperous days did not last, however. New churches and the vexations of dissenters who challenged Bennet—and inspired some of his writings—ultimately made his situation less desirable than it had been. By 1710 he had ample reason to want to call his name to the attention of the heads of the Church who might favor him with appointments, perhaps even in the metropolis of London. Great events were occurring there.

During the first part of the century, religious controversy was at a high level, with crucial political implications. The most conservative wing of the Church of England had suffered grievously in the wake of James II's overthrow. Among the most capable were the Nonjurors, who, though they stoutly affirmed their Anglicanism, were conscience-bound not to swear allegiance to new rulers so long as James still lived. They and their right-wing colleagues, forced to be cautious after the Glorious Revolution, began early in the new century to reassert the power of the Church. In particular, a spellbinding preacher, Dr. Henry Sacheverell, included in his sermons so much that was critical of both the liberal religious faction and the Whig political position that the government of Godolphin and Churchill impeached him for seditious libel. A great show trial in Westminster Hall became the sensation of 1710. The case against Sacheverell was too strong to be denied, but the punishment imposed upon him was so small and the adulation the street crowds heaped upon him so great that the outcome was a virtual victory for the conservatives of the Church and their political allies, the Tories. The result was seen as a defeat for the Whigs, and soon the Tories and the High Church conservatives had captured the government. The great victory appeared to signal an end to toleration, the reinstitution of strict adherence to the Church of England as a condition of holding civil position, and the Church's return to dominance. Actually it was a brief resurgence for a Church that never again would hold so strong a position.[11] But in 1710 feeling ran high indeed. Just then Anthony Collins, a prominent Deist and disciple of John Locke, issued a provocative attack on the authority of the Church in his publication *Priestcraft in Perfection*.[12] Collins's major attack was upon the disparity between copies of the Articles in regard to the Controverted Clause, which, he charged, had been fraudulently inserted into the Articles to expand the Church's power and authority. So monstrous a charge demanded a prompt response. Immediately the conservatives of the Church consulted about a reply and agreed that Hilkiah Bedford, a prominent and able leader of the Nonjurors, should prepare the answer, which was soon published.[13]

By the time of these events, Bennet was often in London. The Church's customary tolerance of multiple appointments allowed him to serve, along with his place at Colchester, as deputy chaplain of Chelsea Hospital and, later, in the London posts of lecturer at St. Olave's and morning preacher at St. Lawrence, Jewry. Particularly after 1711, when he was created doctor of divinity, his connection with Colchester became more and more tenuous. In the lively atmosphere of London, Bennet naturally reacted strongly, as the loyal clergy did in general, to Collins's attack. He suggested to Bedford a line of argument that Bedford did not entirely adopt; worse, Bennet believed that Bedford had gratuitously attacked him in the course of discussing that point in his reply to Collins. From that beginning Bennet resolved to reply to Collins on his own.

Bennet's work, published in April 1715, did not excite great response. Only in 1724 did Collins formally reply, and then Bennet does not seem to have responded at all.[14] Perhaps Bennet's demonstration of loyalty to the Church was one of the factors taken into account when, in 1717, he was appointed to the prosperous London church, St. Giles, Cripplegate. His subsequent career brought him neither further advancement nor great peace. In his new position, however, he achieved a stability that permitted him to marry. For the rest of his career he remained at St. Giles. When he died in 1728, he left a wife and three daughters.

It is appropriate at the end to reframe the original question to take account of its implications. Confirmation of Jackson's assessment, based upon a comparison of Bennet's *Essay* with the actual copies he used as evidence, raises the additional question whether

Bennet did indeed originate analytical bibliography and, further, whether a connection is to be seen between his work and that of the twentieth-century New Bibliographers. No one who has heard of Karl Popper and the black swan is likely to be so foolish as to make an unreserved claim of priority; yet it does seem reasonable on the evidence to put in a limited claim for Bennet. Neither can one find direct connections between Bennet in 1715 and Pollard in 1909. Yet again, the bibliographical tradition of Cambridge is truly extraordinary, including such great names as Henry Bradshaw, the University's librarian, and those associated with Bentley's Trinity College from McKerrow himself to the Trinity librarians, W. Aldis Wright, the Shakespearean editor who used physical evidence as a means of clarifying text, W. W. Greg, probably the most accomplished of all the New Bibliographers, and Philip Gaskell, the present librarian and author of a recent new work that expands upon the topic of McKerrow's classic text. No doubt other universities can name great bibliographers as well, but the Cambridge roster and record is impressive. Bennet, if not connected in a line, shares a tradition.

These questions of Bennet's predecessors and successors, though interesting, are less significant than the broad matter of human creativity involved in trying to understand Bennet's capacities and achievement. If we can understand how he created something new, we come closer to understanding the process of creation itself. We find in Bennet no blazing star of genius but something more encouraging: a talented man motivated by sincere religious faith and also by ambition. With intelligence and strong motivation, he worked within the tradition of inductive scholarship that had come into fashion, but brought to his study new insights derived from the knowledge about printing his life experience had given him. Bennet does indeed seem to have brought something new into the world, not by a magical flash of genius but by diligent pursuit of the insights that came to him in the natural course of events. In this conclusion, we ordinary people can find reason to take comfort and hope.

Notes

1. William A. Jackson, *Records of a Bibliographer: Selected Papers*, ed. William H. Bond (Cambridge: Belknap Press of Harvard University Press, 1967), pp. 214–215. A detailed descriptive account of Bennet's book is in Strickland Gibson, "Thomas Bennet, A Forgotten Bibliographer," *Library*, 5th ser., 6 (June 1951): 43–47.

2. Thomas Bennet, *An Essay on the Thirty Nine Articles of Religion, Agreed on in 1562, and Revised in 1571; Wherein (The Text being first exhibited in Latin and English, and the minutest Variations of 18 the most Ancient and Authentic Copies carefully noted) An Account is given of the Proceedings of Convocation in framing and setling the Text of the Articles; The Controverted Clause of the 20th Article is demonstrated to be genuin; And the Case of Subscription to the Articles is consider'd in Point of Law, History, and Conscience . . .* (London: W. Innys, 1715); Church of England, *Articles Whereupon It Was Agreed by the Archbishoppes and Bishoppes of Both Provinces and the Whole Cleargie, in the Convocation Holden at London in the Yere of our Lorde God, 1562, According to the Computation of the Churche of Englande, for the Avoiding of Diversities of Opinions, and for the Stablishyng of Consent Touching True Religion* (London: Jugge and Cawood, 1571), STC10039.

3. William L. Williamson, "A Quest for Copies of the Articles," *Book Collector* 27 (Spring 1978): 27-39.

4. Bennet, *Essay*, pp. 325-326.

5. Ibid., pp. 317-318.

6. *Dictionary of National Biography*, s.v. "Bentley, Richard," by Richard C. Jebb.

7. Thomas Bennet, *Directions for Studying, I. A General System or Body of Divinity. II. The Thirty-nine Articles of Religion. To which is Added St. Jerom's Epistle to Nepotianus* (London: Knapton, 1714), p. 9.

8. Joseph M. Levine, *Dr. Woodward's Shield: History, Science, and Satire in Augustan England* (Berkeley: University of California Press, 1977). I have profited also from correspondence with John Attig, Pennsylvania State University, who has studied some parallel matters.

9. Donald F. McKenzie, *The Cambridge University Press, 1696-1712, A Bibliographical Study*, 2 vols. (Cambridge: At the University Press, 1966); S. C. Roberts, *The Evolution of Cambridge Publishing* (Cambridge: At the University Press, 1956).

10. *Dictionary of National Biography*, s.v. "Bennet, Thomas," by Alexander B. Grosart.

11. Gareth V. Bennett, *The Tory Crisis in Church and State, 1688-1730: The Career of Francis Atterbury, Bishop of Rochester* (Oxford: Clarendon Press, 1975).

12. Anthony Collins, *Priestcraft in Perfection: or, A Detection of the Fraud of Inserting and Continuing this Clause (The Church Hath Power to Decree Rites and Ceremonys, and Authority in Controversys of Faith) in the Twentieth Article of the Church of England . . .* (London: Printed for B. Bragg, 1710).

13. Hilkiah Bedford, *A Vindication of the Church of England from the Aspersions of a late Libel intituled, Priestcraft in Perfection, &c. Wherein the Controversial Clause of the Church's Power in the XXth Article is shewn to be of equal authority with all the rest of the Articles . . .* (London: R. Wilkin, 1710).

14. Anthony Collins, *An Historical and Critical Essay, on the Thirty Nine Articles of the Church of England . . .* (London: Printed for R. Francklin, 1724).

Book Collector, Bibliographer, and Benefactor of Libraries: Sir William Osler

Mary Kingsbury

William Osler (1849–1919), born and educated in Canada, served on the medical faculties of McGill University and the University of Pennsylvania before his reputation as a teacher and physician led to an invitation to join the faculty of the Johns Hopkins University as its first professor of medicine. A great teacher, a prolific writer, a man with an unusual capacity for friendship, Osler is remembered as the exemplary physician, both a scientist and a humanist in his practice of medicine.

Much has been written about nearly all aspects of Osler's life and career. *An Annotated Checklist of Osleriana* published in 1976 contains over 1,300 items,[1] and the *Index Medicus* shows an average of ten articles per year since then. The purpose of this paper will be to give a few details about Osler as a book collector and benefactor of libraries, and to focus on Osler as a bibliographer.

In "The Collecting of a Library," Osler recalled that the first book he ever brought was the Globe Shakespeare, the second, the 1862 Boston edition of Sir Thomas Browne's *Religio Medici*, a book that held a special place in Osler's life and thinking.

A definite historical and educational purpose guided his collecting.

> I began to buy, first, the early books and pamphlets relating to the profession in America; secondly, the original editions of the

Mary Kingsbury *is associate professor of library science at the University of North Carolina at Chapel Hill.*

Journal of Library History, Vol. 16, No. 1, Winter 1981

great writers in science and in medicine; and thirdly, the works of . . . general authors. . . . My interest got deeper and deeper in the history of medicine and in the lives of the great men of the profession.[2]

By the time he left for England in 1905 to become Regius Professor of Medicine at Oxford, Osler had made a good beginning in gathering the original editions of the great authors in medicine. Together with Dr. Harvey Cushing, he was buying everything of Vesalius that was offered. He found the *Fabrica* impossible to resist and distributed six copies to various libraries.

His Regius chair made him an *ex officio* curator of the Bodleian, and he soon became a member of the Library's Standing Committee that met weekly. "Very soon," he wrote, "there was a feeling that a day had not been well spent if altogether away from Bodley. . . . There are greater libraries, . . . but for solid comfort and 'atmosphere' give me a seat in Duke Humphrey or a table in the Selden End!"[3] Other bookish circles included the Bibliographical Society of London; Osler served as president of the Society from 1913 until his death in 1919.

In *Who's Who*, Osler listed bibliography as his recreation. Delivering a speech at a memorial meeting for John Shaw Billings, he said, "there is no better float through posterity than to be the author of a good bibliography."[4] His own claim to bibliographical immortality rests on the *Bibliotheca Osleriana*, a catalogue of books illustrating the history of medicine and science that he collected, arranged, and, in some cases, annotated. It seems of value here to clarify the story behind its production, how contemporaries received it, and how modern critics judge it.

The more leisurely pace of Oxford plus access to the London book shops and auctions enabled Osler to add to his library. Exactly when he decided to leave his collection to McGill is not known, but a deed of gift, dated 1 October 1911 and signed by Osler, is at the Osler Library. The deed lists the books as follows: "I Manuscripts, II Incunabula, and III The medical works included in the Bibliotheca Prima, Secunda, Biographica, Literaria [*sic*], Bibliographica and Historica. The whole to be known as the Bibliotheca Osleriana." Osler added that before sending out the books he hoped to have a "well prepared catalogue." He may have meant a simple card catalogue; later evidence suggests that he did not yet have a printed catalogue in mind. But he certainly had decided on eight divisions for his library.

According to the Cushing biography, the idea for a printed catalogue evidently had its genesis during a trip to Cambridge in July 1914. Osler planned to stay a few days "to work over the Pepys Library and to preside at the first peripatetic meeting of the Bibliographical Society."[5]

As Osler browsed through the library of the genial Samuel, as he liked to call him, he must have found more than usual interest in the catalogues mentioned so often in the *Diary*. One, the "Bibliotheca Nautica . . . a Chronological Catalogue of the most eminent Mathematicians . . . to the year 1673,"[6] matched Osler's idea for his Bibliotheca Prima, the works of the most eminent contributors to the history of medicine, and may have been the catalyst that prompted him to attempt a book catalogue of his own collection.

If the idea for a printed catalogue did not originate while Osler was actually in the Pepys Library, it may have come during conversations with a new friend, Charles Sayle, librarian at Cambridge and a Browne scholar. Sayle, in a letter to Harvey Cushing written in 1920, described a long talk he had with Osler when he visited Oxford in September 1914.

I saw that his ideal was a library rather like the Pepys Library at Cambridge, and proposed to him the title for his catalogue Bibliotheca Osleriana.
He was evidently pleased with the idea, and I drew him up a scheme for it 'Bibliotheca Prima' 'Bibliotheca Secunda,' etc. rather endeavoring to crystallize his own ideas than to foist my own upon him.
We corresponded a good deal about this.[7]

Sayle may have been mistaken about his role in naming the *Bibliotheca Osleriana*; certainly the 1911 deed of gift would make it appear that he was. We know from the deed that Osler had outlined the eight divisions for his library and called it the Bibliotheca Osleriana. If the catalogue mentioned in the deed was no more than a simple card catalogue, then it is possible that Osler, inspired by the catalogues for the Bibliotheca Pepysiana, talked with Sayle about a printed catalogue for his own library, the Bibliotheca Osleriana. Sayle, in turn, may have crystallized Osler's thought by suggesting the use of the same title for the printed catalogue and demonstrating how Osler's idea for the Prima, Secunda, and so on, could be incorporated into it. Such an explanation reconciles the deed of gift with both the statement in Cushing about the Cambridge visit and the Sayle letter. Cushing evidently based his statement at least partly on that letter; so if Sayle's memory of his talk with Osler were faulty, Cushing's conclusion about the influence of the Cambridge visit may have been equally faulty.

In any case, from September 1914 until his death, Osler made frequent reference to his bibliographic project—a printed catalogue for his library. Moreover, Sayle was correct in saying that they corresponded a good deal about it. But before citing some of their correspondence, it might be well to mention other influences on Osler's concept of bibliography.

At the November 1916 meeting of the Bibliographical Society, Osler as president took a few minutes to pay tribute to the memory of John Ferguson of Glasgow, his mentor in matters bibliographical. Calling Ferguson's manual, *Some Aspects of Bibliography*, the best introduction to the subject he knew, Osler lamented that too often the results of bibliography are recorded in "big tomes of intolerable dullness," and recommended James Atkinson's *Medical Bibliography A and B* and Ferguson's *Bibliotheca Chemica* as being "full of the marrow and fatness of books." The two-letter bibliography, "dedicated to all idle medical students in Great Britain," was a stimulus to a beginning bibliographer, especially one who appreciated Atkinson's Rabelaisian spirit. But it was the *Bibliotheca Chemica* that he prized for its blend of biography with bibliography. "Scarcely a day passes that I do not refer to its pages," he confessed and ended his tribute by expressing his conviction that "upon the author of a really good bibliography the iniquity of oblivion vainly scatters her poppy."[8]

Ferguson had written that as biography follows from the existence of human beings, bibliography is the result of the existence of books. Bibliography is, he said, the biography of books. He noted that "the recent tendency is to introduce bibliographical detail into catalogues."[9] Osler's catalogue, in fact, is an enumerative bibliography that introduces a good deal of bibliographical detail. It includes some features of descriptive bibliography in that the physical description provided for a book goes beyond the minimum sufficient for a strictly enumerative bibliography; the descriptions are restricted, however, to the specific copies held in the Osler collection. And, although Osler did not follow Ferguson's example in every particular, the two were of one mind in their proclivity for placing books in a biographical framework.

So Osler embarked on the preparation of a catalogue that, like the library it was to describe, would be divided into eight parts that could not be made discrete. When his friends warned him of the problems inherent in such an arrangement, his rejoinder was to suggest printing at the top of every page, "Consult the Index first."

Some of the novice bibliographer's trials appear in his letters and postcards to Charles Sayle in the years after their 1914 meeting. Osler wrote speculating about how many ideas of the very first rank have controlled the development of science. The special articles and books illustrating them would come in the first division, the Bibliotheca Prima, he told Sayle.[10] One difficulty was deciding whether a person should be placed in the Prima as a first-rank discoverer or relegated to the Secunda status of those who had made notable contributions, but were not up to the mark of those in Prima. Conrad Gesner presented him with just such a problem, one that he solved in typical Oslerian fashion.

An oft-quoted incident tells of Osler's discussing the catalogue with a friend. When he came to Gesner, he admitted, "I am not sure that this fellow should go into 'Prima'; but I love him so much that I must put him there. Besides, he is the father of Bibliography."[11]

By March 1916 plans for the printed catalogue had been codified in a series of "Notes on the Catalogue of Sir William Osler's Library," evidently typed up by Miss J. F. Willcock, a "practiced bibliographer" who worked with Osler during the war and to whom he had explained his scheme in some detail.[12]

He assured Sayle in May 1916 that "the Library thrives—the revision of the catalogue is nearly complete. . . . The B. Prima grows in mind and shelves." In March of the following year, he shot off a postcard: "B. O. progresses. . . . The B. Litteraria is to be *very* strong. Think for me of the best novels with descriptions of Doctors or of the profession."[13]

It is difficult to reconcile the optimism about the nearly complete revision of the catalogue voiced in 1916 with a request sent off to Sayle in July 1918. "I am not making very rapid progress with my catalogue and should like another worker. Do you know of a good trained man who could come for a year or two?"[14] The seeming lack of progress was no doubt due, in part, to the magnitude of the task but probably even more to the tragedy that struck the Oslers in August 1917 when their only son, Revere, was killed in combat. A few intimates to whom Lady Osler wrote were privy to the shattering effect the loss had on Sir William. In public, however, he appeared the embodiment of his often extolled quality of aequanimitas.

But work on the catalogue did continue. In an attempt to make his collection and catalogue match the scheme he kept elaborating in his mind, he added volumes to the very end. In December 1919, one long-sought volume arrived. Knowing he was dying of pneumonia, he had a note inscribed in it: "All things come to him who waits—but it was a pretty close shave this time!" He died 29 December 1919, in his seventy-first year.

Osler had specified in a memorandum written during his last illness that he hoped the catalogue could be finished before the books were shipped to Montreal. He entrusted the completion of the catalogue to Dr. William W. Francis; Reginald H. Hill of the Bodleian Library; Dr. Archibald Malloch, later to become librarian of the New York Academy of Medicine; an old friend, Leonard Mackall; and his wife, Lady Grace Revere Osler. Work on the catalogue had been for Osler a joy and, during the great tragedy of his life, a consolation. But in the nearly ten years that passed between his death and the completion of the catalogue, what had been for him a stimulating hobby became for others a worrisome burden.

Bill Francis, generally called Osler's nephew but actually the son of Osler's first cousin, had been forced by ill health to give up medical practice. Osler, in recommending him for an editorial position, claimed that "his meticulosity exceeds anything you ever met with."[15] And indeed it did. As the struggle to complete the catalogue dragged on, Francis's excessive concern for details coupled with a seeming lack of concern for working toward a specific completion date brought him into conflict with Lady Osler, once described by her husband as a "woman of push and go."[16]

For the first two years after Osler's death, no one worked full-time on the catalogue. Bill Francis had an editorial job in Geneva; Malloch worked in a London hospital; and Hill had his job at the Bodleian but continued to work on the catalogue at night. Evidently, during the second year Malloch found more time for the catalogue.[17] Then, in January 1922, Bill Francis, his wife, and daughter began living in the Oslers' home, the Open Arms; and Francis took up the work that occupied him the rest of his life—completing the catalogue and serving as the Osler librarian at McGill.

Francis, later described as having had an "infectious enthusiasm" for his task, may have found it overwhelming at first; for in March 1923 Lady Osler reported to Archie Malloch, who had returned to Montreal, that Bill had told someone what a terrible job it was.[18] She obviously expected the catalogue to be completed fairly soon, however, because in May 1923 she went to the Oxford University Press to begin printing arrangements. On this visit, Mr. Hall of the Press sounded a warning note that "Dr. Francis should stop making alterations." But alterations continued, and the cards for the Prima still had not gone to the Press when Leonard Mackall arrived in August.[19]

In desperation, Lady Osler and her sister wrote to Archie Malloch, asking him to return to extricate Bill Francis from his "mires of unmethod." Malloch arrived, spent three months attempting to "alter Francis methods" and went back to Montreal. During his visit, however, Bill Francis evidently agreed to find someone to help him on a full-time basis. Later, when Lady Osler urged him to do so, he told her it was no use, that he was the only one who saw mistakes and that he would have to redo the work. Redoing the work of others, including Reginald Hill, became part of Francis methods—this despite the fact that Hill was the only professional bibliographer working on the catalogue.[20]

Worry about the completion of the Osler biography by Harvey Cushing added to Lady Osler's concerns. Cushing was a favorite of hers, and she welcomed his planned visit to the Open Arms. But as she wrote to Malloch, "Nothing must interfere with Harvey's plan and I would like some of that crowd out of the house. I will help with their rent if necessary." That crowd was, of course, Bill Francis and his wife and child. But by August 1924, the first section was completed. A. W. Pollard and his wife, in Oxford for a meeting, came for tea, and Pollard pronounced the Prima "perfect."[21]

Three years later, however, the catalogue was still unfinished and, despite growing pressure from McGill, the books were still in Oxford. Lady Osler issued an ultimatum in February 1928, telling Bill Francis she wanted the books to reach Montreal for the autumn term. He would make no promises, and his wife told her that "the books would never reach Montreal if the move depends on Bill. All he wants to do is to work here and fuss with the books." In her last letter to Malloch, dated August 18, she wrote, "Bill says he can't finish the catalogue before November. He is poking at the Index now—Hill is furious. . . . "[22] She died suddenly on 31 August 1928.

Finally, after what must have seemed an eternity to all parties concerned, except perhaps Bill Francis, the officers of McGill University presented the Bibliotheca Osleriana, both library and catalogue, to the public on 29 May 1929.

How did contemporary critics evaluate the catalogue? Fielding Garrison recommended it as the "best bibliographic introduction to medical literature since Haller and Boerhaave." A. W. Pollard predicted that the *Bibliotheca Osleriana* would always be a "live catalogue."[23]

Following the publication of the 1969 reprint of the catalogue, F. N. L. Poynter concluded that the increasing interest over the years in the subject of the books described and the greatly enhanced value of even the minor items justified Pollard's original evaluation. Adding a personal note, Poynter said that in nearly forty years of almost daily consultation, the catalogue had been rarely faulted. Lee Ash, reviewing the reprint, said that its reputation had been enhanced by its continuing usefulness, its ability to give pleasure to readers, and its value in the antiquarian trade.[24]

Another bibliographical work, *Incunabula Medica: A Study of the Earliest Printed Medical Books 1467-1480,* bears Sir William Osler's name as the sole author, but he wrote only the draft for the long introductory essay that had served as his presidential speech before the Bibliographical Society in 1914, plus some material included in an appendix. Osler did, however, inspire the work. In July 1911 he accepted an invitation to give the Silliman Lectures at Yale. Preparing the series led to tracing the influence of the introduction of printing on the development of medicine. Calls began going out for information about medical incunabula. In January of 1918 he reported to Archie Malloch that the completed list was being revised at the British Museum, adding that Pollard would not risk any mistake; Victor Scholderer of the British Museum put the bibliography into its final form.[25]

The index to Cushing's biography of William Osler testifies to the importance of libraries in Osler's life; the list of citations takes up an entire page and reads like a Cook's tour. For Osler, the lodestone in any city was the library—from the Khedival Library in Cairo or the Vatican in Rome to the smallest of professional libraries being set up by the local medical societies—he loved them all. In a speech delivered at the dedication of the new building of the Boston Medical Library in 1901, he said that it was hard for him to speak of the value of libraries "in terms which would not seem exaggerated."[26]

The Medical Library Association in 1976 issued a commemorative medal to mark its seventy-fifth anniversary. Because of the role he played in founding the MLA and his influence on medical librarianship, Osler is one of three people portrayed on the medal. He served as second president of the association from 1901 to 1904. In his presidential address, "Some Aspects of American Medical Bibliography," Osler, sounding like a curator of rare books, reminded his listeners that a library should be a storehouse for everything relating to the history of the profession of the locality.[27]

Later, as we know, he was an *ex officio* curator of the Bodleian, serving with more than his usual enthusiasm and devotion the library he so loved. He became the prime mover, for example, in raising the £3,000 needed to buy back the original Bodleian Folio of Shakespeare. Just two days before the deadline, Osler persuaded one of his friends to donate the last £500. When Bodley's librarian, E. W. B. Nicholson, heard the news, he told Osler he deserved a statue in the Bodleian quadrangle.[28]

Falconer Madan credited the start of the *Bodleian Quarterly Record* to Osler's suggestion and his offer to make up any deficit incurred during the first few years of publication. From his earliest days as a teacher, Osler urged his students to develop themselves through research and publication. In fact, one reason he promoted the *Quarterly* was to encourage the younger staff members to get into print.[29]

Throughout his life, Osler turned most of what he did, said, and wrote to educational ends. It is not surprising, therefore, that his interest in libraries extended to library education. As early as 1907, in a letter to President Daniel Gilman of Johns Hopkins, he expressed hopes of interesting Andrew Carnegie in establishing a training program for librarians in connection with the Bodleian and the Clarendon Press. In an unpublished manuscript found among his papers after his death, he enumerated several departments for such a college—the School of Library Economics, the School of Bibliography, and a School of Publication and Printing. He even outlined a course of lectures on libraries, ancient and modern.[30]

Nothing came of his grand plan, but he did not abandon it. Ten years later, on 31 July 1917, he gave the opening address for the Summer School of Library Service at Aberystwyth, Wales. The speech, titled "The Library School in the College," incorporated many of his ideas of library service. Recommending a School of the Book in at least one university in each division of the kingdom, he cited the example of America, where the library school had been the means of furnishing highly trained men and women who, in his own time, had completely changed the atmosphere of the libraries.[31]

Three years later, the School of Librarianship was opened by Sir Frederic Kenyon in connection with the University of London. Although Osler was not mentioned in the prospectus, its organization followed the lines laid down by him. Because Kenyon and Osler were members of several of the same dining clubs and of the Classical Association, it is not unlikely that Kenyon's School of Librarianship profited from Osler's influence.[32]

Just as few outdid Osler in his support of libraries, few surpassed him in his devotion to books and their makers. Others collected more and perhaps collected better, but he can be called a great collector—great in his aim of bringing together a collection for the use of students and historians of medicine and great in the inspiration he provided for other collectors.

But was he a great bibliographer? Certainly not. John Fulton claimed in his *Great Medical Bibliographers* that Osler did much to advance medical bibliography by directing the attention of students into "historical by-ways," but that he could not be judged an "accomplished technical bibliographer." Osler's chief legacy to medical bibliography is the somewhat eccentric catalogue for his personal library, the *Bibliotheca Osleriana*. But, as we have seen, it was left to others to complete what Fulton called "one of the great reference tools of medical history."[33]

In a paper delivered at a symposium celebrating the fiftieth anniversary of the Osler Library, Dr. Charles Roland concluded that Osler's contribution to bibliography was "his remarkable ability of inspiring others to perform first-rate work."[34] The *Bibliotheca Osleriana* would probably never have been completed if Francis, Hill, and Malloch had not had the memory of Osler to keep them going. Osler thought a good bibliography the best ticket to immortality. Lesser people may need such a ticket, but not Osler. "Perhaps less than once in a century," a writer noted recently, "does genetic chance produce a person of the caliber of William Osler."[35] He will be remembered not because he was a great bibliographer—he wasn't; rather, he will be remembered because he was a great man. And it may very well be that the *Bibliotheca Osleriana* will last not because of its bibliographical virtues but because it embodies the humane spirit of that great man.

Notes

1. Earl F. Nation, Charles G. Roland, and John P. McGovern, *An Annotated Checklist of Osleriana* (Kent, Ohio: Kent State University Press, 1976).
2. William Osler, "The Collecting of a Library," in *Bibliotheca Osleriana: A Catalogue of Books Illustrating the History of Medicine and Science Collected, Arranged, and Annotated by Sir William Osler, Bt. and Bequeathed to McGill University*, 2nd ed. (Montreal: McGill–Queen's University Press, 1969), pp. xxvii–xxviii.
3. Ibid., p. xxx.

4. William Osler, "Address: Memorial Meeting in Honor of the Late Dr. John Shaw Billings, April 25, 1913," *Bulletin of the New York Public Library* 17 (July 1913): 518.

5. Harvey Cushing, *The Life of Sir William Osler* (London and New York: Oxford University Press, 1940), p. 416.

6. Henry Wheatley, *Samuel Pepys and the World He Lived In*, 5th ed. (London: Sonnenschein, 1907), p. 93.

7. Charles Sayle to Harvey Cushing, 21 April 1920, Cushing Papers, Osler Library, McGill University.

8. *Transactions of the Bibliographical Society, London* 14 (October 1915-March 1917): 133-135.

9. John Ferguson, *Some Aspects of Bibliography* (Edinburgh: G. P. Johnston, 1900), pp. 9, 47-48.

10. William Osler to Charles Sayle, 29 September 1914, Cushing Papers, Osler Library, McGill University. A series of letters from William Osler to Charles Sayle are hereafter cited as S. L. plus date.

11. William Osler, *Bibliotheca Osleriana*, p. 64.

12. Reginald H. Hill, "W. W. Francis and Oxford, 1919-1929," in *W. W. Francis: Tributes from His Friends on the Occasion of the Thirty-fifth Anniversary of the Osler Society of McGill University* (Montreal: Osler Society, 1956), pp. 40-41. A copy of the *typed* copy of "Notes on the Catalogue: Sir William Osler's Library" is in the Cushing Papers, Osler Library, McGill University.

13. S. L., 27 May 1916 and 31 March 1917.

14. S. L., 2 July 1918.

15. Lloyd G. Stevenson, "Prologue," in *Bibliotheca Osleriana*, p. xi.

16. Archibald Malloch, *Journal*, Sunday, 4 July 1915, Cushing Papers, Osler Library, McGill University.

17. Reginald H. Hill in *Francis Tributes*, p. 41.

18. Charles G. Roland, "Dry, Dusty, Tedious, Accursed, Hateful, Bibliography," paper delivered at a Symposium on the 50th Anniversary of the Osler Library, 29 May 1979, McGill University, Montreal, p. 25; Lady Grace Osler to Dr. Archibald Malloch, 19 March 1923, Lady Grace Osler Papers, Osler Library, McGill University. A series of letters from Lady Osler to Archibald Malloch are hereafter cited as O. L. plus date.

19. O. L., 3 May 1923 and 12 August 1923.

20. O. L., 14 August 1923 and 2 February 1924; Sue Chapin to Malloch, 14 August 1923 and 10 September 1923, Lady Osler Papers.

21. O. L., 2 February 1924 and 2 August 1924.

22. O. L., 2 February 1928 and 18 August 1928.

23. Fielding H. Garrison, "The Osler Catalogue," *Bulletin of the New York Academy of Medicine* 5 (September 1929): 860-863; A. W. Pollard, "Reviews and Notices," *Library* 10 (December 1929): 341-344.

24. F. N. L. Poynter, "Reviews," *Library* 25 (September 1970): 271-272; Lee Ash, "Book Reviews and Journal Notes," *Bulletin of the Medical Library Association* 58 (April 1970): 220-222.

25. William Osler, *Incunabula Medica: A Study of the Earliest Printed Medical Books, 1467-1480* (Oxford: Oxford University Press, 1923).

26. William Osler, "Books and Men," in *A Way of Life and Selected Writings, 12 July 1849 to 29 December 1919* (New York: Dover, 1958), p. 35.

27. William Osler, "Some Aspects of American Medical Bibliography," in

Aequanimitas: With Other Addresses to Medical Students, Nurses and Practitioners of Medicine, 3rd ed. (New York: McGraw-Hill, 1932).

28. Cushing, *Life*, vol. 2, pp. 44–47.

29. Falconer Madan, "The Late Sir William Osler," *Bodleian Quarterly Record* 2 (4th Quarter, 1919): 298; Cushing, *Life*, vol. 2, p. 389.

30. William Osler to Daniel Gilman, 19 February 1907, quoted in Cushing, *Life*, vol. 2, p. 81.

31. William Osler, "The Library School in the College," *Library Association Record* 19 (August–September 1917): 287–308.

32. Cushing, *Life*, vol. 2, 573 n.

33. John F. Fulton, *The Great Medical Bibliographers: A Study in Humanism* (Philadelphia: University of Pennsylvania Press, 1951; reprint ed., Westport, Conn.: Greenwood Press, 1977), p. 78.

34. Charles G. Roland, "Dry, Dusty . . . Bibliography," pp. 27–28.

35. Richard L. Golden, "Medallic Tributes to Sir William Osler and Their Historical Associations," *Journal of the American Medical Association* 242 (28 December 1979): 2862.

The *Cabinets de lecture* in Paris, 1800–1850

James Smith Allen

Among a host of other historical developments in France, a remarkable transition in popular culture began in Paris during the
first half of the nineteenth century. Ordinary Parisian men and
women enjoyed, for example, new kinds of song, drama, and fiction that initially appeared in the course of the 1789 Revolution
and continued to spread rapidly after the revolutionary and Napo-
leonic upheaval. After 1800, folk tales, almanacs, saints' lives,
ballads, and the like were carried less and less in Parisian colporter
baskets; by 1870 the literature of the centuries-old *bibliothèque
bleue* appealed almost exclusively to peasants in the countryside.
In the burgeoning nineteenth-century city of Paris, sentimental
songs, familial melodramas, fictional romances, and dramatic na-
tionalistic histories were displacing an older subliterary world,
drawing the attention of a more socially heterogeneous audience
whose attitudes about political authority, social deference, and the
individual were far different from those of most readers of the
early modern past. Nineteenth-century *chansonniers*, *vaudevilles*,
and *romans noirs* thus represented a shift from traditional folk to
a more "modern" popular culture whose significance historians
are only beginning to explore carefully.[1]
    A number of factors promoted this development.[2] The rapid
spread of literacy produced a large, unsophisticated readership,
one untrained in finer esthetic considerations long before the elaborate educational system of the Third Republic. Responding to a

James Smith Allen *is assistant editor of the* Journal of Family
History, *Clark University.*

Journal of Library History, Vol. 16, No. 1, Winter 1981
    ©1981 by the University of Texas Press   0275-3650/81/010199-11$01.05

growing audience with new tastes developed in the nineteenth-century literary marketplace, authors wrote less for a small coterie of well-educated elite patrons and more for an anonymous mass of plebeian admirers in the streets. Large revenues accrued for those willing to compose *chansonniers* like Pierre-Jean de Béranger, to stage melodramas like Eugène Scribe, or to serialize fiction like Alexandre Dumas. Not only did the book trade acquire titles appropriate to an audience in quest of distraction, it also produced cheaper books and newspapers for readers with comparatively modest incomes. In Paris from 1800 to 1850, as literacy rates increased nearly 50 percent, books and newspapers dropped in price to less than a fourth of what they cost at the end of the eighteenth century. By the Second Empire the new popular literature was circulating easily among hundreds of thousands of readers in Paris, making one important aspect of urban culture a lucrative as well as widespread commercial enterprise.

What role did lending libraries play in the early development and diffusion of the new popular literature in Paris from 1800 to 1850? How did the *cabinets de lecture* act as agents in this major cultural change? What share did they have in the shifting tastes and attitudes of Parisian readers who turned from an older literature expressing a traditional folk *mentalité* to a newer literature embodying a mind-frame more familiar to our own?

In suggesting answers to such important questions, this paper argues that Parisian lending libraries facilitated the early stages of an urban cultural revolution. They served as major distribution centers for the works of authors and publishers anxious to reach a wide audience in the new literacy commerce. Consequently, lending libraries also participated in a much larger historical phenomenon fostered by the development of a new popular literary culture: the new social and political alliance between certain artisan groups and the bourgeoisie who then were reading many of the same serial novels, attending many of the same melodramas, and singing many of the same songs—all readily and cheaply available at the numerous *cabinets de lecture* in Paris. The cultural origins of what Marx termed "false consciousness" among the aristocracy of labor and the lower middle classes in the nineteenth century may be found in the holdings and diverse clientele of the lending libraries: it is the purpose of the present paper to characterize more fully this historical function of the *cabinets de lecture*.[3]

Clearly, these *boutiques à lire* were the most accessible sources of printed matter in Paris in the first half of the nineteenth century. When few public libraries existed and book prices often exceeded the weekly wages of Parisian day laborers, cabinets rented books for nominal fees "by the month, by the year, by the sitting, by the volume, or by the day."[4] For as little as ten, but certainly no more than twenty-five centimes one could secure a single-volume novel overnight at most rental shops. Such modest costs made access to books from 1800 to 1850 cheaper than a kilogram loaf of bread, well within the means of ordinary men and women in the city. Thus, cabinets acted as important cultural intermediaries that made available to a large audience anxious for reading material the books offered by many *libraires* at the excessive standard price of 7 fr. 50 per volume throughout the constitutional monarchies. Even though the cost of books and newspapers decreased remarkably in the period, and many remaindered books appeared in the boxes of the *étalagistes* on the quays for a franc or less, the lending libraries remained consistently inexpensive distributors of both old and new books that were much in demand.

Moreover, Parisian cabinets were not marked by the social barriers of bookstores that continued to cater almost exclusively to elites in the period. Since no *brevet* and little initial capital were required, widows and retired officers on half pay frequently set up business once their fortunes turned for the worse, according to police records. In one 1829 report to the Ministry of the Interior, seven petitioners for permission to operate lending libraries in Paris included an artillery officer's widow, a wigmaker, a retired captain of the Hussars, and other lower middle class figures of "good reputation," whose "morals, politics, even religion" appealed to the authorities. Names and addresses in Sébastien Bottin's *Almanach du commerce de Paris* indicate the rapid increase in the number of cabinets; there were 32 in 1820, 150 in 1830, 189 in 1840, and 226 in 1850. The effective number of lending libraries before mid-century was actually much higher: sources other than Bottin were more sensitive to the many unregistered operations throughout the city. One recent historian, using the records of the police and the Ministry of the Interior, has identified and documented 463 cabinets for the Restoration alone. Although most, like bookstores, were located near the Palais-Royal and the universities, they existed primarily on the east-west and north-south thoroughfares, creating by such a distribution an even greater impact than absolute numbers imply.[5]

Few attained the prestige of Madame Cardinal's cabinet on the rue des Canettes, which maintained a substantial collection of over 20,000 well-chosen titles and was perhaps the best-known lending library in the period. Cabinets in the early nineteenth century generally offered less than 5,000 titles in one or two rooms furnished with "a table, a stuffed chair, a fire, . . . some pens, paper, and ink, and tobacco in the neighboring shops . . . each *habitué* with his own seat." Many lending libraries in fact were much less elaborate, providing books or newspapers but no place to read them. Some set up operations in parks and near cafés with little more than a few crudely constructed shelves and some titles for rent by the hour. Such modest circumstances must have invited a wide circle of readers from nearly every social class in the city, a suggestion attested to by various satires of cabinet clientele written as early as the First Empire. The innocent domestic in quest of a "good" book "with castles, secret passages, old villains, and lovers who marry in the end" was the target of more than one critic of the Parisian cabinets.[6] One lithograph (ca. 1840) by Félix Regamey detailed a worker in his smock and a domestic with her apron, standing with better-heeled borrowers in a lending library, waiting to return or take out books.

Thus, cabinets not only provided cheap and easy access to books in a period when such items were still luxuries produced primarily for the middle classes; they also appealed, by their number and diversity, to a socially heterogeneous clientele. These accessible operations must have promoted the distribution of books and newspapers to a growing literate audience of modest means and social status. Shopkeepers, artisans, domestics, journeymen in the more prosperous trades, even their wives and daughters could easily afford the 10 centimes per volume for the latest *nouveauté* from the neighboring lending library run by a poor widow. Stated one prominent *libraire* and cabinet operator, an astute observer of literary trends during the Restoration, "We must carry popular novels, if I may express myself thus, . . . for the artisan in his shop, for the little seamstress in her humble garret, for the second-hand clothes dealer in her basement. One must carry them for all the common people." Of course, not all lending libraries catered indiscriminately to classes high and low; social barriers surely discouraged the *menu peuple* from visiting many cabinets patronized by more "respectable" people in the Faubourg Saint-Germain on the left bank and in the Faubourg Saint-Honoré on the right. But the increasing assertiveness of the lower orders, especially after the 1830 Revolution, encouraged them to share in a cultural world, including lending libraries, that once belonged exclusively to their social betters. As Frances Trollope remarked in 1835, even the Louvre and the Tuilleries gardens were invaded by "dingy jackets, uncomely casquettes, ragged blouses, and ill-favoured round-caps, that looked like they did duty night and day." The presence of the *menu peuple* was surely felt even more in the far less intimidating *cabinets de lecture* of the Marais and the *quartier* Saint-Jacques.[7]

The impact of this diverse readership on the cabinets can easily be seen in the kinds of books they offered. A quick survey of the last remaining catalogues published by the more prominent operators in Paris reveals a marked emphasis on titles much in demand by such a broad audience.[8] Sentimental novels, adventure fiction, gothic tales, moralizing stories, fictitious memoirs, exotic travelogues, and biographies of notorious public figures formed the core of nearly every cabinet in Paris whose records still exist. The authors most represented were not those still read or studied today, but writers long forgotten and ignored. Pigault-Lebrun, Ducray-Duminil, Defauconpret, Guénard, (Auguste) Lafontaine; women writers like Madames Flahaut, Genlis, and Riccoboni; and translators of Ann Radcliffe, Elizabeth Bennett, and Jane Porter—all had a dozen or more copies of their novels on the shelves of cabinets in Paris between 1820 and 1845. The reading interests of most users of lending libraries included far fewer works by Hugo, Musset, Vigny, Mérimée, Stendhal, Gérard de Nerval, Madame de Staël, Lamartine, and Sainte-Beuve—the creators of the great literature appreciated in the elite *cénacles* and socially respectable salons of the city. Only Chateubriand's *Atala* and *René* and Scott's Waverly novels seem to have enjoyed the same popularity as the flood of new popular fiction produced before 1850 in response to the prevailing tastes of the cabinet's clientele.

A close look at the catalogue to the lending library of one Monsieur Gambard, near the Panthéon in the *quartier* Saint-Jacques, suggests the social diversity of its readers as well as the emphasis on the new literature.[9] In 1826 Gambard's collection of nearly 2,000 titles was available to subscribers at only 3 fr. per month; but as in many other cabinets the subscription for novels was only 2 fr. Individual volumes could also be rented at 10 centimes for a two-day loan if the borrower deposited 7 fr. 50 (about a week's wages for a *journalier* during the Restoration). Whether or not this deposit was demanded of everyone, friends and neighbors alike, is not known. The stock Gambard offered his clientele included complete sets of Greek and Latin classics (Plutarch, Ovid, Petronius, Catullus, Horace, and Virgil) in addition to those of the seventeenth- and eighteenth-century French masters (Corneille, Racine, Molière, Voltaire, and Rousseau). But the heart of this collection was much less serious. Over two-thirds of the cata-

logue's 180 pages were given over to novels; 31 by Ducray-Duminil, 28 by Walter Scott, 21 by DeFaverolle, 27 by Madame Flahaut, 35 by Guénard, 49 by Lafontaine, 26 by Montolieu, and 22
by Pigault-Lebrun. Gambard also kept 56 accounts of voyages, 23
histories of France, and 53 memoirs, including two copies of Las
Cases's depiction of Napoleon's last days on Saint Helena. Though
nearly all readers, high and low, could find something in this lending library, most were probably attracted by the popular works
that appealed to a middling audience with little formal education
and just as little social or literary pretension.

Similar Parisian *cabinets de lecture* played an active role in the
diffusion of popular literature. Of course, lending libraries did not
"make" literary tastes; they responded to popular tastes more
than they shaped them. But cabinets surely facilitated the development of prose fiction in Paris after 1800. Thanks in part to the
lending libraries that satisfied the new literary demands of a broad
readership, the modern novel evolved rapidly into a more plebeian
genre. The simple folktales and *canards* that had been the dominant popular forms in the eighteenth century gave way to sentimental, gothic, and adventure novels, both longer and more appropriate to an increasingly literate audience in the nineteenth
century. By then prose romances had become the staple literature
of Parisian readers, many of whom patronized the cabinets filled
with *romans noirs et terrifiants* as well as sentimental representa-
tions of domestic bliss. However much observers decried popular
prose fiction and its supposed effects on gullible readers, especially
impressionable young women like Flaubert's Emma Bovary, Parisian cabinets encouraged an avid audience for the novel, though
not for the more realistic works by Balzac, Stendhal, and Flaubert, whose presence in the lending libraries was overwhelmed by
the volumes of less accomplished fiction.

At the heart of the nineteenth-century novel, created by greater
and lesser literary lights alike, was essentially a new middle-class
value system whose influence in the period was fostered, in part,
by the Parisian cabinets.[10] The bourgeois nature of the novel is
obvious: it was concerned with private and domestic life in a distinctly urban and commercial social setting. Written about, by,
and for the middle classes, the prose fiction available in the lending libraries was no exception. Moreover, nearly all urban literature after 1800—the songs, melodramas, and histories as well as
the novels—reflected a similar set of social values and expressed
for its more diverse audience a view of the world very different

from that expressed in the chapbooks of the *bibliothèque bleue*. Indeed, the subject matter of the new popular literature appears to mark a shift in the plebeian intellectual outlook, a social change in the mentalities of the literate lower orders who were now reading many of the same works as their social betters. The decline of old folkways among peasants migrating to the city in the nineteenth century coincided with the rapid growth of this literature that heralded not only a new popular culture, but also, and more importantly, the displacement of the traditional superstition, fatalism, fear, and deference expressed by folk culture. Another set of attitudes appeared among the *menu peuple*, whose values were now based more on experience, optimism, empathy, and self-assertion. Much of this waning of early modern mentalities in nineteenth-century Paris can easily be seen in the changes in literature demanded by social groups of decidedly modest status and income in the lending libraries; they clamored less for titles in the nearly timeless subliterature of the colporter baskets now largely consumed only in the countryside, and more for the prose fiction featured by the cabinets proliferating in the city.[11]

The consequences of this new taste and mind-frame are significant. For perhaps the first time in French cultural history since the seventeenth century, the middle classes and the less respectable artisans and shopkeepers shared a common literary interest.[12] The novel, especially, formed an important part of Parisian cultural life, if we are to believe contemporary observers in the nineteenth century. Given the distinctly bourgeois nature of modern fiction, its Parisian audience must have constituted what Herbert Gans terms a middle-class "taste public," a social group with a relatively narrow range of common interests, political as well as literary, in the period.[13] The fact that skilled artisans and their families were demanding a literature written primarily for the bourgeoisie brought all of them closer not only in cultural taste but also in social outlook, implicitly at least. The shared literary and social interest certainly implied as well a shared political interest. It could well be that the middle-class culture, represented by the novel in the lending libraries, promoted an alliance between certain members of the *menu peuple* and the bourgeoisie in the 1830 Revolution, or, more dramatically, in the last stages of the Revolution of 1848.

The shared political values of some artisans and the middle classes can be seen more clearly in the process of politicization among various social strata in modern France: the aristocratic and middle-class elites mobilized first and most pervasively in the eighteenth century to set off the 1789 Revolution that was completed by the *menu peuple* and the peasantry. But the laboring poor, essentially on the margin of social and political life until the nineteenth century, took longer to arrive at such a revolutionary consciousness. By the June days of 1848 the unpropertied classes of Paris became more actively involved in revolutionary politics, and in so doing they contributed to a decisive shift in the sociopolitical structure of Paris. Out of fear and a common interest in political stability, the more "respectable" artisans and shopkeepers who had manned the barricades in times past increasingly identified now with the less revolutionary values of the Parisian *rentiers* and financiers who attempted to contain the recently self-conscious proletariat. After 1848 a political reaction set in among the propertied and middling classes in opposition to the new working-class revolutionary threat.[14]

It is no accident that this well-documented redefinition of social and political class interests in Paris coincided with the development of a more popular bourgeois culture. This included the new literature of the cabinets aimed at a readership far broader than the audience of any elite or plebeian genre in the eighteenth century.[15] Widely available in the lending libraries and later in the *romans-feuilletons*, novels defined a new middle-class audience participating in a common cultural activity that reinforced its political values—values distinct from those of the largely illiterate laboring poor, who neither read prose fiction nor shared in the political reaction of their social betters. To be sure, no one knows exactly what books reached the hands of this or any other social group; the records for such precision simply do not exist. But the reading material most available to the *nouvelles couches sociales* as they evolved in the nineteenth century appears to have distinguished its audience culturally and promoted its overt social and political role during the Second Empire and the Third Republic.

Thus, lending libraries participated, through their particular holdings and clientele, in a major cultural change influencing, albeit indirectly, the class and power structure of Paris in the first half of the nineteenth century. Although the precise contribution of the cabinets to the change in tastes and attitudes of Parisian readers remains obscure, their collections of novels did promote the transition from an older literature expressive of a traditional folk *mentalité* to a newer literature embodying a more modern, middle-class frame of mind. Moreover, their broad social appeal helped establish a new popular culture, and its implicit values must have fostered the creation of a new middle class fashioned by recent financial and industrial innovations.[16] Meanwhile, the illiterate portion of the laboring classes enjoyed something of a counterculture, especially after 1848. Dependent upon face-to-face collective life at work and in the cafés, the new proletariat was still defined by the lack of capital that set it off from the propertied classes. But the divergence in conscious attitudes and values—political, social, and literary—between the cultures of the middle and laboring classes in nineteenth-century Paris surely owes something to the agency of the *cabinets de lecture*; by making the literature of the bourgeoisie available to the *menu peuple*, lending libraries helped redefine the social classes and the nature of political conflict in nineteenth-century Paris.

Notes

The author would like to thank Nancy Barker, Bland Addison, and Nate Therien for their shrewd criticisms in the writing of the present draft.

1. For discussion of these developments, see Maurice Crubellier, *Histoire culturelle de la France, XIXe-XXe siècle* (Paris: Colin, 1974), pp. 8–18; Jean-Jacques Darmon, *Le colportage de librairie en France sous le second Empire: Grands colporteurs et culture populaire* (Paris: Plon, 1972), pp. 159–162; Eugen Weber, *Peasants into Frenchmen: The Modernization of Rural France, 1870-1914* (Stanford, Calif.: Stanford University Press, 1976), pp. 452–470; Robert Mandrou, *De la culture populaire aux XVIIe et XVIIIe siècles; La Bibliothèque bleue de Troyes* (Paris: Stock, 1964), pp. 182–195; and James Smith Allen, *Popular French Romanticism: Authors, Readers, and Books in the Nineteenth Century* (Syracuse, N.Y.: Syracuse University Press, 1980), ch. 1-2.

2. For a more complete discussion of these factors, see John Lough, *Writer and Public in France: From the Middle Ages to the Present Day* (Oxford and New York: Clarendon Press, 1978), pp. 164–274; Jean-Alexis Neret, *Histoire illustrée de la librairie et du livre français des origines à nos jours* (Paris: Lamarre, 1953), pp. 111–198; and Allen, *Popular French Romanticism*, ch. 3-6.

3. Important studies of the cabinets are M. Tirol, "Les cabinets de lecture en France, 1800-1850," *Revue des Bibliothèques* 33 (1926): 77–98, 198–224, 401–423; 34 (1927): 13–25; Claude Pichois, "Pour une sociologie des faits littéraires: Les cabinets de lecture à Paris durant la première moitié du XIXe siècle," *Annales: E.S.C.* 15 (1959): 521–534; Harry E. Whitmore, "The Cabinets de Lecture in France, 1800-1850," doctoral dissertation, University of Wisconsin—Madison, 1975; and Françoise Parent, "Les cabinets de lecture dans Paris: Pratiques culturelles et espace social sous la Restauration," *Annales: E.S.C.* 35 (1979): 1016–1038.

4. Marie-Joseph Pain and C. de Beauregard, "Les cabinets de lecture," *Nouveaux tableaux de Paris, ou Observations sur les moeurs et usages des Parisiens au commencement du XIXe siècle* . . . , 2 vols. (Paris: Pillet ainé, 1828), vol. 1, p. 69.

5. See accounts of lending libraries and their operators in Archives Nationales de France F^18 2162 bis, "Cabinets de Lecture: Demandes d'autorisation,

1816-1830." For the number of cabinets in Paris, see Parent, "Les cabinets de lecture dans Paris." Note that their life in Paris was brief: after 1850 they disappeared almost as rapidly as they had appeared during the first half of the century. For a discussion of their decline and the reasons for it, see Whitmore, "Cabinets de Lecture in France," pp. 135-149.

6. Alphonse Karr, "Imprimeurs, libraires, bouquinistes, cabinets de lecture," *Nouveau tableau de Paris au XIXe siècle*, 5 vols. (Paris: Bechet et al., 1835), vol. 5, p. 71. For satires of Parisian lending libraries, see Robert (P.-Louis Solvet), *Le cabinet de lecture, pièce satirique* (Paris: Egron, 1808); and Mathurin-Joseph Brisset, *Le cabinet de lecture*, 2 vols. (Paris: Magen, 1843), vol. 1, ch. 1, especially.

7. Such remarks in Alexandre Pigoreau, *Petite bibliographie biographico-romancière, ou Dictionnaire des romanciers* . . . , 3 vols. (Paris: Pigoreau, 1823), vol. 2, pp. ii-iv; and Frances Trollope, *Paris and the Parisians in 1835* (New York: Harper and Brothers, 1836), p. 39, are corroborated by secondary studies on the growing consciousness and assertiveness of the working poor. See, for example, Louis Chevalier, *Labouring Classes and Dangerous Classes in Paris during the First Half of the Nineteenth Century*, trans. Frank Jellinek (London: Routledge and Kegan Paul, 1973), pp. 394-408; and Bernard H. Moss, *The Origins of the French Labor Movement, 1830-1914: The Socialism of Skilled Workers* (Berkeley and Los Angeles: University of California Press, 1976), pp. 31-41.

8. See the Q^{28} series of more than seventy uncatalogued boxes of cabinet catalogues at the Bibliothèque Nationale de France in Paris. Unfortunately, many of the sole remaining catalogues are incomplete or merely supplements to nonextant catalogues, a fact that seriously hampers a systematic account of lending library holdings in Paris for the period. A good attempt, however, is Whitmore, "Cabinets de Lecture in France," pp. 56-112.

9. *Catalogue des ouvrages qui se trouvent dans le cabinet de lecture de M. Gambard, libraire, rue Soufflot, No. 3* . . . (Paris: n.p., n.d.), 180 pages. This shop was located by the Panthéon near where day laborers were recruited for work.

10. Middle-class values in the modern novel are discussed well in Priscilla P. Clark, *The Battle of the Bourgeois: The Novel in France, 1789-1848* (Paris: Didier, 1973); Ian Watt, *The Rise of the Novel: Studies in Defoe, Richardson, and Fielding* (Berkeley and Los Angeles: University of California Press, 1957), pp. 35-59; and John Cawelti, *Adventure, Mystery, and Romance: Formula Stories as Art and Popular Culture* (Chicago: University of Chicago Press, 1976), pp. 20-36.

11. See the more complete discussion of this cultural trend among elites in Paul Hazard, *The European Mind, 1680-1715*, trans. J. Lewis May (New York: New American Library, 1963), pp. 335-434; and, among the lower orders, in Weber, *Peasants into Frenchmen*, pp. 485-497. Note the gradual disappearance of colporter literature from Paris discussed in Darmon, *Le colportage de librairie*, pp. 140-144.

12. A major cultural separation between the elite and popular classes in France, for a number of reasons, existed from the middle of the seventeenth century to the end of the eighteenth, a phenomenon that makes the appearance of a new popular culture in the course of the nineteenth century all the more significant. See Peter Burke, *Popular Culture in Early Modern Europe* (New York: Harper and Row, 1978), pp. 270-281; and Philippe Ariès,

Centuries of Childhood: A Social History of Family Life, trans. Robert Baldick (New York: Vintage Books, Random House, 1962), pp. 62–99. On the cultural convergence in the early nineteenth century, see Edmond Goblot, *La barrière et le niveau: Etude sociologique sur la bourgeoisie française moderne*, 2nd ed. (Paris: Alcan, 1965), pp. 86–103.

13. See Herbert J. Gans, *Popular Culture and High Culture: An Analysis and Evaluation of Taste* (New York: Basic Books, 1974), pp. 9–15, 65–93.

14. For discussion of the process of politicization in France, see Georges Lefebvre, *The Coming of the French Revolution, 1789*, trans. R. R. Palmer (Princeton: Princeton University Press, 1947), pp. 1–151; and Richard Cobb, *"La Vie en Marge*: Living on the Fringe of the Revolution," *Reactions to the French Revolution* (London and New York: Oxford University Press, 1972), pp. 128–179. On the shifting political alliances of the middling classes, see Lynn Lees and Charles Tilly, "Le peuple de juin 1848," *Annales: E.S.C.* 29 (1974): 1061–1091; and, more generally, in Charles Tilly, "How Protest Modernized in France, 1845–1855," in *The Dimensions of Quantitative Research in History*, ed. William O. Aydelotte, Allan G. Bogue, and Robert William Fogel (Princeton: Princeton University Press, 1972), pp. 192–255.

15. See Robert Darnton, "Reading, Writing, and Publishing in Eighteenth-Century France: A Case Study in the Sociology of Literature," in *Historical Studies Today*, ed. Felix Gilbert and Stephen R. Graubard (New York: Norton, 1972), pp. 238–280.

16. On the definition and redefinition of the Parisian bourgeoisie, see Adeline Daumard, *Les bourgeois de Paris au XIXe siècle* (Paris: Flammarion, 1970), pp. 93–101, 123–145, 319–327.

Libraries for the General Public in French-Speaking Africa: Their Cultural Role, 1803–1975

Mary Niles Maack

Free tax-supported public libraries have never existed in Francophone Africa, but from the early nineteenth century there have been numerous, if intermittent, attempts to serve the general reader. An inventory of 18 vendémiaire, year XI (1803), indicates that one of the first libraries in the region was a municipal collection in Saint Louis, Senegal, that contained 1,351 volumes on a variety of subjects. Since this time, general readers have been served by a few municipal libraries in other cities, by a variety of small circulating libraries in French posts or *cercles*, and later by collections sponsored by cultural centers, embassies, and private associations. Although these libraries were set up for different reasons and therefore had different goals, it is possible to trace certain dominant ideas that have historically shaped the philosophy of library service in French-speaking Africa.

The cultural role of libraries is one thing in theory, another in law, and yet another in actual practice. This paper will deal with the underlying theory or philosophy of library service as it evolved in this region from the early nineteenth century to the mid-1970s. Eileen Power wrote in a very different context, "The expressed opinion of any age depends on the persons and classes who happen to be articulate in it; and for this reason alone it often represents the views of a small but vocal minority."[1] The vocal minority concerned with library development in French-speaking Africa included colonial administrators, educators, archivists, librarians,

Mary Niles Maack *is assistant professor at the University of Minnesota Library School.*

Journal of Library History, Vol. 16, No. 1, Winter 1981
© 1981 by the University of Texas Press   0275-3650/81/010210–16$01.35

other library association members, and a few African political leaders. It was these individuals who defined goals and objectives for library service. Although some of the specific projects they championed were not realized, their efforts to promote libraries illustrate the changing perception of the cultural role that libraries for the general reader should play in Africa.

Libraries as an Antidote to Exile

During the colonial period the role ascribed to French African libraries was influenced by the nature of library service in France, by changes in French educational and social policy in Africa, and by the unique needs arising from the African environment. Both general and specific needs for books were discussed in the correspondence of early colonial administrators, but prior to 1919 no consideration was given to the particular needs of African readers. Libraries were set up by and for the colonists, who, for the most part, neither encouraged nor arbitrarily restricted library use by Africans.

The library in Saint Louis, which was inventoried in 1803 by Charles Picard, the city clerk, had probably been established sometime after the French Revolution.[2] The commandant of Senegal, Blanchot de Verly, returned to France in 1801 and may have then obtained a part of this collection from the *dépôts* of confiscated books, which were being distributed to French municipal libraries.[3] Picard's inventory of the collection in Saint Louis, in fact, coincided with an 1803 law on French libraries that confirmed two earlier laws (of 1794 and 1796) requiring that public libraries be set up in each provincial capital.[4] Despite this legislation, many French cities were without municipal libraries and might well have envied the small but well-rounded collection of classics, French and European literature, history, philosophy, science, and theology available in this remote colonial outpost.

Although any Saint Louisien was apparently free to use these books, it is doubtful that many inhabitants of the island city would have had enough education to take advantage of such a collection. A 1786 census listed the population of Saint Louis as between 5,000 and 7,000, including: 660 European soldiers, merchants, and administrators; 2,400 free Africans and mulattos; and approximately 3,000 domestic slaves.[5] The slaves would have had little opportunity to learn to read and write French, and Muslim Africans were not especially motivated to acquire this skill since commercial success did not depend on literacy.[6] French fathers sometimes provided their Creole offspring with tutors or sent them to France for schooling, but none of the inhabitants had access to formal Western education in the colony prior to 1816, when the first French school was set up in Saint Louis. This meant that the users of the municipal library were drawn from among the French colonists, and from a small privileged group of Creoles and Africans who were literate in French.

The group of potential library users remained much the same throughout the nineteenth century, when there were few French public schools and little missionary activity. Even after the educational reforms at the turn of the century, the vast majority of Africans under French rule continued to live in a nonliterate society where customs, skills, legends, history, genealogy, and religious practices were passed down through oral traditions. Some nobles and Muslim clerics read Arabic, and a body of Islamic devotional literature written by Africans circulated among a restricted group of readers. Local rulers sometimes had Wolof, Pulaar, and certain other vernaculars transcribed in Arabic characters, but the majority of Africans were peasants, artisans or traders who felt little need for reading or writing.

The French colonists, on the other hand, came from a society where the use of printed books and documents was an accepted part of daily life among the middle classes. The establishment of colonial libraries must therefore be seen as one element in the larger effort of these colonists to transplant French civilization, commerce, and administration to Africa. Thus a demand arose for books to support French culture and thought, to sustain a limited amount of applied scientific research, and to aid in governing the colony.

During the 1820s and 1830s legal works and scientific publications were specifically requested for the colony, but when the library of Saint Louis was mentioned in an 1827 document it was referred to as the "bibliothèque publique."[7] In 1834, after this collection was moved into the new courthouse, a colonial inspector remarked that officials and *habitants* could both profit from works that the public library contained. He included in his report to the minister the following statement: "Your excellency is not unaware that, on the one hand, the laws of the colony are very poorly known, and on the other, the reading of less serious works is absolutely the only diversion in our exile."[8] This is the earliest surviving reference to the role the colonial library played in providing a vicarious escape from the sense of isolation felt by colonists living in a country whose climate many Europeans found enervating, and among peoples whose customs seemed exotic or sometimes incomprehensible.

This theme of alienation in Africa, loneliness for family, and nostalgia for a more familiar landscape was prominent in much French colonial literature. In such an environment, surrounded by an alien culture, reading often fulfills a deep-seated psychological need that goes beyond relaxation or escapism. For these early French colonists, the public library also served as cultural reinforcement by enabling them to maintain touch with an intellectual and literary life absent in the colony. A social role for the library might also be implied in the 1834 report stressing that inhabitants could profit from reading legal works, but the theme of self-improvement through reading was seldom used as a justification for acquiring books in the various appeals made to the ministry during the nineteenth century.

The idea that the colonial library should provide intellectual sustenance to administrators far from home persisted well into the twentieth century. The most eloquent apology for circulating libraries in isolated French posts was written in 1931 by Jules Brévié, a colonial administrator, scholar, and book lover. When Brévié began his African career in 1905, French holdings in the region extending from the southern fringe of the Sahara to the dense tropical forests of Guinea had recently been consolidated into a federation of territories known as Afrique Occidentale Française (the A.O.F.). While serving in Niger and the Ivory Coast, Brévié became familiar with life in distant French outposts where tiny libraries provided the only link with the intellectual life of Europe.

Just one year after becoming governor general of the A.O.F., Brévié sent the lieutenant governors of each colony a circular urging them to foster the development of such libraries in posts and cercles.[9] In his circular Brévié commented that many of these small collections had fallen into disuse and needed to be renovated if they were to once again serve as "instruments for culture and work." Brévié described the library as "valuable and uniquely fruitful" in a setting where it provided for "wholesome relaxation" and for "intellectual well-being" by serving as an antidote against fatigue and nostalgia. He then turned to its educational role, stressing that a small, well-planned collection would enable colonial administrators to renew their intellectual vigor and extend their vision beyond the narrow limitations of their daily tasks. Knowing that not all administrators were interested in bookish pursuits, Brévié emphasized that there was no inherent conflict between a life of action and the life of the intellect. This affirmation of the "administrator-scholar" tradition of his generation was undoubtedly directed toward some of the younger men in the colonial corps who sought a career in Africa to escape from European culture, which they described as "stifling" or "moribund."[10]

Most of Brévié's remarks concerned the reading needs of French personnel, but he did comment that the library should be open to all *habitants* of the *cercle* and should even include children's books. His final argument for the establishment of a local library involved its function as a cultural center that would provide literate persons in the *cercle* with a motive for meeting. Partly because of the social role such libraries might play, Brévié felt they should be sponsored by voluntary associations. Nonetheless he urged the local authorities to provide the library with quarters, and with some funding if possible. He also requested that the lieutenant governors make a survey of existing libraries and send this information to him in Dakar so that the Government General could donate selected works to these libraries and supply them with bibliographies of new works available for purchase.

In their replies to this circular, the lieutenant governors from Senegal, the Ivory Coast, and Dahomey all attributed the absence of libraries in certain *cercles* to the small number of Europeans resident there.[11] None of the four lieutenant governors who responded to Brévié's 1932 survey mentioned whether literate Africans used these small libraries. However, another colonial administrator who served in the early 1940s wrote that the *cercle* library "originally conceived for the European post, sometimes opened its doors to Westernized Africans who had no other source [for reading material] aside from the school library or the private collection of the teacher."[12]

Libraries for Extending French Culture

Prior to the 1930s, a few officials who were asked to report on the colonial library situation did acknowledge that local collections might play a role within the African community. When a library survey was ordered by the Colonial Ministry in 1919, the lieutenant governor of Dahomey mentioned a need for recent books and stressed that these should be chosen with care "because reading has a marked influence on the Westernized native element." Another official, Henri Gaden, commandant of Mauritania, remarked in his 1919 report that the public library which he proposed to attach to the *medersa* (Franco-Islamic school) in Saint

Louis "would constitute an excellent means of French propaganda" among the Maures.[13]

The idea that libraries could serve as a means of propagating French culture was not given much attention until the late 1930s, when the impact of school reforms and increased enrollment became visible in major West African cities. While the percentage of children reached by the A.O.F. school system was still minute (4.3 percent in 1934), the numerical increase in enrollment was impressive—with 16,800 Senegalese children attending French schools in 1937 as compared to 4,200 in 1910. The emphasis of the educational system, however, remained on primary instruction, and in the mid-1930s only 2,000 pupils were attending post-primary programs throughout the entire federation.[14] This policy created a group of young wage earners with limited reading skills and little income to purchase books. André Villard, who was appointed as the A.O.F. archivist in 1936, remarked on the eagerness with which these literate Africans patronized a Dakar bookstore that sold cheap editions of "the best and worst" books.[15]

Villard feared that the French primary school had given most of these young wage earners only a superficial understanding of Western culture; this brief exposure did not enable them to discriminate between works accurately reflecting European life and those giving a badly distorted image. Therefore he urged that popular libraries be set up to counteract the influence of cheap books by providing good literature to shape the taste of impressionable readers. While Villard's concept of popular libraries was certainly paternalistic, it was also rooted in the belief that the library should be a continuation of the school. Villard felt that the "striking success" experienced by public libraries in northern Europe and in the Union of South Africa was due to their close cooperation with the schools.[16]

By 1937 the young archivist had already begun a personal crusade for the creation of small circulating libraries that would attract young African readers and lead them to see that books were not "boredom incarnate"—but were an "inextinguishable source" of understanding and self-knowledge. Yet he realized that his goal of providing attractive, popular, but high-quality literature relevant to the African experience was impossible. In his 1937 report he commented that there were unfortunately no works in French equivalent to the simplified English works used in South Africa.[17] At this time local publishing was almost nonexistent in the A.O.F. and the French book industry had not begun to cultivate the African market. Thus the lack of appropriate literature stood out as one major obstacle, among many, to the growth of the popular library in Africa.

In spite of the numerous problems he foresaw, Villard proceeded to draw up a detailed program for establishing popular libraries throughout the A.O.F.[18] Villard's proposal was modest and ambitious at the same time. It was modest in that he recommended setting up such libraries at a minimal cost by employing local teachers as "librarians," by using already existing buildings, and by offering convenient but limited hours, since the main purpose of such libraries was loaning books rather than providing material for use in a reading room. However, the proposal was terribly ambitious in the sense that it advocated the establishment of libraries throughout French West Africa at a time when very little money was allotted for cultural or educational institutions, when well over 95 percent of the total population was illiterate, and when few Africans (aside from a small group of Muslim leaders) had a precolonial tradition of literacy or a body of written literature in the vernacular.

Nonetheless, Villard's innovative ideas about the cultural role of popular libraries were well received by the governor general and other officials in the A.O.F., where a new vision of a Franco-African culture had recently emerged. One of the chief proponents of this new doctrine was Brévié, who wrote in 1935 "however pressing may be the need for economic change . . . our [first] mission in Africa is to bring about a cultural renaissance, a piece of creative work in human material, an association of two races. . . . "[19] Albert Charton, then inspector general for education in the A.O.F., shared these ideals and frequently referred to the "blending of primitive civilizations with . . . [France's] universally applicable civilization." Although patronizing in his attitude toward African culture, Charton acknowledged that "the peoples of Africa [offered France] an enormous field for research and for the enrichment of our culture." Therefore he viewed France's educational role in Africa as a "moral alliance" rather than a "moral conquest."[20]

Charton's most eloquent expression of the doctrine of association appeared in a speech he gave in 1936 at the time of Governor General Brévié's departure for Indochina. Charton wrote:

> Gentlemen, let us recall the profound and redoubtable words of [the poet] Valéry: We other civilizations, we know now that we are mortal. . . . Eh bien, colonization will not be mortal if it ceases to be simply domination, simply exploitation . . . but

[rather] extends into culture, into influence, into education.
. . . In this, colonization is a humanistic endeavor, a profound
solidarity between two associated peoples.[21]

A generation of administrators imbued with such ideals was not
insensitive to the role of books in extending French culture. Thus
Villard's appeal that good popular libraries might "prepare for the
future by shaping the conscience of an entire country" did not fall
on deaf ears.[22] The intellectual and social climate was favorable
for his proposed undertaking, but the timing could not have been
worse. In 1939, when Villard's library campaign seemed on the
verge of success, France entered World War II and cultural programs in the colonies were abruptly tabled.

After the war, the theme of cultural synthesis was taken up by a
group of African writers led by Léopold Sédar Senghor, a Senegalese poet, scholar, and political leader. The blending of African
culture with the best elements of both French and Islamic civilization remained a central theme in Senghor's writings after he became president of an independent Senegal in 1960.[23]

Following the independence of the fourteen black African colonies, French officials once again turned to the role of French language and culture in maintaining close ties with Africa. During a
debate in the French National Assembly in 1964, Prime Minister
Georges Pompidou stated: "Of all countries, France is the one that
cares most about exporting its language and culture. This is a need
of our thought, perhaps of our genius."[24] Jacques Charbonnel,
Gaullist secretary of state for foreign affairs in the mid-1960s, also
stressed that the key element of French interest in Black Africa
was "the desire to build a firm foundation there for the expansion
of the French language," and Pierre Billecoque, the French secretary of state for national education, remarked at a 1970 meeting of
African ministers of education that "the teaching of French entails
the initiation into a culture."[25]

Between 1959 and 1975 a number of French cultural centers
with circulating libraries were set up; these centers were charged
with the double mission of providing greater access to French
books on all subjects and encouraging African authors to write in
French. To aid in the distribution of French publications a special
office known as the Bureau du Livre was also created in 1963.
During its first decade of existence, this office distributed nearly
600,000 books to the twenty-five cultural center libraries located
in Francophone Africa.[26]

In addition to circulating books for home use, the cultural centers organized book clubs to encourage original writing and to discuss French or African works. Prizes were offered to young African writers and winning works were published by the Bureau du Livre in the hope of stimulating more authors to produce books in French adapted to local interests. Such works could ultimately become an important element in creating a culture inspired by France, but rooted in the African experience. This goal was clearly expressed by one French cultural officer, who wrote:

> the opportunity for France's illuminating influence, [now] as during the Enlightenment resides in her ability to furnish other nations with the cultural instruments for their own flowering. [Our] cooperation. . . . is an aid in the creation of a new culture, a culture which will certainly owe much to our influence but which will be authentically African."[27]

This statement, written in 1969, mirrors the vision of a new Franco-African culture described by Brévié and Charton three decades earlier.

The Movement for Public Libraries

Initiatives to establish a coherent system of library service for general readers can also be traced back to the 1930s. At the time Villard prepared his proposal, several attempts had already been made to set up circulating libraries for African readers in Guinea, the Soudan, the Ivory Coast, and Senegal.[28] The educational service in the Soudan also established a limited system of library service by mail where books were sent free of charge to European and African instructors or administrators working in isolated posts far from the library in the colony's capital. A few of these circulating libraries proved quite successful, and in 1939 the inspector of education for the A.O.F. proposed a system whereby popular lending libraries would be attached to each higher primary school.[29]

This proposal, which could have incorporated many of Villard's recommendations, was never implemented due to the outbreak of World War II. Although there was limited fighting in the A.O.F., the war years were not conducive to the development of libraries. Villard himself returned to France in 1942 and was not replaced for the duration of the war. His successor, Marguerite Verdat, who served from 1945 to 1948, was more concerned with creating a system of *cercle* libraries in each colony, and did not address the special reading needs of literate Africans.

Unfortunately, no overall plan was adopted to promote systematic library development in the A.O.F., and little attention was directed toward African readers during the postwar period. In 1952 when UNESCO initiated a survey of African public libraries, few collections were available in French West Africa aside from nine research libraries that offered limited access to the public.[30] These collections, plus a few small libraries set up by French administrators or by private associations, provided all the "public library service" then available in the A.O.F. with its population of 16,500,000 persons.

In 1953, just prior to UNESCO's Ibadan seminar on public libraries in Africa, André Masson, an inspector general from the Direction des Bibliothèques in Paris, undertook a study-tour in Africa. Drawing on his observations (in Nigeria, Morocco, and the Gold Coast) and on the recommendations of the Ibadan conference, Masson outlined a plan for public library service in Francophone Africa.[31] To justify the establishment of public libraries, he also cited recommendations from the recent meeting of directors of education in tropical Africa, who urged that general libraries be set up in each important town, and that a central lending library be established in each educational district. Masson realized the immensity of such an undertaking and therefore suggested following the procedure used in France, where rural library service had been extended to certain "favorable" areas but had not yet been established in every *département*. The two cities he suggested as the starting point in Africa were Dakar and Tananarive.

Masson was convinced that small isolated collections by themselves were completely ineffectual. He therefore urged the creation of a central public library to serve as the headquarters of a system with branches, bookmobiles, and a service of book boxes for rural areas.

Although the central collection of 36,000 volumes that Masson recommended was roughly half as large as that of the Gold Coast Library Board (which served a population of approximately 4,000,000), it would have represented a large, unprecedented investment on the part of France and the Government General. The A.O.F. authorities, who were preoccupied with several major public works projects and with the rapid expansion of primary schools, took no action on Masson's project, nor did they request UNESCO aid. Their apparent lack of concern for libraries was undoubtedly shaped by their experience with French public libraries, which, prior to World War II, had not been perceived as important cultural or informational resources. When Dr. André Hahn, a second library official from Paris, visited Dakar in 1956, he remarked that one of the major obstacles to the creation of public libraries was the lack of interest, both on the part of Europeans and of French-educated Africans.[32]

Dr. Hahn's mission had been proposed by André Masson, who urged his colleague to look into the possibility of creating a network of public libraries for all kinds of readers—from the newly literate to the university graduate. However, after observing the situation in Dakar, Hahn concluded that it was best to concentrate on library service aimed at young people and adults with at least four years of secondary school. He therefore suggested that the university library include a department for general literature and reference material, which would be open to all readers with enough education to take advantage of such a collection. In addition, Hahn suggested the creation of a similar library nearer Dakar's African residential section.

The rector of the university, who approved both projects, stated that the new general section to be attached to the university library would be an appropriate nucleus for what he hoped to see as "the future public library of Dakar."[33] However, with the advent of independence, funding for the university library was cut back, and no collection was set up for general readers.

Since colonial authorities did not follow through on the proposals made by French library experts, Senegal and its neighbor states attained independence with no public library infrastructure and no tradition of significant government support for any *bibliothèque publique* that was not attached to a research institute. Lacking a model of effective public library service, neither Senegal nor any other former A.O.F. territory (except the Ivory Coast) was willing to invest its resources to experiment with an institution whose value was unproven.

Despite this governmental indifference, the Inter-African Library Association (A.I.D.B.A.) has continuously worked to promote public libraries since its foundation. Originally called the Association for the Development of Public Libraries in Africa, this group was organized by E. W. K. Dadzie, a Togolese archivist who had studied library science abroad during his appointment as a UNESCO fellow.

A visit to Scandinavia introduced Dadzie to Anglo-American concepts of librarianship, and a tour of the Gold Coast deeply im-

pressed him with the potential of free public libraries adapted to
an African environment. In 1956 Dadzie returned to his position
at the Mauritanian archives in Saint Louis, where he began to discuss the promotion of public libraries with African friends—educators, civil servants, and a few doctors, lawyers, and technicians.
These people were soon convinced that there was an urgent need
for public libraries in Africa. In September 1957 fifteen men and
women agreed to form the provisional executive committee for an
association whose goal was the development of "an effective system of public libraries in all African territories where public library service is not officially organized in accordance with the
UNESCO manifesto."[34]
The association held public conferences, sponsored radio programs, and actively lobbied for adequate public library legislation.
Knowing that local authorities would be slow to take action, the
group also hoped to establish a few model public libraries, which
would later be integrated into national library systems as these
came into being. The association's 1958 statutes clearly stated
that such model libraries must give high priority to children's work
and devote at least 30 percent of their budget to children's books.
In addition, the collection was to include manuals for literacy
training and books for the newly literate.[35] In 1962 a library was
set up by A.I.D.B.A. in Saint Louis, but the difficulty in raising
adequate funds resulted in a small collection staffed by volunteers.
Although A.I.D.B.A. continued its campaign for public library
service during the 1960s, it extended its concern to comprehensive
library planning that would include provisions for national, research, special, and academic libraries, for documentation services,
for archival management, and for library education.
In 1962 the first library school in the region was set up in Dakar
with UNESCO aid. Prior to 1964 the school's primary emphasis
was on training African librarians to set up public libraries throughout the Francophone states. Once it became clear that these states
were not ready to devote adequate funds to public libraries, the
school's program was modified to prepare Africans for positions in
a variety of settings including research libraries, documentation
centers, and national archives. Nonetheless, the school continued
to be concerned with the potential role of the African public library and its relationship to traditional African culture.
One of the most perceptive discussions of this theme appeared
in a short paper on the mission of the public library prepared
by Théodore N'diaye, a faculty member of the Dakar Library
School.[36] N'diaye expressed the view that library services should

not be limited to an elite but should reach the masses through use of audiovisual media. Since the newer media are more closely akin to the oral expression of traditional culture and can be used with the illiterate, N'diaye emphasized that these media should be an integral part of the African public library, which should serve as a community cultural center. He wrote:

> In this perspective, the African public library will certainly be a source for information, for self-education, for meeting, [a place] where every member of the community can find a response to his needs; but [the library] will also be a center for literacy training, for artistic endeavors and literary exchange, for reading alone or in a group, for listening to music, for exhibits and other cultural events. The African public library . . . it is simply *l'arbre à palabre* [the traditional tree where the village gathers].

N'diaye based these goals for the public library on the principle that "each civilization's structure calls for its own mode of cultural expression." By creating libraries that would also be communal meeting places like the time-honored "arbre à palabre," N'diaye believed that they could form an integral part of the community life, serving as a source for the preservation and diffusion of African traditions as well as a source for exposure to Western ideas. Thus he foresaw the library as playing a part in the evolution of a new culture that would be both modern and African.

To create the kind of public library that would be a synthesis of African and Western modes of "cultural expression," a wide range of community leaders must be involved and financial support must come from both the local and central government. Obtaining the means to establish such a library system is in turn dependent on political, economic, and cultural priorities that have emerged in the course of African history.

It is difficult to say whether N'diaye's vision of the African public library will ever become a reality in the French-speaking states. However, it is certain that without goals and visions, achievement is impossible.

Not every blueprint for a library becomes a library building, but every library building begins with a blueprint. The grand designs for library service in Africa are much like blueprints. They may not have resulted in new structures, but they reveal in the history of librarianship what blueprints reveal in the history of architecture: a society's unattained goals, which may later be revived, modified, or abandoned.

Notes

1. Eileen Power, *Medieval Women*, ed. M. M. Postan (Cambridge and New York: Cambridge University Press, 1975), p. 9.

2. "Inventaire des papiers du greffe-Bibliothèque, 18 vendémiaire, an XI (1803)," in J95, Dakar, Archives d'Afrique Occidentale Française (henceforth abbreviated AAOF).

3. For a discussion of other possible sources of books, see chapter 1 in Mary Niles Maack, *Continuity and Change: Library Structure in Senegal* (Chicago: American Library Association, 1981). Copyright ©1981 by the American Library Association. Portions of this article were reprinted by permission of the publisher.

4. Maurice Pellisson, *Les Bibliothèques populaires à l'étranger et en France* (Paris: Imprimerie Nationale, 1906), pp. 144–150; and Edward Edwards, *Free Town Libraries, Their Formation, Management and History: In Britain, France, Germany, and America* (New York: J. Wiley and Son, 1869), p. 198.

5. Camille Camara, *Saint-Louis-du-Sénégal: Evolution d'une ville en milieu africain* (Dakar: IFAN, 1968), p. 39.

6. G. Wesley Johnson, *The Emergence of Black Politics in Senegal: The Struggle for Power in the Four Communes, 1900-1920* (Stanford, Cal.: Published for the Hoover Institution on War, Revolution, and Peace, by Stanford University Press, 1971), p. 22. Johnson notes that Paul Benis, an African who could neither read nor write, was known as one of the most successful Saint Louisien merchants on the eve of the French Revolution.

7. Letter from the governor of Senegal to the minister of the navy, 12 December 1927, in *Sénégal* X, 2e, Paris, Archives Nationales, Section d'Outre-Mer.

8. Report of the colonial inspector, 3 November 1834, in J95, AAOF.

9. Circular, governor general of the A.O.F. to MM the lieutenant governors, 26 August 1931 in 16/0-6, AAOF. Reprinted in full in "Notes et informations," *Bulletin du Comité d'Etudes Historiques et Scientifiques de l'A.O.F.* 14 (July–September 1931): 454-455.

10. Robert Randau, a French colonial administrator and novelist, expressed the kind of antipathy toward a bookish life that Brévié was attempting to combat: "Je suis bien emprunté à Paris. J'éprouve dans ses rues la même inquiétude qu'à la visite d'une bibliothèque ou d'un musée. . . . L'enérgie meurt vite en compagnie des livres." Quoted in Jean Nizerugero, "Robert Randau et la vie coloniale en Algérie et en Afrique Occidentale Française" (Brussels: Université de Louvain, September 1964, Mémoire de Licence).

11. Responses to the circular of 26 August 1931 in 16/0-6, AAOF.

12. Robert Cornevin, *Littératures d'Afrique noire de langue française* (Paris: Presses Universitaires de France, 1976), pp. 126-127.

13. Responses to the official telegram from the Ministry of the Colonies, 6 June 1919 in J102, AAOF.

14. Statistics for education in the A.O.F. are drawn from W. Bryant Mumford and Major G. Orde-Brown, *Africans Learn to Be French: A Review of Educational Activities in the Seven Federated Colonies of French West Africa* (London: Evans Brothers, [1937]), p. 158-171. Those for Senegal are taken from Elliot J. Berg, "Education and Manpower in Senegal, Guinea and the Ivory Coast," in Frederick H. Harbison and Charles A. Myers (eds.), *Manpower and Education: Country Studies in Economic Development*, McGraw-Hill Series in International Development (New York: McGraw-Hill, 1966), p. 236.

15. André Villard, "Rapport à M le Gouverneur Général de l'A.O.F.," June 1937, in 16/0-12, AAOF.

16. André Villard, "Etat actuel des bibliothèques de large diffusion en A.O.F., Rapport à M le Gouverneur Général," 1938, in 16/0-12, AAOF.

17. Villard, "Rapport," 14 June 1937.

18. Ibid.

19. Quoted in Mumford and Orde-Brown, *Africans*, p. 96.

20. All preceding quotes from Charton are drawn from Mumford and Orde-Brown, *Africans*, pp. 100, 110, 111.

21. This speech was printed in "Notes et informations—Création de l'Institut Français d'Afrique Noire," *Bulletin du Comité d'Etudes Historiques et Scientifiques de l'A.O.F.* 19 (April-September 1936): 383-384.

22. Villard, "Rapport," 14 June 1937.

23. This doctrine is expanded in Léopold Senghor, *Les Fondements de l'africanité ou negritude et arabité* (Paris: Présence Africaine, 1967).

24. Quoted in William Cohen, *Rulers of Empire: The French Colonial Service in Africa* (Stanford, Cal.: Stanford University Press, 1971), p. 204.

25. Quoted in Edward M. Corbett, *The French Presence in Black Africa* (Washington, D.C.: Black Orpheus Press, 1972), pp. 7 and 13.

26. Régine Fontaine, "Le Problème du livre face au lecteur en Afrique: Quelques lignes d'actions proposées," *Coopération et Développement* no. 48 (1974): 16; and F. Lafon, "Le Bureau du Livre," *Coopération et Développement* no. 42 (1972): 33.

27. Robert Thomas, "A propos des centres culturels," *Coopération et Développement* no. 27 (1969); 5, 8.

28. André Villard, "Compte-rendu de la tournée effectuée à Saint Louis du 16 au 23 octobre 1938," in 16/0-12, AAOF; "Tournée—Conakry," February 1938, in 16/0-12, AAOF; "Tournée—Côte d'Ivoire," March 1938, in 16/0-12, AAOF; "Tournée—Soudan," December 1937, in 16/0-13, AAOF.

29. Circular, M l'Inspecteur de l'Enseignement to MM les Chefs du Service d'Enseignement, in 16/0-12, AAOF.

30. "UNESCO Seminar on the Development of Public Libraries in Africa," *UNESCO Bulletin for Libraries* 6 (November-December 1952): 136, 137.

31. André Masson, "Project de lancement de la lecture publique en Afrique Française avec l'aide du FIDES et de l'UNESCO" (1954), Dakar, Association Pour le Développement de la Documentation, des Bibliothèques, et des Archives (henceforth A.I.D.B.A.), dossier 21; all recommendations discussed below are drawn from this report.

32. A. Hahn, "L'Oeuvre éducative, les bibliothèques et la lecture publique en Afrique Occidentale Française: Impressions de mission," *Bulletin des bibliothèques de France* 1 (November 1956): 513.

33. Ibid., p. 517.

225

34. Association Pour le Développement des Bibliothèques Publiques en Afrique, *Statuts*, article 3b in A.I.D.B.A., dossier 10.

35. Ibid., articles 5 and 6.

36. Théodore N'diaye, *Réflections sur la mission de la bibliothèque publique africaine* (Dakar: EBAD, 1973).

The Reading Habits of the Nineteenth-Century Baltimore Bourgeoisie: A Cross-Cultural Analysis

Larry E. Sullivan

In 1795 several of Baltimore's wealthiest and most influential men joined together for the purpose of ameliorating what they considered a deplorable situation: the city's lack of a quality library. A short while later a library was organized with John Carroll, first Catholic bishop of the United States, as its first president. In the fall of 1796, the library opened its doors. The Library Company of Baltimore was to have a difficult, worried existence of almost sixty years until its demise in 1854. Nonetheless, it was the first quality subscription library in Baltimore and it set the standards of reading in the city during the first half of the nineteenth century.[1]

The purpose of this paper is to study the reading habits of the bourgeoisie who were members of the Library Company and to compare and contrast the selection policy of the library with what was actually read. The collection policy of the Library Company will be compared with the policies of other libraries in the city, chiefly in the pre–Civil War period. This analysis will also reveal the significance of social and educational programming for these libraries.

The Library Company's first catalogue, printed in 1797 with a list of its members and bylaws, is a good indication of the tastes and reading preferences of the late eighteenth century bourgeoisie.[2] The Company had 226 members in 1797, and a study of their occupations indicates their social status in a city that was on the

Larry E. Sullivan *is the librarian of The New York Historical Society.*

Journal of Library History, Vol. 16, No. 2, Spring 1981
©1981 by the University of Texas Press   0022-2259/81/020227-15$01.50

eve of burgeoning into economic distinction. City directories, local histories, tax lists, and obituary files identify the members who paid the stiff initial twenty-dollar subscription fee and five-dollar annual dues as the strategic elites of Baltimore.[3] The obvious leaders were there: Charles Carroll of Carrollton, Bishop John Carroll, Governor John Eager Howard; but also on the lists were the leading merchants of the day, men whose business instincts and money carved out Baltimore's fortunes in the first decades of the nineteenth century. Included were Robert Gilmor, William Patterson, Richard Caton, Robert Oliver, and Solomon Etting.

It was a conservative body and its members included the ruling elite of Baltimore. Our sources allow us to identify the professions of 167, or 74 percent, of the charter members of the Library Company. Of this number, 126, or 75 percent, were engaged in trade. The designations listed in the directories mention only the term "merchant" for many of the people, but local histories describe these merchants as the large-scale commission merchants of the city—the ones who amassed substantial fortunes in the export-import trade. Other professional categories include: attorneys, 8 members or 5 percent; physicians, 13 or 8 percent; clergy, 6 or 4 percent; and statesmen, "gentlemen," and officeholders contributed 14 of their kind, or 10 percent. The latter classification included Charles Carroll; Samuel Chase, judge of the Supreme Court of Maryland; Alexander Furnival, the postmaster; Martin Eichelberger, the weighmaster of the port; John Eager Howard; Luther Martin, attorney general of Maryland; and judges and court clerks. Although clergymen accounted for only 6 members, they had an influence outweighing their small number; for example, Bishop John Carroll was the president of the Library Company for over twenty years and his immediate successor in the presidency was Episcopal Bishop James Kemp.

It is obvious that these men were influential. We can, however, be more specific. Whitman Ridgway in his work *Community Leadership in Maryland* has classified Baltimore leaders of the first and second party eras into four categories of elites according to money, property, office, and other positions of leadership.[4] Of the 221 individuals in his schema, Library Company members accounted for 90 or 41 percent. These were the men who set the trends in business, law, politics, and religion. Did they also determine what the literate public read in their libraries? What types of literature did they read, and how did Library membership and reading habits change over the next half century?

The first Library Company catalogue, issued in 1797, clearly reflected eighteenth-century tastes as shown by Joseph Wheeler's and Richard Beale Davis's studies of pre-Revolutionary Maryland reading interests.[5] The Library had 614 titles, which are classified in table 1.

The preponderance of history and theology titles is nothing extraordinary for late eighteenth century libraries. One of the few catalogues that we have for an eighteenth-century Maryland commercial circulating library—the Annapolis Circulating Library of 1783—shows approximately the same title classification as the later Baltimore library.[6] In addition, recent research on Maryland religion has indicated that piety in no way declined after the Revolution.[7]

The next general catalogue of the Library Company, that of 1809, listed 3,685 titles in a broad range of classifications.[8] Theology, history, and fiction led the field, each having approximately 9 to 10 percent of the titles. Supplements were issued in 1816, 1823, 1831, and 1841.[9] The directors bought in all subjects, but the acquisition policy did reflect the conflict between what the directors considered valuable and lasting literature and what the members demanded, namely novels and romances. For instance, theology comprised 5 percent of the titles in the 1816 supplement, 6 percent in the 1823 issue, declined to 1½ percent in 1831, and went back to 5 percent in 1841. History and biography generally held their own. Novels and romances, however, went from 13 percent in 1816 to 17 percent in 1823, increased to 24 percent of the titles in 1831, and to 28 percent in 1841. Clearly, the members desired the diversionary pleasures to be found in fiction, and the library had to follow suit in its selection policy.

That the Library Company's members preferred fiction is borne out by the circulation statistics for 1800 to 1803.[10] Members borrowed fiction works almost 25 percent of the time, whereas theology accounted for only 6 percent; biography was second in demand with 16 percent, and history third with 14 percent. Although the Library's selection policy was somewhat behind its stockholders' tastes, it does not necessarily follow that the institution was out of step with its times. In fact, I would argue that the collection policy was ahead of other contemporary "quality" libraries in its stated objectives. For instance, we read in the 1802 report of the directors:

> The Directors flatter themselves that the Company will approve the selection of authors, whose works constitute the valuable accession to their literary treasure. In making

TABLE 1

Classification of Titles in the Library Company of Baltimore Catalogue, 1797

Classification	Number of titles	Percentage
Theology	123	20
History and biography	125	20
Novels and romances	71	11.5
Miscellaneous (periodicals, etc.)	59	9.5
Law and politics	49	8
Poetry	50	8
Natural philosophy	48	8
Travel	48	8
Natural history	24	4
Ethics	17	3
	614	100

the selection, the Directors were guided by the intention and desire of enriching the Library with those productions which are esteemed most conducive to encourage Religion and Morality, diffuse correct historical information, and advance the cultivation of the sciences and useful arts. But tho' the Directors appropriated to these purposes, the largest portion of the funds within their management, they were not unmindful of employing a competent share of them for gratifying the taste of genius and providing for the entertainment of those readers who seek amusement and instruction in works of a lighter and less durable kind, but made interesting, by their reference to the events and manners of our own times.[11]

The directors were attempting what they felt was a good balance between value and demand.

We can find contemporary commercial circulating libraries that did not demonstrate as much balance. Many commercial libraries were established in Baltimore during this time but few went beyond the proposal stage.[12] A few catalogues from the second and third decades of the century still exist. The Maryland Circulating Library of 1820 had exactly the same number of titles in theology as in fiction, and each category outnumbered history by two to one.[13] It was only in the 1821 supplement that titles in fiction surpassed those in theology, with history and biography remaining static in percentages.[14] The next year, however, saw the library add thirteen times as many titles in theology as in fiction, and four times more titles than in history.[15] During the same period, Robinson's Circulating Library provided popular literature in the extreme: 90 percent of its titles were in novels and romances, with 10 percent in history.[16] Books on other subjects were not even offered. Robinson's, however popular it was with the literate working classes, was not officially approved by the establishment. A newspaper article of 1816 warned of the evils of such libraries:

Those who are truly jealous of the morals, good habits, and real literary improvements of their family, will do well not to trust indiscriminately the choice of these books to their uninformed and unexperienced children—the least review of their CATALOGUES will show them a very large proportion, or disproportion of bad novels, plays, and infidel tracts, which bear almost in their very title the evidence of mischief they are apt to do to unguarded youths—parents and tutors ought then at least to keep to themselves the management of any subscription to such a catalogue, and never leave to their family the choice of the books to be read, whether for recreation or regular instruction. Libraries were called by the ancients the repositories of the remedies of the soul; but in our times, not all their drugs are elixirs of life or moral beauty—more of poison might pour from many of the phials than the pretended antidotes or other articles could counteract. —More of infectious immorality may be caught from the reading of some of the most generally circulated articles than the good stuffs left on the shelves could remedy—let us say freely that a tolerably numerous set of useful books may be selected *for circulation* from these catalogues—but so many of the worse productions of the press are crowding along with them, that for the whole it is true, that the little good which such speculations confer upon society, bears no proportion to the mischief which it must certainly occasion. . . . [17]

The Library Company's directors were cognizant of what the public, including their own members, wanted to read and therefore took a moderate course by providing novels, even many of the type that were offered by Robinson's. All they had to do was read the newspapers to see the plethora of romances that were advertised by local booksellers. John Uhler's study of book advertisements in Baltimore newspapers from 1815 to 1833 shows that fiction was well ahead of other categories, with biography second, religion third, and history a poor fifth.[18]

The Library Company issued no more catalogues after 1841, but we are fortunate to have manuscript membership lists for 1844 and circulation statistics for part of 1843.[19] These sources permit us to discern if any alteration in the class of membership took place and also exactly what were the reading interests of the members.

The 1830s were years of great change for Baltimore. Between 1800 and 1840 the population quadrupled. The Jacksonian Party was a strong force in the city's political structure; businessmen began looking more to the Western markets for profits rather than to the traditional oceanic trade. This period saw the beginning of the B&O Railroad and the slow rise of manufactures in the city. Ethnic immigration increased dramatically. New leaders, formed by these changing forces, took command of the city.[20]

The Library Company's membership reflects these changes. Of the 315 members in 1844, we can identify 160 of them by profession, as shown in Table 2.

TABLE 2

Professional Classification of Library Company Members, 1844

Profession	Number	Percentage
Merchants	57	36
Attorneys	31	19
Doctors	22	14
Officeholders	14	9
Bankers	12	8
Clergy	11	7
Manufacturers and railroad men	7	4
Architect and engineer	2	1
Craftsmen	2	1
Insurance company president	1	0.5
Farmer	1	0.5
	160	100

Source: Records of the Library Company of Baltimore, MS 80, Maryland Historical Society, Baltimore, Maryland

This breakdown of members coincides generally with the distribution of professions among the leadership of the city. If we use Ridgway's classification of elites during the second party era we see that 53 Library Company members were among the 380 people he listed. Although this number included 14 percent of the elite, a drop from 1800, it is quite respectable considering the increase in population and the dispersion of leadership among the ranks of society. The new breed of bourgeoisie was rising as the old merchant class declined. This fact is evident in city leadership as well as in Library Company membership. The railroad men, the manufacturers, the bankers, the lawyers, and even the Jacksonian craftsmen were represented in the Library Company. Clearly, membership did not remain stagnant and wedded to the past.

If we look at the Library's circulation statistics for the last three months of 1843, we also see a significant change. The members chiefly used the reading room for its service of providing periodical literature. Of the 667 entries in the librarian's book for 1843, 381 or 57 percent of the loans were for the large assortment of newspapers and magazines kept on file. Second in demand was fiction, with 11 percent of the loans, and then history with 8 percent. This trend reflects two related phenomena: the contemporary concern with current issues and the need to spend a large portion of the Library's funds on the increasing number of periodicals while sacrificing new additions to the book collection. The librarian found it extremely difficult to accommodate financially the demands for quality editions of all the new works of fiction and history. In 1844 the librarian asked permission to buy inexpensive editions of new novels. A committee was formed to study the situation and reported that "cheap" editions were ruining private libraries and that there was no reason to compete with the bookseller.[21] The Library Company might offer any type of literature, but it was not going to stock the 1840s equivalent of the paperback.

From this date onward, the Library Company declined until its collection was incorporated into the Maryland Historical Society's holdings in 1854. It went out of existence for a combination of reasons, among them poor management and its failure to take advantage of inexpensive books. It did not fail because it was conservative in the type of literature offered to its readers. A few years ago at another Library History Seminar, William Van Beynum stated that the Book Company of Durham, Connecticut, "gave way to modern times, newspapers and light reading. . . ."[22] This was not the case with Baltimore, for as we have seen the

Library Company assiduously attempted to provide exactly this type of literature. No library of the period before the appearance of the public library could provide for all its demands. An area in which the Library Company did not keep up with the new libraries formed in the 1840s was in the nonreading services offered to their public. The ancillary functions of the new libraries soon became the main appeal for their members, and because some subscription libraries did not diversify their services, they failed to survive. Although they could adapt to new reading interests, they could not adjust to the demand for public programming.

An analysis of the catalogues of the new libraries reveals that selection was based primarily on the same type of collection policy as at the Library Company. A group of merchants and businessmen formed the Mercantile Library in 1839, and shortly thereafter began providing books to that class of clerks and apprentice businessmen whom the bourgeoisie wished to form in their own image.[23] For a nominal subscription and an annual fee, these clerks had access to a relatively well stocked library. The merchants themselves could become honorary members for an annual fee and receive reading and other privileges, but they could not vote in the affairs of the institution. Here, however, among the honorary members were the same influential men who were stockholders in the Library Company, and who were providing for the reading needs of their fledglings. The first printed catalogue of 1851 shows that the number of titles in each classification was almost exactly the same as the Library Company's distribution of twenty years previous.[24] Novels comprised 24 percent of the titles, history and biography 20 percent, and the rest were divided among 18 additional classifications. New periodical titles numbered 26, lower than the Library Company's 41 titles of 1843. The third annual report of the Mercantile Library (1842) states a collection policy that is the logical conclusion of the Library Company's statement of 1802, as it more strenuously justifies the reading of novels and romances and relinquishes selection to the principle of demand:

> Light literature has not been neglected. Though sometime made the subject of unsparing condemnation, the Board venture to express their belief that it is, in its place, harmless and even useful. Those who wrest it from its proper position by making it the sole object of their attention, are undoubtedly chargeable with a species of mental intemperance. But justice forbids us to hold it responsible for the abuse and perversion

it occasionally suffers at the hand of injudicious admirers. Whatever may be the better opinion on this subject, a point not necessary here to decide, it is certain that the presence of fictitious reading in the library is almost indispensable to the ends of an Association like our own. Those of the young, whose taste for reading is not yet confirmed, find in it the attraction which draws them towards books, and often lays the foundation for after love of mental cultivation. Many others seek it as an amusement during the intervals of care and labor, and the most grave are sometimes willing to employ it as a relief from the exhaustion of severer studies. The interests of the Association demand that the taste of all these should be consulted by those to whom the management of its affairs is delegated. It is undoubtedly incumbent upon them to foster, as far as practicable, a taste for solid and instructive reading. But their authority to do so is limited. One of the earliest lessons that the necessity of their office presses upon their notice is, that they must rather follow, than endeavor to force the taste of their readers. They have unquestionably power to place works of a grave and serious character exclusively upon the shelves: but they have no power by which they can cause them to be read.[25]

It was not, however, what the Library stocked on its shelves that differed from the Library Company, but the other services it provided. And here the Library Company suffered in comparison. Other programs were developed to draw in the public in the 1840s, as is the case today. Books were not enough. They were plentiful and inexpensive enough for any avid reader to buy. The Mercantile Library devised lectures and other diversions for its clerks and honorary members. The programs received publicity, were described in the newspapers, and therefore membership grew. But it was never that much larger than the Library Company's.

Libraries became more social. Other associations formed libraries that were more than reading rooms. The large Baltimore German population was the main group to establish substantial libraries. The people who came together in these societies were members of the German haute bourgeoisie who wished to retain elements of their own culture. The chief German organizations were the German Odd-Fellows, with their Wilhelm Tell Bibliothek, the Germania Club, and the Concordia Club. The Odd-Fellows accommodated different segments of the German population, while the planters joined the Germania and the merchants and industrialists entered the Concordia.[26]

The Odd-Fellows Library issued the earliest printed Baltimore German Society catalogue in 1857.[27] As is the problem with using catalogues, it is difficult to ascertain which books were read, although this source does allow us to define the collection policy of the Library. The Odd-Fellows followed the tastes and habits of the older libraries in the city with one obvious difference: a good stock of German literature. The 25 percent fiction in the collection and the titles in the various classifications reflected what was apparently the set distribution of titles in libraries during this period.

The collecting policy of the Concordia was similarly defined. Liberal Germans founded the Concordia in 1848, and it quickly became an exclusive club for German merchants and businessmen. In 1867 it issued its library catalogue.[28] By this time it had become an organization for the German Jewish elite.[29] The Library stocked a selection of literature that coincided with the Odd-Fellows, the Mercantile, and the Library Company, again with the exception of German literature. But the types of titles were similar to those in the other libraries.

The German society libraries suffered through two conflicts in their selection policy. One was the same as the older established libraries: working out a compromise between what was, in their estimation, the valuable and the lasting and what was popular and in demand. Additionally, the libraries needed to maintain some balance between what was German and what was American. After much initial hesitation, they attempted to accept American culture while retaining the Germanic heritage. But this inherent contradiction in their cultural outlook resulted eventually in the almost total demise of Germanic culture as they knew it. Similarly, due to the insistence on the German language being taught in public schools, German language schools died out in Baltimore.[30] When the Society for the History of the Germans Library was formed in the latter part of the century, it is significant to note that a majority of the titles were in English.[31]

The libraries, however important as cultural indicators, were not responsible for the success of these societies. The social and educational programs prolonged their life. The Concordia threw balls, had a choral society, and held countless other events that attracted members of the proper class. The new breed of merchant and industrialist of every ethnic background was torn between the traditional ideal of the well-read gentleman and the social need for organizations. He thought he could combine both. Therefore a compromise was struck not only between the types of literature offered but also in the very character of the libraries. As time passed, the library function tended to become less and less important as the programs grew. Eventually, reading was relegated to an auxiliary role as the truly public library burst on the Baltimore scene in the 1880s.[32]

The advent of the public library has been stressed unduly as the cause of the demise of the subscription and association libraries.[33] Many of the members of these private libraries most likely would not enter the doors of a genuinely public library. They supported them, but can we say how many used them? A confluence of factors was responsible for the end of the subscription library: the availability of literature in inexpensive editions; the proliferation of novels; poor management; the metamorphosis of libraries into social organizations; and the narrowness of the economic base— the latter reason not because the bourgeoisie could not afford the dues but because libraries such as the Library Company no longer provided exclusive services. In other words, the nineteenth-century bourgeois reader demanded more for his money. The few real bibliophiles left were not enough to support most private libraries. The libraries that survived longest either went into programming in a large way or restricted themselves to building up significant special collections made available to a narrow but staunchly supportive public. The ideal of the balanced collection was left to the new public library.

Notes

1. For a brief history of the Library Company, see Stuart C. Sherman, "The Library Company of Baltimore," *Maryland Historical Magazine* 39, no. 1 (March 1944): 6–24 (hereafter cited as *MdHM*). See also Dennis Rankin Clarke, "Baltimore, 1729–1829: The Genesis of a Community" (Ph.D. dissertation, Catholic University of America, 1976): 266–267.

2. *A Catalogue of Books &c, Belonging to the Library Company of Baltimore; to Which are Prefixed the Bye-Laws of the Company and an Alphabetical List of the Members* (Baltimore: John Hayes, 1797).

3. Especially valuable is the Dielman-Hayward Biographical Index at the Maryland Historical Society. See also John Thomas Scharf, *History of Baltimore City and County from the Earliest Period to the Present Day: including Biographical Sketches of Their Representative Men* (Philadelphia: L. H. Everts, 1881); George W. Howard, *The Monumental City, Its Past History and Present Resources* (Baltimore: J. D. Ehlers, 1873); and the Maryland Tax Lists, 1798–1805, MS 807, Maryland Historical Society.

4. Whitman H. Ridgway, *Community Leadership in Maryland, 1790–1840: A Comparative Analysis of Power in Society* (Chapel Hill: University of North Carolina Press, 1979), pp. 214–339.

5. Joseph T. Wheeler, "Booksellers and Circulating Libraries in Colonial

Maryland," *MdHM* 34 (1939): 111–137; "Books Owned by Marylanders, 1770–1776," *MdHM* 35 (1940): 337–383; "Reading Interests of the Professional Classes in Colonial Maryland, 1700–1776," *MdHM* 36 (1941): 181–201, 281–301; "Reading Interests of Maryland Planters and Merchants, 1700–1776," *MdHM* 37 (1942): 26–41, 291–310; "Reading and Other Recreations of Marylanders, 1700–1776," *MdHM* 38 (1943): 37–55, 167–180; "Literary Culture in Eighteenth Century Maryland, 1770–1776," *MdHM* 38 (1943): 273–276; Richard Beale Davis, *Intellectual Life in the Colonial South, 1585–1763*, 3 vols. (Knoxville: University of Tennessee Press, 1978); *A Colonial Southern Bookshelf: Reading in the Eighteenth Century*, Mercer University Lamar Memorial Lectures, no. 21 (Athens, Ga.: University of Georgia Press, 1979).

6. *A Catalogue of the Annapolis Circulating Library* (Annapolis: Frederick and Samuel Green, [1783]). Earlier circulating libraries were founded in Annapolis by William Rind and William Aikman. See Wheeler, "Booksellers and Circulating Libraries in Colonial Maryland"; and David Kaser, *A Book for a Sixpence: The Circulating Library in America*, Beta Phi Mu Chapbook, no. 14 (Pittsburgh: Beta Phi Mu, 1980), pp. 19–23, 36–38.

7. See Thomas O'Brien Hanley, *The American Revolution and Religion: Maryland 1770–1800* (Washington: Catholic University of America Press, 1971).

8. *A Catalogue of the Books, &c. Belonging to the Library Company of Baltimore*... (Baltimore: Edes and Leakin, 1809).

9. *A Supplement to the Catalogue of Books, &c. Belonging to the Library Company of Baltimore, 1816* (Baltimore: J. Robinson, 1816); *A Supplement to the Catalogue of Books*..., *1823* (Baltimore: John D. Toy, 1823); *Third Supplement of Books*..., *1831* (Baltimore: John D. Toy, 1831); *Fourth Supplement of Books*..., *1841* (Baltimore: John D. Toy, 1841).

10. For these early statistics, taken from the Records of the Library Company of Baltimore, MS 80, Maryland Historical Society, see Sherman, "The Library Company of Baltimore," p. 14.

11. Quoted in Sherman, "The Library Company of Baltimore," pp. 2–3.

12. Wheeler, "Booksellers and Circulating Libraries in Colonial Maryland"; Kaser, *A Book for a Sixpence*, pp. 37–85.

13. *Catalogue of Books Belonging to the Maryland Circulating Library* (Baltimore: Frederick G. Shaeffer, [1820?]).

14. *Supplement to the Catalogue of Books, &c. Belonging to the Maryland Circulating Library* (Baltimore: n.p., [1821?]).

15. *No. 2 Supplement to the Catalogue of Books, &c. Belonging to the Maryland Circulating Library* (Baltimore: n.p., 1822).

16. *Catalogue of Robinson's Circulating Library* (Baltimore: n.p., 1816). Similar statistics can be extracted from the *Catalogue of Roach's Circulating Library* [Baltimore: n.p., 1826?] and the *Catalogue of the Baltimore Circulating Library, Kept by William Munday* (Baltimore: John W. Butler, 1807). The Baltimore Circulating Library issued supplements in 1812, 1813, and 1814.

17. *American and Commercial Daily Advertiser*, 6 January 1817.

18. John Earle Uhler, "Literary Taste and Culture of Baltimore: A Study of Periodical Literature in Baltimore, 1815–1833" (Ph.D. dissertation, Johns Hopkins University, 1927), pp. 70–71.

19. Records of the Library Company of Baltimore.

20. For an excellent description of this transitional period, see Gary L. Browne, *Baltimore in the Nation, Seventeen Eighty-Nine to Eighteen Sixty-One* (Chapel Hill: University of North Carolina Press, 1980), esp. pp. 115–196.

21. Wm. Gwynn, Librarian, to J. Meredith, Esq., 7 February 1844, Records of the Library Company of Baltimore. The report was issued in April 1844.

22. William J. Van Beynum, "The Book-Company of Durham," in Martha Jane K. Zachert (ed.), *Library History Seminar No. 3, Proceedings, 1968* (Tallahassee, Fl.: Journal of Library History, 1968), p. 73.

23. *Constitution, Rules, Regulations, &c. of the Mercantile Library Association of the City of Baltimore* (Baltimore: Bull and Tuttle, 1839); Mercantile Library Association Papers, 1839–1873, MS 585, Maryland Historical Society.

24. *Catalogue of the Mercantile Library Association of Baltimore, 1851* (Baltimore: John W. Woods, 1851).

25. *Third Annual Report of the Board of Directors of the Mercantile Library Association, November, 1842* (Baltimore: John Murphy, 1843).

26. Dieter Cunz, *A History of the Germania Club of Baltimore City, Maryland* (Baltimore: Society for the History of Germans in Maryland, 1940); idem, *The Maryland Germans: A History* (Princeton: Princeton University Press, 1948); *Baltimore, Seine Vergangenheit und Gegenwart mit Besonderer Berücksichtigung des Deutschen* (Baltimore: C. C. Bartges, 1887).

27. *Catalog der Deutschen Odd-Fellow Bibliothek* (Baltimore: Th. Kroh, 1857).

28. *Catalog der Bibliothek der Concordia* (Baltimore: C. W. Schneidereith, 1869).

29. Isaac M. Fein, *The Making of an American Jewish Community: The History of Baltimore Jewry from 1773 to 1920* (Philadelphia: Jewish Publication Society of America, 1971), pp. 132–133.

30. Ernest J. Becker, "History of the English-German Schools in Baltimore," *Society for the History of the Germans in Maryland* 25 (1942): 13–17.

31. *List of Books Contained in the Library of the Society for the History of the Germans in Maryland* (Baltimore: C. W. Schneidereith, 1896).

32. The Enoch Pratt Free Library opened in 1886. See Philip A. Kalisch, *The Enoch Pratt Free Library: A Social History* (Metuchen, N.J.: Scarecrow, 1969).

33. This is the view taken by Sherman in "The Library Company of Baltimore." Sidney Ditzion expresses the same opinion concerning mechanics' and mercantile libraries in his "Mechanics' and Mercantile Libraries," *Library Quarterly* 10, no. 2 (April 1940): 192–219. Such library historians as Ditzion and Jesse Shera have generally cited the public library movement as the deciding factor in the decline of association and subscription libraries without, however, taking into consideration regional and cultural differences.

The Modern Library Series and American Cultural Life

Gordon B. Neavill

The Modern Library series was a visible and significant part of American cultural life for half a century. From 1917, when it was founded, to 1970, when it became moribund, it was the leading American series of hardbound reprints of important works of literature and thought. The small, inexpensive volumes were stocked at virtually every bookstore and major department store in the country. There can be few readers of serious books during the Modern Library's long history who did not know and use its volumes.

The series was founded at a time when the United States was undergoing an intense cultural upheaval. Victorian culture, once vigorous and bracing, had ossified and grown brittle; its certainties were being challenged, and its grip was loosening under the assault. This upheaval, as Henry F. May has shown, had been in progress since about 1912.[1] The ideas and tendencies that fueled it came largely from Europe: the important names in the alternative pantheon included writers like Samuel Butler, Henrik Ibsen, Friedrich Nietzsche, George Bernard Shaw, August Strindberg, Leo Tolstoy, and Oscar Wilde. One of the consequences of the upheaval was a considerable Europeanization of American intellectual life.

The Modern Library in its origins was inseparable from the revolt against Victorian culture. It was conceived by Albert Boni, a twenty-five-year-old Greenwich Village bookseller and occasional publisher. Boni was in the thick of the cultural upheaval. His

Gordon B. Neavill *is assistant professor of library service at the University of Alabama.*

Journal of Library History, Vol. 16, No. 2, Spring 1981
©1981 by the University of Texas Press   0022-2259/81/020241-13$01.40

Washington Square Bookshop was a favorite gathering place of Village artists and intellectuals. He was one of the founders of the Washington Square Players. As publisher of the *Glebe*, a little magazine edited by Alfred Kreymborg, he was already active in promoting translations of modern European writers (much to the dismay of Kreymborg, who was interested mainly in discovering and nurturing unknown Americans).[2] Young, Jewish, politically radical, in touch with new writing in Europe and culturally active at home, Boni embodied the European intellectual currents that were beginning to shake American culture. The Modern Library was a fully conscious attempt on his part to transmit these currents to the broader American audience.[3]

The name Modern Library was not chosen by chance. Nor was it an accident that the first title in the series was Oscar Wilde's *The Picture of Dorian Gray*. The books that followed were primarily by post-Victorian British and Continental writers. By 1925, five additional titles by Wilde had found their way into the Modern Library, along with four by Anatole France and three each by Gabriele D'Annunzio, Ibsen, Guy de Maupassant, and Nietzsche. Lord Dunsany, Gustave Flaubert, Walter Pater, Arthur Schnitzler, Strindberg, Tolstoy, Ivan Turgenev, and H. G. Wells had two titles each. There were few Americans in the early years. The only pre-nineteenth-century works were by authors like François Villon and Voltaire whom the modernists claimed as spiritual forebears. As a reprint series, the Modern Library did not introduce any of these works to American readers. What it did was to make them readily available to a large audience at a time when interest in such works was growing, at a price that anyone could afford.[4]

The Modern Library was published in its early years by the new firm of Boni and Liveright. Horace Liveright, who was to make his mark as one of the most important literary publishers of the 1920s, had no publishing experience when he and Boni became partners, and editorial decisions regarding the Modern Library were entirely in Boni's hands.[5] But Boni's connection with the series was short-lived. He and Liveright did not get along, and in the summer of 1918 they flipped a coin to see who would buy out the other. Boni left the firm. Liveright gradually added a few more contemporary American authors like Sherwood Anderson, Theodore Dreiser, and Eugene O'Neill, but in the main the Modern Library remained as Boni conceived it. Titles he had planned to include continued to be added. If anything, Liveright tended to neglect the Modern Library. He preferred publishing exciting new writers to the comparatively unglamorous business of reprint publishing. In 1925, when he needed money, he sold the Modern Library to a young Boni and Liveright vice president who, at the age of twenty-seven, wanted to go into business for himself. His name was Bennett Cerf.

Cerf, together with his friend and partner Donald S. Klopfer, established their firm, The Modern Library, Inc., in August 1925. Their original intention was to publish only the Modern Library. But they soon found that they had time and energy to spare, and in 1927 they started Random House as a subsidiary of the Modern Library to publish, at random, other books that interested them. Random House grew into one of the leading American trade publishers, and the Modern Library eventually became a subsidiary of its offspring.

Cerf and Klopfer set out to invigorate and expand the Modern Library. Poorer-selling titles were discontinued. By the end of the 1930s, only about one-third of the titles from the Boni and Liveright series remained in the Modern Library. At the same time they added new titles at a faster rate than they dropped them. But they did not merely increase the size of the Modern Library; they also altered its scope. Cerf and Klopfer added many more American authors. And, while they maintained a generally modern emphasis, they included older classics as well. In 1931 they launched the Modern Library Giants series. The Giants were larger in format than the compact volumes of the regular Modern Library. They allowed Cerf and Klopfer to include works like Tolstoy's *War and Peace*, Boswell's *Life of Johnson*, and Hugo's *Les Misérables*—books that belonged in the Modern Library but were too long for the regular format. The Giants sold initially for one dollar a copy, only five cents more than the regular volumes. They were an extraordinary bargain, ideally suited to the conditions of the Depression book trade, and they were an immediate success.

The Modern Library's cultural significance was not based on its being a mass-market operation. Modern Library books were not available at every crossroads. Drugstores and other mass-market outlets sold books before the beginning of the paperback revolution in 1939, but the books they sold tended to be popular hardcover reprints issued for this market by specialist reprint publishers like Grosset and Dunlap and Garden City Publishing Company. Cerf never thought that the Modern Library as a whole had much potential for this kind of mass-market sale. Nor did he believe it was geared to small-town markets.[6] There were occasional attempts to persuade Sears, Roebuck and Montgomery Ward to include Modern Library books in their mail-order catalogs, but when these attempts were successful, the sales achieved thereby were disappointing.[7]

The great bulk of the Modern Library's sales came through general bookstores, college stores, and the book departments of major department stores. Here the Modern Library was a staple. But book outlets of this sort did not darken the American landscape in great numbers. The bleak portrait of American bookselling that O. H. Cheney drew in his classic 1931 study of book industry economics remained essentially unchanged until the 1960s.[8] The problem was not merely the shortage of bookstores but the poor quality of most of those that did exist. According to Lewis Miller, the retired vice president and former sales manager of Random House, from the 1920s to the 1950s there were in the entire United States only about one hundred book outlets, including department stores, that met his working definition of a real bookstore: a place where *The Oxford Book of English Verse* would be stocked regularly.[9] Part of the Modern Library's significance lies in the fact that few bookstores, especially before the advent of "quality" paperbacks in the mid-1950s, offered much of intellectual substance other than the Modern Library.

Although the importance of distribution and sales cannot be underestimated, it is in the editorial arena that publishers' reputations are made. Most publishers exercise their chief influence on cultural and intellectual life by determining which manuscripts will be accepted for publication, by working with authors at the editorial stage, and by conceiving ideas for books that they then commission authors to write.[10] The role of the reprint publisher is different. Much of the reprinter's time is spent negotiating with other publishers. There is little contact with authors: commissioning a new introduction to an old book or working with an outside editor on a new anthology is about the extent of it. Yet the reprint publisher also has a capacity to influence cultural life. The reprinter's editorial decisions can affect how widely a work will be circulated. A reprint edition may save a work from going out of print. Sometimes a reprint can give a work overlooked in its original edition a new lease on life.

Alfred A. Knopf, though never primarily a reprint publisher, provides a classic example of the reprinter's influence. Knopf is largely responsible for the American reputation of W. H. Hudson's *Green Mansions* as a minor literary classic. When it was first published in the United States by G. P. Putnam's Sons in 1904 it was a resounding failure. But Knopf liked the book and believed in its stature and potential appeal. When he founded his own firm in

1915, he persuaded Hudson to allow him to reissue it. *Green Mansions* was resurrected in a handsome new format and with an enthusiastic introduction commissioned from John Galsworthy. Knopf did everything he could to promote the book, and this time it caught on.

The possibility of bringing similarly neglected works to the attention of a wider audience appealed to Cerf and Klopfer when they took over the Modern Library. The Modern Library seemed a perfect vehicle for doing this. As an established series of modern classics, stocked by most booksellers in its entirety and with a ready-made audience, any work they chose to include was assured of distribution and notice. One of the first works they tried to popularize was *The House with the Green Shutters* by George Douglas Brown. It was first published in 1901, shortly before its author's early death. A stark, powerful novel of life in a small Scottish town, written at a time when the prevailing view of Scottish common life was sentimental and romantic, it tells a story of meanness and greed, culminating in murder and suicide. Much of the dialogue is written in Scottish dialect. From the beginning it had a small but devoted cult following—a following its original publisher had helped to create by advertising it quietly but repeatedly as a story of limited appeal that only lovers of the best literature would appreciate.[11] Cerf and Klopfer were among its enthusiasts. Cerf considered it one of the best novels of the past thirty years and hoped that the Modern Library edition would greatly increase its popularity.[12] The Modern Library edition was published in April 1927 with a larger-than-average first printing of 8,000 copies. But *The House with the Green Shutters* failed to repeat the born-again popularity of *Green Mansions*. The first printing sold out slowly. Unwilling to give up, Cerf and Klopfer called for a second printing of 1,000 copies. But it still failed to catch on, and they reluctantly dropped it from the series.

Another of the works they tried to popularize was Evelyn Waugh's *Vile Bodies*, which was added to the Modern Library in 1933. Waugh's career was just beginning. *Vile Bodies*, originally published in 1930, was his second novel. When the Modern Library edition was announced, the Modern Library's most experienced salesman told Cerf and Klopfer that he didn't expect it would sell—and didn't expect they did, either.[13] It limped along in the series for seven and a half years until the decision to drop it could be put off no longer. Klopfer still recalls how they hated to let it go.[14]

In the case of John Dos Passos a very different pattern emerges.

In the late 1920s Dos Passos's agent offered the Modern Library reprint rights to *Manhattan Transfer* and *Three Soldiers*. Both offers were declined. In 1927, when *Manhattan Transfer* was offered, Cerf consulted several booksellers and found there was no public demand for it.[15] The following year, when he declined *Three Soldiers*, he explained that, while he personally liked the book, he did not think Dos Passos was quite worthy of the Modern Library.[16] Then Dos Passos's masterpiece, the *U.S.A.* trilogy, began to appear. It confirmed his reputation as a major American writer and greatly expanded his public. Less than a month after the publication of the second volume, Cerf wrote to Dos Passos's publisher about getting a Dos Passos novel for the Modern Library.[17] *Three Soldiers* was published in the Modern Library later that year; it remained in the series for thirty-seven years. In 1937 *The 42nd Parallel*, the first of the *U.S.A.* volumes, appeared in the Modern Library with a new introduction by the author. The entire trilogy came out as a Modern Library Giant in 1939. That edition remained in print for twenty-nine years.

After several failures akin to *The House with the Green Shutters* and *Vile Bodies*, Cerf and Klopfer concluded that the Modern Library was not an instrument that could be used to popularize deserving but little-known works. Thereafter, they generally followed the more cautious approach they used with Dos Passos and restricted themselves to adding titles for which they believed a substantial demand already existed.

Successes and failures of this sort suggest something, I think, about how the Modern Library's audience perceived the series. The series billed itself as "The Modern Library of the World's Best Books," and book buyers expected its contents to be generally acknowledged as belonging in that category. They were not looking for the latest avant-garde writings, or for outstanding books by new authors whose reputations were not yet established, or for sleepers that had been overlooked in the past. At the same time they were looking for something more than relatively ephemeral bestsellers. Popular novels like Edna Ferber's *Show Boat* and Charles Jackson's *The Lost Weekend*, though highly successful in their original editions, were failures in the Modern Library, perhaps because they were seen as not quite meriting inclusion in it. This does not mean, however, that successful titles were unremittingly highbrow. Among the top one hundred titles in terms of sales were such works as Pearl Buck's *The Good Earth* and Daphne Du Maurier's *Rebecca*. W. Somerset Maugham's *Of Human Bond-*

age, with an annual sale of around 10,000 to 12,000 copies, was for years the Modern Library's best-selling title.

Once poorer-selling titles began to be discontinued, the records of titles added to and dropped from the Modern Library provide a fascinating barometer of changing literary taste. Once-popular names like D'Annunzio, France, and Maurice Maeterlinck fade in the late 1920s and early 1930s, and authors like Ernest Hemingway, Aldous Huxley, and Thomas Mann take their place. In the mid- and late 1930s, Erskine Caldwell, James T. Farrell, Clifford Odets, and John Steinbeck enter the ranks. Also at this time are some surprising failures. F. Scott Fitzgerald's *The Great Gatsby* was published in the Modern Library in the fall of 1934. Fitzgerald was then identified almost completely as an author of the 1920s; there was little interest in him, it turned out, in the depths of the Depression. The Modern Library edition of *The Great Gatsby*, with sales of about 700 copies a year, was one of the poorest sellers in the series.[18] It was discontinued after five years, and a substantial portion of its first and only printing of 5,000 copies was remaindered.

It is necessary here to add a cautionary note: one should not assume anything about the popularity of added and dropped titles without knowing the circumstances involved. For example, Thomas Mann's *The Magic Mountain* and *Buddenbrooks* were added to the Modern Library in the 1930s and discontinued five years later. The reason was not that they were failures but because they sold so well that Knopf, who controlled the American rights, decided that it was not in his interest to let the Modern Library keep them, and he declined to renew the reprint contracts. (Cerf may have anticipated this possibility when the books were first included. The reprint agreement he drew up for *The Magic Mountain* did not limit the Modern Library's rights to any period of time; it was Knopf who inserted the customary five-year clause.)[19] Another title dropped at the end of its original five-year contract was Willa Cather's *Death Comes for the Archbishop*, published in the Modern Library in 1931. It was one of the most popular titles in the series. The advance sale had been the largest of any Modern Library title published up to that time.[20] But Cather decided she did not want any of her books in reprint editions, and it had to go.

Sometimes special circumstances accounted for flourishing sales of particular titles. Following Simon and Schuster's publication of Will Durant's enormously successful *The Story of Philosphy* in 1926, sales of the Modern Library's philosophy titles increased by

78 percent over the preceding year.[21] The Second World War produced a rise in book sales of all kinds, but books dealing with
human values seem to have been in special demand. Sales of poetry and philosophy titles in the Modern Library increased at a dis-
proportionate rate, and Cerf reported that the demand for these
titles was especially strong among men in the service.[22] (A similar
phenomenon was observed in Britain, where sales of poetry picked
up during both world wars.)[23] It was presumably also the uncer-
tainties of wartime that caused *Oracles of Nostradamus*, published
in the Modern Library in 1942, to become—to everyone's astonish-
ment—one of the best-selling titles in the series.

Titles discontinued because of poor sales did not always pass
from the Modern Library unlamented. When Stendhal's *The
Charterhouse of Parma* was dropped in 1943, the Modern Library
found itself the object of a storm of protest. There is a tendency,
because publishers deal in things of the spirit and intellect, to
assume that they should not sully their activities with considerations of the marketplace. But publishing is a business. Though
noncommercial motives enter into the decision making of serious
publishers to an amazing extent, it is ultimately on the economics
of profit and loss that a publisher's survival depends. *The Charterhouse of Parma* had been one of the Modern Library's poorest-
selling titles. In 1938, its second year in the series, it sold 307
copies; by 1942, when sales of all titles were booming, it crept up
to 1,083 copies.[24] Paper was scarce during the war, and publishers
felt compelled to allocate supplies to books that were most in demand. Moreover, Cerf and Klopfer had always assured the booksellers who stocked the Modern Library that its commercial via-
bility would be maintained by regular weeding of slow-selling
titles. Under these circumstances it is hard to see how retention of
The Charterhouse of Parma could have been justified. Yet when
the decision to drop it became known, intellectuals reacted as if
they had been betrayed.

The reaction was a measure of the importance of the Modern
Library in the lives of its most ardent audience. Young Americans
had cut their intellectual teeth on Modern Library books for a
quarter of a century. One thinks of Charlie Citrine, the protagonist
of Saul Bellow's *Humboldt's Gift*, wandering in the park as a
young man with his Modern Library books, talking incessantly
about them to his first love, remembered by his boyhood pals as
having had "the largest collection of Modern Library books on the
block."[25] It was readers like this who made the dropping of *The
Charterhouse of Parma* into something of a cause célèbre. An open

letter protesting the decision appeared in the *New Republic*.[26] The little magazine *Pharos*, in a special issue on Stendhal, charged that the publishers of the Modern Library had "committed [a] cultural outrage against their country."[27] James T. Farrell, writing in 1946 about the commercialization of publishing, asserted that a study of Modern Library titles added and dropped in recent years showed that its editors were "gradually watering down their stock."[28] And when Jason Epstein founded Anchor Books, the first "quality" paperback series, in 1953—a decade after the fact— he boldly staked a claim to the intellectual audience by making *The Charterhouse of Parma* his first title.[29] (It lasted twelve years in Anchor Books compared with six and a half in the Modern Library, but when the Anchor edition was dropped in the mid-1960s, no one noticed or cared. By then, the paperback revolution had so expanded the range and number of serious books in print that readers could choose from three other paperback editions. When the Modern Library edition was dropped, the only alternative was an expensive and little-known two-volume edition published by Liveright. *Books in Print* did not yet exist, and most observers assumed the demise of the Modern Library edition meant that *The Charterhouse of Parma* not only ceased to be widely available in the United States but was out of print altogether.)

A major trend of the past century that is reflected in the Modern Library is the increasing academization of American intellectual and cultural life. In 1875, as Arthur E. Bestor, Jr., has noted, "productive scholarship in the United States was not associated in any close or direct way with a career in college teaching."[30] With the founding of American universities on the German model, beginning with Johns Hopkins in 1876, the amateur scholar began to be displaced by the professional academic. By the mid-twentieth century, a person like Edmund Wilson or Lewis Mumford, who led an active and productive scholarly life without any academic connection, was an extreme rarity. At the same time a steady expansion of the university curriculum began. New academic disciplines emerged to study cultural and intellectual activities and other areas of human experience that previously had been carried on without academic scrutiny. American literature, for instance, first became a common subject of study in American colleges and universities in the 1920s. Contemporary literature was accepted into the curriculum even later. (The first course in contemporary fiction at an American university was offered by William Lyon Phelps at Yale as early as 1895/96; Phelps's superiors threatened him with dismissal if he repeated the course, and it was dropped.[31]

Since the Second World War, cultural life itself has been increasingly academized. University programs in creative writing, studio art, and music have drawn large numbers of practitioners in these areas into the university, and more and more of the creative artistic works of our culture are being produced within an academic setting. Younger critically recognized poets and, even more so, composers of contemporary serious music are becoming rare species outside the groves of academe.

These trends are reflected dramatically in the introductions to Modern Library books. In the Boni and Liveright period, nearly all of the introductions were by literary figures, journalists, reviewers, and the like—the sort of person best described by the generic term "man of letters." Only a handful were by academics, and these can usually be accounted for on nonacademic grounds. The chemist Benjamin Harrow, who edited and wrote the introduction to the Modern Library anthology *Contemporary Science* (1921), was married to a daughter of Liveright's cousin. Carl Van Doren, who prepared a collection of Thomas Paine's writings for the Modern Library in 1922, was both a well-known Columbia University professor and a man of letters, serving as literary editor of the *Nation* and, later, the *Century Magazine*. After Cerf and Klopfer took over the series, introductions by academics became more common, but they remained very much the exception. Cerf and Klopfer frequently asked living authors to write introductions to their own books. The majority of the other introductions continued to be by men of letters. Among these were such figures as J. Donald Adams, Brooks Atkinson, Ernest Boyd, Heywood Broun, Henry Seidel Canby, Christopher Morley, George Jean Nathan, and Ben Ray Redman. The academization of the Modern Library began after the Second World War, when the burgeoning college market caused Modern Library books to appear more and more in academic dress. Modern Library College Editions, a paperbound series intended for classroom use, began in 1950. Older introductions were gradually discarded in favor of new introductions commissioned from and directed toward the academic community. Several titles, including Hardy's *Tess of the D'Urbervilles* and Thackeray's *Vanity Fair*, were reset to bring their texts up to acceptable standards. Authors of most Modern Library introductions in the 1950s and early 1960s were highly regarded academics such as Walter Jackson Bate, Cleanth Brooks, Douglas Bush, Northrop Frye, Moses Hadas, Gertrude Himmelfarb, Hajo Holborn, Ricardo Quintana, and Gordon N. Ray.

The Modern Library came under increasing competition from

paperbacks in the 1960s, and in 1970 a decision was made to stop adding new titles to the series. Thereafter, many of the less profitable titles were remaindered or allowed to go out of print. By the mid-1970s, the series had shrunk from 498 titles to fewer than 140. Then, as the prices of both paperback and hardbound books escalated, Random House began to hope that there might again be a market for comparatively inexpensive hardbound editions of classics. In the spring of 1977 thirty-two Modern Library titles were reissued in newly designed jackets and bindings. Each publishing season since has seen a substantial increase in the number of Modern Library reissues in print.

Notes

1. Henry F. May, *The End of American Innocence: A Study of the First Years of Our Own Time, 1912-1917* (New York: Knopf, 1959).
2. Alfred Kreymborg, *Troubadour: An Autobiography* (New York: Boni and Liveright, 1925), p. 211.
3. Albert Boni, interview with J. C. Furnas, 24 February 1971 (notes of interview provided by Furnas).
4. Modern Library books sold initially for 60 cents a copy. Wartime inflation drove up the price to 95 cents by 1920, but that price remained in effect until after the Second World War. When the last new title was added in 1970, Modern Library books were selling for $2.95.
5. Manuel Komroff, "The Liveright Story," p. 35, Komroff papers, Columbia University.
6. Cerf to James L. Crowder, 9 October 1930; Cerf to Robert deGraff, 20 November 1933, Random House archives, Columbia University.
7. James L. Crowder to Cerf, 2 September 1930; Crowder to Cerf, 24 August 1934; Crowder to Cerf, 8 March 1939, Random House archives, Columbia University.
8. O. H. Cheney, *Economic Survey of the Book Industry, 1930-1931: Final Report* (New York: National Association of Book Publishers, 1931).
9. Lewis Miller, interview, 13 June 1978.
10. See Gordon B. Neavill, "Role of the Publisher in the Dissemination of Knowledge," *Annals of the American Academy of Political and Social Science* 421 (September 1975): 23-33.
11. Algernon Tassin, "The Story of Modern Book Advertising," *Bookman* 33 (June 1911): 413.
12. Cerf to Heywood Broun, 26 October 1926, Random House archives, Columbia University.
13. James L. Crowder to Cerf [1933], Random House archives, Columbia University.
14. Donald S. Klopfer, interview, 1 June 1977.
15. Cerf to Bernice Baumgarten (Brandt and Brandt), 25 May 1927, Random House archives, Columbia University.
16. Cerf to Baumgarten, 7 March 1928, Random House archives, Columbia University.

17. Cerf to Robert deGraff (Doubleday, Doran), 9 April 1932, Random House archives, Columbia University.

18. Cerf to Whitney Darrow (Scribner's), 31 January 1940, Random House archives, Columbia University; Donald S. Klopfer, interview, 5 July 1978.

19. Alfred A. Knopf, Inc., to Cerf, 14 May 1931, Random House archives, Columbia University.

20. Cerf to Hugh S. Eayrs (Macmillan Co. of Canada), 2 September 1931, Random House archives, Columbia University.

21. Cerf to Richard Simon, 19 October 1926, Random House archives, Columbia University.

22. "Of Men and Books: Critic John T. Frederick, Guest Bennett Cerf, in a Radio Conversation over the Columbia Broadcasting System," *Northwestern University on the Air* vol. 2, no. 16 (16 January 1943): 4.

23. Mass Observation typescript report no. 46, "Book Reading in Wartime," p. 10; cited in Angus Calder, *The People's War: Britain 1939–1945* (New York: Pantheon Books, 1969), pp. 516–517.

24. Cerf, letter, *New Republic* 109 (29 November 1943): 747.

25. Saul Bellow, *Humboldt's Gift* (New York: Viking Press, 1975), pp. 76, 398.

26. George Mayberry, "An Open Letter: The Modern Library, Inc., New York City," *New Republic* 109 (8 November 1943): 661.

27. *Pharos*, no. 3 (Winter 1945): 71.

28. James T. Farrell, "Will the Commercialization of Publishing Destroy Good Writing? Some Observations on the Future of Books," *New Directions* 9 (1946): 13.

29. Jason Epstein, interview, 19 June 1978.

30. Arthur E. Bestor, Jr., "The Transformation of American Scholarship, 1875–1917," *Library Quarterly* 23 (July 1953): 166. See also Edward Shils, "The Order of Learning in the United States: The Ascendancy of the University," in Alexandra Oleson and John Voss (eds.), *The Organization of Knowledge in Modern America, 1860–1920* (Baltimore: Johns Hopkins University Press, 1979), pp. 17–47.

31. René Wellek, "Literary Scholarship," in Merle Curti (ed.), *American Scholarship in the Twentieth Century* (Cambridge, Mass.: Harvard University Press, 1953), p. 117.

Gathering Enemy Scientific Information in Wartime: The OSS and the Periodical Republication Program

Pamela Spence Richards

The existence and the necessity of the international flow of scientific information has become a commonplace to us. This study, however, focuses on a period when that flow was disrupted, namely World War II. During that conflict, American awareness of the importance of the exact sciences for winning the war elevated the gathering and distribution of scientific information to a matter of high national priority. The story of how an emergency information supply system was set up by this country between 1939 and 1945 to replace nonfunctioning book trade channels is a story with all the suspense of a cloak-and-dagger spy novel, but its importance stretches far beyond the anecdotal. From it we can learn how the foundations were laid for the nation's postwar intelligence collection and library acquisitions policies, and we can also document changing perceptions of the function of libraries—from depositories to active agents—in the organization of information.

To understand the gravity of the information crisis faced by the United States during World War II, it is necessary to understand, first, the importance of Germany as a producer of scientific research, and, second, the collapse of the international book trade in the first few years of the war. Since the nineteenth century, German universities had been centers of the most advanced research in all fields of learning. Of the $1.5 million a year the United States was spending for foreign books and journals in 1939, most was spent for German publications.[1] Immediately

Pamela Spence Richards *is assistant professor of library and information studies at Rutgers University.*

Journal of Library History, Vol. 16, No. 2, Spring 1981
© 1981 by the University of Texas Press   0022-2259/81/020253-13$01.40

upon the outbreak of war in September 1939, American librarians took steps to ensure the continuation of imports. During World War I, the ALA's Importation Service, operating under the Department of State and the War Trade and Censorship Boards, had secured scientific periodicals published in Germany and Austria. There was, thus, a precedent for several of our national library associations to establish the Joint Committee on Importations in October 1939. Fear of losing touch with German science was great: Ralph Munn, president of the ALA, wrote to Secretary of State Cordell Hull: "Germany has made, and is making, many contributions to man's knowledge. . . . The world of scholarship can not afford to be deprived of the German contribution to this knowledge."[2]

Initially chaired by Harry Lydenberg of the New York Public Library, and, after August 1941, by Thomas Fleming of the Columbia Medical School Library, the Joint Committee was at first successful in accomplishing its goal of expediting the receipt of multiple copies of key foreign scientific periodicals and allocating them to industries, research organizations, and libraries. With America neutral, it was not initially difficult to buy the belligerents' publications either from Germany or through agents in another neutral country such as Switzerland. Even the embargo on all German exports announced by the British on 26 November 1939 had little immediate effect on receipts. Although there was great anxiety among U.S. librarians about the British insistence on checking cargoes of German origin at control points like Gibraltar, Bermuda, or Trinidad, and indignation at the demand that a list of German subscriptions be submitted to His Majesty's Government for approval, nonetheless, the supply continued. In the beginning of 1940, the bigger libraries were placing orders as they did before the war, and Fleming wrote in April of that year that "the British have been confiscating no publications sent to American libraries, and that is about all there is to the situation."[3]

The German invasion of the Low Countries in May 1940 ended this period of deceptive normalcy. Not only was the number of neutral countries through which Americans could deal drastically reduced, but the intensified submarine warfare in the North Atlantic increasingly endangered shipping of all kinds. For a while the Committee advised its member libraries to have their orders stored on the Continent, but British area bombing soon made this an unwise alternative. Before Germany's invasion of Russia in June 1941, German publications were successfully shipped via Siberia, but after this route closed, the Committee despaired of any dependable flow. Even had a safe passage been found, importing German publications had by that time become impossible because of the question of payments. By mid-1941 the State Department was forbidding Americans to transfer any money to Germany or to German-occupied territory. Since German publishers were prohibited from exporting materials for which payment had not already been received, the import of European materials by conventional means seemed to be coming to an end six months before the United States entered the war.

During the year following Pearl Harbor there were two separate organizations involved in keeping America supplied with the fruits of European scholarship. In 1942 the activities of Fleming's library-sponsored Joint Committee were in some respects duplicated by the federal government's Interdepartmental Committee for the Acquisition of Foreign Publications (IDC), operated by the now-legendary Office of Strategic Services (OSS). During 1942, while the Joint Committee was authorized by the State Department to spend a quarter of a million dollars to acquire, as best it could, multiple copies of foreign periodicals, the IDC was also collecting foreign journals overseas in order to reproduce them on microfilm and distribute them to government agencies. One of these agencies was the Library of Congress, which sent out copies of the film on request. This dual system of acquisition was inefficient for various reasons: the multiple copies purchased by the Joint Committee were extremely difficult to transport across the torpedo-infested North Atlantic, and, furthermore, the government's 1942 Importations Plan severely limited the number of libraries permitted to subscribe to the enemy periodicals. The IDC-supplied microfilm, on the other hand, while technically available in unlimited copies from the Library of Congress, was cumbersome to use in laboratories.

It was at this point, in late 1942, that a group of prominent librarians and educators urged the Office of the Alien Property Custodian to seize the copyrights of the leading European periodicals and to reprint and distribute them, both in order to prevent large amounts of money from being spent abroad for duplicate copies and to ensure that the journals would be widely disseminated for use in the American war effort. The Office of the Alien Property Custodian (APC) was no stranger to this type of activity. Originally set up in 1917 to seize and administer enemy properties in the United States, the APC operated as part of the Justice Department after 1934, but was recreated as an independent agency by President Roosevelt on 21 April 1942. Immediately thereafter the Custodian (first Leo T. Crowley, and after March 1944 James E. Markham) began seizing and licensing for American publication all enemy-produced items that were normally copyrighted, including books, musical compositions, and movies (the first copyright so seized was that of *Mein Kampf*). The sole criterion for licensing —under which arrangement the Custodian received the royalties normally accruing to the holder of the copyright—was that the republication be in the public interest. After October 1942 the APC was aided in its decisions by the Advisory Committee on the Republication Program, consisting of, among others, Thomas Fleming, Keyes Metcalf (president of ALA), Luther Evans (assistant librarian of Congress), and Paul North Rice (executive secretary of the Association of Research Libraries).

It was essentially the republication, under the APC's license, of the forty-nine volume "Bible" of organic chemistry, Beilstein's *Handbuch der Organischen Chemie*, that inspired the idea of a republication program for periodicals. Published by Edward Brothers, of Ann Arbor, Michigan, at a list price of only $400 (compared to a prewar price of $2,000), the reprinted *Handbuch* struck readers with the quality of its reproduction and led to the question "If books, why not periodicals?" This thought was passed on to the Advisory Committee, which immediately urged the APC to undertake a periodical republication program. In its barest outline, the program called for the selection, with the help of the Advisory Committee, of a list of periodicals to be reprinted, and the acquisition abroad of a single copy of each desired issue by the OSS's Interdepartmental Committee, headed by Frederic G. Kilgour. The reprinting itself was done by photo-offset under contract with Edwards Brothers, which, among eleven bidders, had submitted the most attractive terms to the APC. The APC took care of sending out the announcement of available material, but the reprinted journals themselves were distributed by three established periodical subscription agencies. Clearly, this was a more efficient system than that of the old Joint Committee on Importations. Subscription prices (which ultimately ran about one-quarter of the original) were determined by demand, and there was no limit imposed on the number of subscribers, advantages that Fleming stressed when announcing the APC program to the libraries that had hitherto acquired imported material through his group.[4]

Thus, the mechanics of the operation were established by the early months of 1943. But what was the nature of the journals reprinted, and who ordered them, and why? Of the 116 separate European journals made available, 16 were French, 3 were Dutch,

and 1 was Belgian; the remainder were published in Germany and
Austria. These periodicals covered almost every phase of scientific
development of interest to a nation at war, including acoustics,
aviation, biochemistry, electronics, engineering, enzymology, ex-
plosives, mathematics, pathology, petroleum, plastics, rubber, and
virus research. An analysis done by the APC at the end of the war
indicated that 94 percent of the subscribers used the reprints for
war purposes. That group broke down as follows: 48 percent were
industrial concerns; 33 percent were scientific institutions, universities, or research organizations; 8 percent were U.S. government
agencies; and 5 percent were industries, research institutions, or
government agencies within the British Empire. The remaining 6
percent, who presumably used the journals for nonstrategic purposes, included 8 subscribers from the British Empire, 2 in Hawaii,
and 38 biological, public, and hospital libraries in the United
States. The over 900 subscribers included 36 from Canada, 8 from
Australia, 12 from England, 1 from South Africa, and 1 from New
Zealand.[5]

An adequate history of the APC's periodical republication program has never been written. Two short articles appeared at the
end of the war,[6] and Carol Nemeyer, in her excellent book on
Scholarly Reprint Publishing in the United States (New York:
Bowker, 1972), gives considerable attention to the pioneering
reprint aspects of the program. But the files of the IDC were classified until 1975/76, and those of the APC remain in the possession
of the Justice Department, so these earlier accounts are necessarily
fragmented and incomplete. The publication in 1975 of Kermit
Roosevelt's declassified *War Report of the OSS* began to shed a
little light on the matter, but the whole story of the program as it
emerges from the newly available records is yet to be told. This
paper will limit itself to reconstructing the methods whereby the
original materials were acquired for reprint. For this account the
author is indebted not only to the records of the OSS, now in the
Modern Military Branch of the National Archives, but also to
those individuals involved in the work of the IDC, most particularly its chief, Frederick G. Kilgour, now president of OCLC in
Columbus, Ohio.

The IDC had been set up in 1941 under the Office of the Coor-
dinator of Information, William Donovan, and was orginally
chaired by historian William Langer of Harvard. It was Langer who
had convinced Donovan of the importance of foreign publications
for strategic planning, and when Donovan's operation was reformed as the OSS, reporting to the Joint Chiefs of Staff, the IDC

went with it. The task of the IDC was to keep U.S. government agencies supplied with the foreign publications they needed, whatever the publication's origin. There was a considerable amount of jostling for attention among the different agencies represented on the Committee, all of whom felt their needs should have priority. There was, indeed, so much rivalry between the departments that, when Langer resigned as chairman in 1942, agreement could not be reached as to his successor, and Frederick Kilgour, the twenty-eight-year-old executive secretary of the IDC, gradually evolved into its chief.

Kilgour had left his job at Harvard Library to work for Langer's Washington-based IDC in March 1942. At Harvard, from which he had graduated as a chemistry major in 1935, he had been in charge of Keyes Metcalf's pioneering project of microfilming selected foreign newspapers, and it was this expertise that commended him to Langer. With a staff of 7, which would grow to 150, Kilgour took over the job of juggling departmental intelligence priorities, dispatching orders to agents in the field, recording receipts, abstracting and translating material when necessary, and forwarding material to the appropriate agency. Most of the actual microfilming was done in the field.

The collection mandate of the IDC was from its inception much broader than that of Fleming's Joint Committee, and included not only conventional periodical publications, but also Orientalia and all kinds of strategically important ephemera. German timetables, for example, were ordered by the Air Force, so that fighter planes accompanying B-17 bomber missions could fan out after the raid's completion and hit matériel-laden trains. Even the smallest local German newspapers were important, since total enemy casualty figures could be derived from the number of death notices inserted by the families of deceased officers.

The quality of the material received by the IDC in Washington depended, of course, not only on the orders sent out, but increasingly on the abilities of the field agents to fill or supplement them. These men and women, many of them drawn from academe and the book world, were stationed on the periphery of the Axis-controlled territories: Stockholm, Lisbon, Istanbul, Cairo, and Chungking were the principal cities of activity (the IDC could make little use of cautious, landlocked Switzerland). Orders from Kilgour's office were generally sent via diplomatic pouch to the American consulates in those cities, picked up by the IDC's agents, and filled as local conditions permitted.

In those neutral countries with postal connection with the Axis, the simplest method for obtaining enemy scientific periodicals was subscription. In Stockholm and Lisbon, for example, American operatives entered hundreds of subscriptions to strategically important journals, filmed them on the spot, and sent them by diplomatic pouch to Washington. Sometimes the agents used the names of cooperative locals, but this was not usually deemed necessary. Sweden had the best communications with Germany throughout the war, and Stockholm became the center of European periodical activity (the IDC collected Orientalia for intelligence purposes, but no Asian journals were reprinted). Although the American planes carrying the microfilm had to fly over German-controlled Norway, that country's coastline was too long to control effectively and, as Kilgour recollects, the IDC never lost a shipment.

The efficiency of the subscription system depended, of course, on the willingness of the publishers to keep filling the subscriptions. This, in turn, depended to a great extent on the ability of both the IDC and the Alien Property Custodian to keep the project's strategic importance from the enemy. Nazi policy worked very much in the Allies' favor. It is clear from the nature and quality of the materials printed that throughout the war the German government continued, and in some cases even intensified, its peacetime policy of encouraging publication of scientific information. The advantages of this kind of dissemination as a means of expanding scientific frontiers within Germany and territory occupied by the German government seem to have been considered to outweigh the possibility that such information would become available to the enemies of the Reich.[7]

The American government did its best to limit public awareness of the program at home so that German intelligence would not be alerted to its value. All seven of the circulars sent out by the APC announcing available reprinted periodicals bore the warning: "NOT FOR PUBLICATION! If any publicity is given, it will mean the cessation of the supply of copy and total failure of the enterprise." In fact, the APC only disclosed at the end of the war that it had gotten all of its original copy from the OSS.

Great efforts were also made overseas to protect the "clean" status of the subscriptions. There were instances, for example, when people in the German publishing houses, thinking to aid the Allied cause, began inserting messages in the Swedish-bound periodicals; but the IDC studiously avoided clandestine relations with behind-the-lines publishers, which might have jeopardized the subscriptions. While it is hard to believe that an intelligence machinery as efficient as that of the Germans was unaware of the strategically important reprint program, all the evidence gathered so far seems to indicate that the measures taken to keep it secret were fairly successful. Perhaps future research in the archives of German publishers will yield more information, but so far, evidence of only one instance of German suspicion has been found: apparently, Nazi officials in occupied France asked Portuguese authorities for a list of individuals in Portugal receiving German periodicals, and, although the list finally supplied contained only the names of Portuguese "users," the incident did slow up the IDC's receipt of copy via Lisbon for a short while.[8]

When the Nazis focused their attention on the journals that were destined for reprint, German prestige rather than destination seemed to be their main interest. There is, for example, a long and querulous correspondence between the Nazi-controlled Dutch Department of Cultural Protection (*Kultuurbescherming*) and the editors of Nijhoff's *Physica* concerning the "disappointingly" small proportion of German-language text contained in the wartime issues; it was suggested menacingly that, precisely because of the journal's international orientation, the number of English, Dutch, and French articles be kept to a modest level, and that German summaries be affixed to all articles.[9] The subscription lists, however, were never asked for, and none of the periodical publishers interviewed later recollected having had any problems from the German authorities about subscriptions to Sweden. Nor did any of the publishers interviewed remember having had any awareness during the war that their journals were being collected by the OSS in Stockholm and reprinted, although many of them learned of the program later.

Although the subscription method worked well, the progress of the war made constant adaptations necessary. German publishing proceeded fairly normally during the first four years of conflict, but the air raid of 3 December 1943, when the RAF dropped 1,500 tons of bombs within twenty-five minutes on the center of Leipzig, destroyed the plants of 90 percent of the "book city's" publishers, paper manufacturers, and type founders. By October 1944, Germany was publishing only about 500 periodicals, little more than 10 percent of its prewar production. Air raids, and the shortages of paper, lead, and electricity, had forced the German government to limit publication, either by merger or suspension, to journals regarded as absolutely vital for information.

Not only did the lack of available copy become a problem for the IDC, but the advance of Allied troops after D-Day meant that

some of the reprinted journals were no longer being published behind enemy lines. As the liberation of France and the Low Countries progressed, the Alien Property Custodian's policy had to be
revised. At this time the APC decided not to include in the republication program any volumes of periodicals whose first numbers
were originally issued in those countries after the date of liberation. The 1945 active list was therefore limited to German and
Austrian periodicals; however, by May 1945, no copy of 1945
German journals had been received, and Eugene Tilleux, the head
of the APC's Copyright Administration, speculated that all the
periodicals in the program had been bombed out of existence, and
that "the upper time limit for their republication [had] already
been established by the action of B-17's . . . "[10]

Having now reviewed the background and implementation of
the OSS's work in collecting periodicals and the Alien Property
Custodian's republication program, do we have any evidence that
this tremendous effort made any tangible contribution to winning
the war? It was, of course, unreasonable to expect that the enemy
journals would contain exact specifications for the latest radars or
of such weapons as the V-1 or V-2. Some of the German articles
did, however, contain material of surprising practical value: certain
war issues of the *VDI Zeitschrift*, for example, which covered engineering problems encountered in the construction of German
camps, were utilized directly by our own army engineers. More
frequently, though, the enemy publications served to reveal the
trend of German research, and sometimes presented basic facts
that confirmed previously held theories, thus saving Allied scientists months of painstaking investigation.

Unquestionably the most important strategic contribution of
the program concerned the development of the atomic bomb. The
nuclear program of the Germans, who had first split the uranium
atom at the Kaiser Wilhelm Institute in Berlin in 1938, was way
ahead of that of the Allies. Niels Bohr, the Danish physicist who
in 1943 escaped to England, reported that in October 1941 the
head of the German nuclear laboratory visited him in Copenhagen
and implied strongly that the Nazis were already working on an
atomic bomb. R. V. Jones, wartime scientific advisor to Britain's
MI 6, reported later that his department "had the impression that
the Germans had originally been thinking of a bomb, but had decided that it would not be practicable inside the time span of the
war, since in 1942 they allowed a number of relevant papers to be
published on nuclear work done in the previous two years, which
seemed to have been kept secret while they decided whether to go

for the bomb or not."[11] The articles to which Jones referred, written by Otto Hahn and his associates at the Kaiser Wilhelm Institute and giving detailed descriptions of atomic fission experiments and Uranium 238, consisted of eight papers in the 1942 and 1943 issues of *Zeitschrift für Physik* and three papers in the 1943 issues of *Die Naturwissenschaften*, all of which were reprinted by the APC. So urgently were these articles awaited by atomic scientists working on the Manhattan Project that Thomas Fleming recalls having specific orders to telephone a certain number as soon as his New York unit of the reprint program received microfilm from the IDC, and to announce that "I have received a package." Within five minutes a taxi would draw up outside, and a mysterious "Dr. Cohen" would emerge, have the film copied, and disappear with it, presumably back to the Manhattan Project's laboratories at Columbia University.

The importance of the articles was acknowledged in a statement issued in 1945 by the Atomic Scientists of Chicago that if Hitler had prevented the publication of the first papers on atomic fission, Germany might have remained for a certain period of time in exclusive possession of some fundamental secrets of atomic power.[12] E. J. Crane, wartime editor of *Chemical Abstracts*, told the APC that there was not the least doubt in his mind that "your republication program was one of the factors which made the atomic bomb possible." In a similar vein, Iowa State University, which had received an "E" for its research on the atomic bomb, wrote the APC that "the men working on the splitting of the atom used, to a considerable extent, the periodicals which you have reprinted."[13]

This heightened national awareness of the strategic importance of current published information was to affect both the perception of and the planning for American research libraries in the postwar decades. Before World War II, intelligence gathering was done by military attachés at consulates, and political intelligence was sent through diplomatic dispatches. It had little if anything to do with libraries. Archibald MacLeish initially rejected as inappropriate the idea of basing the IDC at the Library of Congress, but by the end of 1942 he was lobbying—in vain—to transfer Kilgour's unit to his own department.[14] MacLeish's *volte-face* typified the sudden recognition that was taking place of the important role of libraries in the prosecution of the war and of the peace to follow. At the same time, anxiety was spreading about the serious lacunae in the nation's collection of publications pertaining to foreign countries. It was clear to the intelligence community and to many librarians that the lack of European city plans—we lacked many—and the absence of navigational charts of foreign waters had cost the lives of many American soldiers. It was also clear from the material gathered by Kilgour's unit that most of the foreign information vital to the nation's security was available in published form, if only the proper mechanism was set up to gather it. (It became one of the axioms of Sherman Kent's classic 1951 *Strategic Intelligence for American World Policy* that 90 percent of the sources used in constructing such intelligence are "open" —that is, published—and can be acquired by conventional means.)

It is against this background that one must understand the sense of urgency with which the Americans' Cooperative Acquisitions Project combed the rubble of Europe from 1945 to 1948 looking for research materials published during the war, and the aggressiveness with which the Project's members—many of whom had been transferred from the IDC—wrestled large stockpiles of German books and periodicals out of Russian-held Leipzig. With the intensification of the Cold War, the same high priority was given to the Farmington Plan, which in 1948 began its global collection project to assure that there would be in this country at least one copy of every foreign publication of importance to research. The State Department even began assigning Publications Procurement Officers to strategic areas to safeguard the flow. Because of the success of the IDC in collecting, and that of the republication program in disseminating, vital scientific information, the nation's great research libraries had passed in four tumultuous years from the status of "cultural treasures" to that of "national defense priorities." On the value scale of twentieth-century America, this shift must be interpreted as an enormous advance.

Notes

1. U.S. Office of Alien Property Custodian, "Report to the President on the Periodical Republication Program," mimeographed, Washington, 1945.

2. Ralph Munn to Cordell Hull, 2 April 1940, copy lent to author by Thomas Fleming.

3. Thomas Fleming to Eileen Cunningham, 4 April 1940, copy lent by Fleming.

4. Joint Committee on Importations, "Announcement Number Seven," mimeographed, 26 May 1943.

5. APC, "Report to the President."

6. See William F. Jacob, "When Books Are Boomerangs," *Library Journal* 71, no. 3 (1 February 1946): 169; and Eugene A. Tilleux, "Periodical Republication Program of the Office of Alien Property Custodian," *D.C. Libraries* 17 (January 1946): 11–13.

7. APC, "Report to the President."

8. Notes of Edward Chapman, former chief of the APC's Copyright Administration, in possession of author.

9. Departement van Opvoeding, Wetenschap en Kultuurbescherming to N. V. Martinus Nijhoff's Boekhandel en Uitg. Mij., 5 August 1944, Archives of Martinus Nijhoff Publishing Company, The Hague.

10. U.S. Office of Alien Property Custodian, "Withdrawal by the Custodian from the Periodical Republication Program," typewritten, Washington, 25 May 1945.

11. R. V. Jones, *The Wizard War: British Scientific Intelligence, 1939–1945* (New York: Coward, McCann and Geoghegan, 1978), p. 472.

12. David L. Hill, Eugene Rabinowitch, John A. Simpson, Jr., "The Atomic Scientists Speak Up: Nuclear Physicists Say There Is No Secrecy in Atom Bomb and No Defense against It," *Life* 19, no. 18 (29 October 1945): 45.

13. APC, "Report to the President."

14. Interview with Frederick G. Kilgour, Columbus, Ohio, 31 May 1979.

Efficiency, Taylorism, and Libraries in Progressive America

Marion Casey

The same intense sense of urgency that surrounded the word "energy" in the late 1970s was felt in connection with the word "efficiency" in the late nineteenth and early twentieth centuries. Efficiency was a serious word to progressives. It was one of the most important and frequently expressed concepts, whether the person articulating the thought was a president or common citizen, a liberal or conservative, an engineer or librarian. The time had come—indeed, it might be too late—for putting into order the chaos resulting from the technological/industrial revolution. The urgency cut across all lines. No one doubts the presidential devotion to efficiency on the part of Theodore Roosevelt and Woodrow Wilson, but even William Howard Taft, with a reputation for conservatism (perhaps overplayed), in 1909 called for a Commission on Efficiency and Economy to survey governmental bureaucracy, review the budget, and propose changes. Everyone seemed to know, even before philosopher Alfred North Whitehead pointed to the fact, that technological development was what distinguished the nineteenth century from the previous centuries.[1] People who had lived through it did not need to be told. They sensed that time was running out for improving society. There was a frenzy to organize (the formation of the American Library Association is one example), to order society efficiently, to put matters on a scientific basis. The trend even affected personal life. The book *How to Live on 24 Hours a Day*, a work on "scientific dressmaking," and

Marion Casey *is visiting assistant professor of library and information studies at the University of California, Berkeley.*

Journal of Library History, Vol. 16, No. 2, Spring 1981
©1981 by the University of Texas Press   0022-2259/81/020265-16$01.55

an article on how to apply efficiency tests to a church were found in popular literature.[2] There was even a favorite philosopher of the movement, William James, who was lauded for his condemnation of time-wasting in his oft-quoted essay "The Energies of Man." Erroneously, the publication of Frederick W. Taylor's *Principles of Scientific Management* in 1911 is often cited as the beginning of the efficiency craze, but contemporary sources indicate the movement was in full force by then. His ideas and others like them had been public knowledge for a decade or more. Even Taylor admitted his scientific management ideas were but part of a larger efficiency movement. In his preface he chides the reader for not heeding Roosevelt's call for efficiency in 1908 when the president not only urged conservation of water and forestry resources but also called for national efficiency in all areas. Taylor reiterated the president's message and hoped that interest in T. R.'s complete message could be reawakened by applying Taylor's *Principles* "with equal force to all social activities: to the management of our homes; . . . of our farms; . . . of the business of our tradesmen, large and small; of our churches; our philanthropic institutions, our universities, and our government departments." Taylor's message in the *Principles* was that in all aspects of life a scientific approach was far superior than proceeding by "rule of thumb" habit.[3]

People as diverse as Roosevelt, Wilson, Taft, John Dewey, Walter Rauschenbusch, Charles Beard, Jane Addams, Lincoln Steffens, Herbert Hoover, Louis Brandeis, and William Allen White were attracted to anything utilitarian, efficient, or orderly in their respective fields. Two library leaders, the subject of this paper, were no less and at times even more caught up in the movement: Melvil Dewey (1851-1931), revitalizer and acknowledged leader of the public library movement from the 1870s to the first years of the new century, a predecessor of Taylor in his ideas of efficient management, and Charles McCarthy (1873-1921), organizer of the movement for legislative libraries from 1901 to 1921, whose accomplishments run parallel to and gain support from Taylor's ideas. Their two types of libraries are the most representative forms of new library development in the 1876 to 1920 period. In studying the two librarians in their drive for efficiency we are fortunate to witness a blurring of lines between library history and social/economic/political history.

Public libraries needed efficiency when Dewey was formulating his ideas. In that delightful utopian novel of the 1880s *Looking Backward* author Edward Bellamy says in one of the few footnotes in the book how much improved libraries would be in the coming century. The hero in the story, who experienced the 1880s and also the 1980s, digressed, "I cannot sufficiently celebrate the glorious liberty that reigns in the public libraries of the twentieth century as compared with the intolerable management of those of the nineteenth century, in which the books were jealously railed away from the people, and obtainable only at an expenditure of time and red tape calculated to discourage any ordinary taste for literature."[4] It was Dewey's hope that, with applied efficiency measures, one hundred years would not elapse before formation of a better public library system. Other progressives shared the same optimism and *Looking Backward* gave them hope, not for the extremes of socialism detailed in the novel, but at least for a more orderly future. No one wanted to wait one hundred years. It was the intolerable library mismanagement Bellamy detailed in the 1880s that Dewey wanted to correct. Simplified spelling and abbreviation, conversion to the metric system, use of short-hand, a classification system, a well-planned curriculum for library schools, the formation of the ALA, and the establishment of the *Library Journal* were all manifestations of his scheme for ratio-nality. Even when he went into private business he produced stan-dardized materials, cards (7.5 x 12.5 cm), and record forms. He was truly a pioneer in organization twenty years before Taylor's ideas were popularized. In fact there was evidence that Taylor's colleagues, perhaps Taylor himself, were impressed enough by Dewey's library classification system to model industrial classi-fication systems on Dewey's.[5]

Even the preliminary call for a library conference in 1876 issued and signed by Dewey and twenty-seven others declared that the group summoned the session "believing that efficiency and econ-omy in library work would be promoted by a conference."[6] Thus began the American Library Association. Many of his early clashes with ALA members for the next twenty years revolved around Dewey's insistence on exact measurements, decimals, and scien-tific approaches to library procedures. Scholars such as historian Justin Winsor, ALA president for its first nine years (1876–1885), and William Frederick Poole of the Chicago Public Library and the Newberry Library, and second ALA president, were hesitant about the innovative businesslike approach. Poole feared that what a li-brarian lacked "in scholastic style, he [would] make up in sugges-tive helpful devices."[7] This could lead to librarians devoid of scholarship though expert in scientific management of their libraries. Therefore, Poole and other ALA leaders hedged on whole-sale approval.[8]

Dewey's own writings indicate an interest in efficiency from the time he designed his classification system in 1873. Long before Taylor, the Midvale engineer, was prominent, Dewey had respect for an engineer's approach to problems. When critic William I. Fletcher of the Amherst College Library brought what he called "the workship of decimals" into question as early as 1889, Dewey answered that engineers commonly use decimals as well as the metric system, and Dewey evidently thought knowledge of this fact should suffice. Dewey scoffed at those conservatives who thought another "French revolution lurks behind all use of the mighty labor-saving decimals."[9] The respect for the work of engineers and the interest in labor-saving devices antedated Taylor's activity. Dewey did not have to wait until the mechanical engineer began popularizing his theories in the 1890s, but once Taylor's works became known, Dewey was even more convinced of his own beliefs.

Dewey in reviewing late nineteenth century history declared that since 1876, America owed its prosperity to having "adopted standard sizes for machinery parts and other labor saving methods and devices," a direct reference to scientific management. Dewey said that since this "marvelous development" was recognized, labor-saving devices were valued highly for factory, shop, farm, office, and library. Dewey specifically included libraries. Slight improvements in working habits, he wrote, "will readily add ten percent to efficiency. In a working life of fifty years, five full years!" Dewey calculated the time saved when telephone operators and patrons omitted saying "please." He loved to quote William James (as did McCarthy) on the value of automation, and how much the mind could be set free for higher things if the ordinary mechanical duties of life were turned over to automation.[10]

These seemingly innovative ideas met resistance not only from top ALA leaders but from many public librarians who looked upon the approach as unscholarly and somewhat uncultured. (In university libraries this attitude was even more common.) Librarian Theresa Hitchler, of the Brooklyn Public Library, was repulsed by the prominence given to what she termed "shoddy statistics" and she detailed her concerns in the pages of the *Library Journal*. There was "no joy in working which meant only unfailing accuracy. . . ." Hitchler felt the pernicious movement had "seeped" in from the industrial world to the professional world (perhaps this was enough to discredit it with her) and ultimately led to the

"deification of the bookkeeper." She warned that "nervous break-
downs" would be the result among librarians if jobs were reduced
to the monotony of bricklaying.[11]
Detroit librarian Adam Strohm gave a similar message to the annual assembly of the ALA in Ottawa in 1912. In a speech, "The
Efficiency of the Library Staff and Scientific Management," he
warned against overemphasis on statistics and output to the neglect of humanitarian aspects of librarianship. A mechanical, stop-
watch approach unfortunately would be carried over into the type
of service patrons received. A better way to increase efficiency, according to Strohm, was, among other things, to give adequate
wages, paint the rooms pleasant colors, and allow "occasional conversations during working hours."[12]
Others agreed with Hitchler and Strohm when they read of library circulation being compared to output from a shoe factory.
Even Arthur Bostwick, a sympathetic supporter, admitted that
when he adopted individual efficiency forms for each employee
(including a rating for whether the librarian had an appreciation
of literature!) his staff received his experiment with "suspicion,
distrust and dislike of the whole scheme."[13]
Yet some were as caught up in the movement as Dewey. Much
early discussion developed around whether librarians should take
a civil service exam, which was an attempt to standardize positions. An exam would assure the library clientele of "the same degree of efficiency, continuity and development that any employer
would desire in his own private business." Many voices supported
certification; most argued that libraries, as businesses, were ac-
countable to the public and taxes should not be wasted. When the
graduates of his School of Library Economy of Columbia College
and at Albany excelled on the exams, Dewey knew he had planned
well.[14]
Bostwick of the New York and St. Louis public libraries and
president of the ALA in 1907/8, was thoroughly caught up in
the efficiency movement despite his staff. He insisted on scientific
procedure in library management. The public paid for service, he
argued, and was therefore entitled to a fair return for its investment. Otherwise librarians could be accused of squandering public
funds. Idle talk, wasted time, and illegible handwriting were to be
eliminated. "Wasting time is worse than wasting money" he stated
in *Some Principles of Business-Like Conduct in Libraries.*[15] Even
politeness was good business. Organized methods resulted in improved checking systems for completed work, as well as for goods
received, the librarian noted. Bostwick thought that just as a busi-

nessman solicited trade, so too should the librarian "create a demand for his goods where it does not exist," a concept that some scholar-librarians felt was beneath their dignity.[16]

Accountability in libraries took various forms. An examination called an "efficiency test" was designed by the chief librarian at the Queens, New York, library in 1912. Assistant librarians had to fill out detailed charts on their hourly activities, whether cataloguing, mending books, or engaging in any other activity. From this the average rate of speed could be determined for library activities and the completed chart for each worker could be presented to superiors as a "self-recorded statement of the efficiency of each assistant."[17]

Labor-saving devices interested Dewey from the beginning, even before he realized that such devices were a basic element in Taylor's task management. In 1914 there was an exhibit in New York of such items for libraries. Everything was displayed, from typewriters to the model vacuum cleaner used at the John Crerar Library in Chicago. C. Seymour Thompson, a District of Columbia librarian who described the exhibit, made a direct connection with improved output resulting from use of the new items. He hoped that scientific management, of which these labor-saving devices were a part, would not be a fad in libraries. Thompson called for a study of all that had already been done "to secure a truly scientific management of libraries," noting that some libraries had already conducted elaborate time and motion studies.[18]

In concluding the first half of this paper it could be inferred that in public library management in the post-1876 era, the issue of efficiency seemed a controversial topic, around which swirled many heated exchanges at ALA conventions as well as at the circulation desk of the Brooklyn Public Library. Certainly the issue had captivated Melvin Dewey, some would say to the point of mental distraction. Interest in labor-saving devices, simplified work procedures, and an improved classification system all preceded Taylor's ideas and then gained further notoriety when Taylor became widely known.

Perhaps the argument over whether the public library was an elitist institution dedicated to serving the educated class or whether it was enthusiastically dedicated to uplifting the immigrant might be modified by speculating that its motive was to produce an efficient populace, whether upper-class, middle-class, working-class, "new" immigrant or "old," or whatever. At least it was Dewey's overriding concern that efficient organization be brought to libraries and—like others of his generation—the promotion of orderliness and efficiency in society may not have been far from his mind. While this argument can be debated in relation to the public library, when it comes to the second library with which this paper is concerned, the Legislative Reference Library, there is no question. Not only was the library run in a methodical way, but its very purpose was to put government on a more scientific and utilitarian basis through the use of the library's enlightening information.

The second type of library that developed in response to the industrial/technical revolution of the late nineteenth century was the Legislative Reference Library, whose purpose was to assist lawmakers in their attempt to legislate in a scientific manner in a new machine age. Therefore the legislative reference movement is a fitting example of a library springing to life from contemporary circumstances. The idea had been experimented with in England. Charles McCarthy (Massachusetts born, but educated at Brown University and the University of Wisconsin, where he received a Ph.D. in history under Frederick Jackson Turner), originated the American version in Madison, Wisconsin. McCarthy said he was inspired by two Englishmen who lived through the same sort of industrial revolution in their own country: the radical reformer Francis Place (1771–1854), who had an influential private library, and the philosopher of utilitarianism, Jeremy Bentham (1748–1832). The Wisconsin librarian felt that as civilization advanced there was "no reason why we could not make statute law in a more scientific manner."[19] From Wisconsin his movement spread throughout the United States and to other countries.

The words "scientific," "scientific point of view," and "efficiency" form a theme throughout the McCarthy writings. McCarthy was aware of Taylor's experiments from their first popularization and he became personally acquainted with the engineer in 1912 (in contrast to Dewey, who did not know Taylor). The two were mutual supporters from then until Taylor's death in 1915. McCarthy visited Taylor in Pennsylvania. Taylor also visited Madison, Wisconsin, and admitted that his own state was far behind Wisconsin due to the absence of a library such as the Legislative Reference Library. He also noted that everywhere he went in Madison, McCarthy was always mentioned as "something of a storm center,"[20] and this was precisely the role Taylor played in the newly emerging field of scientific management, especially in its relation to labor. McCarthy was trying to organize an effective information center to make law a model of efficiency in a new industrial age. Resistance was encountered in the ultra-conservative "stand-patters" who resented their loss of control. Taylor simultaneously was running industries so that order could be made out of the wasteful habits of the period. Resistance was loud, especially from labor unions, which felt this approach was inhuman. McCarthy was attempting through his information center to do in the area of state government what Taylor was doing in the field of scientific management in industry. Support for each other was welcome at a time when both were under fire. McCarthy was being attacked by die-hard Old Republican elements in Wisconsin, while Taylor was under attack from labor unions.

The library in Madison was an information center in the capitol building that furnished the legislators of Wisconsin, most of whom were inexperienced lumbermen and dairymen, with the most up-to-date information available. Although he collected books of all kinds, McCarthy felt that books could be outdated before they reached the shelves. Hence he perfected an elaborate clipping system whereby material of all varieties was saved: newspaper and periodical articles; letters; court briefs; records of votes; news on pending legislation in other states; political platforms. They were gathered from every possible American and foreign source and were filed under a particular heading. As new information was added, the file expanded. The hardest thing, McCarthy admitted, was keeping "the dead stuff out and the live stuff in,"[21] but it was worth it since the purpose of all the collecting efforts was "to know what the dearly bought experience of other places is."[22] Once this was known, more expert legislation could be proposed. His librarians were encouraged to take courses at the university and continually update their knowledge. Conferences were frequently held with the staff. Bonuses in the form of a week's vacation at a nearby lake were given for good work. All of these practices were similar to Taylor's.

The utilization of efficiency experts was one of the most original parts of the Legislative Reference Library's organization. The services of University of Wisconsin professors (out of state and foreign experts were consulted as well) were sought in gathering ideas for improved legislation. The exchange often took place in the library, where one could find such famous scholars as Richard T. Ely, John R. Commons, and Frederick Jackson Turner giving their views to the librarian and also to legislators. The information center was an intellectual center for the dispensation of enlightenment. This distinctly unique arrangement of using the expertise of university professors to improve legislation was expounded fully by McCarthy in one of the primers of the progressive era,

The Wisconsin Idea.[23] It described the intellectual interchange of the expert and the legislator through the medium of the library, for the purpose of placing government on a more scientific, orderly basis. Henceforth, nothing would have to be decided by "rule of thumb" procedures (Taylor's oft repeated phrase), nor by persistent lobbyists. This idea was very close to Taylor's idea in industry.

While inside the state the conservative opponents of seemingly innovative legislation blamed the library for such radical measures as workmen's compensation and university extension courses, praise was abundant from outside. Approval was given in the form of imitation. Duplicates of McCarthy's library idea appeared not only in the nation's capitol, on state and municipal levels, and in university centers, but also in other countries. The Philippine Islands founded a similar library after reading the account in *The Wisconsin Idea.* Theodore Roosevelt praised McCarthy's innovation and declared that as far as getting rid of disorder "the only solution is that worked out by Mr. Charles McCarthy." The lesson given in Wisconsin of "scientific self help and patient care in radical legislation" should be picked up by other institutions, he declared.[24] One Wisconsin individual, progressive Governor Robert M. La Follette to no one's surprise firmly supported the institution, declaring that it was a money saver worth "many times its cost to the people of the state" in his address to the 1905 assembly.[25]

It was not just in the area of librarianship that McCarthy fought to have Taylor's ideas applied. "You can't turn back scientific organization in agriculture" he declared as he launched a movement in this area.[26] He urged American farmers to follow the lead of Danish, Dutch, and Irish farmers in standardizing of butter, cheese, cream, and flour. Horace Plunkett, leader in the Irish cooperative movement, was one of the many out-of-state experts McCarthy brought to meet legislators. McCarthy dated the instigation of a Wisconsin farmers' dairy cooperative movement and increased interest in standardization from Plunkett's appearance before the legislature in 1911. McCarthy also strongly supported what he called the application of efficiency methods to the marketing of produce.[27]

As librarian in the state capitol McCarthy saw an obvious need for a well-trained corps of elected officials. Hence he was also interested in the training of public officials. He felt they should go through some sort of "civic West Point" where they would be judged and graded on efficiency as well as conduct and atten-

dance.[28] He was closely in touch with the New York Training
School for Public Service, even turning down an offer to head the
institution. Librarians who made a career of aiding legislators
should be well trained also, McCarthy stated. During his period as
chief librarian, he taught courses at the University of Wisconsin
designed for political scientists and librarians. In one course entitled "Comparative Legislation," he compared American, English,
German, and French sources, and hoped to turn out "better and
broader men who are up-to-date and practical."[29]

McCarthy came to the defense of scientific management when
he served as research director of the U.S. Federal Commission on
Industrial Relations in 1912. Since McCarthy was always a strong
labor supporter (he was even chosen by a union official once to
represent the union in a strike settlement in Madison), many labor
leaders could not understand how he could defend a system they
considered dehumanizing. Yet McCarthy did. He was one of the
only vocal labor sympathizers in the period to see anything bene-
ficial in the Taylor system, which shows how thoroughly he was
convinced (misled, his critics would say) that the principles of
scientific management did not ignore human nature. (Taylor argued in this manner but few accepted his arguments.) One is
tempted to think that he was so blinded by his love of efficiency
that he rationalized the benefits of scientific management for
labor. Perhaps it is also likely he was one of the only people who
understood that Taylor also emphasized harmony between worker
and employer, a factor always downplayed by critics.[30]

McCarthy argued before the Commission that Taylor's system
was not so coldly heartless as to disregard the laborer's humanity.
He urged members to visit any of Taylor's plants, as he had. To
appease Taylor, McCarthy told him that his system was a "new
machine and it is meeting with the same reception that new machines usually meet with."[31] When Taylor testified before the
Commission, McCarthy had enlightened the commissioners before-
hand so that Taylor's system was not condemned outright as a
cause of industrial unrest. This feat shows the value McCarthy
placed on Taylor's ideas. Here was one of the few pro-union persons on record who saw enough good in scientific management not
to have it condemned. It shows how far McCarthy would go in
defending Taylorism.[32]

The ideological attraction between McCarthy and Taylor is insightful. McCarthy's endorsement of an efficiency system "for the
good of the laborer" and his application of this same principle to
government for "the good of the people" was typical of a certain

type of progressive mentality. Despite the rhetoric that said "let the people rule," a common phrase in the progressive movement, many progressives, including McCarthy, thought people needed a colossal dose of help to do this. That workers should be kept at a distance from management, that people should be kept at a distance from government was often unsaid but endorsed. Between the two groups came such devices as commissions, scientific management, efficiency studies, scientific determination of the day's work, time and motion studies, and so on. McCarthy's infatuation with Taylor's experiments casts a revealing light not only on the organization of his library but also on his philosophy of government, as well as on the spirit that permeated the era.[33]

This paper has been an attempt to place two types of libraries in the mainstream of the progressive period. Since libraries never exist in a vacuum, where do libraries become indistinguishable from larger social/intellectual/cultural trends? An obvious contact point in the progressive period seems to be in the emphasis on efficiency, before, after, and simultaneously with the onslaught of Taylorism. A secondary motive in writing this paper was the number of complaints in the literature of library management that there is no study of how the innovations of Taylor were applied to library-oriented problems in this early period. Upon closely observing the period, one senses the inadequacy of such a question and the need for a more thoughtful question and a more comprehensive answer.

The three most important persons in this study, Melvil Dewey, Frederick Taylor, and Charles McCarthy, share the same characteristics: the desire to conserve time, energy, and human effort; the desire to organize industry, government, and libraries efficiently; the desire to bring order out of a society torn by technology. Such thoughts typified the age as evidenced in similar ideas found in the larger nonlibrary world of Theodore Roosevelt, Jane Addams, John Dewey, Gifford Pinchot, and others.

Evidence shows that "Tayloresque" solutions were being applied to public library oriented problems by Dewey and others before Taylor fully outlined his program. McCarthy was utilizing efficiency experts before Taylor; there is reference to the fact that Dewey's classification system was studied and adapted by Taylor's circle for industrial classification. Even before *Principles* was declared the Bible of the movement, Dewey's interest in libraries had slackened, though Bostwick was quick to pick up the new ideas. References to Dewey's activities in relation to libraries are not abundant after 1906, but on one rare occasion when he attended a 1912 meeting in Atlantic City, his presence was noted briefly in the *Library Journal.* The talk was appropriately on scientific management, indicating he was still enchanted with the topic.[34]

So the search for the influence of "scientific management" on libraries in this period indicates that library leaders had ideas parallel to Taylor's. A revealing statement was made about McCarthy after his death in 1921, and it could be applied as well to Dewey and Taylor. The *Library Journal* remarked that state and national governments owed much to the legislative reference librarian for "the prevention of much waste of time and effort arising from the duplication of measures to the same purport. . . ."[35] Was that not Taylorism? Was that not Dewey's intention as well? The same reference to not wasting time, not duplicating measure applied to all three. In addition, this was a notable component of the progressive reform movement. In this instance we can witness the often elusive, difficult-to-document phenomenon of library history melding into the social and economic and political history of the era.

Notes

1. Alfred North Whitehead, *Science and the Modern World* (New York: Macmillan, 1925), p. 96.

2. H. H. B. Meyer, "Select List of References on Scientific Management and Efficiency," *Special Libraries* (May 1913): 72–109, is a gold mine of information on the topic. Hundreds of references are listed beginning with the earliest in 1896. Listed are the following: Arnold Bennett, *How to Live on 24 Hours a Day* (New York: George H. Doran [c. 1910]) Antoinette Wakeman and Louise M. Heller, *Scientific Sewing and Garment Cutting, for Use in Schools and in the Home* (New York and Boston: Silver, Burdett, 1898); "How to Apply Efficiency Tests to a Church," *Current Literature* (December 1912): 675–676.

3. Frederick Winslow Taylor, *The Principles of Scientific Management* (New York and London: Harper and Row, 1911), pp. 5–8. The public was informed of Taylor's experiments through his minor writings and publicity well before 1911. Copley states that a scientific management course was instituted at Harvard in 1909 in the newly formed business school after the dean visited the Taylor shop in Pennsylvania. Taylor occasionally lectured on the subject at Harvard. (Frank Copley, *Frederick W. Taylor: Father of Scientific Management*, 2 vols. [New York and London: Harper and Brothers, 1923], 2: 297).

4. Edward Bellamy, *Looking Backward, 2000–1887* (1887; reprint ed., New York: Modern Library, 1951), p. 129.

5. Morris Llewellyn Cooke, "Classification and Symbolization," in *Scientific Management in American Industry* (New York and London: Harper and Brothers, 1929). This chapter notes the influence of the Dewey system. Cooke states, "Carl G. Barth is my authority for the statement that the enormous numbers of charge accounts . . . of the Pullman Car Works were

designated by numbers so arranged as to be largely mnemonic, along the lines of the Dewey system," p. 119. See Copley, *Frederick W. Taylor*, who states, "It would appear that all the industrial systems of classification and symbolization, including Taylor's, owe much to the Dewey decimal system, well known from its use in public libraries," p. 354.

6. "Call for a Library Conference" [n.d.], in Edward G. Holley, *Raking the Historic Coals: The A.L.A. Scrapbook of 1876*, Beta Phi Mu Chapbook, no. 8 (Chicago: Lakeside Press, 1967), pp. 54–55.

7. "The Proceedings at the Southern, St. Louis, Mo., Wednesday–Saturday, May 8–11, 1889," *Library Journal* 14, nos. 5–6 (May–June 1889): 266–294. See also Dennis Thomison, *A History of the American Library Association, 1876–1972* (Chicago: American Library Association, 1978).

8. William F. Poole, "Address of the President," *Library Journal* 11, nos. 8–9 (August–September 1886): 202.

9. William I. Fletcher, "Some Library Superstitions," *Library Journal* 14, nos. 5–6 (May–June 1889): 155–159; Melvil Dewey, "Proceedings," *Library Journal* 14, nos. 5–6 (May–June 1889): 270–271.

10. Melvil Dewey, "Office Efficiency," in Howard P. Dunham (comp. and ed.), *The Business of Insurance* (New York: Ronald Press, 1912), pp. 1–45.

11. Theresa Hitchler, "Efficiency in Library Work," *Library Journal* 38, no. 10 (October 1913): 558–561.

12. Adam Strohm, "The Efficiency of the Library Staff and Scientific Management," *Public Libraries* 17, no. 8 (October 1912): 303–306. None of Strohm's suggestions would have been antithetical to Taylor, either.

13. Arthur Bostwick, "Efficiency Records in Libraries," *Library Journal* 38, no. 3 (March 1913): 132; idem, "An Oral Speed-Test in Mental Response," *Library Journal* 35, no. 10 (December 1910): 555–556; "The Efficiency Rating System of the New York Public Library," *Library Journal* 44, no. 6 (June 1919): 376–377; "Efficiency Rating Scheme of the Brooklyn Public Library," *Library Journal* 44, no. 10 (October 1919): 664.

14. Helen Haines, "The Effect of Civil Service Methods upon Library Efficiency," *Library Journal* 31, no. 10 (October 1906): 699–704; Arthur Bostwick, "New York Library Civil Service Examinations," *Library Journal* 26, no. 7 (July 1901): 391; "Statement of the Committee on Standardization of Libraries and Certification of Librarians," *Library Journal* 42, no. 9 (September 1917): 719–724; "The Brooklyn Public Library Scheme of Library Service," *Library Journal* 29, no. 7 (July 1904): 363–365; Judson T. Jennings, "Municipal Civil Service in Libraries," *Public Libraries* 14, no. 6 (June 1909): 209–212; Judson Jennings, "A Few Grains of Wheat in a Bushel of Chaff," *Public Libraries* 19, no. 5 (May 1914): 224–228; "Civil Service Inadequacy," *Public Libraries* 22, no. 4 (April 1917): 143–144.

15. Arthur E. Bostwick, *Some Principles of Business-Like Conduct in Libraries* (Chicago: American Library Association, 1920).

16. Arthur E. Bostwick, *The American Public Library* (New York and London: D. Appleton, 1910), pp. 3–4.

17. "Notes & News: Queens Borough Public Library," *Library Journal* 37, no. 10 (October 1912): 582.

18. C. Seymour Thompson, "The Exhibit of Labor Saving Devices," *Library Journal* 39, no. 7 (July 1914): 512–520.

19. McCarthy to W. F. Dood, 7 January 1914, Charles McCarthy Papers, State Historical Society of Wisconsin, Madison, Wisconsin.

20. Frederick W. Taylor to McCarthy, 5 May 1914, Frederick W. Taylor

Papers, Stevens Institute of Technology, Hoboken, New Jersey.

21. "Statement of Dr. Charles McCarthy, Wisconsin Reference Department," Congressional Reference Bureau, Hearings before the Committee on the Library, House of Representatives, on Various Bills Proposing the Establishment of a Congressional Reference Bureau, February 26 and 27, 1912 (Washington, D.C.: Government Printing Office, 1912), p. 55.

22. McCarthy to Fred Holmes, 30 March 1909, McCarthy Papers.

23. Charles McCarthy, *The Wisconsin Idea* (New York: Macmillan, 1912).

24. Theodore Roosevelt, "Roosevelt on the Progressive Fight," an interview with H. B. Needham, *Saturday Evening Post* (25 October 1913), 3-4, 28-31.

25. Robert M. La Follette, "Message to the Senate and Assembly," *Assembly Journal*, State of Wisconsin, 12 January 1905, p. 109.

26. McCarthy to Lionel Smith-Gordon, 17 September 1915; McCarthy, "Scientific Management and Standardization," 22 September 1914, McCarthy Papers.

27. Horace Plunkett, "Better Farming, Better Business, Better Living: Two Practical Suggestions," *Outlook* (26 February 1910): 497-502; Horace Plunkett, "McCarthy of Wisconsin: The Career of an Irishman Abroad as it Appears and Appeals to an Irishman at Home," *Nineteenth Century* (June 1915): 1335-1347.

28. McCarthy to Richart T. Ely, 10 August 1916; McCarthy to Delos Kinsman, 11 September 1916, McCarthy Papers.

29. Alva H. Cook, "Training for Future Librarians" [clippings, c. 1903], Legislative Reference Library, Wisconsin State Capitol, Madison, Wisconsin. On the relevance of education, see also McCarthy to Robert La Follette, 18 April 1914, La Follette Papers, Library of Congress, Washington, D.C.

30. "Suggestions of Expert Witnesses: Statement of Mr. Charles McCarthy," *Final Report and Testimony of the U.S. Commission on Industrial Relations*, 11 vols. Senate Document 415, 64th Congress, 1st Session, Washington, D.C., 1916. See vol. 1, p. 386.

31. McCarthy to Taylor, 28 January 1914, Taylor Papers.

32. John A. Fitch, "Mutual Misunderstanding of Efficiency Experts and Labor Men," *Survey* (25 April 1914): 92-93. See also McCarthy to Taylor, December 1913; Taylor to McCarthy, 15 December 1913; McCarthy to Taylor, 10 January 1914; Taylor to McCarthy, 16 January, 22 January 1914, Taylor Papers.

33. For the pioneering study of the efficiency craze in society at large, see Samuel Haber's excellent *Efficiency and Uplift: Scientific Management in the Progressive Era, 1890-1920* (Chicago: University of Chicago Press, 1964). Some helpful information is found in Ruth L. Moore Jackson, "Origin and Development of Selected Personnel Management Functions in the Field of American Librarianship, 1876-1969" (Ph.D. dissertation, Indiana University, 1976).

34. "Bi-state Library Meeting at Atlantic City, March 8-9, 1912," *Library Journal* 37, no. 4 (April 1912): 194-196. In or out of the library world he was active in clubs and groups that promoted usefulness, among them the Efficiency Society of New York. See also letters in which Dewey refers to innovations he introduced decades earlier as well as the importance of efficiency at the time of writing. Some informative letters are: Dewey to Glenn M. Hobbes, 8 February 1915; Dewey to William Alcott, 31 January 1918; Dewey to L. F. Vosburgh, 15 July 1920; "Notes on Efficiency Week

Letter . . . ," (n.d.); Dewey to N. J. Werner, 25 April 1929, Melvil Dewey Papers, Columbia University, New York City, New York.

35. *Library Journal* 46, no. 9 (1 May 1921): 413. Another obituary article making the same point was written by scientific management expert Morris Llewellyn Cooke, a friend of McCarthy's and close associate of Taylor's. See Cooke, "In Death of 'Father of the Wisconsin Idea' Republic Has Lost One of Its Master Builders," *Philadelphia Public Ledger*, 11 April 1921.

Azariah Smith Root and Social Reform at Oberlin College

John Mark Tucker

> What is a man born for but to be
> a Reformer, a Re-maker . . . a
> restorer of truth and good?
>
> Emerson

Azariah Smith Root merits attention not only for his library achievements, but also for his visions of how to reform society. Today there is a growing tendency to separate our private lives from our professional lives: we are hired and promoted solely on the basis of professional progress. Political or philanthropic affiliations are rarely considered. In contrast, Root was one of several Oberlin professors who pursued a wide range of social, political, and religious interests, integrating them into professional activity. A look at Root's family origins, educational background, and professional achievements can inform a discussion of his social purposes.

He was born in Middlefield, Massachusetts, on 3 February 1862, the son of Solomon Francis and Anna Smith Root. A sense of public responsibility and a concern for the rights of others were among the strong traditions handed down by Root's ancestors. The Root, Smith, and Metcalf families were Baptist and Congregational; they opposed slavery, supported equality of the sexes, and contributed financially to the higher education of women.[1]

In 1878 Root moved to Oberlin to complete his preparatory studies. Henry Severance, formerly University of Missouri librar-

John Mark Tucker *is reference librarian and assistant professor of library science at Purdue University.*

Journal of Library History, Vol. 16, No. 2, Spring 1981
©1981 by the University of Texas Press   0022-2259/81/020280-14$01.45

ian, credited Root's choice of Oberlin College at least partially to the influence of Judson Smith, Root's uncle and an Oberlin professor of church history.[2] There were other reasons for attending Oberlin: its pietistic atmosphere, its origins in the culture and ideas of New England, and its historic reputation as a college actively concerned with significant political issues. Root earned B.A. and M.A. degrees and studied law one year each at Boston University and Harvard. In 1885 he assumed a temporary position cataloging Oberlin's library collections. Impressed with his work, the Oberlin faculty in 1887 elected Root college librarian, a position he held until his death forty years later.

With Root's appointment as librarian, the college launched "the building of a first-rate college collection."[3] In 1924 Oberlin possessed the largest college library in the United States, having surpassed many universities as an important research collection.[4]

Appointed professor of bibliography in 1890, Root taught courses in the history of the printed book, book illustration, and library use. He lectured in the library schools at Western Reserve, Atlanta, the New York Public Library, Michigan, and Pratt Institute. He established and directed the American Correspondence School of Librarianship.

The history of printed books provided the focal point for Root's scholarly interests. His study of German facilitated a year of course work at Göttingen under the direction of Karl Dziatzko. Researching the origins of printing, he examined Grolier bindings and Costeriana during trips to Holland and other European countries.

A prolific speaker and energetic organizer, he was active in numerous civic and professional groups. During the academic year 1909/10, for example, he presented forty-two lectures away from the Oberlin campus. He was president of ALA, and twice president of both the Ohio Library Association and the Bibliographical Society of America.[5]

Root's stature in the profession is suggested by William Warner Bishop, who in 1926 was seeking to hire a full professor for the library science faculty at Michigan. Bishop described Root as "the ideal man," stating that "exactly his combination of scholarship, good judgment, remarkable ability in clear presentation, strength of character, and broad sympathies seem what is desirable. . . . I wish most heartily that any one else could be found possessing even the major part of these qualities, and in my study of possible candidates I have endeavored to measure them against Mr. Root. . . ."[6]

Oberlin and Its Traditions

We should consider not only Professor Root and his social philosophy, but also the college, its historic commitment to reformist notions, and the interplay between Root and his Oberlin colleagues. The Oberlin Collegiate Institute was established to train young people as "ministers and pious school teachers."[7] The founders, John Jay Shipherd and Philo Penfield Stewart, envisioned an educational institution in the midst of a Christian community; thus the college and the colony began simultaneously and for related purposes. Shipherd viewed learning as the handmaid of religion, and he saw true religion as a life of action devoted to good deeds.[8] These views held firm throughout the cataclysmic events of the nineteenth century, inspiring a pedagogy of social responsibility and reform.

The college earned George Schmidt's approbation as "one of the most individualistic and influential colleges in the land."[9] In 1837 it became the nation's first coeducational college.[10] Two years earlier it had admitted black students, thereby initiating its widely recognized affiliation with pro-black causes such as abolition.

Social Science and Social Action

Historian James Axtell emphasizes the interdependent relationships between small colleges and their nineteenth-century environments. He urges disavowal of the notion that only large universities responded to the "same general configuration" of newer ideas, social needs, and inherited and imported traditions.[11] Daniel Boorstin argues that the "distinctively American college was neither public nor private, but a *community* institution."[12] Oberlin not only responded to the community and the society, but it actively sought to integrate the study of contemporary social topics into its educational philosophy.

During the last three decades of the nineteenth century, American universities established graduate research programs and placed them on a par with teaching. The growth and differentiation of the social sciences spawned the new disciplines of economics, sociology, and political science. These fields of study came to Oberlin almost as readily as they had come to the universities.

Unlike their colleagues across the country, social scientists at Oberlin were not torn between the personal inclination to reform society and the professional responsibility to act only as dispassionate scholar-advisors. To the contrary, Oberlinians merged scholarly research and social action.

Two professors, John R. Commons and James Monroe, characterize the vitality of the reformist impulse in the social sciences. An Oberlin graduate, Commons joined the faculty after studying at Johns Hopkins under Richard Ely, having adopted Ely's concept of science as "the fusion of the will to act and the command to study."[13] Commons rejected the application of the biological principles of Darwinian thought to human economic behavior, believing instead that an educated elite should guide the masses through inevitable conflict toward social harmony.[14] He taught Oberlin's first courses in sociology and American history, and he compiled a bibliography of sociology that Root published as the first issue of the *Oberlin College Library Bulletin.*[15]

Monroe appeared in the political arena as a state senator, diplomat in the Lincoln administration, and five-term congressman in the United States House of Representatives. At Oberlin he introduced the seminar method of teaching, which featured student presentations on current events. During Monroe's tenure few subjects, if any, rivaled the social sciences in student popularity.[16]

The college community could not fail to be excited by the interchange made possible with major social critics. Oberlin professors founded the Institute of Christian Sociology, whose first president was the social gospel advocate Washington Gladden. In 1895 the institute sponsored a symposium on human poverty bringing together such luminaries as Jane Addams, Samuel Gompers, and Clarence Darrow.

Given his own broad sympathies, Root's response to this environment was one of active identification. In describing Root's philosophy of library education, Richard Rubin emphasizes that Root recommended the study of sociology and general social problems (among other subjects) as appropriate prerequisites for library school courses. "There is no question that Root conceived the library process as one intimately related to the conditions in society. This view, extending from . . . working conditions to the need for theoretical background in sociology, was consonant with the social reform movements associated with Oberlin College."[17]

Prohibition and the Bourgeois Interior

As an ardent prohibitionist, Root was at the forefront of those Oberlin students and faculty who marshaled political support for ordinances designed to destroy saloons and "grog-shops." Meeting in the Spear Library on 24 May 1893, Root and other executive committee members of the Oberlin Temperance Alliance planned a new organization designed to unite church groups and other temperance forces. On June 4 the committee's work was ratified at a mass meeting at Oberlin's First Congregational Church, where Root's presence on the platform symbolized the fledgling organization's nonpartisan character.[18] These meetings brought into existence the Ohio Anti-Saloon League and the Anti-Saloon League of America.

Oberlin graduates Howard H. Russell and Wayne B. Wheeler played key roles in the nation's temperance movement. As ASL director, Russell arranged federation agreements with more than 250 temperance and church groups representing over 9,000,000 people in 40 states and territories.[19] Wheeler was general counsel to the ASL. As he later recalled, the June fourth mass meeting showed him that the new organization was to be aimed at church members, "the genuine altruists and idealists of the nation," and that it would ignore "sectarian, political, racial, sectional," and other subdivisions of people.[20]

Root was more than a founding officer; he was an active temperance worker. He spoke in the Lorain County area; he wrote news items about the movement; and he supplied the pulpit for his former classmate Howard Russell, permitting Russell to expand his prohibition work.[21] Root celebrated the thirty-fourth anniversary of the birth of the ASL by meeting with other charter members. Late in life he complained of the unenforceability of temperance legislation, questioning the practicality of the Volstead Act, designed to enforce the eighteenth amendment.[22] However, taken as a whole, his commitment to the cause cannot be denied.

Historians James Timberlake and Norman Clark place the prohibition movement firmly within the central reform tendencies of the progressive era. Prohibition grew from the same moral idealism that impelled reformers to struggle with problems apparent in the growing power of big business and the mounting discontent of urban industrial workers. Timberlake notes that "if progressivism represented a quickening of the humanitarian impulse, manifested in redoubled efforts of philanthropists and social workers to banish crime, poverty, and disease from the environment, prohibition was an effort to eliminate one factor that caused them."[23]

The ASL was not designed to advocate prohibition in the broadest sense but to rally divided temperance groups around the more modest task of saloon suppression. Saloon life was antithetical to the values of the cohesive nuclear family. Saloons encour-

aged a "defiantly anti-middle class indulgence" that produced
drunkenness, fostered prostitution, and created an undisciplined
and brutal influence amidst home and hearth. Clark sees reform as
a conservative notion, an effort, literally, to re-form or form again,
an attempt by a social class to establish order and stability in a
volatile society.[24]

The "bourgeois interior" as defined by John Lukacs offers a
conceptual framework for understanding temperance groups. Its
characteristics are an emphasis on status as community citizen
(drawn from an earlier connotation of "city-dweller"), on personal
security, and on an interiority of lifestyle. Domesticity, privacy,
and the concept of home and family are its principal achievements. The bourgeois interior accompanied social mobility, which
after the seventeenth century became intertwined with the propagation of education. A proper education inculcated humanistic
commitments to justice and reason, tempered with moderation
and prudence. Without the guidance of the bourgeois interior,
which must be freed from its narrow economic and class connotations, it is difficult to see prohibition as other than repressive or
irrational.[25]

A Public Library and a Presidential Library

Root's professional work and humanitarian interests were
brought together in his planning and administering the new Carnegie library building opened at Oberlin in September 1908. At
Root's instigation the college contracted with the Oberlin Board
of Education to provide public library services in the college library. Approval of this joint arrangement was not difficult since
Root was president of the board that had approval authority.

Root was intensely interested in public access to the library.
Research collections and reference services were open to townspeople. During the first year of operation, circulation of the public
library collection topped 27,000, and seven years later more than
60 percent of the townspeople borrowed books for home use.[26]
In a real sense Root had the unusual distinction of founding a
public library, directing it, supporting it, and promoting its use.

Dee Garrison complains that the "orthodox progressive interpretation" of library history has two extremes that ought to be
avoided: the tendencies to "deemphasize or ignore the patrician
source of much of the library's activities and to greatly exaggerate
the support given the public library by the working class."[27] Even
to determine the existence of a differentiated class structure in a

small turn-of-the-century college town would pose another research problem entirely. That Oberlin bore patrician characteristics
needs simply to be stated. The college assumed the responsibilities
incumbent upon an upper middle class, educated elite to critique
the society and to offer advice for governmental and philanthropic
solutions. Root himself employed no less a term than *noblesse
oblige* to explain why the college should support public library
services.[28]

Root envisioned a library that did much more than simply open
its doors to the public. He saw it as a community center and as a
cultural center, hosting myriad displays, programs, and workshops.
Its materials and facilities would attract groups as disparate as
local historians and radical priests. In order to make the public
library a community cultural center, Root urged librarians to
become public-spirited citizens vitally interested in a wide range
of local affairs.[29]

Garrison further notes that less noble aims motivated public
library founders and trustees, namely the urge to arrest working-
class dissent. In Root's instance, this possibility should be laid
aside until more extensive evidence proves otherwise. Various historians recognize that altruistic concerns were among multiple
motivations behind the founding of public libraries; Root himself
acted as a responsible citizen, having embodied the concepts of
Oberlin's best reform traditions.

Michael Harris asserts that the primary theme in the history of
American librarianship is "the librarian's self-conscious and im-
pelling desire to gain entrance to the professional pantheon—that
elite grouping of vocations" considered essential to the nation's
well-being.[30] This description cannot apply to Root, whose professional identity was secure as a professor and even as an administrator. In fact, in 1893 he joined the Prudential Committee, which
determined college policy and made administrative decisions. Two
times he chaired that committee in the absence of a college president, virtually serving as acting president. In this capacity he led
the Rockefeller matching fund campaign to raise $500,000 during
the year of 1901/2.

Root played a vital role in the development of the Rutherford
B. Hayes Memorial Library in Fremont, Ohio. The guiding spirits
behind the project were Hayes's son, Colonel Webb Hayes, and the
Hayes Historical Society, which Root served as its first secretary.

Root worked on the Hayes project as advisor and consultant
and made book selections based on extensive bibliographies he had
prepared. He developed the collection according to President

Hayes's interests, including postwar reconstruction, the temperance movement, Chinese immigration, and prison and civil service reform. The extent of Root's participation in the project is indicated by Henry Severance, who exuberantly referred to Root as the librarian of the Hayes library.[31]

Root's appreciation of Hayes was consistent with his own system of values. Both were Ohio-bred, liberally educated Republicans committed to prohibition and other reforms. President Hayes's personal integrity and vigorous pursuit of civil service reform naturally appealed to the sense of moral responsibility that pervaded Oberlin.

Henry Churchill King and the Social Gospel

The social gospel has been hailed by historians as one of the most distinctive contributions of American churches to world Christianity. Sydney Ahlstrom modifies this conclusion without questioning the vitality of the movement. He describes the movement as truly bringing news of great joy because it was based on a faith in the perfectibility of human nature and it sought to use the modern church to control social forces. Faith and morality were aimed at the set of problems unleashed by the Gilded Age: the urban dislocations occasioned by the country's unregulated industrial expansion. Ahlstrom identifies the historical continuum from antislavery sentiment to the social gospel: "Both were characterized by a readiness to harness the churches and a tendency to subordinate every other interest of the church to the one great national policy question of the day. The line from Theodore Dwight Weld and Elijah Lovejoy to Washington Gladden and Walter Rauschenbusch must never be ignored."[32]

At Oberlin the line from Weld to Gladden and Rauschenbusch was secure. Weld's fiery sermons were crucial to Oberlin's early acceptance of abolitionism.[33] Gladden and Rauschenbusch were among the steady stream of social gospel advocates appearing at Oberlin during the Progressive Era. Gladden lectured regularly; Rauschenbusch sent his children to Oberlin.

The college's resident theologian on Social Christianity and its president from 1902 to 1927 was Henry Churchill King. He believed that the ideal practice of religion was for man to enter into personal relationships of a high ethical character embodying a sacred respect for the personality of others. "Friendship among men and friendship between man and God were parallels."[34] Man's task was to apply the ethics of Christ to all social problems and the principle of personality was evident in the world "fulfilling the will of God in social service."[35]

King's ideas about personality and social service were echoed in Root's address at the seventy-fifth anniversary celebration of the First Church of Oberlin. Root saw the task of man as to glorify God by doing good deeds, which would be greatly facilitated if college people and townspeople could maintain the intimate friendships that had long characterized their relations. Grounded in mutual respect and democratic instincts, these friendships would halt the tendency of church members to slide into socio-economic class distinctions. He called upon the Christian's sense of responsibility to the social and natural environment and upon the "heroic self-denial" that he said often characterized students and alumni. These qualities should undergird a wide range of community services. Root advocated expanding the town's role in the improvement of sanitation and water purification, landscaping and public parks, school buildings, and cultural facilities. He described progress in these areas, contrasting the contemporary scene with the bleak environment he had observed thirty years earlier.[36] His recommendations for the local community demonstrate an interior sense of order and a moral responsibility consistent with President King's theological views.

Root had no formal theological training, but he frequently accepted ministerial responsibilities: as moral leader and pulpit speaker. A sermon on Congregationalism stressed increased productivity and efficiency in benevolent work. He preached at least once a year at each of Oberlin's black churches. Once an elderly communicant suggested that Root had missed his calling, indicating that he would have made an ideal minister.[37] Garrison's observation that public librarians of the period felt a sense of mission and personal responsibility to do something about the social disorders of their day easily applies to Root. His "identification with the ministry" was a point of strength, especially when combined with the vitality of Social Christianity and the historic traditions of the college.

In summary, Root's contributions as public citizen, college teacher, and professional librarian drew strength from the traditions of his institution and the energetic theological concepts of his era. His own sense of internal order and social obligations were brought to bear on library problems and public policy. His faith that man should exert a positive influence on the community demonstrated his reformist commitments. That the library flourished under his leadership, on the other hand, suggests an environment conducive to professional growth. The idea of the librarian as moral leader, widely accepted from the times of Leland and Leibniz, is seldom as varied or as conspicuous as in the case of Root. The extent to which this energetic, gregarious personality was a product of his situation or the cause of it is a question for the future.

Notes

The author gratefully acknowledges the valuable suggestions and continual encouragement of Dr. D. W. Krummel, professor of library science, University of Illinois at Urbana-Champaign.

1. Marion Metcalf Root, "Azariah Smith Root: An Account Prepared for His Grandson and Also Presented to Keyes D. Metcalf on His Retirement as Director of the Harvard University Libraries" (1956?), p. 1, Azariah Smith Root Papers, Box 11, Oberlin College Archives, Oberlin, Ohio.

2. Henry O. Severance, "Azariah Smith Root, 1862-1927" (1941?), p. 3, Azariah Smith Root Papers, Box 13, Oberlin College Archives.

3. John Barnard, *From Evangelicalism to Progressivism at Oberlin College, 1866-1917* (Columbus: Ohio State University Press, 1969), p. 66.

4. Fremont Rider, *The Scholar and the Future of the Research Library: A Problem and Its Solution* (New York: Hadham Press, 1944), pp. 6-7; *The Place of a Research Library in a Liberal Arts College: Proceedings of a Symposium Held at Bowdoin College, February 21-22, 1963* (Brunswick: Bowdoin College, 1963), pp. 5-7; Eric Moon, "A Place Where You Can Follow the Footnote Back Home," *Library Journal* 88, no. 7 (1 April 1963): 1412-1416; *Encyclopedia of Library and Information Science*, s.v. "College Libraries"; and *Annual Reports of the President and the Treasurer of Oberlin College 1925-26* (Oberlin, Oh.: Oberlin College, 1926), p. 93.

5. Herbert F. Johnson, "Root, Azariah Smith (1862-1927)," in George S. Bobinski, Jesse H. Shera, and Bohdan S. Wynar (eds.), *Dictionary of American Library Biography* (Littleton, Colo.: Libraries Unlimited, 1978), pp. 444-446.

6. William Warner Bishop, "Report to the President, to the Dean of the Graduate School, and to the Dean of the College of Literature, Science and the Arts, on a Possible Faculty for the Department of Library Science" (5 May 1926), School of Library Science, University of Michigan, Ann Arbor.

7. Mary C. Venn, "Additions and Corrections" (1941?), ASR Papers, Box 13, Oberlin College Archives.

8. Robert Samuel Fletcher, *A History of Oberlin College from Its Foundation through the Civil War*, 2 vols. (Oberlin, Oh.: Oberlin College, 1943), 1:64.

9. George P. Schmidt, *The Liberal Arts College: A Chapter in American Cultural History* (New Brunswick, N.J.: Rutgers University, 1957), p. 30; and Malcolm Lyle Warford, "Piety, Politics, and Pedagogy: An Evangelical Protestant Tradition in Higher Education at Lane, Oberlin, and Berea, 1834-1904" (Ed. D. diss., Columbia University, 1973), pp. vi-viii, 68.

10. Ronald W. Hogeland, "Coeducation of the Sexes at Oberlin College: A Study of Social Ideas in Mid-Nineteenth-Century America," *Journal of*

Social History 6, no. 2 (Winter 1972/73): 160-176. For an earlier interpretation, see Frances Juliette Hosford, *Father Shipherd's Magna Charta: A Century of Coeducation in Oberlin College* (Boston: Marshall Jones, 1937).

11. James Axtell, "The Death of the Liberal Arts College," *History of Education Quarterly* 11, no. 4 (Winter 1971): 344.

12. Daniel J. Boorstin, *The Americans: The National Experience* (New York: Random House, 1965), p. 160. The community orientation of American colleges is amplified by David B. Potts in "American Colleges in the Nineteenth Century: From Localism to Denominationalism," *History of Education Quarterly* 11, no. 4 (Winter 1971): 363-380.

13. Jurgen Herbst, *The German Historical School in American Scholarship: A Study in the Transfer of Culture* (Ithaca, N.Y.: Cornell University Press, 1965), p. 44. The popularity of Johns Hopkins among Oberlinians is evidenced by comments in the student newspaper and by enrollment figures. In 1888 more Oberlin graduates entered Johns Hopkins than did graduates from any other school, see Barnard, *From Evangelicalism to Progressivism*, pp. 42-43, 85-91.

14. *Dictionary of American Biography*, s.v. "Commons, John Rogers."

15. Barnard, *From Evangelicalism to Progressivism*, p. 86; and John R. Commons, *A Popular Bibliography of Sociology* (Oberlin, Oh.: Oberlin News Presses, 1892).

16. Likewise the student societies maintained a lively dialogue on important issues of the day. Barnard writes that "child labor, working women, sweat shops, the threat of the trusts, arbitration of industrial conflicts, trade unions, workmen's compensation, profit sharing, socialism, immigrant problems, and city government were the stuff of society debates" (*From Evangelicalism to Progressivism*, pp. 22-24, 54-55, 64-66, and 123).

17. Richard Rubin, "Azariah Root's Concept of Education for Librarianship" (M.L.S. thesis, Kent State University, 1976), p. 15.

18. Barnard, *From Evangelicalism to Progressivism*, pp. 98-99.

19. *National Cyclopedia of American Biography*, s.v. "Russell, Howard Hyde."

20. Justin Steuart, *Wayne Wheeler, Dry Boss: An Uncensored Biography of Wayne B. Wheeler* (1928; reprint ed., Westport, Conn.: Greenwood Press, 1970), pp. 38-42.

21. Russell to Root, 15 July 1886, Azariah Smith Root Papers, Box 9, Oberlin College Archives; and Ernest Hurst Cherrington (ed.), *Standard Encyclopedia of the Alcohol Problem*, 6 vols. (Westerville, Oh.: American Issue, 1925-1930), 1:175-177.

22. Keyes D. Metcalf to the author, 17 April 1980; and Severance, "Azariah Smith Root," p. 14.

23. James H. Timberlake, *Prohibition and the Progressive Movement, 1900-1920* (Cambridge, Mass.: Harvard University Press, 1963), pp. 1-2.

24. Norman H. Clark, *Deliver Us from Evil: An Interpretation of American Prohibition* (New York: Norton, 1976), pp. 31-34, 69.

25. John Lukacs, "The Bourgeois Interior," *American Scholar* 39, no. 4 (Autumn 1970): 616-630; and Clark, *Deliver Us from Evil*, p. 12.

26. *Annual Reports of the President and Treasurer of Oberlin College, 1908-1909* (Oberlin, Oh.: Oberlin College, 1909), p. 345; and Marion Metcalf Root, "Azariah Smith Root," pp. 30-31.

291

27. Dee Garrison, *Apostles of Culture: The Public Librarian and American Society, 1876-1920* (New York: Free Press, 1979), p. xii.

28. Azariah Smith Root, "Community Service by the College Library," Azariah Smith Root Papers, Box 14, Oberlin College Archives.

29. Ibid.

30. Michael H. Harris, "Portrait in Paradox: Commitment and Ambivalence in American Librarianship, 1876-1976," *Libri* 26, no. 4 (December 1976): 283-284.

31. Severance, "Azariah Smith Root," p. 14. Root's Republican preference coincides with his own reformist instincts, but also with his religious affiliation. For example, in his study of eight midwestern townships in the late 1870s, Jensen found that 82 percent of Congregationalists (more than any other denomination) indicated a preference for the GOP. See Richard Jensen, *The Winning of the Midwest: Social and Political Conflict, 1888-1896* (Chicago: University of Chicago Press, 1971), pp. 62-63. See also Watt P. Marchman, "The Rutherford B. Hayes Memorial Library," *College and Research Libraries* 17, no. 3 (May 1956): 224-227.

32. Sydney E. Ahlstrom, *A Religious History of the American People* (New Haven: Yale University Press, 1972), p. 787. Ahlstrom's complaint that the social gospel was indifferent to racial issues has little significance for Oberlin and none for Root. In his seventy-fifth anniversary address at First Church, Root took pride in the presence of both a college professor and a black day laborer on the town council. In 1910 when a student society excluded blacks from membership, the *Cleveland Plain Dealer* quoted Root: "the faculty does not endorse the attitude of the undergraduates in the move to erase the Negro socially from the college map" (quoted in W. E. Bigglestone, "Oberlin College and the Negro Student, 1865-1940," *Journal of Negro History* 56, no. 3 [July 1971]: 204). Root said that the "fundamental principle of the brotherhood of men, of all classes and color, which has been our Oberlin pride for more than seventy-five years, is based upon such fundamental principles of righteousness and justice that it must in the long run command the assent of thoughtful students is the firm conviction of the faculty. . . ." See Marion Metcalf Root, "Azariah Smith Root," p. 57.

33. *Dictionary of American History*, s.v. "Oberlin Movement"; and Wilbur Greeley Burroughs, "Oberlin's Part in the Slavery Conflict," *Ohio Archaeological and Historical Publications* 20 (1911): 273-279.

34. Barnard, *From Evangelicalism to Progressivism*, p. 116.

35. Francis G. Peabody quoted in Henry Churchill King, *Theology and Social Consciousness: A Study of the Relations of the Social Consciousness to Theology* (New York: Macmillan, 1902), pp. 111-112.

36. Azariah Smith Root, "Seventy-Fifth Anniversary Address, First Church of Oberlin," Azariah Smith Root Papers, Box 14, Oberlin College Archives.

37. Marion Metcalf Root, "Azariah Smith Root," p. 58.

Azariah Smith Root (1862–1927); photograph taken about 1890.
Courtesy, Oberlin College Archives.

Oscar G. T. Sonneck: Architect of the "National Music Collection"

Carol June Bradley

Oscar George Theodore Sonneck was born in Lafayette, New Jersey—a little village later incorporated into Jersey City—on 6 October 1873, the son of George C. and Julia (Meyne) Sonneck. His father died while Sonneck was a child. Mrs. Sonneck took the boy to Germany, where she was employed as head of the household of a wealthy, widowed banker in Frankfurt-am-Main. Sonneck was raised as a son in the banker's home; every advantage was his. He was educated in Germany and attended the universities of Heidelberg and Munich, but he never earned a degree. "As a 'free American' [he] would not sit for any academic examination!"[1]

After he left Munich, Sonneck studied privately for a year to improve his musical technique, devoted a year to research in Italian libraries, and then returned to the United States, where he began to research America's musical history. For two and a half years, traveling among some twenty libraries in the eastern coastal states, Sonneck devoted his full time to research. The favorable financial circumstances of his childhood continued, so that instead of earning a living Sonneck was free to spend his time in the manner he found most appropriate.

At the Library of Congress his frequent visits to the newspaper department "attracted the attention of the official in charge . . . who," as Sonneck later related, "supposed that he was writing a history of the early American press." When it became known that his "labors were directed toward musical ends, Sonneck was ad-

Carol June Bradley *is music librarian at the State University of New York, Buffalo.*

Journal of Library History, Vol. 16, No. 2, Spring 1981
©1981 by the University of Texas Press   0022-2259/81/020293-13$01.40

vised to visit the Librarian of Congress, Dr. Herbert Putnam, who at that time was faced with the problem of organizing the Library's musical material."[2]

Putnam had, since his own appointment as Librarian of Congress in 1899, wrestled with the amassed music copyright deposits as well as with a conception of the role of music in relation to the government and the national library. What was the Library's responsibility toward the copyright material? What was the Library's duty toward music generally? Putnam determined

> that Music . . . had a rightful claim to recognition from the National Government; that the expression of it, in composition and in literature, should have a rightful place in the National Library; and that the fervor for it among our people was certain to develop a zeal for exact knowledge and understanding promising studies and research which the National Library might foster as could no other institution.
>
> The duty, then, was to develop the collection on the scholarly side, and to assure a scholarly conduct of it.[3]

But where was the musician/librarian capable of effecting such a concept? Three years elapsed.

> Then one day (in 1902) there strolled into [Putnam's] office a young man who introduced himself as Oscar Sonneck, and his interest as Music. He had under his arm a packet of manuscript which he proffered . . . without recompense—for publication by the government.[4]

Although unable to accept the manuscript—Sonneck's "Bibliography of Early Secular American Music"—for publication by the Library of Congress, Putnam made a counteroffer: Would Sonneck become chief of the Music Division? Sonneck accepted, and official records cite 1 August 1902 as the date on which he formally assumed his duties as chief of the Music Division, replacing the incumbent—Walter Rose Whittlesey—who became his assistant. The next two months Sonneck spent in Europe, where he reexamined outstanding music libraries, studied their classification systems, and visited music dealers. In October 1902, when he actually reported for work in the Library of Congress, he was in charge of a music collection that consisted largely of copyright deposits accessioned and catalogued by composer and title—if the title was distinctive. Bound music and sheet music were shelved separately.

The literature of music was in the stacks, available only from the main reading room. In short, wrote Sonneck, "an accumulation of music . . . rather than a collection; and most assuredly not a 'musical library' in any organic sense!"[5]

Sonneck began by surveying the collection the best he could, considering its inadequate catalogues, and formulating a classification appropriate to LC's unique situation regarding the copyright deposits. A classification for the Library of Congress, unlike those of libraries that purchased their music collections, had to accommodate the copyright laws, which obliged the deposit of all music —whether or not it was desirable for a library. Sonneck appraised the undesirable items as constituting "at least nine-tenths of the entire musical output," music "written largely for forms, for instruments, and instrumental combinations" with which purchasing libraries need not be concerned. His classification, then, would resemble the systematic catalogues of the publishers of that undesirable music, carefully avoiding the indiscriminate interweaving of desirable and undesirable material. Sonneck rejected "simply separating sheet music from book music, and copyrighted from purchased music." The distinctions in the first category were not absolute; the second would result in "two similar collections": the purchased collection one-tenth the size of the copyright collection *and* duplicating one-tenth of it. Sonneck's solution was "a classification which depends merely in detail upon the experience of other institutions, but which in the main is peculiar to the needs and nature of the Library of Congress." His plan for the literature of music was not markedly different from other classifications *except* that instruction materials and methods were classed with literature rather than music. In the music classes the characteristic features were: the separation of original compositions from arrangements, which constitute so much of the undesirable copyright deposits; collections from separate works; multi-movement cyclical forms, that is, sonatas, symphonies, suites, cantatas, and so forth, from single pieces; general from specific; and a systematic arrangement, by instruments and voices, similar to that used in publishers' and dealers' catalogues. Sonneck employed the "running-leaping numbers" of the Königliche Bibliothek in Berlin, which he found "scientific, logical, and practical."[6] The running-leaping numbers were used in numerical sequence but with gaps of unassigned numbers for future use.

After a little more than a year's experimentation, the new scheme was published. It had been satisfactorily applied "to some seven or eight thousand volumes . . . illustrating the history and theory of music, and to more than 150,000 volumes and pieces of music."[7] That great amount of music was classified only, not catalogued. Sonneck used the classification schedule as a finding guide for the individual pieces of music until they were catalogued or re-catalogued, as the case might be.

Appended to Sonneck's first annual report, that for 1902/3, is an evaluative essay on the "Development of the Music Division." That essay is the first written selection and acquisitions policy for an American music library as well as Sonneck's first statement of his goal for the music collections of the Library of Congress.

As a place to study the development of American music . . . the Music Division of the Library of Congress stands without a rival. But until we have produced masters equal to the great European, the study of European music will certainly remain paramount. Today [1903] it is still necessary to go abroad for original and serious research on these lines. Consequently the ideal should be to place at the disposal of the American student a collection so symmetrical and extensive as to dispense him of the necessity of going abroad whatever his line of investigation may be. This ideal probably is beyond reach, but we may approach it by planfully taking steps in the right direction.[8]

His first step was to check every book and composition listed in Hugo Riemann's *Musiklexikon* against LC's holdings. Desiderata lists were prepared and sent to various European dealers for prices on the items they could supply. Those initial purchases filled the most obvious gaps.

Sonneck's essay continued with the individual principles of his policy of "systematic development," the policy to which he would adhere more or less rigidly until his goals for the collection were realized. His principles were separated by American and European music, by literature and musical instruction. By European music Sonneck meant "the musical product of European brain and press [which LC will collect] very much in the same manner as European libraries do or would like to do."[9]

The first specification for European music called for the purchase of all the important critical and historical modern reprints, that is, the *Denkmäler* that, together with Collected Editions, are the heart of any music library. In this first collection policy Sonneck advised the purchase of every available pre–eighteenth-century manuscript and score not held by the Library of Congress. He quickly reconsidered; prior to about 1700, American and

European music did not have a "community of historical interest" so LC would not compete with European libraries for manuscript music or music published before 1700.

> Any such attempt would clearly tend to scatter the scarce and costly works of the old masters still further and give undue prominence to a selfish *museum of costly relics* policy over the best interests of the scholar. What sense would there be, for instance, in paying heavily for possibly unique copies of original editions of a few works by Palestrina, and thus possibly prevent some European institution from putting before the Palestrina specialist a full set of his works? Such a set or even a collection of the original editions representative enough to be of any practical use to the American scholar, the Library of Congress at this late date could never hope to achieve, even if its entire appropriation were given to the Music Division. If such works are of great interest in some other direction, let us say, as characteristic and sufficiently illustrative specimens of early music printing, it is part of our policy to make exceptions to our rule. ... But on the whole, the Library of Congress contents itself at present, so far as music before 1700 is concerned, with acquiring it as reprinted principally in the splendid historical subscription publications undertaken by the foreign governments, learned societies and firms. ...[10]

For the eighteenth century he recommended the selection of prominent composers and the preparation of lists of their desirable works (p. 3), which

> should be placed in the hands of our agents with the instruction to purchase whenever possible the works selected or others by the masters listed. ... Important works by prominent masters should be supplied in copies from the original manuscript if they exist in manuscript only.

The nineteenth century he found "less complicated" and predicted (pp. 3-4) that his success would

> depend more upon our intention to purchase and upon the carefulness with which we lay our plans than upon favorable circumstances.
> In a few decades it will be just as difficult to purchase 19th. century publications as it is now to purchase those of the 18th.

Clearly, it is now the time to purchase with the minimum of cost and trouble all desirable 19th. century publications.

The problems of acquiring the literature on music were more easily solved, and

not so numerous. It will be easy to keep in touch with current publications, and so far as 19th. century publications go I believe that we already possess or have ordered the greater number of important works. Collections of special literature can gradually be developed without much difficulty.

The same guidelines were applied to the acquisition of musical instruction materials.

This extraordinary document articulates for the first time many tenets of American music librarianship. Sonneck was concerned about the quality of the collection available to American scholars, about Europeans' perception of the collection's value and prestige. He recognized the urgency of acquiring current imprints, of acquiring most economically representative selections until such time as LC would buy more comprehensively, of developing special collections both as an aid to scholars and to enhance the prestige of the library. He identified certain techniques such as want lists, with their concomitant reliance upon carefully instructed European agents, and transcripts, that is, handmade copies of otherwise unavailable scores. He emphasized the purchase of music rather than the literature of music when a choice was required.

Sonneck conceived a five-year acquisition plan by which to implement his principles of systematic development. He proposed an annual expenditure of $5,000 for five years, by which time "the collections would be so well developed that a yearly sum of approximately $3,000 would be sufficient to keep the Music Division in the front rank."[11] The five-year plan was prepared in great detail. The first $3,000 each year—that is, the years 1905 to 1909 —was to be spent according to want lists. Those lists were arranged by medium, chronological period, and specific composers. The remaining $2,000 was to be spent in specific dollar amounts for Americana, current imprints of both music and music literature, miscellaneous "modern" music and music literature, and miscellaneous pre-1800 materials; a few hundred dollars were designated "margin." After the five-year period, the $3,000 acquisitions budget would be apportioned among the various classes so that eventually the collections would be sufficiently complete to allow the annual expenditure of $1,000 for rarities.

In the fall of 1904 Sonneck went back to Europe to implement his acquisitions policies for European music. He submitted want lists to publishers and dealers for special en bloc prices. He negotiated with secondhand dealers for the purchase of old scores, literature, and sets of musical periodicals identified on his want lists; each dealer was asked to specialize during the coming fiscal year in specific areas from among those identified in his plan. By block purchasing he realized a 38 percent reduction in net prices; by persuading dealers to use direct mailing, he saved a 5 percent commission fee. He approached various libraries for permission to have old opera scores hand copied for the Library of Congress. His practice of rounding out the collections with manuscript or photographic copies made especially for the Library of Congress was a unique activity. The unavailability of seventeenth- and eighteenth-century opera scores, many of which exist only in manuscript, forced Sonneck to arrange for copies if they were to be added to LC's collections. After the preliminary arrangements were made on the scene in 1904, he prepared a list of the operas to be copied. The project, which continued well into the 1930s after a delay caused by World War I, ultimately brought some 500 otherwise unavailable scores to the Music Division—and the United States.

By December 1908, when Sonneck addressed the annual meeting of the Music Teachers' National Association in Washington, D.C., the Library of Congress was in its fourth year of the five-year plan and Sonneck had identified additional principles or refinements of his collection development policy. More positively than in any earlier statement, he reiterated his intention to build a *"collection of music and books on music sufficiently comprehensive to ultimately release the American scholar of the necessity of consulting European libraries, except for research not bearing directly or indirectly on music in America as a reflex of music in Europe"* (his italics). Particularly, LC would acquire as many old printed books on music as possible "because extremely few of these books have been reprinted and because it is still entirely feasible to form a representative collection at a reasonable cost." Because the Library of Congress "is a reference and research, not a circulating or conservatory library," the purchase of scores would take precedence over orchestral parts. As a rule, arrangements would be bought only when vocal or piano scores were required to take the place of full scores.

Just as he refused to compete with European libraries for pre-
1700 scores, he thought it "folly" to compete with the great European libraries for autographs. But it was "entirely different with
autographs of American masters [which] should be saved from
disappearance and destruction [in] the logical place . . . our National Library."
From his experience he drew four advantages of want lists:
(1)   patiently waiting to check desirable items in publishers'
      and dealers' catalogues was time-consuming, passive;
(2)   the specialist should know where his collections are lacking
      and what will make them symmetrical, "and it is part of his
      business to compile systematic want lists covering the inter-
      ests of his special Division";
(3)   want lists in "the hands of reliable and energetic dealers"
      affect lower prices "than otherwise, and the saving in cleri-
      cal labor, correspondence, and therefore expense of time
      and money, is also considerable"; and
(4)   want lists are a hedge against unexpected monies—"we are
      ready . . . at a moment's notice."
To give an idea of the extent of his commitment to desiderata,
Sonneck revealed that lists he had prepared for the year 1907
filled 350 typewritten pages.
There was also a new term for the current status of LC's collection development. Now he was "working along the lines of carefully laid plans of development in a chronological backward direction" that he called

the theory of *concentric* development. This means that first the
nucleus of a library of moderate size but complete in itself was
formed, what one may call a good working collection. Then we
drew a wider circle, and now the circle which we are drawing
and which is so wide that it will require years to perfect it, reflects "the duty of the National Library to aid the unusual need
with the unusual book."[12]

He had resolved, albeit temporarily, the problem of the copyright deposits, so many of which were undesirable: he simply left
both copies with the Register of Copyrights so that undesirable
material was excluded from the shelves of the Music Division. As
that exclusion did not affect the number of readers using the
Music Division, Sonneck inferred that his readers were "readers of
quality."
Sonneck's practice regarding contemporary composers was

to collect comprehensively the published works of new composers who have "arrived," are about to "arrive," or who have
created controversial discussion of their tendencies. The Library
of Congress has come to be known universally among the co-
gnoscenti as the place where a thorough study of the works of
new men is likely to be possible.[13]

Almost from the beginning Sonneck had urged the development
of a special collection. His 1903 evaluative essay had remarked,
"The time has come to specialize." Evaluation of the extant collections made it clear that opera, or "dramatic music," to use his
phrase, could become "a special feature of pride without very
much difficulty." Five years later (1908) he published a catalogue
of full scores of operas, the first catalogue of a portion of LC's
music collections. But although opera had been "developed sufficiently to warrant the publication of a catalogue," it was "by no
means as comprehensive as planned."[14] Sonneck worked on the
collection until December 1915, when he wrote the preface to his
"practically" complete manuscript of a second edition of the
"Catalogue of Full Scores of Dramatic Music." Publication was
held off so that European purchases delayed in delivery by the war
could be included. But by then Sonneck himself had left LC and
the second edition was never published.
    Before it was widely known that it might be available for pur-
chase, Sonneck negotiated LC's acquisition of the unexcelled
libretto collection assembled by Alfred Schatz of Rostock,
Germany. That purchase, combined with LC's existing libretti,
immediately suggested publication of a catalogue of the combined
collections. The libretto catalogue, published in 1914, may be Sonneck's outstanding bibliographic achievement. Both American and
European critics agreed "to the importance of the subject, the
value of the material set forth, and the erudition displayed. . . ."[15]
Sonneck perceived the librarian's duty to the collections in the historical perspective of the great nineteenth-century European bib-
liographers/librarians who "exploited the resources" of their institutions in terms of published catalogues and bibliographies.
Lamenting the dearth of similar publications appropriate to
American libraries, "where the centers for musical research [were]
few and scattered," Sonneck remarked the "relief" with which
such catalogues would be received "by musical students, for, after
all is said, a card catalogue is but of local value."[16] During his
tenure at LC, Sonneck was responsible for at least eight bibliographic publications that advertised the development of the music

collection, especially in Europe; appraised American scholars of LC's resources; and created reference tools of permanent value.

Sonneck's concept of systematic collection development more than doubled the holdings of desirable music during his fifteen-year tenure. In the place of masses of copyright deposits, some nine-tenths of which he considered to be trash, were approximately 82,500 purchased items. At the time of his resignation on 5 September 1917, he considered the collection second only to Berlin as "a general international collection" while in musical Americana its superiority was "absolute."[17]

America's entry into the First World War understandably distressed Sonneck, the son of German Americans, who had himself been raised and educated in Germany. On the one hand his heart bled for Germany, where his mother still lived; on the other, he was a patriotic American. The circumstances made him uncomfortable in the nation's capital so he accepted Rudolph Schirmer's offer of a position with his music publishing firm in New York City. At first director of the publication department, later vice president, Sonneck remained with G. Schirmer, Inc., until his untimely death on 30 October 1928, one week after an emergency appendectomy. He was only fifty-five years old.

It was difficult for his friends and colleagues to console themselves at his death. Considering the incredible sum of Sonneck's labors, his friend Franklin Peale Patterson may have been right in his conclusion "that Sonneck simply wore himself out with work."[18] He was, in the final tally, responsible for the publication of twenty four books, many of which have been reprinted and/or issued in revised and enlarged editions, innumerable articles, and a group of musical compositions; he also was editor of the *Musical Quarterly* from its inception in 1915 until his death. Although he was removed from Washington, Sonneck never severed his ties with the Library of Congress. He was in regular contact with his successor, Carl Engel, and continued to advise the Library in matters of acquisition policy and collection development.

Sonneck persistently advocated music for all libraries. "Music in Our Libraries," an essay that first appeared in 1917, included seven arguments in support of that belief; three may be considered Sonneck's philosophy of librarianship:

a librarian ought not to content himself with giving to the public what it happens to want, but ought to help create a demand for what the public needs; . . . no self-respecting library can afford to be without certain cultural documents, whether they be consulted frequently or seldom. . . . The needs of one solitary scholarly specialist should weigh with librarians just as heavily as the wants of a hundred "general" and generally superficial and unproductive readers.

After all, it is not the frequency of use that counts, but the use to which a book is put.[19]

Sonneck's influence remains profound, extending to the present time. His classification, the model procedures he instituted at the Library of Congress Music Division, the importance of his studies in American music, his emphasis on published bibliographies and catalogues, and his recognition of the need and appropriateness of American music and musical literature for American libraries combine to lend substance to a perception of Oscar G. T. Sonneck as the father of American music librarianship.[20]

Notes

1. Translated from Carl Engel, "O. G. Sonneck; Ein Charakterbild," in *Studien zur Musikgeschichte, Festschriften für Guido Adler zum 75. Geburtstag* (Vienna: Universal, 1930), p. 217.

2. Otto Kinkeldey, "A Notable Scholar Passes On: Oscar G. T. Sonneck, Musicologist and Editor, Enjoyed A Brilliant Career," *Musical America* 48 (10 November 1928): 18.

3. Herbert Putnam, "O. G. Sonneck: Remarks at the Funeral Services, November 1st, 1928," *Musical Quarterly* 15 (1929): 1-2.

4. Ibid., p. 2.

5. Sonneck, "The Music Division of the Library of Congress," *Library Journal* 40 (August 1915): 587.

6. Quotations from his "Report on the Classification of Music and Literature on Music," 31 October 1902, Music Division Files, Library of Congress, Washington, D.C.

7. Sonneck, "Prefatory Note," in *Classification: Class M, Music; Class ML, Literature of Music; Class MT, Musical Instruction. Adopted December, 1902; as in Force April, 1904* (Washington, D.C.: Government Printing Office, 1904).

8. Sonneck, "Development of the Music Division," appended to typewritten 1902/3 annual report, Music Division Files, Library of Congress, Washington, D.C.

9. Sonneck, "The Music Division of the Library of Congress: Methods, Policies and Resources," *Proceedings* of the Music Teachers' National Association 3 (1908): 270-271.

10. Ibid., p. 271.

11. Appendix II, typewritten 1904 annual report, Music Division Files, Library of Congress, Washington, D.C.

12. Quotations from *Proceedings* of the Music Teachers' National Association 3 (1908): 272, 274, 275, 276.

13. *Report of the Librarian of Congress* (Washington, D.C.: Government Printing Office, 1917), p. 67.

14. Sonneck, "Prefatory Note," in *Dramatic Music (Class M 1500, 1510, 1520); Catalogue of Full Scores* (Washington, D.C.: Government Printing Office, 1908).

15. *Report of the Librarian of Congress*, 1914, p. 115.

16. Sonneck, "The Bibliography of American Music," *Proceedings and Papers* of the Bibliographical Society of America 1 (1905): 58–59.

17. *Report of the Librarian of Congress*, 1917, p. 66.

18. [Patterson], "Personal Recollections of Oscar G. Sonneck," *Musical Courier* 97 (15 November 1928): 8.

19. Sonneck, "Music in Our Libraries," *Art World* 2 (1917); reprinted in his *Miscellaneous Studies in the History of Music* (New York: Macmillan, 1921) and Carol June Bradley (ed.), *Reader in Music Librarianship* (Washington, D.C.: Microcard Edition, 1973).

20. *Dictionary of American Library Biography*, s.v. "Sonneck, Oscar George Theodore."

Frances Newman: Librarian and Novelist

Fay M. Blake

Hardly anyone remembers Frances Newman. In her short life-time her work glittered briefly, then died almost as soon as she did. But we ought to recall, if only for a moment, what an intelligent Southern lady, alienated but not freed from her own time and culture, was impelled to create. She was born in Atlanta on 13 September 1888, the youngest of six children. Her father was a distinguished judge of the Georgia District Court, born in Knoxville, Tennessee, a Confederate soldier at 17, wounded in 1864, a member of the Georgia bar at 23, and married at 28 to Frances Percy Alexander, great-granddaughter of the founder of Knoxville. Frances came into a world of economic comfort, social distinction, and rigid codes of behavior. Frances learned these codes from her mother, her three older sisters, and teachers at a series of the "best" schools: the Calhoun Street School and Washington Seminary in Atlanta, Agnes Scott College in Decatur, Miss Mc-Veagh's School for Young Ladies in Washington, and Mrs. Semple's School near Central Park in New York. A three-month tour of European capitals in 1910 polished the genteel young lady's very proper education, and Frances's mother had reason to expect that she could now settle her youngest daughter into a very proper marriage. But Frances, convinced even as a child that she could never rival her sister's beauty, balked. Somewhere along the way she had discovered that she was clever. After some courses in Italian and Greek at the Summer School of the South, in 1911 she

Fay M. Blake *is senior lecturer in library and information studies at the University of California, Berkeley.*

Journal of Library History, Vol. 16, No. 2, Spring 1981

began the course at the Atlanta Carnegie Library, forerunner of what is now the library school at Emory University. She graduated in June 1912, then worked for a year at Florida State College for Women in Tallahassee and hated it—the place, the work, and the exile from her family. She hurried back to Atlanta from what she called "bondage." In 1914 she joined her sister Isabel for a trip to Algiers, Egypt, Greece, and Italy, then came back to Atlanta and to a job at the Atlanta Library, "stamping red dates on neatly marked pockets in other people's novels." "I became a librarian because I liked books," she once wrote, and she was soon letting everyone at the Atlanta Library know what she thought about books, first in a kind of primitive reader's advisory service, then in reviews in the library's bulletin, where she not only listed but commented on the library's accessions, and then as head of the lending department in signed, and often caustic, reviews. Newman is one of the few librarians whose library work led directly to wider recognition as a writer.

In 1920 her father died, and her mother followed in 1922. Newman set up her own household with Susan Long, the black woman who had helped bring her into the world, and Louis Rucker, her young nephew, orphaned by the death of Newman's sister, whom Newman supported, educated, spoiled, and loved as long as she lived.

Her reviews in the library bulletin soon began appearing in the *Atlanta Constitution* and gradually in such contemporary journals as the *Bookman*, the *Atlanta Journal*, the *American Mercury*, and the *Saturday Review*. When she retired from her review column in the *Atlanta Journal*, she was succeeded by the then young cub reporter Margaret Mitchell, later the author of *Gone with the Wind*. In 1923 Newman and her friend Delia Johnston traveled to Europe together. Newman took a course or two at the Sorbonne and studied French literature with a Mlle. Angela Lovelli. The year 1924 was one of Newman's busiest and most productive. From book reviews she had graduated to a book-length work of criticism, *The Short Story's Mutations*, published in 1924. Her short story, "Rachel and Her Children," published in the *American Mercury* in May, was awarded the O. Henry Memorial Prize. In October Newman was appointed head librarian at the Georgia School of Technology, with Delia Johnston as her assistant. The *Atlanta Constitution*, reporting the appointments, describes Newman as "a popular and attractive member of Georgia society" and Johnston as a member of a family that "is among the oldest and most cultured in America," apparently qualifications as important for their new positions as their education and experience.[1] Newman remained at Georgia Tech for about a year, then took a year's leave of absence and finally left for good in 1926. She had begun work on her first novel and was able to complete *The Hard-Boiled Virgin* during a stay at the MacDowell Colony in Peterborough, New Hampshire, in 1926. The next two years were a restless saga: brief sorties to New York, a tour of Europe with her nephew in 1927; another sojourn at the MacDowell Colony to finish her second novel, *Dead Lovers Are Faithful Lovers*, and work on her last book, a translation of six stories by Jules Laforgue, both published in 1928; back to Europe again in the spring of 1928 and a hurried return when her eyes began to trouble her.

Quite early in her life Newman acquired an eccentricity that developed into a mild monomania. Her passion for the color purple and all of its shades—lavender, mauve, fuchsia, violet, plum, cyclamen—led not only to such esoterica as lavender bedsheets and purple hats but to the need for purplish bindings on her books. "Besides my own personal fondness of purple, so many people associate me with this color that I think it has a real commercial value. If the book has a second printing, can't you make it purple?" she pleaded with her publisher, and like the iron-willed Southern lady she was, she got her way.

On 22 October 1928 Newman died in her rooms at the Hotel Schuyler in New York. Her brother Henry had hurried up from Atlanta and her sister Isabel Patterson of Richmond joined him. It was announced that death had resulted from a cerebral hemorrhage complicated by pneumonia, but the assistant medical examiner of New York announced that death was due to an overdose of veronal.[2] A bizarre incident occurred just before her death, which Newman, characteristically, enjoyed. The magazine *Vanity Fair* informed her they were publishing a parody of her work. In the parody a novelist jumps to her death on October 21, the day before her actual death. The parody appeared in the November 1928 issue of the magazine, but *Vanity Fair* yanked the Covarrubias illustration that was to have accompanied the article, a drawing of Newman in her coffin.[3]

Newman's published fictional work is really too meager to assure her a prominent place in American literature—one short story and two novels. But in her time she represented, alone, the literature by and about Atlantans and, by extension, the literature of the South. Margaret Mitchell writes in a letter dated 4 September 1938, ten years after Newman's death, "We sho' Gawd got a flourishing crop of authors in Georgia now! Not so long ago we could only point to Frances Newman and then hastily brag about Uncle Remus."[4] H. L. Mencken, who detested the Southern literature he called the "Sahara of the Bozart," described Newman as the "violet of the Sahara." To the Baptist Convention of Georgia, Newman's *The Hard-Boiled Virgin* was "blasphemous stuff which reeks with vulgarity and with unmentionable implications," and the novel was banned in Boston, when being banned in Boston still had some consequences, for "obscene, indecent, impure language" and "corrupting the morals of youth." The consequence for *The Hard-Boiled Virgin* was that it immediately hit the bestseller list and established Newman's reputation as a sophisticate.

Newman's South is neither the Georgia of Erskine Caldwell's sharecroppers and mill-workers nor the nostalgic antebellum Georgia of *Gone with the Wind*. During Newman's lifetime, Atlanta's factory workers were notoriously among the lowest paid in the country, but Newman's work never even indicates that she knew of the existence of industrial Atlanta. Rural Georgia, with its desperately poor black and white workers struggling to make the red earth produce, never surfaces in Newman's work. During her lifetime Atlanta was the scene of continuing harsh discrimination against its black population. In 1906 a violent race riot, white mobs rampaging through Atlanta's black neighborhoods, resulted in the deaths of ten blacks and two whites before the National Guard finally restored order, but Frances Newman's fiction barely hints at the existence of either the injustice or the violence. Her own lifelong relationship with Susan Long is a typical Southern arrangement. Mrs. Long, born a slave and a runaway when she was a child of eight, is always her "mammy," tenderly regarded, closer to her than her own mother, a source of comfort and love but a social inferior. Newman's letters whenever she is away from home are full of loving care for Long and injunctions to her nephew to be mindful of her health and comfort, but Newman never questions a black woman's rightful place as a domestic servant. In her fiction blacks never appear except as servants, without names or personalities, differentiated only by color.

> Evelyn Cunningham took a card from the deep primrose-coloured maid whom her mother had lent to her because she could not have cards and platters handed to her daughter by a maid whose darker ancestors must have been unworthy of being brought to Virginia—or who must have been found unworthy of sawing the logs of Virginia or of drawing water from Virginia's wells. . . .[5]

she writes in *Dead Lovers*, and in an unpublished story, "Atlanta Biltmore," the bellboys at the Atlanta hotel are not only in "uniforms as correct as those they have at the New York Biltmore" but, just as correctly, all with "cafe au lait faces," an allusion to the convention that required black domestic servants to have light complexions. We know that Newman was troubled by the prejudice and discrimination against blacks. In a letter to Scott Cunningham, written on 16 January 1927, she says: "Of course, I don't know any new negroes, but I'm far from disliking negroes —in fact, I suffer tortures over their sorrows, because I don't see what can be done about them."[6] We can take this as a cry from the heart, but Newman's fiction does not recognize the existence of black life.

Also in Newman's lifetime, Atlanta was the scene of an ugly lynching that sent shock waves through the country. In 1913 Leo Frank, the Jewish manager of an Atlanta pencil factory, was tried for the rape and murder of a fourteen-year-old girl who worked in the factory. During and after the trial, inflammatory anti-Semitic articles appeared in the *Jeffersonian Magazine*, edited by Tom Watson, and anti-Semitic mobs demonstrated in the streets. An Atlanta lawyer recalls: "I attended every day of the trial. The yokels lined the streets yelling at the jury every night when they went to the hotel, 'Hang the Jew.' You were afraid to walk down the street if you were Jewish."[7] When Frank's death sentence was commuted by the governor of Georgia, Frank was dragged from his cell and hanged by a lynch mob. Not a breath of this case or of the life of Atlanta's Jewish community surfaces in Newman's published work. But the library of the Atlanta Historical Society has a typescript of the story "Atlanta Biltmore," written by Newman in 1924. It describes a dinner party given at the Atlanta Biltmore by Mr. and Mrs. Arthur Hirsch, leaders of Atlanta's Jewish aristocracy and owners of Atlanta's only Rolls Royce limousine. The Hirsches are anxious for a match between their daughter and Henry Minis, scion of a distinguished Savannah Jewish family. Newman is obviously knowledgeable about the lives of the Jewish aristocracy, although she could have had little direct contact with this clannish group—doubly removed from the rest of Atlanta because of their wealth and because of their Jewishness. People who could afford to buy Renoirs and Rolls Royces, who chose their clothes at Mme. Jeanne Lanvin's and M. Paul Poiret's Paris ateliers, and who served as founding directors of Atlanta's opera, did not mingle with most of the rest of Atlanta's population, and Jews, whatever their financial status, were not generally welcome outside of their own society. While Newman's usual ironical style, heavily used in this story, makes her own attitude to the characters somewhat ambiguous, it is clear that the Hirsches, the Minises, the Samuels, the Jonases, and the Lazaruses are people of cultivated tastes. They are not only patrons of the arts, but they know and appreciate Renoir and Titian, Chaliapin and Frances Alda, Bernard Shaw and Georg Kaiser, Adam ballrooms and Chippendale desks. Newman is laughing at their ostentation, their peculiar prohibitions of certain foods, and their uncertain compromises with Eastern European backgrounds, but she is laughing gently and without the virulent dislike and contempt prevalent in her time and place. Only once does Newman explicitly refer to the lynchings that repeatedly occurred in the South, although she manages to avoid any mention of the fact that lynching was most often a weapon of terror against black people. In *Dead Lovers Are Faithful Lovers* Isabel Ramsay, the librarian heroine, recalls her newspaper editor father:

> She always remembered her father's sufferings on the day when he had wanted his words to scream out his horror of a state in which hundreds of young gentlemen from America's oldest state university could stand still and hear another human being scream out of the agony of a body which was burning a slow exit from a world that dozens of virgins' sons had lived and died to save.[8]

The characteristic of her writing of which Newman herself was proudest and on which she worked hardest was her distinctive style. The beginning of the twentieth century was a time of experimentation in prose style, and Newman had read assiduously and reviewed appreciatively such revolutionary stylists as Stein, Hemingway, James, and Joyce as well as Laforgue and Morand. Reviewers commented again and again on her style: "perhaps the most amazing prose style in America" (Burton Rascoe); "a tight, glittering, extremely uncommon style" (H. L. Mencken); "readable for the ingenuity of the style" (*Times Literary Supplement*); or the *Boston Transcript*'s remark on her "peculiar style." It is not peculiar, only different, and so distinctive that it lends itself to parody. Newman uses long involved sentences and insistent repetitions and has an almost obsessive eye for color. She describes the elegant clothes of her characters with careful specific detail and consistently avoids direct conversation:

She sat up on the yellow chaise-longue and carefully slipped off her beautifully clocked black stockings. And then she stood up and slipped off her beautifully embroidered white chemise, and carefully laid it over the mahogany lyre which was the back of a little chair.

She walked across the yellow rug to the little satin-wood dressing-table from which her father's great-grandmother had often risen to put her beautifully arranged hair through the little door of a powdering-closet. And she looked in its experienced mirror at the light brown hair and the dark brown lashes and the delicately concave nose and the white neck. . . .

Then she walked across the yellow rug again, and she looked in her bathroom's long mirror at the hair and the eyes and the nose and the lips. . . . She looked down at the breasts which she would have liked to have remind her of the budding halves of two pomegranates. . . .[9]

A style as distinctive as this is almost crying for a malicious parody, and John Riddell in the *Vanity Fair* article mentioned earlier obliges wickedly. He calls it "Dead Novelists Are Good Novelists."

. . . she walked across the yellow hooked rug into her bathroom, and she looked into the full-length mirror, which had been presented to her by the son of two Chicago packers because it was the precise reflection of her beautifully-tended figure, at the familiar arrangement of hair and eyes and nose and lips, which could be called a face, if you were being general enough. And then she looked down at the delicately curved throat, and the voluptuous arms, and the two round firm white objects which reminded her of two round firm white pint-bottles of cream which the Borden's man left on her doorstep every morning, but which of course were really only her two fists clenched tightly before her, because a heavy golden shell of pain had just burst in the center of her body for fear that John Riddell did not love her.[10]

Newman's most important contribution to American writing, one she was fully aware of, is her perception of the role of women in our society. It is no accident that critic Elizabeth Hardwick, advisory editor for Arno Press's reprint collection called "Rediscovered Fiction by American Women," chose both Newman's novels for reprinting. Newman described *The Hard-Boiled Virgin* as "the

first novel in which a woman ever told the truth about how
women feel" in a letter to her publisher, Horace Liveright,[11] and a
review of *Dead Lovers Are Faithful Lovers* by Isabel Paterson
says, "No man could have written it. Most men will be unable to
read it. It says things men have tried by every social and economic
device to avoid hearing."[12] The main characters in all of Newman's
published fiction are women, and it is through their eyes and
bodies that we view and feel their experiences. They are all women
who are well off, well fed, richly clothed, physically well cared
for. When they work at all, it is not from dire necessity but rather
from a need for some sort of genteel recognition. Isabel Ramsay in
Dead Lovers is a librarián at Atlanta's Carnegie Library, as Newman herself was, but she seems able to slip away frequently to
meet her lover in New York, and her expensive stylish clothes are
not those of the other librarians who work to support themselves.
Both Evelyn Cunningham of *Dead Lovers* and Katharine Faraday
of *The Hard-Boiled Virgin* come from distinguished Southern
families with Confederate generals and railway presidents and lawyers and judges among their forbears. But it is Newman's contention that these cosseted, gently bred Southern ladies are so crippled psychologically by the education they receive and the severe
constraints of the society they live in that their lives are shadowy
half-lives and their loves unfulfilled half-loves. In her column in
the *Atlanta Journal* Newman wrote of *The Hard-Boiled Virgin*:

> I discovered that I was going to write a novel about a girl
> who began by believing every thing her family and her teachers
> said to her, and who ended by disbelieving most of those things,
> but by finding that she couldn't keep herself from behaving as
> if she still believed them—about a girl who was born and bred to
> be a southern lady, and whose mind never could triumph over
> the ideas she was presumably born with, and the ideas she was
> undoubtedly taught.[13]

All of her ladies—Katharine Faraday, Isabel Ramsay, Evelyn Cunningham, and Mrs. Overton of "Rachel and Her Children"—have
been brought up to believe that their own lives could become complete only through the love of their husbands. Katharine and Isabel never marry, Evelyn is so terrified of losing her husband to
another woman that she finds happiness only when her husband
suddenly drops dead and she knows at least he will be a "faithful
lover." Mrs. Overton, married off at seventeen to Colonel Overton,
an elderly widower, finds him an overbearing, bad-tempered

master who jealously watches her every move, even the purchase of a new hat or a visit to the dentist. By the time he dies, Mrs. Overton realizes he has had a long relationship with a "prepossessing colored—just barely colored—nurse who had been the comfort of his declining years," but instead of the freedom she expected from his death, Mrs. Overton finds herself once more a dependent, watched over by her daughter and her lawyer son-in-law. Trapped by marriage and by motherhood into a life in which all her decisions are made by others, Mrs. Overton begins to pine "for a house where a ringing telephone would mean that some one in the world wanted to talk with her badly enough to go through the trouble of getting a telephone number." She is shaking with bitter sobs at her daughter's funeral not because she mourns her daughter but because she is mourning for her own lost life. A brief hope that her daughter's death would let her once more preside over her own tea table is shattered when she realizes that her son-in-law will soon remarry and that she will once more be subordinated to others.[14]

Not only are these women thrashing impotently in a world that denies them independent recognition, but their severely limited education denies them even a sensible knowledge of their own bodies. Katharine Faraday has to learn in secret and with an abiding sense of guilt and shame that her sexual desires are as compelling as a man's. She discovers painfully that her careful training by her mother, her older sisters, and her schools and her immersion in hundreds of romantic novels have filled her head with mistaken claptrap and that her expectations of proper male behavior have absolutely nothing to do with real people's real behavior. She learns that a passionate kiss from a suitor is not an irreparable insult but a normal response to provocative flirtation but she learns it too late. The suitor doesn't return. She learns that a well-liked but profligate brother has died of venereal disease, a fact that is never acknowledged, only whispered. She learns about masturbation, male anatomy, and the sexual act but not about love and she learns what she learns almost accidentally and despite her family, her friends, and her teachers. Finally, she learns how to write, but through painful experiment and not through anything in her formal education. The Southern lady, filling her days with the importance of the color of her gloves or the correct way to hold a bouquet or, most important, the proper game-playing that will net her a rich, distinguished husband, has been rendered incapable of understanding the realities of creativity, of passion, and of love. Southern women's lives are sacrificed to gentility and ignorance. In the 1920s when Frances Newman was creating her psychically crippled gentlewomen the South was certainly not ready for her revelations. Neither was the respectable literary world, although a sense of titillation gave Newman a momentary notoriety. But we have some reason to believe that Newman applied her embittered clarity to her own life. The recognition that she was herself—like Katharine, Isabel, Evelyn, and Mrs. Overton—crippled by her genteel past and no longer capable of an independent and fully loving life may have precipitated the veronal overdose that ended her life at forty.

Notes

1. *Atlanta Constitution*, 28 October 1924, p. 15.
2. *New York Times*, 26 October 1928, p. 4.
3. *New York Times*, 28 October 1928, p. 3.
4. Richard Harwell (ed.), *Margaret Mitchell's "Gone With the Wind" Letters, 1936-1949* (New York: Macmillan, 1976), p. 223.
5. Frances Newman, *Dead Lovers Are Faithful Lovers* (New York: Boni and Liveright, 1928), p. 34.
6. Hansell Baugh (ed.), *Frances Newman's Letters* (New York: Liveright, 1929), p. 240.
7. Eli N. Evans, *The Provincials: A Personal History of Jews in the South* (New York: Atheneum, 1973), p. 273.
8. Newman, *Dead Lovers*, p. 219.
9. Ibid., pp. 47-49.
10. John Riddell, "Meaning No Offense," *Vanity Fair* (November 1928): 89.
11. Baugh, *Newman's Letters*, p. 205.
12. *New York Herald Tribune Books*, 6 May 1928, p. 3.
13. Quoted in Robert Y. Drake, Jr., "Frances Newman: Fabulist of Decadence," *Georgia Review* 14, no. 4 (Winter 1960): 391.
14. Frances Newman, "Rachel and Her Children," *American Mercury* 2, no. 5 (May 1924): 92-96.

Carlos E. Castañeda's Rendezvous with a Library: The Latin American Collection, 1920–1927—The First Phase

Félix D. Almaráz, Jr.

In the seniority of his career—especially after wartime experiences as regional director of President Franklin D. Roosevelt's Committee on Fair Employment Practices—Carlos Eduardo Castañeda definitely achieved distinction as a first-rate historian of the Borderlands. In light of honors and awards that Carlos received in the 1940s and 1950s, few individuals who equated the prestigious *Our Catholic Heritage in Texas* with Castañeda realized that his early career included tenure as librarian of the Benson Latin American Collection at the University of Texas at Austin. Even today, contemporary observers unaware of the contributions Castañeda made to the professions of history and library science conceivably may overlook the cultural significance in the dedication of the Perry-Castañeda building on the Austin campus. The first phase of Castañeda's rendezvous with the library began in 1920 and concluded in 1927, when he assumed responsibility for the Latin American Collection.

Born to a French mother and Mexican father in Camargo, Tamaulipas, in 1896, Carlos E. Castañeda established his cultural roots in the Lower Rio Grande Valley. After attending schools in both Matamoros and Brownsville, excelling in mathematics and foreign languages, Castañeda graduated as valedictorian of the class of 1916. Following graduation from high school, Castañeda remained in Brownsville for nearly a year, working at odd jobs to augment financial support of the family, whose parents had died

Félix D. Almaráz, Jr., *is professor of history at the University of Texas at San Antonio.*

Journal of Library History, Vol. 16, No. 2, Spring 1981
© 1981 by the University of Texas Press   0022-2259/81/020315-15$01.50

in 1909. On the strength of advice from local teachers, Castañeda enrolled at the University of Texas in 1917, seriously contemplating a career in civil engineering. America's involvement in World War I briefly interrupted his studies. Although Castañeda's alien status exempted him from military duty, he enlisted in the army because he believed that it was his patriotic responsibility and that his record of service might expedite an application for naturalized citizenship in the future. With the signing of the Armistice—which Castañeda acknowledged with pride because it coincided with his birthday—he dropped out of school due to lack of finances and accepted employment with an oil company in Tampico.[1]

Early in January 1920, just prior to his departure for the engineering job in Mexico, Castañeda attended the public inaugural ceremony of Governor Pat M. Neff. Among the "colorful delegation" on the platform, representing Mexico's President-elect Alvaro Obregón, was General Manuel Pérez Treviño, whose splendid uniform of chief of staff of the Mexican army contrasted dramatically with the civilian attire of other dignitaries present for the occasion. No one in the audience, let alone Castañeda, could have predicted that from this official visit, within a year, the University of Texas would acquire "the finest and most extensive historical and literary collection of Mexico."[2] When the inauguration ended, Castañeda proceeded into his native Mexico, hardly cognizant that he had taken the initial step in the direction of a rendezvous with a great collection.

The rigors of laboring in the oil fields, not without high adventure and adequate compensation, soon convinced Castañeda that he should return to Austin, where he had come under the influence of two outstanding historians who appreciated his keen intellect and linguistic ability, Eugene Campbell Barker and Charles Wilson Hackett. In the fall semester of 1920, as Castañeda resumed his studies, the next step in his rendezvous with the library occurred in Mexico.

The special interest of the University of Texas in the history and culture of Spanish America originated in 1897, when Professors George P. Garrison and Lilia Casis visited Mexico's Archivo General de la Nación to transcribe handwritten copies of important documents. Subsequently, in 1905, the eminent scholar of the Borderlands Professor Herbert E. Bolton offered the first courses in Latin American history at the Austin campus. Then, between 1915 and 1917, Professor W. E. Dunn visited archives in Spain and Mexico in search of documents for the history of the Southwest. Late in November 1920, reciprocating courtesies extended to General Pérez Treviño, President Obregón invited a delegation from Texas to attend his inauguration. Among those in the Texan party were three members of the University's Board of Regents (H. A. Wroe, H. J. Luther Stark, and J. A. Kemp) and Adjunct Professor Charles W. Hackett of the department of history. In the midst of festivities in Mexico City, Hackett visited the widow of Genaro García, the most prominent historian and bibliophile south of the border, who had recently died. In the conversation Hackett confirmed a rumor that the vast library of the distinguished Mexican scholar was for sale. Disappointed that the Mexican government had manifested little interest in purchasing the collection, the García family, consisting of the widow and ten children, then turned to the United States in search of a buyer.

The Texan delegation, holding a "hurried consultation" in the hotel, agreed to obtain an immediate option to conduct "a more careful investigation" to determine the extent and value of Señor Genaro García's library. In less than a month, Ernest W. Winkler, reference librarian of the University of Texas, journeyed to Mexico City to inventory and appraise the 18,000 printed materials and 200,000 manuscript folios. Winkler submitted a favorable report in February 1921, after which Kemp persuaded the Board of Regents at the May meeting to purchase the García Collection for $100,000 plus other costs. By the end of June 1921, a special train from "the high *mesas* of the central plateau" conveyed the contents of García's library to the Río Grande. Two representatives of the García estate and one from the University of Texas escorted the crates of books and documents through customs and finally to the campus library. The delivery of the García Collection coincided with Castañeda's graduation from the University with a bachelor of arts degree in history.[3]

In the three years after graduation, Castañeda accomplished several personal and professional goals. First, he secured employment as a high school instructor of Spanish in Beaumont, supplementing his salary with night teaching at the local YMCA. Next, during the Christmas holidays of 1921, he married his childhood sweetheart, Elisa Ríos, in San Antonio. An unexpected gift for Castañeda was the publication of his initial article, entitled "The Early Missionary Movement in Texas." At the conclusion of the academic year in Beaumont, the newlyweds relocated in San Antonio. Castañeda then negotiated a teaching assignment in the Spanish department of Brackenridge High School, and periodically commuted to Austin as a part-time graduate student in history. On the day after Christmas 1922, his wife gave birth to a daughter,

Irma Gloria. Finally, late in the summer of 1923, when Castañeda successfully completed all requirements for the master's degree, he and the family moved to Williamsburg, Virginia, where he had accepted a position as associate professor of modern languages at the historic College of William and Mary.[4] Ironically, it was from distant Virginia that Castañeda accelerated his rendezvous with the García Collection.

Although financial problems, coupled with Elisa's frequent illnesses, perennially haunted Castañeda in Virginia, he remained an incurable optimist who discovered redeeming values in every situation. His gregarious, outgoing disposition soon won many friends and acquaintances for the family on and off the campus. Even so, perhaps the isolation he experienced from familiar surroundings prompted him to search for new opportunities for professional growth and advancement. Castañeda maintained close contact with his mentor at the University of Texas, Eugene C. Barker, by mail. In fact, within six months after becoming established at William and Mary, Castañeda accepted Barker's suggestion of translating for publication the journal of Colonel Juan N. Almonte, who inspected Mexican Texas in 1834 prior to the outbreak of the War for Independence. Another research project that Castañeda launched was a study concerning "the early teaching of modern languages in the United States."[5] In the meantime, two of his articles—one on a Texas Franciscan missionary and another on educational innovations in Mexico—appeared in print.[6]

Personal problems notwithstanding, a year later Castañeda welcomed the publication of two additional contributions in the *Southwestern Historical Quarterly* and the *Catholic Educational Review*. The college administration of William and Mary praised his essay on early modern language instruction by reprinting 500 copies for complimentary distribution. Aside from regular teaching responsibilities, Castañeda became enthusiastically involved in planning the college's 1926 summer school program in Mexico in association with the National Autonomous University. Two courses that he introduced into the curriculum and taught himself were Latin American History in English and Government of Spanish America. "If the plan fails," he wrote to Barker, "it will not be for lack of advertisement for I am doing all I can to keep it before the public."[7] By early spring, with the summer school program fairly organized, Castañeda succeeded in getting another article on Argentina's renowned educator Domingo Faustino Sarmiento accepted in *Current History*. Excited about the prospects for the summer, Castañeda informed Barker that he might have an opportunity to confer with Hackett, who would be in Mexico City at approximately the same time.[8] Hardly did Castañeda realize that new horizons beckoned south of the border and in the Lone Star State.

Evidently the summertime experience of teaching in Mexico provided many occasions for Hackett and Castañeda to become reacquainted and to discuss career possibilities at the University of Texas, particularly the management of the García Collection. In the meantime, the Knights of Columbus of Texas, a fraternal organization of Catholic laymen and clergy, inaugurated a comprehensive history project designed to commemorate the Lone Star Centennial, in which Castañeda would play a prominent role. Once back in Austin, Hackett assuredly informed Barker and the library director of his conversations with Castañeda regarding doctoral studies and the likelihood of full-time work. By March of the following year, Ernest W. Winkler of the UT–Austin library broached the subject of employment with Castañeda:

> A vacancy exists in the librarianship of the Garcia Collection. Dr. Hackett informed me that you are planning to continue your studies in history. Does the place named above interest you? It pays an annual salary of $1800. Librarians are required to work seven hours a day, and are allowed four weeks vacation. Besides being work in which you would be very much interested, it would be right in line with your plans, therefore I've ventured to lay it before you.[9]

Given Castañeda's desire to return to Texas under auspicious circumstances, he obviously found the job offer interesting, but the question of salary at the moment seemed an immovable barrier. Nevertheless, the momentum was in Castañeda's favor when the Knights of Columbus state deputy, Joseph I. Driscoll, a lawyer in El Paso, contacted him about their centennial project. Specifically, the Texas State Council of the Knights of Columbus, through the establishment of a Historical Commission to supervise the project, envisioned a full-length study of the Catholic church from the Spanish colonial period "to the present time." "Your name," wrote Driscoll matter-of-factly, "has been mentioned to me as being one well informed touching the archives of Texas, conversant with material for such work and well advised as to the sources." The El Paso attorney then invited Castañeda to submit suggestions on "method of procedure."[10]

As the spring term came to an end at William and Mary,

Castañeda optimistically accepted the directorship of another summer session in Mexico City. Reinforcing his optimism was the publication of another edited translation in the *Southwestern Historical Quarterly* and an upcoming essay in *North American Review*. For expediency, he obtained a letter of introduction to the American consul general in the Mexican capital from a friend in the college's department of biblical literature and religious education.[11] In early June, before leaving Williamsburg, Castañeda mailed Driscoll a detailed memorandum outlining a methodical approach to the acquisition of primary sources and to a systematic arrangement of topics. Informing the lawyer of his itinerary in Mexico City, including residence at Hotel Metropolitano, Castañeda explained the plans of his current research: "I am vitally interested in the historical background of the Church in Mexico and am at present collecting some material on the early relations between the Church and the Government in an endeavor to trace the distant causes for the present trouble in Mexico." He capped the memorandum with an acknowledgement of positive interest in the KC project: "Needless for me to add that I am more than willing to cooperate with you in any way possible. I am a graduate of the University of Texas, and though a Mexican by birth, I feel that I am a Texan in spirit." To cement cordial relations with the state deputy, Castañeda dispatched reprints of his earlier articles on Texas missionaries and his latest effort, an essay entitled "The First Pan-American Congress."[12]

Driscoll capitalized upon Castañeda's presence in Mexico to enlist his services in behalf of the project of the Knights of Columbus. "I feel free to authorize you for the Commission," the deputy wrote, "to secure and send such materials as you may find while in Mexico City bearing on our subject, not covered in the secondary sources of history already available." For Castañeda's benefit in understanding the leadership role of the Historical Commission, Driscoll identified the principal members, the most prominent being the permanent chairman, the Rev. Dr. Paul J. Foik, C.S.C., of St. Edward's University in Austin.[13] Notwithstanding Driscoll's zeal in trying to recruit Castañeda for the KC project, the success of the summer school program in Mexico was of more immediate concern for the administration of William and Mary. To this end Castañeda devoted his boundless energy, traveling in high style in an ocean liner from New York via Havana to Vera Cruz. Then he and the student group boarded a train for Mexico City.[14] As in the previous summer, Castañeda found another opportunity to discuss the library employment situation with

Hackett. Understandably, since Hackett was only an intermediary, nothing definite resulted from the extended conversations, but in any event the seed of an idea had been planted in Castañeda's mind. When he returned to Williamsburg, his colleagues lionized him on account of a timely article, published in the *Catholic World* during his absence, with the provocative title, "The Trouble in Mexico: Both Sides. I. Is Mexico Turning Bolshevik?" The focal point of the article was the bitter power struggle between the Catholic church and anticlerical elements in Mexico's ruling establishment.[15]

From William and Mary, Castañeda maintained contact with influential friends in the history department at the University of Texas. At the beginning of the fall semester he wrote to Hackett, reminding him: "of our last conversation regarding the Garcia Library and the possibility of my securing a position in connection with it. I wish you w[o]uld keep me in mind and take me seriously, as I am very anxious to return to Texas. Of course, I am not set on the library position, but if there is any other possibility, do not fail to keep me in mind. . . ."[16] Whatever else Castañeda may have contemplated concerning employment opportunities, he perceived the librarianship of the García Collection as an avenue for returning home to Texas. Still, the insufficient salary level Winkler had described in early spring disturbed him. The conversations with Hackett in Mexico assuredly gave Castañeda the confidence he needed to open negotiations directly with Ernest Winkler. Addressing the issues forthrightly, Castañeda responded to Winkler's original inquiry: "Needless to say, your proposition interests me deeply, and doubtless the work would be most congenial and pleasant, but there are several considerations I would like to lay before you before I would accept your offer." In rapid order Castañeda outlined the issues from his perspective. First, the duty schedule seemed too long to allow time for "personal work" on doctoral studies. Second, at William and Mary he earned $2,700 a year for three classes a day. The salary Winkler offered was $900 less than his current income. These points, of course, could be adjusted. What concerned Castañeda most, given the fact that the new academic year had begun, was the question of when Winkler expected him to come to Texas. Castañeda's contract at William and Mary required at least a sixty-day notice for the administration to hire a replacement. Under the circumstances, Castañeda admitted, "I could not leave here before December 1st." For him to consider the librarianship offer in earnest, Carlos asked Winkler for a salary of $2,400 and a two-month extension "to make the necessary arrangements for my departure."[17]

Concomitant with the correspondence with Winkler's office, Castañeda enlisted the support of his old mentor at the Austin campus, Professor Eugene C. Barker. "The offer of Mr. Winkler appeals to me very strongly," Castañeda wrote, "but under the present circumstances I could not accept at the salary he suggests and the hours he mentions." He asked Barker to intercede with the librarian in his behalf. Within a week Barker replied: "Winkler wants more time to consider. He is not inclined to shorten the hours, but may come up on the salary. . . . I will try to reconcile him to the better salary." From Barker's vantage point the crucial issue was not the salary. More importantly, for the sake of his protégé, Barker worried about the length of time it would take Castañeda to satisfy the requirements for the doctorate. "The things would drag out interminably if you busied yourself for seven hours a day over eleven months in the year in the Library job. Think soberly about the matter and let me have your conclusions while Winkler is puzzling over it."[18]

In the autumn months of 1926, Castañeda and Winkler, with Barker's friendly intercession, negotiated the details of an employment contract and a reporting date acceptable to the presidents of both institutions. Reflecting long-range planning in recommending Castañeda to the president of the University of Texas, Winkler advocated changing the title of the collection—from García to Latin American—"because it interprets itself and is in keeping with the broadened work required of this librarian." In mid-October, Winkler notified Castañeda of the administration's affirmative decision. "I congratulate you upon this appointment, for if any of my information about you is correct, it means the beginning of a very interesting, valuable and congenial service for you near home."[19] In accepting the librarianship at $200 a month, effective 1 January 1927, Castañeda soon found himself in a quandary with the president of William and Mary, who preferred that Castañeda delay his departure for Texas for another month to coincide with the termination of the fall term.[20] While the presidents deliberated this final point, Castañeda informed a friend in neighboring South Carolina of his imminent farewell to Williamsburg:

The law of compensation is ever present in human life. We must sacrifice some things in order to secure others and it is for us to decide which we prefer. We may choose wrong and regret it all our lives, but we may be fortunate to change our whole future.

> ... I am decided to take this opportunity if the University of
> Texas accedes to my demands. Everything is not definitely set-
> tled, but there are nine chances to one that it will.[21]

Meanwhile, as Castañeda waited for a decision on a suitable departure time, he received a letter from a priest at St. Edward's University. There was no way for Castañeda to know with certitude
that the plans of the Knights of Columbus which Father Paul J.
Foik outlined to him would eventually become intermingled with
his own career as librarian and historian. "Your knowledge of original sources," wrote Foik, "both in Texas and Mexico surely qualify [sic] you to speak with great authority." Although Foik's
letter was merely introductory, he concluded with a tempting invitation: "If you can be of service to me in any way, . . . in the way
of p[l]anning the prospectus of the work . . . I am sure that I will
appreciate your efforts."[22]

Throughout the month of November, Winkler and Castañeda
exchanged letters on the matter of a starting date. With presidential approval, Winkler granted permission fo Castañeda to remain
at William and Mary until the end of the semester, with February
1 scheduled for his initiation and orientation as librarian. In turn,
Castañeda pledged to Winkler that he would arrive "in Austin
about the 28th or 29th" of January for a prompt report to duty.
"I shall be ready for real hard work when I come," Castañeda
assured Winkler, "for I am looking forward with a great deal of
anticipation to my new position."[23] Cognizant of Charles W.
Hackett's role as intermediary in recruiting him for the library,
Castañeda thanked the noted Latin Americanist and admitted his
eagerness "to be among old friends again."[24]

In the midst of preparations to return to Texas, Castañeda briefly enjoyed the attention lavished upon him by colleagues at William and Mary on the occasion of the publication of an editorial
in the *Commonweal* that actually centered on the Spanish Southwest, the cultural region with which, through Hackett, he shared
identification with the Bolton school of historiography.[25] Castañeda took a big step toward his destiny with the Boltonian fraternity when he expressed to Father Foik constructive interest in the
history project of the Knights of Columbus in Texas. Seemingly
uninhibited by shades of regional pride, he informed Foik:

> The need for this has long been felt by many Catholics and his-
> torians in general. Furthermore, our church has not had a more
> interesting history in any other part of this country than in the

Lone Star State. California has made good use of its early missionary history and Texas can do as much, for its history is even
more interesting and nearer being a great epic in the annals of
missionary work than that of California.[26]

Not without some emotion, in January 1927, Castañeda concluded a memorable association at William and Mary with a banquet sponsored by the Spanish Club, which he moderated. In
attendance at the "sumptuous affair" in his honor was the president of the college, who subsequently assessed Castañeda's contributions. J. A. Chandler wrote:

> I consider that you have been very successful in your work.
> . . . Your absence will be felt by the members of the faculty,
> but more so by the students, with whom you worked so closely
> and by whom you were loved. . . . You came to us at the begin-
> ning of the session 1923–1924, and I feel that within this period
> the Spanish [curricular] work has been put on a high plane and
> a firm basis here.
> The summer school in Mexico, which you originated and suc-
> cessfully carried out . . . was an innovation into our curriculum,
> and I feel that it was worth-while.[27]

Describing the event as a "fitting climax" to his career at William
and Mary, Castañeda and the audience heard an address by Antonio Alonso of the Pan American Union in Washington, D.C.
After the banquet, Castañeda carefully completed travel plans. On
January 19, he accompanied his wife and daughter to Richmond,
where they boarded a train for Texas. Two days later, from Williamsburg, he said farewell to his friends and commenced the long
drive by automobile to his alma mater.[28]

On 1 February 1927, Castañeda punctually assumed responsibility for the Latin American Collection at the University of
Texas. To familiarize himself personally with the contents, he
began a comprehensive inventory of the entire holdings. A week
later, with only a fifth of the contents inventoried, he reported to
a friend in Virginia: "Here I am in Texas and in full possession of
one of the most wonderful collection [*sic*] of books in the United
States. Believe me, I feel sort of puffed up, but hard work is about
to take all the puffiness out of me. . . ."[29] Ten days later, to a
friend and former student in Mexico, Castañeda wrote: " I have
been extremely busy ever since my arrival here. This is no soft job,
I want to tell you, yet I like the work much more than teaching

and I will soon get it well in hand. I will then have time to work on my doctorate which is the thing I have been wanting to do for some time."[30]

With the euphoria of the new job behind him, by early March Castañeda found himself deeply immersed in the custodial duties of the collection and in course work for the doctorate. Not surprisingly, Ernest Winkler was anxious to reconcile the current status of the Latin American Collection with the initial inventory compiled when the University purchased Genaro García's library. "Please," he asked Castañeda, "make this check as rapidly and as accurately as possible."[31] Using a checklist Hackett had prepared of "Materials for Spanish History in the Garcia Library at the University of Texas" as a guide, Castañeda complied with Winkler's request in less than two weeks. "The chief difficulty in checking this list," he advised, "was found in the inaccuracy of the authors' names and titles, and the fact that the latter were translated freely to English. Every item has been checked and the books looked up after finding the card and the call number."[32]

For the remainder of the spring, Castañeda busied himself with routine tasks, including requesting awnings for the west windows and rechecking the contents of the collection.[33] What Castañeda may have missed in the library was the social prestige he had enjoyed as a faculty member. To a fellow librarian at William and Mary he admitted that the transition was too "great and too sudden . . . to leave one unbewildered." All the same, he devised compensatory activities to snap him out of the "daze." First, he presented a formal paper, "The Veto in Latin American Constitutions," at a meeting of the Southwestern Association of Political Sciences. Then, thanks to Barker's finesse, he received the distinction of a Fellow of the Texas State Historical Association in recognition of earlier contributions. Finally, "if my wires don't break in pulling them too hard," he anticipated an invitation to join the Texas Historical Commission of the Knights of Columbus. As these activities unfolded, Castañeda initiated numerous tactics in search of "unrestricted publicity." "Things come to him who waits," he acknowledged to a political scientist at Williamsburg, "but while you are waiting you might as well turn you[r] hand to the wheel and keep things moving until results come."[34]

By early summer, after successfully completing one course in the doctoral program, Castañeda reviewed the progress of his work in the Library.

My work here is very pleasant but it certainly takes a great

deal more time than I imagined. It is the most curious phenomenon to me. I thought I would have a great deal of time to read
and study while in the Library but I find that being librarian
means an endless amount of unavoidable routine and trifling
duties that take up all the time and leave very little to show for
your pains. Nevertheless, I like my work and I am learning a
great deal incidentally about library work and bibliography in
general.[35]

Evidently, Castañeda's strategies in gaining "unrestricted publicity," in view of his status as a Mexican national, created a back-
lash effect when the Texas legislature met in special session. An
unexpected result was "some high-handed" pruning in the appropriations for the forthcoming biennial budget. Initially, the version
of the bill that passed the House of Representatives drastically reduced Castañeda's salary by $600, a cut that a conference com-
mittee restored (to the original level of $2,400). The legislative
action so greatly alarmed Castañeda that he "almost regretted
leaving old Virginia." More to the point, the appropriations bill
enacted by the special session eliminated Castañeda's expectations
of a salary advancement for the next two years.[36]

Following the unpleasantness of the special session, in mid-sum-
mer, for the first time in ten years, Castañeda went on vacation to
his hometown of Brownsville, combining family entertainment
and professional field work. Crossing the Río Grande into Matamoros, he spent a week examining the municipal archives. Apparently recognizing the importance of the discovery, Winkler advised
Castañeda to "stay as long as it is worthwhile." As inducement to
mollify the anxiety caused by the Texas legislature, he informed
Castañeda that the Board of Regents had approved plans for enlarging the Library "so you can spread."[37] Castañeda's glowing
description of the archival windfall in Matamoros clearly showed
the direction his career as librarian would take in the years ahead.

They have an excellent collection of archives dating from 1797
to the present and there is a great deal of valuable material for
the history of Texas and the Confederacy, for that matter, for
from 1861 to 1863 [Matamoros] was the only open port for
Southern Cotton. I spent all my time making a careful survey of
the records and separating all those I considered of interest to
have them copied later. . . . The bulk increases as one approaches the Mexican War. All in all, I think I have a gold mine.[38]

Castañeda's discovery of a "gold mine" in the municipal archives of Matamoros closed the first phase of his career as librarian of the Latin American Collection. Prior to that fateful trip to Brownsville, he had concentrated on inventorying the contents of the collection that others before him had acquired. In Matamoros he stood on the threshold of the next phase, in which he would make notable contributions to the Latin American Collection, and in the process considerably enhance his own reputation as a Borderlands scholar. In 1927, Castañeda kept his rendezvous with a library. The odyssey began with his boyhood experiences in the Lower Río Grande Valley; it concluded in the same region when the adult Castañeda returned home to find an archival windfall in his own backyard across the border.

Notes

1. Félix D. Almaráz, Jr., "Carlos Eduardo Castañeda, Mexican-American Historian: The Formative Years, 1896-1927," *Pacific Historical Review* 42, no. 3 (August 1973): 320-323; taped recollections of Rev. Fr. Edward Peters, the Ohio State University, Columbus, Ohio, 1972.
2. Carlos E. Castañeda, "The Human Side of a Great Collection," *Books Abroad* 14, no. 2 (Spring 1940): 116.
3. Ibid., pp. 116-118; Louis C. Moloney, "A History of the University Library at the University of Texas, 1883-1934" (D.L.S. dissertation, Columbia University, 1970), pp. 243-245; Francis Oliver, assistant registrar UT-Austin, to Félix D. Almaráz, Jr., 22 June 1972.
4. Almaráz, "Castañeda," pp. 327-330; Carlos E. Castañeda, "The Early Missionary Movement in Texas," *Missionary* 35 (December 1921): 360-361.
5. Carlos E. Castañeda to Eugene C. Barker, 4 January, 15 February 1924, Barker Papers, 1924-1934, Barker Texas History Center, UT-Austin.
6. Carlos E. Castañeda, "Father Antonio Margil de Jesus," *Missionary* (June-July 1942): 163-164 and 197-199; "The Educational Revolution in Mexico," *Educational Review* 48 (October 1924): 123-125.
7. Castañeda to Barker, 10 February 1925, Barker Papers.
8. Castañeda to Barker, 4 March 1925, Barker Papers; C. E. Castañeda, "Latin America's First Great Educator," *Current History* 22, no. 2 (May 1925): 223-225.
9. E. W. Winkler to Castañeda, 9 March 1926, Castañeda Correspondence, Nettie Lee Benson Latin American Collection, UT-Austin. (Hereinafter citations to Castañeda's correspondence in the Benson Latin American Collection will be identified by the initials BLAC.)
10. J. I. Driscoll to Castañeda, 4 June 1926, Knights of Columbus Correspondence File, Catholic Archives of Texas, Chancery of Austin. (Hereinafter cited as KCCF, CAT.)
11. Rev. W. A. R. Goodwin to Alexander W. Weddell, 9 June 1926, BLAC; Carlos E. Castañeda, "A Trip to Texas in 1828: José María Sánchez," *Southwestern Historical Quarterly* 29, no. 4 (April 1926): 249-288; "The First

Pan American Congress," *North American Review* 223 (June-July-August 1926): 248-255.
12. Castañeda to Driscoll, 12 June 1926, KCCF, CAT.
13. Driscoll to Castañeda, 22 June 1926, KCCF, CAT.
14. Arthur George Williams to Castañeda, 2 July 1926, BLAC.
15. C. E. Castañeda, "The Trouble in Mexico: Both Sides. I. Is Mexico Turning Bolshevik?" *Catholic World* 123, no. 735 (June 1926): 366-372. Charles Phillips, professor of English literature at Notre Dame University, presented the opposing view of the argument ("The Trouble in Mexico: A Reply to the Foregoing Article," *Catholic World*: 372-380).
16. Castañeda to Charles W. Hackett, 10 September 1926, BLAC.
17. Castañeda to Winkler, 13 September 1926, BLAC.
18. Barker to Castañeda, 18 September 1926, BLAC.
19. Castañeda to Barker, 23 September 1926; Barker to Castañeda, 24 September 1926; Winkler to W. M. W. Splawn, 5 October 1926 (first quotation); Winkler to Castañeda, 13 October 1926 (second quotation), BLAC.
20. Castañeda to Barker, 18 October 1926, BLAC.
21. Castañeda to Havila Babcock, 28 October 1928, BLAC.
22. Paul J. Foik to Castañeda, 28 October 1926, BLAC.
23. Winkler to Castañeda, 29 October, 5 November 1926; Castañeda to Winkler, 1 and 9 November 1926 (quotation), BLAC.
24. Castañeda to Hackett, 10 November 1926, BLAC.
25. [C. E. Castañeda], "A Helping Hand to Mexico," *Commonweal* 5, no. 2 (17 November 1926): 37-38.
26. Castañeda to Foik, 5 November 1926, KCCF, CAT.
27. Castañeda to Frank L. Crone, 10 January 1927; J. A. Chandler to Castañeda, 24 January 1927 (quotation), BLAC.
28. Castañeda to Crone, 10 January 1927; Castañeda to W. C. Stynor, 11 January 1927; Castañeda to Lillian Berlin, 4 March 1927, BLAC.
29. Castañeda to Crone, 9 February 1927, BLAC.
30. Castañeda to F. O. Adam, 19 February 1927, BLAC.
31. Castañeda to Berlin, 4 March 1927; Winkler to Castañeda, 9 March 1927 (quotation), BLAC.
32. Castañeda to Winkler, 21 March 1927, BLAC.
33. Castañeda to Winkler, 1 April 1927; Castañeda to Williams, 29 April 1927; Castañeda to Crone, 29 April 1927, BLAC.
34. Castañeda to Herbert L. Ganter, 16 May 1927 (first and second quotations); Castañeda to H. W. Childs, 31 May 1927 (third quotation), BLAC.
35. Castañeda to Babcock, 17 June 1927, BLAC.
36. Castañeda to Crone, 24 June 1927, BLAC.
37. Winkler to Castañeda, 23 July 1927; Castañeda to Crone, 2 August 1927, BLAC.
38. Castañeda to E. G. Swem, 9 August 1927, BLAC.

The Public Library as the Dependent Variable: Historically Oriented Theories and Hypotheses of Public Library Development

Robert V. Williams

Someone has characterized the past thirty years' work of the historical and social science communities as a period in which historians have turned to the social scientists for their methodology and social scientists have relied on the historians for their theories. While this observation appears to have some merit, it is nevertheless an anomalous one. Social scientists have usually been obvious, in some cases embarrassingly so, in stating the theoretical basis of their research and historians have been reluctant to state their generalizations in any structured and rigorous manner. Historians generally prefer to use the phrase "philosophy of history" and to write of specific events and trends, while social scientists search for generalizations, causal relations, and the ability to predict phenomena. Historians generally do not "test hypotheses" but instead attempt to describe unique events as accurately as possible. Social scientists, on the other hand, spend a good deal of their time attempting to evolve a series of interrelated and causally connected propositions that can be empirically tested on a group of data.

Despite these differences, the two fields have been remarkably useful to and dependent upon each other. Louis Gottschalk emphasizes the rich sharing that has taken place in the past and notes that research in both fields could be improved if the historian as social scientist and the social scientist as historian roles were adopted more frequently.[1] Reliance on a totally idiographic approach, where statements can be made only about a specific time and

Robert V. Williams *is assistant professor at the College of Librarianship, University of South Carolina.*

Journal of Library History, Vol. 16, No. 2, Spring 1981
© 1981 by the University of Texas Press   0022-2259/81/020329-14$01.45

place, or a completely nomothetic one, where one attempts to make universal generalizations about phenomena, limits understanding. One needs to seek an understanding of the general patterns in order to understand the significance of the unique event fully. Detailed study of the unique event will also permit the construction of more tightly knit generalizations and exact predictions about the overall phenomena under study.

Within the discipline of library science we have not had an enriching exchange of methods and theories between the library historians and the "nonhistorians." There are probably many reasons for this, not the least of which has been the tendency of library history to be more idiographic than nomothetic. However, even when the work of library historians contains generalizations about library-related phenomena, they are often neglected. Our community of scholars is small and the issues so diverse that the generalizations of one researcher are of limited interest to others in the field and often go unused and unchallenged. In addition, the reviewers and state-of-the-art writers in library history do not systematically follow up on the generalizations that are made in new publications and, instead, content themselves with merely recounting titles and topics.

Library history should have the potential to inform the work of other researchers in our discipline, just as the work of the larger historical community has been of value to the social sciences. This paper is an attempt to encourage this interchange by examining the historical work in one area of library history, public library development. Specifically, the objectives of this paper are: first, to identify those writings in the area of library history that have attempted to state theoretically oriented generalizations or hypotheses about the development of public libraries; second, to assess the extent to which these theories (or near theories) conform to the types of theories used in the social sciences; third, to determine the extent to which these theories or generalizations have been supported by empirical research.

For the purposes of this paper, a theory is defined as a systematic statement of the relationships between variables (or constructs) for the purpose of explaining natural phenomena.[2] The purpose of a theory is to explain. A theory can be used for prediction, control, classification, or to create a sense of understanding. A theory, and its interrelated statements, may take on varying forms, such as set-of-laws, axiomatic, or causal process.[3] Using this definition as a general guide, an attempt will be made to identify those generalizations and explanations about public library development that have the potential for theory.

The specific concern here will be with those historically oriented writings that deal with the *establishment* or *growth* of libraries open to the general public. Writings that focus predominately on the philosophy, nature, and operations of public libraries will not be treated unless in some way these aspects are also related, by their author, to the two issues of establishment and growth. The central geographical focus of the paper will be the American public library, but attention will also be paid to the development of public libraries in Western Europe.

A review of the relevant literature indicates that there are approximately four general patterns of explanation of the problem of public library development. As might be expected, the extent to which these four match the stated definition of theory varies considerably. Some of these explanations have been refined rather carefully, while others are only tentative hypotheses.

The Social Conditions Theory

The first, and most inclusive, explanation is one that attributes the development of public libraries to a variety of social conditions or forces. Dee Garrison calls this the "multiple social forces argument."[4] The writers in this group vary considerably in their use of the argument. Some list several different social conditions as the cause of library development while others list only a few. Some writers indicate the relative importance of their factors and others ignore this concern.

The best-known advocate of the social conditions argument is Jesse Shera, as reflected in his study of the origins of the public library in New England during the period 1629 to 1855. Shera summarizes his conclusions about library development as follows:

> Historical scholarship and the urge to preservation, the power of national and local pride, the growing belief in the importance of universal education, the increasing concern with vocational problems, and the contribution of religion—these, aided by economic ability and encouraged by the example of Europe, were the causal factors in the formation of libraries that would be free to all the people.[5]

A similar type of explanation has been offered by Sidney Ditzion in his study of public library development in the United States during the period 1850 to 1900:

> Certain sociological backgrounds were found to be almost self-evident prerequisites to the establishment of the tax-supported free library. These were the ability of communities to provide financial support to libraries, the necessity for a population sufficiently dense . . . to make service economical, a climate sympathetic to public support of education in general, and a favorable cultural *milieu*.[6]

Shera's nine "causal factors" and Ditzion's four "sociological backgrounds" have been used by many different library historians. For example, Gwladys Spencer's study of the Chicago Public Library used all of these variables and added an additional list of thirty more, for a total of approximately fifty factors.[7]

The usual trend in the historical writings using this pattern of explanation, however, is to reduce this list to only a few variables. Robert Lee maintains, in his study of public libraries in the United States during the period 1833 to 1964, that four factors had to be present in a community before a public library could be established. These factors, in order of importance, were: financial ability, energetic and progressive leaders, a public school system, and a "sufficient number of educated adults."[8] Lee then goes on to say that the growth of the library is dependent on other, unspecified, "societal forces." W. J. Murison's study of public library development in the United Kingdom concludes that education and urbanization were the most important variables.[9] Jean Hassenforder's historical overview of public library development in the United States, the United Kingdom, and France during the period 1850 to 1914 indicates that the three variables of economic growth, advance of democratic ideas, and the expansion of school attendance were related to the rate of growth of public libraries in all three nations.[10] Sidney Jackson, in his summary history of library development in Western Europe, uses education, urbanization, and industrialization as the critical variables.[11] And, finally, Elmer Johnson and Michael Harris's discussion of libraries in the Western world groups the "important prerequisites for library growth" under the three broad headings of social conditions, economic conditions, and political conditions. However, under these three headings, and, presumably, as necessary measures of them, are an additional fourteen variables.[12]

How does this compare with the requirements of theory? The

answer: not very well. The only requirement of theory that is met is the naming of variables. Generally missing in all of these explanations are the following characteristics of theory: relative importance of a variable, relationships between the variables, and an explanation as to *why* these variables affect the establishment and growth of public libraries. As noted earlier, the *why* part of the explanation is critical to theory because it specifies the interrelationships of the variables according to degree of importance and order over time. In general, the writers in this group fail to provide these kinds of explanations. The reader can only assume that these writers believe that all of these factors affect public libraries at the same time and in the same way. Evidence that this assumption is at work can be found in Shera's statement that "much of what is said here with reference to New England is equally applicable elsewhere as economic and social conditions began to approximate those of the northeastern Atlantic seaboard."[13] This view is not only an untested hypothesis, but it also ignores differences in library development that might be the result of the variables of time and region.

The conclusion that this pattern of explanation fails to meet the requirements of theory does not also mean that the findings and conclusions of these writers are not possibly useful to the nonhistorians in library science. Naming variables is an important, and essential, first step on the road to theory construction. And, as has been shown, a large number of variables has been listed by this group of writers. The problem of economy, however, dictates the selection of only a few candidate variables for testing. This problem can be addressed by considering the degree to which one or more have a substantial degree of empirical support.

This apparently simple approach, however, is not so simply accomplished. Upon inspection of many of these historical works, it is obvious that the evidence either is secondary, referring back to some earlier writer in the group, or is not systematically compiled in terms of assessing the actual effect of one or more variables. Certain variables—such as education, urbanization, economic ability, and religion—are mentioned repeatedly by the writers in this group, but the evidence for their effect, over time, is not systematically pursued. And, when some of these variables are systematically analyzed, as Haynes McMullen did (using data on the founding of libraries in the United States before 1876), the results often do not agree with the generalizations made by the writers in the group. For example, McMullen found no relationship between the founding of libraries of all kinds and the variables of economic conditions and population growth.[14]

If the empirical evidence for these "social forces" as variables is weak, why then do library historians continue to use them? The answer is not clear. It appears, however, that we have not managed to move *beyond* Shera's initial generalization that "the emergence and development of the American public library was conditioned, either directly or indirectly, by the totality of forces that constitute the contemporary social *milieu*. . . ."[15]

Shera did, of course, go on to name some specific variables that he considered important to library development, but he did *not* specify their degree of importance and interrelationships. It may be that these two types of specification are not possible given the complexity of the issue and the problem of data collection. Surely, however, the more we attempt to acquire this kind of understanding, the more likely it is that we will understand the manner in which various "social forces" affect public library development.

The Democratic Tradition Theory

The second candidate for theory, labeled here the "democratic tradition," is unquestionably the most popular of all those offered by historians of the public library. Public librarians are particularly fond of it since it places them squarely in the mainstream of the Jeffersonian tradition and permits them to view their work as central to the advancement of democracy.

The argument of this group of historians is fairly straightforward: the development of the American public library is the result of the growth of democracy. The *why* part of the explanation is that the public library came into existence and prospered because citizens needed a place where they could obtain the information they needed for effective and full participation in the democratic tradition. At this "people's university" adults could continue learning once they were past the years of formal education; it provided resources for new immigrants learning the language and laws of their new home; and, later, it would foster in children the habit of lifelong learning and reading.

The problem with this candidate explanation comes when one attempts to understand the nature of the operational measures of the theoretical construct known as democracy. Ditzion, probably the best-known advocate of the variable, fails to define it adequately. Lee also fails to give a clear indication of his definition, and the evidence in his chapter on "Strengthening Democracy" indicates that the variable would probably be more correctly labeled education. Oliver Garceau's study of the public library in the American political system speaks of the "democratic ideal," but no definition is offered. Instead, he shows that *politics* affects the library and he offers the hope that through providing educational information the public library will have a democratizing effect on politics.[16]

The lack of a clearly defined, measurable definition of democracy is the central weakness of this explanation. Such definitions *are* available in the literature (for example, participation in political parties, proportion voting) but have not been used by library historians. Given the evidence available in the literature, one suspects that this explanation is incomplete and that democracy, when adequately defined, should be considered an intervening variable between library development and some other variable, such as education.

The concept of democracy is and has been a useful myth[17] in all of American history and life and it seems to have the same role in library history. The "story" told by public library historians seems to be partially real and partially ideal: real because there is evidence that some public libraries were established as a result of the need for information that could be used for more effective participation in the affairs of government; ideal in that if arguments for establishing a public library were made in the form of an appeal to the "strengthening of democracy" they would be more likely to succeed than any other type of plea. Library historians have not attempted to separate these two different types of stimulus variables and the result is a lack of information about the effects of either one of them.

The Social Control Theory

The third type of explanation of public library development, here given the name "social control," is one that has been offered as an alternative to the democratic tradition interpretation. Essentially, writers in this group argue that while there is much to commend in the interpretations made by the "liberal-progressive" historians of public libraries (that is, the first two candidate theories considered here) one should not neglect to consider the actual motivations of the founders of public libraries. These founders, it is noted, were often wealthy, upper-class aristocrats who used the public library as one of the means by which they could control social change in an orderly manner and thereby insure their position in society.

The causal variables in this explanation are extremely difficult to identify because they are a mixture of variables that are actually present (the wealth and social position of founders and directors) and variables that can be only partially verified (the *motivations* of these founders and directors) using historical data. The *why* part of the explanation, however, is excellent: these founders supported the public library because they thought it was a social institution that encouraged gradual social change through education instead of revolution and chaos.

An early statement of this explanation is found in James Wellard's 1940 study of public library development in the United Kingdom:

> Libraries, we find, were conceived by a small group of socially-minded philanthropists as a social corrective; they were next legislated into being; then presented to or imposed upon sundry communities; then supplied indiscriminately with books—with the emphasis now on reform, now on education, and now on recreation; and finally tacitly accepted as an agreeable community endeavour which was commendable rather than essential.[18]

Unfortunately, Wellard's several assertions about his causal variables are not well supported in this general monograph.

This explanation, and an attempt to document it with empirical evidence, has been worked out in the greatest detail in a series of articles by Harris,[19] and in portions of the recent monograph by Garrison.[20] Harris presents a careful, detailed portrait of George Ticknor, one of the founders of the Boston Public Library, and attempts to show how Ticknor's social philosophy and upper-class attitudes affected the establishment and growth of the library. In Harris's view, Ticknor is an exemplary model of the upper-class patricians who used the American public library as one means for achieving social control and maintaining the status quo.

Garrison's evidence is wider-ranging than Harris's detailed study of one founder of one library. She examines the work and motivations of the founders, board members, and leaders of the library community in a number of different locations in the United States during the period 1876 to 1920. She presents considerable evidence that middle- and upper-middle-class conservative attitudes had direct effects on the founding and growth of public libraries. Much of Garrison's evidence, however, is directed toward arguments about what the contents of a library ought to be and about the nature of the library profession and thus is not directly pertinent to the issues of founding and growth.

Overall, then, the empirical evidence for the social control explanation is mixed. Harris presents a typology, but we have little corroborating evidence that it is applicable to the founders of other public libraries. As Phyllis Dain points out in her response to Harris's writings, we have a number of counter-models of founders, such as Horace Mann, that can be presented as evidence for an entirely different explanation.[21] Dain's comment is also applicable to Garrison's statement that even in political democracies "it is the purpose of ruling elites . . . to perpetuate their power by disseminating their own cultural values. . . ."[22] The exact nature of these values and the ways in which they affected public library development are still not clear.

This mixed picture is particularly evident when one considers the results of the philanthropy of Andrew Carnegie. George Bobinski shows that 521 new libraries (about 22 percent of all public libraries in the United States as of 1923) were established with Carnegie funds.[23] David McLeod's detailed analysis of public library development in Wisconsin concludes, however, that Carnegie's influence "for better or worse, was slight."[24] McLeod asserts that the Carnegie philanthropy, by encouraging the development of independent libraries in small towns that could not afford them, may actually have had a negative impact on public library development in Wisconsin. The critical variable for the establishment and growth of libraries was, in McLeod's view, not philanthropy but the attitudes of the community. Contrary to Garrison's assertion about ruling elites, McLeod also indicates that Carnegie imparted no particular philosophy or service orientation for the libraries he funded, even when directly asked to do so by librarians. If the social control theory of library development were operative, one would have expected it to surface in the philanthropy of Andrew Carnegie. That it did not do so seriously weakens the validity of this explanation.

Clearly, a great deal more empirical work, particularly in smaller communities, needs to be done before the arguments of this group of writers can be said to have provided adequate empirical support for their explanations of public library development. These writers will also have to deal more systematically with the problem of evidence in their work since much of it now approaches "psycho-history" in ascribing certain motivations to library founders.

Influence of Libraries and Librarians

The three candidate theoretical explanations of public library development considered thus far have all treated the library as a dependent variable, subject to factors within the social system but having no direct effect on the social system or, indirectly, on itself. Can the library (and librarians) be considered an independent variable that has an effect on its own development? The logical answer is yes. Construction of an explanation supported by empirical evidence, however, is not quite so simple.

To a certain extent, library historians have advanced all of these explanations. The focus of much of the argument of social control writers centers on the negative effects that white, middle- and upper-class librarians and founders of libraries had on public library development. Garrison gives a convincing portrait of the ways in which the attitudes of librarians and library leaders about social class and sex roles negatively affected public library development, concluding that "the feminization of public librarianship did much to shape and stunt the development of an important American cultural institution."[25] Harris presents an equally compelling argument when he notes that these attitudes may be the reason why so few of the people in the United States considered the public library a place that was open and useful to them.[26]

The alternative view, that the influence of libraries and library leaders had a positive impact on library development, is also backed by valid evidence. McMullen shows that the rate of increase in the number of nonschool libraries in the United States from 1876 to 1974 was 985 percent while the rate of population increase was only 460 percent.[27] Robert Downs shows that increase in collection size and library funding has shown similar growth rates since 1876.[28] These increases appear to exceed changes in any of the variables mentioned by the "social conditions" group of library historians. The positive influence of dynamic and progressive librarians, such as William F. Poole and John Cotton Dana, has also been well documented. William Williamson shows how Poole was effective, as librarian and library consultant, in bringing about increased support and prestige for public libraries in a variety of different communities.[29] And, despite the possible long-term negative consequences of some of Carnegie's library philanthropy, the publicity libraries received as a result of these gifts appears to have had some lasting, positive effect.[30]

It should be obvious that the issue of the library and librarians as independent variables affecting their own future, within a community or within the nation, is a complex one. That is, its relevance as an important variable is not questioned; the study of its effects, however, will be extremely difficult because of its possible indirect influence and the confounding effects that arise as a result of using it as a dependent variable and also as an independent variable. It is not surprising, then, that the explanatory statements about its influence are tentative ones and that the evidence is inadequate.

Conclusion

No one denies that public library development is a complex phenomenon. Historians of the public library have made that quite evident by the variety of explanations they have offered. This paper has examined four of these explanations, showing that all have some merit as theory but that they also all have significant problems. The central weaknesses are the lack of specification about the relationships between the variables and the failure to include a causally oriented statement that explains the *why* of public library development. The merit in these explanations is in naming and tentative validation of a number of specific variables that may affect, either positively or negatively, the founding and growth of public libraries. Such factors as education, urbanization, religion, economic ability, "democracy," and the attitudes of librarians and library founders all appear to have substantive impact on the public library when it is viewed as a dependent variable.

It is possible to conclude, then, that the work of library historians is useful to the work of the "nonhistorian" in library science. Providing the names of variables and evidence to support their validity is an important first step toward theory. What is now required, by library historians as well as by all researchers in library science, is to construct and test statements that explain the interrelationships and relative importance of these and other variables in public library development.

Finally, and somewhat in the manner of a personal epilogue to this paper, some comments need to be made to those library historians who insist that the work and purposes of the historian have nothing to do with testing hypotheses and formulating theory. It should be obvious that the arguments made in this paper are somewhat different. John Colson, in an excellent review of library history writing during the past thirty years, offers a different perspective when he argues against a social science approach to library history.[31] I am sympathetic to that viewpoint but I also believe that library history would be improved if greater attention were devoted to a nomothetic approach instead of an idiographic one. Facts, including "historical facts," take on meaning only within the context of prior knowledge and theory.[32] Historical research, like all research, involves constantly testing generalizations against specific events of time and place. In this manner we manage to improve our understanding of the specific event as well as the general phenomenon under study. My point is that neither approach is necessarily best, but that both are needed in library history and within library science generally. We need to use and learn from each other. As I stated at the beginning of this paper, there is a long tradition of this kind of sharing in the social science and historical communities. Library science may be greatly enriched if we actively encourage a similar type of exchange of methods and theory in our efforts to understand library development.

Notes

1. Louis Gottschalk, *Understanding History: A Primer of Historical Method* (New York: Knopf, 1950), pp. 30–37.

2. Fred N. Kerlinger, *Behavioral Research: A Conceptual Approach* (New York: Holt, Rinehart and Winston, 1979), pp. 10–12.

3. Paul D. Reynolds, *A Primer in Theory Construction* (New York: Bobbs-Merrill, 1971).

4. Dee Garrison, *Apostles of Culture: The Public Librarian and American Society, 1876–1920* (New York: Free Press, 1979), p. xii.

5. Jesse H. Shera, *Foundations of the Public Library: The Origins of the Public Library Movement in New England, 1629–1855* (Chicago: University of Chicago Press, 1949), p. 243.

6. Sidney H. Ditzion, *Arsenals of a Democratic Culture: A Social History of the American Public Library Movement in New England and the Middle States, from 1850 to 1900* (Chicago: American Library Association, 1947), p. 190.

7. Gwladys Spencer, *The Chicago Public Library: Origins and Backgrounds* (Chicago: University of Chicago Press, 1943).

8. Robert E. Lee, *Continuing Education for Adults through the American Public Library, 1833–1964* (Chicago: American Library Association, 1966), p. 3.

9. W. J. Murison, *The Public Library: Its Origins, Purpose and Significance*, 2nd ed. rev. (London: Harrap, 1971), p. 12.

10. Jean Hassenforder, "Comparative Studies and the Development of Public Libraries," *Unesco Bulletin for Libraries* 22, no. 1 (January–February 1968): 13–14.

11. Sidney L. Jackson, *Libraries and Librarianship in the West: A Brief History* (New York: McGraw-Hill, 1974).

12. Elmer D. Johnson and Michael H. Harris, *History of Libraries in the Western World*, 3rd. ed. rev. (Metuchen, N.J.: Scarecrow, 1976), pp. 4–5.

13. Shera, *Foundations of the Public Library*, p. v.

14. Haynes McMullen, "The Prevalence of Libraries in the United States before 1876: Some Regional Differences," Harold Goldstein and John Godeau (eds.), *Library History Seminar No. 4, Proceedings, 1971* (Tallahassee: Florida State University School of Library Science, 1972), pp. 115-138; "More Statistics of Libraries in the Southeast before 1876," *Southeastern Librarian* 24, no. 1 (Spring 1974): 18-28.

15. Jesse H. Shera, *Historians, Books and Libraries: A Survey of Historical Scholarship in Relation to Library Resources, Organization and Services* (Cleveland: Press of Western Reserve University, 1953), p. 95.

16. Oliver Garceau et al., *The Public Library in the Political Process: A Report of the Public Library Inquiry* (New York: Columbia University Press, 1949).

17. Here I use the word "myth" in the sociological sense to mean a "collective belief that is built up in response to the values of the group rather than an analysis of the basis of the wishes," *American College Dictionary* (New York: Random House, 1973).

18. James Howard Wellard, *The Public Library Comes of Age* (London: Grafton, 1940), pp. 97-98.

19. Michael H. Harris, "The Purpose of the American Public Library: A Revisionist Interpretation," *Library Journal* 98, no. 16 (15 September 1973): 2509-2514; "Portrait in Paradox: Commitment and Ambivalence in American Librarianship, 1876-1976," *Libri* 26, no. 4 (December 1976): 281-301; and, with Gerard Spiegler, "Everett, Ticknor and the Common Man: The Fear of Societal Instability as the Motivation for the Founding of the Boston Public Library," *Libri* 24, no. 4 (1974): 249-275.

20. Garrison, *Apostles of Culture.*

21. Phyllis Dain, "Ambivalence and Paradox: The Social Bonds of the Public Library," *Library Journal* 100, no. 3 (1 February 1975): 261-266.

22. Garrison, *Apostles of Culture*, p. xiii.

23. George S. Bobinski, *Carnegie Libraries: Their History and Impact on American Public Library Development* (Chicago: American Library Association, 1969), p. 195.

24. David I. McLeod, *Carnegie Libraries in Wisconsin* (Madison: State Historical Society of Wisconsin for the Department of History, University of Wisconsin, 1968), p. 123.

25. Garrison, *Apostles of Culture*, p. 241.

26. Harris, "The Purpose of the American Public Library," p. 2514.

27. Haynes McMullen, "The Distribution of Libraries throughout the United States," *Library Trends* 25 (July 1976): 23-53.

28. Robert B. Downs, "The Growth of Research Collections," *Library Trends* 25 (July 1976): 55-80.

29. William L. Williamson, *William Frederick Poole and the Modern Library Movement*, Columbia University Studies in Library Service, no. 13 (New York: Columbia University Press, 1963).

30. Bobinski, *Carnegie Libraries*, pp. 190-192.

31. John Calvin Colson, "The Writing of American Library History, 1876-1976," *Library Trends* 25 (July 1976): 7-21.

32. Martin Goldstein and Inge F. Goldstein, *How We Know: An Exploration of the Scientific Process* (New York: Plenum, 1978), pp. 17-18.

Popular Fiction Selection in Public Libraries: Implications of Popular Culture Studies

Robert Wagers

Public libraries have traditionally provided access to the products of elite culture—works of greatest interest to a select group of cultural arbiters whose tastes are regarded by many as exemplary. Librarians have not demonstrated much difficulty in selecting these works since well-known criteria for literary or artistic excellence are available. With a certain amount of reluctance, however, public librarians have recognized that the needs of large segments of their audience were not being served by these elite products. The majority public chose to use the works of the mass media and press, and public libraries responded by forming collections of popular materials that often fell short of the high standards of the cultural tastemakers. In the area of popular fiction—suspense, romances, westerns, science fiction, social melodrama—many librarians responded to the challenge by creating two collections based upon totally different standards. The traditional literate fiction collection was formed on the basis of the usual rationales—vivid characterization, complex, imaginative plotting, nonconventional themes—while the popular fiction collection was built upon known popular authors, bulk acquisition plans, dimly perceived subject interests, and gifts. As a result, great numbers of novels that featured flat, stereotyped characters, repetitious, simplistic plots, conventional moral values, and liberal doses of sex and violence and somehow met the needs and desires of the reading public were acquired in a haphazard fashion.

Robert Wagers *is assistant professor of library science at San Jose State University.*

Journal of Library History, Vol. 16, No. 2, Spring 1981
© 1981 by the University of Texas Press   0022-2259/81/020342-12$01.35

If this distinction is maintained, librarians cannot honor a commitment to standards of selection and explain why they acquired or rejected a work. Most important, they cannot meet the *needs* of identified library publics. Gordon Stevenson has asked if it is the function of librarians "to 'read' cultures—to learn to understand the role of information systems as they support the 'myths' which sustain daily rituals—or is it to change the cultural preferences of people? "[1] Both are big jobs, but the second is monstrous. Even if librarians decide that their mission is to change tastes, they cannot succeed without understanding the ways in which existing works serve the needs of the reading public. I propose that librarians abolish the conflict between high values and "low" tastes by formulating selection plans in which value is instrumental—conditional upon the degree to which a work of fiction meets or fails to meet identified needs. Contemporary students of popular culture have taken precisely this approach to understand the appeal of popular artifacts. Librarians might enrich selection plans by comprehending the methods and findings of these theorists.

Popular culture encompasses all elements of life that are not narrowly intellectual or creatively elitist. These elements are expressed in artifacts that are recognized by a significant percentage of the population. The pervasiveness of ideas and patterns in these artifacts is guaranteed by disseminating them through the mass media. Three important approaches to explaining the impact of these works have been proposed. One method has been to study the mass audiences that consume popular materials. This method has been promoted significantly by Herbert Gans.[2] Theorists taking this approach emphasized the importance of the type of "taste culture" to which a work appeals. Those who saw the crucial elements in popular culture acceptance to be the *vehicle* (following Marshall McLuhan) usually stressed the fact that mass delivery limits the choices available to the public and incorporates controls imposed by the media.[3] Some writers have combined these approaches to urge a unified study of the mechanisms by which common cultural elements are transformed into a form that matches the expectations of use groups.[4] Both of these methods are valuable, but they involve a considerable amount of polling and surveying. Unfortunately, librarians are limited in the time they can devote to such activities. It can be argued, however, that the common patterns discoverable in audience reaction and mass delivery are represented significantly in the common themes, ideas, plots, and characters of specific genres. The assumption is that genres or subgenres such as mysteries and gothic romances will display certain commonalities that can be identified and used to develop selection criteria appropriate to their readership. This approach has several advantages. (1) It is largely free from theoretical assumptions and is, in fact, pretheoretical in emphasizing description and classification of elements. (2) Accordingly, deep structure—underlying or archetypical features—is not a major concern; careful description is the first chore. The effect is to forestall judgment, especially the attacks on "trash" that popular culture works so often inspire. (3) Certain established techniques, such as content analysis, can be used confidently for the purpose of dissecting artifacts. Librarians seeking methods of selecting fiction are definitely served by popular culture researchers. The power of this approach comes from a useful blending of different orders of discovery that enrich accounts of the impact of popular materials.

Popular culture researchers stress three levels of analysis. The first level, generally the foundation for explaining the structure and appeal of popular works, is description. What are the essential elements and patterns of specific genres? To answer this question, researchers apply textual criticism and quantitative measures to the traditional literary units—theme, setting, plot, character, and so forth. Representative of such studies is Gans's finding that contemporary romances and melodramas feature characters with the same attributes. These characters, such as Jennie in Erich Segal's *Love Story* (New York: Harper and Row, 1970), rise out of deprived backgrounds to challenge higher society for position. They show great initiative that sometimes earns them success or is overwhelmed by powerful natural or social forces.[5] Why these patterns persist in the popular representatives of certain genres requires a second level of analysis—explanation. Turning to behavior studies, Thomas Kando argues that characters such as Jennie represent our economic system's assumptions concerning the attributes of success.[6] He predicts that a postindustrial society, such as the ones foreseen by Theodore Roszak and Herbert Marcuse, may favor characters who have transcended material striving. A considerable portion of popular culture studies is devoted to ways to explain the findings of descriptive research. At a still higher level of analysis, researchers critically examine the presuppositions and consequences of these theories of popularity. The results are metatheories providing explanations of popular works based upon major anthropological, linguistic, or literary movements. Throughout these studies, the aim is to explain the sources of popularity and to develop reliable tools for the investigation of these sources.

A good place to start illustrating the use of these tools is with
the work of John Cawelti. In his concept of formulaic structure,
Cawelti provides the discipline with a concrete model for all popular works. His model combines the contributions of the first two
levels of analysis and has provoked a wide range of criticism. On
the basis of exhaustive descriptive studies of westerns and mysteries, he argues that popular genres are marked by the extent of
their adherence to standard formulae. For example, effective detective stories are produced by authors who followed the traditional processes of rational detection and invented an "ingenious
new type of mystification" to engage detective story fans.[7] Careful description of such genres allows researchers to construct formulae that represent the recurring patterns in popular offerings.
For the public librarian, this analysis provides a possible technique
for selecting works that reflect the patterns most favored by their
publics. In particular, likely-to-be-popular, epic contemporary
novels resembling the "blockbusters" of Harold Robbins and Jac-
queline Susann may be identified with some degree of precision.
Cawelti has termed these novels "social melodramas" and offers
this representation of Irving Wallace novels:

> As a consequence of some major public event . . . an oddly
> assorted group of people are brought together and faced with
> circumstances that bring about important crises of decision
> and action in their personal lives as well as in relation to the
> public event that is the occasion for the story. . . . [The] pro-
> tagonist's life has been characterized by initial success followed
> by an increasing sense of failure and frustration. [The events in
> the novel propel this protagonist to a new sense of success.] . . .
> Part of his regeneration comes from [a new sexual fulfillment
> which restores a sense of life whose loss is signified by his un-
> happy marriage, etc.]. . . . Beneath the surface of the public
> event there generally lurks some kind of plot that generates
> a sequence of mysterious puzzles for the protagonist and his
> new associates to investigate and often poses serious physical
> danger to [him]. . . . Two favorite villain figures are the great
> tycoon and the ambitious politician, characters whose total
> commitment to wealth and power contrasts with the protago-
> nist's ultimate realization of the importance of human rela-
> tions.[8]

This formula is typical of social melodramas, which are considerably more diffuse in structure than westerns and mysteries.

These novels contain a distinct stylistic problem since they bounce around from personality to personality, from situation to situation. They require some focus that provides the basis for asserting a moral order. As shown above, Irving Wallace selects major public events and dramatizes the characters' resolutions of past problems and present dilemmas. Harold Robbins brings his characters together at crucial times for the purpose of revealing critical changes in viewpoint. Arthur Hailey bases his multiple subplots on a major social/political institution that usually serves as the life-manipulating villain.[9] In each case, the author affirms "a commonly accepted moral universe in order to give its audiences the pleasure of seeing the sympathetic and virtuous rewarded and the hateful and dastardly punished."[10]

Since this form depends upon the audience's reactions to the relationships among the characters, certain characteristics appear regularly in popular offerings. One finding is that scenes, characters, themes, and situations are usually described in shorthand—a minimum of description and complexity. Erich Segal has even stressed the fact that he wastes no time in describing things, but allows readers to believe that the world remains much as it always was and invites them to draw on their own experiences to fill in the blanks.[11] Gans agrees with this description of *Love Story*, adding that partly delineated characters and soothing messages permit the readers to respond directly to emotions they have helped to create.[12] These stereotyped characters are therefore largely reader-created, endowed with the values and feelings of the audience. Thus a second finding is that in spite of the bizarre lifestyles and plot twists that are pictured, protagonists ultimately represent majority customs and values.[13] Often after experimenting with variant behavior (underworld characters, illicit sex, and so on), characters return to acceptable life-styles. This treatment allows us to "have the vicarious pleasure of playing at deviant behavior without having to give up or revise our existing moral universe."[14] Many of these patterns are made possible because the world of the social melodrama is an imaginary one, formed from the emotions and ideals of the readers. This fact allows expression to cultural taboos since boundaries against certain behavior are temporarily dissolved. As a result, fantasies dominate the events described, fantastic characters move in and out of the plot, and resolutions can avoid mundane realities.

Cawelti concludes that formula literature such as social melodrama utilizes conventions that appeal directly to the reader's experiences. It serves entertainment and relaxation by allowing for appreciation without analysis or comparisons.[15] At the second level of analysis, other researchers have accepted this basic finding, but have sought the mechanisms by which conventional treatments engage the reader. For example, Jan Cohn has theorized that popular authors succeed when they provide a set of guarantees that moral values will not be overturned and the status quo will be supported.[16] In social melodramas such as Judith Krantz's *Scruples* (New York: Crown, 1978), characters are rewarded for kicking and clawing to the top, but only when they do not actually trample on others. If characters violate this "law," they are marked as losers in the game of human relations. In the same way, characters (and readers in fantasy) are permitted to experiment lavishly with all varieties of sexual activities, schemes for success, and near-criminal behavior. The only requirement is that no one is hurt. The readers are protected from traditional moral "scruples" by this omnibus guarantee. It could be argued from Cohn's explanation of the appeal of formula that popular social melodramas cannot be written about unambitious, but high-principled characters or ambitious, seamy ones. The first type offends the readers' need to justify their striving while the second violates their need to believe that one can be decent in the course of battling to the top.

It is important to realize that these levels of research do not exhaust the problems associated with the structure of popular fiction works and the dynamics of reader behavior. In particular, the manner in which authors captivate readers requires study. For example, Linda Busby claims that popular culture artists use "symbols which have a commonly held cultural understanding and require minimum delineation."[17] This useful observation partly explains the value of the concept of formula in explaining popular tastes, but it does not help us to distinguish among formula stories. For this reason, critics have implications of broader theoretical views for the impact of works designed for mass publics. Two recent analyses, an extension of the formula approach by Janice Radway and an attack on the concept by David Feldman, suggest the directions from which deeper understanding of popular fiction dynamics may come.

Radway attempts to explain the differences between elite and popular works of the same genre, for example, any work by Phyllis Whitney and Faulkner's *Sanctuary* (New York: J. Cape and H. Smith, 1931)—two gothic novels. She finds a possible solution in structuralist approaches to linguistics such as those of Merleau-Ponty. Literary works can be seen as language systems and arranged on a continuum according to the number of rules, norms, and conventions they break or observe.[18] In clearly elite works, the artist expresses ideas by deforming language, producing new meaning by altering the syntactic rules governing the language system.[19] In popular works, the writer violates very few conventions, relying instead upon the basic structure of the system. In this case, readers discern meaning immediately on the basis of traditional treatments.[20] Radway tested this view by describing in a detailed manner all the message units in the novels mentioned above and Carson McCullers's *Member of the Wedding* (Boston: Houghton Mifflin, 1946). All three used a standard gothic meaning structure, but Faulkner and McCullers profoundly altered the plotting, themes, settings, and so on, to produce radically different meanings from those common to the genre.

This theory of fiction structure explains the force of formulaic writing in popular novels and the attraction of conventional works for the average reader. In brief, popular novels employ devices resembling those that appear in day-to-day uses of language. In both cases, readers and speakers discern meaning directly on the basis of mutual understanding of traditional treatments. Speech acts and works are "referential" since little room for interpretation or analysis is permitted.[21] In contrast, elite fiction "goes beyond the limits of the language institution itself and . . . constantly adds to the possibilities of expression contained within it."[22] Radway implies that all artistic productions can be compared by the number and magnitude of deformations included, but the fiction selector must know further what characteristics account for popularity.

This question continues to challenge theorists who see formulaic structure as the principal ingredient in popular fiction. If, for example, all mysteries share a common structure, how can we distinguish between the novels of Mickey Spillane and those of Erle Stanley Gardner? Or, if the genre is narrowed to "hard-boiled detective stories" as Cawelti suggests, between Spillane and Raymond Chandler? In terms of Radway's findings, isn't it possible that the appeal of certain popular works lies in their use of the same creative methods that she found in the work of Faulkner and McCullers? David Feldman argues that the differences between such authors lie in their inventional systems—the nonconventional features of popular works. The proper perspective is to view the effects of handling characters, themes, and so forth, within the context of specific types of works with specific audiences. Samuel Beckett shocked audiences with the surrealistic setting of *Waiting for Godot*, but the premises of the play were familiar to contemporary philosophers. In contrast, the writers of "Gun-smoke" arranged for Kitty to have an affair after nineteen years of chaste fidelity to Matt Dillon. Which artifact was the most "inventional"?[23] Feldman does not abandon the use of formula as a concept, but insists that overemphasis on conventional and recurring motifs—cultural values, icons, myths, and archetypes—ignores the main concern of the artist—to use these elements to alter the story's structural system. It is the arrangement of these elements by the author that accounts for a formula's appeal.[24]

Feldman came to this conclusion in an interesting fashion. Studying the works of Russian Formalism, he discovered that by attending to the alteration of structure in "Perry Mason" reruns he could determine 90 percent of the killers.[25] He achieved this feat by noting themes in the story that deviated from the expected. For Feldman, conventional elements were those developments that were fully predictable within the structure of a genre, while inventional elements were all deviations in time sequence, plot, character, and so on, that altered this basic pattern. In order to understand the crime (the basic component of this type of mystery), the reader must pick out the structural changes in the course of events and explain them in terms of required story elements.

This technique followed methods proposed by the Formalists, who had argued, in the twenties, that what distinguished literary productions was their "literariness." They meant that the elements of content in stories did not help to explain the function of any given work. Only by ignoring content and concentrating upon the ways in which specific works were structured for specific effects could the critic explain the audience's perception of a work. The method works in this manner: recognize that an artist takes a "story," a sequence of causal-temporal events, and transforms it into a "plot" by altering this sequence to serve his interests. He does this by shifting bound and free motifs. "Motifs" are the smallest, most irreducible themes of a work, for example, "Raskolnikov kills the old woman," "the hero dies," and so forth. Bound motifs are those parts that are absolutely necessary to the story whereas free motifs are introduced to lead the reader along the paths of the plot that the author wants followed. The arrangement of these inventional motifs helps to explain "how audiences can be conditioned psychologically to embrace themes they would ordinarily reject."[26] Conservative audiences could be led to condone hostility to authority in *The Longest Yard* by carefully transforming ordinary events through free motifs that express the themes desired by the author.[27] By "defamiliarizing" the audience, the author's intent could be transmitted in place of the audience's normal, expected reactions. The critic must reverse this process—"refamiliarize" the plot in order to uncover the structural features that account for the impact of the work.

Feldman illustrates this method with an analysis of Gardner's *The Case of the Blonde Bonanza* (New York: Morrow, 1962). Clearly, the main attraction of a Perry Mason thriller is the chance to deduce the killer. Isolating the motifs of the story reveals that the first eighty-eight pages are strictly chronological, but the author deviates from this order when he has the actual killer recount to Mason a complex description of the events surrounding the murder. The point is that this free motif has no purpose in the novel unless it highlights an action or character who *must* affect the plot in an important way.[28] Through this type of analysis, the critic can ignore conventional content and discover the real excitement of the work in its formal structure.

I suspect that this analysis succeeds especially well with mysteries because their formulaic structure *requires* the author to lead the reader down many false paths. The author necessarily defamiliarizes the story and invites the reader to transform incongruities, apparent free motifs, into acceptable patterns of events—bound motifs. It is possible that other genres without this stress upon demystification will not yield as easily to Feldman's method. Nonetheless, the one common element in the above two treatments of formula literature is their stress on *system*. Fictional works are systematically designed to elicit certain effects. These systems depend upon the common experiences of the intended audience, who are invited to transform their everyday life by means of imaginary manipulation of those experiences. Radway explains the pull of conventionality while Feldman shows why we are not bored by another Perry Mason case. The readers' need to balance danger with security is explained in these treatments. Critics must recreate the mind-sets of audiences by means of formulaic elements and recurring deviations from those elements in order to predict accurately the appeal of a given work.

Free motifs, language systems, conventional treatments, inventional treatments, experimenting with forbidden experiences, realizing ideals in fiction, recreating mythological moral universes, success in human relations—all these findings and theories bring the critic closer to the attraction of popular fiction. The methodology of popular culture studies remains uncomfortably "soft" with continuing debates concerning the basic units of analysis, but even incomplete investigations of specific genres offer new directions for the critic. The librarian is invited to modify significantly such criteria as "original in plot," "unbelievable characters," "avoids sensational themes" along the lines of the factors responsible for popularity.[29] In a recent column, the television critic Ron Miller points out that many situation comedies and soap operas used exactly the *same* source of conflict to complicate situations. For example, in two episodes of "Happy Days" and one of "Alice," characters avoided something bad happening to them by purposely not doing something they always do.[30] Miller mentions three other findings equally interesting for our understanding of the structure of television series. His conclusion, however, is that "the tube gobbles up ideas like the shark in *Jaws*, so writers fall back on the basic plots to meet their deadlines."[31] This may be true, but he misses the importance of conventional plotting for audience satisfaction. Librarians should probe the dynamics of popular treatments in order to avoid this value-laden approach to criticism. The result could easily be collections of popular fiction formed on discovered principles of audience reaction and enhanced theories of popular culture.

Notes

1. Gordon Stevenson, "Popular Culture and the Public Library," in Melvin J. Voigt and Michael H. Harris (eds.), *Advances in Librarianship* 7 (New York: Academic Press, 1977), p. 218.

2. Herbert J. Gans, "*Love Story*: A Romance of Upward Mobility," in William M. Hammell (ed.), *The Popular Arts in America: A Reader* (New York: Harcourt Brace Jovanovich, 1972), pp. 431–436; Herbert J. Gans, *Popular Culture and High Culture: An Analysis and Evaluation of Taste* (New York: Basic Books, 1975).

3. Jeffrey Schrank, *Snap, Crackle, and Popular Taste: The Illusion of Free Choice in America* (New York: Dell, 1977).

4. Pershing Vartanian, "Popular Culture Studies: A Problem in Sociocultural Dynamics," *Journal of Popular Culture* 11, no. 1 (Summer 1977): 281/141–283/143.

5. Gans, "*Love Story*," pp. 433–434.

6. Thomas M. Kando, *Leisure and Popular Culture in Transition* (St. Louis: Mosby, 1975), p. 16.

7. John G. Cawelti, *Adventure, Mystery, and Romance: Formula Stories as Art and Popular Culture* (Chicago and London: University of Chicago Press, 1976), p. 10.

8. Ibid., pp. 285–286.

9. Ibid., pp. 265–267.

10. Ibid., p. 267.

11. Nora Ephron, "Mush," in Hammell, *Popular Arts*, p. 424.

12. Gans, "*Love Story*," p. 435.

13. Schrank, *Snap, Crackle, and Popular Taste*, pp. 21–22.

14. Cawelti, *Adventure, Mystery, and Romance*, p. 289.

15. Ibid., pp. 2-10.

16. Jan Cohn, "The Romances of Mary Roberts Rinehart: Some Problems in the Study of Popular Culture," *Journal of Popular Culture* 11, no. 3 (Winter 1977): 581.

17. Linda J. Busby, "Myths, Symbols, Stereotypes: The Artist and the Mass Media," paper delivered at the National Meeting of the Speech Communication Association, San Francisco, California, 27 December 1976, p. 4.

18. Janice A. Radway, "Phenomenology, Linguistics, and Popular Literature," *Journal of Popular Culture* 12, no. 1 (Summer 1978): 94.

19. Ibid., p. 92.

20. Ibid., p. 95.

21. Ibid.

22. Ibid., p. 91.

23. David N. Feldman, "Formalism and Popular Culture," *Journal of Popular Culture* 9, no. 2 (Fall 1975): 388/36.

24. Ibid., p. 390/38.

25. Ibid.

26. Ibid., pp. 393/41-395/43.

27. Ibid., p. 395/43.

28. Ibid., p. 396/44.

29. Mildred Vick Chatton and James Cabaceiras, *Library Science 214: Selection of Materials*, 2nd ed. (San Jose, Calif.: San Jose State University, 1978), pp. 46-48.

30. Ron Miller, "Worn Plots Keep Coming in TV's Recycling Plan," *San Jose Mercury*, 4 October 1979, p. 9C.

31. Ibid.

Youth, Unemployment, and Work with Young Adults

Miriam Braverman

Introduction

The history of work with young people in public libraries in the last sixty years has been characterized by two cycles, the cultural cycle and the social cycle. The cultural cycle can be defined as the period when the librarian was preoccupied with life as reflected in literature, while the social cycle was characterized by the librarian's concern with the conditions of life of young people in their societal environment.[1] The Depression years of the 1930s and the war and postwar years of the 1940s had a great impact on the thinking and programs of service of young adult librarians, and it was during those years that the social approach was developed. Poor and unemployed young people, with aspirations for improving their lives, were of great concern to young adult librarians, who articulated the need for social responsibility as an essential aspect of work with youth. During the 1950s, a period when poor and minority peoples moved into urban areas, small cities and large in various parts of the country, this orientation changed. Unable to understand the needs of the new population, and further frustrated by rigid administrative patterns and staff shortages, young adult librarians turned inward, "emphasized work on book lists, promoting reading among young people who came into the branches, providing material for school assignments, and giving book talks to classes."[2] Young people's librarians shifted from an

Miriam Braverman *is assistant professor of library service at Columbia University.*

Journal of Library History, Vol. 16, No. 2, Spring 1981
© 1981 by the University of Texas Press   0022-2259/81/020353-13$01.40

emphasis on the library's role in the lives of youth, to a service centered on materials, their selection and promotion.

The 1970s saw a resurgence of interest in relating library service to youth and their particular problems. However, as in the earlier years, the response of young adult librarians to the problems of youth has been pragmatic and impressionistic. There is, therefore, a need to explore the critical problems of youth in society to aid in developing a systematic response based on a knowledge of the complexities of each problem and the possibilities and potentials for library service. By examining the social basis of young people's experience in terms of hard facts and data, young adult librarians could be armed with the knowledge needed for realistic and effective services.

In the last twenty-five years one of the most critical areas affecting youth, and one that has merited little attention in the profession, has been a consistently high and stubbornly persistent unemployment rate. This paper is an exploration of this topic, with a view to developing an approach that will serve as a model for an extended study in this and other areas seriously affecting the lives of youth. I will discuss the dimensions of the unemployment problem, the evolution of the government programs developed to deal with it, and a definition of the role of libraries in relation to it.

Youth Unemployment: Evolution and Contours

Although the unemployment rate for young people[3] has fluctuated since 1954, it has risen steadily, always exceeding by multiples the national unemployment rate.[4] Called "social dynamite" in 1961, the youth unemployment rate was still critical eighteen years later, when, in 1979, it was described as a "ticking bomb."[5] The rise in this period has been particularly serious for black youth. Since 1954 their unemployment rate rose from 16.5 percent to 36.6 percent in 1978. The unemployment rate for white teenagers rose in the same period from 12.1 percent to 13.9 percent.[6] Both of these years were relatively "good" years in the national economy, with 5 percent and 5.2 percent national unemployment rates, respectively.[7]

Although the geographic distribution of youth unemployment varies, it has remained consistently high in relation to the general unemployment rate in any given area. Both white and black unemployment rates for youth are high in poverty areas, but they are high in nonpoverty areas as well. In 1978, with a 5.2 percent national unemployment rate, the unemployment for white youth in poverty areas was 14.6 percent and nonpoverty areas 13.8 percent.[8] For black youth the respective rates were 39.3 percent and 33.8 percent. In states such as Florida and Illinois, with general unemployment rates of 6.6 percent and 6.1 percent, respectively, in 1978, the white youth rates were 20.4 percent in Florida and 15 percent in Illinois, while black youth unemployment rates were 44.6 percent and 44.2 percent in those states.[9] Although the rates of unemployment, thus far, have dropped as the teenager has grown older and has had some job experience, the long-term effects of early joblessness are marked: "being out of school *and* out of work as an adolescent or young adult is more clearly related to later labor market problems."[10] The National Longitudinal Surveys, done by Herbert Parnes of the Ohio Center for Human Resources Research, following the labor market experience of sixteen- to nineteen-year-olds for a period of seven years, beginning in 1966 for males and 1968 for females, found that early joblessness has meant lower earnings and less satisfying work experience in later years.[11]

Youth unemployment is not an exclusively American phenomenon. Since 1974/75, "most of the industrialized countries have experienced a marked increase in youth unemployment."[12] The fact that this development is of more recent origin has not diminished the serious view taken by the experts and the governments in most of the countries of Western Europe and in Japan and Australia. With "prospects [for the future] for young people viewed as limited, . . . stronger fears are expressed about the alienation and radicalization of an entire generation than one hears in the U.S."[13]

Perhaps the most disturbing is the trend revealing that even in the years between 1968 and 1978, when the jobs in the low-wage, labor-intensive sectors that have served as entry-level jobs for youth—for example, sales, clerical work, services, and some blue-collar areas—have increased, there has still been a rise in youth unemployment.[14]

There have been numerous attempts to explain the consistently high unemployment rates for youth, the astoundingly high rates of unemployment for minority youth, and the steady rise in youth unemployment since 1954. What is incontrovertible is that technological innovation has changed the job structure and job content dramatically, and conventional wisdom has it that technological change has meant that "many of the jobs available demand much more skill and training than [young people] now can offer."[15] This has been disputed in several important studies. In 1966 a paper prepared for the National Commission on Technology and the American Economy punctured the myth that technological advance required a new and higher level of skills. "Automation," the report stated, "does not inevitably mean lack of opportunity for the unskilled worker. On the contrary, automated machinery tends to require less operator skill after certain levels of mechanization are achieved."[16]

In a landmark analysis of the job structure in the twentieth century, Harry Braverman explained how automation has extended to other sectors in the economy the process that Taylorism or scientific management had begun in factory production: reducing jobs to a series of specific routine operations in which dexterity rather than skill is required. The intellectual or conceptual components are extracted from jobs, and the whole process is controlled by a tiny group of experts, while the bulk of the jobs is confined to a narrow slice of the total operation. This holds true not only in factories, but in clerical, retail, and service occupations as well[17] — and even, one might add, in some professional areas where technicians and paraprofessionals have assumed many duties once regarded as professional. Braverman's thesis is being ever more widely accepted by students of work and the economy, who see in the future almost all work being defined as "mental" on the one hand and "menial/manual" on the other. Future jobholders, in whatever sector they will be employed, will enter a workplace organized "much like traditional factory work, except that workers will wear white shirts and the work will be performed in an office setting."[18] Let us just note here that a 1973 discussion at ALA concerned the vanishing differences between white- and blue-collar jobs in our profession.

At the same time that automation has embraced ever greater areas of the job structure and reduced the knowledge required in work, the educational level of the general population has steadily increased. In 1952, the median school years completed was 10.9; by 1977 it was 12.6. The median level for whites went up from 11.4 in 1952 to 12.6 in 1977; for blacks from 7.9 in 1952 to 12.2 in 1977. For the total population, men and women, and for all ethnic and racial groups, the median level was over 12.0 by 1977.[19]

This scissors action, a lowering of the skills required on jobs and a rising educational level, was the subject of a study by Ivar Berg, head of the department of sociology at the University of Pennsylvania, in his important book, *Education and Jobs: The Great Training Robbery*. Berg describes how education has no direct relation to job performance. His studies demonstrate that "Americans of diverse educational achievements perform productive functions adequately and perhaps well in all but a few professional occupations."[20] However, the labor supply has been characterized by a large number of college graduates, and between 1940 and 1960 the demand for more highly educated workers within occupational structures has increased 85 percent. Querying management in several industries, Berg found that "to a man, the respondents assured us that diplomas and degrees were a good thing, that they were used as screening devices by which undesirable employment applicants could be identified, and that the credentials sought were indicators of personal commitment to 'good middle-class values,' industriousness, and seriousness of purpose, as well as salutary personal habits and styles."[21] What has been happening, says Berg, is that as the educational level of the population has risen, we are "redefining the requirements for employment, if not the job itself, and thus, in the fashion of Humpty Dumpty, make the content of the work what we say it is," thus "absorb[ing] the more highly educated people."[22]

An interesting commentary on the scissors phenomenon, and perhaps a portent of things to come, is the statement made by David Lilienthal, once head of TVA and former chairman of the Atomic Energy Commission, on a recent visit to the Sequoyah nuclear plant in Tennessee on the occasion of the forty-sixth anniversary of the TVA: "standing before control panels like those filmed in 'The China Syndrome' . . . simulators [at which] T.V.A. trains what it says are the nation's best nuclear operators. . . ." Mr. Lilienthal said, "these trainees, high school graduates who start at $11, 930 a year, represent America's best hope for a safe future."[23]

The simultaneous development of the rise in the population's educational level, the higher educational credentials required for jobs, and the general rise in the unemployment rate, especially among new entrants in the labor force, has produced, since 1950, the "drift down" of college graduates in jobs, blocking off the less educated and the less experienced—which, in today's terms, means high school graduates. By 1978 "one out of four employed college graduates held a job traditionally filled by someone with less schooling. As a result high school graduates had to take lesser skilled jobs."[24] Those who suffer most from the "drift down" are those who are at the bottom, as the data cited have shown: youth, particularly minority youth; women, especially minority young women; and those with lower educational credentials. It is this group that has suffered high unemployment rates even in periods of economic improvement and that, many fear, is forming a permanent, and alienated, underclass. And it is this group that has been a concern for policy makers for the past two decades.

Government Policies and Programs for Youth

In 1961 the National Committee for Children and Youth stated that "the private sector of the economy cannot solve the unemployed youth problem. The public sector should enter the field."[25] The federal government then instituted programs stressing better preparation for jobs: training for school dropouts, functional illiterates, delinquent and handicapped youth, with special emphasis on minority youth over nineteen years of age. Grants were made for special programs, "a key goal [of which] was to make 'unemployable' youth employable."[26]

In 1964 the emphasis shifted somewhat when the Job Corps, the Neighborhood Youth Corps, and work-study programs were initiated, adding to the target group the younger unemployed, sixteen to nineteen years old, and also adding a subsidy component to training and education. All programs, however, considered the unemployed youth "maladjusted" and sought "to help them make an adequate adjustment first to the educational institution, if they are in school or can be induced to return" and then "to adjust the youth to the world of employment, to change him [*sic*] in the direction of employer specifications."[27]

By 1967 it was clear that "the demand side of job development [the job market] has been seriously underemphasized in current manpower and anti-poverty programs."[28] In other words, perhaps the problem was not in youth's attitudes or even lack of skills, but in the lack of jobs for youth. It was felt that the emphasis on training may be misplaced when automated machines tend to require less rather than more skills.[29] In an ironic note, Berg pointed out that supervisors in a company whose work force he studied found the less educated the better workers: there was less absenteeism among them and less turnover.[30]

The provision of jobs has been the toughest area of all for policy makers and program planners to deal with, and for a number of reasons. As the general unemployment rate increases the "drift down," more experienced and educated workers push youth to the back of the queue. Discrimination, identified almost twenty years ago as a major factor in youth unemployment, has not only persisted, but has worsened. Government programs, studies have shown, "do not benefit [black males and black male youths] as much as other sex-ethnic groups," for example, white males and females.[31] Although minority youth have raised their educational level substantially "from 1969 to 1977, while white teenage employment increased, black teenage employment actually fell by 3.1 percent."[32] The higher level of education has not made an appreciable dent in the unemployment rate among black and Chicano youth. Indeed, "significant percentages of young men in these communities have obtained both academic and vocational training without measurable benefit to themselves in the labor market."[33]

After two decades of experience and experimentation, many students of the problem have concluded that there must be more emphasis on the demand side of the labor market equation—the job supply. However, it is recognized that general growth of the economy has not lowered the general teenage unemployment rate so that it approaches the general rate of unemployment in the country. In 1969, during the Vietnam War, when the unemployment rate for full-time male workers over twenty years old was 1.9 percent, the rate for full-time male and female workers was 12.7 percent. For "Negroes and Other Races 16–19 years" the unemployment rate that year was 24.1 percent.[34]

It is evident, then, that general growth of the economy has a limited impact on youth unemployment, and is even more limited in drawing minority young people into the labor market. At the same time, educational and training programs aimed particularly at improving attitudes and habits are out of joint with an economy that on the one hand is characterized by a diminution in the intellectual and skills content of jobs, and on the other by higher educational attainment of young people, with raised expectations, particularly among minority young people, for jobs with high status and pay and good working conditions.

However, public policy seems little affected by these findings, and the current government programs are similar to those first instituted twenty-five years ago, with their emphasis on training and preparation for nonsubsidized employment in the private sector.

The Library's Role

These studies have special importance for librarians. First, because it is important to understand the varying unemployment patterns of different youth populations to be prepared to cope with realities and design more effective programs for the particular population the young adult librarian serves. Second, studies have shown that the most effective components of the government programs have been job counseling and the provision of labor market and occupational information. Placement services have been mentioned in a historical study of the effectiveness of youth programs as "the most effective" of all services offered.[35] It is in this area—labor market information—that librarians can play a crucial role.

Libraries have traditionally provided career materials for young people. Young adult librarians have included job and college selection in their programming. More recently Job Information Centers have been set up in public libraries, which include career materials useful to young people and often government brochures and applications for youth programs. Many have information to steer youth to programs designed for their needs.[36] These Job Information Centers are not geared to the special needs of youth, however. One program that is youth-centered is the New York Public Library's "Learn Your Way Center for Teenagers" in the Nathan Straus Young Adult Library at the Donnell Library Center. Although more involved with education and training than with job information, and located some distance from the neighborhoods with high concentrations of youth unemployment, it is a special service targeted to teenagers.

These programs, like the earlier young adult programs of the 1930s and 1940s, have been inspired by a genuine concern for young people and a commitment to provide the services they need, responding to needs as the librarians perceived them. Like their predecessors, librarians today are responding pragmatically to particular conditions and situations. The flexibility of this approach is a great advantage, as it emphasizes fashioning services to meet needs on a microlevel. However, library services to youth can be more effective when informed by developments on a macrolevel and investigating how the general trends affect the local area. By identifying a critical problem affecting the lives of young people, by probing it in depth, by analyzing its components and exploring the role of the library and librarians in relation to its realities, a distinctive and precise definition of service can be achieved. Applied to the area of employment—and unemployment—librarians need to know general information, such as the current labor market and its trends, particularly in the services, clerical, and retail areas—labor-intensive areas that hire teenagers. Most important, detailed local information in terms of specific jobs, programs, and their requirements is needed. The problem is complex and there are many variables that affect local areas. Employment services list only 30 percent of active job vacancies, and "the closer job development gets to the operational level on a local level, the more serious is the lack of labor market information."[37] Librarians, who are community based, are in the best position to become the local job information centers for youth. They can gather information to answer such questions as: Where are the jobs? What are they? Who works? What is changing in the local labor force and local employment picture? What are the local government programs? What are their eligibility requirements? What are the processes for enrollment? How have they been evaluated by previous participants? What about the armed forces? What types of training programs do they offer? How about the National Guard and what opportunities are given to youth through this avenue? Such information is particularly needed by minority youth, who rely more heavily on public agencies than other youth who have a friends/family network.[38] A survey by the librarian can "identify the availability and accessibility of public school counseling"[39] and government and nongovernment employment agencies that list jobs in areas of teenage employment. An Indianapolis study found that "labor market information available to ghetto blacks is probably of a low quality and insufficient quantity."[40] The informational skills of the librarian can make an important contribution to young people who are starting out in the critical but frustrating world of work.

It is problematical whether either sector, public or private, or both combined, can make substantial inroads toward reducing youth unemployment in other than a defense economy, given the dimensions of the problem and the ineffectiveness of policies and programs until now. Garth Mangum concludes, in his 1978 study, that "no more than marginal improvement can be expected from the best research and the best policy. But that margin is often the difference between the acceptable and the insufferable."[41] Librarians can make a contribution to that margin of difference, can make a difference in individuals' lives, a goal worthy of libraries as well as the larger society. For this we must become knowledgeable in labor market information and skillful in applying that knowledge to local situations.

Notes

1. Miriam Braverman, *Youth, Society and the Public Library* (Chicago: American Library Association, 1979), p. 243. The observations in this in-

troduction are based on a study of young adult work in New York, Cleveland, and Baltimore from 1920 to the early 1960s. The influence of the leaders in these libraries was profound in shaping young adult work nationally.

2. Ibid., p. 247.

3. I will be discussing sixteen- to nineteen-year-olds. The data on four-teen- to sixteen-year-olds is slim, and their patterns and problems differ be-cause they are more likely to be in school. I have also excluded, because of the time and space constraints of this paper, a discussion of the effects of the volunteer armed forces on the youth labor market.

4. U.S. Department of Labor, Bureau of Labor Statistics Tables, com-piled by Bureau of Labor Statistics Library, New York City, unpublished, un-paged.

5. National Committee for Children and Youth, *Social Dynamite: The Report of the Conference on Unemployed, Out-of-School Youth in Urban Areas, May 24-26, 1961* (Washington, D.C.: National Committee for Chil-dren and Youth, 1961); Harvey A. Rubenstein, "Unemployed Youth: A Tick-ing Bomb," *U.S.A. Today* (July 1978).

6. The Bureau of Labor Statistics figures identify as unemployed those who are actively seeking employment. This excludes those who have dropped out of the labor market because of hopelessness, or, in some cases, are operat-ing in the subeconomy. Long-term statistical data for youth other than black or white, for example, Hispanic, American Indian, and Asian American youth, are not available. The unemployment rate for females sixteen to nine-teen years old was almost always consistently lower than that for males of that age from 1948 to 1963, when the female unemployment rate overtook the male rate and, until 1975, was consistently higher. Between 1954 and 1975 black male unemployment rates were higher than those for male and fe-male whites. Black female unemployment rates were higher for the whole period than for all the other groups. The area of unemployment of females in the sixteen- to nineteen-year-old group deserves thorough study (U.S. Depart-ment of Labor, Bureau of Labor Statistics Tables, compiled by Bureau of Labor Statistics Library, New York City, unpublished, unpaged).

7. U.S. Department of Health, Education, and Welfare and the Depart-ment of Labor, *Employment and Training Report of the President* ([Washing-ton, D.C.: Department of Labor, 1979]), table A-6, p. 246.

8. Ibid., table A-11, p. 252.

9. U.S. Department of Labor, Bureau of Labor Statistics, *Geographic Pro-file of Employment and Unemployment* ([Washington, D.C.]: Department of Labor, Bureau of Labor Statistics, [n.d.]), report no. 571, table 1.

10. Bernard E. Anderson and Isabel V. Sawhill, "Policy Approaches in the Years Ahead," in *Youth Employment and Public Policy*, The American As-sembly, Columbia University, Background papers for the Arden House As-sembly on Youth Employment, August 1979 (Englewood Cliffs, N.J.: Pren-tice-Hall, 1980), p. 141.

11. Rubenstein, "Unemployed Youth," p. 46.

12. Beatrice G. Reubens, "Review of Foreign Experience," in *Youth Employment and Public Policy*, p. 112.

13. Ibid., p. 113.

14. United States Bureau of Labor Statistics, *Educational Attainment: Some Trends from 1973 to 1978*, Special Labor Force Report no. 225, re-printed from *Monthly Labor Review* (February 1979). Blue-collar jobs up

from 3.5 percent to 6.6 percent of labor force; sales and clerical up 11.2 percent to 13.6 percent; services up 1.1 percent to 2.1 percent (p. 56).

15. President of the United States, *The Challenge of Jobless Youth: [Report and Recommendations of President's Committee on Youth Employment, April 1963]* (n.p., [1963]), p. iv.

16. James R. Bright, "The Relation of Increasing Automation and Skill Requirements," in *The Employment Impact of Technological Change*, appendix, vol. 2 of *Technology and the American Economy*, U.S. National Commission on Technology, Automation, and Economic Progress (Washington, D.C.: U.S. Government Printing Office, 1966-   ); quoted in R. A. Nixon, *The Labor Market Framework of Job Development: Some Problems and Prospects* (New York: Center for the Study of Unemployed Youth, Graduate School of Social Work, New York University, Fall 1967), p. 30.

17. Harry Braverman, *Labor and Monopoly Capital: The Degradation of Work in the Twentieth Century* (New York: Monthly Review Press, 1975), passim.

18. William Serrin, "U.S. Labor: Post-Meany," *New York Times* 12 January 1980, 25:1.

19. U.S. Department of Labor, Bureau of Labor Statistics, *Handbook of Labor Statistics 1978*, bulletin 2000, table 12, pp. 60-62.

20. Ivar Berg, *Education and Jobs: The Great Training Robbery* (Boston: Beacon Press, 1971), p. 41.

21. Ibid., p. 78.

22. Ibid., p. 68.

23. Howell Raines, "In T.V.A. Country, Contentment Is a Nuclear Plant," *New York Times*, 18 May 1979, 1:2.

24. U.S. Bureau of Labor Statistics, *Educational Attainment of Workers: Some Trends from 1973 to 1978*, Special Labor Force Report no. 225, reprinted from *Monthly Labor Review* (February 1979): 58.

25. National Committee for Children and Youth, *Social Dynamite*, p. 123.

26. National Child Labor Committee, New York, National Committee on Employment and Youth, *Youth Employment Programs in Perspective* (Washington, D.C.: Department of Health, Education, and Welfare, Office of Juvenile Delinquency and Youth Development, 1965), p. 4.

27. Ibid., p. 11.

28. R. A. Nixon, *Labor Market Framework*, p. 31. See also, Richard B. Freeman, "Why Is There a Youth Market Problem? " in *Youth Employment and Public Policy*, pp. 6-32.

29. Nixon, *Labor Market Framework*, p. 30.

30. Berg, investigating the relationship between education and occupational skills in blue-collar, white-collar, and professional categories, found that often there was an inverse relationship between them. See *Education and Jobs*, ch. 5, 6, 7.

31. Ernst W. Stromsdorfer, "The Effectiveness of Youth Programs: An Analysis of the Historical Antecedents of Current Youth Initiatives," in *Youth Employment and Public Policy*, pp. 88-111.

32. Richard B. Freeman, "Why Is There a Youth Market Problem? " in *Youth Employment and Public Policy*, p. 26.

33. Paul Bullock, *Aspiration vs. Opportunity: "Careers" in the Inner-City*, Policy Papers in Human Resources and Industrial Relations, 20 (Ann Arbor, Mich.: Institute of Labor and Industrial Relations, University of Michigan—Wayne State University, 1973), p. 69.

34. Bureau of Labor Statistics Tables, Bureau of Labor Statistics Library, New York City, unpublished, unpaged.

35. Stromsdorfer, "Effectiveness of Youth Programs," pp. 4-20. See also, "Unemployed Youth: A Post-Secondary Response," unpublished paper by Fund for the Improvement of Post-Secondary Education (Department of Health, Education, and Welfare, and Department of Labor, 1979), p. 5; Garth L. Mangum and Stephen F. Seninger, *Coming of Age in the Ghetto: A Dilemma of Youth Unemployment*, Policy Studies in Employment and Welfare, no. 33 (Baltimore, Md.: Johns Hopkins University Press, 1978), pp. 90-91; Nixon, *Labor Market Framework*, ch. 2; Bullock, *Aspiration vs. Opportunity*, p. 167.

36. Brochures from some of the thirty-two Job Information Centers in New York State: Buffalo and Erie County Public Library, Nioga Library System, Rochester Public Library, Brooklyn Public Library, Clinton-Essex-Franklin Library System. Other libraries—Queens Borough Public Library, Seattle Public Library, White Plains (N.Y.) Public Library—had materials, bibliographies, and some forms for applying for government programs.

37. Nixon, *Labor Market Framework*, p. 16.

38. Bullock, *Aspiration vs. Opportunity*, p. 30.

39. Mangum and Seninger, *Coming of Age in the Ghetto*, p. 91.

40. Ibid., p. 40.

41. Ibid., p. 102.

Library History in Britain: Progress and Prospects

Paul Sturges

In 1959 Dr. W. A. Munford published one of his many pleasant essays in which he drew up a list of subjects for future work in Britain on library history.[1] His list included: concise histories of the National Libraries of Britain and more detailed histories of particular periods of their past; histories of the newer university and college libraries; a history of public libraries as well as centenary histories of individual public libraries; histories of nonmunicipal public libraries in the nineteenth century; a history of the Library Association and histories of some of its branches and groups; and biographies of librarians. Since he was thinking in terms of categories of libraries, he could have added learned and special libraries. What he did not mention was the study of themes such as professionalization or the role of women. Munford's essay can be seen as anticipating the modern period of British library history writing, which reached something of a peak with the Library Association Centenary of 1977. Looking back on the period it can be seen that categorization in the style of Munford is still relevant and that branching out from writing about types of library to writing about themes in librarianship has hardly occurred. The retrospective part of this paper is intended to amplify this claim through a brief survey of the literature.

To take Munford's first category, the National Libraries, there has been some excellent work done, though it is not particularly what he envisaged. No comprehensive history of the Bodleian,

Paul Sturges *is lecturer in library and information studies at Loughborough University, Leicestershire.*

Journal of Library History, Vol. 16, No. 2, Spring 1981
© 1981 by the University of Texas Press   0022–2259/81/020365–16$01.55

Cambridge University Library, National Library of Wales, or National Library of Scotland has emerged during the period, nor has a history of the British Library. The only comprehensive history is of a comparatively recent institution, the National Central Library.[2] Filon, the author, was for many years the librarian of this predecessor of the British Library Lending Division.

Miller's excellent history of the British Museum has much on the library departments and his biography of Panizzi will be considered later, along with other works on that most famous of British Museum librarians.[3] Apart from Panizzi, Sir Frederick Madden is the person from the library departments who has attracted most attention. This is not merely owing to his contribution in the Manuscripts Department, but because he kept a voluminous and informative diary from 1817 to 1872. Its forty-three volumes are now available in microform.[4]

Another venture into the publication of source materials in a more traditional manner is the edition of the diary of Humphrey Wanley produced by the Wrights.[5] The two magnificent volumes present the text of the diary with a lengthy introduction, a plethora of valuable footnotes, and other scholarly apparatus. As library-keeper to Robert Harley, first earl of Oxford and Edward, the second earl, Wanley was responsible for the Harleian Library, which formed a vital keystone of the British Museum collections. His day-to-day comments on the world of collecting and scholarship in the early eighteenth century are of unfailing interest. However, all this leaves the field of national libraries in Britain surprisingly open to historical enterprise.

Other learned and special libraries are more numerous and varied, with a certain amount of literature devoted to them. The best of this is probably that which deals with medieval ecclesiastical or academic libraries. The libraries of the medieval period have been very much the preserve of one scholar—N. R. Ker. His *Medieval Libraries of Great Britain: List of Surviving Books* (1964) is a key work. This and other contributions, including those on parochial libraries (1959), Oxford college libraries (1959), and cathedral libraries (1967), established him as a dominating figure in the study of earlier periods of British library history.[6] Subsequent periods are less well served, though one can mention Thornton's books on the collectors and libraries in the medical and scientific fields and an excellent account of the modern industrial special library in Margaret Marshall's 1972 article.[7]

Undoubtedly the major category into which writings on British library history fall is that of modern, rate-supported public libraries. Their predecessors and contemporaries, the commercial and proprietary subscription and circulating libraries, are also favored subjects and should perhaps be dealt with as a preface.

The chief contributions on subscription and circulating libraries include many from Dr. Paul Kaufman, an American. Most of his various pioneer articles on what he calls "community libraries" have been collected in a single volume published in 1969.[8] However, it is important to note that certain of the articles were shorn of their appendices for this collection and might still need to be consulted in their original form. Guinevere Griest, another American, in her 1970 account of Mudie's Library is as much concerned with the influence of Mudie's on the nineteenth-century novel as she is with the library itself.[9] As an example of the treatment of the library in its literary context this book deserves special mention. Contemporary with Mudie's but still in existence is the London Library, the fee-charging lending library to the London literary community. Gillam has written both on the library's 125th anniversary and on Hagberg Wright, its most famous librarian.[10]

The Act of Parliament of 1850, which inaugurated the period of public libraries in the local government structure, was celebrated by Munford in his *Penny Rate* (1951), a brief centenary history of public libraries.[11] Though so much has been published since, this is still read and indeed remains a worthy summary of the first 100 years. As libraries were founded under the provisions of the Act in the years after 1850, so the years since 1950 have seen a steady output of centenary and other histories of individual library systems. Of individual public library histories as a form, the best that can be said of them is that their cumulative effect is to provide building materials for history on a broader plan.

That we now have an extremely substantial history of rate-supported public libraries we owe to Dr. Thomas Kelly. His first major work was his *History of Adult Education in Great Britain* (1962).[12] This inevitably touched on libraries, reading rooms, and book clubs as instruments of adult education. Kelly's command of the literature on libraries and his sympathetic understanding of them was such that the Library Association asked him to write the history of public libraries. At his own request he began by working on the precursors of the rate-supported libraries and what was intended as quite a small book became his *Early Public Libraries* (1966).[13] Again what impresses is his mastery of a very large and miscellaneous literature covering the period from medieval ecclesiastical libraries to the sophisticated commercial and institutional libraries of the first half of the nineteenth century. The breadth of coverage and sheer variety of detail are impressive, but the book is also extremely enjoyable and coherent.

The prefatory work complete, Kelly then turned his attention to the main task and in 1973 the first edition of his *History of Public Libraries in Great Britain* appeared.[14] In 1977 a second revised edition with the coverage extended from 1965 to 1975 appeared as one of the LA Centenary volumes. If *Early Public Libraries* could happily be a little diffuse because of the diversity of institutions it treated, then the task in the second book was harder because, despite the supposed homogeneity of the rate-supported libraries, a coherent theme in their past is often hard to discern. That Kelly succeeds as far as he does is remarkable.

A good number of other writers have also chosen general public library topics. Legislation, for instance, has been taken up by two recent writers. Pemberton, in a 1977 work, is concerned with the political activity in the library profession over library legislation and concentrates on the twentieth century. The examination of the whole corpus of relevant law is the task undertaken by Morris, also in 1977.[15] He takes the legislation bill by bill, act by act, discussing the investigating committees, their reports, the parliamentary debates, the amendments, and the implementation of new laws.

Not all books on public library history are learned monographs. Two publications consisting chiefly of pictures appeared in 1977. Of the two, Ball's book on London public libraries, though on a narrower topic, is the more enjoyable. The illustrations cluster several to the page and constitute a richly nostalgic impression of the first age of public libraries. The variety is tremendous: prints, posters, handouts, and cartoons as well as photographs, covering such topics as buildings, opening ceremonies, interiors, fittings, and staff groups. All are enhanced by Ball's witty and observant text. The second book, by Dr. Kelly and Mrs. Kelly, tries to span the whole of British public library history and despite great numbers of fascinating pictures has a considerably slighter impact.[16]

The Library Association itself was one of Munford's suggested categories for future work, and in the end he himself wrote its history.[17] The materials available, in the form of minute books, newspapers, and journal materials, were unpromising as the meat of lively history. The result is a very respectable example of institutional history. The branches, sections, and activities of the LA also merit attention, and some books have been written on these. Ramsden's 1973 account of the Association of Assistant Librarians, though based on minutes, annual reports, and the Association's published journal, the *Assistant Librarian*, is lively and readable, with the personalities involved emerging in a lifelike way.[18]

Biography of librarians is perhaps the second richest variety of British library history. This is largely owing once again to Munford. Besides his main book-length studies of librarians he has written various articles in a biographical vein. His debut was in 1960 with his life of William Ewart, the nineteenth-century parliamentary champion of library legislation. By Munford's account he had some difficulty finding a commercial publisher for this life of a man little-known to any except students of one or two minor fields (libraries included). According to one publisher, the book lacked some kind of sex interest, but unfortunately Ewart had the most blameless sex life. However, the book was published and remains a useful work. Munford's *Edward Edwards* (1963) is much more substantial from the library historian's point of view.[19] Edwards made major contributions to the development of librarianship as an art and, through his work with Ewart, to the passing of the Public Libraries Act of 1850. Fortunately, materials in the form of correspondence and diaries were available for a full and sympathetic portrait of the unfortunate library pioneer.

A further notable contribution to the biography of public librarians is Ollé's account of Ernest Savage (1977). Ollé was previously best known for his textbook on library history but also has written a number of articles with a biographical slant.[20]

Also an extremely enjoyable book is Miller's account of Panizzi (1967). Panizzi, apart from his unrivaled contribution to the making of the British Museum Library into a worthy national library, was a character on a noble scale with an interesting and varied life beyond the Library's walls. Miller has fitted this life into a richly described background of the times and writes ably enough to keep the attention of the reader even through the more technical aspects of his career as a librarian. Panizzi was commemorated in spring 1979, one hundred years after his death, by a special exhibition in the British Museum. This was done with the Museum's usual professionalism and must have brought Panizzi to the attention of an unusually varied public from the Museum's visitors. To coincide with the exhibition, an issue of the *British Library Journal* was given over almost entirely to articles on various aspects of Panizzi's life.[21]

Finally it must be noted that historical approaches pervade the general literature of librarianship in Britain. For illustration of the point one can turn to James Thompson's *History of the Principles of Librarianship* (1977).[22] That an attempt to distill the principles that lie behind what librarians think about their craft should be made by historical investigation rather than by an examination of current practice or by a survey of the views of active librarians is typically British. From his exploration of the literature, early to recent, Thompson feels able to state the main principles of librarianship. The seventeen principles that emerge, from "Libraries are created by society" to "A library must have a subject catalogue," sometimes seem rather trite. They are unlikely to receive universal approbation, but their chief virtue is that other contributions on this topic seem likely to be drawn out by Thompson's bold excursion. Thompson, in writing on theory, is really quite unusual in British terms, for British library historians seem happy to avoid such questions. They also retain a surprising methodological innocence in the face of all of modern historiographical writing. A glance at a few contributions in this area will illustrate the point.

In 1958 R. Irwin's essay "Does Library History Matter?" gave a response to this question that was almost mystical, offering to the student of library history "inner satisfaction and joy" or even "supreme happiness" rather the more mundane benefits one might have expected.[23] His best known book, *Origins of the English Library*, appeared in an enlarged edition in 1966 as *The English Library*, with an introductory chapter incorporating much of the 1958 essay.[24] Lest it seem Irwin's approach is all vague ideals, it must be stressed that this introduction contains much that is practical. For instance the following—"A history of libraries, whether regional or national, can acquire vitality only if it is intimately related to the literature that libraries contain and the social circumstances of the people who use them. Such a history must be treated as one aspect of both social studies and literary history and it will not come to life unless this is recognised" (p. 22).

Other British contributions to the theory of library history have been few and slight. Cutcliffe, in 1967, summed up some relevant arguments to justify the practice of library history. As his ultimate justification he falls back on the "sheer interest" of the subject, arguing that any benefits arising from its study are purely incidental. Thomas Kelly in 1975 had a good deal of value to say on his research techniques and offered some cautionary remarks on the danger of writing the history of individual libraries insulated from period background. The present writer took up the question of context in 1976 and attempted to illustrate from the case of Derby in the eighteenth century the argument that period background is not enough. The history of a library or libraries also needs a firm institutional and social context.[25]

To sum up the current state of the literature, it is strongest in scholarly and painstaking institutional histories and biographies. While there are some good treatments of groups of libraries, there is a lack of attention given to themes in library history, and also a lack of theoretical and methodological work.

Turning to the prospects for library history in Britain, they can be seen as depending on three main factors. These are: a good organizational base for the discipline; good teaching and supervision of student library historians; and the availability of suitable source materials.

The first of these we have had in Britain since a separate Library History Group of the Library Association was formed in 1963. This has a large and growing membership. It first communicated with its members through a newsletter, but in 1967 was able to launch *Library History*.[26] This journal has been lucky in its first two editors, Peter Hoare and P. S. Morrish, who have maintained high standards of scholarship and readability. It is unusual among publications of LA sections in that it circulates very widely among nonmembers, a tribute to its quality. Besides one or two main articles per issue it has book reviews, a narrative bibliography entitled "Notes on other Recent Publications," and other material including notes on archives. The section's work does not stop at the journal, for three volumes of an excellent annotated bibliography have appeared under the editorship of Denis F. Keeling.[27]

On the teaching of library history in the library schools it is less possible to be confident. It tends to be narrative and short on social context. However, there is a small but steady flow of theses on library history. Two separate listings, one of FLA theses by L. J. Taylor (1979) and one of university librarianship theses by P. J. Taylor (1976), give some of the story.[28] The numbers of theses submitted on library history topics increased in the second half of the 1960s from approximately one each per year to the LA and to universities, to something like six each per year. Thus for over ten years approximately twelve new recruits to the writing of library history have been made each year. Additionally many undergraduate students of librarianship write long essays on library history topics, which may be the start of a research interest. Since theses and dissertations are the main means by which people come to study library history, the role of supervisors in assisting the choice of worthwhile topics and directing students toward appropriate techniques is crucial. There is perhaps too little sign yet of a move away from the typical thesis topic of a study of a particular library, to something broader and more valuable. There needs to be some hard thinking in library schools on the purposes of library history, the theoretical framework of research, and the methods adopted.

The third factor, good source material, is essential for any kind of history, weak or strong. A glance at the notes on archives that have appeared in *Library History* on various occasions will show that record offices and libraries in Britain do have many fascinating and valuable documents, some of which are so far unused. However, a question of some urgency that has been too little discussed is the provision modern libraries are making for the preservation and care of their records. Such records are clearly the substance of library history research in the future. A small survey of British public library administrative records has been carried out for the purposes of this paper. Since local government reorganization in the early 1970s, there are 166 authorities providing the public library service for the whole of England, Wales, Scotland, and Northern Ireland. This makes a postal survey of the kind described here much less expensive and difficult than when there was a multitude of small independent public libraries. Bearing in mind the unpopularity of questionnaires, this one was brief, just six questions with one or two subquestions in most cases (see appendix 1). It was sent to 162 of the 166 authorities and the remaining 4 (2 counties and 2 cities) were visited to provide some kind of a check on the findings from the questionnaire.

The response to the questionnaire was good. In addition to the 4 visits, 101 questionnaires were returned completed, 1 other informative response was received, and there were only 5 refusals. This represents information from 63 percent of the library authorities. For comparative purposes the responses were divided into 5 groups: English and Welsh counties (32 responded out of 47, 68 percent); London boroughs (21 out of 34, 61 percent); English and Welsh metropolitan and other district libraries (22 out of 40, 55 percent); Scottish districts and regions (28 out of 40, 70 percent); and the Northern Ireland Education and Library Boards (2 out of 5, 40 percent). The response was fairly consistent throughout the groups.

What emerged in general was that while a few libraries have clear-cut archives policies resulting in well-ordered and useful bodies of records, there is a widespread lack of such policies. Some authorities are well aware of this and have policies under consideration, for example, Sheffield City, whose "Archive Division has recently established a records management programme for the Authority as a whole and is at the moment about to turn its attention

373

to the records of the Libraries Department."[29] Others seem either to have little interest or to have adopted a philosophy unsympathetic toward the retention of archival material. This philosophy was identified by one interviewee as the philosophy of modern management: we live in the present and the future, not the past; precedent is of little importance; new ideas, new methods are all.[30] Any records that are kept, are kept solely for their continuing usefulness to the organization. In cases where the basic philosophy of the organization is not inimical to records retention there often seems to be a curious blind spot: librarians, to whom all kinds of information are worthy of preservation, fail to see the records of their own organization in the same light. This last attitude results in a great unevenness in preservation, storage, organization, and availability of records.

A little or a lot may survive under such conditions. What does survive is often in dark corners of cupboards, attics, or basements. The major finding of the survey is that there is much scope for the education of librarians in enlightened policies toward the records of their own organizations. Libraries are after all just as worthy of being the object of future historical study as any other kind of organization.

Virtually all the responding libraries admit to retaining some material after its immediate use is over. But a small number, such as Enfield, which retains "very few," or Dunfermline, which retains records "only very exceptionally and if of historical significance," are clearly quite ruthless about this.

A good many authorities have records going back into the nineteenth century, and this is most common with the large city libraries whose foundation followed the 1850 Public Libraries Act (see appendix 2). Equally naturally, a majority of county libraries have records beginning in the 1920s and 1930s when they were formed. Some counties by virtue of having absorbed municipal libraries have nineteenth-century material. A surprisingly high number of all kinds of libraries only have material from the 1960s or 1970s, but in most cases this is due to their having been created as new authorities in that period.

Most libraries regard current materials as being 1970s material only, with the curious exception of the London boroughs, which have a majority keeping "current" material from the 1960s. A few libraries have material in their current files dating back to the 1940s and in a couple of cases back to the 1920s.

The vagueness of archive policies in the libraries responding to the survey emerges very clearly in their attitudes to weeding and discarding. Sixty-seven percent of the libraries avoided having a definite period laid down for the beginning of this process. The minority with policies weed and discard after anything from a one-year to a ten-year period.

There is tremendous variety in the categories of material retained and the decision as to whether to retain them in full or in part. Minutes are more or less universally kept, often in printed form, but for other categories—correspondence, internal reports, staff records, loan records, donations registers, and so forth—there are as many different policies as libraries.

Storage of records is very seldom in one single place (32 percent overall). Scottish libraries are unusual in having 53 percent with unified storage of records, while for English and Welsh libraries the figure is 24 percent. The chief cause of separation of material is the keeping of current material in the administrative office and older material in some other store. Reorganization of authorities is responsible for some decentralization of records. English and Welsh counties have 56 percent reporting records still held by authorities absorbed, and English and Welsh districts with 54 percent are similarly placed. However, the London boroughs have only 14 percent of their number reporting records retained by constituent authorities, and Scottish libraries are similar with 18 percent. The difference probably stems from geographical compactness in the case of the London boroughs and the fact that many of the Scottish authorities have not undergone the process of amalgamation. The difficulty of the counties is shown in the response of one authority to the question of whether absorbed libraries kept their own records: "They should not, but you can bet that some of the silly b. . . . . .s still do unofficially." Nearly half of the libraries had some of their records looked after by an official archive repository; sometimes part of the same department, sometimes a separate department of the authority. This figure is somewhat distorted by the infrequency with which the Scottish libraries followed this practice, 21 percent compared with 57 percent for English and Welsh libraries.

The lack of consistent archives policy is once again illustrated by the designation of someone with responsibility for records. Only 53 percent of libraries have someone whose responsibilities formally include this role, and, whereas with the English and Welsh counties the figure is 65 percent, the London boroughs 57 percent, and the English and Welsh districts 54 percent, the figure falls to 35 percent with the Scottish authorities. The responsible person quite frequently has a high standing in the hierarchy, such as an assistant chief librarian or head of administrative services. Sometimes the responsibility is split between an administrative officer for current material and an archivist for the older material. However in several cases the person responsible is quite junior, for example the chief librarian's secretary, the filing clerk, or the chief typist. This all represents a very inconsistent view of the importance of overseeing the fate of record material.

This impression is borne out by the extent to which libraries have lists and indices for their records. The percentages that do are very similar to those for designating a responsible person. The overall figure is 56 percent, that for English and Welsh counties 59 percent, London boroughs 61 percent, English and Welsh districts 73 percent, Scottish libraries 32 percent. The standard practice is probably similar to that of the London borough of Hammersmith and Fulham, which for current material has typescript lists in alphabetical order under subject headings referring to the location of the files, and for older material has cards listing the contents of the records of each of the authorities that now form part of the borough. Many libraries have only indexes to the contents of minutes or an index of files according to Stewarts Tabulation.[31] The most fascinating response came from a library where "our filing index, designed by the Chief, is based on Ranganathan and is most exciting to use because there are at least 2 and sometimes 6 locations possible for each item."

Most libraries, something like 67 percent (worthwhile figures are difficult to produce because of the variety of responses to this question), have a fairly open attitude to the availability of their material for research. Recent staffing records are understandably almost universally closed, and a small minority of libraries would keep all their records closed. Perhaps the most open attitude is that of Hampshire, which allows "free access to any material available." Practical difficulties do intervene even when there is an open attitude, as with Derbyshire, where problems could be "related to hours of access, removal from site, etc.," but are "unlikely to be related to 'sensitivity.'" Other authorities adopt a very cautious policy, such as that of Birmingham, where "exceptions would be made in special circumstances, otherwise documents would not be available." Clearly a tactful approach and the right credentials would be an advantage in every case, but in some they are even more vital than in others.

This examination of public library administrative records leaves out of consideration other types of source that would also repay attention from librarians and researchers. Oral history has been rather neglected, though David Gerard of the College of Librarianship, Wales, has taped some distinguished librarians, and made the tapes available for sale.[32] There is still material in private hands, and more such material will no doubt reward the diligent researcher. Museum objects and library ephemera await the efforts of some dedicated collector who will bring us the much needed museum of libraries and librarianship.

The prospects for library history in Britain remain open and inviting. There is much to do in both library schools and libraries themselves, but the consistent level of interest in the subject from librarians and students of librarianship, coupled with the excellent work of the Library History Group, makes possible an optimistic view of the future.

Appendix 1: The Questionnaire

The basic questions asked, minus the boxes for yes, no, and further information, are as follows:
Name of library
1. Does your library keep files of administrative documents?
   (a)   only during the period they have immediate use?
   (b)   even after their immediate use is over?
2. 1   From what year do your earliest records date?
   2   From what year do your earliest currently used files begin?
   3   Is there a deliberately chosen period, after which records begin to be discarded or weeded?
      If so, after how many years?
3. What categories of material are retained after immediate use has ended?
4. 1   Are your records kept
      (a) in a single store?
      (b) in various locations?
   2   Do other libraries absorbed by amalgamation still retain their own records?
   3   Are any records kept in an archive repository?
5. 1   Is a particular member of the library's staff responsible for internal records?
   2   If so, what is the name of the post?
      Are there any lists, inventories or indices to your records?
6. Would your records ever be made available for research?

Appendix 2: The Earliest Material Held by Library Systems

Some libraries did not provide any data on this, and therefore the total number here is not the full 106. The numbers in the columns represent libraries whose earliest material dates from the period indicated. Thus 3 county libraries have their earliest material dating from the 1970s.

	English and Welsh counties	London boroughs	English and Welsh metropolitan and other districts	Scottish district and regional libraries
1970–1979	3		3	5
1960–1969	4	7	1	1
1950–1959	1	1		1
1940–1949	1		1	1
1930–1939	6	1		2
1920–1929	5			4
1910–1919	1	1		
1900–1909	1	2	2	3
1890–1899		3	1	1
1880–1889	1	1	2	1
1870–1879	2		5	2
1860–1869	1			1
1850–1859	1		2	1

Notes

1. W. A. Munford, "Our Library Inheritance," *Library Review* 17, no. 130 (Summer 1959): 101–106.

2. S. P. L. Filon, *The National Central Library: An Experiment in Library Co-operation*, centenary volume (London: Library Association, 1977).

3. Edward Miller, *That Noble Cabinet: A History of the British Museum* (London: Deutsch, 1973; Athens, Oh.: Ohio University Press, 1974); idem, *Prince of Librarians: The Life and Times of Antonio Panizzi of the British Museum* (London: Deutsch, 1967; Athens, Oh.: Ohio University Press, 1967).

4. F. Madden, *The Diaries of Sir Frederick Madden*, 17 reels of 35mm microfilm (London: World Microfilm Publications, 1974).

5. C. E. Wright and Ruth C. Wright (eds.), *The Diary of Humphrey Wanley, 1715–1726*, 2 vols. (London: Bibliographical Society, 1966).

6. N. R. Ker, *Medieval Libraries of Great Britain: List of Surviving Books*, Royal Historical Society Guides and Handbooks, no. 3, 2nd ed. (London: Office of the Royal Historical Society, 1964); idem (ed.), *The Parochial Li-*

braries of the Church of England . . . (London: Faith Press, 1959); idem, "Oxford College Libraries in the Sixteenth Century," *Bodleian Library Record* 6, no. 3 (January 1959): 459-515; idem, "Cathedral Libraries," *Library History* 1, no. 2 (Autumn 1967): 38-45.

7. John L. Thornton, *Medical Books, Libraries, and Collectors: A Study of Bibliography and the Book Trade in Relation to the Medical Sciences*, 2nd ed. rev. (London: Deutsch, 1966): John L. Thornton and R. I. J. Tully, *Scientific Books, Libraries, and Collectors: A Study of Bibliography and the Book Trade in Relation to Science*, 2nd ed. rev. (London: Library Association, 1962); Margaret R. Marshall, "British Industrial Libraries before 1939," *Journal of Documentation* 28, no. 2 (June 1972): 107-121.

8. Paul Kaufman, *Libraries and Their Users: Collected Papers in Library History* (London: Library Association, 1969).

9. Guinevere L. Griest, *Mudie's Circulating Library and the Victorian Novel* (Newton Abbot: David and Charles; Bloomington, Ind.: Indiana University Press, 1970).

10. Stanley Gillam, "125 Years of the London Library," in Robert L. Collison (ed.), *Progress in Library Science, 1966* (London: Butterworths, 1966; Hamden, Conn.: Archon Books, 1967), pp. 162-173; idem, "Hagberg Wright and the London Library," *Library History* 1, no. 1 (Spring 1967): 24-27.

11. W. A. Munford, *Penny Rate: Aspects of British Public Library History, 1850-1950* (London: Library Association, 1951).

12. Thomas Kelly, *History of Adult Education in Great Britain* (Liverpool: Liverpool University Press, 1962).

13. Thomas Kelly, *Early Public Libraries: A History of Public Libraries in Great Britain before 1850* (London: Library Association, 1966).

14. Thomas Kelly, *A History of Public Libraries in Great Britain, 1845-1875*, 2nd ed. rev. (London: Library Association, 1977).

15. John E. Pemberton, *Politics and Public Libraries in England and Wales, 1850-1970*, centenary volume (London: Library Association, 1977); R. J. B. Morris, *Parliament and the Public Libraries: A Survey of the Legislative Activity Promoting the Municipal Library Service in England and Wales, 1850-1976* (London: Mansell, 1977).

16. A. W. Ball, *The Public Libraries of Greater London: A Pictorial History, 1856-1914* (London: Library Association, London and Home Counties Branch, 1977); Thomas Kelly and Edith Kelly, *Books for the People: An Illustrated History of the British Public Library* (London: Deutsch, 1977).

17. W. A. Munford, *History of the Library Association, 1877-1977*, centenary volume (London: Library Association, 1976).

18. Michael J. Ramsden, *History of the Association of Assistant Librarians, 1895-1945* ([Falkirk]: Association of Assistant Librarians, 1973).

19. W. A. Munford, *William Ewart, M.P., 1798-1869: Portrait of a Radical* (London: Grafton, 1960); idem, *Edward Edwards, 1812-1886: Portrait of a Librarian* (London: Library Association, 1963).

20. James G. Ollé, *Ernest A. Savage: Librarian Extraordinary*, centenary volume (London: Library Association, 1977); idem, *Library History: An Examination Guidebook* (London: Bingley, 1967).

21. *British Library Journal* 5, no. 1 (Spring 1979).

22. James Thompson, *A History of the Principles of Librarianship* (London: Bingley; Hamden, Conn.: Linne Books, 1977).

23. Raymond Irwin, "Does Library History Matter?" *Library Review* no. 128 (Winter 1958): 510-513.

24. Raymond Irwin, *Origins of the English Library* (London: Allen and Unwin, 1958); idem, *The English Library: Sources and History* (London: Allen and Unwin, 1966).

25. M. R. Cutcliffe, "The Value of Library History," *Library Review* 21, no. 4 (Winter 1967): 193-196; Thomas Kelly, "Thoughts on the Writing of Library History," *Library History* 3, no. 5 (Spring 1975): 161-169; R. Paul Sturges, "Context for Library History: Libraries in 18th Century Derby," *Library History* 4, no. 2 (Autumn 1976): 44-52.

26. *Library History* 1967—two issues per annum, Spring and Autumn.

27. R. J. Busby et al. (comps.), Denis F. Keeling (ed.), *British Library History: Bibliography* (London: Library Association), 1962-1968 vol. (1972); 1969-1972 vol. (1975); 1973-1976 vol. (1979).

28. L. J. Taylor, *FLA Theses: Abstracts of All Theses Accepted for the Fellowship of the Library Association from 1964* (London: British Library, Library Association Library, 1979); Peter J. Taylor, *Library and Information Studies in the United Kingdom and Ireland, 1950-1974: An Index to Theses* (London: Aslib, 1976).

29. Letter from R. F. Atkins, Director of Sheffield City Libraries, 2 January 1980.

30. Interview with Geoff Hare, Assistant County Librarian (Organisation and Development), Nottinghamshire County Library, 4 January 1980.

31. James D. Stewart, *A Tabulation of Librarianship: Classified Tables for the Arrangement of All Material Relating to Library Economy* (London: Grafton, 1947).

32. Tapes available through College of Librarianship, Wales, Aberystwyth.

The British Library: Phenomenon of the Seventies or Prototype of National Library Planning

F. Dolores Donnelly

On 27 July 1972, Royal Assent was given to the British Library Act, bringing to fulfillment the effort of years of concerted action aimed at providing a solution to Britain's national library problem. The Act gave effect to the more detailed proposals formulated in a Government White Paper prepared under Viscount Eccles, then paymaster general and minister for the arts in Britain's Department of Education and Science. The White Paper, published in January 1971,[1] was followed by long and searching debate in both Houses with subsequent amendments to the proposed British Library Bill.[2] Outside Parliament, an Organizing Committee was engaged in exploring all the practical aspects of implementing the proposals. On 1 July 1973—the appointed "Vesting Day"—the formality of the involved transfers was observed and the new British Library came into existence.

The Act provided for the establishment of "a national library for the United Kingdom under the control and management of a new Board and incorporating the Library of the British Museum. . . ." In effect, it provided the enabling legislation for the proposals contained in the Government White Paper to create an apex for a national library system in Great Britain by bringing together into a single organization four of Britain's prominent library institutions spanning a range of separation in their years of existence, organizational set-ups, goals, and objectives. These were: the British Museum Library, including the more recently established National

F. Dolores Donnelly *is professor of library science at the University of Toronto, Canada.*

Journal of Library History, Vol. 16, No. 2, Spring 1981

Reference Library of Science and Invention; the National Central Library; the National Lending Library for Science and Technology; and the British National Bibliography. The Act referred to "a comprehensive collection of books, manuscripts, periodicals, films and other recorded matter, whether printed or otherwise," which the British Library would seek to encompass. It explicitly gave the Board powers to contribute financially to the expenses of library authorities and others providing library facilities, and to carry out and sponsor research. On the whole, the legislation was drafted in what Lord Eccles described as "wide-ranging terms" so as to allow latitude for development and change in planning and policy to meet future demands without having recourse to "radical amendments."

In its legislation, the composition and powers of its Board, and its implied and articulated understanding of the role and responsibilities of a National Library in the seventies and beyond, the British Library might justifiably be discussed as a prototype of modern national library planning. On the other hand, since the British Library began its existence from a vantage point not accessible to other national libraries already in existence in the developed countries, and certainly beyond the reach of those in developing countries, it may be viewed rather as a phenomenon of the seventies. The British Library inherited from the British Museum one of the finest and most comprehensive collections of printed books and manuscripts in the world. Moreover, beyond the advantage of material resources, Britain's National Library was established at the right time in the historical evolution of understanding the role and responsibilities of a national library. Britain, therefore, was in a position to plan policies and services in accordance with changed concepts and ascertained expectations.

National Library Perceptions

In 1934, Arundell Esdaile, writing in the preface to his first edition of *National Libraries of the World*, remarked that for over a century the idea of a national library had been expanding, with such prestigious pioneers as Bignon, Panizzi, Korf, and Putnam each adding "some fresh and valuable element" to the functions of the institutions under their charge. What their successors would do, he could not foresee.[3] Esdaile was formerly an assistant keeper and later secretary to the trustees of the British Museum Library. He must have been aware that the "fresh and valuable element" brought to the British Museum Library by Sir Anthony Panizzi needed refueling. As Sir Frank Francis, one of Panizzi's distinguished successors in more modern times, has perceptively observed: "It would be no exaggeration, I think, to say that the Library continued to run on the impetus imparted to it by Panizzi for nearly seventy years after his retirement [in 1866]." Although the library staff was highly qualified and academic in its interests, and the library appeared to function to the satisfaction of the scholars who used it, there was no responsible effort to continue the innovative achievement of Panizzi.[4] In 1947, Dr. J. H. P. Pafford, Goldsmiths Librarian at the University of London (one of the most prestigious library posts in the United Kingdom), took the lead in advocating that the British Museum Library should make fuller use of its resources by extending its services and even adding new ones, which would bring it into touch with other libraries in the country. Pafford declared that the British Museum Library should "concentrate rather more on work for its readers of the present and immediate future and rather less on work for those of a dim and distant posterity."[5]

In 1952 at a session of the IFLA Council in Copenhagen, a special section for national and university libraries was founded in response to a call from Frank Francis, then keeper of the Department of Printed Books and later director of the Museum. He called on national libraries to examine their functions in the light of present and future needs and to adjust their philosophy and policy making to the modern world.[6] For example, the idea of comprehensiveness within a single library, on which older national libraries had been founded and which was the pattern set by Panizzi at the British Museum, was no longer tenable because of developments in science and technology and the changed methods of scholarly research. No modern library, however great or rich, could systematically collect the literature of the world as the nineteenth-century institutions had attempted to do. Collaboration and cooperation among libraries of all kinds as well as with other information and documentation centers provided the key to modern services.

In 1958, the UNESCO Symposium on National Libraries, held in Vienna, consolidated this concept. This marked the beginning of an active, ongoing interest in national libraries and their functions. Frank Francis was again in the forefront as he insisted in his paper on "The Organization of National Libraries" that national libraries must make a determined effort to organize a system of national cooperation "if it is not to be forced on them by circumstances."[7] During the next ten years, international conference papers by authorities in the library field labored to enunciate definitions of the role and functions of a national library in the overall structure of a country's library services. One of the most quoted writers on the subject was Dr. Kenneth Humphreys, then librarian of the University of Birmingham, who examined the functions of national libraries or their counterparts in major countries of the world and compiled categories of their perceived responsibilities.[8] In the light of subsequent understandings, Humphrey's perceptions appear cautious and limited, although his emphasis on the "prime mover" function of a national library is still highly relevant.[9]

The Parry Report

Kenneth Humphreys was himself a "prime mover" when in 1963 the University Grants Committee of Great Britain set up a Committee on Libraries under the chairmanship of Dr. Thomas Parry "to assess how greater use might be made of shared facilities among the universities themselves and between them and outside library systems and institutions." The report, completed in 1967, stated in a chapter attributed to Humphreys that it was extremely difficult "to relate the position of the university library to the national library scene for a variety of reasons of which the fundamental one is that there is no true apex to the library system of the country. In comparison with the organization of libraries in other countries which have a national library, Britain is especially wanting. . . . " The report recommended that "the British Museum should become the National Library" but suggested that the Museum could fully carry out the range of functions proper to a national library only when a new library building was completed and the library departments were reconstituted and housed as a unit.[10] The recommendation of the Parry Report in this regard was indeed a significant factor in the ultimate government decision to appoint a special committee to consider possibilities. Other complex issues in the meantime contributed to the same end.

The Bloomsbury Crisis

Despite the international outlook and innovative perceptions of a few British Museum officials such as Sir Frank Francis, within the British Museum system the antiquarian emphasis seemed to predominate. The Board of Trustees, consisting almost entirely of elderly peers and eminent scholars, was a power to itself in decid-

ing museum and library policy. One of the Library's most acute
problems was the extreme need of more adequate accommodation
for books, readers, and staff—a need considered urgent even at the
time of the Royal Commission on Museums and Galleries in 1928.
The trustees vigorously resisted the idea of separating the Library
from the rest of the Museum on the grounds that it would destroy
the unity of library and museum collections, which traditionally
had been deemed the ideal. Again to quote Sir Frank Francis: "it
is not at all unlikely that Panizzi's brilliant solution to his space
problem in the 1850's, by putting the Reading Room and its surrounding bookstacks in the inner quadrangle of the Museum, gave
rise, though unconsciously, to the idea of the Library as the heart
of the Museum." Instead, the Library had become "more like a
prisoner confined within a strait-jacket that would inevitably
strangle its efforts to expand and develop."[11]

Recognition of the problems accumulating within the British
Museum Library came only gradually with the development of the
dilemma about a site for a new building. In the postwar County of
London Development Plan, the Bloomsbury site for the new building had been designated and approved by the minister of housing
in 1955. Two distinguished architects, Sir Leslie Martin and Mr.
Colin St. John Wilson, were commissioned to prepare preliminary
specifications, which in turn were approved by the Conservative
government in 1964. In the meantime, the Ministry of Public
Buildings and Works began negotiations to acquire the separate
properties that would be needed to provide accommodation for
the proposed edifice on the south side of Great Russell Street
facing the front of the Museum. The trustees' insistence that the
unity of the Museum and Library collections must be preserved
with the closest possible proximity prevailed throughout all the
controversies over the site. It was expected that the new building
would begin in the 1970s and would be phased over a ten-year
period. In October 1967, however, a new (Labour) government,
apparently without due consultation with the trustees of the British Museum, served notice that because of the housing situation in
the London Borough of Camden (in which the Bloomsbury site
was located); the need to preserve buildings of historical and/or
architectural importance; and the objections of existing business
and resident occupants of the borough, the government had decided not to go ahead with the Bloomsbury building plan. In
reaching its decision, the government declared that it also had in
mind that "the present pattern of national library service was a
patchwork which had developed piecemeal over the years under

different institutions." The recent Parry Report had drawn attention to some of the problems. The government, therefore, had decided "to set up a small, independent committee to examine the organization and functions of the British Museum Library in providing national library facilities and to consider whether, in the interests of efficiency and economy, such facilities should be brought into a unified framework."[12]

The Dainton Committee

In December 1967, the government appointed the National Libraries Committee under the chairmanship of Dr. F. S. Dainton (later Sir Frederick Dainton), vice chancellor of the University of Nottingham, eminent scientist, and scholar. The six members of his committee were distinguished members of business and the professions, but it did not include a single member of the library profession, nor any member of the Civil Service having library experience. The Committee's terms of reference were: "to examine the functions and organization of the British Museum Library, the National Central Library, the National Lending Library for Science and Technology, and the Science Museum Library, in providing national library facilities; to consider whether in the interests of efficiency and economy such facilities should be brought into a unified framework and to make recommendations."

The Dainton Committee took over eighteen months to complete its work, during which time visits were made to all the principal institutions concerned and evidence taken from more than sixty university and college libraries, from the Library Association, and from other related bodies and individuals. The secretary of the Committee also visited libraries in the United States and France to make observations. Among the many briefs and memoranda that emerged in the course of the hearings, a majority favored the idea of a National Reference Library to be developed from the British Museum Library and most were uncompromising in their insistence that the site should remain in Bloomsbury.[13] The idea of a single, all-purpose National Library serving as an *apex* to the library system of Great Britain (such as had been suggested by the Parry Report) did not appear palatable to many of the libraries concerned. Several proposed that a more realistic approach would be through a national body coordinating the national lending, reference, and bibliographic facilities and taking into account the libraries already operating at the national level in specific fields.

The Library Association (Great Britain)

The Library Association of Great Britain may take credit for an earlier definition of the need for a national center to coordinate reference, information, and bibliographical services as well as for attributing responsibility to the government of Britain for the efficient organization of information. In 1964 the National Reference Services Subcommittee of the Library Research Committee produced a report entitled "Access to Information: a National Bibliographical Service." In it the committee reviewed the new responsibilities just assumed by Britain's Department of Education and Science as a result of the Libraries and Museums Act of 1964, and the recent involvement of the government in proposals for a scientific documentation organization (from which emerged in 1965 the Office of Scientific and Technical Information—OSTI). The document took cognizance of the establishment of the National Lending Library for Science and Technology and the National Reference Library of Science and Invention as "other welcome examples of government action in this field." It noted that the National Central Library, although recognized as the center for interlending, was far from adequate as a bibliographical information center. Its union catalogues did not include the holdings of major national, university, and research libraries, irrespective of whether their materials were available for interlending or not. The situation for reference resources was just as inadequate. "National subject libraries" such as the Science Library, the Patent Office Library, the Board of Trade Library, the Library of the Royal Institute of British Architects, and so many others possessed enormous reference potential, but there existed no formal machinery to tap such resources. What was needed, therefore, was a national institution with clearly designated responsibilities for formulating national policy in this field and coordinating activities. Among its "proposals for action," the *Access to Information Report* called for a national bibliographical center that would establish and control a full national bibliography, current and retrospective; coordinate library activities on a national level; carry out research and serve as a clearinghouse of research in progress and completed.[14]

The Dainton Report

It is not surprising that the Dainton Report, published in June 1969, concluded that the inadequacies in library service revealed by the submissions to the National Libraries Committee could not be dealt with in a positive way while there existed no centralized body responsible for achieving the required degree of coordination among different units and services (p. 17). It recommended, therefore, that the existing administrative responsibilities of the British Museum Library, the National Central Library, the National Lending Library for Science and Technology, the National Reference Library of Science and Invention, and the British National Bibliography should be terminated and that they should become the responsibility of a new statutory body to be known as the National Libraries Authority. In addition, this Authority should assume full administrative responsibilities for the functions and services of OSTI. Dainton recommended a two-tier system of administration for the National Libraries Authority; a management board on which heads of the functional units would *not* be represented; and an executive committee composed of heads of the functional units. As it turned out, neither the National Libraries Authority, *per se*, nor the two-tiered board was adopted when the new institution finally came into existence. Nevertheless, the National Libraries Committee under the chairmanship of Dr. F. S. Dainton presented the government with an innovative proposal for a feasible and functional amalgamation of four of Britain's independent national institutions. In so doing they provided the preliminary blueprint for the establishment of the British Library.[15]

The British Library as Prototype

A change in government shortly after the National Libraries Committee had presented its report on 27 March 1969 provided a circumstance that was to have a significant bearing on the shaping of the legislation that would ultimately guide the new national library system in Great Britain. In 1970, the Rt. Honourable Viscount Eccles, a long-time member of Britain's Conservative Party and a trustee of the British Museum, was appointed minister for the arts in the Department of Education and Science. Included in his ministry was the Arts and Libraries Branch whose recently appointed under-secretary, Dr. H. T. Hookway (now Sir Harry Hookway), had previously been the chief scientific officer at the Department of Education and Science and in this capacity had been charged with the establishment and direction of OSTI in 1965. It was to Lord Eccles and his small and experienced ministry that the responsibility fell for drafting the White Paper for the proposed British Library. He was in a strategic position to initiate the proceedings. Lord Eccles knew the library situation at the British

Museum as a long-term member of the Board of Trustees and its chairman until 1970. He knew the thinking behind the appointment of the Dainton Committee and had participated in one of the most heated debates on record in the House of Lords during the controversy that ensued over the previous government's decision not to develop the Bloomsbury site.[16] Almost singlehandedly he had drafted the memorandum presented to the Dainton Committee on behalf of the trustees of the British Museum in which he laid out proposals later incorporated into the Dainton Report. Lord Eccles was spokesman in the House of Lords during the debate on the British Library Bill. He was ultimately credited with the decision to name the new national institution the *British Library* as a compromise for those who wanted the old British Museum Library title preserved.

The British Library Board

During the period of legislative debate on the White Paper, considerable discussion was given to the structure and format of the British Library Board. The two-tier system recommended by Dainton was rejected. The Act finally provided for "not less than eight nor more than thirteen" members in addition to the chairman who would be appointed by the secretary of state. It also made provision for any of these members including the chairman to be part-time appointees. The choice was between a full-time chairman, or a part-time chairman and a full-time chief executive (National Librarian) who would also be deputy chairman. The latter option was adopted. The structure and composition of the British Library Board reflected Lord Eccles's philosophy of management: a modern national library must be governed by a board with powers similar to that of any other corporation responsible for the good government and expansion of a business. It had to have sufficient flexibility to move with change and the widest possible terms of reference to interpret its mandate. Moreover the main divisions of the institution should be represented on the board by voting members who would provide open channels of communication with their staffs. Accordingly, the three directors general of the principal areas of the Library's operations—reference, lending, and bibliographic services—were appointed as full-time voting members of the Board. Nine part-time outside members were nominated on the basis of representation and related areas of public concern. Since each member was expected to make a definite commitment, it was decided that part-time members would receive a salary rather than just reimbursement for expenses incurred. Board members would hold office for not less than three years, or more than seven. A further assurance of communication and exchange between the Library and its users was effected in the constitution of "Advisory Councils with responsibility for providing advice to the Board, or to any department of the British Library" (sec. 2 [3]). From this provision emerged the appointment of an advisory council and five advisory committees, representing an impressive range of experience and expertise in public life: libraries, universities, learned societies, business, and the professions—all calculated to serve as links between the British Library and the publics of its constituent parts.

Coordination of Resources

One of the most widely debated issues presented as background evidence to the Dainton Committee by scholars and their institutions was the British Museum Library's right to preserve its reference function unhampered by any diversion of its resources into the lending stream. It was argued that the BML's "heritage of published material" must be permanently available for reference use not only to satisfy a national obligation but also to fulfill its responsibilities to international scholarship.[17] On the other hand, library institutions repeatedly stressed the need for coordination of resources and services with other research libraries such as the British Library of Political and Economic Science (the London School of Economics), the School of Oriental and African Studies (SOAS) of the University of London, the various types of specialized library institutions such as the Royal Society of Medicine, the Royal Institute of British Architects, and others. The extension of lending functions on the part of national and paranational collections was foreseen as part of a total response to an integrated information service within the structures of the proposed national institution. The Dainton Report specifically named Oxford and Cambridge in recommending that additional lending responsibilities be undertaken by an "inner circle" of relatively large libraries. Dainton suggested that "a national libraries organization should be able to make grants to cooperating libraries in recognition of their national responsibilities."[18]

It is precisely within this purview that the ensuing British Library legislation created a prototype. It provided a flexible approach to the coordination of library resources in allowing the British Library to negotiate the terms of particular cooperative agreements with the libraries concerned, without infringing their autonomy and the priorities due to their specific clienteles, and with due regard for the costs involved. The brilliantly drafted legislation thus enabled the National Lending Library at Boston Spa— in its own right a national achievement of first significance—to utilize on a contractual basis the resources of libraries that had not previously cooperated to any extent in interlending. The whole concept of a national central lending library of first resort, supplemented by the national resources of subsidized "back-up" libraries, offers an attractive and feasible model to national libraries elsewhere in the world seeking to equalize access to library resources without making unfair demands upon so-called net lending libraries. Significant in a lesser vein is the arrangement with the British Library Reference Division (the original British Museum Library) whereby the lending division may pass on to the reference division requests for photocopies of materials not otherwise available, thus bringing the benefits of lending services to the user without compromising the cherished prerogative of the British Reference Library.

The Research and Development Function

In April 1974, the functions of OSTI were transferred, as had been recommended by Dainton, from the Department of Education and Science to the British Library, thus forming the nucleus of the British Library Research and Development Department. The Department has since undertaken a systematic program to promote and support research related to library and information operations in all subject fields as well as the experimental development of interactive library systems. Its exceptional resources, accruing from the absorption of OSTI and continued by annual budget allotments amounting in recent years to over one million pounds sterling, have accorded the British Library a unique role in identifying priorities for library-related research. Team and individual research projects mounted in university and library education faculties, libraries, and information institutions include such categories as scholarly publishing, humanities research, library user education, telecommunications, interactive library systems, bibliographic exchange projects, and many other related investigations. Particularly important is the responsibility assumed by the Department for the publication and dissemination of results. The Research and Development Department has become, in fact, a cata-

391

lyst in British Library relationships on a local, regional, national, and even international level.

Epilogue

It is beyond the scope of this conference paper to review the current functions of the British Library in the context of its enabling legislation—or even to attempt to offer detailed support for the thesis of this article. A few general observations are in order by way of conclusion. The establishment of the British Library was indeed a phenomenon of its times, growing out of the concern for a national approach to an integrated national library system. However, the British Library may also be viewed as a prototype of National Library planning inasmuch as it made visible the multi-dimensional role of a National Library in the context of the nation's library and information services. Although conceived as an apex to the nation's library system, the British Library skillfully shifted its image and function from *apex* to *hub* while maximizing its role and responsibility for leadership, planning, and coordination of resources. This is not to ascribe to the British Library the overall objectives of a national organization such as the U.S. National Commission on Libraries and Information Science. The psychological climate of the British library environment does not favor a government-mandated body with sweeping responsibilities. One can speculate that had the recommendation of the Dainton Committee for the creation of a National Libraries Authority been followed to the letter by the government of the day, the institution that is now the British Library would have had enhanced power to do for the development and coordination of library and information services what a number of fragmented agencies are endeavoring to do at the present time. There are those, now, who recognize the need for "some coordinated approach to library development in its widest all embracing sense and would welcome the establishment of a high level body given statutory powers to monitor and advise on all aspects of library provision and development."[19] Proposals and recommendations are currently under consideration to provide a more unified focus for library concerns, beyond the mandate of the British Library Act.

In the meantime the fact of the matter is that, despite the vicissitudes which have plagued Great Britain economically and politically in recent years and which have adversely affected the implementation of building plans, British librarians are willing to admit that the new institution has "achieved much in its comparatively short existence and has considerably increased access to the nation's library resources."[20] Based on the record, this writer would be less cautious in assessing the British Library as an ongoing national library system that, given favorable circumstances in the next decade or so, may ultimately have no parallel in the world.

Notes

1. *The British Library*, presented to Parliament by the Paymaster General, by Command of Her Majesty, January 1971 (London: Her Majesty's Stationery Office, 1971), cmnd. 4572.
2. An interesting and highly relevant range of background information pertaining to the establishment of the British Library is contained in the debates conducted in both the House of Lords and the House of Commons: Gt. Britain, Parliament, House of Lords, *Parliamentary Debates*, 2 March 1971; 28 March 1972; 25 April 1972; 9 May 1972; 16 May 1972; 27 July 1972; Gt. Britain, Parliament, House of Commons, *Parliamentary Debates*, 14 June 1972; 15 June 1972; 18 July 1972.
3. Arundell Esdaile, *National Libraries of the World: Their History, Administration and Public Services*, 1st ed. (London: Grafton, 1934), pp. v-vii.
4. Sir Frank Francis, "The British Museum in Recent Times: Some Reflections," in A. T. Milne (ed.), *Librarianship and Literature: Essays in Honour of Jack Pafford* (London: Athlone Press, 1970), pp. 9, 10.
5. J. H. P. Pafford, "The British Museum Library," *Library Association Record*, series 4, vol. 49, no. 2 (February 1947): 32-38.
6. F. C. Francis, "The Contribution of the National Library to the Modern Outlook in Library Services," *Aslib Proceedings*, 10, no. 11 November 1958): 267-275.
7. F. C. Francis, "The Organization of National Libraries," in *National Libraries: Their Problems and Prospects*, Symposium on National Libraries in Europe, Vienna, 8-27 September 1958, UNESCO Manuals for Libraries, no. 11 (Paris: UNESCO, 1960), pp. 21-26.
8. K. W. Humphreys, "National Library Functions," *Unesco Bulletin for Libraries* 20, no. 4 (July-August 1966): 158-169.
9. Ibid., p. 169.
10. University Grants Committee [Dr. Thomas Parry, chairman], *Report of the Committee on Libraries* (London: H.M.S.O., 1967), ch. 7.
11. Francis, "The British Museum in Recent Times," pp. 8, 9.
12. Gt. Britain, Parliament, House of Commons, *Parliamentary Debates*, 26 October 1967, p. 1801. (The House of Lords, to which several members of the Board of Trustees of the British Museum belonged, responded to this unwelcome news with full-scale and vitriolic debates in their own House: see Gt. Britain, Parliament, House of Lords, *Debates*, 13 December 1967, pp. 1113-1240.)
13. Most of the submissions were compiled and published under the title: *Principal Documentary Evidence Submitted to the National Libraries Committee*, 2 vols. (London: H.M.S.O., 1969).
14. "Access to Information: A National Bibliographic Service," *Library Association Record* 67, no. 4 (April 1965): 131-134.

15. National Libraries Committee [Dr. Frederick Dainton, chairman], *Report Presented to Parliament by the Secretary of State for Education and Science by Command of Her Majesty*, June 1969 (London: H.M.S.O., 1969), cmnd. 4028.

16. Gt. Britain, Parliament, House of Lords, *Debates*, 13 December 1969, pp. 1114-1240.

17. Chapter 12 of the *Report of the Committee on National Libraries* addresses itself to the British Museum Library's reference function and related arguments.

18. *Report of the Committee on National Libraries*, pp. 68, 119.

19. "W. A. G. Alison Grasps the Nettle" [presidential address to the Library Association Conference at its annual meeting in Nottingham, 1979], *Library Association Record* 81, no. 10 (October 1979): 473.

20. Ibid.

Libraries and Adult Education: The Russian Experience

Boris Raymond

I was particularly happy to note throughout many of the excellent papers presented at this Library History Seminar the thread of concern for the socioeconomic and cultural context in which, I firmly believe, the historical evolution of libraries must be placed. And it is within this wider institutional setting that I would like to locate my own contribution to these proceedings.

The general concern of my paper is with the development of adult education in Russia, a process that occurred in the second half of the nineteenth century, in response to the country's modernization needs. Its specific focus is on how public libraries were utilized as instruments of adult education, both before the revolution and especially during the first decade of the Soviet rule.

The transition of a society from one that is predominantly rural, agricultural, and traditional to one that is in the main urban, industrial, and contractual, in addition to its economic development, involves a vast increase of popular political participation. It also requires a massive diffusion of technical skills and a substantial spread of scientific knowledge among the population. The impetus for such a transition has, in every known case, come from a minority within the nation. This minority, be it the commercial and industrial entrepreneurs of eighteenth-century England, or the coterie of brilliant young reformers surrounding the Emperor Meiji in nineteenth-century Japan, has invariably imprinted its own specific coloration on the forms that the modernization process of the society assumed.

Boris Raymond *is associate professor of library service at Dalhousie University, Nova Scotia.*

Journal of Library History, Vol. 16, No. 2, Spring 1981
© 1981 by the University of Texas Press   0022-2259/81/020394-11$01.30

In Russia, pressure for a break with the traditional past accelerated after the defeat in the Crimean War in 1856, which was felt most acutely by the small, educated group of the minor nobility who were the tsar's civil servants and junior military officers. For them Westernization, minus the unwelcome side effects of individualistic capitalism, seemed to offer the best way out for their country's military weakness and political backwardness.

Fueled additionally by the guilt it felt toward the peasantry, who were still serfs, this modernizing minority turned to a form of socialist populism advocating the emancipation of the serfs, as well as favoring a vast effort at educating them to a level where they would be able to participate in the political life of the nation.

In a predominantly traditional society such as Russia before the middle of the last century, the knowledge that most adults obtained came from the church, the community, and family sources. These sources were primarily oral, and required little if any ability to read or write. And, indeed, the country's illiteracy rate was close to 80 percent. It was therefore quite natural that the *kul'-turniki*, as the adherents of the popular education movement called themselves, would lay particular stress on the need to bring literacy and rudimentary education to the peasant masses, whom they hoped to enlist in their struggle to modernize the country's political system.

According to Olga Kaidanova, one of the young activists who spent a large part of her life as an adult educator, there grew up in the minds of the *kul'turniki*, "the image of the people as a younger brother, suffering from economic want, from a lack of culture, a lack of rights. . . . [This] image became a dominant one, and merged with a passionate desire to help this younger brother, and to participate in the improvement of his lot."[1]

However, popular education activists often encountered obstacles and even persecution from tsarist police officials, who considered them to be politically dangerous. As a result, while some stubbornly persevered with their efforts to spread the benefits of education to the Russian masses, others came to the conclusion that nothing fundamental could be accomplished as long as the tsar remained in power. They became convinced that a revolution was necessary before any significant progress in popular enlightenment would be possible.

By the 1870s, a major split had developed between these two wings of the populist movement. The *kul'turniki* favored a nonrevolutionary strategy, one designed to create a democratic foundation for Russian society through popular enlightenment; the revolutionaries, on the other hand, were intent on overthrowing the tsar as a first step in any program of political progress.

Despite open admiration on the part of more moderate members of the Russian intelligentsia for the revolutionary martyrs who were executed or exiled by the tsarist authorities, the *kul'-turniki* were convinced that it was "impossible to lead an uncultured, more than half illiterate population onto the road of a broad, sociopolitical life."[2] For them, without lengthy preliminary educational work, freedom and democracy in Russia could not be sustained even if these were somehow temporarily attained through a revolution. Furthermore, they accused the revolutionaries of needlessly endangering institutions of popular education that had been built by insisting on using these institutions—such as libraries and Sunday schools—for subversive propaganda purposes that, when discovered, inevitably led to their closure by the police.

However, although there was constant friction between these two fundamentally different perspectives on how to effect social change in their country, the two groups also tended to cooperate with one another. This was the case with Krupskaia, Lenin's wife, who for five years worked as a volunteer Sunday school teacher while also being an active member of an underground revolutionary society.

As a result of the political concessions made by the tsarist government after the 1905 revolution, many of the existing restrictions on adult educational activities were removed. Because of this new freedom, the years that followed until the outbreak of the First World War saw major progress in establishing libraries and adult literacy associations. Thus the first legal workers' education circles were organized in St. Petersburg in 1906.[3] In 1908 the first All-Russian Conference of Popular Education Societies met, and in 1911 the first All-Russian Congress of Librarians was held. In 1913 the first All-Russian Congress of Popular Education met in the capital and proclaimed that "a successful development of economic, political, and social life is possible only on condition that there be a high cultural level among the whole population."[4] Because existing schools could not accomplish this goal on their own, the Congress urged that adult education be given a major place in the country's educational system. In addition, the Congress also argued that adult education had to be based upon a voluntary, individualized approach that could best be promoted through reading and through public libraries.

Thus, as a result of efforts by literally thousands of volunteers over several decades, a vast adult educational infrastructure had been created in the country before the Bolshevik revolution of 1917. This infrastructure included over 14,000 public libraries, 1,000 cultural clubs, and numerous literacy centers. Also during this period, many programs for popular reading were elaborated, and a large variety of techniques was developed to study readers' needs as well as to perfect readers' guidance procedures. One of the leaders of this effort was a young radical bookman by the name of Nicholas Rubakin, who originated the theory of bibliopsychology.[5]

As Kaidanova puts it, the Soviet government was thus able to inherit the "rich spiritual content that filled the whole of the pedagogical work of the prerevolutionary period," as well as an organized network of public libraries.[6]

Lenin and the Communist Party came to power in an underdeveloped country. This circumstance forced the Bolshevik leaders to act both as a modernizing elite and as agents of the Marxist revolution. In order to fulfill both roles, they had to place a heavy emphasis upon achieving high levels of popular culture—all essential prerequisites to modernization and socialism. Thus Lenin insisted in 1921 that "it is not enough to abolish illiteracy, it is necessary to build up Soviet economy, and for that literacy alone will not carry us very far. We must raise culture to a much higher level. . . . The ability to read and write must be made to serve the purpose of raising the cultural level."[7]

For the Soviet leadership, adult education was to serve as an instrument of political socialization. It was expected to instill in the population a scientific Marxist world view, to disseminate information about the new government, to help raise industrial production, and, most urgently, to reduce adult illiteracy. In order to underscore the urgency of this last problem—over half of the country's adults were illiterate—Lenin declared in 1921, "I can say that so long as there is such a thing as illiteracy in our country, it is too much to talk about political education . . . an illiterate person stands outside of politics; without that there are rumors, gossip, fairy-tales and prejudices, but not politics."[8] And returning to the same theme is his last article, the dying leader warned that "without universal literacy, without a proper degree of efficiency, without training the population sufficiently to acquire habits of book-reading, and without the material basis for this . . . we shall not achieve our object [socialism]."[9]

Lenin's emphasis upon adult education as the very essence of postrevolutionary development makes subsequent Soviet efforts in this field understandable: they were aspects of a far wider endeavor to build an egalitarian socialist society, based upon highly developed technology and a politically sophisticated population. Seen from the perspective of the immediate requirements of the new regime, adult education had the additional task of providing the new industrial recruits with a modicum of literacy and with rudimentary technical knowledge.

The role that libraries were called upon to play in this effort was a significant one. As early as the 1922 Congress of Political Education Committees, library work with readers was singled out as a most important area of the adult education effort. For Soviet libraries this decision meant that "the library must cease being an institution for storing books, and for lending them; it must rather become a weapon for the propaganda of communism."[10]

A few months later, in April 1923, the 12th Congress of the Communist Party reinforced these decisions by creating a special All-Russian Commission on Independent Learning, as well as by establishing local Independent Learning Commissions throughout the country. Their task was to aid the literacy campaign, and to insure continued assistance to public libraries from local organizations.

As the independent learners' movement gathered momentum, Soviet public libraries inevitably were drawn ever deeper into this work. The first results of their experiences were brought together in 1925 at the All-Union Conference on Independent Learning. Members of this conference decided to launch a massive campaign among the country's libraries in order to encourage them to promote independent learning through reading.

These decisions had a landmark effect upon libraries, and after another year of experimentation with different methods of work, Soviet library leadership arrived at two principal conclusions:

> 1—public libraries should continue working in such a way as to render maximum assistance to existing adult education commissions; and
> 2—they also needed to establish their own independent participation in this work through the method that was unique to libraries: readers' guidance.[11]

Thus by the mid-twenties, two distinct lines of activity were delineated for Soviet libraries. They were to serve as resources for adult educators and also as self-contained centers of independent learning, carrying out their own educational activities through the medium of readers' guidance.

There were two groups of learners being served by libraries: those with only a rudimentary level of education and those who had had some previous education and who consequently possessed wider intellectual interests. The former group was typically organized by Soviet librarians into "readers' circles," which followed very specific and guided programs of reading. Individuals in the latter group were able to learn at a faster pace, and therefore required less detailed assistance on the part of librarians.

The center of this self-educational work was the library's "corner for independent learning," where the various readers' aids, as well as tools used for readers' guidance, were located. Another function of these corners was to provide a place for bulletin boards displaying announcements and posters. Such material was divided into two separate sections: "how to read" and "what to read," with the latter section carrying information about the latest books on political matters and the social and natural sciences. Recommended lists of readings on current events were also placed on these boards. All lists were arranged in a sequence, beginning with the most general and the simplest materials, and then materials increasing in difficulty. They were called "reading trails," because they attempted to guide the readers into predetermined reading patterns. They were frequently illustrated with book covers chosen from among the titles that were included, and they were posted in conspicuous places. Their popularity with Soviet librarians was based upon the premise that "the library is responsible for providing its patrons with a program of reading on all important themes; to convince the readers to follow these programs, and to teach them the most rational way of using books."[12]

Another standard Soviet library practice was the acquisition of a core of self-educational books, which was also kept in these special corners. This core collection consisted of

> selected books on questions of interest to the average reader;
> books for the reading programs of existing independent learners' circles of a particular library;
> books for the programs carried out by adult education courses in neighboring schools;
> books needed for correspondence courses;
> special textbooks for independent learners; and
> periodicals devoted to the methodology of independent learning.[13]

However, recommended bibliographies and core collections

alone were not considered sufficient. Consultations on a one-to-one basis between the independent learner and the librarian were the real basis of this work. The content of these consultations typically consisted of the librarians answering questions that were posed by readers and giving general advice about additional useful books on a given topic. Consultation work was also provided by local specialists who had volunteered for such service.[14] When the number of readers was so great that individual consultations had to be restricted, readers' circles were established to enable librarians to reach all the people who wanted to engage in independent reading. Soviet librarians were constantly urged to advertise their independent learning services to the public; indeed their professional work was evaluated primarily by their success in recruiting new readers and learners to their libraries. Oral publicity took such forms as talks with individual patrons, publicly reading books on the library's premises, and library-sponsored readers' conferences with authors. Graphic publicity was carried out through posters, wall catalogues, and book displays.

Finally, Soviet librarians were seldom allowed to forget the ultimate purpose behind all of their techniques for helping independent learners. Exhortations to relate educational work to the policies of the Communist Party abounded.

Thus, by the end of the 1920s, adult education in the Soviet Union had been extended to the work of museums, workers' clubs, cinema and drama circles, adult evening and Sunday schools, and public libraries. For Soviet educational authorities, the book was the primary tool of enlightenment. Because of this, they did not hesitate to allocate large sums of money for the maintenance of special labor-intensive services such as readers' guidance, or to sponsor the publication of numerous self-educational textbooks and periodicals. Insofar as the public libraries were concerned, by the end of the decade it had become firmly established that they were not only the principal channel for the distribution of books among the population, but also the main locus of independent learning in the country.

As long as the educational institutions were under the leadership of Lunacharskii, the commissar of education, and Krupskaia—his deputy commissar—the broad educational policies originally laid down by Lenin were carried out. However, after 1929, with the establishment of Stalin's personal dictatorship, Soviet libraries were purged of all books that had been written by Lenin's former collaborators who had opposed Stalin, and the independent learners' movement was reduced to a machine for the mass indoctrination of readers with the Party line. Unfortunately, due to space restrictions, I cannot discuss these developments here.

I would, however, like to end this presentation by pointing to the relevance, both for developing countries and for North American public librarianship, of the experience of Russian libraries with adult education. In the developing countries of the Third World, the general social and economic conditions are remarkably similar to the conditions that existed both in tsarist Russia and during the early years of the Soviet state. The general level of literacy in these countries is quite low; the diffusion of technical skills and of scientific knowledge among the population is very thin. As a rule, political participation in the affairs of the national government is restricted to an educated elite. Given these conditions, the utilization of all available resources for adult education is a practical imperative. Here the Russian example of relying upon libraries as one of the instruments of modernization can be instructive.

In the industrialized nations there are also pockets of illiteracy, and on the part of large sections of the population, there is a noticeable lack of awareness of the basic processes that determine how their societies function. Here the Russian example of assigning to public libraries a major role in upgrading the level of scientific, technical, cultural, and political awareness among the general population may deserve some thought on the part of public librarians. Taken selectively, without the distortions that were injected into the adult educational role of libraries by Stalin and his followers, the Russian experience in the use of public libraries as an explicitly educational instrument with its own special techniques is one that we may well wish to study further.

Notes

1. Olga Kaidanova, *Ocherki po istorii narodnogo obrazovaniia v rossii i v S.S.S.R.*, vol. 2, part 2 (Brussels: imp. E. Gelezniakoff, 1939), p. 8.

2. Ibid., p. 21.

3. S. Elkina, *Ocherki po agitatsii, propagande, i vneshkol'noi rabote v dorevoliutsionnoi rossii* (Moscow: Gosizdat, 1930), p. 160.

4. E. N. Medynskii, *Vneshkol'noe obrazovanie* (Moscow: Nauka, 1917), p. 9.

5. For a brief account of Rubakin's work in the English language, see Sylva Simsova (ed.), *Nicholas Rubakin and Bibliopsychology* (Hamden, Conn.: Archon Books, 1968).

6. Kaidanova, *Ocherki po istorii narodnogo obrazovaniia*, p. 106.

7. V. I. Lenin, *Collected Works*, 45 vols. (Moscow: Progress Publishers, 1964-1975), 33:75.

8. Ibid.

9. Ibid., p. 470.

10. *Sputnik politprosvetrabotnika* (Moscow: Krasnaia nov', 1923), p. 51.
11. S. Palatnik (ed.), *Samoobrazovanie i politprosvetrabota: Sbornik statei* (Moscow: Doloi negramotnost', 1927), p. 46.
12. Ibid., p. 31.
13. B. Bank, "Na novyi put'," *Krasnyi bibliotekar'* 12 (December 1925): 31-39.
14. Palatnik, *Samoobrazovanie i politprosvetrabota*, pp. 31-32.

Additional References

Azrael, Jeremy R. "Soviet Union." In James S. Coleman (ed.), *Education and Political Development*. Princeton, N.J.: Princeton University Press, 1965.

Bank, B. "Biblioteka i samoobrazovanie." In S. Palatnik (ed.), *Samoobrazovanie i politprosvetrabota*. Moscow: Doloi negramotnost', 1927.

————. "Kruzhki chitatelei-aktivistov i samoobrazovanie," *Pomoshch' samoobrazovan'iiu*, 4 (1927): 16-21.

————. "Rabota s samouchkami v biblioteke." *Pomoshch' samoobrazovaniiu* 1 (1927): 42-43.

Bank, B. and A. Vilenkin. *Rabochii chitatel' v biblioteke*. Moscow: Rabotnik prosveshcheniia, 1930.

Brooks, Jeffrey. "Readers and Reading at the End of the Tsarist Era." In William Mills III, *Literature and Society in Imperial Russia, 1800-1914*. Stanford, Calif.: Stanford University Press, 1978.

Brower, Daniel R. *Training the Nihilists: Education and Radicalism in Tsarist Russia*. Ithaca, N.Y.: Cornell University Press, 1975.

Coleman, James S. (ed.). "Education and Political Development." In James S. Coleman (ed.), *Education and Political Development*. Princeton, N.J.: Princeton University Press, 1965.

Counts, George S. *The Challenge of Soviet Education*. New York: McGraw-Hill, 1957.

Frid, L. S. *Ocherki po istorii razvitiia politiko-prosvetitel'noi rabote v dorevoliutsionnoi rossii*. Moscow: Gosizdat, 1930.

Gurganus, Jane W. "Nadezhda Krupskaia and Political Socialization, 1917–1930." (Ph. D. dissertation, Emory University, 1973).

Harper, Samuel N. *Civic Training in Soviet Russia*. Chicago: University of Chicago Press, 1929.

Hayashida, Ronald H. "The Third Front: The Politics of Soviet Mass Education, 1917-1918." Ph.D. dissertation, Columbia University, 1973.

Inkeles, Alex and Raymond A. Bauer. *The Soviet Citizen: Daily Life in a Totalitarian Society*. Cambridge, Mass.: Harvard University Press, 1959.

Ivanova, A. M. "Organization of the Campaign to Abolish Adult Illiteracy in the U.S.S.R." *Fundamental and Adult Education*. Paris: UNESCO, 11:3 (1959): 131-192.

Karatygin, F. "Biblioteki i osnovnye zadachi samoobrazovaniia." *Pomoshch' samoobrazovaniiu* 4 (1927): 87-91.

Katz, Zev. "Party-Political Education in Soviet Russia." *Soviet Studies* 7:3 (January 1956): 237-244.

Khavkina, Lydia. "Individual'nye konsul'tatsii." *Pomoshch' samoobrazovaniiu* 4 (1927): 92-97.

Lilge, Frederic. "Lenin and the Politics of Education." *Slavic Review* 27 (June 1968): 230-257.

————. *Lunacharskii o narodnom obrazovanii*. Moscow: n.p., 1958.

McClelland, James. "Bolshevik Approaches to Higher Education." *Slavic Review* 30 (March 1971): 818–813.
Michiewicz, Ellen P. "Adult Political Education in the U.S.S.R." Ph. D. dissertation, Yale University, 1965.
Mokhov, N. J. "Libraries as Means of Education and Enlightenment." *Libri* 20:4 (1970): 300-317.
Nearing, Scott. *Education in Soviet Russia.* New York: International Publishers, 1926.
Neiman, B. "Metodika raboty s knigoi." *Pomoshch' samoobrazovaniiu* 1 (1927): 34-35.
Nevskii, V. *Praktikum po vneshkol'nomu obrazovaniiu.* Kostroma: tip. Severnyi rabochii, 1920.
Pethybridge, Roger W. *The Social Prelude to Stalinism.* London: Macmillan, 1974.
Pinkevitch, Albert P. *The New Education in the Soviet Republic.* Ed. George S. Counts. Trans. Nucia Perlmutter. New York: John Day, 1929.
Pye, Lucian W. and Sidney Verba (eds.). *Political Culture and Political Development.* Princeton, N.J.: Princeton University Press, 1965.
Rabinovich, M. "Biblioteka i samoobrazovanie." *Pomoshch' samoobrazovaniiu* 4 (1927): 49-51.
Rassudovskaia, N. M. "Perepiska N. A. Rubakina s chitatel'iami iz naroda po voprosam samoobrazovaniia." *Sovietskaia bibliografiia* 2 (78) (1963): 76-82.
Rosen, Seymour M. *Education and Modernization in the U.S.S.R.* Reading, Mass.: Addison-Wesley, 1971.
Rubakin, N. A. *Etudy o russkoi chitaiushchei publike.* St. Petersburg: tip. N. P. Karbasnikova, 1895.
Rudneva, E. I. *Pedagogicheskaia sistema N. K. Krupskoi.* Moscow: izd. Moskovskogo universiteta, 1968.
Tsaregradskii, I. "Massovye biblioteki i samoobrazovanie," *Pomoshch' samoobrazovaniiu* 4 (1927): 11-13.
———. *Vneshkol'noe obrazovanie* 4-6 (Moscow: n.p., 1919).
Zvezdin, V. "Pomoshch' samoobrazovaniiu cherez biblioteku." In M. A. Smushkova (ed.). *Massovaia rabota bibliotek: Sbornik statei.* Moscow: Doloi negramotnost', 1927.

Meanings of Literacy in the Third World: The Concepts and Consequences of the Rijchary Reform Movement in Highland Peru

Dan C. Hazen

The twentieth century has seen a marked extension of literacy throughout the Third World. Libraries, however, still play a small role for the people of these regions. In an area like highland Peru, existing collections are either private accumulations of members of the educated elite or institutional collections bequeathed to municipalities or schools by the same relatively wealthy individuals. These libraries, which tend to focus on belles lettres and regional publications, may eventually become meaningful to the masses. For the present, they only serve as totems of prestige and symbols of elite status.

In many respects, libraries and literacy alike reflect the North Atlantic impulse toward democratic societies and informed citizenries. Ideologies of mass education have embodied both idealistic and pragmatic aspirations, and have for the most part simply taken for granted that literate societies are better than illiterate ones.

Peru's intellectual and bureaucratic preoccupation with mass education dates back at least to the positivist vogue of the late nineteenth century. The eventual result has been a dazzlingly ramified educational bureaucracy; a solid rhetorical commitment to literacy and schooling; the entrenchment of cadres of administrators and teachers who are essentially, necessarily, and naturally conservative; and practical consequences, at least in the highlands, of very dubious value. Formal schooling has penetrated slowly, but population pressure and the steady encroachment of urban

Dan C. Hazen *is Latin American Librarian at Cornell University*.

Journal of Library History, Vol. 16, No. 2, Spring 1981

and coastal values have precipitated massive migratory movements toward both coast and city. A wrenching modernization-by-movement has substituted for the more controlled process anticipated through education.

Indigenous modes of information acquisition and usage have little to do with contemporary Western models. The nonliterate culture of the Andean highlands is founded in concepts of ritualized reciprocity and self-sufficient agriculture. Information transfer has occurred through word and example, and traditional needs have generated little pressure for the more abstract approaches of the "developed" world. Until recently, the advantages associated with literacy in highland Peru differed significantly from those expected in the developed world. The identification of education with an alien and often competing culture further clouded the entire process.

While many elements have contributed to the lackluster performance of Peru's official schools, almost all reflect an absence of concern for local cultures and needs. Standardized programs developed in Lima, urban teachers often prejudiced against Indian students and demoralized by the conditions of rural life, perpetually inadequate physical plants, and an administrative structure rife with politics and personal favoritism have all limited the impact of education. Short-lived experiments with more conciliatory pedagogical approaches have comprised a staccato of exceptions that only proves the general rule of indifference and inefficiency.

In the specific context of the Department of Puno, it became apparent at least with the Seventh-Day Adventist incursions of the 1910s and 1920s that successful programs could be mounted when the Indians perceived education as directly advantageous. The circumstances of such enthusiastic participation generally revolved around a basic impulse for cultural and physical survival. The early twentieth century was a time in which legal chicanery and naked force, were used to seize native land and property. The judicial and administrative systems were both geared to transactions of Spanish-speaking literates. Here, as in other areas, the Indians soon recognized that self-preservation required mastery of the exploiters' weapons. Education in Spanish might seem to imply the destruction of indigenous culture. In fact, it often appears to have been embraced for self-defense.

Mestizos, who typically comprise Peru's provincial elite, are normally identified as exploiters. The government shares this image. Not surprisingly, thus, the mestizo advocates of any official program can only rarely generate the intensity of response that has characterized many nongovernmental initiatives. Exceptional sacrifice and sustained identification with Indian concerns are among the requisites for indigenous confidence.

This essay will examine some of the conditions necessary for successful educational activity of the sort that would lay the basis for meaningful library development. Highland structures of social and productive relations have long obstructed official efforts. The relative success of the Rijchary movement, active in the Department of Puno through much of the 1930s and 1940s, can suggest by contrast some of the elements that have both stirred and responded to indigenous aspirations.

Peru's Department of Puno is a heavily Indian area fronting on Lake Titicaca and Bolivia. Census results from 1940 showed its population second only to Lima's. The same census reported over 83 percent monolinguals in native languages, and 86 percent illiteracy.[1] Perhaps the Department's outstanding physical characteristic is altitude: the Altiplano, or high plain, which comprises most of its populated area, lied at about two and a half miles above sea level. Corn, trees, and wheat are almost impossible to grow. The area's essentially agrarian economy revolves around potatoes, high-altitude grains like *cañihua* and *quinoa*, sheep, alpaca, and llamas.

The Altiplano's large population, abundance of alpaca, and highly elaborated systems of access to products from different altitudes and climates led it to be accounted rich before the Spanish Conquest. Today, however, it is considered one of the world's poorest regions. A centuries-long stagnation, which followed the colonial mining boom, was broken only in the late 1800s. A railroad from the coast provided easy transportation, and rising wool prices provoked an active capitalist incursion. The ensuing social conflict set the context for a generalized indigenous impulse for defense and progress. Education and literacy were prominent within this thrust.

Formal expressions of Indian interest in education date from at least 1901.[2] Starting around 1910, North American Seventh-Day Adventist missionaries achieved notable successes in the Aymara-speaking Provinces of Chucuito and Huancané. Church-sponsored schools formed a cornerstone for this activity, and the Adventist educational establishment outweighed its official counterpart until the late 1920s.

The Great Depression affected the Altiplano no less than other parts of the world. Wool exports continued to stagnate after their sharp decline from record levels in the early 1920s. Pressure on pasturelands eased as wool prices subsided, though a few ranchers sought to rationalize their operations by fencing pastures and evicting resident shepherds. Peru's national government faced an era of tight budgets. National politics were extremely unstable, and civil war between military dictators and the reformist Aprista movement appeared a real possibility. Financial stringency and political repression were watch-words of the time.

One break in this gloomy climate was provided by the Rijchary movement. Its history shows the limitations inherent in official and quasi-official efforts, the consequences of indigenous responsiveness to programs perceived as valuable, the role of the charismatic individual in sustaining reform, and the interplay of social groups on the Altiplano. It thus illuminates both the possibilities and the obstacles affecting reform.

Dr. Manuel María Núñez Butrón, founder of the Rijchary movement, was a small-town mestizo from the Altiplano.[3] Following university education in Arequipa, Núñez Butrón proceeded first to Lima and then to Spain for medical training. Subsequent autobiographical passages reveal a youthful obsession to pass as white, a desire rebuffed each time Núñez moved to a more cosmopolitan center and was again labeled "Indian." Ambivalence over his part-Indian heritage may have ultimately influenced Núñez Butrón's personal and professional commitment to this universally subordinate group.[4]

Soon after his Spanish medical credentials were validated in Lima, in 1925, Núñez Butrón was appointed *médico titular—* doctor-in-residence—for Puno's Azángaro Province. This nomination conferred formal control over the province's public health. The incumbent, often an area's only qualified physician, would traditionally reside in the provincial capital and concentrate on its mestizo clientele. The Indian mass was difficult to reach, highly dispersed, and just too large for effective action by one doctor. Moreover, Indian society was already replete with *curanderos* and folk healers, and mestizo authorities intervening for any reason were objects of suspicion and resistance. High rural mortality—fed by recurrent epidemics of typhus, smallpox, and whooping cough —remained the rule.

Núñez Butrón at first seems to have conformed to the normal routine of the *médico titular*. He addressed occasional teacher workshops and held conferences on hygiene and rudimentary medicine, but did little more. By the early 1930s he had been transferred to the geographically smaller and physically more accessible

Province of San Román, centered on the commercial city of Juliaca. Early efforts to reach the indigenous population, however,
failed to generate effective contact.

Núñez responded with innovative programs designed at once to
enforce and to elicit improved rural health. Vaccination certificates were instituted, with mixed results. More fruitfully, Núñez
devised a kind of voluntary medical extension service. He approached Indian *curanderos*, cultivated their friendship, and persuaded them to supplement their traditional practices with his
teachings. He taught basic hygiene and simple cures in weekly
meetings at his Juliaca home, and gradually widened the content
to include preventive medicine. As more and more interested Indians supplemented the medicine men in attendance, the Sunday
sessions were moved to Juliaca's plaza.

The first "Sanidad Rural 'Rijchary'" was inaugurated in the
community of Isla (population about 1,500) in 1933. The keynote
lay in the Quechua word *Rijchary*, meaning "Awaken!" The Rijchary movement, while it required the acceptance of traditional
curers, was more immediately based upon local volunteers charged
with preaching and then enforcing the principles of basic hygiene.
Many of these volunteers were army veterans, whose horizons had
widened during their military service. Five to ten workers would
be assigned specific sectors in each locality. Red Cross bracelets,
and certificates signed by Núñez Butrón, were the symbols of authority. The volunteers gave periodic reports on medical problems
and on general social and sanitary conditions. They were ordered
in a hierarchy running from the community leaders, the Tucuy
Ricuy, up to Jatun Rijchary, the Great Awakener, or Núñez Butrón himself.

Official backing was no less critical than community participation. Núñez Butrón enjoyed the full support of the director of
public health through most of the 1930s. He was especially authorized to divide the salary that would have been paid an official
sanitation officer between four peripatetic assistants who vacci-
nated and proselytized in the countryside. San Román's subprefect, the province's highest official, attended various Rijchary
ceremonies, and in 1935 even helped pass out Red Cross bracelets
to Indian volunteers.

Public health was the Rijchary movement's initial emphasis, and
it always remained a core concern. Nonetheless, the movement
was most significant for the breadth of its approach. Núñez Butrón argued that the ills afflicting Puno's Indians were not just to
be combated with vaccinations and improved hygiene. Rather,

high morbidity and poor sanitation were symptoms of a deep-seated complex of poverty, ignorance, and repression. Alcoholism and coca abuse, widespread illiteracy, and a propensity toward extended litigation over minor disputes were additional symptoms of the Altiplano's social malady. As Núñez Butrón declared, "prevention rather than cures" were needed. This prevention implied education and awareness on a number of levels. Herein lies the movement's relevance to literacy and library development.

The movement's tactics and approach were apparent in its annual celebrations of Indian Day, June 24.[5] Marathon races, parades, dances, speeches, and demonstrations of basic hygiene highlighted the observances. Individual and corporate donations of soap, combs, and scissors were distributed to participants. Schoolteacher Eustaquio Aweranka, Núñez Butrón's chief assistant, taught inspirational songs and a native-language version of the national anthem. Indian sanitary officials compared clean and dirty children from the audience. Núñez Butrón, Indian workers, and local authorities all admonished the assembly on patriotic rights and duties, and on the need for reformed habits.

Other activities also reflected the movement's breadth. Núñez Butrón constructed a small furnace to delouse Indian clothing and to demonstrate visually some of the consequences of poor hygiene. Local authorities were encouraged to refuse audiences with unwashed Indians, and railroad employees were asked to ignore Indians lacking a vaccination certificate. Within the urban environment of Juliaca, Núñez Butrón founded a small hospital and other medical facilities. He was prominent in the Red Cross, and he actively championed school construction and improvements. A short-lived "Centro Cultural Rijchary," inaugurated around 1935, sponsored programs of Indian song and dance, meetings, and festivities.

Public health, hygiene, patriotism, and literacy were recurrent Rijchary themes. Complementary activities also developed. Private classes, often conducted by former conscripts who had learned some Spanish and the rudiments of literacy, were far from rare during the early twentieth century. In many cases, though, the volunteers eventually tired of their unpaid labor or were forced to return to their fields and flocks. The Rijchary movement formalized such spontaneous efforts by establishing tuition-supported private schools. In addition to the eight or more such private institutions, three government elementary schools affiliated with the movement.

The Rijchary concern with schooling was by no means limited

to the classroom. The movement received free subscriptions to the Lima newspaper *La Crónica*, as well as pamphlets from the "League of Hygiene and Prophylaxis," official sanitary publications, and other newspapers. These materials formed the basis for a traveling library. Literates would read aloud to the uneducated, engendering an unprecedented awareness of the world beyond the Altiplano.

A major source of movement publicity was its intriguing journal, *Runa Soncco*. The title translates as "Heart of the Indian," implying an appeal to the indigenous soul, but also suggesting movement leaders' total dedication to the Indian cause. The journal itself purported to both reflect and direct indigenous aspirations. Ten issues were published, seven between 1935 and 1937, and the last three between 1945 and 1948. An editorial in the first number explained the Rijchary movement in the following terms:

> In the midst of our solitude, lacking other company than our fields and our animals, we seek the fellowship of a friend to speak with us, to guide us, to attack our faults, and to show us the way to our social betterment. SHOULD THIS HAPPEN, WE MIGHT NOT BE SO NEGLECTED.
>
> Runa Soncco will bring us sanitary lessons to improve our health. It will teach us to read and write, to no longer be deaf-mutes. It will guide us along the path of hygiene, morality, and progress.
>
> Runa Soncco is an alarm calling us to "AWAKEN!" and end the slumber of our ignorance.[6]

Billed as a publication by and for Indians, *Runa Soncco* combined passages on rudimentary hygiene, public health, and specific diseases with admonitions against alcohol and coca abuse, excessive litigation, and illiteracy. Articles in rustic Spanish detailed movement-related activities in the communities; Rijchary ceremonies were described at length; trilingual lessons and songs were published. Eustaquio Aweranka and Anselmo Molleapasa—the latter subsequently prominent in the government program of "Indian Culturization Brigades"—supplemented Núñez Butrón's contributions. A number of community Indians appear to have written as well, though pseudonyms abounded, and many of the articles may have come from the core editorial staff.

Runa Soncco's "Social Notes" section dealt with the everyday aspects of Indian life, and in some ways captured the essence of the Rijchary endeavor. This section also helped attract urban attention. Fighting families and neighbors were admonished to mend their ways; marriages and trial marriages were announced and applauded; students leaving for school were congratulated.[7] Advertisements were similarly *campesino*-(countryman)oriented, offering wares ranging from bricks to guitars. While *Runa Soncco*'s effect on the Indian population is nearly impossible to assess, the journal constitutes the most tangible chronicle of Núñez Butrón's efforts.

Núñez Butrón complained of landowner and elite obstructionism in an open letter of 1937. Those profiting from Indian lawsuits allegedly sought to divide his followers with rumors that he was embezzling government funds; those who lived by writing letters and interpreting for illiterate monolinguals were also upset. Both groups allegedly painted him as a dangerous extremist. At about the same time, the subprefect of San Román denied permission for a Rijchary private school in Isla. Despite a mild publicity campaign and some vocal champions in Lima, Núñez Butrón was transferred to the jungle province of Ucayali. He ultimately relocated in the highland province of Angaraes, Department of Huancavelica, and was reported back in Juliaca by February 1939.

From this time through 1945, or during the full length of Manuel Prado's administration, Núñez Butrón made no apparent effort to revive the Rijchary movement. He represented San Román in a 1939 fair in Lima, and helped organize such Juliaca ceremonies as observations for "Indian Day" in 1942. Núñez had once again been named *médico titular* by 1943, and he both held a class in his home and visited communities to encourage popular participation during a 1944 literacy campaign. In the same year, he penned a newspaper report that effusively praised another doctor for undertaking a short trip to the countryside. In January 1945, Lima's Red Cross sent Núñez Butrón 100 *soles* to set up showers for Juliaca-area *campesinos*.

Eustaquio Rodríguez Aweranka, perhaps Núñez Butrón's closest associate, had been dismissed as a state schoolteacher around 1940. Happily, he soon found employment in a private school.[8] Anselmo Molleapasa likewise remained pedagogically active, through the Brigadas de Culturización Indígena. Some of the Indians earlier touched by the Rijchary movement also sustained their commitment during Núñez Butrón's quiescence.

Occasional statements in *Runa Soncco* after its reappearance in September 1945 indicated strong official pressure against Núñez Butrón during the Prado regime. Núñez was instructed to confine his activities to public health (fighting lice), and to renounce all campaigns against alcoholism and excessive litigation. Thus his references to "a long period of enforced silence."

The last three numbers of *Runa Soncco*, which appeared between 1945 and 1948, echoed the content of previous issues. The tone, however, was much harsher: Indian ills were more vigorously denounced, and mestizo authorities were broadly attacked. One "riddle" in the September 1945 issue, for instance, pondered the time wasted by an Indian during eight years of biweekly pilgrimages to petition authorities for a state school. *Runa Soncco*'s last issue, published in 1948, explicitly denounced *gamonalismo* (abusive bossism) and crooked courts in the Province of Azángaro—and reportedly provoked a lawsuit in return.

The postwar years were those of José Luis Bustamante y Rivero's relatively liberal regime, and official support was again apparent. Puno's prefect warmly applauded the movement in his 1946 annual report, and Núñez was named "Traveling Doctor and Sanitarian" for the Department's reorganized public health service. Subsequent local documents indicated an approach in many ways compatible with the Rijchary endeavor.[9]

The Rijchary movement dissolved shortly after the 1948 issue of *Runa Soncco*. Movement fortunes again reflected shifts in the national government, which veered sharply to the right with Manuel Odría's anti-Aprista military coup. Núñez Butrón lapsed into semi-obscurity, maintaining contact with only his closest Rijchary associates between 1948 and his death in 1952.

Posthumous recognition was significant. Local newspapers that had scarcely mentioned him while he was alive eulogized Núñez and lauded his efforts. A school was named after him in Juliaca as was, several years later, Puno's new hospital. A series of Peruvian medical conferences paid formal tribute to his energy and achievements. Even today, sporadic books and articles continue to admire his work.

Repercussions of the Rijchary movement also lingered among the *campesinos* of San Román. In 1953, former assistants met a sanitary official and accompanied him to Putina (Azángaro Province) to inaugurate a public health center. Another group of sympathizers collected money for a bridge over the Cabanillas River. As late as 1960, an "Instituto Cultural de Rijcharismo" was reported active in Juliaca.

This thumbnail sketch of the Rijchary movement suggests the impact that a program designed to address Indian needs, implemented with Indian assistants, and addressing both the causes and the symptoms of poverty might carry. While we lack statistics to assess the degree of real change resulting from Rijchary activities, our sources are unanimous in praising the movement's efforts and approach.

The movement's pedagogical underpinnings, though not explicitly defined, merit particular attention. Educational psychologists have argued that the degree of redundancy in lessons and programs plays a key role in the effectiveness of instruction: where new material is embedded in the context of the familiar, learning performance improves. The Rijchary movement placed considerable emphasis on bilingual and trilingual materials. Teachings in Spanish employed the rustic dialect used on the Altiplano rather than a polished literary style. Where possible, analogies and examples were drawn from familiar rural contexts. Whether inspired by instinct or science, the result was an approach far more effective than that of official efforts—even in the relatively few cases where official programs sought the same progressive ends.

The Rijchary movement's appeal to local values and local cooperation clearly bolstered its impact. Other components were no less crucial. Most obviously, the gaps in Núñez Butrón's activities suggest the difficulties of conducting any kind of action-oriented program in the absence of government support or high-level patronage. Rijchary efforts proceeded only in times of official toleration. The government's intervening experiment with the "Indian Culturization Brigades," which both subsumed many movement goals and borrowed some of its materials, suggests that successful initiatives might well be coopted. While official concern would thus be demonstrated, actual change could be tightly limited and strictly controlled.

Educational and reform efforts that have enjoyed some measure of success—Seventh-Day Adventist schools, various private endeavors, the Rijchary movement—addressed the whole texture of Indian life. This approach necessarily implied a conflict with the local status quo. The response might include both terrorism (burning schools, and beating or jailing schoolteachers—both most common early in the century) and official repression (anti-Adventist measures in the late 1920s, the pressures against Núñez Butrón during the early 1940s). When reformist activities did persist, support from the central government was essential. The complaints of local landowners and politicians could be ignored whenever political expedience or principle so dictated. As the Rijchary movement's 1937 shutdown indicates, the same complaints could be cited at will when it was deemed desirable to prohibit some activity.

Successful reform efforts on the Altiplano, epitomized by the Rijchary movement, have embodied a kind of proto-conscientization in their theory and evolution. Conscientization refers to the philosophical and pedagogical approach articulated most fully by Paulo Freire with regard to literacy activities in Northeastern Brazil. According to Freire, education is only meaningful when linked to students' immediate needs. Full awareness of these needs provides the context for literacy, but this awareness also implies an analysis of the causes of poverty and oppression. Literacy's political context and content are thus explicit, and the implicit consequence is social change. Núñez Butrón failed to elaborate a detailed philosophy of communal self-analysis, just as he failed to articulate fully his pedagogical assumptions. The movement's preoccupation with the sources of sickness and poverty was nonetheless critical.

Our conceptualizations of education and literacy must go beyond the lessons and expectations and ideologies of the North Atlantic world. We commonly think of schooling as an enlarging process for both individual and society, and of information as an absolute and self-sufficient good. There is increasing evidence that education and literacy function as much to perpetuate existing values as to form a citizenry capable of full participation in change. Moreover, the value of information is heavily dependent on the transactional context in which it is embedded. The social and political implications of the school are both more and less than what our ideology would suggest. The circumstances of schooling in an area like highland Peru do much to elucidate the dynamic.

Libraries depend upon readers. The conditions of Andean library development, along with the situation of schooling, reveal how both literacy and libraries can serve as trappings of the elite and symbols of the status quo. As the Peruvian example suggests, the implicitly revolutionary consequences of readily accessible information can contrast sharply with official manipulation of information, of the tools for receiving it, and of the vehicles for conveying it. The checkered career of the Rijchary movement illustrates the degree and implication of such influence, and suggests that we must take a critical stance in evaluating either literacy or libraries in the Third World.

Notes

1. Perú, Ministerio de Hacienda y Comercio, Dirección Nacional de Esta-

dística, *Censo nacional de población y ocupación de 1940*, 9 vols. (Lima: Imp. Torres Aguirre, 1944), vol. 1, pp. 152-163, 189; vol. 8, pp. 3, 8.

2. See, for instance, [Santiago Giraldo (ed.)], *La raza indígena en los albores del siglo XX. II Opúsculo* (Lima: Imprenta de Victor A. Torres, 1903), or the report of Alejandrino Maguiña in *Memoria que el Ministro de Gobierno, Sr. Leonidas Cárdenas, presenta al Congreso Ordinario de 1902. Anexos* (Lima: Imprenta del Estado, 1902).

3. Among the most important and accessible sources on Núñez Butrón and the Rijchary movement are: David Frisancho, *Jatun Rijchary; Dr. Manuel Núñez Butrón, Precursor de la sanidad rural en el Perú* (Puno: Editorial "Los Andes," 1958); *Runa Soncco* Año 1, no. 1 to Año 14, no. 10 (28 de abril de 1935-24 de junio de 1948); Manuel Núñez Butrón, "Una obra de apostolado médico," *Medicina social* 2, no. 3 (mayo-junio 1944): 9-10; "Laudable campaña sanitaria," *Revista de la Cruz Roja*, tercera época, no. 12 (mayo-diciembre 1937): 20-25; Luis A. Ugarte, "Una trascendental labor médico-social en el Perú," *Informaciones sociales* 3, no. 2 (febrero 1939): 125-128.

4. This dilemma, which may have been reflected in Núñez's youthful practice of identifying the relatively cosmopolitan center of Arequipa as his birthplace, parallels that of Peruvian anthropologist and novelist José María Arguedas. Arguedas's novels vividly depict the conflict and its possible effects.

5. "Indian Day" coincided with festivals significant in both the autochthonous and Catholic ritual calendars.

6. *Runa Soncco* 1, no. 1 (28 de abril de 1935): 1. Emphasis in the original.

7. Only the first grades of elementary education were available in the countryside, and even then in only a few communities. Most would-be students had to leave home.

8. Rodríguez Aweranka reinstated the "Rodríguez"—an unmistakably Spanish patronym—during this period of official emphasis on Peru's European heritage. Census results from 1940, by combining the "white" and "mestizo" categories, also sought to dispel the image of Peru as an Indian country.

9. See early issues of *Altiplanía: Boletín bimensual de sanidad rural*, Organo de la Sanidad Departamental de Puno, 1, no. 1 to 3, no. 5 (diciembre 1946-setiembre 1949).

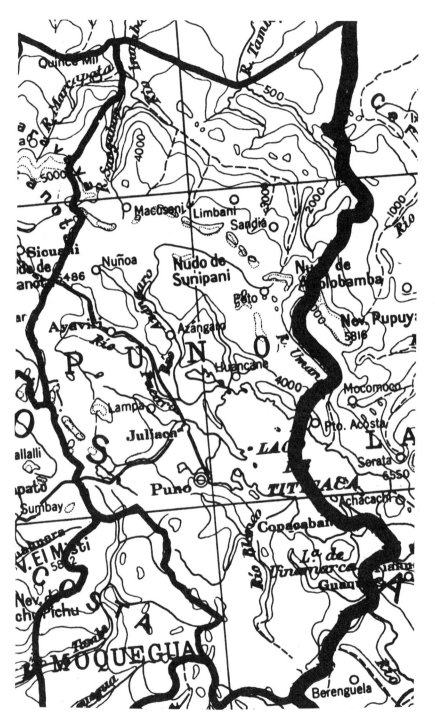

Detail from Sheet 13, "South America," World 1:5000000 series, reprinted with the permission of the American Geographical Society.

Chinese Libraries during and after the Cultural Revolution

Lee-hsia Hsu Ting

In spite of the general acknowledgement of the importance of China, our knowledge of libraries and library services in the People's Republic of China is extremely limited. None of the English books on contemporary China I have read mentions libraries. About a dozen or so articles have appeared in professional journals in the 1970s, mostly Australian and British; almost all of them are records of impressions from brief visits by foreign librarians who had to rely on interpreters. Even though the interpreters could be "well informed" and "a number of the [Chinese] librarians were familiar with English library terminology," as one American librarian claimed,[1] reports of this kind are necessarily superficial and cannot reflect the truth that the Chinese government under the Gang of Four (Chiang Ch'ing, Chang Ch'un-ch-iao, Yao Wen-Yüan, and Wang Hung-Wen) kept carefully hidden from all foreigners during those years. One librarian from Australia, in fact, went as far as to assert that the Cultural Revolution had "affected library services hardly at all."[2] We do look back now at such statements with surprise, but during those years almost all well-meaning visitors to China were similarly deceived. Most recent travelers to the People's Republic, especially those who can speak Chinese and have friends and relatives there, cannot help but share the feeling of Arthur Miller, who, after an extensive tour of China, wondered about "the question of how it happened that this 'fascist' government [during the Cultural Revolution] managed to so

Lee-hsia Hsu Ting *is associate professor of library science at Western Illinois University.*

Journal of Library History, Vol. 16, No. 2, Spring 1981
© 1981 by the University of Texas Press   0022-2259/81/020417-19$01.70

charm correspondent after correspondent into a kind of reportage that left no impression of the real magnitude of the Chinese disaster."[3]

Since available printed information on Chinese libraries during those tumultuous years is also scarce in Chinese,[4] this paper is based primarily on the data I collected during my visit to the libraries in the People's Republic of China in July 1978,[5] my subsequent correspondence with the Chinese librarians, and the printed materials they have kindly mailed to me since then.[6] It is a brief account of the history of Chinese libraries in contemporary China, as carefully documented as possible. In the section on Chinese libraries after the great fiasco, I will try to describe how they are meeting the challenges of a culture moving away from anti-intellectualism to scientific and technological researches, and what their salient problems are.

Before the Cultural Revolution, 1949–1966

The Cultural Revolution broke out in 1966, and ran rampant for more than ten years until October 1976, when the Gang of Four were arrested.[7] Its effects on Chinese libraries were truly catastrophic, especially since in the first seventeen (particularly the first ten) years of the People's Republic the government had worked hard to develop libraries.

To be sure, Soviet influence was very strong during these years. Lenin's views on libraries as a means of mass education and indoctrination profoundly influenced Chinese policies. The purposes of the library were described as "to serve politics, production, workers, peasants, soldiers, and scientific studies."[8] As in the Soviet Union, Chinese libraries were divided into three principal systems: the public libraries (under the supervision of the Ministry of Culture), the Academy of Science libraries (under the Chinese Academy of Science), and the academic libraries (under the Ministry of Higher Education).[9]

Village libraries (reading rooms) and labor union libraries were the two new kinds of libraries that developed most rapidly during these years. By the end of 1956, there had been 182,960 village libraries, and the number was on the increase as villages merged into communes after 1958.[10] Libraries run by labor unions, located in both cities and countryside, numbered 35,000 with collections totaling 34,000,000 volumes by the end of 1958.[11] Through these small libraries or reading rooms, library services were extended to the peasants and workers, hitherto rare visitors to libraries. Besides, there were the university and provincial or municipal libraries, situated mostly in East and South China, which the new government had inherited from the ancien regime. To serve readers better, many academic libraries installed some new facilities in 1956, such as "department of science" and "faculty reading rooms."[12]

Late in 1957, with the encouragement of Premier Chou En-lai, Chinese libraries took a great leap forward and started the library coordination program, which designated two main library centers (Peking and Shanghai), and nine secondary library centers (Wuhan, Shenyang, Kwangchow, Chengtu, Sian, Tientsin, Harbin, Lanchow, Nanking).[13] Vertically, large public libraries were instructed by the Ministry of Culture to help the smaller ones in the same jurisdiction. Through book-lending and other experimental projects, the provincial libraries had the responsibility to assist county libraries in that province, municipal libraries to assist district libraries, the county (or district) libraries to assist those at a lower level, and so on. Many small libraries worked hand in hand with local cultural halls, bookstores, and museums to form a cultural network in the villages. Public libraries were designated as coordination centers. Nanking Library, for instance, organized all libraries in the three principal systems in the province of Kiangsu according to their specialties. Larger libraries in one system were made to assist smaller ones of the same kind. Nanking Engineering College Library was thus made to assist technical school libraries and libraries specialized in mining technology in the province. Horizontally, local library coordination committees, composed of representatives from local libraries, met regularly to discuss problems of mutual concern. To train librarians, some libraries combined efforts to establish departments of library science in local colleges, with experienced practicing librarians serving as part-time instructors. National bibliographies, union catalogs, indexes, and so forth, were being compiled; limited centralized cataloging and interlibrary loans were instituted. In some areas, certain readers could receive a library borrowing card good for all the libraries in that area. In the spirit of cooperation, many large libraries transferred books in their own collections to their "brother libraries." For instance, libraries in Shanghai, which for many years had been the cultural and publishing center of China, transferred 500,000 volumes to help small libraries in six remote provinces, such as Kansu and Sinkiang.[14]

As new libraries of different levels came into existence, holdings of the older libraries were greatly increased. The acquisitions of

the National Peking Library, for instance, jumped from 30,000
volumes a year in 1949 to 300,000 volumes a year in the seventeen years, and exchanged publications with more than 3,000 institutions in more than 120 countries.[15] Besides the multitude of
volumes for indoctrination, readers in those days could have free
access to technical books; the ideologically "incorrect" or "pernicious" works, which may not be readily available to ordinary
readers, were still well preserved in the stacks.

The Cultural Revolution, 1966-1976

The situation changed completely in 1966, when the thunder-
storm of the Cultural Revolution broke out. Control of cultural
and intellectual activities had certainly been increasing in stringency since 1962, when Mao Tse-tung regained supremacy and
delegated more power to his wife Chiang Ch'ing. In 1963, Chiang
Ch'ing began to dominate the cultural activities. Scholarly and
professional journals and other publications had been suspended
one after another. But the witch-hunt did not become an open,
mass movement rampaging throughout the vast land until 1966.
Following Mao's instructions that class struggle had to be continued perpetually in order to sustain revolutionary fervor, young
radicals searched the country for remnants of "bourgeois" ideology and "revisionism" and destroyed without scruples whatever appeared objectionable to them. Their chief targets were the old
revolutionary leaders of the moderate faction within the Party,
and the specialists in cultural and educational circles who valued
professional competence above ideological commitment. The
"Sixteen-Point Directive Decision of the Central Committee on
the Great Proletarian Cultural Revolution," which they professed
to support, maintained that China had reached "a new stage in the
socialist revolution" that required a total transformation of public
opinion by "the *destruction of the entire old civilization.*" The old
civilization was specified as the "four olds"—old ideas, old culture,
old customs, and old habits of the "exploiting classes." To achieve
this goal, they were urged to "totally topple, smash, and expose
the counter-revolutionary revisionists, the bourgeois rightists, and
the reactionary bourgeois academic savants," who "must never be
allowed to rise again!"[16] Led by self-styled radicals, headed by the
Gang of Four, who were actually interested only in establishing
absolute control and eliminating all obstacles to the seizure of
power, the Red Guards terrorized the populace for years. The

tyranny of the ignorant and the self-righteous plunged China into an unprecedented disaster.

For over a decade, therefore, methods learned from European fascism, as is now widely admitted in China, were employed to buttress traditional feudalism and despotism. It was not just enough to destroy people who were labeled "rightists, counter-revolutionaries," "capitalist roaders," or "class enemies." All books and publications that might inspire independent thinking and help produce offenders had to be burnt or stashed away forever so that a new generation, blind and pliant tools of their leaders' will, might be born. Almost all the classical heritage of China, as well as that of the West, was marked for extinction because, as the Gang of Four declared, they "prefer workers without culture to exploiters with culture and intellectual aristocrats."[17] According to librarians in Kwangchow, Chiang Ch'ing believed that from the Renaissance in Europe to the Cultural Revolution in China the cultures of the whole world should be called a total blank.[18] Chang Ch'un-ch'iao, I was told in Shanghai, spoke contemptuously of libraries, claiming that only two shelves of books (meaning those pertaining to Marx, Lenin, and Mao) out of the millions should be allowed to exist.[19] He believed that "it would be better for the intellectuals to forget everything they had learned from primary school to college." Yao Wen-yüan clamored that the Chinese intellectuals had "the sham academic knowledge of the bourgeoisie." Once one "acquires knowledge, one becomes bourgeois" and "one who acquires professional competency forgets the dictatorship of the proletariat."[20] All intellectuals were thus condemned as "careerist," "freaks and monsters," "exploiters and intellectual aristocrats." Punishments dealt out to intellectuals included public humiliation at the mass rallies, home arrests, detention in office, imprisonment, endless interrogations and criticisms, and torture. Even after they had confessed their own "erroneous acts and crimes," they still had to be exiled to work farms far away from home and constantly to confess their "crimes." Those who could commit suicide were the fortunate ones. The majority did not dare to take their own lives in order that their children might not be penalized for the parents' "cowardice." Their homes were of course searched at will over and over again, and their private libraries and other belongings trucked away, destroyed, or confiscated.[21]

A regime hostile to accumulated knowledge could not be expected to spare the libraries, which were then supposed to be—

like the army, the police, and the courts—tools for the promotion
of fascist-feudalist policies. Only government propaganda, Communist classics, Mao's thoughts, and formula stories expounding
radical doctrines could be published and read. All libraries were
closed for periods of various lengths of time. Yüan Ting reported
in 1979 that "for exactly five years, many libraries were closed
and had no new acquisitions."[22] Shanghai Library was closed from
1967 to 1970. Even after it reopened its doors in 1970, the card
catalog and most of its Chinese books, except for a small number
containing "correct thoughts," were off limits to the general reader. The Western-languages section was nominally open, but no one
dared to use it for fear of being labeled "admirers of the West, and
trucklers to foreigners." Even scientific and technological books
published before the Cultural Revolution were banned. No book
could be checked out. Few readers ever came to the library, since
everyone had the works of Marx, Lenin, and Mao at home.[23] Collections in some libraries, such as those in Yunnan, a librarian in
Kwangchow told me, were simply put to the fire.[24]

Academic libraries suffered even more. As the students—now
composed solely of workers, peasants, and soldiers—took command, called for short and relevant courses, and spent their energy
"making revolution," knowledge, technological know-how, and
publications all became targets of scorn. Libraries that served in-
structional and research needs were accused of being "the center
of feudalism, capitalism, and revisionism"; "the tool of the bour-
goisie intellectuals for the control of the school"; "the scene of
crime where bourgeois intellectuals achieve their fames"; and "the
weapon of imperialist aggressions in China." In short, they were
doomed for destruction. Many libraries with a long history and
good collections were thus closed. Under the pretext of saving foreign exchange, subscriptions to foreign periodicals were suspended. In 1975, when the Gang of Four were most influential, many
libraries were forced to abolish faculty reading rooms and forbidden to assist instructors in research.[25]

The Academy of Science libraries were also in disarray, since
basic scientific research was virtually abandoned, as Fang I, the
head of the Chinese Academy of Sciences, admitted in 1977.[26]
As it was a crime to possess the " black products" of "feudalism,
capitalism, and revisionism, " that is, materials containing the so-
called incorrect thoughts, many libraries tried to get rid of such
materials by burning or destroying them. Some gave them the so-
called technical treatment, by cutting off or blackening out un-

desirable parts of these books or journals.[27] No record was kept of such irretrievable losses.

Librarians were all labeled "watch dogs" of the imperialists, and many were persecuted too.[28] One of the conspicuous examples happened in the Shanghai Library: Ku T'ing-lung—its director, a famous calligrapher, bibliographer, and author of several books—committed a "crime" by teaching Chinese calligraphy to staff members of the library's rare book department at their lunch breaks. Shanghai Library incurred the most official wrath because it housed a more complete collection of Chinese books, periodicals, and newspapers published during the 1930s when Chiang Ch'ing was active in Shanghai as a third-rate actress, and Chang Ch'un-ch'iao a minor writer. Because of these publications, a well-known incident took place as follows. Many Chinese publications of the 1930s contained writings by an author with the pen name of Ti K'e, which toed the Kuomintang line. Among these writings was a one-act play entitled *Fei-ch'ü chih yeh* (One Night in the Bandit-Occupied Areas), coauthored by Ti K'e and Ho Yung-Jen, a known Kuomintang secret agent, which attacked the Chinese Communists as murderers. An article in Ti K'e's name in the March 1937 issue of *Chiang-hsi min-tsu wen-i* (Kiangsi Nationalist Literature) also criticized Lu Hsün, the undisputed leader of the Leftist Writers' Union. In 1967, in response to a reference question, Ko Cheng-hui, a librarian of Shanghai Library, discovered from an article by Lu Hsün that Ti K'e had been the pen name of Chang Ch'un-ch'iao. When his discovery was known to the authorities, Ko was arrested and repeatedly questioned about the number of people who knew the same information. Ko asked his interrogators to turn to Chang himself for denial or confirmation of Lu Hsün's remarks, but was imprisoned instead for five years and three months. Many of his colleagues in the library, including many young pages, were also imprisoned. As a result, about one-seventh of the library's 360 staff members at that time were jailed or sent to work farms, and numerous others were persecuted in subtler ways.

Ko was not the only librarian who displayed heroism under duress. The name plate over the front door of the Shanghai Library was written by Ch'en Yi, a general and high official known for intelligence and integrity and bitterly opposed to the Gang of Four. The extremists ordered the library to destroy the plaque. But an old warehouse clerk preserved it by burying it secretly underground at great personal risk.[29]

Peking Library was perhaps the only one whose collection did not suffer much during the Cultural Revolution. But many staff members, afraid of being labeled reactionaries or backward elements "contemptuous of workers, peasants, and soldiers," "restorers of the old," dared not perform their duties. Its large collection was thus never fully utilized.[30]

The above stories, many confided to me orally by Chinese librarians in July 1978, present vivid accounts of woes in individual libraries. A recently published article in Chinese draws a general picture of these evil days for libraries in the whole country. Here is the pertinent passage:

> Because of wanton destruction by Lin Piao and the Gang of Four, many libraries were undermined, and their staff members exiled to the countryside. The collections that had been accumulated over a period of many years in some libraries were subjected to destructions on an unprecedented scale. In 1965, before the Cultural Revolution, there were 1,100 public libraries at or above the county level. After eleven years [that is, in 1976], instead of increasing, the number decreased by one-third. Similar situations can be found in libraries of other systems. Academic and labor union libraries suffered even worse devastation. So, in the last decade or so, the history of our libraries is not one of stagnation, but one of enormous devastation and [tragic] retrogression. . . . On account of the years of consistent disruption by the Gang of Four, in the hundreds of thousands of nationalized industries and other enterprises, very few could keep their union libraries open and operative.[31]

At the end of the Cultural Revolution, according to 1977 statistics, there were only 851 public libraries. Not all provinces had a provincial library; only 32 percent of the districts had libraries at the district level, and 27 percent of the counties had libraries at the county level. Although 75 percent of the large cities had municipal libraries, only 7 percent of the districts under their jurisdiction had libraries. No one knows how many of the more than 50,000 communes, 680,000 production brigades, and 4,000,000 production teams had libraries of their own. The Chinese Academy of Science and the universities fared better. Generally speaking, each of the 100 plus scientific research institutions and 800 plus institutions of higher education had some sort of library. But of the more than 200,000 secondary schools and 1,000,000 elementary schools, only a small fraction had libraries. The number of trade union libraries, as has been pointed out before, had also been greatly reduced.[32]

After the Cultural Revolution, 1976–

When the Gang of Four were arrested on 6 October 1976, people in China were so elated that, according to both newspaper and oral reports, they bought up all the cheap liquor in Peking to celebrate their liberation. The country was then actually in shambles, especially in the areas of science and technology, higher education, and industrial development. Under the Gang of Four, production figures and other achievements had been greatly inflated. People had been conditioned to live on lies and act like robots. To reset the priority of the nation, the central government under the moderate pragmatists tried to redress the past wrongs, acknowledge its own backwardness, and concentrate on the "four modernizations." As the intellectuals rose from one of the lowest classes during the Cultural Revolution to regain respect and prestige, libraries also came back to the foreground. In his report to the First Session of the Fifth National People's Congress, Chairman Hua Gongfeng called for the "development of all types of libraries in order to organize a library network to serve scientific research and the masses."[33] The functions of Chinese libraries are now again defined as serving the following: (1) mass education, (2) scientific and technological research, (3) dissemination of information, and (4) preservation of books.[34]

To meet the demand of the nation, dedicated librarians have worked hard to pick up the pieces. Those at the Shanghai Library put their reference skills and unique collection to work to look for evidence to disgrace the Gang of Four. They searched enthusiastically for many days and nights through the publications of the 1930s, and uncovered 365 articles and books to discredit the notorious clique. Among their important discoveries was the fact that Chiang Ch'ing had pledged allegiance to the Kuomintang in 1935 when she was arrested by Chiang Kai-shek's agents.[35]

In libraries that have survived the disaster, catalogs and collections are again made available to the public. Local library coordination committees in large cities are meeting again regularly. Large libraries, such as National Peking Library and Shanghai Library, now again shoulder the responsibility of providing reference and bibliographic services to other libraries, preparing exhibits, photoduplication service, interlibrary loans, and so forth. Peking Library, the national library, is also responsible for centralized cataloging and providing catalog cards for new books to libraries in the nation. It now exchanges publications with 2,000 libraries in 120 countries, including the Library of Congress.[36] Contacts with foreign libraries are being increased and strengthened. Many activities, such as the compilation of national and other union catalogs, special or subject bibliographies, and indexes, have been resumed.

One of the most ambitious projects now actively undertaken is the compilation of the national bibliography of rare books in Chinese classics. This is a project suggested by the late Premier Chou En-lai in October 1975, but thwarted by the Gang of Four. After their fall, some libraries in Peking, Shanghai, Nanking, and Hangchow received instructions from the Museum and Archaeological Materials Administration, which now supervises all public libraries, to make necessary preparations really to begin the project. In March 1978, an editorial meeting was held in Nanking, and decided on the scope, treatment, and classification of this work. A census of the rare books was to be taken in the nation. Workshops were to be set up in various provinces, municipalities, and autonomous regions to train young workers. Many people have sent their own treasured volumes, which were buried underground during the reign of terror, to local agents for examination. In November 1978 and again in March 1979, two more meetings were held in Chengtu and Kwangchow, to work out the details. The ambitious bibliography is now being compiled.[37]

Realizing the importance of professionalism, library science journals have been revived.[38] On 9-16 July 1979, more than 200 libraries of all nationalities in China, representing libraries of all systems, from 29 provinces, municipalities, and autonomous regions, met in Taiyuan to announce the birth of the Society of Chinese Libraries. This is a professional association for the Chinese librarians with the purpose of promoting libraries and library science in order to subserve the four modernizations. Liu Chi-p'ing, director of National Peking Library, is now its first president. In order to strengthen the role of the leadership in library development, a new Bureau of Library Administration has been set up under the Ministry of Culture.[39]

In their efforts for recovery, Chinese libraries of course encounter many difficulties. Besides inadequacy in number, they also face other serious problems resulting from the sabotage by the extreme radicals, among which is the recruitment of new personnel. Professional librarians are now mostly older people; few young librarians have been trained in the past dozen years. Some library science courses are being offered at Peking University and Wuhan University, and more recently in Shanghai Normal University, but they do not turn out enough graduates. Some libraries have to offer on-the-job training to new staff members.[40] Local library coordination committees, such as those in Shanghai and Peking, also sponsor workshops for library personnel with experienced librarians as instructors. In November 1978, in a preparatory meeting of the Society of Chinese Libraries, the Provincial Szechuan Library was instructed to compile a series of fifteen textbooks in library science for training library assistants in secondary schools.[41]

The most serious problem inherited from the reign of terror is perhaps the restoration of academic freedom. How librarians can forget their fears and once again engage in free inquiry seems to be uppermost in the minds of Chinese librarians, as may be seen in the various articles in the *Tushuguanxue Tongxun.*[42] This problem is actually shared by all the people in China. The present administration has been trying hard to assure the people that the terrors of yesterday will not afflict them again by enacting new laws, introducing free elections at lower levels, and rehabilitating innocent victims of the Cultural Revolution. Like many other people, all the librarians I met in China hailed the liberal measures and exhibited high morale. The possibility of the return of radicalism now seems very remote, but few can be sure what the future has in store.

Another problem is the shortage of space. After years of enforced closure, so many Chinese readers are now scurrying back to the fountains of knowledge that the libraries do not have enough space to accommodate them and must limit their services. National Peking Library, for instance, has fifteen reading rooms with a seating capacity of over 700. But more than 2,000 readers use the library everyday, although admission is highly selective. As for borrowers, only government agencies, their employees, and diplomatic corps personnel may have the privilege when they can demonstrate a need.[43] Others have to borrow through interlibrary loans. To solve the problem, the library is now planning a new building in a western suburb of Peking.[44] Shanghai Library has a total seating capacity of 1,000, but each day it has to accommodate about 3,000 readers and circulate 6,000 volumes. No wonder readers often have to queue up at the peep of dawn in order to find a seat. It also plans for a new building in the 1980s.[45] Peking University Library has had a new building since 1975, and is not worried yet about spacing.

Still another problem is that of updating their holdings. Take, for instance, prose fiction. One English teacher complained that "there is hardly even anything about this century" in the Chinese libraries.[46] What he said about British and American novels is also true of many other subject fields. While short in scientific and technological publications (the most popular area with users) and Chinese novels produced before the Cultural Revolution, especially those of the 1930s (the next in line in popularity), most of the Chinese libraries are nevertheless overstocked with the worthless propaganda and formula stories printed during the period of the Gang of Four. The junk that nobody cares to read now has become a big burden for the staff. How to weed the collections and dispose of the numerous duplicates they were once forced to buy remains a serious issue.[47]

Cataloging also bothers Chinese librarians because there is as yet no standard method for organizing library catalogs. Most libraries have separate catalogs for Chinese books and foreign-language books. For the Chinese books, there is usually the author catalog and perhaps also the title catalog, both arranged by the radicals of Chinese characters. For the subject approach, classified catalogs are used, and arranged according to classification number. If more than one book is in a class, then the cards may be arranged in one of the following ways:

(1) Chronologically by the author (especially for the classics).

(2) According to the author number. (Before 1958, some large libraries, following the example of the Cutter alphabetical table, compiled an author number table.) This is the classified author catalog.

(3) By the Four-Corner number of the title. This is the classified title catalog.

(4) By the chronological order of the accession of the book by the library.

Although the author number or accession order seems to be used by most libraries, debates are still going on as to the advantages and disadvantages of each method.[48]

But the thorniest problem for catalogers is again one inherited from the nation's irrational past. So many library materials were wantonly destroyed or carelessly misplaced without records during the Cultural Revolution that in most cases the catalog does not accurately represent the holdings in a library. How to make the two match is certainly a big headache for the large libraries.

Another most complex problem is in classification. Many libraries, especially those in the public library system, adopted the

Chinese Library Classification in 1974, when libraries closed their old classified catalogs. All materials cataloged after that date have been classified under the new scheme. To connect the old and new catalogs, "see also" references are used. The Chinese Library Classification was devised collectively for more than ten years from 1960 by representatives from many libraries all over the country (draft edition, 1960–May 1963; tentative edition, 1963–March 1974; first edition, March 1974–October 1975).[49] Like the Library of Congress classification, it uses mixed notations—the letters used in the Pinyin system and arabic numbers. According to Marxist, Leninist, and Maoist doctrines, all knowledge is divided into five principal groups that comprise 22 main classes, and further divided into 20,000 subclasses, divisions, and subdivisions. Class A is reserved for works on Marxism, Leninism, and Maoism. There has been a great deal of criticism of this scheme, mainly because it clearly reflects the influence of the Gang of Four—especially in philosophy and the social sciences, where unique subclasses and divisions were invented to suit the extremists' ideas.[50] In a revision meeting held in March 1979 in Changsha, attended by ninety librarians, it was decided that, in view of the fact that thousands of libraries had already adopted the system, the main classes and notation system will be kept, but necessary revisions will be made to purge the influence of the Gang of Four.[51]

One problem having little to do with political ideology is that of computerization. Chinese librarians are keenly interested in using computers, although those I met all admitted that they did not have sufficient knowledge in this area, and expressed a desire to learn more about this subject.

As in the Soviet Union, library and information sciences were at first separated in China.[52] Beginning in September 1977, the leadership role of the main library at the Academy of Science over other libraries in its subordinate research institutes and branch offices has been restored. The Academy of Science libraries have now been given the responsibility for scientific information retrieval.[53] At the time Chairman Hua called for building up a library network to serve scientific research and the public, Fang I, vice premier in charge of scientific research and technological affairs, was advocating another network of information retrieval: "to build up within eight years enough data bases and terminals to form an on-line bibliographic and information retrieval network."[54] This seems to be a very ambitious plan, especially because no library is yet known to possess a computer.[55] The enormous costs that the design and development of library automation would entail should be a serious deterring factor. Before in-depth indexes are compiled, problems of converting large files with Chinese characters to machine-readable records are solved, and the telecommunication system in the country is greatly improved, I feel it would be premature to institute library automation or on-line bibliographic searching. Recent reports from China indicate that some technical problems in treating Chinese characters in a computer are being tackled.[56]

Financing, the worst bugaboo for Western librarians, is on the other hand not a serious concern to their Chinese counterparts. Though China is still a poor country, the government has been as generous to libraries as may be expected. Consequently, in all libraries, book budgets have been on the increase since 1976. If a clear need is demonstrated, additional funds may be granted over and above the regular budget. For instance, in connection with promoting tourism, libraries such as Shanghai Library were getting supplemental funds to acquire materials in this area, and even ordered works on cold permanent waves at readers' requests. If any cuts have to be made in the budget, I was told, they are always made in the administrative funds rather than book-purchasing funds. The purchase of foreign books and periodicals, handled through China Book Import Company, in Peking, has been a heavy drain on Chinese libraries.[57] Since so many materials are badly needed in China, the libraries have to be very selective in acquisition.

Conclusion

To sum up, because of its anti-intellectualism, the Cultural Revolution did almost irreparable damage to Chinese libraries, as it did to all other educational institutions. After the removal of the ultraradical leaders, libraries in China have been making strenuous efforts for recovery and expansion. Their problems are numerous and not all immediately solvable, but with determination and adequate financial support, they ought to be removed or at least alleviated in time. If the intelligent and dedicated librarians can have a bigger share in policy making and really be allowed to pursue more stable goals, libraries in the People's Republic of China will have a very bright future.

Notes

1. Josephine Riss Fang, "Chinese Libraries Carry Out Chairman Mao's

431

Dictum: 'Serve the People,'" *Wilson Library Bulletin* 49, no. 10 (June 1975): 745. The standard procedures for foreign librarians to obtain information from their Chinese counterparts and to become instant experts on Chinese libraries in a matter of hours are described in ibid, p. 746. The same article is reprinted with slight revision in *The Bowker Annual of Library and Book Trade Information* (New York: Bowker, 1976), pp. 382–387.

2. S. W. Wang, "Impressions of Chinese Libraries and the Chinese Book Market," *Australian Academic and Research Librarian* 5, no. 1 (March 1974): 24.

3. Inge Morath and Arthur Miller, *Chinese Encounters* (New York: Farrar, Straus, Giroux, 1979), excerpted in *Book Digest* (February 1980): 64.

4. From about 1963 to 1977, not much besides Marxism, Leninism, Maoism, formula stories, and the like was published. With few exceptions, all scholarly journals were suspended during this period.

5. In China, I visited National Peking Library, the national library and also the largest library in China, on July 23, and met Pao Chen-hsi (deputy director of the Functional Department), Chu Yen, and Huang Chün-Kuei; Shanghai Library, a municipal library and the second largest library, on July 12 and 13, and talked at length with eight senior librarians: Ku T'ing-lung (director), Yüan Hsüeh-kuang (deputy director), Lu T'iao-wen, Shen Chin, Wang Ch'eng-hsien, Sun Ping-liang, Han Ching-hua, and Yang Chen-ying; Sun Yat-sen Library in Kwangchow, a provincial library and the sixth largest, on July 5 and July 24, and met T'ung Te-shan (director), Huang Yu-cheng, Au Ch'ang-wei, Tsou Ts'ai-ying, and Huang Tao; Peking University Library, the largest university library, on July 22, and talked with Liang Ssu-chuang (deputy director). Unless otherwise indicated, all information regarding these four libraries was obtained from these interviews. As for romanization in this paper, the Wade-Giles system is used unless I know a journal or person's preferred form of name.

6. The assistance from all the Chinese librarians named above, especially Pao Chen-hsi of National Peking Library, and Yüan Hsüeh-kuang of Shanghai Library, is hereby acknowledged with deep gratitude.

7. See Chairman Hua Guofeng's speech on the First Session of the Fifth National People's Congress on 26 February 1978, *Hung-ch'i* (The Red Flag) no. 3 (1978): 3.

8. "Libraries in New China—A Survey of the Past Ten Years," by the Committee on the History of Libraries (in Chinese), *Pei-ching ta-hsüeh hsüeh-pao: Jen-wen Ko-hsüeh (Bulletin of Peking University: The Humanities)* no. 18 (October 1959): 107. Hereafter this article will be referred to as *PTJ*.

9. The Academy of Science Library was first founded in 1951. At the end of 1958, there were 113 libraries in this system, with holdings totaling 6,000,000 volumes. Two hundred thirty-two of the 663 staff members and 1,750,000 volumes of the total holdings were in the main library in Peking. There were 82 public libraries at or above the county level in 1952, 400 in 1957, and 848 in April 1959. Academic libraries numbered 229 in 1958. See *PTJ*, pp. 96, 97, 102, 103.

10. *PTJ*, p. 96. According to incomplete statistics, in December 1958, there were 35,659 commune libraries in the province of Honan, and 67,685 in the province of Kwangtung (*PTJ*, p. 101).

11. *PTJ*, p. 104.

12. *PTJ*, p. 97.

432   JLH/*Chinese Libraries*

13. Peking Library Center, the first national center, was established on 14 December 1957, and decided on (1) a cooperative acquisition program: National Peking Library would concentrate on the humanities, especially Chinese rare books and publications in Asian countries, Chinese Academy of Science Library would concentrate on science and technology; (2) the compilation of union catalogs, and the establishment of a centralized cataloging center in National Peking Library beginning from 1958 to provide catalog cards for libraries in the nation. Other programs to be implemented were: international exchange, photo-duplication, interlibrary loans, and librarian training (*Jen-min jih-pao*, 15 March 1959). See also Du Ke, "A Preliminary Probe into Establishing a Network of Libraries in Our Country" (in Chinese), *Tushuguanxue Tongxun* (*Bulletin of Library Science*), no. 1 (1979): 23. Hereafter this issue of the journal will be referred to as *BLS*.

14. *PTJ*, pp. 97, 100, 104-105.

15. Yüan Ting, "Shift the Focus of Library Service to Socialist Modernization" (in Chinese), *BLS*, p. 10.

16. Robert S. Elegant, *Mao's Great Revolution* (New York: World, 1971), p. 205. Italics mine.

17. Hsin-hua News Agency, 17-18 July 1977; quoted in Leslie Evans, *China after Mao* (New York: Monad Press, 1978), p. 131.

18. Interview with librarians of Sun Yat-sen Library in Kwangchow, 24 July 1978.

19. Interview with librarians of Shanghai Library, 13 July 1978.

20. Hsin-hua News Agency, July 17-18, quoted in Evans, *China after Mao*, p. 131.

21. According to a Museum and Archaeological Materials Administration spokesman in Peking, during the Cultural Revolution rare books, which were regarded as "old culture," were sent to garbage dumps, paper factories, or the 72 warehouses scattered all over the city. Millions of rare books were recycled and made into paper to print Mao's "Little Red Book." In 1979, after the government changed its policy, it returned 2,000,000 volumes of confiscated rare books to their rightful owners. It also recovered 314 tons of books with historical significance, among which was a set of 700-year-old *The Thirteen Classics* (in 120 volumes). See *China Daily News* (New York, in Chinese), 17 December 1979.

22. Yüan Ting, "Focus of Library Service," p. 9.

23. Interview with librarians of Shanghai Library, 13 July 1978.

24. Interview with librarians of Sun Yat-sen Library, 24 July 1978.

25. Yüan Ting, "Focus of Library Service," p. 9.

26. *New York Times*, 3 January 1978. Yü Kuang-yüan's speech to the Chinese Library Association in 1979. See *Chung-kuo t'u-shu-kuan hsueh-hui ch'eng-li ta-hui chuan-chi* (*The Founding of the Society of Chinese Libraries, A Special Bulletin;* August 1979): 23-26, 32. Hereafter this publication will be referred to as *CKTSK*. Yü is a deputy director of the Chinese Academy of Social Science.

27. T'an Hsiang-chin, "Some Problems Facing the Peking Library" (in Chinese), *BLS*, p. 14. T'an is a deputy director of National Peking Library.

28. Yüan Ting, "Focus of Library Service," pp. 10, 12.

29. Interview with librarians of Shanghai Library, 13 July 1978. The plate has now been dug out and restored to its original place.

30. T'an Hsiang-chin, "Some Problems Facing the Peking Library," p. 13.

31. Du Ke, "A Preliminary Probe," pp. 24-25.

32. Ibid., p. 25.

33. *Hung-ch'i* no. 3 (1978): 21. The entire text of the speech is reprinted in this issue on pp. 3-30.

34. Ding Zhi-gang, "A Message to the New Bulletin" (in Chinese), *BLS*, p. 7. Ding is a deputy director of National Peking Library.

35. Interview with librarians of Shanghai Library, 13 July 1978.

36. More than 3,000 libraries bought 6,850,000 printed catalog cards from National Peking Library in 1978 (*Beijing Tushuguan Jianjie* [*A Short Guide to the National Library of Beijing*; Peking: National Peking Library, 1979], pp. 11, 12). However, there is still a great deal to be desired as far as library cooperation is concerned. Cf. Liu Chi-p'ing's speech to the Society of Chinese Libraries in 1979 (*CKTSK*, p. 15). Liu is the director of National Peking Library.

37. Xue Dian-xu, "The National Bibliography of Chinese Old and Rare Books in Active Preparation" (in Chinese), *BLS*, pp. 60-61.

38. *Tushuguanxue Tongxun* (the organ of the Society of Chinese Libraries) and a journal devoted to information science both began publication in 1979. There had been no professional journal at the national level since the suspension of *Tushuguan* (*The Library*) in 1965. Some libraries publish their own journals and circulate them nationwide (Ding Zhi-gang, "Message to the New Bulletin," p. 6).

39. It was first suggested in 1956, and then again in 1978, to organize such an association. The chief functions of the Society are: (1) to organize library science research and other professional activities, (2) to publish professional periodicals and other materials, (3) to disseminate basic knowledge as well as Chinese and foreign research results of library science, (4) to develop international cooperation and friendship with foreign librarians. All library associations at the provincial, municipal, and autonomous regional levels and the other library systems devoted to certain specialties may be corporate members. Only those experienced librarians (1) who are at or above the instructor or assistant researcher level, (2) who have worked in libraries, library research, or library education for at least three years, (3) who have worked in the field for five years with demonstrated research ability or academic qualifications, or (4) who have made important contributions to the field may join the Society as individual members upon the approval of the board of directors. Officials in related government agencies who are interested in library work and have contributed to the field and other qualified persons specifically invited by the board of directors may also become individual members. The present board of directors comprises sixty-nine members (*CKTSK*, pp. 23-26, 32). All except three provincial and municipal library associations were founded after 1978 (Hsü Wen-hsü, "Library Associations Are Being Founded" [in Chinese], *BLS*, p. 5; also Pao Chen-hsi's letter to me dated 28 July 1980).

40. Warren Tsuneishi, "U.S. Librarians Visit the People's Republic of China," *LC Information Bulletin* 38, no. 48 (30 November 1979): 488. Cf. Fu Yang, "On Building Up Public Libraries in Large Cities" (in Chinese), *BLS*, p. 30.

41. "News about Chinese and Foreign Libraries" (in Chinese), *BLS*, p. 93.

42. Ding Zhi-gang, "Message to the New Bulletin," p. 8; Yüan Ting, "Focus of Library Service," p. 12; Liu Chi-p'ing, *CKTSK*, pp. 18-19.

434   JLH/*Chinese Libraries*

43. Interview with librarians of National Peking Library, 23 July 1978.
44. The new building will have more than 1,500,000 square feet, about 3½ times as large as the present building (*China Daily News*, 3 September 1979). For photographs showing the architects' design, see the inside front and back covers of *BLS*.
45. Interview with librarians of Shanghai Library, 13 July 1978.
46. Derek Bryan, a British subject who taught English in China, told reporters in Hong Kong ("Teaching English in China," *Ta kung pao Weekly Supplement*, Hong Kong, 8 November 1979). Cf. Tsuneishi, "U.S. Librarians," p. 488, in regard to the shortage of twentieth-century music books.
47. Interview with librarians of Shanghai Library, 13 July 1978. Fu Yang (*BLS*, p. 29) reports that, during the Cultural Revolution, one commune library received 500 copies of one novel for its slightly over 1,000 readers, and 200 or 250 copies each of some other novels favored by the extremists.
48. Wang Chang-bin, "Library Bibliographies and Catalogues, Their Present, Past, and Future" (in Chinese), *BLS*, pp. 52-53. Cf. also Huang Jue-sheng, "Present Task of the Society of Chinese Libraries" (in Chinese), *BLS*, p. 4.
49. Interviews with librarians of Sun Yat-sen Library, 5 July 1978; and with librarians of Shanghai Library, 13 July 1978; Yüan Hsüeh-kuang's letter to me dated 16 August 1979; Editorial Board of Chinese Library Classification (ed.), *Chung-kuo t'u-shu-kuan t'u-shu fen-lei-fa (Chinese Library Classification*; Peking: Scientific and Technological Documents Publishing Co., October 1975) is now still "for internal reference" only. Some Academy of Science Information Retrieval Centers have adopted "Chinese Information Classification," a scheme similar to this one (Song Ke-qiang, "On the Appraisal of Classification—A System in Use in Chinese Libraries" [in Chinese], *BLS*, pp. 49-50).
50. Ibid., pp. 47, 48.
51. "News about Chinese and Foreign Libraries" (in Chinese), *BLS*, p. 92.
52. Hsin Hsi-meng, "On the Merging of Library and Information Sciences in the Chinese Academy of Science" (in Chinese), *BLS*, p. 21; Huang Jue-sheng, "Present Task of the Society of Chinese Libraries," p. 3.
53. Hsin Hsi-meng, "On the Merging of Library and Information Sciences," pp. 18-19. The functional office of the Academy of Science Library now has six departments (acquisition, cataloging, readers service, information, research, and publication) and three sections (library automation preparation, public relations, internal information service), ibid., p. 21.
54. Du Ke, "A Preliminary Probe," p. 26; Huang Jue-sheng, "Present Task of the Society of Chinese Libraries," p. 3.
55. Cf. Liu Chi-p'ing, *CKTSK*, p. 15.
56. *China Daily News*, 13 October 1979; 19 January 1980; 28 January 1980.
57. Interview with librarians of Shanghai Library, 13 July 1978.

Prolegomena to the History of International Librarianship

Michael Keresztesi

In the closing decades of the twentieth century, the history of international librarianship is still largely uncharted territory. No comprehensive treatment of the subject exists apart from a short historical sketch by Wormann dated 1968, which remains a landmark because of the broad perspective in which pertinent facts and developments are presented.[1] Although narrow in focus, a more recent and ambitious undertaking was Coblans's monograph published in 1974, concentrating on the measures taken by international organizations to improve the state of the art in bibliography and documentation.[2] The panoramic view he offers in this significant work and the integrative method he employs show how disparate and often inchoate elements have combined to result in substantial advancement.

Aside from the above, however, there is no more than a smattering of articles covering the activities and accomplishments of several major international organizations in the field of librarianship appearing in professional journals and in the *Encyclopedia of Library and Information Science.*[3]

Evidence of Interest in International Librarianship

The scarcity of writings on the history of international librarianship is by no means due to a lack of interest in the subject. There is ample evidence to indicate that collaboration among librarians

Michael Keresztesi *is associate professor of library science at Wayne State University.*

Journal of Library History,Vol. 16, No. 2, Spring 1981
©1981 by the University of Texas Press   0022-2259/81/020435-15$01.50

of various countries has a long tradition and that a great deal of effort has been invested over the years to maintain this tradition. The annual conference of IFLA, FID, and other professional forums have been well attended in past years. American involvement in international library activities and the role played in the various international library assistance programs by the American Library Association and its International Relations Office are well documented.[4] The recent launching of the *ALA World Encyclopedia of Library and Information Services* can be seen as a response to manifest interest in library affairs on an international scale. Reflecting the same trend, the number of American library schools that offer courses in international library affairs has grown from five in 1965 to forty-five in 1973.[5]

The Subject and Scope of International Librarianship

An analysis of the objectives and contents of courses dealing with international library matters as reported by Boaz reveals a complete lack of consensus on the subject matter of international librarianship.[6] Most commonly, international librarianship is thought to be coterminous with comparative librarianship, or to be an aspect and, in some instances, a branch of it.

A loss of direction in this matter is evident wherever one turns for guidance and clarification. The professional indexing tool, *Library Literature*, for example, denies the existence of international librarianship as an autonomous field and refers the reader to "comparative librarianship" and "librarianship—international aspects" for relevant reading material. Nor does the *Encyclopedia of Library and Information Science* contain a separate substantive discussion of this subject. Instead there is an eighteen-page essay entitled "International and Comparative Study in Librarianship, Research Methodology" in which the author treats the terms "international" and "comparative" as if the one were no more than an aspect of the other.[7] Moreover, the writer of the article "Comparative Librarianship" in the *Encyclopedia* defines the scope of the topic by alluding to the fact that: "Comparative librarianship is also closely related to efforts aimed at international understanding and cooperation in librarianship, but its lively concern with and usefulness to these activities grows out of its basic preoccupation with the systematic search for accurate understanding and interpreting of library practices and results in differing cultural contexts."[8] The writer's consideration of international aspects is limited to passing references to UNESCO, IFLA, FID, and OAS as producers of data for the study of comparative librarianship.[9]

The pervasive coupling of international librarianship and comparative librarianship into a common intellectual domain strikes one as a logical incongruity. Comparative librarianship is essentially a method of inquiry. The domain of comparative librarianship consists of the results of the application of this particular method. Without the method the domain cannot be said to exist.

Even more illustrative of the prevailing conceptual and terminological ambiguity is a collection of seventeen generally informative and erudite essays brought together and edited by John F. Harvey in 1977 under the title *Comparative and International Library Science*.[10] The compilation appears to be a veritable Procrustean bed for a bewildering array of topics and issues hoarded together under the term "comparative and international librarianship."

International librarianship, however, as defined by J. Stephen Parker, and interpreted in a systematic critique and analysis written by J. Periam Danton in the lead article of Harvey's work,[11] comes closest to a logical formulation: "International librarianship consists of activities carried out among or between governmental or nongovernmental institutions, organizations, groups or individuals of two or more nations, to promote, establish, develop, maintain and evaluate library, documentation and allied services, and librarianship and the library profession generally, in any part of the world."[12]

For the historian, this formulation has a great deal of merit because it divorces international librarianship from comparative librarianship and places international organizations in the center of inquiry. International bodies are established as the key protagonists carrying out a multitude of systematic efforts on a global or regional scale, organized for the benefit of library and information services and their allied professions everywhere. International librarianship thus has an autonomous existence independent of any kind of investigative approach. It is to this discrete reality that the attention of historical research should be directed.

The core of Parker's definition is on target, but for the historian the contours of the scope become a little diffuse on the fringes. The first difficulty arises when one considers the role of "groups and individuals." If international librarianship consists of the activities of international organizations, then the activities coming under the purview of a study of international librarianship would be those that have been carried out directly on behalf of, or in the organizational or program framework of, international bodies.

Consequently, a UNESCO expert's teaching activity, for example, in a member state requesting assistance, is international librarianship, but an American Fulbright scholar's similar endeavor in a host country is not.

The contention here is that those individual or group activities taking place in a structured, multilateral organizational context broadly construed are legitimate subjects of investigation for writers of the history of international librarianship. The term "broadly construed" as a modifier of "multilateral organizational context" would allow, for example, including a case where librarians from several countries initiate steps to improve cooperation among themselves. Even though this initiative would ultimately not become institutionalized in a supranational body, the intent of the initiative is clearly multilateral in character.

A further problem with Parker's definition stems from the interpretation of the term "international." The word is used here to indicate two or more nations, although in actuality, activity that affects only two parties could more accurately be described as "bilateral."

Bilateral library relations should not be considered germane to the history of international librarianship for two main reasons. First, because such relations have seldom become permanent and have not culminated in the creation of a jointly controlled supranational organization in charge of administering pertinent library programs. Second, bilateral relations in library matters after World War II usually involved situations in which one party was donor and the other recipient. This type of relationship is antithetical to the principle of library organization at an international level. Such organization calls for participation on an equal basis on many different tiers in the interest of all. In this kind of relationship, sharing is an inherent right of each constituent member.

To put it more concretely, collaboration in library matters between the United States and Mexico, for example, is not international librarianship in a strict sense. Such collaboration should be relegated to respective national histories, subsumed under the rubrique "international relations." If, on the other hand, there is evidence of the intervention of a supranational body affecting in any way the conduct of collaboration, or, conversely, if the collaboration exerts influence on a regional or global organization of the profession, then these relations do belong to the realm of international librarianship.

Similarly, the activities of ALA's International Relations Office, with all of its impressive accomplishments in many parts of the

439

world, are the concern of the historian of international librarianship only insofar as they contribute to the formation, destinies,
and policies of international professional organizations and institutions. The rest is national library history in America and in the
impacted country.

Thus, the proper subject matter for the history of international
librarianship is the multilateral, supranational organizations and
institutions that were brought into existence through some joint
effort with a view to promoting and developing library and information services, as well as the profession as a whole, all over the
world.

**Hypotheses Underlying Historical Investigation in International
Librarianship**

The accurate delineation of the scope and subject matter of
international librarianship is dictated by the hypotheses around
which substantive historical inquiries can be mounted. The researcher must be guided by the realization that the emergence of
supranational structures in librarianship has opened a new chapter
in the history of the profession. Their presence has created a qualitatively different environment in which library, information, and
professional problems can be approached and solved.

The advent of supranational organizations also reflects a maturation of library and information service issues as international
concerns. The maturation process has progressed along three distinct but interrelated lines: professional, scientific, and political.
The professional line was an expression of practitioners themselves
in the form of collaboration of individual librarians, groups, or
library associations of various nations for the purpose of advancing
their art. The evolutionary path in the realm of the sciences and
humanistic scholarship led to wide-range coordination of activities
in bibliographical and informational matters linking together librarianship, information and documentation, and the scientific
disciplines through the creation of specialized summit bodies. "Politicization" began with the establishment of global and regional
organizations of governments, such as the League of Nations,
United Nations, UNESCO, the Organization of American States,
and others. Politicization has involved the handling of bibliothecal matters in an international public forum under some form of
collective jurisdiction, with decisions having implications for all
member states.

This evolutionary pattern explains the history, relationships, and functional alignments of the numerous international organisms active on the library scene. Taken together, they make up a global web of channels, forums, rallying points, linking devices, and multilevel transmission mechanisms that elevate librarianship to a social and cultural force. International organizations have been especially effective instruments for the diffusion of advanced library thought and techniques. They have been shaping the profession for decades. The accumulated intellectual and operational experience derived from these activities constitutes the domain designated as "international librarianship."

Sorting out the organizations involved would be a difficult task, owing to their large number. Coblans studied the role of forty major organizations that have contributed to the improvement of international bibliographic control and documentation in recent times, in one way or another.[13] This is, of course, far from being a complete census. The current edition of the *Yearbook of International Organizations* identifies more than 150 bodies in the field of librarianship and in the various branches of information service. Our own estimate, arrived at by a comprehensive survey of library literature from 1876 through the middle of 1979, indicates that during this period hundreds of international bodies with primary and subordinate library and information concerns have come into being and carried out a variety of activities.[14] A number of them have already outlived their usefulness and have disappeared from the scene. But the growing complexity of the field, compounded by a relentless pressure toward narrower specialization, as well as tendencies toward decentralization and regionalization, has given birth to new constellations of organizations and institutions, incessantly.

Sources of the History of International Librarianship

The presence of international organizations looms large in professional literature. Although the indexing tools omit the distinct subject headings under which writings on the topic could be clustered, it is possible to identify relevant material indirectly. An initial attempt to inventory the literature yielded an estimated 10,000 entries covering the past hundred years.[15] Conceivably, a number of these entries may have been duplications and may have been counted separately under different subject headings. But the fact remains that international librarianship as an autonomous field of study possesses a sizable body of literature of its own. Much of this literature consists of published proceedings of meetings and conferences, and post-facto accounts in respective national library periodicals, written by participants.

Few of the organizations have maintained an official journal. For communication, humbler formats have usually been resorted to, such as bulletins, newsletters, news releases, announcements, and others. Together with the requisite annual reports these materials are extremely useful for historical research. But the indispensable primary resources, without which no close-range analyses of policies, events, political context, and the impact of individuals is possible, reside in the internal files of the organizations.

The nature of these primary resources varies from case to case. Occupying a pivotal place among international intergovernmental organizations, UNESCO produces the greatest volume of official papers. The *Reports* of the various advisory bodies and field missions, the briefing materials, working papers, agendas and the accounts and resolutions of regional conferences, and the official summaries of the proceedings of seminars and meetings of experts are normally in the public domain but often receive "limited" distribution. These documents could provide insight into the operational philosophy and methods of UNESCO and also shed some light on the origin of programs and projects.

Although UNESCO public documents are generally accessible, the nature of these documents presents some barrier to historical analysis. For one thing, they are designed primarily for the record and to facilitate the business of the organization. Corporate logic and cost considerations contribute to a documentary policy that only summarizes official happenings. Obviously, such records have limited value for an in-depth and detailed academic study.

Furthermore, as an intergovernmental body, UNESCO and its executive arm conduct their relations and communications according to the standards and protocol of international diplomacy. This is reflected in the tone, style, and language of published documents. Official pronouncements carry no critical statements or allusions to negative facts. Plans, formulation of programs, and the launching of projects are announced, but results are seldom reported and they are not, as a rule, evaluated substantively. The tone is businesslike, pervaded by institutional anonymity with lapses into "officialese." The *Programmes and Budgets* and the *Reports of the Director-General* contain a plenitude of figures, quantifiable facts, and data, but they relate to the allocation of resources, not to the returns.

What is more, internal files are confidential. For all practical purposes, this material is not available to researchers for a system-

atic study. Similar provisions regulate the use of archival materials. Much of the stock, especially communications between
UNESCO and governments of member states, remain closed for
thirty years from the date of origin. Further, few if any depositories in the United States have in hand a complete file of UNES-
CO published documents that deal with the full range of the organization's activities in the field of libraries, documentation, and
archives.[16]

Presumably, the state of documentation and access to the files
at other intergovernmental bodies is similar. The condition of
documentary resources at nongovernmental organizations is yet
to be examined. It seems, therefore, that the immediate task confronting historical scholarship in international librarianship is a
thorough exploration of the state of archival and contemporary
records maintained in the offices of international organizations.

Eliciting biographical material presents a special problem. A
preliminary study revealed that the number of men and women
of various nationalities who have held important positions over
the past hundred years in international organizations, assemblies,
and their subordinate bodies can be counted in the thousands.[17]
Often, not even painstaking research can discover anything about
these people beyond their barest identification. Searching for biographical and career information in the national library or reference
literature is normally a hopeless task, since few of the countless
internationally active librarians have been memorialized in their
respective national pantheons. For this reason, it should be a
legitimate goal that in the global interest of the profession, international organizations and institutions routinely gather, preserve,
and disclose meaningful biographical data on their influential contributors.

Agenda for Historical Scholarship

Opening up the field of international librarianship as a sovereign
intellectual domain is contingent upon the availability of applicable conceptual and methodological tools, including a variety of
auxiliary instruments for research. These, however, do not exist
at the present time. Thus, the first item on the agenda, after identifying the relevant organizations and institutions according to
the proposed definition, is a call for the bibliographical organization of the already censused literature and an inventory of the
primary resources, along the lines of a specially constructed thesaurus reflecting the structure of the field. The structure of such

a thesaurus must grow out of the intrinsic logic of the subject matter.

Establishing the fundamental facts and data would involve fitting the material into a chronological and thematic frame, or some other relational context that would readily exhibit the parameters of the corporate concerns, spheres of jurisdiction, and activities of the organizations encompassed. This kind of elaboration would call for a reference-work format for the easy conspectus of events, programs, and people, suitably arranged in chronology, synchronistic tables, and topical and biographical dictionaries.

Our knowledge of international organizations is so filled with gaps that at this juncture plain descriptive works, even chronicles, could perform a useful service in educating the public. For example: a mere cataloging of UNESCO, IFLA, and FID programs could give working librarians and cultural policy makers a better grasp of the wide scope and diversity of the undertakings of these organizations.

But beyond reconstructing past events and factually presenting contemporary developments, the task of historical scholarship is total analysis, the interpretation of facts and a search for their meaning.[18] In attempting to respond to this challenge, the historian faces many dilemmas and choices. The issue-centered inquiry, of which Coblans supplied a fine example, can be pitted against the method of weaving parallel histories into majestic annals.[19] Both approaches have their virtues and drawbacks. Or, it may be more fruitful to organize the history of international librarianship around landmark conferences and meetings, an approach that could bring the forces, ideologies, and personalities into sharper relief than other modes of treatment.

Then, there is the problem of balance; first, the balance between the intergovernmental international organizations on the one hand, and the nongovernmental international professional associations and regional agglomerates on the other. What relative weights should be given to the International Institute of Intellectual Cooperation of the League of Nations, UNESCO, the Organization of American States, the European Communities' League of Research Libraries, and the Eastern European Socialist Block's professional arm? Should center stage perhaps be given to the profession's own umbrella organizations: the International Federation of Library Associations, the International Federation for Documentation, and the International Council on Archives?

The problem of balance crops up at practically every stage of the historian's work. Which of the three main lines of the profession: librarianship, information science, or archives administration, should occupy the center stage? The proliferation of international bodies, institutions, and programs within these three main lines of professional pursuits reflects the diversification and fragmentation of the profession by type and level of service and by type and function of library. The picture is further complicated by the fact that in many instances other organizations have moved in to fill functions not performed by library organizations.

While all these have particular pertinence and value for the clienteles they serve, they are not all of equal value to international librarianship as a whole. How does one establish a hierarchy among them that does not reflect the writer's own experience in the field?

Stated in general terms: is there a primacy among the panoply of international agencies, and what criteria should be used in establishing it? And, how can a proper place be found for all these innumerable international structures and programs in the longer perspective of history?

Related to the effort to establish a proper historical perspective is the problem of setting matters into the right context. Should analysis and discussion proceed in a narrow professional and technical framework, or should a history of international librarianship move on broad-gauged tracks embedded in the context of contemporary sociopolitical, cultural, and intellectual currents? Should such a history concentrate solely on the internal evolution of international organizations, or should the historian be more interested in examining the attitudes, and responses of the respective organizations of the profession to the central issues of the day to see how these issues were translated into professional concerns and actions?

The Uses of the History of International Librarianship

What purpose would historical scholarship in international librarianship serve? What would motivate the researcher? The student of the history of international librarianship with an idealistic bent would be inspired by the prime import that can be attached to the subject. The inherent majesty of the theme would bring a broader dimension to the generally technical preoccupations of the profession. A history of even the technical aspects of the profession, a subject rarely discussed on a philosophical plane, when viewed from the global vantage point that a history of international librarianship can offer, will inform us of the profession's collective search for instrumentation of increasing sophistication to improve its services to society. Such a study will lead to the recognition of the profoundly international character of librarianship, affirming Ranganathan's dictum: "library service, bibliographic organization, and library classification recognize no national or political boundaries."[20] Over the centuries, librarianship has evolved everywhere through the conscious transmission of professional traditions and sharing "the bibliographic dreams and efforts."[21]

Thus, the history of international librarianship can serve as a mirror for the profession. Bringing the past to the consciousness of the present gives a sense of continuity and reflects the process of professionalization on a global scale, uneven as it may have been. An objective analysis of pertinent historical facts will evidence the steady rise of information issues and the diffusion of knowledge through library channels as vital societal concerns. The ensuing elevation of the status of the profession will create or reinforce an esprit de corps transcending national frontiers and raise the morale of its practitioners.

A growing social awareness of the significance of the profession's contribution on the one hand, and the profession's own improved self-image on the other, will produce a general atmosphere in which transnational communication and expressions of commonality of interests become easier and the desire for sharing more keen.

But the impact may be felt even more strongly on the domestic front. The multiple perspectives provided by the history of international librarianship give wider scope to national library activity and induce a deeper understanding of professional issues within national boundaries.

Another important justification for researching the history of international librarianship is the academic uses such a history would serve. Professional experience magnified through systematic international analysis and examined in chronological depth allows generalization on a higher level. Diagnostic, predictive, and methodological conjectures assume greater force when distilled from practice in different environments. Because international library organizations must integrate the various national experiences as part of the organizations' rationale for existence, they are in a position to gain cululative knowledge on all important bibliothecal phenomena. Library and information science may claim scientific legitimacy only to the extent they are capable of formulating universally valid propositions. A history of international librarianship would contribute directly and indirectly to the broadening of the theoretical base of the library and information disciplines.

But beyond the morale-building, improvement of corporate self-image, and scientific uses, the writing of the history of international librarianship is necessitated by practical considerations. It is a fact of life today that nowhere can libraries insulate themselves from international developments. The issues with which international organizations deal inevitably affect all librarians.[22] Therefore, it would seem imperative that librarians everywhere involve themselves in international activities, "or at least demand accountability from those who would speak for them in such fora."[23]

This, however, is easier said than done. For one thing, the international agencies of the profession have not escaped the general tendency toward bureaucratization with its potential stultification, manipulation, and impenetrability. But the sine qua non of effective participation in the activities of international organizations is informed judgment based on a full understanding of issues. Only the analysis and broad syntheses stemming from the toil of historical scholarship can supply the ingredients to practitioners.

On a higher plane, such syntheses are also needed to guide those who are in charge of policy making, program development, and coordinating activities in the international agencies and governments themselves. Indeed, without the perspectives provided by historical syntheses, the diplomatics of librarianship will be continued groping in the dark. True international library statesmanship needs the vistas that only the history of international librarianship can open up.

Notes

1. Curt D. Wormann, "Aspects of International Library Co-operation—Historical and Contemporary," *Library Quarterly* 38, no. 4 (October 1968): 338-351.

2. Herbert Coblans, *Librarianship and Documentation: An International Perspective* (London: Deutsch, 1974), 142 pp.

3. See: P. Havard-Williams, "The History of the International Federation of Library Associations and Institutions," *Unesco Bulletin for Libraries* 31, no. 4 (July–August 1977): 203–209; Charles Kecskemeti, "International Council on Archives (ICA)," *Encyclopedia of Library and Information Science* (New York: Marcel Dekker, 1974) 12: 361–372; Helmut Arntz, "International Federation for Documentation (FID)," *ELIS*, 12: 377–407; Ana Maria Clark and Jane Wilson and Marietta Daniels Shepard, "Organization of American States (OAS)," *ELIS*, 21: 16–35.

4. The most comprehensive treatment of the subject is Beverly J. Brewster, *American Overseas Library Technical Assistance, 1940–1970* (Metuchen, N.J.: Scarecrow Press, 1976), 445 pp.

5. J. Periam Danton, *The Dimensions of Comparative Librarianship* (Chicago: American Library Association, 1973), p. 4.

6. Martha Boaz, "The Comparative and International Library Science Course in American Library Schools," in John F. Harvey (ed.), *Comparative and International Library Science* (Metuchen, N.J.: Scarecrow Press, 1977), pp. 167–180.

7. Richard Krzys, "International and Comparative Study in Librarianship, Research Methodology," in *ELIS*, 12: 325–343.

8. Dorothy G. Collings, "Comparative Librarianship," in *ELIS*, 5: 492–502, quote on p. 493.

9. Ibid., p. 496.

10. John F. Harvey (ed.), *Comparative and International Library Science* (Metuchen, N.J.: Scarecrow Press, 1977), 286 pp.

11. J. Stephen Parker, "International Librarianship—A Reconnaissance," *Journal of Librarianship* 6, no. 4 (October 1974): 219–232; J. Periam Danton, "Definitions of Comparative and International Library Science," in *Comparative and International Library Science*, pp. 3–14.

12. Parker, "International Librarianship," p. 221.

13. Coblans, *Librarianship and Documentation*, pp. 137–138.

14. This estimate was arrived at by analyzing entries under names of organizations and an assortment of subject headings in Cannons's *Bibliography of Library Economy* (1910; reprint ed., New York: Burt Franklin, 1970) and all issues of *Library Literature* (New York: H. W. Wilson) beginning with 1921 to the middle of 1973.

15. Cannons's *Bibliography* . . . and *Library Literature* were searched under the names of organizations, conferences, types of libraries, and generic terms of varied library functions, which were often subdivided into "international aspects."

16. This writer could not locate in the United States a complete collection of the numbered documents issued by the former Division of Documentation, Libraries, and Archives of UNESCO. Even the U.N. Dag Hammarskjold Library had little such material in the early 1970s beyond the main official series of UNESCO.

17. Beyond elected, appointed, and staff officers of organizations, the term "important office" includes high-visibility roles and functions, such as membership in a panel, advisory board, committees, and others where a member was in a position to influence the formulation of policy and to affect decisions. The term also covers participation in any form in the implementation of a program or a project.

18. The term is borrowed from R. Krzys and represents one of the research categories in international and comparative study in librarianship. See Richard Krzys, "International and Comparative Study in Librarianship, Research Methodology," *ELIS*, 12: 328.

19. Coblans, *Librarianship and Documentation*.

20. S. R. Ranganathan, "Colon Classification and Its Approach to Documentation," in Jesse H. Shera and Margaret E. Egan (eds.), *Bibliographic Organization: Papers Presented before the Fifteenth Annual Conference of*

the Graduate School, July 24–29, 1950 (Chicago: University of Chicago Press, 1951), pp. 94–105.

21. Robert Vosper, "Librarianship: The International Horizons," *PNLA Quarterly* 42, no. 4 (Summer 1978): 18.

22. The reasons why American librarians ought to get interested in the activities of international organizations were forcefully articulated in an article by S. Michael Malinconico, "International Indirection," *Library Journal* (15 December 1979): 2629–2631.

23. Ibid., p. 2631.

The Evolution of an International Library and Bibliographic Community

Boyd Rayward

The thesis of this paper is that the present far-reaching scope
and variety of bibliographic and library activity at the international level, as manifested in the work of a great many different
kinds of international organization, are possible only because of
the emergence after the First World War of an international community that did not previously exist. It suggests why it was that,
in our areas of professional interest, the League of Nations Organization for Intellectual Cooperation became the symbol of and
the center for this community rather than the Palais Mondial or
Mundaneum created by Paul Otlet and Henri LaFontaine in Brussels over twenty years before; for the Mundaneum may be described as a predecessor in many respects of the League of Nations
Organization. From the point of view presented here, the League
of Nations Organization was clearly a success, though it ultimately
failed in most of the specific library and bibliographic tasks it
undertook and was disbanded after years of relative impotence.
The Palais Mondial, on the other hand, was clearly a failure,
though some of the achievements of the International Institute
of Bibliography, which was one of its component organizations,
have had a lasting impact through the International Federation for
Documentation into which the Institute developed.

The paper will have four parts. First I will examine the objectives and functions of international library and bibliographic
organizations. Next I will analyze the idea of community; I will

W. Boyd Rayward *is dean and associate professor of library science
at the University of Chicago.*

Journal of Library History, Vol. 16, No. 2, Spring 1981
©1981 by the University of Texas Press   0022-2259/81/020449-14$01.45

argue that the notion of a center is of paramount importance to its existence, and describe the present international library and bibliographic community. Third, I will discuss attempts by Otlet and La-Fontaine to create a great international library and bibliographic center in Brussels before the First World War and describe how this grew in size and complexity to become what was called the Palais Mondial or Mundaneum. Finally, I shall discuss the League of Nations and the emergence of a center and a community that represent the beginning of our modern period of international bibliographic organization and control, indicating why the League Organization for Intellectual Cooperation transcended and perhaps displaced the organization in which Otlet and LaFontaine had invested their hope and so much of their work for a better world.

International Organizations

International organizations have proliferated during the twentieth century more than during any earlier period, and they have left practically no area of human endeavor untouched. Many necessarily have crystallized around activities that involve both the creation and dissemination of knowledge. Underlying the work of most international organizations in the latter area are a number of interconnected questions. How can knowledge be shared? What mechanisms can be devised to encourage and to regulate the transmission of knowledge internationally? How can effective use of knowledge be stimulated at the same time as its integrity is maintained and legitimate interests in it are protected? How can nations be encouraged to play their part in sharing with others the knowledge generated within their borders and expressed in their own languages? How can they be encouraged to deploy effectively for their national benefit potentially useful knowledge available to them outside their borders in languages other than their own?

Answers to these and similar questions are not simple, for they must penetrate the intricate web of cultural, economic, political, linguistic, and technological relations that constrain the intercourse of states and nations. Such questions, however, are simplified in practice in two ways: first, a concern for knowledge in its broadest, most abstract sense is replaced by a practical orientation toward providing information about what is known in limited subject areas; second, what is known in these subject areas is considered primarily to lie in the grasp of experts or to be recorded in documents. These documents still appear principally in printed form as books, journals, and reports, but they are also increasingly assuming a nonprint form as films, audiodiscs and cassettes, and computer tapes and discs.

There are, then, international organizations devoted to the substantive development of our knowledge of the arts, humanities, social sciences, and the pure and applied sciences. These organizations attempt to achieve their goal by means of international meetings, cooperative research projects, the education of students, the international exchange of expert personnel, and publishing programs, either involving journals and books or indexing and abstracting services. This last activity, where it exists, brings the organizations concerned with the content of our knowledge into the realm of another group, which may be described as library or bibliographic organizations whose central concern is the dissemination or exploitation of that knowledge. These organizations are primarily interested on the one hand in the physical documents embodying what is known and on the other in the surrogates of various kinds, completeness, and intended uses (indexes or abstracts) that have been devised to facilitate the acquisition of different levels of knowledge about these documents.

Among functions falling within the purview of library and bibliographic international organizations are: (1) the lending and exchange of documentary materials; (2) the control of international commerce related to these materials (postal and tariff regulations, copyright agreements, publishing and distribution rights, and censorship); (3) the generation, standardization, exchange, and publication of machine-readable bibliographic data for books and nonbook materials and of indexing and abstracting data for journal articles and related materials; (4) the creation, maintenance, and operation of international information systems; (5) the provision of moral, technical, and financial assistance to developing countries utilizing existing documentary materials and information systems; (6) the publication of a technical literature necessary to the management of such international systems and agreements as exist; (7) the publication of a support literature consisting of general reports, manuals, directories, monographs, and proceedings about international desiderata, agreements, systems, and procedures, a literature that represents the deliberations of expert bodies or personnel about problems of international interest.[1]

The fulfillment of these functions is seen not merely as intrinsically desirable by those who create the organizations, but as related to a central value or good, the sharing of knowledge, whose nature and importance are supported by common beliefs. The existence of these beliefs allows the international community to become a reality.

The Nature of Community

For a community to exist in the sense I mean there must be a relatively stable and permanent membership; there must be orderly, differentiated activity by members; there must be formal modes of communication; and there must be a center.

Membership implies the recognition of one or more common goals and a willingness to circumscribe the independence of organizational action in the service of these goals and objectives. Moreover, membership must be relatively stable and permanent if a community is to exist through time and allow its members variety and continuity of action within it. Orderliness and differentiation of activity are consequences of the independence of members, for in a community every member is different from every other and not every member can do the same, or yet entirely different, things; that is to say, cooperation is a prerequisite of community. For cooperation to be possible there must be accepted forms of regular communication. Among the purposes of communication are affirmation of common interests and negotiation by members about their activities as they relate to these interests. The center is an embodiment, which can be both symbolic and organizational, of these interests. Contact with the center is sought by members of the community as a source of support for and validation or legitimation of their communal activities. The purposes of the center are to initiate, encourage, focus, coordinate, and reward activity by members of the community it represents.

If this is a plausible description of a form of community, then it is proper to speak of an international bibliographic and library community. Its members, relatively stable and permanent, are predominately international organizations (themselves communities of individual, national, and other international organizational members). The existence and independence of these international organizations as members of the international community are represented by their statutes, rules of procedures, and carefully documented programs of work to which their own members formally subscribe.

These organizations are of different kinds and their work takes place to different degrees within the context provided by the international community. Some are nongovernmental, such as the International Federation of Library Associations and Institutions

(IFLA), the International Federation for Documentation (FID), and the International Association of Agricultural Librarians and Documentalists (IAALD). Some are intergovernmental and are created for a single specific purpose, such as the Berne copyright union; others have a more general, amorphous function, such as the Information Policy Group of the Organization for Economic Cooperation and Development. Most intergovernmental organizations when they assume bibliographic responsibilities do so as part of a broader mission. In recent years, for example, a number of international information systems have been set up, such as INIS (the International Nuclear Information System) of the International Nuclear Energy Agency or AGRIS (Agricultural Information System) of the Food and Agricultural Organization of the United Nations. A number of other systems with similarly acronymic names (DEVSIS, ARCHISIST, for example) are under development.[2] Because of the nature of their parent organizations, these systems represent especially stable services provided within the international library and information community. As a result of creating and maintaining these systems, the parent organizations, though previously not part of the community and though now the main thrust of their work may still be elsewhere, constitute an important part of this community.

Although the members or parts of the international bibliographic and library community are independent, all share common goals, seek to cooperate, and communicate regularly and formally. Above all, either they turn for direction to a common center, or this center deliberately reaches out to bring them within the orbit of its influence. The center nowadays is UNESCO.

While I do not propose to examine in detail the nature of the links with UNESCO that exist between the various international organizations constituting part of the membership of the international bibliographic and library community, any study of their work will at some point conduct one directly to UNESCO, and UNESCO will be seen as fulfilling one or more of the functions of a center that I have described: a source for initiating, encouraging, concentrating, coordinating, and rewarding work.

In practice, it seems clear that such a center can do little else beyond these functions. To be effective it must achieve its goals through the members of the community it represents. To undertake large-scale independent programs of substantive work would bring it into direct competition or conflict with other organizations; it could then be considered just another organization, and the uniqueness of its central position in the international community would be jeopardized.

Thus far I have argued that it makes sense nowadays to speak of an international library and bibliographic community. Its members are international library and bibliographic organizations that are held together, in essence, by the existence of a common center that both is symbolic of a form of organization for the community and provides a basis for it. In the third part of my discussion, I want to take a historical leap to the turn of the century to study an attempt to achieve a version of this international center that, embracing bibliographic work and eventually much more as well, was intended to serve as the foundation for an international community. The attempt failed but was a prelude to the emergence after the First World War of such a center, which had the complex functions I have described, sponsored by the League of Nations.

The World Palace

In 1895 Paul Otlet and Henri LaFontaine founded the International Institute of Bibliography.[3] Its aims were complex, but they turned on the development of a universal catalog and the creation of a classification system (which was eventually called the Universal Decimal Classification) that would allow for the cooperative compilation of the catalog by collaborators from around the world. The headquarters for the catalog was the International Office of Bibliography in Brussels, which was in part supported by the Belgian government (I shall henceforward speak of the International Institute of Bibliography as comprising without further distinction the International Office of Bibliography). While various ancillary technical and publicity functions were carried on in this headquarters, its central aim was the preparation and consultation of the universal catalog, which was no more and no less than an attempt to obtain bibliographic control over the entire spectrum of recorded knowledge.

Participation in the international bibliographic center that Otlet and LaFontaine created in Brussels was by and large predicated on contribution to the vast classified catalog growing inside it. An attempt was made, however, to stimulate the creation of national centers that would be linked to the international center. In these centers portions or even the whole of the catalog would be duplicated. The centers, in their turn, would attempt to collect and transmit to Brussels bibliographic data about the national literature. Thus consultation and use of the cooperatively assembled central record of all knowledge known to be embodied in documents would be facilitated by a measure of decentralization. In the event only one national center of any scope or permanence emerged: the Bureau Biblooographique de Paris. The symbol of the work at the International Institute of Bibliography was its most important tool, the Universal Decimal Classification. It may well be no accident that it is this system that has always been most closely associated with the International Institute of Bibliography, eventually to become the International Federation for Documentation, and that in later years it was not uncommon for aficionados to make rather self-congratulatory references to the brotherhood of the "décimalistes."[4]

As the years went by, attempts were made to increase the range of activities and the effectiveness of the International Institute of Bibliography as an intellectual center. These attempts took several forms. New bibliographical works were developed and institutionalized: a form of encyclopedia comprising a vast collection of files of brochures and newspaper and magazine clippings, a catalog of pictorial material, and an international library were all arranged by the Universal Decimal Classification. The last was created by uniting the library collections of various national and international societies located in Brussels.

Another development was the subject offices founded within the secretariat of the Institute and supported by existing or specially created international associations. Within these offices attempts were made not merely to elaborate the bibliography of their subjects but to synthesize the content of a variety of documentary sources about them. There were offices for hunting, fishing, aeronautics, and polar regions; they seem to have had little effective life apart from the flurry of activity surrounding their creation.

Two attempts to obtain increased support for the center and extend its influence were directed to governments. First, Otlet was an active member of a commission appointed in 1906 to plan a huge architectural complex to house a number of Belgian cultural and artistic institutions in Brussels (the Mont des Arts), and he was able to gain recognition of the International Office of Bibliography as one of these institutions. Unfortunately the planning took decades to become a physical reality and by that time his influence in government circles had declined and the institutes under his care were no longer seen as having much, if any, national importance. Second, an attempt was made in 1908 through the good offices of the Belgian government to have the International

Institute of Bibliography raised to the status of an intergovernmental organization, by creating through governments an International Union for Documentation. Such an organization would
by its very nature have a permanence, an assurance of support, and
an international acceptance of its work hitherto lacking. The governments of the world responded to the Belgian initiative with a
marked lack of enthusiasm and nothing came of it.

The last of the evolutions sustained by the International Institute of Bibliography that I wish to mention here was the creation
of an international center of nongovernmental international organizations embracing all fields of knowledge. This was set up as the
Union of International Associations after a world conference of
these organizations on the occasion of the International Exhibition (or World's Fair) in Brussels in 1910. To the existing bibliographical components of the center were added an international
museum (its subject departments were to be maintained by appropriate international associations, its national sections by governments) and the secretariats of many of the associations. The organization of the center was completed immediately after the First
World War by the foundation of what was misleadingly called an
International University. All of these elements—universal catalog,
"encyclopedia," library, museum, secretariats, and university—
were brought together at the expense of the Belgian government
and housed by its leave in one of the huge buildings erected for
the 1910 exhibition. This complex was given the name Palais Mondial (World Palace). Later the name was changed to a Latinate
form, Mundaneum.

This was the state of affairs at the beginning of the period immediately after the First World War. I turn now to the fourth and
final part of my discussion.

The League of Nations

The most important institution for the world of knowledge and
learning after the war took an organizational form different from
any that had preceded it. For many the war marked the end of the
old order of international politics and diplomacy and the emergence of a new order in which the cooperation and to some degree
the regulation of states and nations would be secured in a League
of Nations. Perhaps no international body has ever had such hope
invested in it. Among those who worked for its realization were
some, like Otlet and LaFontaine, who believed its spheres of interest should encompass not merely political, juridical, and eco-

nomic matters but moral and intellectual ones as well. Expressed first at the meetings in Paris in 1919 at which the League's covenant was drawn up, this notion was then ignored. But in 1922 the Council of the League created an International Committee on Intellectual Cooperation and appointed to it twelve eminent scholars from a variety of disciplines and countries. Among their number were Marie Curie, Polish-French radiological scientist; Henri Bergson, French philosopher; Gilbert Murray, Australian-British classicist; George Hale, American astronomer; and Albert Einstein, German-Swiss physicist, who did not at once take his seat on the Committee.

From its inception the Committee received inadequate financial support from the League, and in 1924 the Council gave it permission to appeal directly to governments for assistance. The French government offered to create in Paris and in part maintain what would be an executive arm and headquarters organization for the Committee, the International Institute for Intellectual Cooperation, frequently referred to as the Paris Institute. Together the Committee and the Institute, which was inaugurated in 1926, were known as the League Organization for Intellectual Cooperation.

Among a wide range of urgent work identified by the International Committee for Intellectual Cooperation were the improvement of the conditions of intellectual life in the war-devastated areas of central Europe, the revision of existing agreements for the international exchange of publications and the protection of copyright, and the coordination of bibliography. In defining its preliminary program the Committee was guided both by the "peculiar urgency" of particular problems and by their capability for "relatively easy and immediate solution."[5] It proceeded to set up subcommittees to facilitate discussion of problems and to identify specific activities to be attempted. Among these first subcommittees was one for bibliography, its membership comprising in equal proportions representatives of the International Committee on Intellectual Cooperation and outside library experts.

The question relevant to our discussion here is not why the League of Nations Committee on International Intellectual Cooperation was set up (which is a real and interesting question). Rather it is, why was an administrative center supported by the French government necessary? And why was it necessary for the League Committee to set up as one of its first subcommittees, an indication of the priority of the subject, a subcommittee on bibliography? After all, there in Brussels on the one hand was the Palais Mondial occupying locations supported by the Belgian

government, and on the other the Institute of Bibliography forming an important component of this organization and having members of various kinds scattered throughout the learned world.
Certainly Otlet and LaFontaine had hoped that the institutes
of the Palais Mondial and the intellectual equipment they contained would be adopted by the League of Nations and elevated
to the status of a technical organ for its work for intellectual cooperation, especially as a section of the League's Covenant provided
for the League to adopt existing international (governmental) organizations. And indeed, the League Communications and Transit
Organization grew out of an existing organization, and another
was intended to become the basis for the Health Organization,
though the opposition of the United States prevented an unofficial
agreement to this effect from being translated into action.

In the hope of gaining recognition and support from the newly
created international body, Otlet had in its first days sought to
draw the attention of League officials to the Palais Mondial and
its work. There was much correspondence between Otlet and
members of the League secretariat, including Sir Eric Drummond,
the secretary general, who visited the Palais Mondial on several occasions. The Council of the League, however, was very careful in
its dealings with Otlet and his colleagues. It responded to Otlet
and LaFontaine's overtures by what may be considered both cau-
tion and a ploy: it requested that the secretary general study the
work of the Union of International Associations and report on it.
The report was accurate and positive in tone but did not envisage
any great role for the League in the Union's work. Asked by Otlet
and LaFontaine for subsidy for and patronage of the first session
of the International University in 1920, the Council offered moral
support and permission for members of the General Secretariat to
participate in its meetings.

Otlet had vigorously urged the creation of an agency for intellectual work within the League both during and immediately after
the First World War. Quite rightly, he saw himself as a leading proponent of the League Committee on Intellectual Cooperation.
Once in existence, however, the Committee—even in the area of
bibliography—having carefully studied the situation in Brussels,
decided not to adopt the methods, programs, or secretariat of the
International Institute of Bibliography. Rather it decided to confine to the Institute a series of partially subsidized tasks of a limited nature, and signed a formal agreement to this effect, which
was never fully implemented. Otlet was bitterly disappointed
when his institutes were, as he interpreted it, rejected by the

League, for, as he had been quick to point out, underlying the Palais Mondial was "the very conception of the League of Nations," and his criticisms of the early work of the Organization for Intellectual Cooperation were almost denunciatory.[6]

There are a variety of reasons why the League's Organization for Intellectual Cooperation went in different directions from the International Institute of Bibliography and the Union of International Associations. Some of them relate to the incompatible personalities in conflict and there was a great deal of this kind of conflict. But the most cogent reason was the isolation of the World Palace from the League, an isolation arising because the impossibility of the World Palace or any of its constituent organizations functioning as a true international center of the kind I described at the beginning of this paper.

From the outset the League Organization for Intellectual Cooperation had seen itself in just this way—as an agency to stimulate, facilitate, and coordinate work; an agency providing a forum for discussion, in which desiderata for international action could be formulated in close consultation with as many interested parties as possible. A major statement of the philosophy guiding the work of the League Organization was provided in 1927, six months after the International Institute in Paris had begun operation and a pattern to its activity had begun to emerge. The study of substantive matters related to the content of disciplines was explicitly eschewed. "The Organization is concerned with problems of organization alone. Its business is to find practical means of promoting international cooperation in the production and circulation of intellectual works." The statement goes on: "Further, the Organization will deal with all of these matters only so far as they are not already being dealt with by others; its particular role will be to encourage and help on the undertakings of interested bodies and, where necessary, to coordinate this action. *Suggestion, encouragement, coordination to improve the conditions of intellectual labour: these are, and must be, the only duties of the Organization of Intellectual Cooperation.*" Moreover, early experience in the Institute for Intellectual Cooperation suggested that "most of the institutions and bodies with which the Organization has so far had dealings desired this systematic form of contact, found it an encouragement and a support ... in brief, *the new institution is a valuable rallying sign*, and would be useful as such though it were useless otherwise."[7]

In line with these principles the Institute actively encouraged the formation of the International Federation of Library Associations and supported its development in 1926 and later as an independent international organization through which library matters could be pursued at the international level. The League Organization also tried seriously over a long period and in a variety of ways to work out a collaborative arrangement with the International Research Council that was founded in Brussels in 1919 and reorganized to become the International Council of Scientific Unions in 1931. A formal agreement was not signed until 1937, though much in the way of informal consultation between the two bodies had by then already taken place. And, of course, there were the attempts to draw the International Institute of Bibliography into the Organization's network of contacts, meetings, and publications. Neither Otlet nor LaFontaine participated to any degree, but after the International Institute of Bibliography was restructured in 1924, limited but cordial relations were established in the late 1920s and during the 1930s between the Paris Institute and the new personnel of the IIB.

By way of contrast, Otlet presented two papers at the Prague conference in 1926 from which we generally date the birth of the IFLA, but did not in any way follow this initial association through. Much earlier, in 1919, before the League was active or its Intellectual Organization had come into existence, he had participated in the constitutive meeting of the International Research Council. He drew up draft statutes, which were accepted by the meeting, for an International Union of Documentation to be created from the IIB. This was to take its place beside the other new subject unions, such as the International Union of Pure and Applied Chemistry and the International Union of Astronomy. But again, he seems to have made no attempt to go beyond this result, and the International Research Council's published records show no further attempt to develop an International Union of Documentation from these draft statutes.

The curious dilemma faced by the Palais Mondial was that to become effective as an intellectual and international center in the new postwar world, it was necessary for it to surrender the work that the institutes comprising it had been performing for more than a quarter of a century. Participation in these institutes required a commitment to special programs and special methods, and many were opposed to the programs, the methods, and the philosophy that they embodied so imperfectly. Before the war these institutes—and the Palais Mondial as a whole—despite the conferences and articles and books and correspondence of their founders, were just other organizations struggling for survival in an arena where there was little law and order, where there was not much cooperation and strength in association because there were so few shared beliefs; that is to say, there was not a community. After the First World War, Otlet and his colleagues could not respond to the new order. They were universalists, centralists, tied to particular programs and methods rationalized in the headiest of abstractions that led them and their work to be mocked and rejected by many, or to become the objects of the passionate but usually ineffective conviction of a few.

The League Organization for Intellectual Cooperation, on the other hand, tried to identify and draw together what already existed into an international community, a task facilitated, as Otlet and the others were vitally aware, by the existence of the League of Nations itself, which was something quite new in the history of human association. Like its parent body, the Organization for Intellectual Cooperation was internationalist in orientation. It was commited necessarily to the independence of states and nations and of organizations and individuals, the cooperation of all of whom in different ways was its general object. Actual programs were formulated only after the closest consultation and involvement with the members of the community that the Organization represented and served.

Most of the programs were unsuccessful: the work on agreements for international exchanges of publications and the protection of copyright, the attempts to coordinate various kinds of subject bibliography, and the efforts to draw libraries into an international network all had to be resumed after World War II. Yet the situation at the end of the Second World War was quite different from that at the end of the first. None of the international bibliographic ventures that flourished in the period before the First World War survived it in a vigorous or lasting way. This is as true of the International Institute of Bibliography as it is of the Concilium Bibliographicum or the International Catalogue of Scientific Literature. Though—unlike the last two ventures—the International Institute of Bibliography's actual existence was maintained, it was forced gradually to relinquish much of what it had previously tried to do. It had to become a new organization, and ultimately only the organization itself—known as the FID—and the Universal Decimal Classification remained as the irreducible residue of its founders' ambitions. Yet after the Second World War there was an orderly and immediate resumption of what was universally accepted as interrupted work, of international relations between members of the international library and bibliographic community, and the emergence in UNESCO of a center for that community that was similar in some ways to the one created by the League of Nations between the wars. This is why I see our modern period of bibliographic organization and control at the international level as deriving from the creation through the League of Nations Organization for Intellectual Cooperation of an international library and bibliographic community and why, despite its failure in many of the tasks it undertook, I judge it a success. This is why, despite the survival of the FID and the UDC, I see the brave experiment begun in Brussels as the International Institute of Bibliography in 1895, and attaining an extraordinary extension and scope by 1914 as the Palais Mondial, as ultimately a grand but almost complete failure.

Notes

1. See W. Boyd Rayward, "The Literature of International and Comparative Librarianship," in Joel M. Lee and Beth A. Hamilton (eds.), *As Much to Learn as to Teach: Essays in Honor of Lester Asheim* (Hamden, Conn.: Linnet Books, 1979), pp. 217–235.

2. For a useful survey of a wide range of these organizations, see the articles that follow W. Boyd Rayward's article, "International Library and Bibliographic Organizations," Robert Wedgeworth (ed.), *ALA World Encyclopedia of Library and Information Services* (Chicago: American Library Association, 1980), pp. 264–268.

3. The information for this section of this paper is contained in W. Boyd Rayward, *The Universe of Information: The Work of Paul Otlet for Documentation and International Organisation*, Fédération International de Documentation Publication no. 520 (Moscow: VINITI, 1975), passim.

4. For example, see Georges Lorphèvre, "Otlet, Paul," *Biographie Nationale* (Brussels: Académie des Lettres et des Beaux Arts, 1964) 32: 533–556; and his "Donker Duyvis et la Classification décimale Universelle," in *F. Donker Duyvis, His Life and Work* (The Hague: Netherlands Institute for Documentation and Filing, 1964), p. 24.

5. "The Work of the International Committee on Intellectual Cooperation," Annex 416b (A.137.1922.xii), *League of Nations Official Journal* (November 1922): 1313.

6. For the work of the League of Nations as it impinged on the International Institute of Bibliography and the Palais Mondial, see Rayward, *Universe of Information*. The standard history of the League is F. P. Walters, *A History of the League of Nations*, 2 vols. (London and New York: Oxford University Press, 1952). An important, and so far unique, study is S. Steven Falk, "The International Committee on Intellectual Co-operation: Its Work for Bibliography" (M.A. thesis, University of Chicago Graduate Library School, 1977).

7. The quotations are from: *The International Institute of Intellectual Cooperation* (n.p., September 1927), pp. 10–11; the italics are in the original.

Index

PREFACE TO SUBJECT INDEX

This subject index includes names of individuals, libraries, and locations mentioned where significant to the authors' discussions. Alphabetization is letter by letter, with acronyms listed before all other entries. Terminology and form of entry are based on the *National Union Catalog*, authors' usage, Library of Congress subject headings, and the previously published index to volumes I-IX of the *Journal of Library History*, with emphasis on ease of access.

This index was prepared as a project for the Fall 1980 Indexing and Abstracting class of the Graduate School of Library and Information Science, University of Texas at Austin. The indexers were Jim Kelly, Marietta Portigal, Karen Stanley, and Linda Wedel.

SUBJECT INDEX

INTERNATIONAL ORGANIZATIONS. *See also* Names of
particular organizations, e.g., ORGANIZATION OF
AMERICAN STATES
—And librarianship, 437–442, 443
INTERNATIONAL RESEARCH COUNCIL, 460
INTERNATIONAL UNION OF DOCUMENTATION, 460
IRWIN, R., 370

JACKSON, W. A., 177, 180, 184–185
JAMES, HENRY, 41
JAMES, WILLIAM, 266, 268
JEFFERSON, THOMAS, 11
JEWETT, CHARLES COFFIN, 158–159, 160, 161, 162
JEWISH HISTORY, 167–175
—In Atlanta, Ga., 19th century, 309–310
JEWISH IMMIGRATION. *See* IMMIGRATION TO UNITED
STATES, 19TH AND 20TH CENTURIES
JEWISH LABOR BUND ARCHIVES, NEW YORK, N.Y.,
167–175
JEWS
—In fiction, 309–310
JOHNSTON, DELIA, 306–307
JOINT COMMITTEE ON IMPORTATIONS, 254, 255

KAIDANOVA, OLGA, 395
KAISER WILHELM INSTITUTE, BERLIN, GERMANY, 261–262
KANDO, THOMAS, 344
KANFER, STEFAN, 174–175
KAUFMAN, PAUL, 367
KAYSERBERG, DR. *See* GEILER, JOHANNES, VON
KAISERBERG
KELLY, THOMAS, 367–368
KEMPINSKI, HILLEL, 174
KER, N. R., 366
KILGOUR, FREDERIC G., 256, 257–259, 262–263
KING, HENRY CHURCHILL, 287–288
KLOPFER, DONALD S., 243–250, passim
KNIGHTS OF COLUMBUS OF TEXAS, 319–320, 323, 325
KOBERGER, ANTHONI, 136, 138, 139
KOEVARY, HANNAH, 174
KÖNIGLICHE BIBLIOTHEK, BERLIN, GERMANY, 295
KOPELSON, TSEMAKH, 168, 173
KRUPSKAIA, NADEZHDA KONSTANTINOVA, 396, 400

PARRY, THOMAS, 383
PAUL II, POPE, 124-125, 129
PEPPER, STEPHEN C., 107-108
PEREZ TREVIÑO, MANUEL, 316-317
PERIODICAL REPUBLICATION PROGRAM, 256, 257
PERIODICALS, SCIENTIFIC
—In Germany, 253-263, passim
PERU
—Indians of, 405-413, passim
—Literacy in, 404-414, passim
—Map of, 416
—Puno, Department of, 405-414, passim
PHRYGIUS DODO, AUGUSTINUS, 139
PICCOLOMINI LIBRARY, PIENZA, ITALY, 124
PINELLI, GIAN VINCENZO, 143-150
PINELLI COLLECTION, 143-150
PIUS II, POPE, 123-125, 129
PIUS III, POPE, 124
PLATINA, BARTOLOMEO SACCI DE PIADENA, 123, 125-126, 128
PLATO, 93
PLATT, ANTHONY, 39
PLUNKETT, HORACE, 273
POOLE, WILLIAM FREDERICK, 267-268
POPES. *See* Names of individual popes, e.g., SIXTUS IV, POPE, etc.
POPULAR CULTURE
—In Baltimore, Md., 19th century, 227-238
—Literary analysis of, 342-351
—In Paris, France, 1800-1850, 199-207
PRINTING INDUSTRY. *See also* PUBLISHERS AND PUBLISHING
—Practices, 179-180, passim
PRIVATE LIBRARIES
—In Italy, 16th century, 143, 146
PROGRESSIVE ERA AND CULTURE, 37
PROHIBITION, 283-285
PUBLIC LIBRARIES
—In French Africa, 218-223
—In Great Britain
—Histories of, 366-371
—And records management, 372-375
—In Italy

Z
665
L67
1980

Library History 52352
Seminar (6th :
1980 : Austin,
Texas)
    Libraries & cul-
ture